Lecture Notes in Computer Science 10590

Commenced Publication in 1973
Founding and Former Series Editors:
Gerhard Goos, Juris Hartmanis, and Jan van Leeuwen

More information about this series at http://www.springer.com/series/7412

Sebastiano Battiato · Giovanni Maria Farinella
Marco Leo · Giovanni Gallo (Eds.)

New Trends in Image Analysis and Processing – ICIAP 2017

ICIAP International Workshops, WBICV, SSPandBE, 3AS, RGBD, NIVAR, IWBAAS, and MADiMa 2017
Catania, Italy, September 11–15, 2017
Revised Selected Papers

 Springer

Editors
Sebastiano Battiato ⓘ
University of Catania
Catania
Italy

Marco Leo ⓘ
University of Catania
Catania
Italy

Giovanni Maria Farinella ⓘ
University of Catania
Catania
Italy

Giovanni Gallo ⓘ
University of Catania
Catania
Italy

ISSN 0302-9743   ISSN 1611-3349 (electronic)
Lecture Notes in Computer Science
ISBN 978-3-319-70741-9   ISBN 978-3-319-70742-6 (eBook)
https://doi.org/10.1007/978-3-319-70742-6

Library of Congress Control Number: 2017959619

LNCS Sublibrary: SL6 – Image Processing, Computer Vision, Pattern Recognition, and Graphics

Printed on acid-free paper

This Springer imprint is published by Springer Nature
The registered company is Springer International Publishing AG
The registered company address is: Gewerbestrasse 11, 6330 Cham, Switzerland

Preface

This volume contains the 46 papers accepted for presentation at the workshops hosted by the 19th International Conference on Image Analysis and Processing (ICIAP), held in Catania, Italy, September 11–15, 2017.

ICIAP is the conferences organized every two years by the GIRPR, the Italian group of researchers affiliated with the International Association for Pattern Recognition (IAPR). The aim of the conference is to bring together researchers working on image processing, computer vision, and pattern recognition from around the world.

Seven individual workshops – four full-day and three half-day – were selected by the workshop chairs, Giovanni Maria Farinella and Marco Leo, to complement ICIAP 2017 in Catania:

- First International Workshop on Brain-Inspired Computer Vision (WBICV) 2017;
- Social Signal Processing and Beyond (SSPandBE) 2017;
- Automatic Affect Analysis and Synthesis (3AS) 2017;
- Background Learning for Detection and Tracking from RGBD Videos (RGBD) 2017;
- Natural Human–Computer Interaction and Ecological Perception in Immersive Virtual and Augmented Reality (NIVAR) 2017;
- First International Workshop on Biometrics As-a-Service: Cloud-Based Technology, Systems, and Applications (IWBAAS) 2017;
- Third International Workshop on Multimedia-Assisted Dietary Management (MADiMa) 2017.

The International Workshop on Brain-Inspired Computer Vision (WBICV) organized by George Azzopardi (University of Malta, Malta), Laura Fernández-Robles (University of León, Spain), and Antonio Rodríguez-Sánchez (University of Innsbruck, Austria) provided a forum for researchers of diverse fields in the context of the modelling different phenomena of the visual system of the brain.

The Workshop on Social Signal Processing and Beyond (SSPandBE) organized by Mariella Dimiccoli (University of Barcelona, Spain), Petia Ivanova Radeva (University of Barcelona, Spain), and Marco Cristani (University of Verona, Italy) provided an interdisciplinary forum to bring together researchers and professionals studying social signal processing and social behavior to present novel ideas and discuss future directions in the field.

The Workshop on Automatic Affect Analysis and Synthesis (3AS) organized by Nadia Berthouze (University College London, UK), Simone Bianco (University of Milan-Bicocca, Italy), Giuseppe Boccignone (University of Milan, Italy), and Paolo Napoletano (University of Milan-Bicocca, Italy) considered the research field that tries to endow machines with capabilities to recognize, interpret, and express emotions.

The Workshop on Background Learning for Detection and Tracking from RGBD Videos (RGBD) organized by Massimo Camplani (University of Bristol, UK), Lucia Maddalena (ICAR-CNR, Italy), and Luis Salgado (Universidad Politècnica de Madrid, Spain) aimed to bring together researchers interested in background learning for detection and tracking from RGBD videos.

The scope of the NIVAR workshop organized by Manuela Chessa (University of Genoa, Italy), Fabio Solari (University of Genoa, Italy), and Jean-Pierre Bresciani (Université de Fribourg, Switzerland) has been to provide a forum for researchers and practitioners from both academia and industry, interested in studying and developing innovative solutions with the aim of achieving a natural human–computer interaction and an ecological perception in VR and AR systems.

The International Workshop on Biometrics As-a-Service: Cloud-Based Technology, Systems, and Applications (IWBAAS) organized by Silvio Barra (University of Cagliari, Italy), Arcangelo Castiglione (University of Salerno, Italy), Kim-Kwang Raymond Choo (University of Texas, USA), and Fabio Narducci (University of Molise, Italy) solicited work and ideas on cloud-based biometric systems and services.

The International Workshop on Multimedia-Assisted Dietary Management (MADiMa) organized by Stavroula Mougiakakou (University of Bern, Switzerland), Giovanni Maria Farinella (University of Catania, Italy), and Keiji Yanai (The University of Electro-Communications, Tokyo, Japan) aimed to bring together researchers from the diverse fields of engineering, computer science, and nutrition who investigate the use of information and communication technologies for better monitoring and management of food intake.

We thank all the workshop organizers who made possible such an interesting pre-conference program.

August 2017

Giovanni Maria Farinella
Marco Leo

Organization

General Chairs

Sebastiano Battiato   University of Catania, Italy
Giovanni Gallo   University of Catania, Italy

Program Chairs

Raimondo Schettini   University of Milano-Bicocca, Italy
Filippo Stanco   University of Catania, Italy

Workshop Chairs

Giovanni Maria Farinella   University of Catania, Italy
Marco Leo   ISASI- CNR Lecce, Italy

Tutorial Chairs

Gian Luca Marcialis   University of Cagliari, Italy
Giovanni Puglisi   University of Cagliari, Italy

Special Session Chairs

Carlo Sansone   University of Naples Federico II, Italy
Cesare Valenti   University of Palermo, Italy

Industrial and Demo Chairs

Cosimo Distante   ISASI – CNR Lecce, Italy
Michele Nappi   University of Salerno, Italy

Publicity Chairs

Antonino Furnari   University of Catania, Italy
Orazio Gambino   University of Palermo, Italy

Video Proceedings Chair

Concetto Spampinato   University of Catania, Italy

US Liaison Chair

Francisco Imai   Canon US Inc., USA

Asia Liaison Chair

Lei Zhang   The Polytechnic University, Hong Kong

Steering Committee

Virginio Cantoni   University of Pavia, Italy
Luigi Pietro Cordella   University of Napoli Federico II, Italy
Rita Cucchiara   University of Modena and Reggio Emilia, Italy
Alberto Del Bimbo   University of Firenze, Italy
Marco Ferretti   University of Pavia, Italy
Fabio Roli   University of Cagliari, Italy
Gabriella Sanniti di Baja   ICAR-CNR, Italy

About This Book

This book constitutes the refereed proceedings of seven workshops held at the 19th International Conference on Image Analysis and Processing, ICIAP 2017, in Catania, Italy, in September 2017: the First International Workshop on Brain-Inspired Computer Vision – WBICV 2017; Social Signal Processing and Beyond – SSPandBE 2017; Automatic Affect Analysis and Synthesis – 3AS 2017; Background Learning for Detection and Tracking from RGBD Videos – RGBD 2017; Natural Human–Computer Interaction and Ecological Perception in Immersive Virtual and Augmented Reality – NIVAR 2017; First International Workshop on Biometrics As-a-Service: Cloud-Based Technology, Systems, and Applications – IWBAAS 2017; Third International Workshop on Multimedia-Assisted Dietary Management – MADiMa 2017.

Contents

Automatic Affect Analysis and Synthesis (3AS)

Brain-Inspired Computer Vision
(WBICV)

A New Objective Supervised Edge Detection Assessment Using Hysteresis Thresholds

Hasan Abdulrahman$^{(\boxtimes)}$, Baptiste Magnier, and Philippe Montesinos

Ecole des Mines d'Alès, Parc Scientifique Georges Besse, 30000 Nîmes, France
`Hasan.abdulrahman@mines-ales.fr`

Abstract. Useful for the visual perception of a human, edge detection remains a crucial stage in numerous image processing applications. Therefore, one of the most challenging goals in contour extraction is to operate algorithms that can process visual information as humans need. Hence, to ensure that it is reliable, an edge detection technique needs to be severely assessed before being used it in a computer vision tools. To achieve this task, a supervised evaluation computes a score between a ground truth edge map and a candidate image. Theoretically, by varying the hysteresis thresholds of the thin edges, the minimum score of the measure corresponds to the best edge map, compared to the ground truth. In this study, a new supervised edge map quality measure is proposed, where the minimum score of the measure is associated with an edge map in which the main structures of the desired objects are distinctive.

Keywords: Edge detection · Supervised evaluation · Hysteresis

1 Introduction on Edge Detection and Thresholding

Edge detection is an important field in image processing because this process frequently attempts to capture the most important structures in the image. Hence, edge detection represents a fundamental step concerning computer vision approaches. Furthermore, edge detection itself could be used to qualify a region segmentation technique. Additionally, the edge detection assessment remains very useful in image segmentation, registration, reconstruction or interpretation. Hence, it is hard to design an edge detector which is able to extract the exact edge with good localization and orientation from an image. In the literature, different techniques have emerged and, due to its importance, edge detection continues to be an active research area [1]. The best-known and useful edge detection methods are based on gradient computing first-order fixed operators [2,3]. Oriented operators compute the maximum energy in an orientation [4–6] or two directions [7]. Typically, these methods are composed of three steps:

1. Computation of the gradient magnitude and its orientation η, see Fig. 1.
2. Non-maximum suppression to obtain thin edges: the selected pixels are those having gradient magnitude at a local maximum along the gradient direction η which is perpendicular to the edge orientation.

© Springer International Publishing AG 2017
S. Battiato et al. (Eds.): ICIAP 2017 International Workshops, LNCS 10590, pp. 3–14, 2017.
https://doi.org/10.1007/978-3-319-70742-6_1

3. Thresholding of the thin contours to obtain an edge map.

Thus, Fig. 1 exposes the different possibilities of gradient and its associated orientations involving several edge detection algorithms compared in this paper.

The final step remains a difficult stage in image processing, however it represents a crucial operation to compare several segmentation algorithms. In edge detection, the hysteresis process uses the connectivity information of the pixels belonging to thin contours and thus remains a more elaborated method than binary thresholding. Simply, this technique determines a contour image that has been thresholded at different levels (low: τ_L and high: τ_H). The low threshold τ_L determines which pixels are considered as edge points if at least one point higher than τ_H exists in a contour chain where all the pixel values are also higher than τ_L, as represented with a signal in Fig. 1. Thus, the lower the thresholds are, the more the undesirable pixels are preserved.

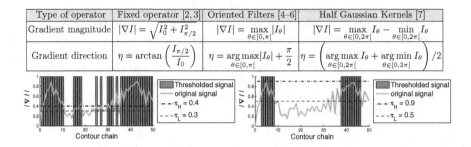

Type of operator	Fixed operator [2,3]	Oriented Filters [4–6]	Half Gaussian Kernels [7]
Gradient magnitude	$\|\nabla I\| = \sqrt{I_0^2 + I_{\pi/2}^2}$	$\|\nabla I\| = \max\limits_{\theta \in [0,\pi[} \|I_\theta\|$	$\|\nabla I\| = \max\limits_{\theta \in [0,2\pi[} I_\theta - \min\limits_{\theta \in [0,2\pi[} I_\theta$
Gradient direction	$\eta = \arctan\left(\dfrac{I_{\pi/2}}{I_0}\right)$	$\eta = \arg\max\limits_{\theta \in [0,\pi[} \|I_\theta\| + \dfrac{\pi}{2}$	$\eta = \left(\arg\max\limits_{\theta \in [0,2\pi[} I_\theta + \arg\min\limits_{\theta \in [0,2\pi[} I_\theta \right)/2$

Fig. 1. Gradient magnitude and orientation computation for a scalar image I and example of hysteresis threshold applied along a contour chain. I_θ represents the image derivative using a first-order filter at the θ orientation (in radians).

Usually, in order to compare several edge detection methods, the user has to try some thresholds to select the ones that appear visually as the best edge maps in quality. However, this assessment suffers from a main drawback: segmentations are compared using the threshold (deliberately) chosen by the user, this evaluation is very subjective and not reproducible. Hence, the purpose is to use the dissimilarity measures without any user intervention for an objective assessment. Finally, to consider a valuable edge detection assessment, the evaluation process should produce a result that correlates with the perceived quality of the edge image, which relies on human judgment [8–10]. In other words, a reliable edge map should characterize all the relevant structures of an image as closely as possible, without any disappearance of desired contours. Nevertheless, a minimum of spurious pixels can be created by the edge detector, disturbing at the same time the visibility of the main/desired objects to detect.

In this paper, a novel technique is presented to compare edge detection techniques by using hysteresis thresholds in a supervised way, being consistent with the visual perception of a human. Indeed, by comparing a ground truth contour map with an ideal edge map, several assessments can be compared by varying the parameters of the hysteresis thresholds. This study shows the importance to penalize stronger the false negative points, compared to the false positive points, leading to a new edge detection evaluation algorithm. The experiment using synthetic and real images demonstrated that the proposed method obtains contours maps closer to the ground truth without requiring tuning parameters and outperforms other assessment methods in an objective way.

2   Supervised Measures for Image Contour Evaluations

A supervised evaluation criterion computes a dissimilarity measure between a segmentation result and a ground truth obtained from synthetic data or an expert judgment (i.e. manual segmentation) [11–14]. In this paper, the closer to 0 the score of the evaluation is, the more the segmentation is qualified as good. This work focusses on comparisons of supervised edge detection evaluations and proposes a new measure, aiming at an objective assessment.

2.1   Error Measures Involving only Statistics

To assess an edge detector, the confusion matrix remains a cornerstone in boundary detection evaluation methods. Let G_t be the reference contour map corresponding to ground truth and D_c the detected contour map of an original image I. Comparing pixel per pixel G_t and D_c, the 1st criterion to be assessed is the common presence of edge/non-edge points. A basic evaluation is composed of statistics; to that end, G_t and D_c are combined. Afterwards, denoting $|\cdot|$ as the cardinality of a set, all points are divided into four sets (see Fig. 3):

- True Positive points (TPs), common points of G_t and D_c: $TP = |D_c \cap G_t|$,
- False Positive points (FPs), spurious detected edges of D_c: $FP = |D_c \cap \neg G_t|$,
- False Negative points (FNs), missing boundary points of D_c: $FN = |\neg D_c \cap G_t|$,
- True Negative points (TNs), common non-edge points: $TN = |\neg D_c \cap \neg G_t|$.

Several edge detection evaluations involving confusion matrix are presented in Table 1. Computing only FPs and FNs [7] or their sum enables a segmentation assessment to be performed. The complemented *Performance measure* P_m^* considers directly and simultaneously the three entities TP, FP and FN to assess a binary image and decreases with improved quality of detection.

Another way to display evaluations is to create Receiver Operating Characteristic (ROC) [19] curves or Precision-Recall (PR) [18], involving *True Positive Rates (TPR)* and *False Positive Rates (FPR)*: $TPR = \frac{TP}{TP+FN}$ and $FPR = \frac{FP}{FP+TN}$. Derived from TPR and FPR, the three measures Φ, χ^2 and F_α (detailed in Table 1) are frequently used. The complement of these measures enables to translate a value close to 0 as a good segmentation.

These measures evaluate the comparison of two edge images, pixel per pixel, tending to severely penalize a (even slightly) misplaced contour, as illustrated in Fig. 2. Consequently, some evaluations resulting from the confusion matrix recommend incorporating spatial tolerance. Tolerating a distance from the true contour and integrating several TPs for one detected contour can penalize efficient edge detection methods, or, on the contrary, advantage poor ones (especially for corners or small objects). Thus, from the discussion below, the assessment should penalize a misplaced edge point proportionally to the distance from its true location (some examples in [14], and, as shown in Fig. 2).

Table 1. List of error measures involving only statistics.

Performance measure [15]	$P_m^*(G_t, D_c) = 1 - \frac{TP}{|G_t \cup D_c|} = 1 - \frac{TP}{TP+FP+FN}$
Complemented Φ measure [16]	$\Phi^*(G_t, D_c) = 1 - \frac{TPR \cdot TN}{TN+FP}$
Complemented χ^2 measure [17]	$\chi^{2*}(G_t, D_c) = 1 - \frac{TPR-TP-FP}{1-TP-FP} \cdot \frac{TP+FP+FPR}{TP+FP}$
Complemented F_α measure [18]	$F_\alpha^*(G_t, D_c) = 1 - \frac{PREC \cdot TPR}{\alpha \cdot TPR+(1-\alpha) \cdot PREC}$, with $PREC = \frac{TP}{TP+FP}$ and $\alpha \in]0;1]$

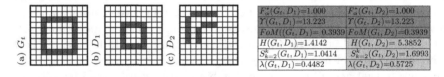

$F_\alpha^*(G_t, D_1)$=1.000	$F_\alpha^*(G_t, D_2)$=1.000
$\Upsilon(G_t, D_1)$=13.223	$\Upsilon(G_t, D_2)$=13.223
$FoM((G_t, D_1)$= 0.3939	$FoM(G_t, D_2)$=0.3939
$H(G_t, D_1)$=1.4142	$H(G_t, D_2)$= 5.3852
$S_{k=2}^k(G_t, D_1)$=1.0414	$S_{k=2}^k(G_t, D_2)$=1.6993
$\lambda(G_t, D_1)$=0.4482	$\lambda(G_t, D_2)$=0.5725

(a) G_t (b) D_1 (c) D_2

Fig. 2. Different D_c: FPs and number of FNs are the same for D_1 and for D_2.

2.2   Assessment Involving Distances of Misplaced Pixels

A reference-based edge map quality measure requires that a displaced edge should be penalized in function not only of FPs and/or FNs but also of the distance from the position where it should be located. Table 2 reviews the most relevant measures involving distances. Thus, for a pixel p belonging to the desired contour D_c, $d_{G_t}(p)$ represents the minimal Euclidian distance between p and G_t. If p belongs to the ground truth G_t, $d_{D_c}(p)$ is the minimal distance between p and D_c. On the one hand, some distance measures are specified in the evaluation of over-segmentation (i.e. presence of FPs), like: Υ, D^k, Θ and Γ. On the other hand, Ω measure assesses an edge detection by computing only an under segmentation (FNs). Other edge detection evaluation measures consider both distances of FPs and FNs [9]. A perfect segmentation using an over-segmentation measure could be an image including no edge points and an image having most undesirable edge points (FPs) concerning under-segmentation evaluations (see Fig. 3). Also, another limitation of only over- and under-segmentation evaluations are

Table 2. List of error measures involving distances, generally: $k = 1$ or $k = 2$.

Error measure name	Formulation	Parameters
Pratt's FoM [20]	$FoM\,(G_t, D_c) = 1 - \frac{1}{\max(|G_t|, |D_c|)} \cdot \sum\limits_{p \in D_c} \frac{1}{1 + \kappa \cdot d^2_{G_t}(p)}$	$\kappa \in\ ]0; 1]$
FoM revisited [21]	$F\,(G_t, D_c) = 1 - \frac{1}{|G_t| + \beta \cdot FP} \cdot \sum\limits_{p \in G_t} \frac{1}{1 + \kappa \cdot d^2_{D_c}(p)}$	$\kappa \in\ ]0; 1]$ and $\beta \in \mathbb{R}^+$
Combination of FoM and statistics [22]	$d_4\,(G_t, D_c) = \frac{1}{2} \cdot \sqrt{\frac{(TP - \max(|G_t|, |D_c|))^2 + FN^2 + FP^2}{(\max(|G_t|, |D_c|))^2} + FoM\,(G_t, D_c)}$	$\kappa \in\ ]0; 1]$ and $\beta \in \mathbb{R}^+$
Symmetric FoM [14]	$SFoM\,(G_t, D_c) = \frac{1}{2} \cdot FoM\,(G_t, D_c) + \frac{1}{2} \cdot FoM\,(D_c, G_t)$	$\kappa \in\ ]0; 1]$
Maximum FoM [14]	$MFoM\,(G_t, D_c) = \max(FoM\,(G_t, D_c), FoM\,(D_c, G_t))$	$\kappa \in\ ]0; 1]$
Yasnoff measure [23]	$\Upsilon\,(G_t, D_c) = \frac{100}{|T|} \cdot \sqrt{\sum\limits_{p \in D_c} d^2_{G_t}(p)}$	None
Hausdorff distance [24]	$H\,(G_t, D_c) = \max\left(\max\limits_{p \in D_c}(d_{G_t}(p)), \max\limits_{p \in G_t}(d_{D_c}(p))\right)$	None
Maximum distance [11]	$f_2 d_6\,(G_t, D_c) = \max\left(\frac{1}{|D_c|} \cdot \sum\limits_{p \in D_c} d_{G_t}(p), \frac{1}{|G_t|} \cdot \sum\limits_{p \in G_t} d_{D_c}(p)\right)$	None
Distance to G_t [13,25]	$D^k\,(G_t, D_c) = \frac{1}{|D_c|} \cdot \sqrt[k]{\sum\limits_{p \in D_c} d^k_{G_t}(p)}, \quad k = 1$ for [25]	$k \in \mathbb{R}^+$
Oversegmentation [26]	$\Theta\,(G_t, D_c) = \frac{1}{FP} \cdot \sum\limits_{p \in D_c} \left(\frac{d_{G_t}(p)}{\delta_{TH}}\right)^k$	For [26]: $k \in \mathbb{R}^+$ and $\delta_{TH} \in \mathbb{R}^+_*$
Undersegmentation [26]	$\Omega\,(G_t, D_c) = \frac{1}{FN} \cdot \sum\limits_{p \in G_t} \left(\frac{d_{D_c}(p)}{\delta_{TH}}\right)^k$	For [26]: $k \in \mathbb{R}^+$ and $\delta_{TH} \in \mathbb{R}^+_*$
Symmetric distance [11,13]	$S^k\,(G_t, D_c) = \sqrt[k]{\frac{\sum\limits_{p \in D_c} d^k_{G_t}(p)) + \sum\limits_{p \in G_t} d^k_{D_c}(p)}{|D_c \cup G_t|}}, \quad k = 1$ for [11]	$k \in \mathbb{R}^+$
Baddeley's Delta Metric [27]	$\Delta^k(G_t, D_c) = \sqrt[k]{\frac{1}{|T|} \cdot \sum\limits_{p \in I} |w(d_{G_t}(p)) - w(d_{D_c}(p))|^k}$	$k \in \mathbb{R}^+$ and a convex function $w : \mathbb{R} \mapsto \mathbb{R}$
Edge map quality measure [28]	$D_p\,(G_t, D_c) = \frac{1/2}{|I| - |G_t|} \cdot \sum\limits_{p \in D_c} \left(1 - \frac{1}{1 + \alpha \cdot d^2_{G_t}(p)}\right) + \frac{1/2}{|G_t|} \cdot \sum\limits_{p \in G_t} \left(1 - \frac{1}{1 + \alpha \cdot d^2_{G_t \cap D_c}(p)}\right)$	$\alpha \in\ ]0; 1]$
Magnier et al. measure [29]	$\Gamma(G_t, D_c) = \frac{FP + FN}{|G_t|^2} \cdot \sqrt{\sum\limits_{p \in D_c} d^2_{G_t}(p)}$	None
Complete distance measure [14]	$\Psi(G_t, D_c) = \frac{FP + FN}{|G_t|^2} \cdot \sqrt{\sum\limits_{p \in G_t} d^2_{D_c}(p) + \sum\limits_{p \in D_c} d^2_{G_t}(p)}$	None

that several binary images can produce the same result (Fig. 2). Therefore, as demonstrated in [9], a complete and optimum edge detection evaluation measure should combine assessments of both over- and under-segmentation.

Among the distance measures between two contours, one of the most popular descriptors is named the Figure of Merit (FoM). Nonetheless, for FoM, the distance of the FNs is not recorded and are strongly penalized as statistic measures (see above). For example, in Fig. 3, $FoM(G_t, C) > FoM(G_t, M)$, whereas M contains both FPs and FNs and C only FNs. Further, for the extreme cases:

- if $FP = 0$: $FoM\,(G_t, D_c) = 1 - TP/|G_t| = 1 - (|G_t| - FN)/|G_t|$,
- if $FN = 0$: $FoM\,(G_t, D_c) = 1 - \frac{1}{\max(|G_t|, |D_c|)} \cdot \sum_{p \in D_c \cap \neg G_t} \frac{1}{1 + \kappa \cdot d^2_{G_t}(p)}$.

When $FN > 0$ and FP constant, it behaves like matrix-based error assessments (Fig. 2). Moreover, for $FP > 0$, the FoM penalizes the over-detection very low compared to the under-detection. On the contrary, the F measure computes the distances of FNs but not of the FPs, so F behaves inversely to FoM. Also, d_4 measure depends particularly on TP, FP, FN and FoM but penalizes FNs like the FoM measure. $SFoM$ and $MFoM$ take into account both distances of FNs and FPs, so they can compute a global evaluation of a contour image. However, $MFoM$ does not consider FPs and FNs at the same time, contrary to $SFoM$. Another way to compute a global measure is presented in [28] with the edge map quality measure D_p. The right term computes the distances of the FNs between the closest correctly detected edge pixel, i.e. $G_t \cap D_c$. Finally, D_p is more sensitive to FNs than FPs because of the coefficient $\frac{1}{|I|-|G_t|}$.

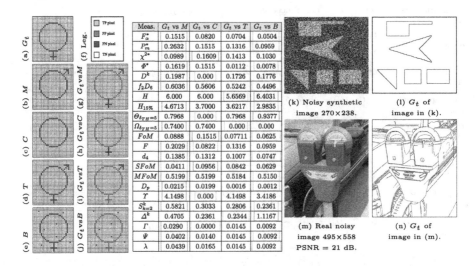

Meas.	G_t vs M	G_t vs C	G_t vs T	G_t vs B
F_α^*	0.1515	0.0820	0.0704	0.0504
P_m^*	0.2632	0.1515	0.1316	0.0959
χ^{2*}	0.0989	0.1609	0.1413	0.1030
Φ^*	0.1619	0.1515	0.0112	0.0078
D^k	0.1987	0.000	0.1726	0.1776
$f_2 D_6$	0.6036	0.5606	0.5242	0.4496
H	6.000	6.000	5.6569	6.4031
$H_{15\%}$	4.6713	3.7000	3.6217	2.9835
$\Theta_{\delta_{TH}=5}$	0.7968	0.000	0.7968	0.9377
$\Omega_{\delta_{TH}=5}$	0.7400	0.7400	0.000	0.000
FoM	0.0888	0.1515	0.07711	0.0625
F	0.2029	0.0822	0.1316	0.0959
d_4	0.1385	0.1312	0.1007	0.0747
$SFoM$	0.0411	0.0956	0.0842	0.0629
$MFoM$	0.5199	0.5199	0.5184	0.5150
D_p	0.0215	0.0199	0.0016	0.0012
Υ	4.1498	0.000	4.1498	3.4186
$S_{k=2}^k$	0.5821	0.3033	0.2806	0.2361
Δ^k	0.4705	0.2361	0.2344	1.1167
Γ	0.0290	0.0000	0.0145	0.0092
Ψ	0.0402	0.0140	0.0145	0.0092
λ	0.0439	0.0165	0.0145	0.0092

(a) G_t
(b) M
(c) C
(d) T
(e) B
(f) Leg.
(g) G_t vs M
(h) G_t vs C
(i) G_t vs T
(j) G_t vs B

TP pixel
FP pixel
FN pixel
TN pixel

(k) Noisy synthetic image 270×238.

(l) G_t of image in (k).

(m) Real noisy image 495×558 PSNR = 21 dB.

(n) G_t of image in (m).

Fig. 3. Results of evaluation measures and images for the experiments.

A second measure widely computed in matching techniques is represented by the Hausdorff distance H, which measures the mismatch of two sets of points [24]. This max-min distance could be strongly deviated by only one pixel which can be positioned sufficiently far from the pattern (Fig. 3). To improve the measure, one idea is to compute H with a proportion of the maximum distances; let us note $H_{15\%}$ this measure for 15% of the values [24]. Nevertheless, as pointed out in [11], an average distance from the edge pixels in the candidate image to those in the ground truth is more appropriate, like S^k or Ψ. Eventually, Delta Metric (Δ^k) [27] intends to estimate the dissimilarity between each element of two binary images, but is highly sensitive to distances of misplaced points [8,14].

A new objective edge detection assessment measure: In [14] a measure of the edge detection assessment is developed: it is denoted Ψ (Table 2) and

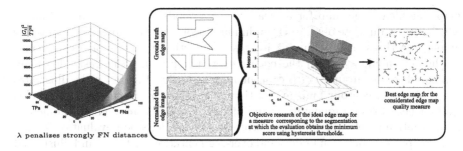

Fig. 4. Number of FNs penalizes λ and computation of a measure minimum score.

improvements the over-segmentation measure Γ, by combining both d_{G_t} and d_{D_c}, see Fig. 3. Ψ gives the same weight for d_{G_t} and d_{D_c} in its assessment of errors. Thus, using Ψ, a missing edge remains not enough penalized contrary to the distance of FPs which could be too important. Another example, in Fig. 3, $\Psi(G_t, C) < \Psi(G_t, T)$ whereas C must be more penalized because of FNs which does not allow to identify the object (also Fig. 5). The solution proposed here is to penalize stronger the distances of the FNs depending on the number of TPs:

$$\lambda(G_t, D_c) = \frac{FP + FN}{|G_t|^2} \cdot \sqrt{\sum_{p \in D_c} d_{G_t}^2(p) + \min\left(|G_t|^2, \frac{|G_t|^2}{TP^2}\right) \cdot \sum_{p \in G_t} d_{D_c}^2(p)} \quad (1)$$

The term influencing the penalization of FN distances can be rewritten as: $\frac{|G_t|^2}{TP^2} = \left(\frac{FN+TP}{TP}\right)^2 = \left(1 + \frac{FN}{TP}\right)^2 \geqslant 1$, ensuring a stronger penalty for $d_{D_c}^2$, compared to $d_{G_t}^2$. When $TP = 0$, the min function avoids the multiplication by infinity; moreover, the number of FNs is large, corresponding to a strong penalty with the weight term $|G_t|^2$ (see Fig. 4 left). When $|G_t| = TP$, λ is equivalent to Ψ and Γ (see Fig. 3, image T). Also, compared to Ψ, λ penalizes more D_c having FNs, than D_c with only FPs, as illustrated in Fig. 3 (images C and T). Finally, the weight $\frac{|G_t|^2}{TP^2}$ tunes the λ measure by considering an edge map of better quality when FNs points are localized close to the desired contours D_c.

The next subsection details the way to evaluate an edge detector in an objective way. Results presented in this communication show the importance to penalize stronger the false negative points, compared to the false positive points because the desired objects are not always completely visible by using ill-suited evaluation measure, and, λ provides a reliable edge detection assessment.

2.3   Minimum of the Measure and Ground Truth Edge Image

Dissimilarity measures are used for an objective assessment using binary images. Instead of choosing manually a threshold to obtain a binary image (see Fig. 3 in [9]), the purpose is to compute the minimal value of a dissimilarity measure by varying the thresholds (double loop: loop over τ_L and loop over τ_H) of the thin edges (see Table in Fig. 1). Thus, compared to a ground truth contour map, the ideal edge map for a measure corresponds to the desired contour at which the evaluation obtains the minimum score for the considered measure among the thresholded (binary) images. Theoretically, this score corresponds to the thresholds at which the edge detection represents the best edge map, compared to the ground truth contour map [8,12,30]. Figure 4 right illustrates the choice of a contour map in function of τ_L and τ_H. Since small thresholds lead to heavy over-segmentation and strong thresholds may create numerous false negative pixels, the minimum score of an edge detection evaluation should be a compromise between under- and over-segmentation (detailed and illustrated in [8]).

As demonstrated in [8], the significance of the ground truth map choice influences on the dissimilarity evaluations. Indeed, if not reliable [31], an inaccurate ground truth contour map in terms of localization penalizes precise edge detectors and/or advantages the rough algorithms as edge maps presented in [9,10]. For these reasons, the ground truth edge map concerning the real image in our experiments is built in a semi-automatic way detailed in [8].

3   Experimental results

In these experiments, the importance of an assessment to penalize stronger the false negative points is enlightened, compared to the false positive points. In order to study the performance of the contour detection evaluation measures, the hysteresis thresholds vary and the minimum score of the studied measure corresponds to the best edge map. The thin edges of both synthetic and real noisy images are computed by five or six edge detectors: Sobel [2], Canny [3], Steerable Filters of order 1 (SF_1) [4] or 5 (SF_5) [5], Anisotropic Gaussian Kernels (AGK) [6] and Half Gaussian Kernels (H-K) [7]. Figure 5 presents the results for 14 measures with their associated scores (bars) according to the hysteresis parameters. In the one hand, we must take into account the obtained edge map, and on the other hand the measure score. Generally, the optimal edge map for FoM, $SFoM$, $f_2 d_6$, Ψ and λ measures allows to distinct the majority of the desired edges for each contour detection operator (except Sobel), whereas for the other assessments, contours are too disturbed by undesirable points or distinguished with high difficulty (especially Ψ which does not penalizes enough FNs). Note that $SFoM$ measure does not classify the Sobel algorithm as less efficient. Concerning the experiment with a real image in Fig. 6, 8 measures are compared together. For FoM, H, Δ^k and S^k, the ideal edge maps concerning Sobel edge detector are highly corrupted by undesirable contours, the main objects are not recognizable. The other segmentations are also disturbed by undesirable pixels for FoM, H and Δ^k. Moreover, the higher score for Δ^k (AGK) does not represent the more disturbed map. Ultimately, using λ, the essential structures are visible in the optimal contour map for each edge detector (objects are easily recognizable). Moreover, contrary to H, FoM, d_4, Δ^k and S^k measures, the scores of λ are coherent, in relation to the obtained segmentations (Sobel and H-K results).

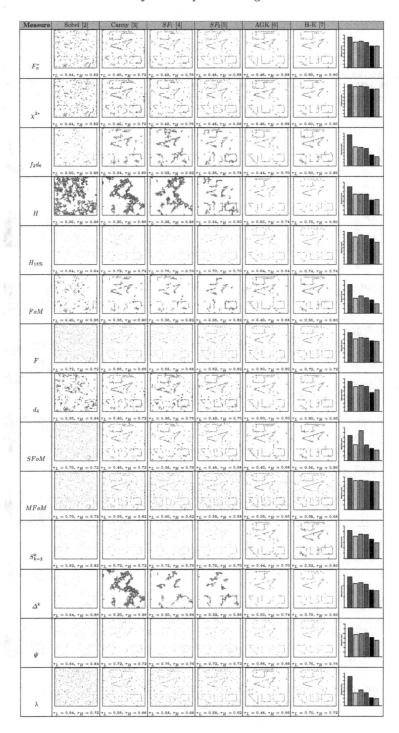

Fig. 5. Comparison of best maps and minimum scores for different evaluation measures. The bars legend is presented in Fig. 6. G_t and original image are available in Fig. 3.

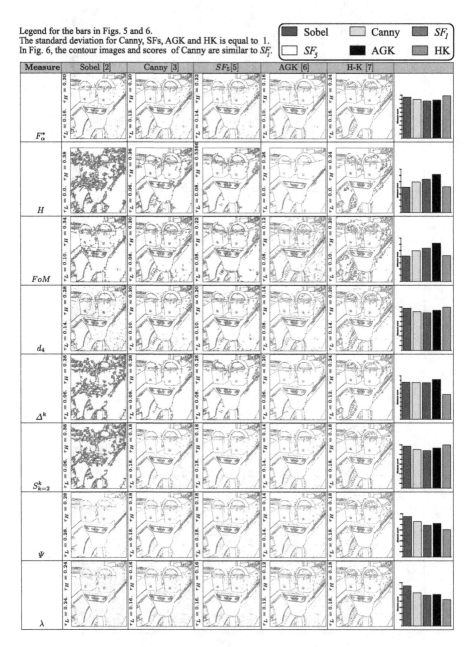

Fig. 6. Comparison of best maps and minimum scores for different evaluation measures. G_t and the original real image are presented in Fig. 3.

4 Conclusion and Future Works

This study presents a new supervised edge detection assessment method λ which enables to assess a contour map in an objective way. Based on the theory of the dissimilarity evaluation measures, the objective evaluation allows to evaluate 1st-order edge detectors. Indeed, the segmentation which obtains the minimum score of a measure is considered as the best one. Theory and experiments prove that the minimum score of the new dissimilarity measure λ corresponds to the best edge quality map evaluations, which is similarly closer to the ground truth, compared to the other methods. On the one hand, this new measure takes into account the distances of false positive points, in the other hand, it considers the distance of false negative points tuned by a weight. This weight depends on the number of false negative points: the more it is elevated, the more the segmentation is penalized. Thus, this enables to obtain objectively an edge map containing the main structures, similar to the ground truth, concerning a reliable edge detector. Finally, the computation of the minimum score of a measure does not require tuning parameters, which represents a huge advantage. For this purpose, we plan in a future study to deeply compare the robustness of several edge detection algorithms and use the new measure in object recognition.

Acknowledgements. The authors thank the Iraqi Ministry of Higher Education and Scientific Research for funding and supporting this work and reviewers for their remarks.

References

1. Arbelaez, P., Maire, M., Fowlkes, C., Malik, J.: Contour detection and hierarchical image segmentation. IEEE TPAMI **33**(5), 898–916 (2011)
2. Sobel, I.E.: Camera models and machine perception. Ph.D. thesis, Stanford University (1970)
3. Canny, J.: A computational approach to edge detection. IEEE TPAMI **PAMI–8**(6), 679–698 (1986)
4. Freeman, W.T., Adelson, E.H.: The design and use of steerable filters. IEEE TPAMI **13**, 891–906 (1991)
5. Jacob, M., Unser, M.: Design of steerable filters for feature detection using Canny-like criteria. IEEE TPAMI **26**(8), 1007–1019 (2004)
6. Geusebroek, J.-M., Smeulders, A.W.M., van de Weijer, J.: Fast anisotropic Gauss filtering. In: Heyden, A., Sparr, G., Nielsen, M., Johansen, P. (eds.) ECCV 2002. LNCS, vol. 2350, pp. 99–112. Springer, Heidelberg (2002). https://doi.org/10.1007/3-540-47969-4_7
7. Magnier, B., Montesinos, P., Diep, D.: Fast anisotropic edge detection using Gamma correction in color images. In: IEEE ISPA, pp. 212–217 (2011)
8. Abdulrahman, H., Magnier, B., Montesinos, P.: From contours to ground truth: how to evaluate edge detectors by filtering. In: WSCG (2017)
9. Martin, D., Fowlkes, C., Tal, D., Malik, J.: A database of human segmented natural images and its application to evaluating segmentation algorithms and measuring ecological statistics. In: IEEE ICCV, vol. 2, pp. 416–423. IEEE (2001)

10. Heath, M.D., Sarkar, S., Sanocki, T., Bowyer, K.W.: A robust visual method for assessing the relative performance of edge-detection algorithms. IEEE TPAMI **19**(12), 1338–1359 (1997)
11. Dubuisson, M.-P., Jain, A.K.: A modified Hausdorff distance for object matching. In: IEEE ICPR, vol. 1, pp. 566–568 (1994)
12. Chabrier, S., Laurent, H., Rosenberger, C., Emile, B.: Comparative study of contour detection evaluation criteria based on dissimilarity measures. EURASIP J. Image Video Process. **2008**, 2 (2008)
13. Lopez-Molina, C., De Baets, B., Bustince, H.: Quantitative error measures for edge detection. Pattern Recogn. **46**(4), 1125–1139 (2013)
14. Abdulrahman, H., Magnier, B., Montesinos, P.: A new normalized supervised edge detection evaluation. In: Alexandre, L.A., Salvador Sánchez, J., Rodrigues, J.M.F. (eds.) IbPRIA 2017. LNCS, vol. 10255, pp. 203–213. Springer, Cham (2017). https://doi.org/10.1007/978-3-319-58838-4_23
15. Grigorescu, C., Petkov, N., Westenberg, M.: Contour detection based on nonclassical receptive field inhibition. IEEE TIP **12**(7), 729–739 (2003)
16. Venkatesh, S., Rosin, P.L.: Dynamic threshold determination by local and global edge evaluation. CVGIP **57**(2), 146–160 (1995)
17. Yitzhaky, Y., Peli, E.: A method for objective edge detection evaluation and detector parameter selection. IEEE TPAMI **25**(8), 1027–1033 (2003)
18. Martin, D.R., Fowlkes, C.C., Malik, J.: Learning to detect natural image boundaries using local brightness, color, and texture cues. IEEE TPAMI **26**(5), 530–549 (2004)
19. Bowyer, K., Kranenburg, C., Dougherty, S.: Edge detector evaluation using empirical ROC curves. In: CVIU, pp. 77–103 (2001)
20. Abdou, I.E., Pratt, W.K.: Quantitative design and evaluation of enhancement/thresholding edge detectors. Proc. IEEE **67**, 753–763 (1979)
21. Pinho, A.J., Almeida, L.B.: Edge detection filters based on artificial neural networks. In: Braccini, C., DeFloriani, L., Vernazza, G. (eds.) ICIAP 1995. LNCS, vol. 974, pp. 159–164. Springer, Heidelberg (1995). https://doi.org/10.1007/3-540-60298-4_252
22. Boaventura, A.G., Gonzaga, A.: Method to evaluate the performance of edge detector (2009)
23. Yasnoff, W.A., Galbraith, W., Bacus, J.W.: Error measures for objective assessment of scene segmentation algorithms. Anal. Quant. Cytol. **1**(2), 107–121 (1978)
24. Huttenlocher, D.P., Rucklidge, W.J.: A multi-resolution technique for comparing images using the Hausdorff distance. In: IEEE CVPR, pp. 705–706 (1993)
25. Peli, T., Malah, D.: A study of edge detection algorithms. CGIP **20**(1), 1–21 (1982)
26. Odet, C., Belaroussi, B., Benoit-Cattin, H.: Scalable discrepancy measures for segmentation evaluation. In: IEEE ICIP, vol. 1, pp. 785–788 (2002)
27. Baddeley, A.J.: An error metric for binary images. In: Robust Computer Vision: Quality of Vision Algorithms, Proceedings of the International Workshop on Robust Computer Vision, pp. 59–78. Bonn, Wichmann (1992)
28. Panetta, K., Gao, C., Agaian, S., Nercessian, S.: A new reference-based edge map quality measure. IEEE Trans. Syst. Man Cybern.: Syst. **46**(11), 1505–1517 (2016)
29. Magnier, B., Le, A., Zogo, A.: A quantitative error measure for the evaluation of roof edge detectors. In: IEEE IST, pp. 429–434 (2016)
30. Fernández-Garca, N.L., Medina-Carnicer, R., Carmona-Poyato, A., Madrid-Cuevas, F.J., Prieto-Villegas, M.: Characterization of empirical discrepancy evaluation measures. Pattern Recogn. Lett. **25**(1), 35–47 (2004)
31. Hou, X., Yuille, A., Koch, C.: Boundary detection benchmarking: beyond F-measures. In: IEEE CVPR, pp. 2123–2130 (2013)

Learning Motion from Temporal Coincidences

Christian Conrad[1]([⊠]) and Rudolf Mester[1,2]

[1] Visual Sensorics and Information Processing Lab (VSI),
Computer Science Department, Goethe University, Frankfurt, Germany
conrad@vsi.cs.uni-frankfurt.de
[2] Computer Vision Laboratory, Electrical Engineering Department (ISY),
Linköping University, Linköping, Sweden
mester@isy.liu.se

Abstract. In this work we study unsupervised learning of correspondence relations over extended image sequences. We are specifically interested in learning the correspondence relations 'from scratch' and only consider the temporal signal of single pixels. We build on the Temporal Coincidence Analysis (TCA) approach which we apply to motion estimation. Experimental results showcase the approach for learning average motion maps and for the estimation of yaw rates in a visual odometry setting. Our approach is not meant as a direct competitor to state of the art dense motion algorithms but rather shows that valuable information for various vision tasks can be learnt by a simple statistical analysis on the pixel level. Primarily, the approach unveils principles on which biological or 'deep' learning techniques may build architectures for motion perception; so TCA formulates a hypothesis for a fundamental perception mechanism. Motion or correspondence distributions as they are determined here may associate conventional methods with a confidence measure, which allows to detect implausible, and thus probably incorrect correspondences. The approach does not need any kind of ground truth information, but rather learns over long image sequences and may thus be seen as a continuous learning method. The method is not restricted to a specific camera model and works even with strong geometric distortions. Results are presented for standard as well as fisheye cameras.

1 Introduction and Related Work

Estimating the relation between images, e.g., from multiple cameras or between subsequent frames in a video sequence is one of the most fundamental tasks in visual pattern recognition. Taking a biology-oriented view on vision, we may ask how processing architectures that successfully unveil the inherent structure of a video signal can evolve almost automatically. Conventional approaches to correspondence estimation between images are almost exclusively based on detecting, matching, or tracking *spatial features*. In this paper, we take a complementary

C. Conrad and R. Mester—This work was in parts supported by the ELLIIT programme funded by the Swedish Government.

© Springer International Publishing AG 2017
S. Battiato et al. (Eds.): ICIAP 2017 International Workshops, LNCS 10590, pp. 15–25, 2017.
https://doi.org/10.1007/978-3-319-70742-6_2

position and analyse the relation between images by looking at the *temporal* course of single pixel signals. It has already been shown previously [3] that by employing this approach (Temporal Coincidences Analysis, TCA), it is possible to reliably estimate the geometric and photometric [4] relations between images taken from a set of arbitrarily oriented cameras looking at the scene from very different view points [5], as well as for a moving stereo rig [3]. It is important to note that our approach is not applicable to single image pairs but requires a long stream of images. Therefore, our method targets vision systems in robotics, driver assistance and other multi-camera systems where long image streams are naturally available from which the regarded system can/should autonomously learn. This learning process can be scaled down almost arbitrarly in time (while increasing learning time) and thus can act as a lightweight subordinated task on a vision system.

In the present paper, we address motion *within* a monocular stream of images taken from a (not necessarily) moving camera. There is an abundance of algorithms to estimate optical flow, ranging from local to global methods such as the classical work by Lucas and Kanade [13] and Horn and Schunck [9]. Since then, the basic idea of brightness constancy and/or locally constant motion have been used and extended many times to design highly optimised algorithms (see [1,16] for an overview). However, these methods do not explain how motion perception may evolve and may be learnt over time. We emphasise strongly that this paper is not about computing individual motion vector fields connecting two particular images of a sequence, but about estimating the *statistics* of such motion vector fields without explicitly computing motion vectors. Furthermore, we address the problem of extracting meaningful *hidden variables* which have a large importance in describing the overall structure of a complex spatio-temporal pattern. In the present paper, we specifically look at variables which are closely coupled to the perception of lateral ego-motion. Learning of motion patterns (persistent motion) has found attention in the computer vision community, especially for video surveillance. Here, the goal is to model and extract persistent or normal motion patterns, which may be used to detect abnormal behaviour or may be used as a prior in a tracking application. Motion patterns are extracted based on the 3D structure tensor [18], from object tracks [7], or based on clustered sparse or dense optical flow fields [10]. Compared to these approaches, we never build object tracks and we never explicitly compute the optical flow. Instead, we apply TCA and solely rely on the temporal difference of single pixels and aggregate motion/correspondence candidates over time.

In the vision community, learning optical flow is mainly addressed by estimating the parameters of a specific model from ground truth data. The focus clearly lies on designing methods that advance the state-of-the-art by means of accuracy and/or running time on, e.g., the Middlebury benchmark [1]. Sun et al. [17] learn a statistical model of the spatial properties of optical flow by learning the parameters of the model based on ground truth data. They show that the model captures the statistics of optical flow and outperforms several standard methods. In contrast to this, we are interested in exploring how the statistics of optical flow may be learnt from scratch without any supervision or ground truth. Roberts et al. [15] learn a subspace of dense optical flow and show how the learnt subspace may be used to infer a dense motion map from sparse measurements and to estimate the ego-motion of a moving platform. Based on [15], Hardtweck and Curio [8] estimate the platform heading from monocular visual cues. They infer the *Focus of Expansion* (FoE), and require sparse flow and incremental platform motion for training. The FoE is computed based on the divergence of the optical flow field. In contrast to this, we present experimental results for inferring the hidden variables proportional to the yaw rate of a moving camera without the need for platform motion data.

To summarise, we will present the applicability of the Temporal Coincidence Analysis approach for learning statistics of image motion. The method can adapt to the computational power available while being easily parallelised if desired.

2   Temporal Coincidence Analysis of Motion

The fundamental idea of the Temporal Coincide Analysis approach for correspondence estimation builds upon the observation that the short-time temporal signature of *corresponding* pixels in different images should be similar. Signatures need to be significantly above usual noise fluctuations in order to be associable across images. In [3] Conrad et al. show how pixel correspondences may be learned in a binocular camera setup by a *Temporal Coincidence Analysis* (TCA), i.e., by the detection and matching of signal changes (temporal coincidences) from long image sequences. As in a spatial approach, matching is done based on features with high information content. In TCA, rare signal changes (events) are detected at a regarded pixel location and subsequently are matched with similar signal changes occurring at a different pixel location. The detection and matching of events is performed over many frames and accumulated; this way the empirical distribution of the correspondence relation is obtained. This correspondence distribution, in turn, can be characterised by a set of attributes, such as its first and second order statistics and thus allow to assess the learning progress in a statistically principled way.

Temporal coincidence analysis is not restricted to the multi-camera or stereo case, but is also applicable when the correspondence relation between pixels in the *same* video stream is explained by optical flow. For reasons that will be explained later, in general only the *average* correspondence relation, or the *distribution* of that correspondence may be learned by TCA. However, experimental results will show that the principle of TCA may also be used to estimate differential motion parameter.

2.1   Approach

We regard monocular image sequences $I_t \in \mathbb{R}^{m \times n}, t = 0, .., T$, where corresponding pixels between two time steps are encoded by means of the optical flow. For a fixed 2D pixel location s (*seed* pixel) and time t, an '*event*' is fired if the grey value difference between time $t - 1$ and t is above some event threshold T_e:

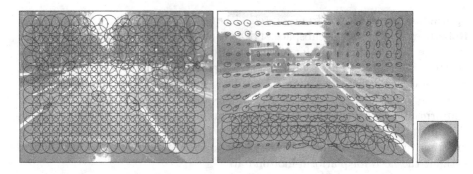

Fig. 1. Learnt flow vectors with associated confidence and color wheel: Sparse flow (blue arrows) and corresponding confidence encoded by means of a (green) covariance error ellipse, at (left) initialisation with maximum uncertainty and (middle) after having processed 24000 frames for sequence GUCar. (right) Color wheel used to visualise direction and magnitude of 2D vectors (cf. [1]). Best viewed in color. (Color figure online)

$$|I_t(\boldsymbol{s}) - I_{t-1}(\boldsymbol{s})| \geq T_e. \tag{1}$$

Next, we identify those pixel locations which show a similar grey value change within time t and $t + 1$. Typically there will be a set of pixels showing a similar event, and without taking further information into account it is in general not possible to identify the single true correspondence between two time steps. Instead we have a set of possibly corresponding pixels which showed a similar event:

$$\Omega_{\boldsymbol{s}_t} = \{\boldsymbol{y} \in I_{t+1} : |I_t(\boldsymbol{s}) - I_{t-1}(\boldsymbol{s})| \geq T_e \tag{2}$$
$$\wedge \quad |(I_{t-1}(\boldsymbol{s}) - I_t(\boldsymbol{y})| < \epsilon \quad \wedge \quad |(I_t(\boldsymbol{s}) - I_{t+1}(\boldsymbol{y})| < \epsilon\},$$

where $\epsilon = 2\sigma$ accounts for the noise standard deviation. The set of possible correspondences per time step are add up in one accumulator array $\boldsymbol{A_s}$ per seed pixel $\boldsymbol{s}$. If nothing is known about the scene layout, the true correspondence may be located at any valid pixel location. Thus, in general the accumulator would need to be of the same size as the image itself. However, the range of typical motion is usually known and it is almost always much smaller than the overall image size. The search area, i.e., the area in which events are matched may therefore be restricted to a window of size $w_x \times w_y$ centred on the regarded seed pixel with $\boldsymbol{A_s} \in \mathbb{R}^{w_x \times w_y}$. As we accumulate correspondence candidates over time, it becomes clear that in general we may only learn the average correspondence relation and thus the average optical flow at pixel location $\boldsymbol{s}$. Imagine a stereo setup where the scene depth does *not* vary. Then the correspondence relation is explained by a disparity map which is constant over time. In this case, the average correspondence coincides with the true disparity. However, given that the scene depth varies, the correspondence relation is given by a time-varying disparity map where correspondences are restricted to lie on the epipolar ray. Given that the scene depth varies, TCA will in general learn parts of the epipolar rays. For similar reasons, the optical flow observed at a specific scene point typically varies such that only the average flow can be learned. TCA is not meant as a competitor to classic stereo or flow algorithms tailored to return instantaneous (per frame) correspondences but may be seen as a prior generator. TCA is an approach to continuously learn and update the distribution of a correspondence relation which allows to guide a higher level process, restrict search areas, or generate confidence information.

2.2 Accumulator Analysis

After a sufficient number of frames have been processed, the accumulator will encode the average correspondence and thus the average optical flow observed within the sequence at location s. We then extract the most likely correspondence m as the location of the accumulator mean and compute a confidence measure as the accumulator covariance matrix C:

$$m = \begin{bmatrix} m_x \\ m_y \end{bmatrix} = \begin{bmatrix} \sum_x x_i \sum_y A_s(x_i, y) \\ \sum_y y_i \sum_x A_s(x, y_i) \end{bmatrix}, \tag{3}$$

$$C = \begin{bmatrix} \sum_x \hat{x}_i^2 \sum_y A_s(x_i, y) & \sum_{x,y} \hat{x}_i \hat{y}_i A_s(x_i, y_i) \\ \sum_{x,y} \hat{x}_i \hat{y}_i A_s(x_i, y_i) & \sum_y \hat{y}_i^2 \sum_x A_s(x, y_i) \end{bmatrix}, \tag{4}$$

where the accumulator is assumed to be normalised to sum to 1 with $\hat{x}_i = x_i - m_x$ and $\hat{y}_i = y_i - m_y$. From an eigenvalue analysis we obtain eigenvectors v_1, v_2 and eigenvalues λ_1, λ_2 with

$$Cv_1 = \lambda_1 v_1, \quad Cv_2 = \lambda_2 v_2, \tag{5}$$

where $\lambda_1 \leq \lambda_2$. The eigenvectors encode the direction of highest and lowest confidence scaled by their associated eigenvalue. The eigenvectors define the principal axes of the 'error ellipse' which will be used in the following to visualise the confidence about a learnt flow vector. In general, the structure of the accumulator content may be (a) scattered, (b) line like or (c) point like which results in (a) a large error ellipse and high uncertainty in all directions, (b) an oriented error ellipse with high confidence along the direction of eigenvector with smaller eigenvalue and (c) a small error ellipse encoding high certainty in all directions.

In order to visualise the confidence for a *dense* flow map, we adopt a color encoding, similar to the color coding of flow vectors (cf. Sect. 3 for details). Regarding the computational complexity, our method has $\mathcal{O}(n)$ complexity in the number of seed pixels and $\mathcal{O}(n^2)$ complexity in the size of the accumulator where the same holds for the memory consumption.

2.3 Instantaneous Image Motion

Besides learning *average* optical flow, we may also estimate *parameters of instantaneous image motion* by applying TCA in a specific manner. Specifically we show, how the yaw rate (rotation about the downward facing Y axis of the camera coordinate system, Z axis towards the image plane) may be inferred by analysing the correspondence samples, i.e., the sets Ω_{s_t} available within two time steps for a specific set of seed pixels.

It is well known that the instantaneous image motion vector $(U(x, y), V(x, y))^T$ of a general rigid 3D scene can be modeled as [11,12]:

$$\begin{pmatrix} U(x,y) \\ V(x,y) \end{pmatrix} = \begin{bmatrix} \frac{\tau_Z x - \tau_X}{Z} - \omega_Y + \omega_Z y - \omega_Y x^2 + \omega_X xy \\ \frac{\tau_Y y - \tau_Y}{Z} + \omega_X - \omega_Z x - \omega_Y xy + \omega_X y^2 \end{bmatrix}, \quad (6)$$

where $(U(x, y), V(x, y))^T$ denotes the image motion vector at location (x, y), $\tau_{\{X,Y,Z\}}$ denote translational velocities in direction X, Y or Z, and $\omega_{\{X,Y,Z\}}$ denote the angular velocities about the three axis respectively, with $x = X/Z$ and $y = Y/Z$. From Eq. (6) we see that the optical flow at any pixel within the image is a superposition of two independent flow fields: a flow field which only depends on the translational velocities and a flow field which only depends on the angular velocities. Consider the case where the camera pitch and roll rates are zero (or sufficiently small), then from Eq. (6) we obtain:

$$\begin{pmatrix} U(x,y) & V(x,y) \end{pmatrix}^T = \begin{bmatrix} \frac{\tau_Z x - \tau_X}{Z} - \omega_Y - \omega_Y x^2 & \frac{\tau_Y y - \tau_Y}{Z} - \omega_Y xy \end{bmatrix}^T. \quad (7)$$

Next, assume that for the translational velocities it holds that $|\tau_{\{X,Y,Z\}}| \ll Z$, then the translational velocities will vanish and we obtain:

$$\begin{pmatrix} U(x,y) & V(x,y) \end{pmatrix}^T = \begin{bmatrix} -\omega_Y - \omega_Y x^2 & -\omega_Y xy \end{bmatrix}^T \quad (8)$$

$$= \begin{bmatrix} -\omega_Y - \omega_Y (\frac{X}{Z})^2 & -\omega_Y \frac{X}{Z}\frac{Y}{Z} \end{bmatrix}^T. \quad (9)$$

From Eq. (9) we see that (scaled) camera yaw corresponds to the observed image motion of pixels where the pixel's corresponding scene point lies at infinity (or sufficiently far away from the camera):

$$\begin{pmatrix} U(x,y) & V(x,y) \end{pmatrix}^T = \begin{bmatrix} -\omega_Y & 0 \end{bmatrix}^T. \quad (10)$$

Now we can infer the current yaw rate based on TCA as follows: We detect and match events for those pixels where the corresponding scene point lies sufficiently far away from the camera. From the above derivations we have that the true correspondence for each pixel lying at infinity is given by $-\omega_y$. We then add up all correspondence sample sets Ω_{s_t} and build the *mother accumulator* A_m for time step $t + 1$. Given that the yaw rate is the dominant image motion, the mother accumulator then shows a distinct peak at the location of the true (but typically scaled) yaw differential. In Sec. 3 we present an approach for selecting pixels at least approximately lying at infinity.

3   Experiments

In this section, we present experimental results of the proposed method and show its applicability for several real world sequences publicly available

Fig. 2. Dense flow and confidence maps: for sequence GUCar after 50000 processed frames. (left) Colour coded dense flow map, (middle) eigen vector corresponding to the smaller and (right) larger eigenvalue of the accumulator's covariance matrix. Colour encoding according to colour wheel (cf. Fig. 1). Best viewed in colour. (Color figure online)

or recorded by us. In all experiments, no ground truth was used; all information has been learnt from scratch. The experiments were performed based on a straight forward **python** implementation. Depending on the computational resources available and the number of seed pixels chosen, the method can operate in real time. In order to recover dense flow fields, the scheme should be applied within a multi scale framework; an initial coarse map is then refined, making use of an optimal accumulator size given by the estimated flow from a previous level. Furthermore the scheme may easily be parallelised. However, for the results presented we make use of a baseline implementation without coarse to fine and/or parallel computations. In the first experiment, we learn dense average flow maps for sequences GUCar, KITTI-Odo, GUOmni and Virat. All sequences are converted to grayscale if needed. Sequence GUCar recorded by our group consists of roughly 50.000 frames with a spatial resolution of 640×480 pixels and a temporal resolution of 30 fps. The event threshold was set to $T_e = 20$ with $\sigma = 3$ and the accumulator size was set to $w_x = w_y = 40$ pixels. Figure 1 shows a subset of the learnt flow vectors at initialisation and after having processed 24000 frames, respectively. The average flow for each pixel is extracted as the coordinates of the mean of its associated accumulator. The location of the mean then encodes the actual flow vector learnt and is visualised as a blue arrow in Fig. 1. With each learnt flow vector, a measure of confidence is provided by the accumulator covariance matrix (cf. Sect. 2.2). The confidence is then visualised as a green error ellipse, defined by the eigenvalues and eigenvectors of the accumulator's covariance matrix. During initialisation, the uncertainty reflected by the ellipse is maximal (Fig. 1 (left)) and becomes smaller as more frames are processed (Fig. 1 (middle)). Figure 2 (left column) shows a dense flow map, learnt after 50000 frames. The direction and magnitude of a flow vector is converted into a color and saturation value respectively, typically given by the 'Middlebury' color wheel (shown in Fig. 1 (right)). In the early learning phase (first few hundred frames), the dense flow learned will usually be noisy and the confidence for large parts of the flow map is low. As the learning continues, the flow map becomes more smooth, the uncertainty decreases and as expected the dense flow map shown in Fig. 2 converges to the expected average flow field observed by a camera moving through a natural street scene. The orientation of the flow vectors in the left half of the map lie within $[90°, 270°]$ while in the right half the orientation lies in $[90°, -90°]$. Note the area where the flow vectors have a low magnitude. This area corresponds to the average focus of expansion [2], i.e., the location where all points seem to emanate. Figure 2 (middle and right column) visualises the colour coded first and second eigenvector of the accumulator's covariance matrix respectively, scaled by the associated eigenvalue. Throughout all figures the colour coded flow vectors are normalised to the maximal possible flow (as given by the accumulator size). Similarly, the confidence maps are normalised as well. From these confidence maps it can be seen that within the area directly in front of the car, the confidence about the learnt flow vector is rather low in all directions. This is to be expected, as this area corresponds to the safety clearance, where most of the time only the homogenous road surface is visible and no events are generated. Highest confidences is attained in the upper half of the image, were most of the events are generated. In Fig. 3 we show results for sequence KITTI-Odo taken from the KITTI benchmark dataset [6] (specifically sequence 00 from the odometry dataset). The sequences contain 4.500 frames with a resolution of 1246×374 pixels recorded with 30 fps. The parameters of

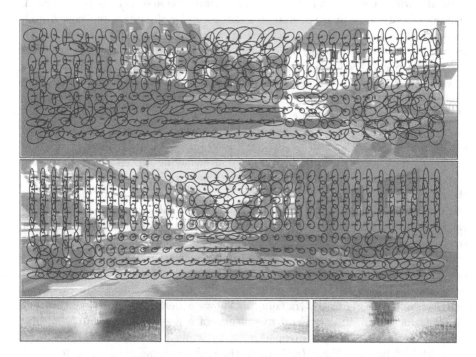

Fig. 3. Learnt flow vectors and associated confidence: Sparse flow and corresponding confidence encoded by means of a covariance error ellipse, learnt after (top) 500 and (middle) 4500 frames for sequence KITTI-00. (bottom) Dense flow map learnt after 4500 frames and associated confidence maps. Best viewed in color and upscaled. (Color figure online)

the method are set as described for sequence GUCar before. From the figures, we can basically draw the same conclusions as before. However, the flow maps are considerably more noisy which is due to the low number of frames available.

Figure 4 (top) shows a learnt dense flow map for sequence GUOmni, recorded by our group. The sequence consists of 12.500 frames with a spatial resolution of 640×480 pixels at 30 fps. The camera is equipped with a fish-eye lens and moves through an indoor office environment. It can be seen, that the proposed method may also be used for non standard camera models. The presented approach may of course be applied to static cameras as well. In Fig. 4 (bottom) we show results for sequence Virat, taken from the Virat data set [14]. Average flow maps for static cameras are of special interest in surveillance scenarios, where typical and abnormal behaviour is to be detected. To summarise, the first experiment shows that average flow maps can be learnt by just looking at the temporal change of single pixels. These flow maps may subsequently be used as a prior for other flow algorithms. Learning over very long image sequences (not large amounts of ground truth!) clearly is in contrast to the still lasting trend in the vision community to solve a specific problem on short sequences or even still images. The results demonstrate that by only looking at the temporal signal of single pixels useful information may be learnt without any supervision.

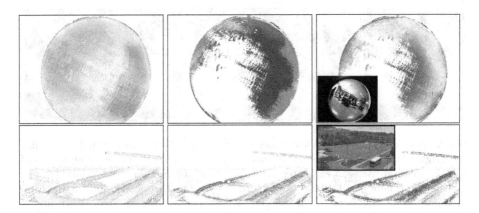

Fig. 4. Dense flow and confidence maps: (top row) (left) Dense flow map learnt after 12500 frames for sequence GUOmni and (middle, right) associated confidence maps (bottom row) Dense flow map learnt after 30000 frames for sequence Virat and associated confidence maps. Best viewed in color. (Color figure online)

3.1   Inferring Instantaneous Motion

Next, we show how instantaneous (differential) image motion can be estimated via TCA as well. Recall from Sect. 2.3 that we may infer the yaw rate from a set of pixels lying at infinity. Pixels at infinity are those for which the average flow is small; they can be determined by first learning the average flow map and the local flow dispersion. However, for the street scenes used in the previous experiment, we can select pixels as follows: We subdivide the image in 4 sectors by two diagonal lines which pass roughly through the focus of expansion. The upper sector can be well used for estimation of the horizontal shift and hence the yaw rate, since the rotational part does not contribute significantly in vertical direction. Figure 5 visualises the selected pixels for some sample images of sequence GUCar, where the car turns left, goes straight and turns right. Figure 5 also shows the associated mother accumulators. It can be seen that left and right turns show up as a distinct peak within the accumulator in the opposite direction. To extract the actual yaw rate, we pool the accumulator (=sum up) vertically to obtain a more robust estimate. When vertical motion is not the dominant motion, or if only a few number of selected pixels show an event, the mother accumulator will be scattered. However, this can easily be detected, e.g. by an eigen value analysis as for the normal accumulators. We found that left and right turns can be detected with high confidence (by means of the accumulator statistics as described), given that the analysis is carried out on a sufficiently large number of active pixels. Forward and backward motion can not directly be read off the mother accumulator, as it will in general be scattered for both types of motion. To summarise, this experiment has shown that TCA can also be used to estimate differential motion.

Fig. 5. Inferring current yaw rate: Car turns left (left) goes straight (middle) and (right) turns right. From pixels within the upper triangle the current yaw rate is to be inferred. At each time step only the pixels showing an event are taken into consideration, here marked blue. At each time step a mother accumulator is build by summing up all Ω_{s_t} from which the current yaw rate can be inferred shown in the lower right part of every image. See text for details. (Color figure online)

4   Conclusion

We demonstrated that *temporal coincidence analysis (TCA)* is able to autonomously learn to 'perceive' and quantify motion without using any of the elaborated techniques currently used in image analysis. The architecture is able to successfully learn the local mean and dispersion of motion maps and can also be used to perform inference on global 'hidden variables' (here: global motion parameters). The method can deal with different camera models in a principled manner. Learning is done completely unsupervised without the need for any ground truth data.

References

1. Baker, S., Scharstein, D., Lewis, J., Roth, S., Black, M.J., Szeliski, R.: A database and evaluation methodology for optical flow. IJCV **92**, 1–31 (2011)
2. Ballard, D.H., Brown, C.M.: Computer Vision. Prentice Hall, Upper Saddle River (1982)
3. Conrad, C., Guevara, A., Mester, R.: Learning multi-view correspondences from temporal coincidences. In: CVPR Workshops (2011)
4. Conrad, C., Mester, R.: Learning relative photometric differences of pairs of cameras. In: Advanced Video and Signal based Surveillance. IEEE (2015)
5. Eisenbach, J., Conrad, C., Mester, R.: A temporal scheme for fast learning of image-patch correspondences in realistic multi-camera setups. In: CVPRW (2013)
6. Geiger, A., Lenz, P., Urtasun, R.: Are we ready for autonomous driving? the KITTI vision benchmark suite. In: CVPR (2012)
7. Grimson, E., Stauffer, C., Romano, R., Lee, L.: Using adaptive tracking to classify and monitor activities in a site. In: CVPR (1998)
8. Herdtweck, C., Curio, C.: Monocular heading estimation in non-stationary urban environment. In: MFI (2012)
9. Horn, B.K., Schunck, B.G.: Determining optical flow. In: AI (1981)
10. Hu, M., Ali, S., Shah, M.: Learning motion patterns in crowded scenes using motion flow field. In: International Conference on Pattern Recognition, pp. 1–5 (2008)
11. Irani, M., Anandan, P.: Video indexing based on mosaic representations. In: Proceedings of IEEE (1998)
12. Longuet-Higgins, H.C., Prazdny, K.: The interpretation of a moving retinal image. Proc. R. Soc. Lond. B **208**, 385–397 (1980). https://doi.org/10.1098/rspb.1980.0057
13. Lucas, B.D., Kanade, T., et al.: An iterative image registration technique with an application to stereo vision. IJCAI **81**, 674–679 (1981)
14. Oh, S., Hoogs, A., Perera, A., et al.: A large-scale benchmark dataset for event recognition in surveillance video. In: CVPR (2011)
15. Roberts, R., Potthast, C., Dellaert, F.: Learning general optical flow subspaces for egomotion estimation and detection of motion anomalies. In: CVPR (2009)
16. Sun, D., Roth, S., Black, M.J.: Secrets of optical flow estimation and their principles. In: CVPR (2010)
17. Sun, D., Roth, S., Lewis, J., Black, M.: Learning optical flow. In: ECCV (2008)
18. Wright, J., Pless, R.: Analysis of persistent motion patterns using the 3D structure tensor. In: Workshops on Application of Computer Vision (2005)

The Fusion of Optical and Orientation Information in a Markovian Framework for 3D Object Retrieval

László Czúni[(⊠)] and Metwally Rashad

University of Pannonia, Veszprém 8200, Hungary
`czuni@almos.uni-pannon.hu`
`http://keplab.mik.uni-pannon.hu`

Abstract. In this paper we introduce a new 3D object retrieval model inspired by some well-known mechanisms of the human brain: viewer-centric recognition, Markovian estimations, and fusion of information originating from the visual and vestibular subsystems. We have built a Hidden Markov Model (HMM) framework where 2D object views correspond to states, observations are coded by compact edge and color sensitive descriptors, and orientation sensors are used to secure temporal inference by estimating transition probabilities between states. Our first evaluation results, over a database of 100 3D objects, are very encouraging: the fast and memory efficient new method outperformed previous models.

Keywords: Object retrieval · Information fusion · HMM Viewer-centric models

1 Introduction and Motivation

We introduce an efficient bio-inspired 3D object retrieval approach which can be implemented with very limited memory and processing power. Our motivation is to use ideas (viewer-centric object models with Markovian inference and information fusion) originating from the operation of the brain but also to avoid the complexity of hierarchical deep neural networks as it would be a direct copy of nature's successful mechanisms. In our research we focus on a relatively simple task: how to recognize/retrieve 3D objects by several 2D views taken from different directions.

Humans have only access to a limited subset of reality due to the limitation of attentional capacity and of sensitivity. As a result our experiences do not replicate the real world but rather create a construction or representation of it with prediction and estimation. One example is the temporal difference (TD) learning algorithm which has received attention in the field of neuroscience a long time ago [16]. TD mechanisms consider that subsequent predictions are correlated in some sense: TD learning adjusts predictions to match other predictions about the future. Evaluation of Markovian processes can be considered

© Springer International Publishing AG 2017
S. Battiato et al. (Eds.): ICIAP 2017 International Workshops, LNCS 10590, pp. 26–36, 2017.
https://doi.org/10.1007/978-3-319-70742-6_3

as a rough approximation of this, moreover Hidden Markov Models are able to make efficient predictions considering the difference between the real world and its sensations with the help of probability functions. How we make representations of uncertainty greatly depends on the integration of data over time. The extent to which past events are used to represent uncertainty seems to vary over the cortex: primary visual cortex responds to rapid perturbations in the environment, while frontal cortices encode the longer term contexts within which these perturbations occur [9].

Information fusion is also very important in the creation of the brain's representations. Several examples for this are the different phenomena of vestibular and visual information co-processing. For example during long-drawn head rotations with the eyes closed, the elasticity of the cupula (a structure in the vestibular system providing the sense of spatial orientation) gradually restores it to its upright position. Thus the drive to the optokinetic response stops (misleadingly informing the brain that there is no motion). When opening the eyes in such situations, the world is seen moving and people feel giddy.

While the exact mechanisms of interaction between the different modalities are not always clear for the researchers, we will fuse orientation and visual information in a viewer-centered object recognition model. In cognitive science the recognition of objects from different views are described by two competing theories: according to the so-called object-centered approach [1] the structural description of simple parts play important role without explicit object representation from the different views. This can be imagined similar to the computer vision algorithms for object recognition with SIFT-like features [12]. In contrary, viewer-centered theory, supported e.g. by [7], suggests that this is done based on matching specific views to a set of templates, which requires explicit viewer-specific object representations.

Convolutional Neural Networks have very strong biological motivation and have been extensively used for image-based recognition, detection, retrieval, and image segmentation. However, their complexity (also energy and memory requirements) is quite large to be applied for real-time image based recognition in embedded or mobile systems. What we knew before and has been shown experimentally in recent developments is that simple approximations to input or internal data representations can still result in satisfactory performance. For example the so called XNOR-Networks, where both the filters and the input to convolutional layers are binary, run 58× faster convolutional operations and show 32× memory savings [15].

Following the above bio-inspired concepts we introduce a retrieval model with the following features:

- it is viewer-centered with the storage of very limited number of 2D views,
- it fuses visual and orientation information,
- it utilizes the inference in temporal sequences of signals (Markovian),
- the relation of observations and hidden model states can be estimated with simple correlations,

- it relies on compact descriptors computed very fast,
- it can be successfully used for real-time video object retrieval with lightweight devices.

There are two main reasons we are not using deep neural network models. First, we can implement the aimed concepts (Markovian inference, information fusion, viewer-centric object models) very efficiently in a HMM framework. Second, we have knowledge of efficient compact descriptors, and can use the orientation information directly in the Markovian model for the temporal support (as explained later), i.e. there is no need for time consuming training and optimization of millions of parameters of the neural structures.

In the next Section we give a short overview of related papers. Then the proposed object views, as hidden states of a Markov model, state transitions, observable features, and the decoding and retrieval steps are defined in consecutive subsections. Section Experiments and Evaluations contains experimental data and analysis followed by Summary.

2   A Brief Overview of Related Papers

Optical object retrieval and recognition is a very large topic with thousands of theoretical articles and applications, now we focus only on some which are closely related to our aims and motivations.

HMMs are often used in different recognition problems such as speech, musical sound, or human activity recognition but we relatively rarely meet them in the recognition of 2D or 3D visual objects. This is natural since ordered sequences of features are needed to construct HMM models. In [10] affine invariant image features are built on the contours of objects, and the sequence of such features are fed to the HMM. This approach is interesting but seemed to be too unnatural to have later followers.

In [5] authors presented an approach for face recognition using Singular Values Decomposition (SVD) to extract relevant face features, and HMMs as classifier. In order to create the HMM model the 2 dimensional face images had to be transformed into 1 dimensional observation sequences. For this purpose each face image was divided into overlapping blocks with the same width as the original image and a given height, and the singular values of these blocks were used as descriptors. A face image was divided into seven distinct horizontal regions: hair, forehead, eyebrows, eyes, nose, mouth and chin forming seven hidden states in the Markov model. While the algorithm was tested on two standard databases, the advantage of the HMM model over other approaches was not discussed.

The method of Torralba et al. [17] seems to be more close to a real-life temporal sequence: HMM was used for place recognition based on the sequences of visual observations of the environment created by a low-resolution camera. It was also investigated how the visual context affects the recognition of objects in complex scenes. There is no doubt that this approach has real cognitive motivation and relevance compared to those above.

Gammeter et al. [8] used accelerometer and magnetic sensor to help the visual recognition of the landscape. Clustered SURF (Speeded Up Robust Features) features were quantized using a vocabulary of visual words, learnt by k-means clustering. For tracking objects the FAST corner detector was combined with sensor tracking. Because of the small storage capacity of the mobile device a server-side service was used to store the necessary information for the algorithm.

It is obvious that video gives much more visual information about 3D objects than 2D projections. Local feature descriptors (like SIFT, FAST, etc.) are often used for view-centered recognition. In [14] the underlying topological structure of an image set was represented as a neighborhood graph of local features. Motion continuity in the query video was exploited for the recognition of 3D objects.

The most similar viewer-centered HMM based 3D object retrieval method to ours was published by Jain et al. [11]. However, there are many differences to our work and many ambiguous details in [11]: it is not clear how the crucial emission and transition probabilities were estimated and also the dimension of the applied image descriptor (13) seems to be too small for real-life applications. The dataset in their tests included only gray-scale CGI without texture and no orientation sensor was used during the recognition.

Our early work, to utilize orientation information for object retrieval, can be found in [3]. Later we modified our method [4] to maximize a fitness function over a sequence of observations, based on the Hough transformation paradigm. While, as we have demonstrated by the above examples, the use of HMMs for object recognition is often a bit unnatural, turning our previous Hough framework to HMM is obvious and is also biologically motivated. As will be shown, our recent HMM model has better hit-rate and smaller complexity and encapsulates the bio-inspired concepts described above.

3   Object Retrieval with HMM

To achieve object retrieval will need to build HMM models for all elements of the set of objects (M). Then, based on observations, we find the most probable state sequence for all objects models. The state sequence among these, which is the most similar to the observation sequence, will belong to the object being retrieved.

3.1   Object Views as States in a Markov Model

Let $S = \{S_1, \cdots, S_N\}$ denote the set of N hidden states of a model. In each t index step this model is described as being in one $q_t \in S$ state, where $t = 1, \cdots, T$.

In our approach the states can be considered as the 2D views (or the average of some neighboring views) of a given object model. This can be easily imagined as a camera is targeting towards and object from a relative elevation and relative azimuth. The number of possible states should be kept low, otherwise the state transition matrix ($\mathbf{A}$) would contain too small numbers and finding the most probable state sequence would be too unstable. On the other hand, small number of states would mean that quite different views of some objects should be represented by the same descriptors, resulting in decreased similarity of model these views and actual test observations. Thus it is easy to see that the generation of states should be designed carefully. Often Gaussian mixtures are used to combine the views of similar directions. Now we use static subdivision of the circle of 360°, into 2, 4, 6, and 8 uniform parts with 180°, 90°, 60°, and 45° correspondingly, with surprisingly good results as given in Sect. 4.

We define the initial state probabilities $\pi = \{\pi_i\}_{1 \leq i \leq N}$ based on the orientation range of states:

$$\pi_i = P(q_1 = S_i) = \frac{\alpha(S_i)}{360} \tag{1}$$

where $\alpha(S_i)$ is the size of orientation aperture of state S_i given in degree.

3.2 State Transitions

Between two steps the model can undergo a change of states according to a set of transition probabilities associated with each state pairs. In general the transition probabilities are:

$$a_{ij} = P(q_t = S_j | q_{t-1} = S_i) \tag{2}$$

where i and j indices refer to states of the HMM, $a_{ij} \geq 0$, and for a given state $\sum_{j=1}^{N} a_{ij} = 1$ holds. The transition probability matrix is denoted by $\mathbf{A} = \{a_{ij}\}_{1 \leq i,j \leq N}$.

To build a Markov model means learning its parameters (π, $\mathbf{A}$, and emission probabilities introduced later) by examining typical examples. However, our case is special: the probability of going from one state to an other severely depends on the user's behavior, interest and also on the frame rate of the camera. Thus we can not follow the traditional way, to use the Baum-Welch algorithm for parameter estimation based on several training samples, but can directly compute transition probabilities based on geometric probability as follows.

First define $\Delta_{t-1,t}$ as the orientation difference between two successive observations:

$$\Delta_{t-1,t} = \alpha(o_t) - \alpha(o_{t-1}). \tag{3}$$

Now define R_i as the aperture interval belonging to state S_i by borderlines:

$$R_i = [S_i^{min}, S_i^{max}[. \tag{4}$$

The back projected aperture interval is the range of orientation from where the previous observation should originate:

$$L_j = [S_j^{min} - \Delta_{t-1,t}, S_j^{max} - \Delta_{t-1,t}[. \tag{5}$$

Now we have arrived to estimate the transition probability by the geometrical probability concept applied on the intersection of L_j and R_j:

$$a_{ij} = P(q_t = S_j | q_{t-1} = S_i) = \frac{\alpha(L_j \cap R_i)}{\alpha(L_j)}. \tag{6}$$

Please see Fig. 1 for illustration.

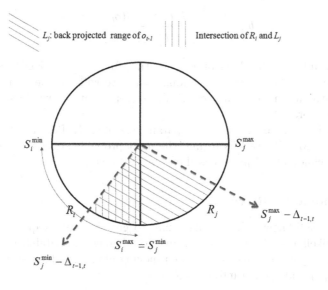

Fig. 1. Geometrical interpretation of transition probabilities.

3.3   Hidden States Approximated by Observations with Compact Descriptors

The appearance of objects may significantly differ from those made during model generation under controlled circumstances. The changes in illumination, color balance, viewing angle, geometric distortion and image noise can result in heavily distorted feature descriptors. Thus observations only resemble the descriptors of the model states. Let $O = \{o_1, o_2, \cdots, o_T\}$ denote the set of observation sequence. The emission probability of a particular o_t observation for state s_i is defined as

$$b_i(o_t) = P(o_t | q_t = S_i) \tag{7}$$

In [4] we have shown that the CEDD (Color and Edge Directivity Descriptor) [2] is a robust low dimensional descriptor for object recognition. Being area based, pixels are classified into one of 6 texture classes (non-edge, vertical, horizontal, 45 and 135° diagonal, and non-directional edges). For each texture class a (normalized and quantized) 24 bin color histogram is generated, each bin representing colors obtained by the division of the HSV color space, resulting in feature vectors of dimension 144 (6×24). The similarity of CEDD vectors is computed by the Tanimoto coefficient:

$$T(e_i, c_j) = \frac{e_i^T c_j}{e_i^T e_i + c_j^T c_j - e_i^T c_j} \tag{8}$$

where e_i^T is the transpose vector of the query descriptor and c_i denotes the descriptors of object views. Rotational invariance can be achieved as given in [3]. Now Eq. 7 can be rewritten as:

$$b_i(o_t) = \frac{T(C(S_i), C(o_t))}{\sum_{j=1}^{N} T(C(S_j), C(o_t))} \tag{9}$$

where C stands for the descriptor generating function of CEDD. Since each model state can cover a large directional range we will use the average CEDD vector, of available model samples within, to represent the whole state with a single descriptor.

Now we have the complete set of parameters of all HMMs denoted by $\lambda_k = (\mathbf{A}, b, \pi)$, $k \in M$. The task is to find the most probable state sequence $\hat{S}_k$, for all possible candidate objects, based on observations.

3.4 Decoding for Retrieval

We use the well-known Viterbi algorithm to get the state sequence with the maximum likelihood. The variable δ_t gives the highest probability of producing observation sequence $o_1, o_2, \cdots, o_t$ when moving along a hidden state sequence $q_1, q_2, \cdots, q_{t-1}$ and getting into $q_t = S_i$, i.e.

$$\delta_t(i) = \max P(q_1, q_2, \cdots, q_t = S_i, o_1, o_2, \cdots, o_t | \lambda) \tag{10}$$

It can be calculated inductively as

1. Initialization:
$$\delta_1(i) = \pi_i b_i(o_1), \quad 1 \leq i \leq N \tag{11}$$

2. Recursion:
$$\delta_{t+1}(j) = b_j(o_{t+1}) \max_i [a_{ij} \delta_t(i)], \quad 1 \leq j \leq N \tag{12}$$

Finally, we can choose the most probable state $\hat{i}$ ending at T:

$$\hat{i} = arg \max_i [\delta_T(i)] \tag{13}$$

To achieve object retrieval we have to find the most probable state sequence $\hat{S}_k$ with the above steps for all possible candidate objects. Now, to select the winner object, we have to compare the observations with the most probable state sequence:

$$\hat{k} = arg \max_{\forall k \in M} \left(\frac{\sum_{i=1}^{N} T(C(o_i), C(\hat{S}_{k,i}))}{N} \right) \tag{14}$$

4 Experiments and Evaluations

4.1 Test Dataset

The COIL-100 dataset [13] includes 100 different objects; 72 images of each object were taken at pose intervals of 5°. We evaluated retrieval with clear and heavily distorted queries using Gaussian noise and motion blur. The *imnoise* function of Matlab, with standard deviation $sd = 0.012$, was used to generate

Fig. 2. First three lines: clear samples from COIL-100. 4th line: example queries loaded with Gaussian additive noise. 5th line: example queries loaded with motion blur.

additive Gaussian noise (GN) while motion blur (MB) was made by *fspecial* with parameters $len = 15$, and angle $\theta = 20°$. Some examples of the queries are shown in Fig. 2.

For different tests different numbers (2, 4, 6, 8) of hidden states were generated by equally dividing the full circle. Each state was represented with its average CEDD descriptor vector.

To estimate the relative orientation of the camera we used the same built in IMU (Inertial Measurement Unit) sensor as in [4] with around 4.5° average absolute error with a 5.25° variance. The evaluation of our method with textured and varying backgrounds is for future work.

4.2   Hit-Rate

The hit-rate of retrieval is measured by taking the average of 10 experiments with all 100 objects with randomly generated queries (the orientation angle of subsequent queries were increased monotonically). As shown in Fig. 3 for different quality queries, as the number of queries increases the hit-rate increases monotonically. It is also true that higher number of states gives better results. We tested no more states than 8, where it reached the maximum performance in most cases.

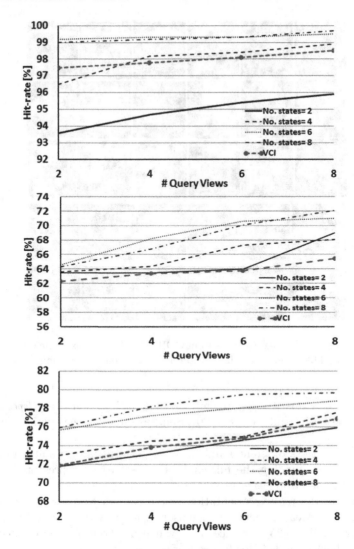

Fig. 3. First graph: average hit-rate with clear samples from COIL-100. Second graph: queries loaded with Gaussian additive noise. Third graph: queries loaded with motion blur.

For comparison with the method of [4] we included the best results of the Voting Candidates algorithm denoted by VCI. There is an obvious 2–6% gain over VCI observable. Please note, that the same visual descriptors and orientation sensor was used by VCI in previous tests.

4.3 Running Time and Memory Requirements

Tests were run on a Samsung SM-T311 tablet equipped with Android 4.2.2 Jelly Bean, 1 GB RAM, and ARM Cortex A9 Dual-Core 1.5 GHz Processor. No code optimization or parallelism was carried out and only the CPU was used during calculations. As given in Table 1 even for 8 queries the whole processing chain is within 1 second on the specified mobile computing hardware. This is a fraction of the complexity of VCI [4].

The advantage of using compact descriptors is the very limited memory requirement of object models. A CEDD descriptor occupies 144 Bytes in memory and orientation can be stored in 4 Bytes. For 100 objects and 8 states we need to store roughly 120 KB ($100 \times 8 \times 148$ Bytes).

Table 1. Running times in seconds for the retrieval of one object from 100.

Phase	Number of query views (N_f^q)			
	2	4	6	8
CEDD generation	0.08	0.16	0.24	0.32
HMM evaluations	0.11	0.15	0.18	0.23
SUM	0.19	0.31	0.42	0.55

5 Summary

The main purpose and contribution of our paper is twofold:

- building a bio-inspired object retrieval framework with Markovian inference and multimodal information fusion in a viewer-centric model, and
- showing that its implementation is robust and resource efficient to be used in mobile devices.

We presented our first results over a dataset of 100 3D objects with 7200 views using clear and noisy queries. While results are better than with our previous model, still there is a lot to do: we are developing a clustering technique to build optimal states instead of the uniformly distributed states and should work also on automatic object segmentation and tracking.

Acknowledgements. The work and publication of results have been supported by the Hungarian Research Fund, grant OTKA K 120367 and by the framework of Széchenyi 2020 Programme, within project EFOP-3.6.1-16-2016-00015.

References

1. Biederman, I.: Recognition-by-components: a theory of human image understanding. Psychol. Rev. **94**(2), 115 (1987)
2. Chatzichristofis, S.A., Boutalis, Y.S.: Accurate image retrieval based on compact composite descriptors and relevance feedback information. Int. J. Pattern Recogn. Artif. Intell. **24**, 207–244 (2010)
3. Czúni, L., Metwally, R.: View centered video-based object recognition for lightweight devices. In: International Conference on Systems, Signals and Image Processing (IWSSIP), pp. 1–4 (2016)
4. Czúni, L., Metwally, R.: The use of IMUs for video object retrieval in lightweight devices. J. Vis. Commun. Image Represent. **48**, 30–42 (2017)
5. Dinkova, P., Georgieva, P., Milanova, M.: Face recognition using singular value decomposition and Hidden Markov Model. In: 16th WSEAS International Conference on Mathematical Methods, Computational Techniques and Intelligent Systems (MAMECTIS 2014), pp. 144–149 (2014)
6. Edelman, S., Blthoff, H.H.: Orientation dependence in the recognition of familiar and novel views of three-dimensional objects. Vis. Res. **32**(12), 2385–2400 (1992)
7. Fang, F., He, S.: Viewer-centered object representation in the human visual system revealed by viewpoint aftereffects. Neuron **45**(5), 793–800 (2005)
8. Gammeter, S., Gassmann, A., Bossard, L., Quack, T., Van Gool, L.: Server-side object recognition and client-side object tracking for mobile augmented reality. In: 2010 IEEE Computer Society Conference on Computer Vision and Pattern Recognition Workshops (CVPRW), pp. 1–8 (2010)
9. Harrison, L., Bestmann, S., Rosa, M.J., Penny, W., Green, G.G.: Time scales of representation in the human brain: weighing past information to predict future events. Front. Hum. Neurosci. **5**, 37 (2011)
10. Hornegger, J., Niemann, H., Paulus, D., Schlottke, G.: Object recognition using hidden Markov models. Pattern Recogn. Pract. IV: Multiple Paradigms Comp. Stud. Hybrid Syst. **16**, 37–44 (1994)
11. Jain, Y.K., Singh, R.K.: Efficient view based 3-D object retrieval using Hidden Markov Model. 3D Res. **4**(4), 5 (2013)
12. Lowe, D.G.: Object recognition from local scale-invariant features. In: The Proceedings of the Seventh IEEE International Conference on Computer Vision, vol. 2, pp. 1150–1157 (1999)
13. Nene, S.A., Nayar, S.K., Murase, H.: Columbia object image library (COIL-100), Technical report CUCS (1996)
14. Noor, H., Mirza, S. H., Sheikh, Y., Jain, A., Shah, M.: Model generation for video-based object recognition. In: Proceedings of the 14th ACM International Conference on Multimedia, pp. 715–718 (2006)
15. Rastegari, M., Ordonez, V., Redmon, J., Farhadi, A.: XNOR-Net: ImageNet classification using binary convolutional neural networks. In: Leibe, B., Matas, J., Sebe, N., Welling, M. (eds.) ECCV 2016. LNCS, vol. 9908, pp. 525–542. Springer, Cham (2016). https://doi.org/10.1007/978-3-319-46493-0_32
16. Schultz, W., Dayan, P., Montague, P.R.: A neural substrate of prediction and reward. Science **275**(5306), 1593–1599 (1997)
17. Torralba, A., Murphy, K.P., Freeman, W.T., Rubin, M.A.: Context-based vision system for place and object recognition. In: Proceedings of Ninth IEEE International Conference on Computer Vision, vol. 1, pp. 273–280 (2003)

Modelling of the Poggendorff Illusion via Sub-Riemannian Geodesics in the Roto-Translation Group

B. Franceschiello[1(✉)], A. Mashtakov[2], G. Citti[3], and A. Sarti[1]

[1] Center of Mathematics, CNRS—EHESS, Paris, France
benedetta.franceschiello@gmail.com, alessandro.sarti@ehess.fr
[2] CPRC, Program Systems Institute of RAS, Pereslavl-Zalessky, Russia
alexey.mashtakov@gmail.com
[3] Department of Mathematics, University of Bologna, Bologna, Italy
giovanna.citti@unibo.it

Abstract. We present a neuro-mathematical model for the well-known Poggendorff illusion, where an illusory contour appears as a geodesic in some given metric, induced in the primary visual cortex V1 by a visual stimulus. Our model extends the cortical based model by Citti and Sarti of perceptual completion in the roto-translation space SE(2), where the functional architecture and neural connectivity of V1 of mammalians is modelled as principal fiber bundle of SE(2) equipped with a sub-Riemannian (SR) metric. We extend the model by taking into account a presence of a visual stimulus (data adaptivity), which is done by including an appropriate external cost modulating the SR-metric. Perceptual curves appear as geodesics, that we compute via SR-Fast Marching.

1 Introduction

In this paper, we present a neuro-mathematical model for the Poggendorff illusion, a well-known geometrical optical illusion [14,33,34], in which the presence of the central bar induces a misalignment of an oblique transversal [10,31]. See Fig. 1, left. Our interest is to provide a model that takes into account the neurophysiology of the visual process, starting from the investigation of Hubel and Wiesel [19]. They discovered the hypercolumnar structure of the primary visual cortex V1, meaning that for each point of the retina a whole set of cells in V1 sensitive to all possible orientations (hypercolumn) spikes. This structure induced a great interest among scientists from many communities: first neuromathematical model for the functionality of V1 of mammalians have been presented in [2,6,18,21,25].

We base our model on [6], where the functional architecture and neural connectivity of V1 is modelled as a principal fiber bundle of the roto-translation space SE(2) equipped with a sub-Riemannian (SR) metric. In particular, the latter provides a justified model of perceptual completion through surfaces, ruled in geodesics. As a consequence, an illusory contour appears as a geodesic in the

© Springer International Publishing AG 2017
S. Battiato et al. (Eds.): ICIAP 2017 International Workshops, LNCS 10590, pp. 37–47, 2017.
https://doi.org/10.1007/978-3-319-70742-6_4

metric defined in the cortex. In this work, we propose a new SR-metric in SE(2), with a neuro-physiological basis and directly induced by data-adaptivity to a visual stimulus. The polarized SR metric obtained in this way is presumably responsible for the misperception in such type of illusions. In particular, illusory curves arise as geodesics of the considered metric.

We compute globally optimal geodesics (length-minimizers) via SR Fast-Marching(SR-FM) [28], a fast accurate numerical method for solving SR-eikonal system. The solution is a SR distance map and minimizers are recovered through back-tracking on it. We show that illusory contours are well approximated by length-minimizers of SE(2), meaning that the perceptual phenomena is naturally explained by the geometry of V1. This hypothesis is verified qualitatively for the Poggendorff illusion in Sect. 4.1.

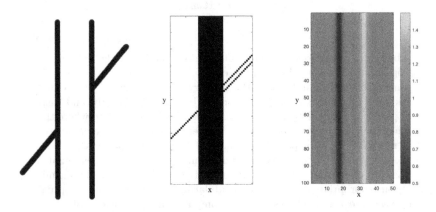

Fig. 1. Left: The Poggendorff illusion: a transversal line, obstructed by a surface, appears to be misaligned. **Center:** the initial stimulus with a second transversal corresponding to the perceptual completion. **Right:** A level set of $\mathcal{C}(x,y,\theta)$ for $\theta = 0$.

2 Preliminaries

2.1 Gabor Filters

The visual process is the result of several retinal and cortical mechanisms which act on the visual signal. The retina is the first part of the visual system responsible for the transmission of the signal, which passes through the Lateral Geniculate Nucleus and arrives in the visual cortex, where it is processed. The receptive field (RF) of a cortical neuron is the portion of the retina which the neuron reacts to, and the receptive profile (RP) $\psi(\chi)$ is the function that models its activation when a stimulus is applied to a point $\chi = (\chi_1, \chi_2)$ of the retinal plane. Let us notice that $\chi = (\chi_1, \chi_2)$ denotes the local portion of the retina, centered at $\eta = (x, y)$, to which the neuron reacts to, while $\eta = (x, y)$ refers to the global coordinates system of the retina $\mathbb{R}^2$. Simple cells of V1 are sensitive to position and orientation of the contrast gradient of an image. Their properties have been experimentally described by De Angelis in [11]. Considering a basic geometric model, the set of simple cells RPs can be obtained via translation of vector $\eta = (x, y)$ and rotation of angle θ from a unique mother profile $\psi_0(\chi)$. As pointed out by Daugmann in [9] and Jones and Palmer in [20], Gabor filters are a good model of receptive profiles and they provide a good estimation of the spiking responses. In our contribution, odd part of Gabor filters are employed to detect orientation and polarity of contours and to identify the presence of surfaces. A mother Gabor filter is given by

$$\psi_0(\chi) = \psi_0(\chi_1, \chi_2) = \frac{\alpha}{2\pi\sigma^2} e^{\frac{-(\chi_1^2 + \alpha^2 \chi_2^2)}{2\sigma^2}} e^{\frac{2i\chi_2}{\lambda}}, \tag{1}$$

where $\lambda > 0$ is the spatial wavelength of the cosine factor, $\alpha > 0$ is the spatial aspect ratio and $\sigma > 0$ is the standard deviation of the Gaussian envelope. Translations and rotations can be expressed as:

$$A_{(x,y,\theta)}(\chi) = \begin{pmatrix} x \\ y \end{pmatrix} + \begin{pmatrix} \cos\theta & -\sin\theta \\ \sin\theta & \cos\theta \end{pmatrix} \begin{pmatrix} \chi_1 \\ \chi_2 \end{pmatrix}. \tag{2}$$

Hence a general RP can be expressed as:

$$\psi_{(x,y,\theta)}(\chi_1, \chi_2) = \psi_0(A_{(x,y,\theta)}^{-1}(\chi_1, \chi_2)).$$

2.2   Output of Receptive Profiles

The retinal plane is identified with $\mathbb{R}^2$, see [6]. When a visual stimulus of intensity $I(x, y) : M \subset \mathbb{R}^2 \to \mathbb{R}^+$, activates the retinal layer of photoreceptors, the neurons whose RFs intersect M spike and their spike frequencies $O(x, y, \theta)$ can be modelled (taking into account just linear contributions) as the integral of the signal I with the set of Gabor filters. Indeed we assume the treated visual stimulus I to be integrable, i.e. $I \in L^1(\mathbb{R}^2)$. The expression for this output is:

$$O(x, y, \theta) = \int_M I(\chi_1, \chi_2)\, \psi_{(x,y,\theta)}(\chi_1, \chi_2)\, d\chi_1 d\chi_2. \tag{3}$$

In the right hand side of the equation, the integral of the signal with the real and imaginary part of the Gabor filter is expressed. These last model two families of simple cells which have different shapes, hence they detect different features.

2.3   Sub-Riemannian Structure on SE(2)

The Lie group SE(2) of planar roto-translations is identified with the coupled space of positions and orientations $\mathbb{R}^2 \times S^1$, and for each $\eta = (x, y, \theta)$, $\eta' = (x', y', \theta') \in \mathbb{R}^2 \times S^1$ one has left multiplication

$$L_\eta \eta' = (x' \cos\theta + y' \sin\theta + x, -x' \sin\theta + y' \cos\theta + y, \theta' + \theta). \tag{4}$$

Via the push-forward $(L_\eta)_*$ one gets the left-invariant frame $\{X_1, X_2, X_3\}$ from the Lie-algebra basis $\{A_1, A_2, A_3\} = \{\partial_x|_e, \partial_\theta|_e, \partial_y|_e\}$ at the unity $e = (0, 0, 0)$:

$$X_1 = \cos\theta\,\partial_x + \sin\theta\,\partial_y, \quad X_2 = \partial_\theta, \quad X_3 = -\sin\theta\,\partial_x + \cos\theta\,\partial_y. \tag{5}$$

A SR manifold is given by a triple $(\mathrm{SE}(2), \Delta, \mathcal{G})$, where Δ is a subbundle of the tangent bundle, and $\mathcal{G}$ is a metric defined on Δ. For a general introduction to SR-geometry see [24]. If we define the horizontal distribution $\Delta = \mathrm{span}(X_1, X_2)$, the length of a curve $\gamma : [0, T] \mapsto \mathrm{SE}(2)$ whose derivative belongs to the distribution Δ is defined as

$$\dot\gamma(t) = u_1(t)\,X_1|_{\gamma(t)} + u_2(t)\,X_2|_{\gamma(t)}, \quad l(\gamma) := \int_0^T \sqrt{\mathcal{G}_{\gamma(t)}(\dot\gamma(t), \dot\gamma(t))}\,dt \tag{6}$$

Here $\mathcal{G}$ is a diagonal metric, represented in the form $\mathcal{G} = \mathrm{diag}(\frac{1}{C}, \frac{1}{C})$, with respect to the chosen basis $\{X_1, X_2\}$. The Riemannian approximation of $\mathcal{G}$ is $\mathcal{G}^\epsilon$, formally defined over $T\mathrm{SE}(2)$, with respect to the basis $\{X_1, X_2, X_3\}$. C is a strictly positive function, called external cost. In this framework, given a starting point η_0 and a terminal point η_1, the geodesic problem is to find a Lipschitzian curve γ with $\dot\gamma \in \Delta$ almost everywhere on an unknown interval $[0, T]$ with controls $u_1, u_2 : [0, T] \to \mathbb{R}$ in $L^\infty[0, T]$ that minimizes the distance between the two given points [24]:

$$d(\eta_0, \eta_1) = \min_{\substack{\gamma \in \mathrm{Lip}([0, T], \mathrm{SE}(2)), \\ \dot\gamma \in \Delta|_\gamma, \ \gamma(0) = \eta_0, \ \gamma(T) = \eta_1}} l(\gamma). \tag{7}$$

SR-geodesics and their application to image analysis were also studied in [4, 17, 22]. For explicit formulas of SR-geodesics in $\mathrm{SE}(2)$ in the particular case of uniform external cost $C = 1$, see [27]. One of the most efficient method to compute geodesics in the Euclidean setting is Fast-Marching, introduced by Sethian in [30]. The method allows to compute a distance map, viscosity solution (in the sense by [7,8]) of the eikonal equation, which in the SR setting has the following expression:

$$\begin{cases} \|\nabla_{\mathcal{G}} W(\eta)\|_{\mathcal{G}} = 1 \text{ for } \eta \neq e, \\ W(e) = 0. \end{cases} \tag{8}$$

The fast-marching method has been extended in the case of Riemannian metric by Mirebeau, [23], and in [3] was developed in the $\mathrm{SE}(2)$ equipped with a SR metric, with arbitrary external cost. The theoretical counterpart for viscosity solution of the Eikonal equation in the sub-Riemmanian case can be found in [12]. In the current study we use method [3] to compute geodesics. It is based on Riemannian approximation of SR-structure. To compute the minimizers, a Riemannian limit [15] is applied, where d is approximated by Riemannian distance d^ϵ induced by a Riemannian metric $\mathcal{G}^\epsilon = \mathrm{diag}(\frac{1}{C}, \frac{1}{C}, \frac{1}{C\epsilon^2})$, for $0 < \epsilon \ll 1$, and then the SR gradient $\nabla_{\mathcal{G}} W(\eta) = C(\eta)\left(X_1 W(\eta)\,X_1|_\eta + X_2 W(\eta)\,X_2|_\eta\right)$ is used to find geodesics via steepest descent on $W(\eta) := d^\epsilon(e, \eta)$.

In particular, in [3] it was shown that if $\eta_1 \neq e$ be chosen such that there exists a unique minimizing geodesic $\gamma_\epsilon : [0, T] \to \mathrm{SE}(2)$ of $d^\epsilon(e, \eta_1)$ for $\epsilon \geq 0$ sufficiently small, that does not contain conjugate points (i.e. the differential of the exponential map of the Hamiltonian system is non-degenerate along γ_ϵ, cf. [1]), then $\gamma_0(t)$ is given by $\gamma_0(t) = \gamma_b(T - t)$ and the backtracking equation writes as:

$$\begin{cases} \dot{\gamma}_b(t) = -\nabla_{\mathcal{G}} W(\gamma_b(t)), \quad t \in [0, T] \\ \gamma_b(0) = \eta_1, \end{cases} \tag{9}$$

with $W(\eta)$ the viscosity solution of the eikonal system (8).

3 Neuro-Mathematical Model for the Poggendorff Illusion

3.1 Perceptual Curves as SR-length Minimizers

The Poggendorff illusion consists in an apparent misalignment of two collinear, oblique, transversals separated by a rectangular surface (Fig. 1, left). Psychological elements contributing to this misperception have been presented in [10, 26, 31]. It is largely accepted that cortical connectivity propagates the output of the cells $O(x, y, \theta)$, defined in (3), through the metric of the cortex, and is responsible for visual completion and appearance of illusory contours [6]. First model of boundary completion in a contact structure has been presented in [25]. As proved in [5, 29], cortical mechanisms of completion induces minimal surfaces ruled in geodesics. Hence it is possible to look for an illusory contour as minimizer of the geodesic problem in SE(2) with a SR metric. Here we develop the idea that the metric is modulated by the output of the cells $O(x, y, \theta)$ induced by the presence of a stimulus $I(x, y)$: cells already activated by the output are more sensitive to cortical propagation. In this way we can define a polarizing term which will be maxima is correspondence of edges of the visual stimulus:

$$\mathcal{C}(x, y, \theta) = 1 + \mathrm{Im}(O(x, y, \theta)). \tag{10}$$

Imaginary part of the output corresponds to the response of Odd Gabor filters, responsible for detecting polarity of a surface in an initial stimulus. Polarity means that contours with the same orientation but opposite contrast are referred to opposite angles. In the Poggendorff illusion (1, left) the contribution of odd Gabor receptive profiles, responsible for the detection of surfaces, indeed plays a role. For this reason we assume that the orientation θ takes values in $[-\pi, \pi)$. Furthermore the contribution of odd receptive profiles over a straight line is null. Then the inverse of the metric $\mathcal{G}$ in Sect. 2.3, polarized by the output of odd simple cells and expressed in Euclidean coordinates, is given by the following:

$$\mathcal{G}^{-1}(x, y, \theta) = \mathcal{C}(x, y, \theta) \begin{pmatrix} \cos^2 \theta & \sin \theta \cos \theta & 0 \\ \sin \theta \cos \theta & \sin^2 \theta & 0 \\ 0 & 0 & 1 \end{pmatrix}, \tag{11}$$

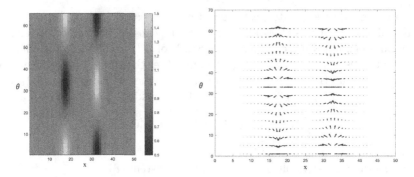

Fig. 2. Left: Representation of a section of $(x, y, \theta, \mathcal{C}(x, y, \theta))$, graph of $\mathcal{C}(x, y, \theta)$, for y fixed. $\mathcal{C}(x, y, \theta)$ is the output positively shifted of odd receptive profiles of simple cells. $\mathcal{C}(x, y, \theta)$ is constant along y. **Right:** $\nabla \mathcal{C}(x, y, \theta)$ is visualized in correspondence of the contours of the central bar, projected onto the (x, θ) plane. We represent x, and θ component of $\nabla \mathcal{C}$, since the y component vanishes.

where $\mathcal{C}(x, y, \theta)$ is given by (10). Let us also observe that the analysis of Fig. 1 (center) can be reduced to the processing of a stimulus in which we neglect the contribution of $\mathcal{C}(x, y, \theta)$ over the entry trasversals. These last are employed to recover θ boundary condition for the experiments. The resulting idea is that the metric mainly depends on the vertical bar and the perceptual curves are obtained as geodesics of the polarized metric (11).

3.2 Implementation

In order to test the model, first the convolution of the initial image with a bank of odd Gabor filters is performed. A response $\text{Im}(O)$ is produced, corresponding to the polarization of our SR metric, which is shifted to positive values $\mathcal{C}(x, y, \theta)$ and used as weight for the connectivity (Fig. 2, left). The SR geodesic that solves (7) is obtained in two steps: 1) computation of the distance map by solving (8) via SR-FM, 2) computation of the geodesic by steepest descent (9). In such a way, we construct a metric in $\mathbb{R}^2 \times S^1$, Riemannian approximation of the SR metric, weighted by external cost $\mathcal{C}(x, y, \theta)$. When switching from image coordinates to mathematical coordinates one should take care of correctly evaluating ξ, which represents the anisotropy between the two horizontal direction, $\xi \Delta x = \Delta \theta$, where $\Delta x, \Delta \theta$ are the discretization steps along x and θ. Then equation (11), adding the Riemannian approximation of the metric, becomes:

$$(\mathcal{G}^\epsilon)^{-1}(x, y, \theta) = \mathcal{C}(x, y, \theta) \begin{pmatrix} \xi^{-2}(\cos^2\theta + \epsilon^2\sin^2\theta) & \xi^{-2}(1-\epsilon^2)\sin\theta\cos\theta & 0 \\ \xi^{-2}(1-\epsilon^2)\sin\theta\cos\theta & \xi^{-2}(\sin^2\theta + \epsilon^2\cos^2\theta) & 0 \\ 0 & 0 & 1 \end{pmatrix}.$$

where ϵ is a parameter of Riemannian approximation (note $\epsilon = 0$ in SR-case). In the experiments we set $\epsilon = 0.1$. As was shown in [28], this value is taken sufficiently small to give an accurate approximation of the SR-case.

4   Results

In this section we discuss the results obtained through the method presented in Sect. 3.1 and implemented in Sect. 3.2.

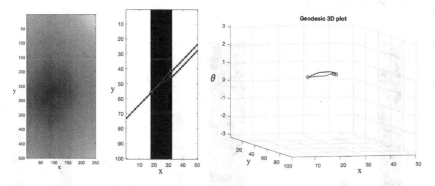

Fig. 3. From left to right: (1) minimum of distance map $W(\eta)$ from the boundary value condition (initial seed) of Eq. 8, along the direction θ, computed through SR-Fast-Marching. (2): 2D projection of the computed geodesics. The perceptual curve is blue, the actual completion of the left side transversal is the red curve. (3): 3D plot of the computed geodesics. (Color figure online)

4.1   Poggendorff Simulation and Comparison with Quantitative Psychophysical Results

Manipulating the elements of Poggendorff to understand how to magnify the illusory phenomenon has been done in many works [10,32]. In [32], the authors performed psychophysical experiments to obtain quantitative measures of the magnitude of the illusion: the illusory effects increased linearly with increasing separation between the parallels as well as increasing the width of the obtuse angle formed by the transversal. Here we consider odd Gabor filters with the following values: $\alpha = 1.5$, $\theta \in [-\pi, \pi]$ (65 values), $\sigma \in \{2, 4\}$ (pixels), $\frac{\sigma}{\lambda} = 2$. This means that for each point of the image (of dimension 50×100 pixels) we took 65×2 receptive profiles. The scale parameter σ is chosen in relationship with the mentioned image resolution. In this example we took the mean between the filter responses for $\sigma = 2$ and for $\sigma = 4$. As initial test we chose $\theta = \pi/4$ and width = 15 pixels, see Fig. 3 (center): the SR-length of the red curve is 2.0480 (correct transversal), and the SR-length of the blue curve is 1.8094 (perceptual completion). The shortest curves implemented through this model are the perceptual ones. Then we tested the following widths for the central surfaces, 15, 25, 9 pixels (see Fig. 4) and the following angles for the transversals $\theta = \pi/4, \pi/10, \pi/2$. Keeping fixed the width of the bar, we varied the angle of the transversal, to create an increased obtuse angle effect ($\theta = \pi/10$ and a non illusory effect ($\theta = \pi/2$). In Fig. 4 (left), a 2D projection of computed geodesics for transversal oriented at $\theta = \pi/2$ is presented. In this case no illusion is shown and the geodesic is a straight line. In the center a 2D representation of the correct transversal (red one), called *actual geodesic*, and the *perceptual* one (blue) is shown, for $\theta = \pi/4$ and width = 25 pixels. Right, same 2D plot for $\theta = \pi/4$ and width = 9 pixels.

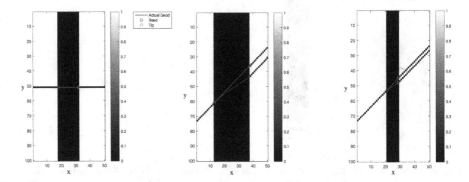

Fig. 4. From left to right: 2D projection of the experiment for $\theta = \pi/2$ and central width = 15 pixels. Experiment for $\theta = \pi/4$ and central width = 25 pixels, 2D projection. Right, $\theta = \pi/4$ and central width = 9 pixels. (Color figure online)

Discussion. In this paragraph we show a table reporting the collected data concerning the SR lengths of the computed curve. It refers to the change of length varying the widths and angles, underlining the observed phenomena.

Type of curve	Width = 9 pixels	Width = 15 pixels	Width = 25 pixels
Percep. curve $\theta = \pi/4$	1.0366	1.8094	3.1113
Actual curve $\theta = \pi/4$	1.1369	2.0480	3.5354
Percep. curve $\theta = \pi/10$	2.1033	3.4719	4.9411
Actual curve $\theta = \pi/10$	2.8925	4.4927	7.3924
Percep. curve $\theta = \pi/2$	1.0320	1.4412	2.5196

4.2 Round Poggendorff Illusion

Now we consider a variant of the Poggendorff illusion, called Round Poggendorff, see Fig. 5, left. The presence of the central surface induces a misperception: the arches do not seem cocircular and the left arc seems to be projected to some point with a certain orientation on the left bar.

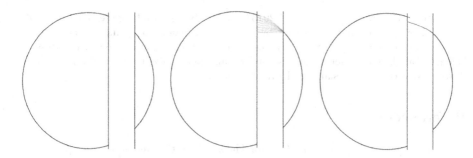

Fig. 5. Left: Round Poggendorff illusion, courtesy of Talasli and Inan see [31]. **Center:** A family of geodesics starting from (x_0, y_0, θ_0) with multiple endpoints. The aim is to determine (y, θ) minimizing the length of the perceptual curve. **Right:** A minimizer has end point $(y, \theta) = (0.88, -0.27)$

Computation of shortest curve with terminal manifold. The seed is fixed at the crossing point between the right arc and the right bar, $\xi = 2.5$. In order to compute the corrected perceptual completion curve we provide a terminal set to the SR-Fast Marching (SR-FM). Possible terminal orientations belong to $[-\pi/10, 0]$, where $\theta = 0$ is the angle corresponding to the orthogonal projection over the left bar and $\theta = -\pi/10$ is the boundary condition of the circle at crossing point with the left bar. In an analogous way we take a discretization between possible values of the y coordinate and run SR-FM, which is able to identify the minimizer connecting a certain seed with multiple end (terminal) points. The aim is to identify the correct angle θ and coordinate y for the end point of the perceptual curve. The SR length of the minimizing geodesic is 1.32668 and the corresponding computed end point is $\{0.3, 0.88, -0.27\}$.

5   Conclusion

In this paper a neuro-mathematical model for the perceptual Poggendorff phenomenon is presented, based on the functional architecture of V1. Perceptual curves arise as geodesics of a polarized metric in SE(2), directly induced by the visual stimulus. The geodesics are computed through SR-FM and the perceptual curves result to be shorter (w.r.t. SR-metric) than the corresponding geometrical continuation. The model has been compared with psychophysical evidences which explain how the effect varies depending on the width of the central surface and the angle of the transversal. Our measurements are in accord with those studies. Such approach can be extended to other illusions such that Hering, Zollner and Wundt illusions ([16]). Improving the understanding of these phenomena is very important because it can lead to insights about the behaviour of the visual cortex [13], allowing new applications to be developed.

Acknowledgment. The research leading to these results has received funding from the People Programme (Marie Curie Actions) of the European Union's Seventh

Framework Programme FP7/2007-2013/ under REA grant agreement n607643. Section 2 of this paper was written by Mashtakov, Sects. 1,3, 4 and 5 were written by Franceschiello, Citti and Sarti. The work of Mashtakov is supported by the Russian Science Foundation under grant 17-11-01387 and performed in Ailamazyan Program Systems Institute of Russian Academy of Sciences.

References

1. Agrachev, A.A., Sachkov, Y.: Control Theory From the Geometric Viewpoint, vol. 87. Springer-Verlag, Berlin Heidelberg (2004)
2. August, J., Zucker, S.W.: The curve indicator random field: curve organization via edge correlation. In: Boyer, K.L., Sarkar, S. (eds.) Perceptual Organization for Artificial Vision Systems. Springer, Heidelberg (2000). https://doi.org/10.1007/978-1-4615-4413-5_15
3. Bekkers, E.J., Duits, R., Mashtakov, A., Sanguinetti, G.R.: A PDE approach to data-driven sub-riemannian geodesics in SE (2). SIAM J. Imaging Sci. **8**(4), 2740–2770 (2015)
4. Ben-Yosef, G., Ben-Shahar, O.: A tangent bundle theory for visual curve completion. IEEE Trans. Pattern Anal. Mach. Intell. **34**, 1263–1280 (2012)
5. Citti, G., Franceschiello, B., Sanguinetti, G., Sarti, A.: Sub-riemannian mean curvature flow for image processing. SIAM J. Imaging Sci. **9**(1), 212–237 (2016)
6. Citti, G., Sarti, A.: A cortical based model of perceptual completion in the roto-translation space. J. Math. Imaging Vis. **24**(3), 307–326 (2006)
7. Crandall, M.G., Ishii, H., Lions, P.L.: User's guide to viscosity solutions of second order partial differential equations. Bull. AMS **27**(1), 1–67 (1992)
8. Crandall, M.G., Lions, P.L.: Viscosity solutions of Hamilton-Jacobi equations. Trans. Am. Math. Soc. **277**(1), 1–42 (1983)
9. Daugman, J.G.: Uncertainty relation for resolution in space, spatial frequency, and orientation optimized by two-dimensional visual cortical filters. JOSA A **2**(7), 1160–1169 (1985)
10. Day, R., Dickinson, R.: The components of the poggendorff illusion. Br. J. Psychol. **67**(4), 537–552 (1976)
11. DeAngelis, G.C., Ohzawa, I., Freeman, R.D.: Receptive-field dynamics in the central visual pathways. Trends Neurosci. **18**(10), 451–458 (1995)
12. Dragoni, F.: Metric Hopf-Lax formula with semicontinuous data. Discrete Continuous Dyn. Syst. **17**(4), 713 (2007)
13. Eagleman, D.M.: Visual illusions and neurobiology. Nat. Rev. Neurosci. **2**(12), 920–926 (2001)
14. Gibson, J.J.: The concept of the stimulus in psychology. Am. Psychol. **15**(11), 694 (1960)
15. Gromov, M.: Carnot-Carathéodory spaces seen from within. In: Bellaïche, A., Risler, J.J. (eds.) Sub-Riemannian Geometry, pp. 79–323. Springer, Heidelberg (1996). https://doi.org/10.1007/978-3-0348-9210-0_2
16. Hering, E.: Beiträge zur Physiologie. I. Vom Ortsinne der Nethaut. Leipzig, Germany: Engelmann (1861)
17. Hladky, R., Pauls, S.: Minimal surfaces in the roto-translation group with applications to a neuro-biological image completion model. JMIV **36**, 1–27 (2010)
18. Hoffman, W.C.: The visual cortex is a contact bundle. Appl. Math. Comput. **32**(2), 137–167 (1989)

19. Hubel, D.H., Wiesel, T.N.: Receptive fields, binocular interaction and functional architecture in the cat's visual cortex. J. Physiol. **160**(1), 106–154 (1962)
20. Jones, J.P., Palmer, L.A.: An evaluation of the two-dimensional gabor filter model of simple receptive fields in cat striate cortex. J. Neurophysiol. **58**(6), 1233–1258 (1987)
21. Koenderink, J.J., van Doorn, A.J.: Representation of local geometry in the visual system. Biol. Cybern. **55**(6), 367–375 (1987)
22. Mashtakov, A., Ardentov, A., Sachkov, Y.: Parallel algorithm and software for image inpainting via sub-riemannian minimizers on the group of rototranslations. Numer. Math. Theory Methods Appl. **6**, 95–115 (2013)
23. Mirebeau, J.M.: Anisotropic fast-marching on cartesian grids using lattice basis reduction. SIAM J. Numer. Anal. **52**(4), 1573–1599 (2014)
24. Montgomery, R.: A Tour of Subriemannian Geometries, Their Geodesics and Applications. Mathematical Surveys and Monographs (2002). http://bookstore.ams.org/surv-91-s
25. Petitot, J., Tondut, Y.: Vers une neurogéométrie. Fibrations corticales, structures de contact et contours subjectifs modaux. Math. Informatique et Sci. Humaines **145**, 5–102 (1999)
26. Robinson, J.O.: The Psychology of Visual Illusion. Courier Corporation, Chelmsford (2013)
27. Sachkov, Y.: Cut locus and optimal synthesis in the sub-riemannian problem on the group of motions of a plane. ESAIM C. Opt. Calc. Var. **17**, 293–321 (2011)
28. Sanguinetti, G., Bekkers, E., Duits, R., Janssen, M.H.J., Mashtakov, A., Mirebeau, J.-M.: Sub-riemannian fast marching in SE(2). In: Pardo, A., Kittler, J. (eds.) Progress in Pattern Recognition, Image Analysis, Computer Vision, and Applications. LNCS, vol. 9423, pp. 366–374. Springer, Cham (2015). https://doi.org/10.1007/978-3-319-25751-8_44
29. Sanguinetti, G., Citti, G., Sarti, A.: Image completion using a diffusion driven mean curvature flowin a sub-riemannian space. VISAPP **2**(8), 46–53 (2008)
30. Sethian, J.A.: Level Set Methods and Fast Marching Methods, 2nd edn. Cambridge University Press, Cambridge (1999)
31. Talasli, U., Inan, A.B.: Applying Emmert's law to the Poggendorff illusion. Front. Hum. Neurosci. 9, October 2015. Article no. 531
32. Weintraub, D.J., Krantz, D.H.: The Poggendorff illusion: amputations, rotations, and other perturbations. Percept. Psychophys. **10**(4), 257–264 (1971)
33. Westheimer, G.: Illusions in the spatial sense of the eye: geometrical-optical illusions and the neural representation of space. Vis. Res. **48**(20), 2128–2142 (2008)
34. Williams, L.R., Jacobs, D.W.: Stochastic completion fields: a neural model of illusory contour shape and salience. Neural Comput. **9**(4), 837–858 (1997)

High-Pass Learning Machine: An Edge Detection Approach

Alan L.S. Matias, Saulo A.F. Oliveira, Ajalmar R. da Rocha Neto, and Pedro Pedrosa Rebouças Filho[(✉)]

Programa de Pós-Graduação em Ciência da Computação, Instituto Federal do Ceará, Fortaleza, Brazil
pedrosarf@ifce.edu.br

Abstract. This paper describes an approach using a neural network structure which is able to generalize the detection of high frequency transitions in non-noisy signals and noisy signals in a linearly separable problem. The neural network performs an adaptive filtering on the signal acting as a high-pass filter for edge detection from linear environment, and estimates its training patterns from user-defined parameters. Such generalization is possible due to the hidden layers use a parametric approximation of the input vector, so that it is approximate knowledge of the patterns of the network, i.e., the training patterns that were estimated by the neural network. Once the network has learned through these patterns, the parametric approach held causes the input vector can be generalized in a linear environment. Considering the accuracy, f-score, PNSR and SSIM, our proposal achieved results quite similar to their counterparts methods, Prewitt, Sobel and Canny filters, using different settings. Thus, our proposal can replace traditional edge detectors in their applications in a optimization way due to the flexibility in a range of applications.

Keywords: Image processing · Edge detection · High-pass filter Neural networks

1 Introduction

The feedforward neural network models have been proposed in recent decades providing a broad range of solutions to a even vast set of problems. These problems may require the ability to generalize large amounts of data from natural or artificial phenomena that require high complex nonlinear mappings - for example, pattern classification problems and regression.

These models focus on different treatments to the network behaviour, ranging from the learning process, to how the input is treated to produce the output. The Least-Mean-Square (LMS), proposed by Widrow and Hoff [1] is the foundation for adaptive filtering. For the Perceptron network, the LMS behaves as a low pass filter, attenuating high frequency components and passing up the

© Springer International Publishing AG 2017
S. Battiato et al. (Eds.): ICIAP 2017 International Workshops, LNCS 10590, pp. 48–59, 2017.
https://doi.org/10.1007/978-3-319-70742-6_5

low-frequency components; however, the Perceptron is only able to solve problems linearly separable. In fact, algorithms more complex than LMS, based upon Backpropagation [2] and some variations, such as, Quickprop [3] and RPROP [4], through the addition of more than one hidden layer, provide the ability to solve nonlinear problems. However, according to their training set size, the training phase.

In recent years, neural network models have been proposed for edge detection in images. In [5], a competitive self-organized neural network is used to qualify the types of edges which are derived from the sum of the magnitudes of the differences from the central pixel in a mask size of 3×3 applied to grayscale images. The output is a fuzzy system used to map the pixels used as edge and non-edge. A similar approach is held in [6] where a feedforward neural network is used with n neurons in the input layer, $2n + 1$ neurons in the hidden layer and a single neuron in the output layer. An error retro-propagation algorithm is used as a learning rule. Furthermore, a fuzzy logic system is adopted to improve the generalization capability of the network. In [7] is used a feedforward neural network which uses the backpropagation algorithm as learning rule. In such work, the image is first binarized and then pass through edge detection process. Differently from the previous approaches, the masks of size 2×2 are used for feature extraction and pixel classification is divided into two classes: border and no border.

From the point of view of image processing, edge detection is given by a two-dimensional high-pass filtering. In addition to the neural networks models, there are classical models which are based on the calculation of the gradient luminosity function or on the estimation of corresponding masks to the derivative of the second order, as in the case of the Laplacian operator [8]. Among the methods that use the calculation of the gradient, we can cite the well-known edge operators, such as, Sobel, Prewitt [9] and Roberts. Moreover, Canny [10] proposes an approach that seeks to improve how the edge is determined through a paradigm that defines that a point marked as edge is the closest as possible to the center of a real edge, so that a single edge must have only one point. Canny uses a high-pass filtering with a mask estimated from the first order derivative vertical and horizontal. In possession of those vertical and horizontal images, the method follows its course by calculating the brightness gradient generating the magnitude image as output.

In this context, in this paper we propose a model along with RBF that behaves just like an adaptive high-pass filter. In addition, we will address its usage in image processing with focus on edge detection. Our proposal will be able to estimate a single mask, the weight vector, considering a linearly separable problem. To demonstrate its effectiveness and flexibility, we compare our proposal with traditional edge detectors, such as, Prewwit, Sobel and Canny.

2   One-Dimensional Approach

Our main goal is through a method be able to distinguish between two types of features in signal behavior: (i) high-frequency transition behavior and; (ii) low frequency signal. In addition, the method must maximize the first case, and subdue the second one.

For this to be possible, we will consider five paradigms previously determined, including: (i) filtering the signal held by the method is adaptive in the sense that it considers neighboring from the point being processed; (ii) the mask is estimated from a binary linear system, i.e., a hyperplane between high and low frequency features must be enough to distinguish them; (iii) the mask should be versatile, with the possibility of different amounts of neighbors from the point that is being processed; (iv) the method performs a transformation in the input signal f so that f can be distinguish by the mask; (v) the problem is defined by a noisy Gaussian distribution.

In signal processing, we say that the convolution is the answer to an impulse that was inferred as input into a system. The discrete convolution is given by:

$$h(k) = \sum_{n=-\infty}^{\infty} f(n)g(k-n) \tag{1}$$

where g is the filter that moves to the right relative to the signal f at each iteration.

In this article, the equation of convolution should be extended to the matrix form so that f is partitioned into several inputs of same size of g, the mask that determines the neighborhood towards the current point. Consider a signal $f = (x_1, \ldots, x_m)$ and $\mathbf{g} = (g_1, \ldots, g_n)$, responsible for making the adaptive high-pass filtering. Thus, the signal will be partitioned in m feature vectors $\mathbf{f}_i$ so that each $\mathbf{f}_i$ has size n. Lets take a example with $m = 4$ and $n = 5$:

$$\mathbf{h} = \mathbf{F}\mathbf{g} = \begin{bmatrix} 0 & 0 & x_1^* & x_2 & x_3 \\ 0 & x_1 & x_2^* & x_3 & x_4 \\ x_1 & x_2 & x_3^* & x_4 & 0 \\ x_2 & x_3 & x_4^* & 0 & 0 \end{bmatrix} \begin{bmatrix} g_1 \\ g_2 \\ g_3 \\ g_4 \\ g_5 \end{bmatrix} \tag{2}$$

where the x_j^* is the point being processed. Note that, with a mask of size $n = 5$, the point x_j^* will have four neighbors and its value after adaptive filtering will be a inner product of $\mathbf{f}_i$ with $\mathbf{g}$. By observing the Eq. (2), we can define the convolution in matrix form as a linear system, in which $\mathbf{g}$ acts as an adaptive filter in $\mathbf{F}$ and each line $\mathbf{f}_i$ in $\mathbf{F}$ acts as a feature vector.

It is straightforward to realize that the adaptive filter $\mathbf{g}$ is equivalent to the unknown variables of a linear system which in the neural networks context refer to the weight vector $\mathbf{w}$, see Eq. (2). Kohonen and Ruohonen [11] proposed OLAM (*Optimal Linear Associative Memory*) a model that estimates the weight vector $\mathbf{w}$ through the pseudo-inverse of the feature matrix. Furthermore, OLAM has a extremely fast learning ability for a totally linear separable problem. The calculation of the weight vector by OLAM is performed based on matrix operations, as can be seen in Eq. (3), in which, $\mathbf{X}^+ = (\mathbf{X}^T\mathbf{X})^{-1}\mathbf{X}^T$ is called the pseudo-inverse of the features matrix $\mathbf{X}, \mathbf{D}$ is the matrix that contains the label for each line of $\mathbf{X}$, and $\mathbf{W}^*$ is the matrix of optimal weights.

$$\mathbf{XW} = \mathbf{D}$$
$$\mathbf{X^T XW} = \mathbf{X^T D}$$
$$\mathbf{(X^T X)W} = \mathbf{X^T D}$$
$$\mathbf{(X^T X)^{-1}(X^T X)W} = \mathbf{(X^T X)^{-1} X^T D} \quad (3)$$
$$\mathbf{IW} = \mathbf{(X^T X)^{-1} X^T D}$$
$$\mathbf{W} = \mathbf{(X^T X)^{-1} X^T D}$$
$$\mathbf{W^*} = \mathbf{X^+ D}.$$

Thus, we can conclude that:

$$\mathbf{h} = \mathbf{Fg}$$
$$= \mathbf{FW^*} = \mathbf{F[(X^T X)^{-1} X^T D]}, \quad (4)$$

where the training patterns $\mathbf{X}$ and their labels $\mathbf{D}$ should be determined during the training.

As the homogeneous regions can be translated into low frequency signals in the feature space, we denote them by a vector of length n which has only values equal to 1 in its structure. Moreover, as we want to attenuate low frequency signals, we define their label to 0. Once defined the features of the homogeneous region, it is straightforward to consider the inverse for a high frequency region. In this case, it is given by the difference in relation to the neighboring point being processed. Therefore, we represent our pattern as a vector of length n filled with zeros, but with its center with value 1. From these statements, we obtain:

$$\mathbf{X} = \begin{bmatrix} 0_{11} & 0_{12} & \dots & 1_{1\lceil n/2 \rceil} & \dots & 0_{1n-1} & 0_{1n} \\ 1_{21} & 1_{22} & \dots & 1_{2\lceil n/2 \rceil} & \dots & 1_{2n-1} & 1_{2n} \end{bmatrix} \text{ and } \mathbf{D} = \begin{bmatrix} 1_1 \\ 0_2 \end{bmatrix} \quad (5)$$

where the first line of $\mathbf{X}$ and $\mathbf{D}$ represents, respectively, the high-frequency feature and the high-frequency label – the second line is the representation for low-frequency feature and label. In this sense, the high-frequency points will tends to 1 and the low-frequency points will tends to 0.

In fact, we can not compute the pseudo-inverse on $\mathbf{X}$, because it is a non-singular matrix. To overcome this issue, we must apply a regularization term λ which is multiplied by the identity matrix $\mathbf{I}$. Therefore, we obtain the equation

$$\mathbf{h} = \mathbf{F[(X^T X + \lambda I)^{-1} X^T D]} \quad (6)$$

It is noteworthy that the central feature in the two patterns in $\mathbf{X}$ has its values equal to 1 on purpose, because these values are the bias. This approach is extremely important for the development of the our proposal in its final state, as will be presented next.

2.1 Signal Transformation

So far we have covered the first three predefined paradigms, which, in a nutshell, define that: (i) the filter is adaptive; (ii) the mask is estimated from a binary linear system, and; (iii) the mask is versatile with respect its size n. However, despite our method estimate the filter from a linear system, the edge detection problem is not linear. In this sense, our proposal must take it into consideration. For solve this problem, our proposal makes a transformation in each line $\mathbf{f}_i$ in $\mathbf{F}$ so that $\mathbf{f}_i$ can be solved by $\mathbf{g}$.

Thus, we consider a Gaussian radial basis function in which the point being processed acts as its mean $\mu_i = x_j^*$. That said, we can then define our transformation as:

$$\Phi_{ij}(x_j, \mu_i, \sigma) = \exp\left(\frac{-\|x_j - \mu_i\|}{2\sigma^2}\right) \tag{7}$$

where σ is the standard deviation, x_j is a neighbor of x_j^*, and Φ_{ij} is a kernel function which performs the transformation in the signal through a Gaussian radial basis function. Now, using the $\mathbf{F}$ matrix in Eq. (2) as example, we can extend it to:

$$\mathbf{F} = \begin{bmatrix} 0 & 0 & \Phi_{11}^* & \Phi_{12} & \Phi_{13} \\ 0 & \Phi_{21} & \Phi_{22}^* & \Phi_{23} & \Phi_{24} \\ \Phi_{31} & \Phi_{32} & \Phi_{33}^* & \Phi_{34} & 0 \\ \Phi_{42} & \Phi_{43} & \Phi_{44}^* & 0 & 0 \end{bmatrix} \tag{8}$$

It is noteworthy that the transformation of $\mathbf{f}_i$ behaves differently for different values of σ. When $\sigma \to +\infty$, the signal is considered to be homogeneous, regardless of having high-frequency regions. In contrast, when $\sigma \to 0$ it is considered that all different neighbors x_j^* have values close to zero. Such behavior results in multiple high-frequency regions when in fact they are not.

It is important to realize that this approach is extremely sensitive to noise. Thus, to overcome this situation, it is necessary to apply a low-pass filter to smooth the signal before passing it to our method. However, the low-pass filter must allow to find the center of the edge and maximize it. Therefore, we must consider that the center of the edge is formulated in such a way that it can be represented by $\left[0_1, \ldots, 1_{\lceil n/2 \rceil}, \ldots, 0_n\right]$.

Intuitively, we can predict that the way to maximize the center of the edge in such conditions is to in the high frequency transition, the transition center is in equal distance on the two extremes. Thus, Gaussian filtering becomes mandatory because it performs a smoothness eliminating noise and smoothing edges.

The 1-D Gaussian filter can be obtained from:

$$G(x, \sigma) = \exp\left(\frac{-x^2}{2\sigma^2}\right) \tag{9}$$

It is depicted in Figs. 1 and 2 examples of approximation of homogeneous and high frequency transition regions, respectively. As one can see in Fig. 1, the low frequency region $\mathbf{f}_i$ is close to zero values, however, after signal transformation values were approximated from a vector containing only values equal to 1. According to the $\mathbf{X}$ and $\mathbf{D}$ matrix in Eq. (5), the point $x_j^* \in \mathbf{f}_i$ being processed will be attenuated by $\mathbf{g}$. In Fig. 2, the signal processed by the Gaussian filter is translated so that the network recognizes $x_j^* \in \mathbf{f}_i$ as a transition high frequency and will maximize it.

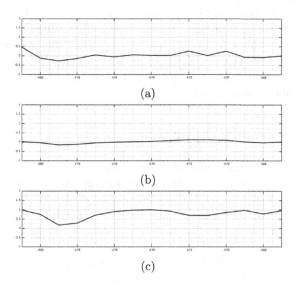

Fig. 1. From top to bottom: (a) low frequency input $\mathbf{f}_i$, (b) signal smoothing using Gaussian filtering and (c) input transformation by our proposal.

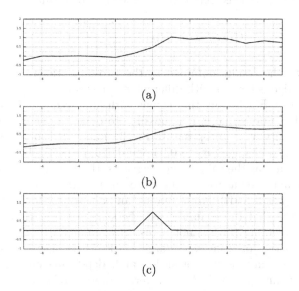

Fig. 2. From top to bottom: (a) high frequency input $\mathbf{f}_i$, (b) signal smoothing using Gaussian filtering and (c) input transformation by our proposal.

Once formulated our proposal, we observe their behavior in relation to how it is parameterized. We perform two operations using Gaussian – Gaussian filtering and low-pass parametric approach – we must define two values of variance, where σ_1 represent the variance in Eq. (9) and σ_2 represent the variance in Eq. (7). Furthermore, the mask size is defined by n, which preferably should always be defined with valuesodd in order to preserve the central point x_j^*, and the same number of neighbors on both sides.

3   Two Dimensional Approach

From 2D approach, the mask should not be defined only in relation to the horizontal direction, but also considering the vertical and diagonal directions. With that in mind, we now have to deal with a matrix of size $m \times n$. However, our proposal is quite flexible because we just have to transform the 2D mask $m \times n$ into a 1D vector of size $m \cdot n$. This way, our matrix $\mathbf{X}$ can be defined by:

$$\mathbf{X} = \begin{bmatrix} 0_{11} \ 0_{12} \ \cdots \ 1_{1\lceil n/2 \rceil} \ \cdots \ 0_{1(m \cdot n)-1} \ 0_{1(m \cdot n)} \\ 1_{21} \ 1_{22} \ \cdots \ 1_{2\lceil n/2 \rceil} \ \cdots \ 1_{2(m \cdot n)-1} \ 1_{2(m \cdot n)} \end{bmatrix} \tag{10}$$

thereby, a mask with 8-connected neighbors ($m = 3$ and $n = 3$) would be incorporated into a vector of size 9, in which the currently point being processed is located at the position 5. Thus, for our proposal become two-dimensional, this is the only modification to be made. Moreover, the Gaussian filter must also be extended into a two-dimensional format, which can be estimated by:

$$G(x, y, \sigma) = \exp\left(\frac{-(x^2 + y^2)}{2\sigma^2}\right) \tag{11}$$

Following to the results obtained in the two-dimentional approach, Fig. 3 illustrates the edge detection with different parameters.

As presented in Fig. 3, only the regions with high frequency transition were classified as edge. Furthermore, it is possible to detect lower frequency regions due to the flexibility of our proposal. In Fig. 3(c) and (d) is depicted some edge detection results by changing σ_2 to 0.05 and 0.025, respectively.

One can see that as the value of σ_2 decreases, the local maxima representing the edges are maximized as well as the more image details are detected. Besides the mask 3×3 (Fig. 3(b–d)), larger masks can be used, as shown in Fig. 3(f–h). – it is noteworthy that the examples use the same mask at the low-pass filter and the edge detection, which is not necessarily required.

The disadvantage of using very large masks is because in the smoothing process, the image may lose information and, depending on the application, this information may be critical. However, the advantage, as can be seen in Fig. 3 is the local maximum of the edges, i.e., the centers, are more exposed. Such advantage is handy if we need to find the centers of the edges due to the maximized exposure of such the local maxima.

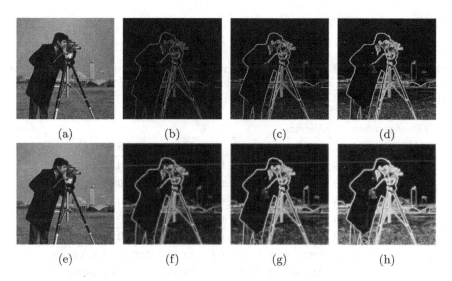

(a)   (b)   (c)   (d)

(e)   (f)   (g)   (h)

Fig. 3. Edge detection by our proposal using $m = n = 3$ (b, c, d) and $m = n = 15$ (f, g, h), and $\sigma_1 = 1$, with different values for $\sigma_2 = \{0.1, 0.05, 0.025\}$.

4   Results and Discussion

In this section we briefly compare our proposal to three widespread methods in image processing literature; among them: (i) Prewitt; (ii) Sobel, and; (iii) Canny. We should emphasize that, in relation to these methods, our proposal performs a kind of estimate of the magnitude images. Thus, for a fairer comparison in relation to the Canny method, we only used the calculation of the magnitude image, which is based on two filterings performed by an estimated mask by computing the first derivative Gaussian in horizontal and vertical directions, and then we compute the gradient from these two images.

In order to improve our evaluation and discussion when comparing our proposal to the State-of-art, we employed four statistical measurements. The four statistical measurements are the accuracy (ACC), F-Measure (F_β), the PSNR (*Peak Signal-to-Noise Ratio*) and SSIM (*Structural Similarity*) [12].

Tables 1 and 2 shows a comparison of our results with the methods Prewitt, Sobel and Canny. The comparison is carried out by adopting the output from the such methods as ground truth, so the metrics can be computed. The results show the configuration of our proposal for analysis. The parameter values used are $m = \{3, 9\}, n = \{3, 9\}, \sigma_1 = \{1, 10\}$ and $\sigma_2 = \{0.025, 0, 05, 0.075, 0.1, 0.250\}$. We used an image dataset with 12 images and we compute the mean and standard deviation for each metric and each configuration.

Table 1. Results of our proposed method with different configurations (σ_1 and σ_2) for the metrics, ACC, F_β, PSNR and SSIM, adopting Prewwit (P), Sobel (S) and Canny (C) as Ground Truth (GT).

Configuration			*Metrics*				
$m = n$	σ_1	σ_2	ACC	F_β	PNSR	SSIM	GT
3	1	0.025	0.82 ± 0.10	0.11 ± 0.04	11.42 ± 2.04	0.35 ± 0.14	P
		0.050	0.94 ± 0.03	0.27 ± 0.11	16.95 ± 2.15	0.62 ± 0.11	
		0.075	0.97 ± 0.01	0.46 ± 0.13	21.80 ± 1.96	0.72 ± 0.04	
		0.100	0.98 ± 0.01	0.62 ± 0.13	26.34 ± 1.55	0.73 ± 0.04	
		0.250	0.99 ± 0.01	0.71 ± 0.13	25.91 ± 2.11	0.38 ± 0.11	
		0.025	0.82 ± 0.10	0.11 ± 0.04	12.13 ± 2.00	0.43 ± 0.12	S
		0.050	0.94 ± 0.03	0.28 ± 0.11	18.35 ± 2.07	0.67 ± 0.07	
		0.075	0.97 ± 0.01	0.47 ± 0.12	23.92 ± 1.70	0.70 ± 0.04	
		0.100	0.98 ± 0.01	0.63 ± 0.13	27.69 ± 1.30	0.64 ± 0.05	
		0.250	0.99 ± 0.01	0.78 ± 0.13	22.20 ± 2.03	0.26 ± 0.11	
		0.025	0.82 ± 0.01	0.17 ± 0.08	12.00 ± 2.13	0.40 ± 0.15	C
		0.050	0.94 ± 0.02	0.36 ± 0.11	17.52 ± 1.93	0.66 ± 0.10	
		0.075	0.97 ± 0.00	0.48 ± 0.08	21.51 ± 1.11	0.68 ± 0.03	
		0.100	0.98 ± 0.00	0.49 ± 0.12	23.81 ± 0.63	0.62 ± 0.04	
		0.250	0.98 ± 0.01	0.12 ± 0.09	22.20 ± 1.41	0.28 ± 0.09	
	10	0.025	0.83 ± 0.09	0.11 ± 0.04	11.64 ± 2.04	0.36 ± 0.14	P
		0.050	0.94 ± 0.02	0.27 ± 0.10	17.27 ± 2.15	0.62 ± 0.10	
		0.075	0.97 ± 0.01	0.43 ± 0.11	22.15 ± 1.96	0.71 ± 0.04	
		0.100	0.98 ± 0.01	0.59 ± 0.11	26.41 ± 1.55	0.70 ± 0.04	
		0.250	0.99 ± 0.01	0.66 ± 0.15	25.37 ± 2.06	0.36 ± 0.12	
		0.025	0.83 ± 0.09	0.12 ± 0.05	12.36 ± 1.89	0.44 ± 0.13	S
		0.050	0.94 ± 0.02	0.28 ± 0.10	18.67 ± 1.88	0.66 ± 0.07	
		0.075	0.97 ± 0.01	0.44 ± 0.11	24.07 ± 1.53	0.68 ± 0.04	
		0.100	0.98 ± 0.01	0.60 ± 0.11	27.00 ± 1.48	0.60 ± 0.06	
		0.250	0.99 ± 0.01	0.64 ± 0.15	21.83 ± 2.01	0.25 ± 0.11	
		0.025	0.83 ± 0.08	0.18 ± 0.08	12.25 ± 2.01	0.42 ± 0.15	C
		0.050	0.94 ± 0.02	0.37 ± 0.09	17.92 ± 1.70	0.67 ± 0.09	
		0.075	0.97 ± 0.01	0.50 ± 0.08	21.89 ± 0.86	0.68 ± 0.02	
		0.100	0.98 ± 0.01	0.51 ± 0.11	23.88 ± 0.65	0.61 ± 0.04	
		0.250	0.98 ± 0.01	0.12 ± 0.09	22.08 ± 1.50	0.27 ± 0.09	

Table 2. Results of our proposed method with different configurations (m, n, σ_1 and σ_2) for the metrics, ACC, F_β, PSNR and SSIM, adopting Prewwit (P), Sobel (S) and Canny (C) as Ground Truth (GT).

Configuration			*Metrics*				
$m = n$	σ_1	σ_2	ACC	F_β	PNSR	SSIM	GT
9	1	0.025	0.63 ± 0.16	$\hat{0}.05 \pm 0.02$	7.54 ± 1.37	0.14 ± 0.08	P
		0.050	0.82 ± 0.07	0.10 ± 0.03	11.09 ± 1.40	0.29 ± 0.14	
		0.075	0.90 ± 0.03	0.17 ± 0.05	13.90 ± 1.35	0.40 ± 0.15	
		0.100	0.94 ± 0.02	0.25 ± 0.06	16.36 ± 1.31	0.46 ± 0.15	
		0.250	0.98 ± 0.01	0.48 ± 0.08	25.20 ± 1.50	0.48 ± 0.13	
		0.025	0.63 ± 0.16	0.05 ± 0.02	7.94 ± 1.33	0.17 ± 0.08	S
		0.050	0.82 ± 0.07	0.10 ± 0.04	11.70 ± 1.35	0.33 ± 0.14	
		0.075	0.90 ± 0.03	0.17 ± 0.05	14.71 ± 1.29	0.41 ± 0.15	
		0.100	0.94 ± 0.02	0.25 ± 0.06	17.30 ± 1.26	0.45 ± 0.15	
		0.250	0.98 ± 0.01	0.48 ± 0.08	23.35 ± 1.99	0.37 ± 0.13	
		0.025	0.63 ± 0.15	0.09 ± 0.05	7.94 ± 1.42	0.17 ± 0.08	C
		0.050	0.82 ± 0.07	0.16 ± 0.08	11.66 ± 1.42	0.36 ± 0.14	
		0.075	0.90 ± 0.03	0.25 ± 0.09	14.60 ± 1.27	0.47 ± 0.15	
		0.100	0.94 ± 0.01	0.33 ± 0.10	17.13 ± 1.10	0.53 ± 0.13	
		0.250	0.97 ± 0.01	0.27 ± 0.10	23.77 ± 1.06	0.43 ± 0.10	
	10	0.025	0.71 ± 0.05	0.06 ± 0.02	8.73 ± 0.68	0.23 ± 0.12	P
		0.050	0.86 ± 0.03	0.11 ± 0.02	12.83 ± 0.86	0.37 ± 0.11	
		0.075	0.92 ± 0.02	0.17 ± 0.04	16.12 ± 1.07	0.44 ± 0.09	
		0.100	0.94 ± 0.01	0.23 ± 0.06	18.85 ± 1.07	0.47 ± 0.10	
		0.250	0.98 ± 0.01	0.36 ± 0.08	24.38 ± 1.97	0.39 ± 0.14	
		0.025	0.71 ± 0.05	0.06 ± 0.02	9.36 ± 0.66	0.24 ± 0.12	S
		0.050	0.86 ± 0.03	0.11 ± 0.02	13.31 ± 0.85	0.36 ± 0.11	
		0.075	0.92 ± 0.02	0.17 ± 0.04	16.51 ± 0.89	0.40 ± 0.10	
		0.100	0.94 ± 0.01	0.23 ± 0.05	18.89 ± 0.78	0.40 ± 0.11	
		0.250	0.98 ± 0.01	0.36 ± 0.06	21.48 ± 2.15	0.29 ± 0.13	
		0.025	0.72 ± 0.05	0.10 ± 0.05	9.16 ± 0.65	0.27 ± 0.12	C
		0.050	0.86 ± 0.02	0.16 ± 0.06	13.39 ± 0.73	0.42 ± 0.10	
		0.075	0.92 ± 0.01	0.21 ± 0.08	16.65 ± 0.88	0.47 ± 0.09	
		0.100	0.94 ± 0.01	0.24 ± 0.09	19.14 ± 0.90	0.48 ± 0.10	
		0.250	0.97 ± 0.01	0.19 ± 0.10	22.22 ± 1.88	0.32 ± 0.12	

Observing Tables 1 and 2, it is possible to notice the flexibility of our proposal against Prewitt, Sobel and Canny. We obtain results that depending on the initial configuration, may or may not be close to the results from other methods. In Table 1, where the mask is 3×3 ($m = n = 3$), regarding the SSIM, we highlight a greater similarity to the Prewitt method when $\sigma_1 = 1$ and $\sigma_2 = 0.1$. With respect to the PSNR metric, the noise is less significant compared the Sobel method when $\sigma_1 = 1$ and $\sigma_2 = 0.1$. However, when $\sigma_2 = 0.25$, we get closer results for ACC and F_β, except for the Canny method, which concentrated the best results for ACC and F_β when $\sigma_2 = 0.1$.

Observing Table 2, where the mask is 9×9 ($m = n = 9$), we see lower scores if we take into account the similarity with the resulting images. This is an advantage of our proposal due to no restriction results in its magnitude image. In all cases the results have distinction, whether or not discrepancy.

Regarding the algorithm execution time, we stored the time that the model took to train, group the data and process the information. Also, in our simulations we used Matlab version R2014b. For the mask 3×3 we achieved in average 2.15 s to carry out our simulations. As for the mask 9×9, the average time was around 3.5 s. This is expected because a mask 9×9 results in a feature vector of size 81 against 9 when a mask 3×3 is adopted.

What most distinguishes our proposal from methods based on gradient, and we consider it an advantage in its usability, is the flexibility with respect to it can adapt depending on the current application need, so feasible results can be generated through the parameter tuning. This flexibility is built into the system, especially with the variation of the initial variable σ_2 as well as the variation of the mask size. This ability to cover a lot of possible outcomes makes it possible to open new possibilities for different applications in imaging context.

5   Conclusion

It was presented in this paper a neural network capable of estimating an adaptive high-pass filter for signal processing based on an parametric approximation held in the hidden layer. Moreover, our proposal was employed for detecting edges in images. With its flexibility, one can obtain different results allowing its use for various kinds of applications. Two key features of their flexibility are in: (i) the ability to estimate the training patterns, providing freedom to choose the size of the mask being used at the signal filtering and (ii) the choice of σ_2 values, which may affect the network to a more restricted parametric regression, or less restricted.

As future works, we intent to create an efficient post-processing method which is able to determine the edges of the central pixel while maintaining the integrity of the segment edges in the images.

Acknowledgment. The authors would like to thank FUNCAP (*Fundação Cearense de Apoio à Pesquisa*) for the academic support.

References

1. Widrow, B., Hoff, M.E.: Adaptive switching circuits (1960)
2. Rumelhart, D.E., Hinton, G.E., Williams, R.J.: Learning representations by back-propagating errors. Cogn. Model. **5**(3), 1 (1988)
3. Fahlaman, S.: Fast-learning variations on backpropagation: an imperical study. In: Proceedings of the Connecionist Models Summer School (1998)
4. Riedmiller, M., Braun, H.: A direct adaptive method for faster backpropagation learning: the RPROP algorithm. In: IEEE International Conference on Neural Networks, pp. 586–591. IEEE (1993)
5. Wang, R., Gao, L.-q., Yang, S., Liu, Y.-C.: An edge detection method by combining fuzzy logic and neural network. In: International Conference on Machine Learning and Cybernetics, vol. 7, pp. 4539–4543. IEEE (2005)
6. Mihalache, C.R., Craus, M.: Neural network and fuzzy membership functions based edge detection for digital images. In: 16th International Conference on System Theory, Control and Computing (ICSTCC), pp. 1–6. IEEE (2012)
7. Mehrara, H., Zahedinejad, M., Pourmohammad, A.: Novel edge detection using BP neural network based on threshold binarization. In: Second International Conference on Computer and Electrical Engineering, ICCEE 2009, vol. 2, pp. 408–412. IEEE (2009)
8. Gonzales, R.C., Woods, R.E., Eddins, S.L.: Digital Image Processing Using MAT-LAB. Pearson Prentice Hall, Upper Saddle River (2010)
9. Prewitt, J.M.S.: Object enhancement and extraction. Picture Process. Psychopictorics **10**(1), 15–19 (1970)
10. Canny, J.: A computational approach to edge detection. IEEE Trans. Pattern Anal. Mach. Intell. **6**, 679–698 (1986)
11. Kohonen, T., Ruohonen, M.: Representation of associated data by matrix operators. IEEE Trans. Comput. **100**(7), 701–702 (1973)
12. Wang, Z., Bovik, A.C., Sheikh, H.R., Simoncelli, E.P.: Image quality assessment: from error visibility to structural similarity. IEEE Trans. Image Process. **13**(4), 600–612 (2004)

Adaptive Motion Pooling and Diffusion for Optical Flow Computation

N.V. Kartheek Medathati[1], Manuela Chessa[2]([⊠]), Guillaume S. Masson[3],
Pierre Kornprobst[1], and Fabio Solari[2]

[1] INRIA, Biovision Team, Sophia Antipolis, France
{kartheek.medathati,pierre.kornprobst}@inria.fr
[2] Department of Informatics, Bioengineering,
Robotics and System Engineering - DIBRIS, University of Genoa, Genova, Italy
{manuela.chessa,fabio.solari}@unige.it
[3] Institut de Neurosciences de la Timone, CNRS, Marseille, France
guillaume.masson@univ-amu.fr

Abstract. We propose to extend a state of the art bio-inspired model
for optic flow computation through adaptive processing by focusing on
the role of local context indicative of the local velocity estimates reliability. We set a network structure representative of cortical areas V1,
V2 and MT, and incorporate three functional principles observed in primate visual system: contrast adaptation, adaptive afferent pooling and
MT diffusion that are adaptive dependent upon the 2D image structure
(*Adaptive Motion Pooling and Diffusion*, AMPD). We assess the AMPD
performance on Middlebury optical flow estimation dataset, showing that
the proposed AMPD model performs better than the baseline one and its
overall performance is comparable with many computer vision methods.

Keywords: Brain-inspired computer vision · Optic flow
Spatio-temporal filters · Motion energy · Contrast adaptation
Population code · V1 · V2 · MT · Middlebury dataset

1 Introduction

Dense optical flow estimation is a well studied problem in computer vision with
several algorithms being proposed and benchmarked over the years [1,7]. Given
that motion information can be used for serving several functional tasks such as
navigation, tracking and segmentation, biological systems have evolved sophisticated and highly efficient systems for visual motion information analysis. Understanding the mechanisms adopted by biological systems would be very beneficial
for both scientific and technological reasons and has spurred a large number of
researchers to investigate underlying neural mechanisms [5].

Psychophysical and neurophysiological results on global motion integration in
primates have inspired many computational models of motion processing [17,19].
However, gratings and plaids are spatially homogeneous motion inputs such that

S. Battiato et al. (Eds.): ICIAP 2017 International Workshops, LNCS 10590, pp. 60–71, 2017.
https://doi.org/10.1007/978-3-319-70742-6_6

spatial and temporal aspects of motion integration have been largely ignored by these linear-nonlinear filtering models. Dynamical models have been proposed [3] to study these spatial interactions and how they can explain the diffusion of non-ambiguous local motion cues [4]. Moreover, the bio-inspired models [12] are barely evaluated in terms of their efficacy on modern computer vision datasets with the notable exceptions such as in [2] (with an early evaluation of spatio-temporal filters) or in [4] (with evaluations on Yosemite or Middlebury videos subset).

In this paper, we propose to fill the gap between studies in biological and computer vision for motion estimation by building our approach on results from visual neuroscience and thoroughly evaluating the method using standard computer vision dataset (Middlebury). It is worth noting that the main interest of this work is not to compete with the state of the art (resulting from more than 20 years of intense research by computer vision community) but to show where a classical model from neuroscience stands with respect to computer vision approaches. The paper is organized as follows. In Sect. 2, we present a brief overview of the motion processing pathway of the primate brain, on which our model is based, and we describe a state of the art model (i.e. a baseline to be improved) for optical flow estimation based on V1-MT feedforward interactions (see [20] for more details). In Sect. 3, we propose the AMPD model, which extends the baseline one through principles inspired by functions of the visual system of the brain by taking into account both image structure and contrast adaptive pooling and ambiguity resolution through lateral interactions among MT neurons. In Sect. 4, the proposed model is evaluated using the standard Middlebury dataset, and Sect. 5 is left for the conclusion.

2 Biological Vision Solutions and a State of the Art Model

Cortical hierarchy. In visual neuroscience, properties of low-level motion processing have been extensively investigated in humans and monkeys [13]. Local motion information is extracted locally through a set of spatiotemporal filters in area V1. Direction-selective cells project directly to the motion integration stage. Neurons in the area MT pool these responses over a broad range of spatial and temporal scales, becoming able to extract the direction and speed of a particular surface, regardless its shape or color [5]. Context modulations are not only implemented by center-surround interactions in areas V1 and MT, but other extra-striate areas such as V2 or V4 project to MT neurons to convey information about the structure of the visual scene, such as the orientation or color of local edges [12].

Receptive fields: a local analysis. Receptive fields (RFs) in the visual field are first small and become larger going deeper in the hierarchy [13]. The small RF size of V1 neurons, and their strong orientation selectivity, poses several difficulties when estimating global motion direction and speed. In particular, any local motion analyzer will face the three following computational problems [5]:

- Absence of illumination contrast is referred to as blank wall problem, in which the local estimator is oblivious to any kind of motion.
- Presence of luminance contrast changes along only one orientation is often referred to as aperture problem, where the local estimator cannot recover the velocity component along the gradient.
- Presence of multiple motions or multiple objects with in the RF, in which case the local estimator has to be selective to arrive at an accurate estimation.

In terms of optical flow estimation, feedforward computation involving V1 and MT could be sufficient in the case of regions without any ambiguity. On the contrary, recovering velocity at regions where there is some ambiguity such as aperture or blank wall problems imply to pool reliable information from other, less ambiguous regions in the surrounding. Such spatial diffusion of information is thought to be conveyed by the intricate network of lateral connections – short-range, or recurrent networks, and long-range – (see [9] for reviews).

Contrast adaptive processing. The structure of neuronal RFs adapts to the local context of the image [18]. and, for instance, orientation-tuning in area V1 and speed tuning of MT neurons are sharper when tested with broad-band texture inputs, as compared to low-dimension gratings [8]. Moreover, spatial summation function often broadens as contrast decreases or noise level increases. Surround inhibition in V1 and MT neurons becomes stronger at high contrast and center-surround interactions exhibit a large diversity in terms of their relative tunings. Moreover, the spatial structure of these interactions is different from the Mexican-hat structure [5]. Lastly, at each decoding stage, it seems nowadays that tuning functions are weighted by the reliability of the neuronal responses, as varying for instance with contrast or noise levels. Still, these highly adaptive properties have barely been taken into account when modeling visual motion processing. Here, we model some of these mechanisms to highlight their potential impact on optic flow computation. We focus on both the role of local image structure (contrast, textureness) and the reliability of these local measurements in controlling the diffusion mechanisms. We investigated how these mechanisms can help solving local ambiguities, and segmenting the flow fields into different surfaces while still preserving the sharpness and precision of natural vision.

2.1 Baseline Model (FFV1MT)

In this section, we briefly introduce the FFV1MT model proposed in [20], in which we revisited the seminal work by Heeger [19] using spatio-temporal filters to estimate optical flow. FFV1MT model is a three-step approach, corresponding to area V1, area MT and decoding of MT response. In term of notations, we consider a grayscale image sequence $I(x, y, t)$, for all positions $p = (x, y)$ inside a domain Ω and for all time $t > 0$. Our goal is to find the optical flow $v(x, y, t) = (v_x, v_y)(x, y, t)$ defined as the apparent motion at each position p and time t.

- *Area V1: Motion Energy.* Area V1 comprises simple and complex cells to estimate motion energy. Complex cells receive inputs from several simple cells
and their response properties have been modeled by the motion energy, which
is a non linear combination of afferent simple cell responses.
Simple cells are characterized by the preferred direction θ of their contrast
sensitivity in the spatial domain and their preferred velocity v^c in the direction orthogonal to their contrast orientation often referred to as component
speed. The RFs of the V1 simple cells are modeled using band-pass filters in
the spatio-temporal domain: the spatial component of the filter is described
by Gabor filters h and temporal component by an exponential decay function k. Denoting the real and imaginary components of the complex filters h
and k as h_e, k_e and h_o, k_o respectively, and a preferred velocity v^c we introduce the odd $g_o(p, t, \theta, v^c) = h_o(p, \theta, f_s)k_e(t; f_t) + h_e(p, \theta, f_s)k_o(t; f_t)$, and
even $g_e(p, t, \theta, v^c) = h_e(p, \theta, f_s)k_e(t; f_t) - h_o(p, \theta, f_s)k_o(t; f_t)$ spatio-temporal
filters, where f_s and f_t denote the peak spatial and temporal frequencies.
Using these expressions, we define the response of simple cells, either odd or
even, with a preferred direction of contrast sensitivity θ in the spatial domain,
with a preferred velocity v^c and with a spatial scale σ by

$$R_{o/e}(p, t, \theta, v^c) = g_{o/e}(p, t, \theta, v^c) \overset{(x,y,t)}{*} I(x, y, t) \tag{1}$$

The complex cells are described as a combination of the quadrature pair
of simple cells (1) by using the motion energy formulation, $E(p, t, \theta, v^c) = R_o(p, t, \theta, v^c)^2 + R_e(p, t, \theta, v^c)^2$, followed by a normalization. Assuming that
we consider a finite set of orientations $\theta = \theta_1 \ldots \theta_N$, to obtain the final V1
response

$$E^{V1}(p, t, \theta, v^c) = \frac{E(p, t, \theta, v^c)}{\sum_{i=1}^{N} E(p, t, \theta_i, v^c) + \varepsilon}, \tag{2}$$

where $0 < \varepsilon \ll 1$ is a small constant to avoid divisions by zero in regions with
no energies which happen when no spatio-temporal texture is present.
- *Area MT: Pattern Cells Response.* MT neurons exhibit velocity tuning irrespective of the contrast orientation. This is believed to be achieved by pooling
afferent responses in both spatial and orientation domains followed by a nonlinearity. The responses of an MT pattern cell [17,19] tuned to the speed v^c
and to direction of speed d can be expressed as follows:

$$E^{MT}(p, t; d, v^c) = F\left(\sum_{i=1}^{N} w_d(\theta_i)\mathscr{P}(E^{V1})(p, t; \theta_i, v^c)\right),$$

where $w_d(\theta) = \cos(d - \theta)$, $d \in [0, 2\pi[$, represents the MT linear weights that
give origin to the MT tuning, $F(s) = exp(s)$ is a static nonlinearity chosen
as an exponential function [14,17], and $\mathscr{P}(E^{V1})$ corresponds to the spatial
pooling.
Cosine function shifted over various orientations is a potential function that
could satisfy this requirement (i.e. smooth function with central excitation

and lateral inhibition) to produce the responses for a population of MT neurons [11]. The spatial pooling term is defined by

$$\mathscr{P}(E^{V1})(p,t;\theta_i,v^c) = \frac{1}{\bar{N}} \sum_{p'} f_\alpha(\|p-p'\|)E^{V1}(p',t;\theta_i,v^c) \qquad (3)$$

where $f_\mu(s) = \exp(s^2/2\mu^2)$, $\|.\|$ is the L_2-norm, α is a constant, and $\bar{N}$ is a normalization term (here equal to $2\pi\alpha^2$). The pooling defined by (3) is a simple spatial Gaussian pooling.

- *Sampling and Decoding MT Response: Optical Flow Estimation.* In order to engineer an algorithm capable of recovering dense optical flow estimates, we still need to address problems of sampling and decoding the population responses of heterogeneously tuned MT neurons. In [20], we proposed a new decoding stage to obtain a dense optical flow estimation from the MT population response. In this paper, we sample the velocity space using two MT populations tuned to the directions $d = 0$ and $d = \pi/2$ with varying tuning speeds. Here, we adopt a simple weighted sum approach to decode the MT population response [15].

$$\begin{cases} v_x(p,t) = \sum_{i=1}^{M} v_i^c E^{MT}(p,t,0,v_i^c), \\ v_y(p,t) = \sum_{i=1}^{M} v_i^c E^{MT}(p,t,\pi/2,v_i^c). \end{cases} \qquad (4)$$

3   Adaptive Motion Pooling and Diffusion Model (AMPD)

The baseline model FFV1MT is largely devised to describe physiological and psychophysical observations on motion estimation when the testing stimuli were largely homogeneously textured regions such as moving gratings and plaids. Hence the model is limited in the context of dense flow estimation for natural videos as it has no inherent mechanism to deal with associated sub problems such blank wall problem, aperture problem or occlusion boundaries. Building on recent results summarized in Sect. 2 we model some of these mechanisms to highlight their potential impact on optic flow computation. Considering inputs from area V2, we focus on the role of local context (contrast and image structure) indicative of the reliability of these local measurements in (i) controlling the pooling from V1 to MT and (ii) adding lateral connectivity in MT.

3.1   Area V2: Contrast and Image Structure

Our goal is to define a measure of contrast, which is indicative of the aperture and blank wall problems, by using the responses of spatial Gabor filters. There exist several approaches to characterize the spatial content of an image from Gabor filter (e.g., in [10] the authors propose the phase congruency approach which detects edges and corners irrespectively of contrast in an image). In dense optical flow estimation problem, region with texture are less likely to suffer blank wall and aperture problems even though edges are susceptible to aperture problem. So phase congruency approach cannot be used directly and we propose the following simple alternative approach.

Let h_{θ_i} the Gabor filter for edge orientation θ_i, we define

$$R(p) = (R_{\theta_1}(p), \ldots, R_{\theta_N}(p)) \text{ where } R_{\theta_i}(p) = |h_{\theta_i} * I|(p).$$

Given an edge orientation at θ_i, R_{θ_i} is maximal when crossing the edge and ∇R_{θ_i} indicate the direction to go away from edge.

Then the following contrast/cornerness measure is proposed as follows, taking into consideration the amount of contrast at a given location and also ensuring that contrast is not limited to a single orientation giving raise to aperture problem:

$$\mu(R(p)) = \frac{1}{N} \sum_i R_{\theta_i}(p), \tag{5}$$

$$C(p) = H_\xi(\mu(R(p))(1 - \sigma^2(R(p))/\sigma^2_{max}), \tag{6}$$

where $\mu(R(p))$ (resp. $\sigma^2(R(p))$) denote the average (resp. variance) of components of R at position p, $H_\xi(s)$ is a step function ($H_\xi(s) = 0$ if $s \leq \xi$ and 1 otherwise) and $\sigma^2_{max} = \max_p \sigma^2(R(p))$. The term $H_\xi(\mu(R(p))$ is an indicator of contrast as it measures the Gabor energies: in regions with strong contrast or strong texture in any orientation this term equals to one; in a blank wall situation, it is equal to zero. The term $(1 - \sigma^2(R(p))/\sigma^2_{max})$ measures how strongly the contrast is oriented in a single direction: it is higher when there is only contrast in one direction and lower when there is contrast in more than one orientation (thus it is an indicator of where there is aperture problem).

3.2   Area MT: V2-Modulated Pooling

Most of the models currently pool V1-afferents using a linear fixed RF size, which does not adapt itself to the local gradient or respect discontinuities in spatio-temporal reposes. This might lead to degradation in the velocity estimates by blurring edges/kinetic boundaries. Thus it is advantageous to make the V1 to MT pooling adaptive as a function of texture edges.

We propose to modify the pooling stage as follows

$$E^{MT}(p, t; d, v^c) = F\left(\sum_{i=1}^{N} w_d(\theta_i)\tilde{\mathscr{P}}(E^{V1})(p, t; \theta_i, v^c)\right),$$

where the spatial pooling become functions of image structure.

We propose the following texture-dependent spatial pooling:

$$\tilde{\mathscr{P}}(E^{V1})(p, t; \theta_i, v^c) = \frac{1}{\tilde{N}(p, \theta_i)} \sum_{p'} \tilde{W}(p, p') E^{V1}(p', t; \theta_i, v^c), \tag{7}$$

where $\tilde{W}(p, p') = f_{\alpha(\|R\|(p))}(\|p - p'\|)g_i(p, p')$, and where $\bar{N}(p, \theta_i) = \sum_{p'} \tilde{W}(p, p')$ is a normalizing term. Note that the weight $W(p, p')$ has two components which depend on image structure as follows. Term $f_{\alpha(\|R\|(p))}(\|p - p'\|)$ is an isotropic weight setting the size of the integration domain. The variance of the distance term α depends on the structure R_{θ_i}:

$$\alpha(\|R\|(p)) = \alpha_{max} e^{-\eta \frac{\|R\|^2(p)}{r_{max}}}, \tag{8}$$

where η is a constant, $r_{max} = \max_{p'}\{\|R\|^2(p')\}$. Term $g_i(p, p')$ is an anisotropic weight enabling anisotropic pooling close to image structures so that discontinuities could be better preserved. Here we propose to define g_i by

$$g_i(p, p') = S_{\lambda, \nu}\left(-\frac{\nabla R_{\theta_i}(p)}{\|\nabla R_{\theta_i}\| + \varepsilon} \cdot (p' - p)\right), \tag{9}$$

where $S_{\lambda, \nu}(x) = 1/(1 + \exp(-\lambda(x - \nu)))$ is a sigmoid function and ε a small constant. Note that this term is used only in regions where $\|\nabla R_{\theta_i}\|$ is greater than a threshold. Figure 1 gives two examples of the pooling coefficients at different positions.

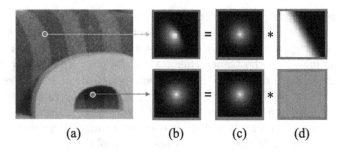

$$\text{(a)} \qquad\qquad \text{(b)} \qquad\qquad \text{(c)} \qquad \text{(d)}$$

Fig. 1. Example of pooling weights at different positions: (a) Sample input indicating two different positions p (see red and blue dots) at which we show: (b) the final pooling weight $W(\cdot, p)$ which is obtained by multiplying (c) the isotropic term by the (d) anisotropic term (see text). (Color figure online)

3.3   MT Lateral Interactions

We model the lateral iterations for the velocity information spread (from the regions where there is less ambiguity to regions with high ambiguity, see Sect. 2) whilst preserving discontinuities in motion and illumination. To do so, we propose an iterated trilateral filtering defined by:

$$u^{n+1}(p) = \frac{1}{\bar{N}(p)} \sum_{p'} W(p, p') u^n(p'), \tag{10}$$

$$c^{n+1}(p) = c^n(p) + \lambda(\max_{p' \in \mathcal{N}(p)} c^n(p') - c^n(p)) \tag{11}$$

$$u^0(p) = E^{MT}(p, t; \theta_i, v^c), \tag{12}$$

$$c^0(p) = C(p), \tag{13}$$

where

$$W(p,p') = c^n(p')f_\alpha(\|p - p'\|)f_\beta(c^n(p)(u^n(p') - u^n(p)))$$
$$f_\gamma(I(p') - I(p))u^n(p'), \quad (14)$$

and $\mathcal{N}(p)$ is a local neighborhood around p. The term $c(p')$ ensures that more weight is given naturally to high confidence estimates. The term $c(p)$ inside f_β ensures that differences in the MT responses are ignored when confidence is low facilitating the diffusion of information from regions with high confidence and at the same time preserves motion discontinuities or blurring at the regions with high confidence.

4 Results

In order to test the proposed method, a coarse-to-fine multi-scale version of both the baseline approach FFV1MT and approach with adaptive pooling AMPD are considered. The method is applied on a Gaussian pyramid with 6 scales, the maximum number of scales that could be reliably used for the spatio-temporal filter support that has been chosen.

A first test was done on the Yosemite sequence (without clouds) as it is widely used in both computer vision and biological vision studies (see Fig. 2, first row). For FFV1MT we have AEE $= 3.55 \pm 2.92$, and for AMPD AAE $= 2.94 \pm 2.00$, where AAE is the average angular error (with associated standard deviations) [1]. This can be compared to what has been obtained with previous biologically-inspired models such as the original Heeger approach [2] (AAE $= 11.74°$) and the neural model proposed in [3] (AAE $= 6.20°$), showing an improvement. One can do comparisons with standard computer vision approaches such as Pyramidal Lucas and Kanade (AAE $= 6.41°$) and Horn and Schunk (AAE $= 4.01°$), showing a better performance.

The results on the Middlebury training set show improvements of the proposed method (see Table 1): in particular, AMPD improves the results of 18%, by considering the average AAE (aAAE) for all the sequences (aAAE $= 7.40°$), with respect to FFV1MT (aAAE $= 9.05°$). By considering state of the art computer vision approaches [16], our model (average EPE for all the sequences, aEPE $= 0.71$ pixel) performs better than some algorithms, e.g. FlowNetC (aEPE $= 0.93$ pixel), but other algorithms outperform it, e.g. SPyNet (aEPE $= 0.33$ pixel).

For qualitative comparison, sample results are also presented in Fig. 2. The relative performance can be understood by observing δAAE (last column of Fig. 2), difference between the FFV1MT AAE map and the AMPD AAE map: the improvements are prominent at the edges.

In order to assess the influence of the two cortical mechanisms (the V2-Modulated Pooling and the MT Lateral Interactions, see Sects. 3.2 and 3.3, respectively) on the optic flow computation, we have alternatively removed one of the two mechanisms from the AMPD model: the relative contribution of the

Table 1. Error measurements, AAE and EPE (endpoint error), on Middlebury training set

Sequence	FFV1MT		AMPD	
	AAE ± STD	EPE ± STD	AAE ± STD	EPE ± STD
grove2	4.28 ± 10.25	0.29 ± 0.62	3.71 ± 8.95	0.25 ± 0.54
grove3	9.72 ± 19.34	1.13 ± 1.85	9.42 ± 18.41	1.00 ± 1.62
Hydrangea	5.96 ± 11.17	0.62 ± 0.96	5.83 ± 11.41	0.51 ± 0.71
RubberWhale	10.20 ± 17.67	0.34 ± 0.54	6.69 ± 10.92	0.24 ± 0.34
urban2	14.51 ± 21.02	1.46 ± 2.13	11.91 ± 18.98	1.01 ± 1.41
urban3	15.11 ± 35.28	1.88 ± 3.27	11.31 ± 29.73	1.24 ± 2.17

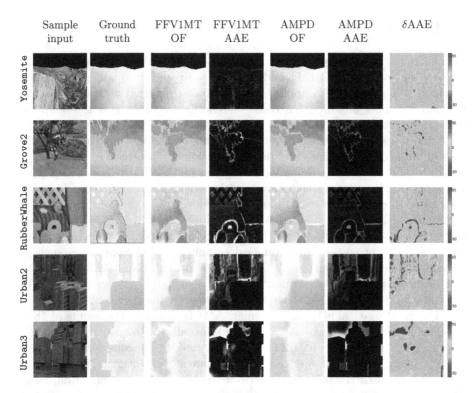

Fig. 2. Sample results on Yosemite sequence and a subset of Middlebury training set. $\delta AAE = AAE_{FFV1MT} - AAE_{AMPD}$

V2-Modulated Pooling (aAAE = 8.32°) and of the MT Lateral Interactions (aAAE = 8.31°) is similar, which corresponds to an improvement of 8%. In order to qualitatively highlight the relative contribution of the different neural mechanisms on optic flow computation, Fig. 3 shows an enlarged region of the RubberWhale sequence. It is worth noting that the main effect of the two devised mechanisms is on borders and discontinuities.

FFV1MT OF	FFV1MT AAE	V2-mod OF	V2-mod AAE	MT lat OF	MT lat AAE	AMPD OF	AMPD AAE

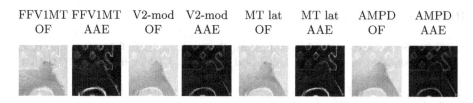

Fig. 3. Comparison of the effects on optic flow computation of the different neural mechanisms considered: in particular "V2-mod" refers to the V2-Modulated Pooling and "MT lat" to the MT Lateral Interactions.

5 Conclusion

In this paper, we have proposed the new brain-inspired algorithm AMPD that incorporates three functional principles observed in primate visual system, namely contrast adaptation, image structure based afferent pooling and ambiguity based lateral interaction. The AMPD is an extension of the state of the art algorithm FFV1MT [20], which is appreciated by both computer vision and biological vision communities. Contemporary computer vision methods to Heeger et al. [19], such as Lucas and Kanade and Horn and Schunck, which study local motion estimation and global constraints to solve aperture problem, have been revisited by the computer vision with great interest [6] and a lot of investigations are being carried out to regulate the information diffusion from non-ambiguous regions to ambiguous regions based on image structure. Very few attempts have been made to incorporate these ideas into spatio-temporal filter based models, and given the recent growth in neuroscience, it is very interesting to revisit this model incorporating the new findings and examining the efficacy. Differently from FFV1MT and Spynet [16], which only rely on scale space for diffusion of non-local cues, our AMPD model provides a clue on the potential role played by the recurrent interactions in solving the blank wall problem by non local cue propagation. It is also worth noting that bilateral filtering based techniques are gaining popularity in semantic segmentation using convolutional neural networks. Here, we show how neural modulation based on local context amounts to such bilateral filtering and a promising direction to explore even for dense optical flow.

The AMPD improves the flow estimation compared to FFV1MT and it has opened up several interesting sub problems, which could be of relevance to biologists as well, for example to investigate what could be afferent pooling strategy of MT when there are multiple surfaces or occlusion boundaries within the MT RFs, or if we could recover a better dense optical flow map by considering decoding problem as a deblurring problem due the spatial support of the filters.

References

1. Baker, S., Scharstein, D., Lewis, J., Roth, S., Black, M.J., Szeliski, R.: A database and evaluation methodology for optical flow. Int. J. Comput. Vis. **92**(1), 1–31 (2011)
2. Barron, J., Fleet, D., Beauchemin, S.: Performance of optical flow techniques. Int. J. Comput. Vis. **12**(1), 43–77 (1994)
3. Bayerl, P., Neumann, H.: Disambiguating visual motion through contextual feedback modulation. Neural Comput. **16**(10), 2041–2066 (2004)
4. Bouecke, J.D., Tlapale, E., Kornprobst, P., Neumann, H.: Neural mechanisms of motion detection, integration, and segregation: from biology to artificial image processing systems. EURASIP J. Adv. Sig. Process. **2011**, 6 (2011)
5. Bradley, D.C., Goyal, M.S.: Velocity computation in the primate visual system. Nat. Rev. Neurosci. **9**(9), 686–695 (2008)
6. Bruhn, A., Weickert, J., Schnörr, C.: Lucas/Kanade meets Horn/Schunck: combining local and global optic flow methods. Int. J. Comput. Vis. **61**(3), 211–231 (2005)
7. Butler, D.J., Wulff, J., Stanley, G.B., Black, M.J.: A naturalistic open source movie for optical flow evaluation. In: Fitzgibbon, A., Lazebnik, S., Perona, P., Sato, Y., Schmid, C. (eds.) ECCV 2012. LNCS, vol. 7577, pp. 611–625. Springer, Heidelberg (2012). https://doi.org/10.1007/978-3-642-33783-3_44
8. Freeman, J., Ziemba, C.M., Heeger, D.J., Simoncelli, E.P., Movshon, J.A.: A functional and perceptual signature of the second visual area in primates. Nat. Neurosci. **16**(7), 974–981 (2013)
9. Ilg, U., Masson, G.: Dynamics of Visual Motion Processing: Neuronal, Behavioral, and Computational Approaches. Springer, New York (2010). https://doi.org/10.1007/978-1-4419-0781-3. Springer e-Books
10. Kovesi, P.: Image features from phase congruency. Videre: J. Comput. Vis. Res. **1**(3), 1–26 (1999)
11. Maunsell, J.H., Van Essen, D.C.: Functional properties of neurons in middle temporal visual area of the macaque monkey. I. Selectivity for stimulus direction, speed, and orientation. J. Neurophysiol. **49**(5), 1127–1147 (1983)
12. Medathati, N.V.K., Neumann, H., Masson, G.S., Kornprobst, P.: Bio-inspired computer vision: towards a synergistic approach of artificial and biological vision. Comput. Vis. Image Underst. **150**, 1–30 (2016)
13. Orban, G.A.: Higher order visual processing in macaque extrastriate cortex. Physiol. Rev. **88**(1), 59–89 (2008)
14. Paninski, L.: Maximum likelihood estimation of cascade point-process neural encoding models. Netw.: Comput. Neural Syst. **15**(4), 243–262 (2004)
15. Rad, K.R., Paninski, L.: Information rates and optimal decoding in large neural populations. In: Shawe-Taylor, J., Zemel, R.S., Bartlett, P.L., Pereira, F.C.N., Weinberger, K.Q. (eds.) NIPS, pp. 846–854 (2011)
16. Ranjan, A., Black, M.: Optical flow estimation using a spatial pyramid network. In: IEEE Conference on Computer Vision and Pattern Recognition (CVPR), July 2017
17. Rust, N.C., Mante, V., Simoncelli, E.P., Movshon, J.A.: How MT cells analyze the motion of visual patterns. Nat. Neurosci. **9**(11), 1421–1431 (2006)

18. Sharpee, T.O., Sugihara, H., Kurgansky, A.V., Rebrik, S.P., Stryker, M.P., Miller, K.D.: Adaptive filtering enhances information transmission in visual cortex. Nature **439**(7079), 936–942 (2006)
19. Simoncelli, E.P., Heeger, D.J.: A model of neuronal responses in visual area MT. Vis. Res. **38**(5), 743–761 (1998)
20. Solari, F., Chessa, M., Medathati, N.K., Kornprobst, P.: What can we expect from a V1-MT feedforward architecture for optical flow estimation? Sig. Process. Image Commun. **39**, 342–354 (2015)

Ventral Stream-Inspired Process for Deriving 3D Models from Video Sequences

Julius Schöning$^{(\boxtimes)}$ and Gunther Heidemann

Institute of Cognitive Science, University of Osnabrück, Osnabrück, Germany
juschoening@uos.de

Abstract. The reconstruction of complex 3D objects from video sequences captured by surveillance, smartphone, and other cameras is a common technique in Hollywood blockbusters and TV series. Unfortunately, the automatic or interactive 3D object reconstruction from this kind of videos is not yet possible in the real world. Enabling computers to recognize the actual 3D shape of objects from complex video sequences, we developed a bio-inspired processing architecture, motivated by findings in the area of human object recognition. By utilizing viewpoint-specific object recognition, changes in position and size of the object of interest in video sequences can be eliminated to a great extent. The result is a representation, comprised of multiple pictures showing 2D projections of the object of interest (OOI) from different viewpoints. Based on this representation, a 3D point cloud (PC) from the object can be obtained. After a detailed description of our architecture and its similarities to the human view-combination scheme, we demonstrate its potency by reconstructing several OOI from complex video sequences. Because some processing modules of the architecture cannot yet be fully automatized, we introduced interactive modules instead. Thus the prototypical implementation of our approach could be realized. Based on the resulting PC, we evaluate our architecture and consider more analogies between human and computer vision, which improve image-based 3D reconstruction.

1 Introduction

In London, UK, we are being filmed by at least 300 different surveillance cameras on a daily basis [18]. With surveillance playing such a big part in our lives, non-experts usually believe that video-based 3D reconstruction of e.g. a bag someone is carrying is already possible in a similar manner as in blockbusters and TV series. Even with state of the art technologies, however, these tasks are usually still tough, especially if the videos are showing moving objects in their natural context. With the nowadays exponentially increasing amount of video sequences uploaded to video-sharing platforms the ability to reconstruct 3D objects from any videos would offer a valuable addition to existing methods of exploring and utilizing these large databases for a multitude of implementations. In contrast to the computer, the recognition of the 3D shape of an OOI within video sequences

© Springer International Publishing AG 2017
S. Battiato et al. (Eds.): ICIAP 2017 International Workshops, LNCS 10590, pp. 72–83, 2017.
https://doi.org/10.1007/978-3-319-70742-6_7

is quite easy for humans, even if the videos do not show the OOI from every side, or if the OOI is partially occluded.

For the purpose of enabling computers to reconstruct 3D models of any OOI, which is shown from all angles, in their natural environment in one or several video sequences, we developed, implemented and evaluated a bio-inspired processing architecture. With our general architecture for deriving 3D models from video sequences, we are moving computer vision from controlled environments with specific data sets, conditions, setups, etc., into real world scenarios. The real world scenarios present challenges, such as semantic object recognition, which are not yet completely solvable with fully-automatic approaches. Thus, to facilitate a prototypical implementation of our process architecture, some of the processing modules of our architecture are interactive.

One or several video sequences showing the same OOI from different specific viewpoints suffice as input data, for our proposed bio-inspired architecture. The extraction of all viewpoint-specific representations of a certain OOI is the essential part of our architecture. Therefore, 2D object recognition algorithms are applied for recognizing the OOI and separating it from the background in every frame. As a result, multiple 2D viewpoint-specific representations of the 3D OOI are extracted from the input data. Using multiple view geometry (MVG) algorithms, these viewpoint-specific representations are used for creating solid viewpoint-invariant geometrical watertight 3D models. These models are beneficial for many technical use cases, e.g. in any computer-aided design (CAD) task [13,19], but on the other hand, these models do not reflect the representation of 3D objects in the brain [6,25]. From viewpoint-specific representations of an OOI, any MVG algorithm, such as structure from motion (SfM) algorithms, calculates the corresponding 3D PC as the basis for the virtual meshed 3D model. It should be noted that so far the generation of virtual viewpoint-invariant 3D models is only inspired by their technical use cases since current psychophysical evidence suggests that "humans encode 3D objects as multiple viewpoint-specific representations that are largely 2D" [6]. Apart from that, some other theories promote the usage of viewpoint-invariant representations in the human brain, such as viewpoint-invariant 3D model representations [15] or combinations of viewpoint-invariant geon structural descriptions [11]. Independent of their overall conclusion, most theories suggest viewpoint-invariant representation at some stage in the process, such that the low-level modules of our architecture emulate the visual information processing in the human brain on a high-level basis.

2 Viewpoint-Specific Object Recognition for Deriving 3D Models from Videos

Our 3D reconstruction architecture [23] which is powered by viewpoint-specific object recognition consists of six processing modules (cf. Fig. 1) and can reconstruct a 3D model of an OOI from any video sequence, recorded by a normal monocular camera. The first four bio-inspired processing modules recognize the viewpoint-specific 2D projection of the OOI on each frame of every video sequence. They are functioning similarly to the main processing direction of the ventral stream pathway of the visual cortex [26,27] and are responsible for the viewpoint-specific object recognition. Thus, these four modules are sequential, straightforward and bottom-up organized in our architecture. The following two processing modules reconstruct the viewpoint-independent virtual 3D model of the OOI by using the recognized 2D projection. These last two modules are mainly technically-inspired and can be compared with SfM approaches [13,21]. The answer to why we motivated our architecture with the ventral visual stream [26,27] of the visual cortex, which is associated with object recognition and not with the dorsal stream [26,27], which is responsible for the spatial aspect "where" the object is located, is simple. The most relevant information for reconstructing a sole object is "what" the object looks like and not "where" the object is located. So the context around an object is irrelevant, in our opinion, for recognizing its 3D shape. Nevertheless, for recognizing the identity of objects, the real world context is relevant [16]. By recognizing and separating the OOI on every frame, where the OOI is visible, apriori real world knowledge is added to the video sequences.

I. Reading input videos as pixel cuboid translates the video sequences into a processable data format. In our case, video sequences of any format are translated into 3D cuboids of pixels $C_1, C_2, \ldots C_n$, where n is the number of available video sequences $S_1, S_2, \ldots S_n$ showing the OOI. For each $i = 1, \ldots, n$, the dimensions of cuboid C_i are defined by the horizontal resolution h_i, by the vertical resolution v_i and the number of frames f_i of each video sequence, thus C_i has $h_i \times v_i \times f_i$ pixels. Furthermore, every pixel $p_i(x, y, t)$ is given as a triple of the additive primary colors.

II. Annotating pixels of cuboids states, whether or not a pixel $p_i(x, y, t)$ belongs to the OOI. Based on a pixel-accurate viewpoint-dependent object recognition in natural scenes, this module provides further information like whether the OOI is occluded and if parts of the OOI are outside the frame.

III. Annotation-based pixel nullification sets the pixels mark as not belonging to the OOI to null. Thus, this module returns the cuboids $C_1, C_2, \ldots C_n$ represent the 2D projection of the OOI.

IV. Creating multiple pictorial representations is the processing module that extracts and crops all non-empty frames from the cuboids based on the minimum bounding rectangle. The resulting sequence of views $V_1, V_2, \ldots, V_z$ show the OOI from different viewpoints. The different projections are caused by the moving OOI and the moving camera. Note, the temporal ordering of the views gain further information and is also extracted.

V. Building a PC based on all views $V_1, V_2, \ldots, V_z$. Due to the prior bio-inspired modules **I** to **IV**, any MVG approach should be able to calculate a dense PC of the OOI based on the multiple pictorial representations. Thus this module is the interface between the bio-inspired and technologically-inspired modules for creating a 3D model.

VI. Meshing the PC creates the watertight surface of the OOI based on its PC. From the several different approaches that exist, we suggest the ball-pivoting algorithm by Bernardini et al. [2], because it does not interpolate points of the PC, thereby its preserving their position during meshing. However, unlike, for example, the Poisson meshing [12], the resulting mesh is mostly not watertight.

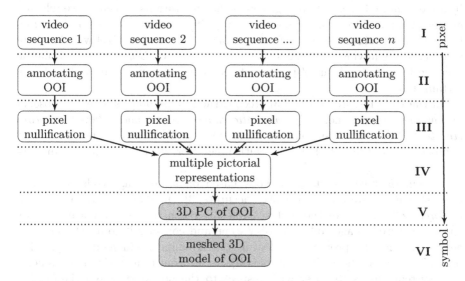

Fig. 1. Overview of our bio-inspired architecture [23] for deriving 3D models powered by viewpoint-specific object recognition; consists of six modules: **I** reading input videos as pixel cuboid, **II** annotating pixels of cuboids—viewpoint-specific pixel-accurate recognition, **III** annotation-based pixel nullification, **IV** creating multiple pictorial representations, **V** building a PC, and **VI** meshing PC. Non-filled modules are bio-inspired; gray marked modules are technology-inspired for creating 3D models.

3   Related Work

Giving a brief overview, only the major topics: image segmentation and annotation tools, and image-based 3D reconstruction techniques are mentioned below.

Fully automatic and pixel-accurate OOI detection, as well as segmentation from images especially from image sequences, seems far from being solved. In general, it can be observed that the performance scores of segmentation algorithm drop significantly from easier data sets, i.e. showing the complete OOI, to natural data sets, i.e. showing a partially occluded OOI [4]. Even the run-time of segmentation methods [4] is, in our opinion, not applicable for high-resolution images. Overcoming the obstacle of inaccurate segmentation, interactive algorithms like interactive graph cut [5] are promising approaches.

Annotation tools for polygon-shaped labeling of OOI can be seen as an extension of interactive segmentation algorithms. Thus, existing video annotation tools could be used for the implementation of processing modules **I** and **II** of our proposed architecture. According to a review [8] of seven video annotation tools, only one tool, the Video and Image Annotation tool (*VIA*, provides pixel-accurate OOI annotations. The quite popular Video Performance Evaluation Resource (*ViPER*) [9] perform object labeling process which can be speeded up by an automatic linear 2D propagation of the annotations. Recently, we released an open source video annotation tool—*iSeg* [20]. It came with a novel interactive and semi-automatic segmentation process for creating pixel-wise labels of several objects in video sequences. The latest version of *iSeg* provides a semantic timeline for defining if an object is not, partially, or completely occluded in a certain frame.

In the wide research area of 3D reconstruction techniques, one can observe two main strategies, i.e. *fully automatic reconstruction* and *interactive reconstruction*. For our bio-inspired architecture, only those 3D reconstruction approaches are relevant that work with images or videos captured by monocular cameras.

Automatic reconstruction methods based on large image collections have been shown to produce sufficiently accurate 3D models [13,21]. The *photo explorer* [24], as one of the first scalable 3D reconstruction application, uses an unstructured image collection of a scene and converts it to a 3D model. In near real-time, the probabilistic feature-based online rapid model acquisition tool [17] reconstructs freely rotatable objects, in front of a static video camera. This system guides the user with respect to the necessary manipulation, i.e. "please rotation of the object clockwise", needed for the object reconstruction.

Often challenging for these automatic reconstruction techniques are the handling of delicate structures, textureless surfaces, hidden boundaries, illumination, specularity, and even dynamic or moving objects, etc., but they usually occur in natural video sequences. Motivated by these issues, Kowdle et al. [13] came up with a semi-automatic approach, which embeds the user in the process of reconstruction. Other interactive approaches are based on the presence of common geometric primitives, i.e. human-made architecture [1] for reconstruction. Usually, such approaches are designed out of automatic pre-processing steps followed by interactive processing steps.

All of the techniques as mentioned earlier have in common that the reconstructed 3D objects are monolithic and not semantically split into their parts or rather subparts. Today, monolithic 3D models are sufficient for indoor navigation, reconstruction of urban environments, etc., but for more complex tasks, the detailed reconstruction of objects including their subparts might be necessary [19]. As a consequence, further research in 3D reconstruction should also focus on semantic part detection in 3D models, as well as from the input data.

4   Analogies to the Ventral Stream

During the implementation of our bio-inspired architecture with all modules illustrated in Fig. 1, we recognize many analogies of our system to the view-combination scheme by Ullman [25].

Ullman stated, in the view-combination scheme, that "recognition by multiple pictorial representations and their combinations constitutes a major component of 3D object recognition" [25, p. 154] of humans and "unlike some of the prevailing approaches... object recognition... is simpler, more direct, and pictorial in nature. " [25, p. 154]. The first four processing modules **I–IV** of our bio-inspired architecture reduce the complexity of the input information, from unclassified pixels over segmented pixels to multiple pictorial representations without any contextual information (cf. [23, Fig. 3]). This process is similar to the statement that "cells along the hierarchy from $V1$ to $V4$ also show an increasing degree of tolerance for the position and size of their preferred stimuli" [25, p. 152]. "An object appears to be represented in IT by multiple units, tuned to different views of the object" [25, p. 152] describing the general idea of SfM, comparable to our processing module **V**.

One can see a strong analogy between the bottom-up idea of the view-combination scheme and our architecture, up to processing module **V** including. The processing module **VI** might be a part of the top-down process, representing an internal object model. In our definition, however, it cannot be mapped to Ullman's scheme.

5   Application of the Architecture

In order to evaluate the performance of our architecture, we processed two natural video sequences [14] showing a red *car* and four computer-generated video sequences [7,10] showing a *table* and *desk*. Based on the artificial video sequences, we can evaluate the resulting virtual 3D models against a known ground truth. Using a ground truth allows us to analyze the performance on a quantitative level, although the artificial nature of the dataset calls for further investigation on how the results will generalize to real world scenarios. In contrast, for the natural video sequences, we do not have a ground truth. Thus, the performance evaluation can still be conducted on a qualitative level by visual inspection. Comparing both phases gives a comprehensive perspective on the general performance of our implementation and the applicability of the underlying architecture.

5.1   Natural Video Sequences

The qualitative analysis is conducted on natural, real-world video sequences, for which our bio-inspired architecture is designed. In our case, we choose the first two video sequences of a benchmark data set for evaluating visual analysis techniques for eye tracking data from video stimuli [14]. These two sequences show the same rigid OOI, a red *car*, driving along roads. Both video sequences provide a resolution of 1080p at a frame rate of 25 fps, and exemplary frames are shown in Fig. 2(a – b). With a duration of 25 s, the first sequence contains, in addition to object motion, camera movement. Furthermore, it also contains frames, where the OOI is partially occluded, completely occluded or off the frame. The second sequence, with a duration of 28 s, contains motion of the OOI only. The number plate of the car is blurred in each video sequence.

5.2 Computer-Generated Sequences

Video sequences, rendered on virtual 3D models of two indoor scenes, are used for quantitative analysis of the proposed architecture. Therefore, the RGB image sequences [7] of the *living room*—cf. Fig. 2(c – d)—and the *office*—cf. Fig. 2(e – f)—are converted to video sequences. The resulting video sequence provides, at a frame rate of 25 fps, a resolution of 640 × 480 pixels and a duration of about 90 s. As rigid OOI, the *table* in the living room scene and the *desk* in the office scene are picked, which were on several frames partial occluded, complete occluded or from the frame. In these sequences, only camera movement occurs. As 3D ground truth for quantitative evaluation, the *table* is extracted from the geometry of the scene [10].

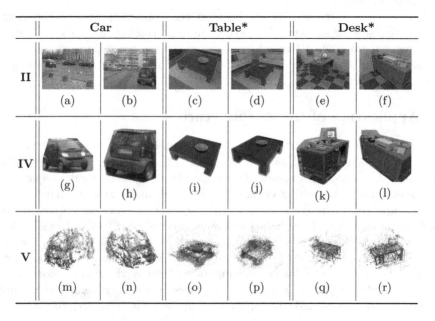

Fig. 2. Exemplary frames of the six video sequences after being processed by the modules **II**, **IV** and **V**. Always two video sequences shown one OOI, here **car**, **table** and **desk**.(a), (b), (c), (d), (e), (f): recognized and annotated OOI in multiple frames; (g), (h), (i), (j), (k), (l): extracted viewpoint-dependent pixel-accurate pictorial representations of the OOI; (m), (n), (o), (p), (q), (r): resulting viewpoint-invariant PC; Note that (f) and (l) show only a partially visible OOI. *computer-generated video sequences rendered from virtual 3D models of indoor scenes.

5.3 Experimental Application

As illustrated by a yellow bounding polygon in Fig. 2(a – f), the OOI is recognized in an interactive process in all six video sequences, using our altered version of *iSeg.* After viewpoint-dependent recognition of the OOI, all sequences including their pixel-wise labels of the OOI are stored in our *mkv*-based exchange format [22], which provides the opportunity to visualize the recognized OOI. The video sequences, including the corresponding OOI annotations, can be found can be found at the project homepage[1].

Using these files, pixel nullification generates a viewpoint-dependent pictorial representation, as seen in Fig. 2(g – l). Note that in case the OOI does not occur on a frame, no pictorial representation is created. Out of the multiple viewpoint-dependent pictorial representations of the recognized OOI, a SfM software [28] computes the PC of the OOI, show in Fig. 2(m – r).

In order to evaluate whether viewpoint-dependent pixel-accurate object recognition improves 3D reconstruction from videos, we also compute the corresponding PC based on the complete, non-nullified frames, where the OOI occurs. Therefore, the stored OOI annotations are only used to assess whether or not the OOI is on a frame. The resulting PC are illustrated in Fig. 3.

(a)   (b)   (c)

Fig. 3. Resulting viewpoint-invariant PC if non pixel-accurate pictorial representations of the OOI (a) **car**, (b) **table**, and (c) **desk** are used for computing the PC; one could recognize that without viewpoint-dependent pixel-accurate object recognition more than just the OOI is represented by the PC.

Obtaining measurements of the accuracy of the proposed architecture, the resulting PC of the *table*, and in Fig. 2(o – p) as well as the result PC without pixel-accurate object recognition, see Fig. 3(b), is compared to the ground truth. Therefore a ground truth PC with 10, 000 vertices was derived from the model of the *table*. Using the open source software *CloudCompare*, the PC are aligned to the ground truth PC. In order to get meaningful information from the dense PC, the resulting PC and the PC of the ground truth are compared with the resulting cloud defined as the reference, as seen in Fig. 4.

6   Results

A first qualitative analysis is conducted by focusing on the last row of Fig. 2. Here, our architecture can reconstruct PC of the OOI. Furthermore, the resulting

---

[1] https://ikw.uos.de/%7Ecv/projects/bi3D.

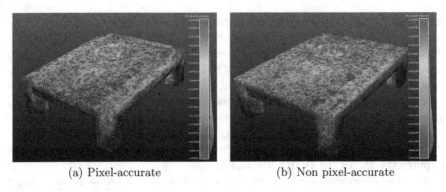

(a) Pixel-accurate   (b) Non pixel-accurate

Fig. 4. Point cloud comparison between the ground truth PC and the resulting PC with and without pixel-accurate object recognition. Note that for the comparisons, the resulting PC is defined as reference; the global coordinate system is scaled on meters.

PC still show an enormous amount of noise, both within the volume of the OOI and also externally, such that it would be even hard for humans to guess the OOI from the PC if the color values of the cloud were omitted. In terms of the qualitative analysis on whether or not pixel-accurate object recognition boosts 3D reconstruction, the last row of Fig. 2 is compared with the PC of Fig. 3. This shows that the PC of the *car* generated from the natural video sequences does not provide a viewpoint-independent 3D model of the *car*. Instead, it only provides a 3D model of the scene, in which the *car* is being driven. Focusing on the computer-generated scene, the OOI are represented in the PC by more points. Thus, the reconstruction result without pixel-accurate object recognition delivers denser PC representation of the OOI.

Due to the missing ground truth, the quantitative analysis can only be done on the artificial, computer-generated video sequences. As seen in Fig. 4, the distribution of cloud to cloud absolute distance between corresponding points is almost identical with a mean value $\mu \approx 0.03\,\mathrm{m}$ at a standard deviation $\sigma \approx 0.018\,\mathrm{m}$. It is striking that by the direct comparison of the PC heat maps, the PC generated by pixel-accurate object recognition, cf. Fig. 4(a), indicates a larger difference to the ground truth.

7   Discussion

In considering the qualitative performance of our bio-inspired architecture using viewpoint-specific object recognition as the key feature, we show that our architecture works exceptionally well. Focusing on the computer-generated video sequences only, one can see that pixel-accurate object recognition indicates a slightly lower performance in accuracy compared to the ground truth, as well as in a number of points in the PC. In our opinion, this effect is caused by i) the number of insufficient feature points within the extracted pictorial representation from the artificial video sequences and ii) due to the static scene without any OOI movement. These circumstances explain the potency of our architecture on the nature video sequences, where the *car* is only reconstructed successfully with viewpoint-dependent pixel-accurate object recognition. As a consequence, our approach could be improved by more sophisticated image features, which generate a high number of features even on textureless and/or shiny surfaces. Finally, note that the 3D reconstruction without pixel-accurate object recognition does not reconstruct the OOI separately, but rather it reconstructs the OOI and the scene jointly. Thus, the OOI must be recognized again, but now in 3D space, before one can start any OOI meshing.

The resulting PC of the OOI are still quite sparse and cannot be meshed into watertight models, yet. This fact might be generated by the transition of the bio-inspired processing modules **I–IV** into the technologically-inspired module **VI**. The module **V** is somehow both and appears in slightly altered versions in human [6,25,26] and computer [13,28] vision. To accompany this transition, the bio-inspired and technically-inspired modules should be interconnected in module **V**. Therefore the module **VI** should be replaced with a top-down approach, e.g. a wireframe [30] or a CAD [29] model-based object fitting based on the created PC. The resulting architecture can derive a complete meshed CAD-ready 3D model from video sequences. In our opinion, such a top-down implementation of module **VI** is possible due to an incredibly huge knowledge database containing generic 3D models. However, by reflecting the conceptual idea of Biederman [3], i.e. that any 3D object can be described by a set of geometrical primitives, symmetry relations and some kind of grammar, it might be possible to generate 3D models from PC, without huge databases.

In conclusion, viewpoint-dependent object recognition, embedded in our architecture, significantly improves 3D object recognition from one or several video sequences. Hence, 3D reconstruction becomes possible even if the camera and the OOI are moving. The creation of a CAD-ready 3D model for technical use, which can be applied for simulation tasks and reverse engineering, is not yet possible since the resulting 3D PC are sparse and not noise-free. For implementing our architecture as a fully automatic process, the problem of pixel-accurate OOI recognition and annotation must be solved.

References

1. Arikan, M., Schwärzler, M., Flöry, S., Wimmer, M., Maierhofer, S.: O-Snap: optimization-based snapping for modeling architecture. ACM Trans. Graph. **32**(1), 6:1–6:15 (2013)
2. Bernardini, F., Mittleman, J., Rushmeier, H., Silva, C., Taubin, G.: The ball-pivoting algorithm for surface reconstruction. Trans. Vis. Comput. Graph. **5**(4), 349–359 (1999)
3. Biederman, I.: Recognition-by-components: a theory of human image understanding. Psychol. Rev. **94**(2), 115–147 (1987)
4. Borji, A., Cheng, M.M., Jiang, H., Li, J.: Salient object detection: a benchmark. Trans. Image Process. **24**(12), 5706–5722 (2015)
5. Boykov, Y., Jolly, M.P.: Interactive graph cuts for optimal boundary and region segmentation of objects in N-D images. In: ICCV, pp. 105–112. IEEE (2001)

6. Bulthoff, H.H., Edelman, S.Y., Tarr, M.J.: How are three-dimensional objects represented in the brain? Cereb. Cortex **5**(3), 247–260 (1995)
7. Choi, S., Zhou, Q.Y., Koltun, V.: Robust reconstruction of indoor scenes. In: CVPR, pp. 5556–5565. IEEE (2015)
8. Dasiopoulou, S., Giannakidou, E., Litos, G., Malasioti, P., Kompatsiaris, Y.: A survey of semantic image and video annotation tools. In: Paliouras, G., Spyropoulos, C.D., Tsatsaronis, G. (eds.) Knowledge-Driven Multimedia Information Extraction and Ontology Evolution. LNCS, vol. 6050, pp. 196–239. Springer, Heidelberg (2011). https://doi.org/10.1007/978-3-642-20795-2_8
9. Doermann, D., Mihalcik, D.: Tools and techniques for video performance evaluation. In: ICPR, vol. 4, pp. 167–170. IEEE (2000)
10. Handa, A., Whelan, T., McDonald, J., Davison, A.: A benchmark for RGB-D visual odometry, 3D reconstruction and SLAM. In: ICRA, pp. 1524–1531. IEEE (2014)
11. Hummel, J.E., Biederman, I.: Dynamic binding in a neural network for shape recognition. Psychol. Rev. **99**(3), 480–517 (1992)
12. Kazhdan, M., Hoppe, H.: ACM Trans. Graph. Screened poisson surface reconstruction **32**(3), 29:1–29:13 (2013)
13. Kowdle, A., Chang, Y.J., Gallagher, A., Batra, D., Chen, T.: Putting the user in the loop for image-based modeling. Int. J. Comput. Vis. **108**(1), 30–48 (2014)
14. Kurzhals, K., Bopp, C.F., Bässler, J., Ebinger, F., Weiskopf, D.: Benchmark data for evaluating visualization and analysis techniques for eye tracking for video stimuli. In: Workshop on BELIV, pp. 54–60. ACM (2014)
15. Marr, D., Nishihara, H.K.: Representation and recognition of the spatial organization of three-dimensional shapes. Proc. Roy. Soc. Lond. B: Biol. Sci. **200**(1140), 269–294 (1978)
16. Oliva, A., Torralba, A.: The role of context in object recognition. Trends Cogn. Sci. **11**(12), 520–527 (2007)
17. Pan, Q., Reitmayr, G., Drummond, T.: ProFORMA: probabilistic feature-based on-line rapid model acquisition. In: BMVC, pp. 112:1–112:11 (2009)
18. Pillai, G.: Caught on camera: You are filmed on cctv 300 times a day in london. International Business Times March 2012. www.ibtimes.co.uk/britain-cctv-camera-surveillance-312382
19. Schöning, J.: Interactive 3D reconstruction: new opportunities for getting CAD-ready models. ICCSW. OASIcs, vol. 49, pp. 54–61 (2015)
20. Schöning, J., Faion, P., Heidemann, G.: Semi-automatic ground truth annotation in videos: an interactive tool for polygon-based object annotation and segmentation. In: K-CAP, pp. 17:1–17:4. ACM (2015)
21. Schöning, J., Heidemann, G.: Evaluation of multi-view 3D reconstruction software. In: Azzopardi, G., Petkov, N. (eds.) CAIP 2015. LNCS, vol. 9257, pp. 450–461. Springer, Cham (2015). https://doi.org/10.1007/978-3-319-23117-4_39
22. Schöning, J., Faion, P., Heidemann, G., Krumnack, U.: Providing video annotations in multimedia containers for visualization and research. In: WACV. IEEE (2017)
23. Schöning, J., Heidemann, G.: Bio-inspired architecture for deriving 3D models from video sequences. In: Chen, C.-S., Lu, J., Ma, K.-K. (eds.) ACCV 2016. LNCS, vol. 10117, pp. 62–76. Springer, Cham (2017). https://doi.org/10.1007/978-3-319-54427-4_5
24. Snavely, N., Seitz, S.M., Szeliski, R.: Photo tourism: exploring photo collections in 3D. ACM Trans. Graph. **25**(3), 835–846 (2006)
25. Ullman, S.: High-Level Vision: Object Recognition and Visual Cognition, 2nd edn. MIT press Cambridge, MA (1997)

26. Ungerleider, L.G.: "What" and "where" in the human brain. Curr. Opin. Neurobiol. **4**(2), 157–165 (1994)
27. Ungerleider, L., Mishkin, M.: Two cortical visual systems. In: Ingle, D., Goodale, M., Mansfield, R. (eds.) Analysis Visual Behavior, pp. 549–586. MIT Press, Boston (1982)
28. Wu, C.: VisualSfM: a visual structure from motion system July 2017. http://ccwu.me/vsfm/
29. Xiang, Y., Mottaghi, R., Savarese, S.: Beyond PASCAL: a benchmark for 3D object detection in the wild. In: WACV, pp. 75–82. IEEE (2014)
30. Zhang, Z., Tan, T., Huang, K., Wang, Y.: Three-dimensional deformable-model-based localization and recognition of road vehicles. Trans. on Image Process. **21**(1), 1–13 (2012)

Social Signal Processing and Beyond (SSPandBE)

Indirect Match Highlights Detection with Deep Convolutional Neural Networks

Marco Godi[1], Paolo Rota[2], and Francesco Setti[1,3(✉)]

[1] Department of Computer Science, University of Verona, Verona, Italy
francesco.setti@univr.it
[2] Pattern Analysis and Computer Vision (PAVIS),
Italian Institute of Technology, Genova, Italy
[3] Institute of Cognitive Science and Technology,
National Research Council, Trento, Italy

Abstract. Highlights in a sport video are usually referred as actions that stimulate excitement or attract attention of the audience. A big effort is spent in designing techniques which find automatically highlights, in order to automatize the otherwise manual editing process. Most of the state-of-the-art approaches try to solve the problem by training a classifier using the information extracted on the tv-like framing of players playing on the game pitch, learning to detect game actions which are labeled by human observers according to their perception of highlight. Obviously, this is a long and expensive work. In this paper, we reverse the paradigm: instead of looking at the gameplay, inferring what could be exciting for the audience, we directly analyze the audience behavior, which we assume is triggered by events happening during the game. We apply deep 3D Convolutional Neural Network (3D-CNN) to extract visual features from cropped video recordings of the supporters that are attending the event. Outputs of the crops belonging to the same frame are then accumulated to produce a value indicating the Highlight Likelihood (HL) which is then used to discriminate between positive (*ie* when a highlight occurs) and negative samples (*i.e.* standard play or time-outs). Experimental results on a public dataset of ice-hockey matches demonstrate the effectiveness of our method and promote further research in this new exciting direction.

1   Introduction

Sport video summarization, or highlights generation, is the process of creating a synopsis of a video of a given sport event that gives the viewer a general overview of the whole match. This process incorporates two different tasks: (1) to detect the most important moments of the event, and (2) organize the extracted content into a limited display time. While the second point is a widely-known problem in the multimedia and broadcasting community, the definition of *what is a highlight* has different interpretations in the community. According to [9], highlights are "those video segments that are expected to excite the users the most". In [22], the focus relaxes from excitement to general attention, and thus salient moments are

© Springer International Publishing AG 2017
S. Battiato et al. (Eds.): ICIAP 2017 International Workshops, LNCS 10590, pp. 87–96, 2017.
https://doi.org/10.1007/978-3-319-70742-6_8

the ones that attract audience attention the most. These two definitions would imply to explicitly design specific models for extracting excitment from the crowd in one case and attention on the other. In this paper we overcome this problem by automatically learn visual features using deep architectures that discriminate between highlights and ordinary actions.

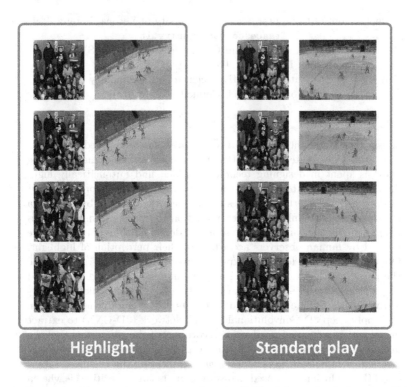

Fig. 1. Example video sequences of a goal event (left) and standard play time (right).

Traditionally, extracting sport highlights has been a labor intensive activity, primarily because it requires good judgment to select and define salient moments throughout the whole game. Then, highlights are manually edited by experts, to generate a video summary that is significant, coherent and understandable by humans. State-of-the-art artificial intelligence is still far away from having solved the whole problem.

In the last years, there has been an increasing demand for automatic and semi-automatic tools for highlights generation, mainly due to the huge amount of data (*i.e.* sport event videos) generated every day and made available through the Internet. Specialized broadcasters and websites are able to deliver sport highlights minutes after the end of the event, handling thousands of events every day. As a consequence, there has been extensive research in this area, with the development of several techniques based on image and video processing [1,2,8,9,13,19,22]. More recently, many works started using additional sources of information to increase performances, including audio recordings [15,21], textual narratives [17], social networks [7,10,18], and audience behavior [4–6,14]. Despite some solutions are already present on the market, performances are in general still fairly poor and we believe there is room for new research on this topic.

While previous work attempted to detect in sport videos actions that stimulate excitement [8] or attract attention [22] of the audience, in this paper we reverse the problem by analyzing the audience behavior to identify changes in emotions, that can only be triggered by highlights on the game field.

Specifically, we present a novel approach for sport highlight generation which is based on the observation of the audience behavior. This approach is based on the analysis of a set of space-time cuboids using a 3D-CNN architecture. All the samples are trained singularly, the result for each cuboid at a certain time step is then processed through an accumulator which generates a sort of highlight probability for the whole audience that will be used to perform the final ranking.

The rest of the paper is organized as follows: in Sect. 2 we briefly present the state-of-the-art in automatic highlight detection. In Sect. 3 we detail the proposed methodology, while in Sect. 4 we show some qualitative and quantitative results on a public dataset of hockey matches. Lastly, in Sect. 5 we draw some conclusions and perspectives for future works.

2   Related Work

Money and Angius [12] provide an extensive literature survey on video summarization. According to the taxonomy proposend in that paper, related work can be classified into three categories: (1) internal summarization techniques; (2) external summarization techniques; and (3) hybrid summarization techniques. By definition, *internal summarization techniques* rely only on information provided by the video (and audio) streams of the event. These techniques extract low-level image, audio, and text features to facilitate summarization and for several years have been the most common summarization techniques. *External summarization techniques* require additional sources of information, not contained in the video streams. These are usually user-based information –*i.e.* information provided directly from users– and contextual information –such as the time and location in which the video was recorded. As for *hybrid summarization techniques*, both internal and external information are analyzed, allowing to reduce the semantic gap between the low level features and the semantic concepts.

Social networks. According to Hsieh *et al.* [10], the quantity of comments and re-tweets can represent the most exciting moments in a sport event. A highlight can be determined by analyzing the keywords in the comments and observing if the number of comments and re-tweets passes a certain threshold. Fião *et al.* [7] uses emotions shared by the spectators during the match via social networks to build a system capable of generating automatic highlight videos of sports match

TV broadcasts. Auxiliary sources of information are TV broadcast videos, the audio, the analysis of the movement and manual annotations (when available). The system also allows for the user to query the video to extract specific clips (*e.g.* attacking plays of a specific team).

Text. In [17], Suksai and Ratanaworabhan propose an approach that combines on-line information retrieval with text extraction using OCR techniques. This way, they are able to limit the number of false positives.

Audio. Rui *et al.* [15] presents a method that uses audio signals to build video highlights for baseball games. It analyzes the speech of the match announcer, both audio amplitude and voice tone, to estimate whether the announcer is being excited or not. In addition, the ambient sound from the surrounding environment and the audience are also taken into considerations. Built on this work, Xiong *et al.* [21] handpicked the highlight events and analyzed the environment and audience sounds at each of those highlight events. They discovered that there exists a strong correlation between loud and buzzing noise and some major highlight events. This correlation exists in all the three sports being analyzed: baseball, golf, and soccer.

Audience. Peng *et al.* [14] propose the Interest Meter (IM), a system able to measure user's interest and thus use it to conduct video summarization. The IM takes account attention states (*e.g.* eye movement, blink, and head motion) and emotion states (*e.g.* facial expression). These features are then fused together by a fuzzy fusion scheme that outputs a quantitative interest score, determine interesting parts of videos, and finally concatenate them as video summaries. In [4], Conigliaro *et al.* use motion cues (*i.e.* optical flow intensity and direction entropy) to estimate the excitement level of audience of a team sport event and to identify groups of supporters of different teams. In [5], these features are used to identify highlights in team sport events using mean shift clustering.

3   Method

The proposed highlights detection methodology uses a 3D Convolutional Neural Network (3D-CNN) to extract visual features from video recordings of the audience of the event, and classify them in positive samples (*i.e.* when a highlight occurs) and negative samples (*i.e.* standard play or timeouts).

From empirical observations, the audience reaction of a highlight (*e.g.* a goal) lasts for at least the 10 s that follows the event itself. For this reason, temporal resolution is not a critical parameter and downsampling the video from 30 to 3 fps allowed us to reduce the computational burden without losing the informative part of the video. The 3D-CNN cuboid is extracted from a manually selected rectangular area that roughly contained the bulk of the audience, using a uniform grid with fixed spatial dimension of 100×100 pixels, while the temporal resolution has been set to 30 frames. These parameters are the result of an a priori intuition that each block should be able to represent a portion of spectators which should not be too large, in order to reduce the computational burden, but

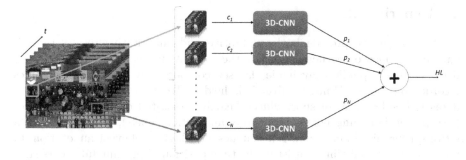

Fig. 2. Sketch of the overall method.

at the same time it should not be too small since this would bring to be too much location dependent. For our model we used a sliding window with a stride of 50 pixels resulting in a maximum overlap between two crops of 50%

In order to detect and rank the most important moments in the video sequence we follow the idea of Conigliaro et al. [3], where information accumulators along time have been proposed to segment supporters of the two different playing teams. Our goal is however different: unlike them, we are interested in a global analysis of the excitement of the audience regardless of the supporting preference at a certain time. For this reason we are using an accumulator strategy over the whole audience location in the scene. Each spatio-temporal cuboid C_i, $i = 1, ..., N$ represents a sample that is fed into a 3D-CNN and analyzed independently; then, for each time instant the related probability score p_i, $i = 1, ..., N$ of being a positive class is accumulated over all the samples in the spatial dimension, generating a scalar value representing the *Highlight Likelihood* (HL) that is a score representing how likely a particular instant can be considered an highlight or not. A sketch of the overall system is shown in Fig. 2.

3.1 Network Architecture

Inspired by earlier works on action recognition [11,20], we use a 3D Convolutional Neural Network composed by 4 convolutional and 3 fully connected layers.

The network takes as input video cuboids of $100 \times 100 \times 30$, where the first two numbers refer to the spatial dimension while the third is the temporal depth (number of frames). The first two convolutional layers are composed 12 filters $3 \times 3 \times 3$, to capture spatio-temporal features from the raw data. These are followed by a $2 \times 2 \times 2$ max pooling layer to detect features at different scales. In the latter two convolutional layers, 8 $3 \times 3 \times 3$ convolutional filters have been used. In all convolutional layers the ReLU activation has been used. The network is then unfolded with a flatten layer followed by three fully connected layers of decreasing dimensionality (32, 8, and 2 neurons respectively). The final classification task is achieved by a softmax layer that outputs the probability of a test sample to belong to each of the two classes: "highlight" and "standard play".

4   Experiments

In this section we provide both qualitative and quantitative results to validate our proposed methodology. For the evaluation we adopted the S-Hock dataset [16], a publicly available dataset composed by 6 ice-hockey games recorded during the Winter Universiade held in Trentino (Italy) in 2013. This dataset, besides a set of short videos heavily annotated on low level features (*e.g.* people bounding boxes, head pose, and action labels), it provides also a set of synchronized multi-view full matches with high-level event annotation. In these games, the labeling consist in the time position of meaningful events such as goals, fouls, shots, saves, fights and timeouts.

In this work we considered only two matches: the final match (Canada-Kazakhstan) which is used for training the neural network, and the semi-final match (USA-Kazakhstan), used for testing.

4.1   3D-CNN Training Procedure

As mentioned briefly earlier, the positive class is named "highlights" and it represents all the spatio-temporal cuboids starting when a team scores a goal while the negative class (*i.e.* "standard play") includes other neutral situations happening during the game. In this work we excluded all the other significant annotated events (fouls, fights, etc.) to reduce the number of classes[1]. In training phase the samples belonging to the two classes have been balanced to avoid dataset bias.

The S-Hock dataset provides a set of synchronized videos of the games including several views of the audience, at different resolution/zoom level, and of the complete game footage. The video acquisition is done from different points of view (frontal and slightly tilted to the side), in this work we used all these views to ensure a more robust model of training that is able to learn features that are more possibly scale and position invariant. Positive and negative samples are then splitted into training and validation sets with a ratio of 70%-30%. Data augmentation procedure has been performed (horizontal flips in the spatial dimension) not only to increase the amount of training data but also to augment the invariance of the network.

The final optimization is proposed as a classification problem, minimizing the categorical cross-entropy between the two classes. For this procedure we used the *RMSprop* algorithm, a generalization of the resilient backpropagation *rprop* algorithm that extends the ability to use only the sign of the gradient and to adapt the learning rate separately for each weight, to improve the work with minibatches. In our experiments we use minibatches of 64 samples each. A Dropout layer with 50% probability to disconnect the link is applied before the first two fully connected layers to reduce overfitting. The procedure iterates over the whole dataset until convergence, usually reached after about 10

---

[1] These events are indeed generating different types of excitement, we could not investigate further for lack of annotated data, but this is an argument that we consider worthed of further research.

epochs. The whole training procedure takes about 2 h on a machine equipped with a NVIDIA Tesla K-80 GPU, using Keras/TensorFlow framework. The whole resulting dataset is composed of a total of 32,000 training samples.

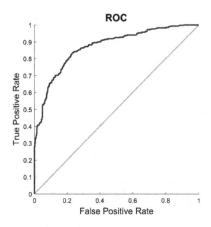

Fig. 3. ROC curve

4.2   Quantitative Results

Here we report a quantitative performance evaluation of the 3D-CNN in detecting positive and negative highlight samples. From the second period of the testing game, we randomly selected 3000 positive samples as well as the same number of negative samples and we fed them into the trained network. In Fig. 3 the ROC curve is reported. The Area Under the Curve (AUC) is 0.87. Binary classification is performed by assigning the sample to the class corresponding to the higher score; under this conditions the network reaches 78% of accuracy, 69% of precision and a recall of 84%. Results themselves are quite good considering the difficulty of the task, however, our goal is different, since we are using those results in a more sophisticated framework to infer and rank interesting events during the whole game. Consequently we expect a certain amount of noise in such prediction since in many cases the sample may be partially filled with empty seats (see Fig. 5), producing a wrong or at least biased prediction toward the negative class. However, this problem is minimized with the use of the accumulator approach and due to the fact that the empty-seats location will be very little informative in the whole sequence, while the crowded locations, where most of the spectators are situated, will convey most of the information used for the final decision.

4.3   Qualitative Examples

We also provide qualitative results to validate our approach. Figure 4 shows the HL score, summed over all the cuboids, at every non overlapping 10-second slice

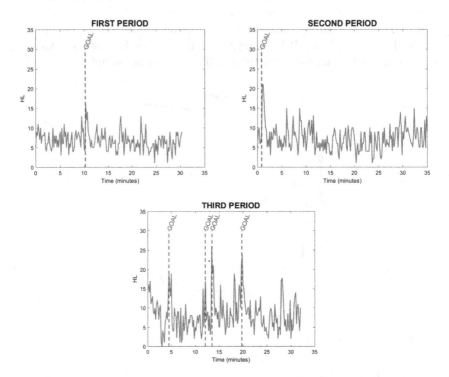

Fig. 4. Summed probabilities of highlights over all the crops in the scene. As visible, peaks in the curve nicely corresponds to a highlight.

(a) Highlight   (b) Standard play

Fig. 5. Probability scores given by a subset of the crops (chosen to be non overlapping for visualization purposes); each dot represents a crop which describes part of the scene. Green dots represent crops classified as people reacting to an highlight (*e.g.* cheering) while the red dots represent the crops classified as people with a "standard" behavior. (Color figure online)

during an entire match (3 periods of 20 min plus timeouts). Goals are clearly identified in the first two periods, while in the third one other events also trigger the audience behavior; in particular, there are two prominent events that don't correspond to goals at 18:45 (which is caused by a player almost scoring) and at 28:15 (which is caused by a foul in front of the goaltender, and the resulting penalty). We can easily see that there is a correlation between HL score and important events in the game and that goals usually cause the biggest reaction on the spectators.

5   Conclusions

In this paper we propose a method to temporally locate highlights in a sport event by analyzing solely the audience behavior. We propose to use a deep 3D convolutional neural network on cuboid video samples to discriminate between different excitement of the spectators. An spatial accumulator is used to produce a score which is proportional to the probability of having an interesting highlight in that precise time location. This enables the model to identify goals and other salient actions.

Despite being very simple, the model we present provides good preliminary result on a public dataset of hockey games, encouraging further research based on this approach. In our opinion, the main limit of this model is in the way we take into account the temporal information; indeed we extend a standard CNN to work with 3D data, where the third dimension is time. A more sophisticated model, such as recurrent neural networks (RNN) and long-short term memory (LSTM), could benefit the final inferential results. As future work we intend to replace the accumulator with such a temporal model, expanding the classification to a multiclass problem in order to detect different events. In order to do so, the dataset has to be enlarged possibly on a different location to make sure the network is learning more general discriminative features.

References

1. Bertini, M., Del Bimbo, A., Nunziati, W.: Model checking for detection of sport highlights. In: ACM SIGMM International Workshop on Multimedia Information Retrieval (2003)
2. Chauhan, D., Patel, N.M., Joshi, M.: Automatic summarization of basketball sport video. In: International Conference on Next Generation Computing Technologies (NGCT), pp. 670–673 (2016)
3. Conigliaro, D., Rota, P., Setti, F., Bassetti, C., Conci, N., Sebe, N., Cristani, M.: The S-hock dataset: analyzing crowds at the stadium. In: IEEE Conference on Computer Vision and Pattern Recognition (CVPR), pp. 2039–2047 (2015)
4. Conigliaro, D., Setti, F., Bassetti, C., Ferrario, R., Cristani, M.: ATTENTO: ATTENTION observed for automated spectator crowd analysis. In: International Workshop on Human Behaviour Understanding (HBU) (2013)
5. Conigliaro, D., Setti, F., Bassetti, C., Ferrario, R., Cristani, M.: Viewing the viewers: a novel challenge for automated crowd analysis. In: International Conference on Image Analysis and Processing (ICIAP) (2013)

6. Conigliaro, D., Setti, F., Bassetti, C., Ferrario, R., Cristani, M., Rota, P., Conci, N., Sebe, N.: Observing attention. In: FISU Winter Universiade Conference (2013)

7. Fião, G., Romão, T., Correia, N., Centieiro, P., Dias, A.E.: Automatic generation of sport video highlights based on fan's emotions and content. In: International Conference on Advances in Computer Entertainment Technology (ACE), ACM (2016)

8. Hanjalic, A.: Generic approach to highlights extraction from a sport video. In: IEEE International Conference on Image Processing (ICIP) (2003)

9. Hanjalic, A.: Adaptive extraction of highlights from a sport video based on excitement modeling. IEEE Trans. Multimedia 7(6), 1114–1122 (2005)

10. Hsieh, L.C., Lee, C.W., Chiu, T.H., Hsu, W.: Live semantic sport highlight detection based on analyzing tweets of Twitter. In: IEEE International Conference on Multimedia and Expo (ICME) (2012)

11. Ji, S., Xu, W., Yang, M., Yu, K.: 3D convolutional neural networks for human action recognition. IEEE Trans. Pattern Anal. Mach. Intell. 35(1), 221–231 (2013)

12. Money, A.G., Agius, H.: Video summarisation: a conceptual framework and survey of the state of the art. J. Vis. Commun. Image Represent. 19(2), 121–143 (2008)

13. Nguyen, N., Yoshitaka, A.: Soccer video summarization based on cinematography and motion analysis. In: IEEE International Workshop on Multimedia Signal Processing (MMSP) (2014)

14. Peng, W.T., Chu, W.T., Chang, C.H., Chou, C.N., Huang, W.J., Chang, W.Y., Hung, Y.P.: Editing by viewing: automatic home video summarization by viewing behavior analysis. IEEE Trans. Multimedia 13(3), 539–550 (2011)

15. Rui, Y., Gupta, A., Acero, A.: Automatically extracting highlights for TV baseball programs. In: International Conference on Multimedia (ACM-MM), ACM (2000)

16. Setti, F., Conigliaro, D., Rota, P., Bassetti, C., Conci, N., Sebe, N., Cristani, M.: The S-Hock dataset: a new benchmark for spectator crowd analysis. In: Computer Vision and Image Understanding (2017)

17. Suksai, P., Ratanaworabhan, P.: A new approach to extracting sport highlight. In: International Computer Science and Engineering Conference (ICSEC) (2016)

18. Tang, A., Boring, S.: #EpicPlay: crowd-sourcing sports video highlights. In: SIGCHI Conference on Human Factors in Computing Systems (2012)

19. Tjondronegoro, D., Chen, Y.P.P., Pham, B.: Highlights for more complete sports video summarization. IEEE MultiMedia 11(4), 22–37 (2004)

20. Tran, D., Bourdev, L., Fergus, R., Torresani, L., Paluri, M.: Learning spatiotemporal features with 3D convolutional networks. In: IEEE International Conference on Computer Vision (ICCV) (2015)

21. Xiong, Z., Radhakrishnan, R., Divakaran, A., Huang, T.S.: Audio events detection based highlights extraction from baseball, golf and soccer games in a unified framework. In: IEEE International Conference on Acoustics, Speech, and Signal Processing (ICASSP) (2003)

22. Zhu, G., Huang, Q., Xu, C., Xing, L., Gao, W., Yao, H.: Human behavior analysis for highlight ranking in broadcast racket sports video. IEEE Trans. Multimedia 9(6), 1167–1182 (2007)

Signal Processing and Machine Learning
for Diplegia Classification

Luca Bergamini[1]([✉]), Simone Calderara[1], Nicola Bicocchi[1], Alberto Ferrari[2],
and Giorgio Vitetta[1]

[1] Department of Engineering "Enzo Ferrari", University of Modena
and Reggio Emilia, Via Vivarelli 10, 41125 Modena, Italy
179844@studenti.unimore.it
[2] Department of Electrical, Electronic and Information Engineering
"Guglielmo Marconi", University of Bologna,
viale Risorgimento 2, 40136 Bologna, Italy

Abstract. Diplegia is one of the most common forms of a broad family of motion disorders named *cerebral palsy* (CP) affecting the voluntary muscular system. In recent years, various classification criteria have been proposed for CP, to assist in diagnosis, clinical decision-making and communication. In this manuscript, we divide the spastic forms of CP into 4 other categories according to a previous classification criterion and propose a machine learning approach for automatically classifying patients. Training and validation of our approach are based on data about 200 patients acquired using 19 markers and high frequency VICON cameras in an Italian hospital. Our approach makes use of the latest deep learning techniques. More specifically, it involves a multi-layer perceptron network (MLP), combined with Fourier analysis. An encouraging classification performance is obtained for two of the four classes.

1 Introduction

Cerebral palsy (CP) is a broad family of non curable disorder of the voluntary muscular system, which appears in human's early childhood; this disorder is characterized by a great variety of symptoms, including stiff muscles, tremors and a general loss of coordination. CP is treatable but it is not curable; its symptoms could become more noticeable, but they do not worsen during lifetime. Common treatments include the effort of therapists and rehabilitation specialists, and the use of physiotherapy, antispastic drugs, orthosis and devices and functional surgery. Several classifications have been proposed for CP and are based on different aspects of this disorder. One of the most used classification relies on the identification of muscle tone anomalies as well on the type of the prevailing neurological symptom. This classification identified three classes as: (1) *spastic*, characterized by constant muscle tightness and stiffness; (2) *dyskinetic*, affecting patients unable to control involuntary movements; (3) *ataxic*, associated with shakiness and lack of coordination.

© Springer International Publishing AG 2017
S. Battiato et al. (Eds.): ICIAP 2017 International Workshops, LNCS 10590, pp. 97–108, 2017.
https://doi.org/10.1007/978-3-319-70742-6_9

Another classification relies on the somatic location of the prevailing neuro-logical symptom: (1) *tetraplegia* if all four limbs are affected; (2) *hemiplegia* if only one side of the body is afflicted; (3) *diplegia* if it involves symmetrical parts of the body.

A good classification system separates patients into clinical clusters char-acterized by sharing comparable prognosis, thus easing choice of treatment and communication of the expectations on autonomy level during child growth. With this goal, Ferrari *et al.* [7] have proposed a new classification of spastic forms of CP, which divides diplegia into other 4 forms (see Table 1), aimed at quickly conveying a "clinical snapshot" of a child by cross-referring to histories of other patients with similar motor impairments and dysfunctions therefore easing the choice of providing specific indications about the treatment to be adopted and about the disorder evolution over time. Moreover, it has been first validated in [4], analyzing a group of 467 subjects affected by CP (213 suffering from diplegia and 115 from tetraplegia), and characterized by significant correlations between identified walking forms. Further validation results, referring to the classification of spastic diplegia and involving 50 children and adolescents followed by profes-sionals of rehabilitation, have been illustrated in [14]. This validation activities have evidenced that the less and the most severe forms of CP are the most easily identifiable, whereas the remaining two being more challenging.

In this work an automatic classification tool able to identify the 4 forms of spastic diplegia defined in [7] is illustrated. This tool combines frequency domain processing of the measurements acquired by means of multiple markers and high frequency VICON cameras with state of the art deep learning techniques. This work falls within the broad category of social signal processing, intended as the analysis of one ore more subjects as it interacts with another or with the environment. In this field techniques have shown competitive performance in classifying people interaction in crowd, as shown in [17]), but also in small groups [16] and in pairs [13].

The remaining part of this manuscript is organized as follows. In Section 2 previous work on the classification of diplegia is illustrated. In Sect. 3 gait analysis is introduced, and the sensors and methods employed for collecting measurements are illustrated; moreover, some indications about the adopted pre-processing techniques are provided. In Sect. 4 the architecture of the employed deep network is described. In Sect. 5 some numerical results are shown. Finally, Sect. 6 offers some conclusions.

2   Related Work

As far as we know, this is the first attempt of building a system based on the classification proposed in [7]. In the following previous work on diplegia classi-fication is illustrated. However, note that most of it aims at discerning between healthy patients and patients affected by diplegia.

In [6] previous work on children affected by CP has been analysed. The considered methods include traditional data analysis systems and more recent machine learning techniques.

Table 1. Diplegia forms from Ferrari et al. [7]

Form	Traits
Form I-forward leaning propulsion	Antepulsion of trunk, walking on toe tips. Requires constant support of four point canes
Form II-tight skirt	Pronounced knee flexion in midstance, loaded knee behavior, short and frequent steps
Form III-tight rope walkers	Frontal trunk swinging and use of upper limbs to keep balance, presence of a dysperceptive disorder causing fearing feeling of falling and fear of open spaces without anything to cling on
Form IV-dare devils	Mainly a motor deficit. Increased talipes equinus at start of walking. Inability to stop walking abruptly without falling in early age

In [9] a *support vector machine* (SVM) for identifying spastic diplegia is proposed. A dataset of 3D points acquired by a six-camera Vicon System is analyzed; a group of 88 children affected by spastic diplegia and a control group of 68 children has been considered. Four features (namely, stride length, cadence, leg length and age) have been extracted from raw data. The best results have been achieved using only stride length and cadence (normalized on the basis of leg length and age) and adopting a radial basis function as kernel. In particular, an overall accuracy of 96.80% with 10-fold stratified cross validation has been achieved.

In [11] an *artificial neural network* is employed to combine traditional patient information with the analysis of heart rate variability. The proposed method is tested using a dataset that concerns healthy subjects and patients diagnosed with central coordination disturbances. Data have been acquired employing a 24-h ECG-Holter monitor; moreover, a shallow network consisting of a single hidden layer with 12 neurons has been employed.

In [1] a *Self-Organizing Map* (SOM) for unsupervised learning has been employed. The dataset collects information about three-dimensional joint angles, moments and powers and refers to 129 gait cycles from 18 subjects not affected by movement disorders; moreover, the *quantisation error* (QE) of the differences between normal and abnormal gaits is computed.

In [15] a rich dataset, referring to more than 900 patients affected with various pathologies, is exploited; data acquisition is based on a VICON 370 system consisting of high resolution infrared cameras. Moreover, the available data are processed to estimate hip rotation and the movements of other junctions, and then employed to train a SVM *classifier*. Since different disorders were included in the dataset, a binary classification algorithm for each of them against all the others has been trained.

Finally, the *principal component analysis* (PCA) has been employed in [3] to identify relevant information for classification of healthy and diplegic subjects.

3   Gait Analysis

Gait analysis plays a key role not only in the study of the muscular system, but also in that of the nervous and the sensory ones. Since this analysis involves the study of locomotion and of body mechanics, various devices are needed to simultaneously control the motion of multiple human joints; some of these devices are listed in Table 2. Gait analysis is usually accomplished in dedicated laboratories, called *motion analysis labs* (MALs).

Table 2. Devices commonly used for *gait analysis*

Devices	Description
Opto-electronic devices	Reflecting markers applied to the patient's skin in defined anatomical landmarks able to provide 3D motion of human segments
Force plates	Plates placed on the ground, used to measure the ground reaction force to body weight
Electromyography	Skin electrodes capable of acquiring the electrical signal generated by the contraction of muscles
Video systems	Cameras to record a patient during his/her trial

3.1   Data Format

One of the most advanced protocol for the storage of bio-mechanical data is the Total3DGait [2], which relies on the C3D format. A C3D file is composed by a *header* (which contains not only information about the considered patient such as his/her height or age, but also data useful for the remaining part of the file) and a *body*, which contains the position of every marker for each frame, along with the validity of the data itself, where the special value -1 indicates an invalid acquisition, and the precision of the measure. The order of the 3D positions is specified in the header. An insight in the single marker point is provided in Table 3.

3.2   Acquisition Method

As the gait analysis involves data referring to several distinct joints, a large number of markers needs to be applied to the skin of the considered patient. The *Davis protocol* [5] is one of the leading methodologies for acquiring not only 3D motion data, but also useful information about the considered patient, such as his/her weight and age; these data are collected before applying the opto-electronics markers for capturing kinematic, dynamic and electromyography measurements. Measurements are acquired as the patient walks at normal speed through the room hosting a MAL; the data usually refer to a variable number of trials (usually between 4 and 6).

Table 3. C3D frame

Word	Content (signed integer format)
1	X coordinate of point divided by POINT:SCALE factor
2	Y coordinate of point divided by POINT:SCALE factor
3	Z coordinate of point divided by POINT:SCALE factor
4	Byte 1: cameras measuring the considered marker (1 bit per camera). Byte 2: average residual divided by POINT:SCALE factor

3.3 Data Pre-processing

Our dataset refers to 1121 trials acquired from 178 patients affected by diplegia. The acquisition frame rate (100 frames/sec) provided by the employed VICON system is too large; for this reason every walk has been subsampled by a factor 2, so dropping the frame rate to 50 frames/sec. Moreover, trials not containing one or more of the 19 markers listed in Table 4 or trials referring less than two consecutive steps have been discarded. As the foot strikes were included as meta-data in every trial, multiple consecutive steps have been considered as a *sequence*. Our dataset evidences an heterogeneous distribution of the available measurements over the classes (see Table 6). This reflects, on the one hand, the incidence of different forms of this disorder in the population; on the other hand, it shows the difficulty for patients suffering from the most severe symptoms to sustain multiple trials. As it is fundamental to have a complete separation between the train set and the test set, our dataset has been split according to the proportion 0.75:0.25 patient-wise for each class. In Table 6 the resulting numbers are given for each class; note that the numbers indicated in bold refer to the case of data augmentation by repetition (this has been employed for the first class only, since it was substantially poorer than the remaining three classes).

Following [12], we have transformed the acquired measurements from the time domain to the frequency domain; in fact, this form of processing, implemented through the *fast Fourier transform* (FFT), has been shown to be extremely useful in discerning abnormal gaits from normal ones. Since the overall number N of steps performed by patients in their trials is highly variable among the four classes, only one coefficient every N was retained in the FFT output; this removes the dependence from the temporal length of the sequence. Moreover, only the first 20 coefficients selected in this way have been processed by our classification algorithm (apart from the first one, they have been normalized).

Moreover, before FFT processing, the following tasks have been accomplished:

1. The acquired xyz points have been projected onto two of the three human body's planes (in particular, the longitudinal and trasversal planes, with the third one corresponding to the floor plane). The use of these projections is fundamental to refer every trial to the same system of 3D coordinates. We also

Table 4. Markers: identifiers and positions

Name	Marker position	Name	Marker position
C7	c7 vertebra	LPSIS	Right hip joint
LA	Left shoulder	RGT	Right knee joint
RA	Right shoulder	LGT	Left knee joint
REP	Right elbow	RLE	Right ankle joint
LEP	Left elbow	LLE	Left ankle joint
RUL	Right wrist joint	RCA	Right heel joint
LUL	Left wrist joint	LCA	Left heel joint
RASIS	Right hip joint	RFM	Right foot
LASIS	Left hip joint	LFM	Left foot
RPSIS	Right hip joint		

swept two axes if the patient was to hindered to walk along the main side of the room hosting the MAL.

2. The absolute xyz coordinates have been transformed into a set of 27 three-dimensional angles, as shown in Table 5; each angle has been projected on every plane, as angles represent meaningful information in the classification of diplegia [7].

4   Classification Algorithm Based on a Multi Layer Perceptron Network

4.1   MLP Architecture

The base unit of a *multi layer perceptron* (MLP) network is called *perceptron*. Perceptrons have an high degree of similarity with the mammals brain cells, as they propagate or soften the incoming input from others. Stacking this units forms a layer, which could also be concatenated to others to obtain a network, where every layer is fully connected with the previous and the next one. To model the neuron activity on the incoming signal, a mathematical variable named weight is used for every connection, plus a bias is introduced to shift every output if it's needed. On the layer's output a non-linear function is then applied to map the layer's input to a new domain, which could be the network final output or the input of the next layer. This relation can be expressed as

$$y = f(W \circ x + b) \tag{1}$$

where x is the layer's input and the new output y, W and b are the weight matrix and the biases of the layer, respectively, $\circ$ is the dot product and f a continuous and differentiable function.

The initial values of the weight are drawn from a random distribution, which could be a Gaussian or some more complex models, while the bias are set to a

Table 5. Absolute xyz collected coordinates have been transformed into 27 three-dimensional angles, as most of the clinical signs of diplegia in all its forms are heavily related on angles instead of positions

Marker I	Marker II	Marker III
LGT	LPSIS	LLE
LLE	LGT	LCA
LCA	LLE	LFM
LEP	LA	LUL
LEP	C7	LUL
LLE	LASIS	LFM
LA	C7	LEP
RGT	RPSIS	RLE
RLE	RGT	RCA
RCA	RLE	RFM
REP	RA	RUL
REP	C7	RUL
RLE	RASIS	RFM
RA	C7	REP
LPSIS	LGT	RGT
LASIS	LGT	RGT
LPSIS	LLE	RLE
C7	LA	RA
C7	LEP	REP
RPSIS	LGT	RGT
RASIS	LGT	RGT
RPSIS	LLE	RLE
C7	LUL	RUL
LASIS	C7	LPSIS
RASIS	C7	RPSIS
LA	LASIS	RASIS
RA	LASIS	RASIS

small value (typically zero). To compare the output of the last network layer, which have a size equals to the classes number, with the labels, a mapping

$$y_{encode} = [\mathbf{0} \ldots \mathbf{0}, \mathbf{1}, \mathbf{0} \ldots \mathbf{0}] \tag{2}$$

$$with \begin{cases} y_{encode}[i] = 1 & if \quad i == class(y) \\ y_{encode}[i] = 0 & otherwise \end{cases} \tag{3}$$

called *one-hot encoding*, is required.

Table 6. Distribution of patients, trials and sequences over the four classes before and after data augmentation. The partitioning we adopted for training and test phases is also shown.

Class	Train		Test	
	Patients	Trials	Patients	Trials
0	9	47(**94**)	4	16
1	36	183	13	83
2	25	174	9	49
3	58	372	20	114

The base architecture of the MLP network we employed is composed by a single layer containing a number of perceptrons equal to the classes. We then added other layers to the first one; the number of hidden units included in each layer was twice that of the previous layer, starting from 32 units contained in the first additional layer (i.e., in the second layer of the network). To avoid a potential overfitting, a *dropout layer* [18] has been also employed; this randomly turns off some perceptrons during the training set, forcing the network not to rely on the same weights to produce a specific output.

The network providing the best results is represented in Fig. 1, (its accuracy scores are given in Sect. 5). Since a probabilistic interpretation of the output was required, a *softmax layer* was also used at the bottom of the network and Adam was used as optimizer [10]. In the following, unless differently stated, the accuracy metric refers to the single patient's trial only.

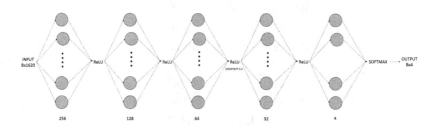

Fig. 1. Architecture of the proposed MLP network.

4.2 Training Phase

Using a part of the total dataset called train set, the MLP follows an iterative process of two steps. During the first one, called *forward propagation*, the train set is fed to the network until it reaches the last layer and the loss score is computed. In our work we used the *categorical cross entropy loss*

$$L = -\frac{1}{N * M} \sum_{n=0}^{N} \sum_{m=0}^{M} (y_{t[n,m]} * ln(y_{p[n,m]})) \tag{4}$$

given the prediction $y_{p[n,m]}$ and the ground truth $y_{t[n,m]}$ for the n-th sample and the m-th class (M and N denote the overall number of classes and samples, respectively).

In the second step, called *backward propagation*, the loss score is used to update the network weights and the biases, in accordance with the gradient direction. The general algorithm, known as Stochastic Gradient Descent (SGD), for updating a weight w is shown in 5

$$w - \alpha * \frac{\nabla L}{\nabla w} \tag{5}$$

where $\frac{\nabla L}{\nabla w}$ is the gradient *w.r.t.* to w and α is a small constant called *learning rate*.

While the SGD is still widely used in the community, several optimized variants have been proposed in the past years [10].

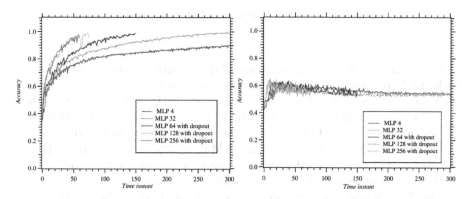

Fig. 2. Accuracies achieved by different MLP networks on both the training (left) and test (right); distinct networks are characterized by different numbers of hidden units in the most populated layer (see the labels of the curves).

5   Results

In Fig. 2 the trends of the accuracies achieved during both train and test phases for a set of MLP networks are shown. The networks are numbered with the hidden units of the most populated layer, and have been trained for an average of 500 epochs on an Nvidia GTX-1060. The network with 256 hidden units on the top layer has been the best performer, with about **0.603** on the test trials, while the other score lower results. While the accuracy reported refers to the single trial, in Table 7 the class with the top frequency among the patient's trials is used as an accuracy meter, where every trial contributes to the final class prediction of the patient. The Accuracy of the MLP is tested against a baseline obtained using a Support Vector Machine Classifier [8] with radial basis kernel functions. While on the classes 0, 1 and 3 the results suggest a validation of the proposed classification system, the prediction on the class 2 are unreliable even with the top two scores using the MLP. The reason could lie in the main trait of this form being a perceptual disturb [7], which of course does not emerge from the motion data, remaining outside from the network knowledge.

Table 7. Accuracy scores (test set).

Class	MLP		SVM	
	Top one	Top two	Top one	Top two
0	0.75	0.75	0.0	0.15
1	0.846	1.0	0.461	0.615
2	0.111	0.333	0.0	0.777
3	0.6	0.9	0.9	0.95
Overall	0.595	**0.816**	0.537	0.761

The conclusion confirms the existence of the classification in accordance with the human's perception, since the classifier performs better on opposite classes which should have very different traits, as shown in Table 8. Among the other two classes, the number 2 is the most difficult to be classified, being often confused with the second and the fourth in the top one and top two predictions. In accordance with the experts in [14] this could be related to some forms of Diplegia being partially overlapped and thus having some common traits difficult to be discerned. The small size of the dataset makes difficult to validate several aspects of the learning process, such as the presence of overfitting on the train set.

Table 8. Confusion Matrix of the patients for MLP.

```
                    Predicted
                    3  1  0  0
    Ground Truth  0 11  2  0
                    0  4  1  4
                    0  7  1 12
```

6 Conclusion

In this work we proposed a method to tackle a four class problem using the state of the art deep learning techniques, which could aid in the development of more specific treatments for muscular system's pathologies, such as the Diplegia. We made use of a MLP (Multilayer Perceptron) on a dateset of 1121 trials from 178 patients, gathered in the last ten years at LAMBDA, Laboratorio Analisi del Movimento del Bambino Dis-Abile, Azienda Ospedaliera Arcispedale S. Maria Nuova and University of Modena and Reggio Emilia, Reggio Emilia, Italy. After a pre-processing step to extract Fourier coefficients of 3D angles motions, we fed these data to train a MLP able to identify 4 different Diplegia classes. Experimental results have been encouraging in 3 out of 4 classes. We make a commitment to release the full anonymized dataset to the machine learning community in future publications.

References

1. Barton, G., Lisboa, P., Lees, A., Attfield, S.: Gait quality assessment using self-organising artificial neural networks. Gait Posture **25**(3), 374–379 (2007)
2. Benedetti, M.G., Manca, M., Ferraresi, G., Cervigni, G., Berti, L., Leardini, A.: A new protocol for complete 3D kinematics analysis of the ankle foot complex in stroke patients. J. Foot Ankle Res. **1**(1), O30 (2008)
3. Carriero, A., Zavatsky, A., Stebbins, J., Theologis, T., Shefelbine, S.J.: Determination of gait patterns in children with spastic diplegic cerebral palsy using principal components. Gait Posture **29**(1), 71–75 (2009)
4. Cioni, G., Lodesani, M., Pascale, R., Coluccini, M., Sassi, S., Paolicelli, P.B., Perazza, S., Ferrari, A.: Eur. J. Phys. Rehabil. Med. **44**(2), 203–211 (2008)
5. Davis, R.B., Õunpuu, S., Tyburski, D., Gage, J.R.: A gait analysis data collection and reduction technique. Hum. Mov. Sci. **10**(5), 575–587 (1991)
6. Dobson, F., Morris, M.E., Baker, R., Graham, H.K.: Gait classification in children with cerebral palsy: a systematic review. Gait Posture **25**(1), 140–152 (2007)
7. Ferrari, A., Alboresi, S., Muzzini, S., Pascale, R., Perazza, S., Cioni, G.: The term diplegia should be enhanced. Part I: a new rehabilitation oriented classification of cerebral palsy. Eur. J. Phys. Rehabil. Med. **44**(2), 195–201 (2008)
8. Hearst, M.A., Dumais, S.T., Osuna, E., Platt, J., Scholkopf, B.: Support vector machines. IEEE Intell. Syst. Appl. **13**(4), 18–28 (1998)
9. Kamruzzaman, J., Begg, R.K.: Support vector machines and other pattern recognition approaches to the diagnosis of cerebral palsy gait. IEEE Trans. Biomed. Eng. **53**(12), 2479–2490 (2006)
10. Kingma, D., Ba, J.: Adam: a method for stochastic optimization. In: International Conference on Learning Representations, pp. 1–13 (2014)
11. Lukić, S., Ćojbašić, Ž., Jović, N., Popović, M., Bjelaković, B., Dimitrijević, L., Bjelaković, L.: Artificial neural networks based prediction of cerebral palsy in infants with central coordination disturbance. Early Hum. Dev. **88**(7), 547–553 (2012)
12. Mostayed, A., Mazumder, M.M.G., Kim, S., Park, S.J.: Abnormal gait detection using discrete fourier transform. In: International Conference on Multimedia and Ubiquitous Engineering, MUE 2008, pp. 36–40 (2008)

13. Palazzi, A., Calderara, S., Bicocchi, N., Vezzali, L., di Bernardo, G.A., Zambonelli, F., Cucchiara, R.: Spotting prejudice with nonverbal behaviours. In: Proceedings of the 2016 ACM International Joint Conference on Pervasive and Ubiquitous Computing, pp. 853–862. ACM (2016)

14. Pascale, R., Perazza, S., Borelli, G., Bianchini, E., Alboresi, S., Paolicelli, P.B., Ferrari, A., Cioni, G.: The term diplegia should be enhanced. Part III: interobserver reliability of the new rehabilitation oriented classification. Eur. J. Phys. Rehabil. Med. **44**, 213–220 (2008)

15. Salazar, A.J., De Castro, O.C., Bravo, R.J.: Novel approach for spastic hemiplegia classification through the use of support vector machines. In: 26th Annual International Conference of the IEEE Engineering in Medicine and Biology Society, IEMBS 2004, vol. 1, pp. 466–469. IEEE (2004)

16. Setti, F., Russell, C., Bassetti, C., Cristani, M.: F-formation detection: individuating free-standing conversational groups in images. PLoS ONE **10**(5), e0123783 (2015)

17. Solera, F., Calderara, S., Cucchiara, R.: Socially constrained structural learning for groups detection in crowd. IEEE Trans. Pattern Anal. Mach. Intell. **38**(5), 995–1008 (2016)

18. Srivastava, N., Hinton, G., Krizhevsky, A., Sutskever, I., Salakhutdinov, R.: Dropout: a simple way to prevent neural networks from overfitting. J. Mach. Learn. Res. **15**, 1929–1958 (2014)

Analyzing First-Person Stories Based on Socializing, Eating and Sedentary Patterns

Pedro Herruzo, Laura Portell, Alberto Soto, and Beatriz Remeseiro[✉]

Departament de Matemàtiques i Informàtica, Universitat de Barcelona,
Gran Via de les Corts Catalanes 585, 08007 Barcelona, Spain
pedro.herruzo@ub.edu, portell.laura@gmail.com, alsoba13@gmail.com,
bremeseiro@uniovi.es

Abstract. First-person stories can be analyzed by means of egocentric pictures acquired throughout the whole active day with wearable cameras. This manuscript presents an egocentric dataset with more than 45,000 pictures from four people in different environments such as working or studying. All the images were manually labeled to identify three patterns of interest regarding people's lifestyle: socializing, eating and sedentary. Additionally, two different approaches are proposed to classify egocentric images into one of the 12 target categories defined to characterize these three patterns. The approaches are based on machine learning and deep learning techniques, including traditional classifiers and state-of-art convolutional neural networks. The experimental results obtained when applying these methods to the egocentric dataset demonstrated their adequacy for the problem at hand.

Keywords: First-person stories · Wearable cameras
Egocentric lifelogging · Annotation tool · Deep learning
Machine learning

1 Introduction

Egocentric lifelogging is a recently new research field that consists in capturing daily experiences of people from continuous records taken by them [5]. Egocentric vision is the next step on the development of the lifelogging technology, since it provides additional visual information taken from wearable cameras using a first person point-of-view. Egocentric visual data analysis can generate useful information about a person on different areas such as social interaction [2,3], food localization and recognition [6], sentimental analysis [24], etc.

Three different kinds of groups are interested in egocentric data analysis. First audience corresponds to people that want to quantify their lifestyle, the so-called quantified self community. The second group are professionals, such as doctors that use this technology to observe active aging of older people or to create cognitive exercises for patients with Alzheimer's disease [11]. The last

---

P. Herruzo, L. Portell and A. Soto—These authors contributed equally to this work.

S. Battiato et al. (Eds.): ICIAP 2017 International Workshops, LNCS 10590, pp. 109–119, 2017.
https://doi.org/10.1007/978-3-319-70742-6_10

group is formed by influential people, such as elite athletes who wear head-mounted cameras like GoPro[1] to remember their emotional experiences [13].

The egocentric vision field is an emerging field that has recently become increasingly active. There are several works that try to face different topics in this area of research. For the analysis of social interactions, Alletto et al. [3] build a model that estimates head pose and 3D location in egocentric video sequences; and Aghaei et al. [2] exploit the distance and the orientation of the appearing individuals using pictures. Regarding activities of daily living, Cartas et al. [8] explore their classification in 21 categories, that includes eating and socializing activities, using egocentric images and convolutional neural networks.

The performance of any machine learning and/or computer vision method depends on the quality and quantity of the training data. However, there are not many proposed datasets for egocentric vision, specially, datasets with low temporal resolutions. Some examples of egocentric datasets include: GTEA [12], a dataset of videos acquired with a GoPro camera and captured by four different subjects, which contains seven types of daily activities and each video is labeled with the list of objects involved and background segmentations; EDUB-Seg [10], a low-temporal resolution egocentric dataset acquired by the Narrative Clip camera, which includes 18,735 images captured by seven users during 20 days and includes indoor and outdoor scenes with numerous foreground and background objects manually annotated to provide a temporal segmentation ground-truth; and Egocentric Food [6], the first dataset of egocentric images for food-related objects localization and recognition that contains 5,038 images collected using the Narrative Clip camera, 8,573 bounding boxes and 9 different food classes.

In order to analyze people's lifestyle patterns during long periods, it is necessary to take pictures for at least 10 hours periods. Taking that into account, we present an egocentric dataset composed of more that 45,000 images taken from four people who wore the camera during active hours. In addition, we propose a research methodology to extract useful information about three different patterns: socializing, eating and sedentary. The proposed methodology should be able to quantify the following information: (1) social patterns, such as time spent with other people; (2) eating patterns, such as timing of meals and duration; and (3) sedentary lifestyle patterns, such us time spent sitting at a desk. Furthermore, these three patterns can be combined allowing to determine information such as time spent eating alone or with other people.

The remainder of the paper is organized as follows: Sect. 2 presents the egocentric dataset and the proposed methods for pattern classification, Sect. 3 presents the experimentation performed and the validation results, and finally, Sect. 4 includes the conclusions and future lines of research.

---

[1] https://gopro.com/.

2   Materials and Methods

In this section, first we present our egocentric dataset and the adapted annotation tool that allowed us to set the ground truth for each image. Second, we explain the different approaches that we used to achieve our objectives.

2.1   Egocentric Dataset

Due to the lack of first-person images to analyze socializing, eating and sedentary lifestyle patterns, we have created a dataset called LAP. It is made of egocentric pictures taken from a Narrative Clip[2] camera and contains 45,297 images taken from four different people in consecutive days with a frame rate of 2 fpm. Each person took the pictures in very different contexts such as working, studying or vacation. All the images were manually labeled according to the three following patterns:

- Eating pattern, three labels: eating (E), food related non eating (FRNE), non food related (NFR). Whereas other works can only distinguish between food or not food, this dataset allows to discard false positives when there is an image containing food but the subject is not eating.
- Socializing pattern, two labels: socializing (S), not socializing (NS). This problem was simplified as being with a person or not. As a limitation of this approach, we cannot distinguish the false positives when there are people around the subject who are not interacting with him/her.
- Sedentary pattern, two labels: table (T), no table (NT). This problem was simplified by determining if he/she is in front of a table or not, which is strongly related to the sedentary pattern of being sat in front of a table.

Each picture had to be assigned with three labels, one per each of the previous sets. As labeling all pictures requires a reasonable amount of time, we have built LAP annotation-tool, a specialized annotation tool with many keyboard shortcuts, which has been developed by adapting the web-based tool for image annotation known as LabelMe [21,25]. LAP annotation-tool allows to load pictures and select N sets of labels, and then it creates an environment with N keys to switch between the target labels. For the problem at had, three different sets of labels were needed ($N = 3$) and so we used three keys (numbers 1, 2, and 3) to switch between the different labels, setting always one label per set. Figure 1 shows three representative images of the LAP dataset with their respective assigned labels. Note that the LAP annotation-tool can be used for any image annotation problem with multiple labels per image, and it is available for download from our Github[3].

During the process of labeling, a set of rules for data integrity was established to avoid different labels in images that represent the same scene:

---

[2] http://getnarrative.com/.
[3] https://github.com/alsoba13/LAP-Annotation-Tool.

Fig. 1. Example of three egocentric images of the LAP dataset, each one with different labels (see the top of each picture).

- Eating pattern: E is used when there is food in the image and the person is eating, FRNE is used when there is food in the image but the subject is not eating, and NFR is used when there is no food in the image.
- Socializing pattern: S is only used when a person appears in the image, regardless of the distance.
- Sedentary pattern: T is only used when a table appears in the image and it is not far from the camera wearer.

Regarding noisy or black pictures, instead of discarding them, they were assigned the default labels NFR-NS-NT. In this manner, the trained model should be able to consider this situation that frequently occurs in real environments.

Table 1 shows some statistics for the LAP dataset taking into account all the possible combinations among the three sets of labels. First insights of data show that the dataset is highly imbalanced. This fact was expected since, in real life, people do not spend the same amount of time socializing than alone, or eating than doing other daily routines or activities. If the different combinations of labels are analyzed, it can be observed that there are several combinations poorly represented. Note that only 4 out of the 12 combinations represent over the 92% of the total number of images acquired.

For experimental purposes, the LAP dataset has been split in training, validation and test sets: the training set contains a 70% of the images, whilst the validation and test sets contain, each one, a 15%.

2.2   Methods

Given an input image, the goal is to classify it in order to determine the three patterns of interest: socializing, eating and sedentary. Accordingly, the following sets were defined: $Eating := \{E, FRNE, NFR\}$, $Socializing := \{S, NS\}$, and

Table 1. Distribution of classes in the LAP dataset.

Id	Labels	%	#Images
0	NFR-NS-NT	46.49	21,058
1	NFR-NS-T	12.97	5,877
2	NFR-S-NT	21.53	9,755
3	NFR-S-T	11.46	5,194
4	FRNE-NS-NT	0.41	187
5	FRNE-NS-T	0.48	218
6	FRNE-S-NT	0.94	425
7	FRNE-S-T	1.49	673
8	E-NS-NT	0.19	88
9	E-NS-T	1.20	543
10	E-S-NT	0.53	242
11	E-S-T	2.29	1,037
	Total	100	45,297

Sedentary := $\{T, NT\}$. All the possible combinations of the three sets are considered, resulting in the cartesian product *Eating* × *Socializing* × *Sedentary*, a set with $3 \times 2 \times 2 = 12$ classes. Therefore, we have a 12-class classification problem for which two different approaches have been considered based on machine learning and deep learning techniques. The two approaches are subsequently presented.

Machine Learning Approach. The first approach is depicted in Fig. 2 (top) and consists in using machine learning (ML) algorithms to classify an input image into one of the 12 target categories.

Applying classical ML methods directly to images requires the use of a feature extraction step before the classification. For this task, we have used the incremental principal component analysis (IPCA) technique [4], which projects the data into a reduced space computing the projection matrix iteratively. Next, three well-known algorithms were used for classification, which were selected aiming to analyze different approaches of the supervised learning process:

- k-nearest neighbors (kNN) [16]: this method assigns the class label of the majority of the k nearest patterns in the data space, based on the idea that the nearest patterns to a target one deliver useful information.
- Support vector machines (SVM) [7]: they are based on the statistical learning theory and revolve around the notion of a *margin*, either side of a hyperplane that separates two classes.
- Gradient boosting machines (GBM) [18]: they are powerful techniques for both regression and classification problems, which can be seen as ensembles of weak prediction models, typically decision trees.

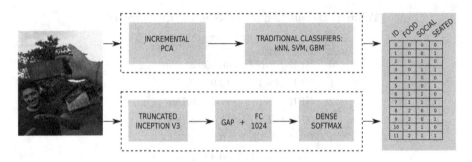

Fig. 2. Workflow of the machine learning (top) and deep learning (bottom) approaches.

Deep Learning Approach. The second approach is illustrated in Fig. 2 (bottom) and aims at classifying an input image using deep learning algorithms.

Convolutional neural networks (CNNs) were considered in this case and, more specifically, the deep architecture known as InceptionV3 [23]. It is a general model for any kind of images with an only assumption about their size: the dimensions of the input layer are $299 \times 299 \times 3$, allowing to compute all convolutions with a valid size after the reductions made by pooling layers.

This model was first pre-trained on a large dataset called ImageNet [20]. Then, the last layers were adapted to our 12-class classification problem. Basically, the last fully connected, pooling and vectorizing layers were removed from the original model; whilst a global average pooling (GAP) and a 1024-unit fully connected (FC) layers were added before the last fully connected layer with a softmax. Additionally, batch normalization [14] and dropout [22] were added to our deep learning approach to avoid the overfitting shortcoming of the CNNs.

The binary cross entropy [17] was used in our model as the loss function. In order to fix the problem of imbalanced classes, described in Sect. 2.1, we combined the use of weights with the loss function. The weights were defined as:

$$w_i = \frac{M}{N_i} \tag{1}$$

where N_i is the number of images in class i ($i \in Eating \times Socializing \times Sedentary$), and M is the number of pictures of the major class ($M = \max_i N_i$).

3   Experiments and Discussion

This section includes the evaluation of our methods using the LAP dataset previously presented, in addition to some details about the experimental setup and the performance measures considered.

3.1   Experimental Setup

Experimentation was carried out on a Intel© Core™ i7-6700 CPU @ 8M Cache, 3.40 GHz with RAM 32 GB DDR4. For the deep learning approach, a NVIDIA TITAN Xp GPU was also used.

Regarding the machine learning approach, the Scikit-learn library [19] was used to train the three classifiers. Their configuration parameters were selected by merging the training and validation sets, and then applying grid search and 3-fold cross validation. The following configuration was finally used: kNN classifier with number of neighbors $k = 3$, SVM with linear kernel and penalty parameter $C = 100$, and GBM with regression trees as weak prediction models.

With respect to the framework for the deep learning approach, we used Keras [9], a Python deep learning library for Theano and TensorFlow. In particular, we run it on top of TensorFlow [1]. Model selection of the CNN approach was made by training the network over the training set and selecting the parameters that make a better score and less overfitting over the validation set. The architecture and training details are as follows: a stochastic gradient descent for optimization half of the epochs and Adam [15] the rest, both with learning rate of 0.001, a momentum of 0.9, and a batch size of 128 images. Additionally, the CNN was trained over 50 epochs, and data augmentation was applied with flipping, Gaussian noise, and a rotation from -30 up to $30°$.

In order to match the model requirements of Inception V3, the images of our dataset were reduced from $1944 \times 2592 \times 3$ to $299 \times 299 \times 3$. Note that this reduction of the input images was applied in both approaches in order to get a fair comparison of the results.

3.2   Performance Measures

Three different metrics were used to evaluate the adequacy of the proposed methods for the classification of the socializing, eating and sedentary patterns:

- F1-score: the harmonic mean of precision and recall.
- Accuracy: the percentage of correctly classified samples.
- Normalized accuracy: the weighted accuracy in which each class contributes with the ratio of correct predictions over the total of images, normalizing by the number of classes.

It should be pointed out the relevance of the normalized accuracy since the dataset is highly imbalanced, and so this metric allows us to know how good is the method classifying each class in a more precise way.

3.3   Results

Table 2 shows the classification results for the task of predicting the class of an input image. Note that the best results appear in bold face.

Regarding the machine learning approach, based on incremental PCA and traditional classifiers, kNN and SVM have a quite similar behavior in terms of performance with a F1-score over 0.3 and an accuracy over the 40%. The best result obtained in this case corresponds to GBM, with a F1-score close to 0.5 and an accuracy over the 53%. If the normalized accuracy provided by the three classifiers is analyzed, the results are quite poor due to the imbalance of the dataset (a normalized accuracy of 15.11% in the best case). In particular, the images labeled as *NFR-NS-NT* correspond to the 46.5%, so it could be said that this class is mainly the only one learned by these models. Note that this behavior is also related with the low F1-score, due to the poor precision obtained when comparing the major class with the others.

Table 2. Results for the machine learning (ML) and deep learning (DL) approaches.

	ML approach			DL approach	
	*k*NN	SVM	GBM	non-weights	weights
F-1 score	0.355	0.368	0.490	0.309	**0.64**
Accuracy (%)	49.25	42.52	53.72	46.75	**60.53**
Normalized acc. (%)	10.11	9.69	15.11	8.59	**57.55**

With respect to deep learning, the results obtained without considering the weights are quite similar to the ones provided by the classical machine learning methods. As a matter of fact, the use of GBM as classifier in the ML approach outperforms the basic DL approach despite the fact that IPCA only does a space reduction on raw pixels data instead of getting more abstract representations. However, when using the proposed weights as part of the binary cross entropy loss function, in order to face the problem of imbalanced classes, these measures are noticeably improved. In particular, the F1-score obtained is 0.64 and the accuracy surpasses the 60%. With respect to the normalized accuracy, it is almost aligned with the accuracy since it reaches the 57%. This result should be highlighted since it is almost four times better than the maximum normalized accuracy obtained in the best configuration of the ML approach (15.11%) and almost seven times better than the one obtained in the first DL approach (8.59%), which demonstrated the key role played by our proposed weights.

Figure 3 displays the confusion matrix of the deep learning approach when the weights are used as part of the binary cross entropy loss function. As can be seen, most of the error comes from misclassifications on the *Eating* pattern. For example, class 11 (*E-S-T*) is often classified as 7 (*FRNE-S-T*), so the model just makes a mistake with the *Eating* component of the triplet. This fact also happens with classes 5 (classified as 1 and 9), 6 (classified as 2 and 10), 7 (classified as 3 and 11) and 10 (classified as 6). All those errors form visible lower and upper diagonals in the confusion matrix. After a more careful analysis, it can be also observed that this trend has an exception since our model correctly classifies most of the samples from classes 8 (*E-NS-T*) and 9 (*E-NS-NT*). Images of these two classes have in common that contain food (*E*) but no people (*NS*). Therefore, it can be said that, when classifying an image of any of these two classes, the model has a strong belief on the person is eating (*E*) as he/she is alone. On the other hand, food in *S* images may be from the subject itself or from any of his/her companions, which makes that these images are sometimes misclassified as *FRNE*. Figure 4 shows two images from the LAP dataset with both the ground truth and the predicted labels.

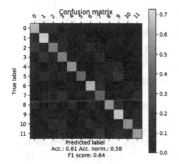

Fig. 3. Confusion matrix of the deep learning approach using our proposed weights to classify input images into the 12 classes (see Table 1 for a detailed explanation of each *id*).

Fig. 4. Two images of the LAP dataset with the ground truth and the predicted labels: (left) a correct classification of an image from class 9; and (right) a misclassification of an image labeled as S, so the food in it may correspond to food being eaten by the subject (E) or by other people (FRNE).

4   Conclusions

First-person cameras are inherently linked to the ongoing experiences of the people who wear them. Pictures acquired by this type of cameras allow to analyze the visual world with respect to the wearer's activities and behaviors.

In this context we present LAP, an egocentric dataset composed of 45,297 pictures taken from four subjects using a wearable camera. In addition to the first-person images, the dataset contains three labels per picture that correspond to the three patterns of interest: socializing, eating and sedentary. Furthermore, we present a simple, yet very useful annotation tool based on LabelMe that allows us to label pictures with more than one label in a very reasonable time.

Regarding the research methodology, we have proved that we can estimate socializing, eating and sedentary patterns of a subject from egocentric pictures by combining different powerful methods and adapting them to our problem. More specifically, a preliminary comparison of two approaches was presented, one of them based on classical machine learning algorithms and the other one on state-of-art deep learning techniques. Both approaches were evaluated over the LAP dataset using three performance measures: F1-score, accuracy and normalized accuracy. The obtained results demonstrated the adequacy of the proposed methods to solve this multi-class problem. It should be highlighted that the deep learning approach outperforms the classical machine learning methods due to the complexity of the problem, with 12 classes and a highly-imbalanced dataset. In particular, the use of the proposed weights in conjunction with the binary cross entropy loss function allows us to achieve the most competitive results, with a normalized accuracy over 57%.

As future work, we plan to explore a multi-task approach in order to predict the socializing, eating and sedentary patterns. On the other hand, the problem of estimating the sedentary lifestyle of a person, i.e. if he/she is sitting or walking, is very difficult to predict in short-term. For this reason, the future research also includes to introduce time dependency in our models. Finally, we would like to increase the labels of the LAP dataset by including new information such as the number of hours spent with a smartphone.

Acknowledgements. This work was partially funded by TIN2015-66951-C2-1-R, SGR 1219, and CERCA Programme/Generalitat de Catalunya. Beatriz Remeseiro acknowledges the support of the Ministerio de Economía y Competitividad of the Spanish Government under *Juan de la Cierva* Program (ref. FJCI-2014-21194). The funders had no role in the study design, data collection, analysis, and preparation of the manuscript.

The authors gratefully acknowledge the support of NVIDIA Corporation with the donation of the Titan Xp GPU used for this research.

References

1. Abadi, M., Barham, P., Chen, J., Chen, Z., Davis, A., Dean, J., Devin, M., Ghemawat, S., Irving, G., Isard, M., et al.: TensorFlow: a system for large-scale machine learning. In: OSDI, vol. 16, pp. 265–283 (2016)
2. Aghaei, M., Dimiccoli, M., Radeva, P.: With whom do I interact? Detecting social interactions in egocentric photo-streams. In: 23rd International Conference on Pattern Recognition, pp. 2959–2964 (2016)
3. Alletto, S., Serra, G., Calderara, S., Solera, F., Cucchiara, R.: From ego to nosvision: detecting social relationships in first-person views. In: Proceedings of the IEEE Conference on Computer Vision and Pattern Recognition Workshops, pp. 580–585 (2014)
4. Balsubramani, A., Dasgupta, S., Freund, Y.: The fast convergence of incremental PCA. In: Advances in Neural Information Processing Systems, pp. 3174–3182 (2013)
5. Bolanos, M., Dimiccoli, M., Radeva, P.: Toward storytelling from visual lifelogging: an overview. IEEE Trans. Hum.-Mach. Syst. **47**(1), 77–90 (2017)
6. Bolanos, M., Radeva, P.: Simultaneous food localization and recognition. In: 23rd International Conference on Pattern Recognition, pp. 3140–3145 (2016)
7. Burges, C.J.: A tutorial on support vector machines for pattern recognition. Data Min. Knowl. Disc. **2**(2), 121–167 (1998)
8. Cartas, A., Marín, J., Radeva, P., Dimiccoli, M.: Recognizing activities of daily living from egocentric images. In: Alexandre, L.A., Salvador Sánchez, J., Rodrigues, J.M.F. (eds.) IbPRIA 2017. LNCS, vol. 10255, pp. 87–95. Springer, Cham (2017). https://doi.org/10.1007/978-3-319-58838-4_10
9. Chollet, F., et al.: Keras: deep learning library for theano and tensorflow (2015). https://keras.io/

10. Dimiccoli, M., Bolaños, M., Talavera, E., Aghaei, M., Nikolov, S.G., Radeva, P.: SR-clustering: semantic regularized clustering for egocentric photo streams segmentation. Comput. Vis. Image Underst. **155**, 55–69 (2017)
11. Doherty, A.R., Moulin, C.J., Smeaton, A.F.: Automatically assisting human memory: a sensecam browser. Memory **19**(7), 785–795 (2011)
12. Fathi, A., Ren, X., Rehg, J.M.: Learning to recognize objects in egocentric activities. In: IEEE Conference On Computer Vision and Pattern Recognition, pp. 3281–3288 (2011)
13. Hoshen, Y., Peleg, S.: An egocentric look at video photographer identity. In: Proceedings of the IEEE Conference on Computer Vision and Pattern Recognition, pp. 4284–4292 (2016)
14. Ioffe, S., Szegedy, C.: Batch normalization: accelerating deep network training by reducing internal covariate shift. In: International Conference on Machine Learning, pp. 448–456 (2015)
15. Kingma, D.P., Ba, J.: Adam: a method for stochastic optimization. CoRR abs/1412.6980 (2014)
16. Kramer, O.: K-nearest neighbors. In: Kramer, O. (ed.) Dimensionality Reduction with Unsupervised Nearest Neighbors, pp. 13–23. Springer, Heidelberg (2013). https://doi.org/10.1007/978-3-642-38652-7_2
17. Lei Ba, J., Swersky, K., Fidler, S., et al.: Predicting deep zero-shot convolutional neural networks using textual descriptions. In: Proceedings of the IEEE International Conference on Computer Vision, pp. 4247–4255 (2015)
18. Natekin, A., Knoll, A.: Gradient boosting machines, a tutorial. Front. Neurorobotics **7**, 1–21 (2013). Article no. 21
19. Pedregosa, F., Varoquaux, G., Gramfort, A., Michel, V., Thirion, B., Grisel, O., Blondel, M., Prettenhofer, P., Weiss, R., Dubourg, V., et al.: Scikit-learn: machine learning in Python. J. Mach. Learn. Res. **12**(Oct), 2825–2830 (2011)
20. Russakovsky, O., Deng, J., Su, H., Krause, J., Satheesh, S., Ma, S., Huang, Z., Karpathy, A., Khosla, A., Bernstein, M., Berg, A.C., Li, F.: Imagenet large scale visual recognition challenge. Int. J. Comput. Vis. **115**(3), 211–252 (2015)
21. Russell, B.C., Torralba, A., Murphy, K.P., Freeman, W.T.: LabelMe: a database and web-based tool for image annotation. Int. J. Comput. Vis. **77**(1), 157–173 (2008)
22. Srivastava, N., Hinton, G.E., Krizhevsky, A., Sutskever, I., Salakhutdinov, R.: Dropout: a simple way to prevent neural networks from overfitting. J. Mach. Learn. Res. **15**(1), 1929–1958 (2014)
23. Szegedy, C., Vanhoucke, V., Ioffe, S., Shlens, J., Wojna, Z.: Rethinking the inception architecture for computer vision. In: Proceedings of the IEEE Conference on Computer Vision and Pattern Recognition, pp. 2818–2826 (2016)
24. Talavera, E., Strisciuglio, N., Petkov, N., Radeva, P.: Sentiment recognition in egocentric photostreams. In: Alexandre, L.A., Salvador Sánchez, J., Rodrigues, J.M.F. (eds.) IbPRIA 2017. LNCS, vol. 10255, pp. 471–479. Springer, Cham (2017). https://doi.org/10.1007/978-3-319-58838-4_52
25. Torralba, A., Russell, B.C., Yuen, J.: Labelme: online image annotation and applications. Proc. IEEE **98**(8), 1467–1484 (2010)

Serious Games Application for Memory Training Using Egocentric Images

Gabriel Oliveira-Barra[1], Marc Bolaños[1(✉)], Estefania Talavera[1,2],
Adrián Dueñas[1], Olga Gelonch[3], and Maite Garolera[3]

[1] Universitat de Barcelona, Barcelona, Spain
marc.bolanos@ub.edu
[2] University of Groningen, Groningen, The Netherlands
[3] Consorci Sanitari de Terrassa, Terrassa, Spain

Abstract. Mild cognitive impairment is the early stage of several neurodegenerative diseases, such as Alzheimer's. In this work, we address the
use of lifelogging as a tool to obtain pictures from a patient's daily life
from an egocentric point of view. We propose to use them in combination
with serious games as a way to provide a non-pharmacological treatment
to improve their quality of life. To do so, we introduce a novel computer
vision technique that classifies rich and non rich egocentric images and
uses them in serious games. We present results over a dataset composed
by 10,997 images, recorded by 7 different users, achieving 79% of F1-
score. Our model presents the first method used for automatic egocentric
images selection applicable to serious games.

Keywords: Lifelogging · Serious games · Egocentric vision
Mild cognitive impairment · Machine learning · Computer vision

1 Introduction

Dementia can result from different causes,
the most common being Alzheimers disease
(AD) [10], and it is often preceded by a
pre-dementia stage, known as Mild Cognitive
Impairment (MCI), characterized by a cognitive decline greater than expected by an
individual's age, but which does not inter-
fere notably with their daily life activities
[11,19]. Currently, medical specialists design
and apply special activities that could serve
as a treatment tool for cognitive capabilities
enhancement. Even though, these activities
are not specially designed for the patients,
which limits their engagement in some cases
(Fig. 1).

Fig. 1. Person using the Narrative
Clip camera.

© Springer International Publishing AG 2017
S. Battiato et al. (Eds.): ICIAP 2017 International Workshops, LNCS 10590, pp. 120–130, 2017.
https://doi.org/10.1007/978-3-319-70742-6_11

Fig. 2. Examples of egocentric images recorded by the Narrative Clip camera.

A possible alternative to the application of generic exercises would be the use of personalized images of the daily life of the patients acquired by lifelogging devices. Lifelogging consists of a user continuously recording their everyday experiences, typically via wearable sensors including accelerometers and cameras, among others. When the visual signal is the only one recorded, typically by a wearable camera, it is referred to as visual lifelogging [4]. This is a trend that is rapidly increasing thanks to advances in wearable technologies over recent years. Nowadays, wearable cameras are very small devices that can be worn all-day long and automatically record the everyday activities of the wearer in a passive fashion, from a first-person point of view. As an example, Fig. 2 shows pictures taken by a person wearing such a camera.

Recent studies have described wearable cameras or lifelogging technologies as useful devices for memory support for people with episodic memory impairment, such as the one present in MCI [8,15]. The design of new technologies to be applied on this field requires to take into account people capabilities, limitations, needs and the acceptance of the wearable devices, since it can directly affect the treatment. So far, some studies have deeply focus into the factors associated to the use of these devices [13,24].

Lifelogging and privacy: In terms of privacy, in 2011, the European Union agency ENISA evaluated the risks, threats and vulnerabilities of lifelogging applications with respect to central topics as privacy and trust issues. In their final report, they highlighted that lifelogging itself is still in its infancy but nevertheless will play an important role in the near future [3]. Therefore, they recommended further and extensive research in order to influence its evolution to be better prepared to mitigate the risks and maximize the benefits of these technologies. In addition, other researchers have also evaluated the possible ethical risks involved on using lifelogging devices on medical studies [7].

Serious games for MCI: Serious games (also known as games with a purpose) are digital applications specialized for purposes other than simply entertaining, such as informing, educating or enhancing physical and cognitive functions. Nowadays they are widely recognized as promising non-pharmacological tools to help assess and evaluate functional impairments of patients, as well as to aid with their treatment, stimulation, and rehabilitation [21]. Boosted by the publication of a Nature letter showing that video game training can enhance cognitive control in older adults [2], there is now a growing interest in developing serious games specifically adapted to people with AD and related disorders. Preliminary evidence shows that serious games can successfully be employed to train physical and cognitive abilities in people with AD, MCI, and related disorders [17]. [18] performed a literature review of the experimental studies conducted to date on the use of serious games in neurodegenerative disorders and [21] studied recommendations for the use of serious games in people with AD and related disorders, reporting positive effects on several health-related capabilities of MCI patients such as voluntary motor control, cognitive functions like attention and memory or social and emotional functions. For instance they can improve their mood and increase their sociability, as well as reduce their depression.

Our contribution: Different studies have proven the benefits of directly stimulating the working memory. Our contribution in this paper consists in using as stimuli the autobiographical images of the MCI patients that was acquired by the wearable cameras. By doing this, we intend to accomplish the goal of enhancing their motivation and at the same time treat them in a more functional and multimodal manner [1,9,16]. The application, which will allow the user to exercise either at the sanitary center or at home, will be composed by serious games where the patient has to observe a series of images and interact with them.

Although the stimuli provided by egocentric images can be of greater importance than non-personal images, it is important to note both, that egocentric images are captured in an uncontrolled environment, and that wearable cameras usually have free motion that might cause most images to be blurry, dark or empty of semantic content. Considering this important limitations together with the limited capabilities of MCI patients, we propose the development of an egocentric rich images detection system intended to select only images with semantic and relevant content. Our hypothesis is that, by using personal daily life rich images, the motivation of the patient will increase, and as a consequence, the health-related benefits provided by the treatment.

This paper is organized as follows. We describe the proposed serious game and model for rich images selection in Sect. 2 and Sect. 3, respectively. In Sect. 4, we describes the experimental setup and show quantitative and qualitative evaluation. Finally, Sect. 5 draws conclusions and outlines future works.

2 Proposed Serious Game: "Position Recall"

MCI patients experiment problems in their working memory [23], therefore, it is of high importance to do exercises for stimulating it. All this under the neuroplasticity paradigm, which has proven that it is possible to modify the brain capabilities and the hypothesis of "use it or lose it", which are the basis of the studies related to the cognitive stimulation of elderly people [22]. Thus, in this work, we introduce a serious game that we name as "Position Recall", which was designed by neuropsychologist of Consorci Sanitari de Terrassa for improving the working memory. The mechanics of this game follow this scheme:

The first screen explains to the patient the instructions of the game and in the second the patient is informed that, before starting the game, there will be some practice examples that will serve to understand its logic. To start, the patient must select his preferred level of difficulty (Level 1, 2 or 3).

- **Level 1** shows 3 images of the patients' day during 8 s and they are asked to remember their positions. Immediately after they disappear, a single "target" image is shown and they are asked to select in what position it was placed. After some trials the number of images displayed are increased to 4 and then to 5.
- **Level 2** follows the same procedure as the 1st level, but the timespan between the moment where the images disappear and the target image is shown is increased. During this timespan, called latency time, a black screen is shown.
- **Level 3** follows the same procedure as the 2nd level, but now a distractor image is shown instead of a black screen during the latency time. The distractor image is also an image belonging to the patients' day.

The reward system of the game are points that are given after each level, and are calculated as $100 x number\ of\ correct\ answers$. There are 10 trials per level translating into a maximum of 1000 points per level and maximum of 3000 points per game. Figure 3a and b show the mechanics of the developed game.

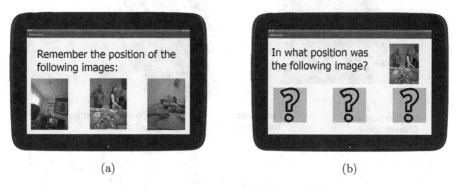

(a)   (b)

Fig. 3. (a) A predefined number of pictures of the patient is shown to him during few seconds at random positions in the screen. (b) After a certain time passed, the patient is asked to recall in what position one of the pictures, picked up randomly, was placed before.

The images to be shown during the serious games should be significant for the patient. We propose to use images that represent past moments of the user's life, i.e. from the egocentric photostreams recorded by the patient. On the following section, we describe the proposed model for rich images selection.

3   What Did I See? Rich Images Detection

The main factor for providing a meaningful image selection algorithm is the fact that the proposed serious games intend to work on cognitive and sentiment enhancement. Considering the free-motion and non-intentionality of the pictures taken by wearable cameras [4], it is very important to provide a robust method for images selection.

Two of the most important and basic factors that determine the memorability of an image [5,14] can be described as (1) the appearance of human faces, and (2) the appearance of characteristic and recognizable objects. In this paper, we focus on satisfying the second criterion by proposing an algorithm based on computer vision. Our proposal consists in a rich images detection algorithm, which intends to detect images with a high number of objects and variability and at the same time avoids images with low semantical content, understanding as rich any image that is neither blur, nor dark and that contains clearly visible non-occluded objects. In Fig. 4 we show the general pipeline of our proposal.

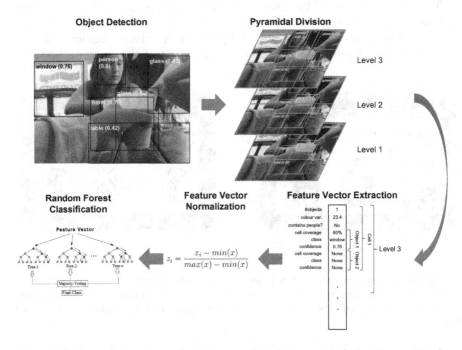

Fig. 4. Scheme of the proposed rich images detection model. (color figure online)

Our algorithm for rich images detection (consists in 1) objects detection: where the neural network named YOLO9000 [20] is applied in order to detect any existent object in the images and their associated confidences c_i. (2) the image is divided in a pyramidal structure of cells, (3) a set of richness-related features are extracted, (4) the extracted features are normalized and (5) a Random Forest Classifier (RFC) [6] is trained to distinguish the differences between rich or non-rich images. When extracting features, the image is divided in a pyramidal structure of cells with different sizes at each level. The set of extracted features are:

- **Numbers of objects the cell contains.**
- **Variance of color in the cell.**
- **Does the cell contain people?**
- **Object Scale.** Real number between 0 and 1.
- **Object Class.** Class identifier that varies between 1 and 9418.
- **Object Confidence** c_i.

where all features are repeated for each cell and the last three kinds of features are repeated for each object appearing in the cells. The image cell divisions applied are $1x1$, $2x2$ and $3x3$, the maximum of objects selected per cell are 5, 3 and 2, respectively and all objects are sorted by their confidence c_i before selection. If the number of objects is less than the maximum number are found, the feature value in that specific position is set to 0.

The pyramidal division of the images helps us consider smaller objects at higher levels (more cells) and bigger objects at lower levels (less cells). Thus, both small and big objects will be considered for the final prediction.

In order to define the feature "Does the cell contain people?" We manually selected a set of person-related objects detected by the employed object detection method. The concepts representing people that we selected are "person", "worker", "workman", "employee", "consumer", "groom" and "bride".

4 Results

This section describes the results obtained in a quantitative and qualitative form. We compare the results obtained by variations of the proposed method on a self-made dataset of rich images.

Dataset: The dataset used for evaluating our model was acquired by the wearable camera Narrative Clip 2[1], which takes a picture every thirty seconds automatically. The camera was worn during 15 days by 7 different people. Considering that on average the camera takes 1,500 images per day, our dataset consists of 10,997 photographs.

The resulting data was labeled by neuropsychologist experts on MCI cognition following the criteria that any rich image has to be (1) properly illuminated, (2) not blurry and (3) contain one or more objects that are not occluded. After this manual selection the acquired images where split in 6,399 rich images and 4,598 non-rich images.

---

[1] www.getnarrative.com.

In Fig. 5a we can see some examples of egocentric rich images and in Fig. 5b non-rich images. We observe that rich images show people or recognizable places. However, non-rich images are meaningless or dark images (that can hardly be seen), including pictures of the sky, ceilings or floor.

(a)   (b)

Fig. 5. (a) Rich images and (b) Non-rich images

The resulting data was divided in training, validation, and test. Considering the pictures taken during the same day can be very similar, we proceeded to randomly separate the different days into the three different sets. First, the training set consists of 60% of the days, in this case 9. Second, 20% of the days, in this case 3, were defined as the validation set. Finally, the remaining 20% was used for the test set.

Evaluation Metrics: In order to evaluate the different results and compare them to get the best one, we make use of the F1-score (or F-measure) metric:

$$F1 = 2 * \frac{1}{\frac{1}{precision} + \frac{1}{recall}} = 2 * \frac{precision * recall}{precision + recall}$$

where *precision* is the quotient between the number of True Positives objects and the number of predicted positive elements; and *recall* is the quotient between the number of True Positives objects and the number of real positive elements.

Quantitative Results: Currently, there are no previous works addressing the challenge we introduce in this work. Thus, in order to compare the performance of our proposed model, we have defined and compared several variations to our main pipeline (see results in Table 1).

As an alternative to our proposed approach (1), we tested an alternative feature vector representation by means of using the (2) Word2Vec word embedding [12]. This word characterization is a 300-dimensional vector representation created by Google that represents words in space depending on their semantic meaning (i.e. words with similar definitions will be represented close in space).

The Word2Vec representation was used in two ways. On the one hand was used for defining the set of concepts related to "person" in the feature described as "Does the cell contain people?". Thus, we computed the similarity between the word "person" and any other concept detected in the image by the object detection and the maximum similarity achieved was used as an alternative to a 0/1 representation. On the other hand, the feature described as "Object Class" was replaced by the 300-dimensions Word2Vec representation.

In the test setting (3) we additionally applied a PCA dimensionality reduction to the Word2Vec representation. Finally, in (4) we used a Support Vector Machine (SVM) classifier instead of a Random Forest Classifier. We applied a Grid Search on the variables C and *gamma* for parameter selection over the validation set.

Table 1. Comparison of the results

		Precision	Recall	F1-score
(1)	RFC	0.79	0.79	0.79
(2)	RFC + Word2Vec	0.78	0.78	0.78
(3)	RFC + Word2Vec + PCA	0.74	0.75	0.75
(4)	SVM	0.68	0.67	0.68

In conclusion we can see that using an RFC classifier (1) obtains better results than SVM (4) and at the same time none of the Word2Vec representations (2) and (3) helped improving the base results.

Fig. 6. Example of rich (left) images selection, vs non-rich images rejection. From an egocentric photostream composed by 972 images, 221 were considered rich.

Qualitative Results: Examples of the selected images by the proposed algorithm are shown in Fig. 6. On one hand, we can observe that rich images (left) are clearer, without shadows and with people or focused objects, which allows the user to infer what is happening in the scene. On the other hand, non-rich images (right) are discarded since they are not illustrative and make difficult the scene interpretation.

Images selected by the proposed model are rich in information and memory trigger. We can foresee that the proposed model cannot only be used for serious games images selection, but also as a tool for images selection for autobiographical memories creation.

5   Conclusions

In this work, we have introduced a novel type of wearable computing application, aiming to provide non pharmacological treatment for MCI patients and to improve their life quality. We discussed lifelogging pictures obtained from wearable cameras combined with serious games as a channel for personalized treatments. We also introduced and tested a novel computer vision technique to classify rich and non rich images obtained from first-person point of view. We obtain 79% F1-score, promising results that will be further studied.

As future work, we will implement more serious games to be included in the application tool. Specialists will use it for MCI patients, aiming to prove the memory reinforcement hypothesis introduced in this work, as well as the motivation experienced by the subjects increase when using personalized rich images and serious games. Furthermore, in [25], positiveness from egocentric images was addressed. Moreover, we will go deeper on the analysis of users acceptance over the proposed technology, their willingness to use it, and the factors that determine their acceptance toward it. Further improvements of the methodology will be developed in order to obtain more accurate results.

Acknowledgements. This work was partially founded by Ministerio de Ciencia e Innovación of the Gobierno de España, through the research project TIN2015-66951-C2. SGR 1219, CERCA, *ICREA Academia 2014*, Grant 20141510 (Marató TV3) and Grant FPU15/01347. The funders had no role in the study design, data collection, analysis, and preparation of the manuscript. The authors gratefully acknowledge the support of NVIDIA Corporation with the donation of the Titan Xp GPU used for this research.

References

1. Alves, J., Alves-Costa, F., Magalhães, R., Gonçalves, Ó.F., Sampaio, A.: Cognitive stimulation for Portuguese older adults with cognitive impairment: a randomized controlled trial of efficacy, comparative duration, feasibility, and experiential relevance. Am. J. Alzheimer's Dis. Other Dement.® **29**(6), 503–512 (2014)
2. Anguera, J.A., Boccanfuso, J., Rintoul, J.L., Al-Hashimi, O., Faraji, F., Janowich, J., Kong, E., Larraburo, Y., Rolle, C., Johnston, E., et al.: Video game training enhances cognitive control in older adults. Nature **501**(7465), 97–101 (2013)
3. Askoxylakis, I., Brown, I., Dickman, P., Friedewald, M., Irion, K., Kosta, E., Langheinrich, M., McCarthy, P., Osimo, D., Papiotis, S., et al.: To log or not to log?-Risks and benefits of emerging life-logging applications (2011)

4. Bolaños, M., Dimiccoli, M., Radeva, P.: Toward storytelling from visual lifelogging: an overview. IEEE Trans. Hum.-Mach. Syst. **47**(1), 77–90 (2017)
5. Carné, M., Giro-i-Nieto, X., Radeva, P., Gurrin, C.: Egomemnet: visual memorability adaptation to egocentric images
6. Criminisi, A., Shotton, J., Konukoglu, E., et al.: Decision forests: a unified framework for classification, regression, density estimation, manifold learning and semi-supervised learning. Found. Trends® Comput. Graph. Vis. **7**(2–3), 81–227 (2012)
7. Doherty, A.R., Hodges, S.E., King, A.C., Smeaton, A.F., Berry, E., Moulin, C.J., Lindley, S., Kelly, P., Foster, C.: Wearable cameras in health. Am. J. Prev. Med. **44**(3), 320–323 (2013)
8. Doherty, A.R., Pauly-Takacs, K., Caprani, N., Gurrin, C., Moulin, C.J., O'Connor, N.E., Smeaton, A.F.: Experiences of aiding autobiographical memory using the sensecam. Hum.-Comput. Interact. **27**(1–2), 151–174 (2012)
9. Flak, M.M., Hernes, S.S., Skranes, J., Løhaugen, G.C.: The memory aid study: protocol for a randomized controlled clinical trial evaluating the effect of computer-based working memory training in elderly patients with mild cognitive impairment (MCI). Trials **15**(1), 156 (2014)
10. Fratiglioni, L., Grut, M., Forsell, Y., Viitanen, M., Grafström, M., Holmen, K., Ericsson, K., Bäckman, L., Ahlbom, A., Winblad, B.: Prevalence of Alzheimer's disease and other dementias in an elderly urban population relationship with age, sex, and education. Neurology **41**(12), 1886–1886 (1991)
11. Gauthier, S., Reisberg, B., Zaudig, M., Petersen, R.C., Ritchie, K., Broich, K., Belleville, S., Brodaty, H., Bennett, D., Chertkow, H., et al.: Mild cognitive impairment. Lancet **367**(9518), 1262–1270 (2006)
12. Goldberg, Y., Levy, O.: word2vec explained: deriving Mikolov et al.'s negative-sampling word-embedding method. arXiv preprint arXiv:1402.3722 (2014)
13. Gurrin, C., Smeaton, A.F., Doherty, A.R., et al.: Lifelogging: personal big data. Found. Trends® Inf. Retr. **8**(1), 1–125 (2014)
14. Khosla, A., Raju, A.S., Torralba, A., Oliva, A.: Understanding and predicting image memorability at a large scale. In: Proceedings of the IEEE International Conference on Computer Vision, pp. 2390–2398 (2015)
15. Lee, M.L., Dey, A.K.: Lifelogging memory appliance for people with episodic memory impairment. In: Proceedings of the 10th International Conference on Ubiquitous Computing, pp. 44–53. ACM (2008)
16. Li, H., Li, J., Li, N., Li, B., Wang, P., Zhou, T.: Cognitive intervention for persons with mild cognitive impairment: a meta-analysis. Ageing Res. Rev. **10**(2), 285–296 (2011)
17. Manera, V., Petit, P.D., Derreumaux, A., Orvieto, I., Romagnoli, M., Lyttle, G., David, R., Robert, P.H.: Kitchen and cooking, a serious game for mild cognitive impairment and Alzheimer's disease: a pilot study. Front. Aging Neurosci. **7** (2015)
18. McCallum, S., Boletsis, C.: Dementia games: a literature review of Dementia-related serious games. In: Ma, M., Oliveira, M.F., Petersen, S., Hauge, J.B. (eds.) SGDA 2013. LNCS, vol. 8101, pp. 15–27. Springer, Heidelberg (2013). https://doi.org/10.1007/978-3-642-40790-1_2
19. Petersen, R.C., Smith, G.E., Waring, S.C., Ivnik, R.J., Tangalos, E.G., Kokmen, E.: Mild cognitive impairment: clinical characterization and outcome. Arch. Neurol. **56**(3), 303–308 (1999)
20. Redmon, J., Farhadi, A.: Yolo9000: better, faster, stronger. arXiv preprint arXiv:1612.08242 (2016)

21. Robert, P.H., König, A., Amieva, H., Andrieu, S., Bremond, F., Bullock, R., Ceccaldi, M., Dubois, B., Gauthier, S., Kenigsberg, P.A., et al.: Recommendations for the use of serious games in people with Alzheimer's disease, related disorders and frailty. Front. Aging Neurosci. **6** (2014)
22. Salthouse, T.A.: Mental exercise and mental aging: evaluating the validity of the use it or lose it hypothesis. Perspect. Psychol. Sci. **1**(1), 68–87 (2006)
23. Saunders, N.L., Summers, M.J.: Attention and working memory deficits in mild cognitive impairment. J. Clin. Exp. Neuropsychol. **32**(4), 350–357 (2010)
24. Sellen, A.J., Whittaker, S.: Beyond total capture: a constructive critique of lifelogging. Commun. ACM **53**(5), 70–77 (2010)
25. Talavera, E., Strisciuglio, N., Petkov, N., Radeva, P.: Sentiment recognition in egocentric photostreams. In: Alexandre, L.A., Salvador Sánchez, J., Rodrigues, J.M.F. (eds.) IbPRIA 2017. LNCS, vol. 10255, pp. 471–479. Springer, Cham (2017). https://doi.org/10.1007/978-3-319-58838-4_52

Implicit Vs. Explicit Human Feedback for Interactive Video Object Segmentation

Francesca Murabito, Simone Palazzo, Concetto Spampinato$^{(\boxtimes)}$,
and Daniela Giordano

Pattern Recognition and Computer Vision (PeRCeiVe Lab),
Department of Electric Electronic and Computer Engineering,
University of Catania, Catania, Italy
{fmurabito,palazzosim,cspampin,dgiordan}@dieei.unict.it

Abstract. This paper investigates how to exploit human feedback for interactive object segmentation in videos. In particular, we present an interactive video object segmentation approach where humans can contribute by either explicitly clicking on objects of interest in videos or implicitly while looking at video sequences. User feedback is then translated into a set of spatio-temporal constraints for an energy-based minimization problem. We tested the method on standard benchmarking datasets when using both eye-gaze data and user clicks. The results indicated how our method outperformed existing automated and interactive methods regardless of the type of human feedback (explicit or implicit), and that click-based feedback was more reliable than eye-gaze one.

1 Introduction

The recent progress in digital imaging and smartphone technologies, followed by their relatively low cost and the explosion of social networks, have favoured the generation and sharing of an impressive amount of visual data content over the internet (to give an idea, 80% of all consumer Internet traffic in 2019 will be due to video data[1]). Millions of videos and images are shared daily on Youtube, Facebook, Twitter, Flickr, etc., and now represent the primary source of information and communication.

Nevertheless, this massive visual data can be seen as an added value only if it is possible to analyze and effectively understand it, thus turning raw data into meaningful information needed for several applications: from security to surveillance to ecology monitoring to marketing strategies. This highlights the importance of automated analysis methods that, as a consequence, are proliferating. Unfortunately, such methods are not always capable of satisfying application requirements, especially in terms of expected accuracy. A key role in the understanding process may be played by humans, who, on one hand, have an extraordinary ability in performing high-level tasks with unreachable performance for

---

[1] http://www.cisco.com/c/en/us/solutions/collateral/service-provider/
ip-ngn-ip-next-generation-network/white_paper_c11-481360.html.

© Springer International Publishing AG 2017
S. Battiato et al. (Eds.): ICIAP 2017 International Workshops, LNCS 10590, pp. 131–142, 2017.
https://doi.org/10.1007/978-3-319-70742-6_12

machines, and, on the other hand, have limited processing/computation capabilities, making it impossible to analyze visual data at a large scale. Combining and integrating effectively humans and machines is, therefore, highly desirable, as also witnessed by the recent research front that aims at involving actively humans in the machine learning loop [4,16,20–22,25,29,31].

Through this paper we intend to contribute to the research on humans in the loop for video understanding by attempting to answer the question "what is the most suitable and effective way to exploit human capabilities in analyzing visual data while keeping efforts as low as possible?". This question has a two-fold implication related to human exceptional performance in understanding the visual world: (a) visual scene understanding in humans involves implicit and involuntary processing, such as eye movements, that, if exploited by automated methods, despite being rather noisy information, would allow to reduce significantly human intervention (given the involuntary nature of the feedback); (b) explicitly annotating visual data, e.g., by providing per-frame bounding boxes, is an easy task for humans but extremely tedious and time-consuming, and requires, at large scale, a collective effort.

To support the answer to this research question, we propose an interactive method for video object segmentation, which extends existing interactive methods [2,6,17,26] to work with several interaction modalities converting user feedback into spatio-temporal constraints for the segmentation process. However, the main contribution is the comparison between (a) implicit eye gaze data recorded through an eye-tracker while subjects look at video sequences, and (b) explicit user clicks collected while people play a web game for video object segmentation. We tested our approach on standard video benchmarks and compared the performance of the two interaction modalities, beside comparing it to state-of-the-art automated and interactive video object segmentation methods.

2   Related Work

In this paper we propose a video object segmentation approach posed as a binary labeling task (i.e., background/foreground segmentation) solved through MRF energy minimization as in [8,13,19]. The difference between those methods and ours is that we involve humans in the segmentation loop; therefore, our approach falls within the interactive video segmentation research area [2,6,17]. Interactive video object segmentation methods aim at converting human input (often in the form of drawn lines or strokes) into constraints for spatio-temporal segmentation, so that manual annotations can be propagated to multiple frames. Our paper draws inspiration from these methods but extends them in the way humans and their feedback are included into the video object segmentation process. Indeed, in our work, user feedback is obtained either explicitly by asking multiple users to click on video sequences through a *web-game* or by simply asking single users to look at video sequences and then recording *eye-gaze* data through an eye-tracker.

Games have been already employed for collecting human annotation with the purpose to train and test machine learning methods as interactive segmentation

or annotation of images [5,15,23,29,30]. Analogously, eye-gaze has been adopted
(a) for identifying the most viewed image regions and their visual descriptors to
be used for image tagging [31] and image indexing/retrieval [3] and (b) as a
tool for human implicit feedback in a video object segmentation scenario with
promising results [27]. As an alternative to eye-gaze, brain activity data recorded
through EEG has been utilized as implicit feedback for supporting interactive
image annotation [16].

Interactive image and video annotation is an active research area both in
multimedia and computer vision, and the existing approaches can be classified
into two main categories: (a) methods requiring explicit user feedback as either
lines and strokes or user clicks [2,5,6,15,17,23,30], and (b) approaches exploiting implicit user feedback (eye gaze or EEG) [3,16,27,31]. However, the main
limitation of these methods is on how user feedback is incorporated into the
interactive annotation process, i.e. how to effectively translate user data into
spatio-temporal constraints for visual data analysis. Furthermore, most of these
methods are thought for image annotation/tagging/segmentation and only few
for video object segmentation and, so far, no one of them has compared the
performance of implicit vs. explicit feedback.

3   The Interactive Video Segmentation Method

Our interactive video segmentation method is based on [26] with the difference
that we make it generic (thus removing some terms which were very application-
specific) and able to work with different interaction modalities including eye-gaze
data. The whole approach relies on (1) a spatial frame segmentation method
which takes into account both visual cues and user input and (b) a spatio-
temporal module able to consider spatio-temporal links between image parts in
consecutive frames.

3.1   Spatial Frame Segmentation

The first step of the algorithm performs image segmentation at the frame level,
which is treated as a binary pixel labeling task (background and foreground). We
start from *superpixel* segmentation [1] and then group superpixels through minimization of an energy cost which enforces spatial and visual coherency between
superpixels as well as including user feedback, as constraints, in the labeling cost.
The underlying idea is that superpixels "selected" by users (either by clicking
on them or by simply looking at them) should be defined as hard constraints in
the energy minimization problem.

Let $P = \{(x_1, y_1), \ldots, (x_n, y_n)\}$ be user feedback in the form of (x, y) points
for frame F. We define an energy function over the set of F's superpixels S
able to model superpixels "selected" by users, and at the same time, to enforce
spatial constraints on visual smoothness at the frame level. The energy function
for spatial segmentation is based on the assumptions that superpixels identified
by multiple users can be considered as hard constraints for segmentation as well

as unselected superpixels that are spatially-close and visually-similar to selected ones; and single superpixels should be ignored as possibly noisy. In particular, it is defined as:

$$E_1(\mathcal{L}) = \alpha_1 \sum_{s \in S} F_1(s, l_s, P) + \sum_{(s_1, s_2) \in \mathcal{N}(S)} F_2(s_1, s_2, l_{s_1}, l_{s_2}) \tag{1}$$

where $\mathcal{L} = \left\{ l_{s_1}, l_{s_2}, \ldots, l_{s_{n_S}} \right\}$ is the superclick label assignment (l_{s_i} is the binary superclick label for superpixel s_i), $\mathcal{N}(S)$ is the set of pairs of neighbor superpixels (that is, having part of boundary in common; we will also use the notation $\mathcal{N}(s)$ to denote the set of neighbors of the single superpixel s), and α_1 is a weighing factor.

F_1 takes into account if a superpixel s should be part of an object or not. As this depends on how many users have selected it and on neighboring superpixels, it is given by two contributions:

- **User feedback f_s on superpixel s:** the more a superpixel has been selected by users, the more it is likely to be an object part. The score f_s for superpixel s is:

$$f_s = \frac{|P \cap s|}{\max_{t \in S} |P \cap t|} \tag{2}$$

where $P \cap s$ is the set of user data hitting superpixel s and $|\cdot|$ is set cardinality. The term takes into account how many times superpixel s has been selected by users.

- **Adjacency A_s:** if superpixel s has not been selected by users but it is adjacent to superpixels which did, it is safe to consider it as foreground as well.

  The proximity term A_s is computed as the fraction of neighbor superpixels with $I_{s_n} > \theta$, with $s_n \in \mathcal{N}(s)$ and $\theta = 0.6$:

$$A_s = \frac{|\{s_n \in \mathcal{N}(s) : I_{s_n} > \theta\}|}{|\mathcal{N}(s)|} \tag{3}$$

The sum of f_s and A_s (clipped to 1 if necessary) is the likelihood that a superpixel s is part of the foreground objects, $P_{s,1} = \min(f_s + A_s, 1)$, while $P_{s,0} = 1 - P_{s,1}$ is the probability that s is "not a part" of the foreground. In the energy function E_1, F_1 encodes the cost of assigning a certain label to each superpixel and is the negative log-likelihood of $P_{s,1}$ and $P_{s,0}$:

$$F_1(s, l_s, C) = \begin{cases} -\log P_{s,1} & \text{if } l_s = 1 \\ -\log P_{s,0} & \text{if } l_s = 0 \end{cases} \tag{4}$$

F_2 is instead the cost of assigning different labels to two adjacent and visually similar superpixels s_1 and s_2 and in our case is computed as:

$$F_2(s_1, s_2, l_{s_1}, l_{s_2}) = KL(H_{s_1}, H_{s_2}) \mathcal{I}(l_{s_1} \neq l_{s_2}) \tag{5}$$

where KL is Kullback-Liebler distance, H_{s_i} is the RGB color histogram of super-pixel s_i, and $\mathcal{I}$ is an indicator function which returns 1 if the arguments is true, and 0 otherwise. The per-frame segmentation is then obtained by minimizing $E_1(\mathcal{L})$ through graph cut; examples are given in Fig. 1 (first row).

Fig. 1. Output examples: (first row) segmentation masks when using only spatial information; (second row) segmentation refinement by including temporal constraints. Blue dots are user input in the form of clicks in the example. (Color figure online)

3.2   Spatio-Temporal Segmentation

The previous step converts user-provided (x, y) points into a set of potential foreground superpixels, but it does not take into account any temporal link between superpixels in consecutive frames, which, instead, is necessary to cope with per-frame segmentation errors. To do that we used the idea proposed in [26] which is based on the assumption that if a set of adjacent superpixels is selected in consecutive frames, then it is very likely that it is part of an object. Nevertheless, superpixel extraction is often not consistent in presence of large motion. This aspect is addressed by including a temporal-based segmentation part, which links superpixels in consecutive frames according to their visual similarity; and makes an hypothesis on the position of superpixels in consecutive frames through optical flow [14]. More specifically, superpixels are linked in consecutive frames by introducing pairwise potentials on all pairs of superpixels $\{s_t, s_{t+\xi}\}$ such that s_t contains at least one pixel p_t whose projection $p_{t \rightarrow t+\xi}^{v_{p_t}} = p_t + v_{p_t}$ into frame $t+\xi$ under the motion vector v_{p_t} (i.e., v_{p_t} is the motion vector computed between frame t and frame $t+\xi$ for location p_t) is part of superpixel $s_{t+\xi}$ in frame $t+\xi$. Thus, we did not consider only linking between two consecutive frames as in [26] since user feedback can be faster than clicks as in the case of eyes.

The energy term encoding spatio-temporal constraints uses (as in the original work) a batch of $2T+1$ consecutive frames from $t-T$ to $t+T$ and is defined as:

$$E_2(\mathcal{L}) = \sum_{\tau=t-T}^{t+T} \left[\sum_{s \in S^\tau} F_1(s, l_s, l_s^\tau) \right] +$$

$$+ \sum_{\tau=t-T}^{t+T} \left[\sum_{(s_1, s_2) \in \mathcal{N}(S^\tau)} F_2(s_1, s_2, l_{s_1}, l_{s_2}) \right] + \qquad (6)$$

$$+ \sum_{(s_1, s_2) \in \mathcal{N}_T(\cup_{\tau=t-T}^{t+T} S^\tau)} F_2(s_1, s_2, l_{s_1}, l_{s_2})$$

The first two lines of Eq. 6 are, respectively, a unary potential for each identified superpixel (first line) and a pairwise potential for each pair of superpixels belonging to the same frame (second line). The last term (third line), instead, aims at enforcing temporal smoothing through a pairwise potential defined over the set $\mathcal{N}_T(\cup_{\tau=t-T}^{t+T} S^\tau)$, i.e. the set of all pairs of superpixels in the $2T+1$ "temporally linked" frames, as described above. F_1 models whether superpixel s is more likely to be background or foreground: if s was labeled as foreground in the frame-segmentation we expect it to be more likely that it is foreground (with a cost lower than being background), and vice versa. F_1 is therefore computed as:

$$F_1(s, l_s, l_s^\tau) = \begin{cases} \gamma_1 & \text{if } (l_s = 1 \wedge l_s^\tau = 1) \vee (l_s = 0 \wedge l_s^\tau = 0) \\ \gamma_2 & \text{otherwise} \end{cases} \qquad (7)$$

with $\gamma_1 < \gamma_2$.

F_2 is computes the similarity between "temporally-adjacent" superpixels in consecutive frames as in Sect. 3.1. E_1, E_2 are minimized through graph cut. Segmentation examples are shown in the second row of Fig. 1: compared to those of the first row, these examples highlight how including temporal-based refinement enhances segmentation performance.

4   Experimental Results

Experiment settings. We tested our method using two user interaction modalities: (1) eye-gaze data recorded by a Tobii T60 eye tracker (with a capture frequency of 60 Hz) while subjects looked at video sequences, and (2) user clicks collected through a web game on the same set of videos.

The eye-gaze experiments involved sixteen (16) subjects, who were asked to watch a set of short videos with the goal of following moving objects. For the click-based experiment we re-adapted (and used the source code released by the authors) the web-based game proposed in [11], changing only the displayed video sequences and leaving the underlying gamification strategy unchanged. In practice, the game consists of several levels, with each level displaying one or more video sequences. Twelve (12) users were asked to click on moving objects and, accordingly, were rewarded with a score reflecting click accuracy.

Datasets and baselines. Performance evaluation and comparison between the two considered interaction modalities was carried out on 9 video sequences, with pixelwise annotations, taken from three challenging visual benchmarks for video object segmentation: SegTrack v2 [12], FBMS-59 [18], and VSB100 [7]. The selected videos included features such as: camera motion, slow object motion, object-background similarity, non-rigid deformations and articulated objects. The comparison between our approach and automated methods was performed over the Youtube-Objects dataset [24]. The automated video object segmentation methods were tested using public source code and default parameters. As for interactive segmentation methods, we did not perform any accuracy comparison since, to the best of our knowledge, all of them require interaction times not compatible with large scale analysis. For example, labeling 10 video frames enough to achieve an F_1 accuracy of 0.7 took about 50 s with our approach, and more than 1,000 s with [17].

Collected data. Each of the 12 subjects for the web game experiment spent approximately 9.5 min playing the game, which resulted in the collection of 40.4 clicks per frame, on average, for a total engagement time of 115 min. Instead, each eye-gaze experiment took 2 min per subject, and provided on average 35.7 points per frame in 32-min user engagement time. This difference in the amount of time required to collect similar amounts of data was expected, due to the higher acquisition rate of the eye-tracker compared to human clicking speed.

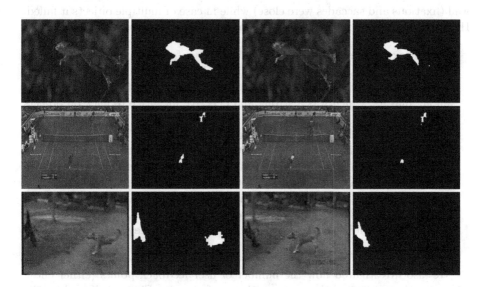

Fig. 2. Segmentation output examples. (First two columns) User clicks and (second two columns) and eye-gaze on sample frames and related output segmentation masks. (Color figure online)

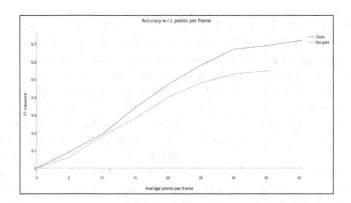

Fig. 3. F1 accuracy w.r.t. user feedback points per frame.

Results and discussion. Table 1 reports pixelwise average F_1-measure achieved by our method using different feedback modalities. It is possible to see how click-based feedback (see Clicks$_M$ column in Table 1) outperformed the eye-gaze–based one; a visual comparison in terms of output segmentation masks between click and eye-gaze–based interaction is given in Fig. 2.

The primary reason behind the lower performance of the eye-gaze–based approach lies in the noisy nature of eye movements: eye gaze, indeed, involves both fixations and saccades with the latter spanning the whole visual scene from fixation to fixation. Thus, in case of isolated objects it tended to perform fairly well (fixations and saccades were close) while in case of multiple objects it failed. Higher performance of the click-based approach was also due to the following:

- In both experiments, top-down saliency was enforced since all participants were instructed to follow moving objects; however, in the web-game, user behaviour was driven by game rewards and consequently by competition among players, which was a strong and effective incentive to click on objects accurately;
- Since users were allowed to play the game several times, after the first time they had a prior knowledge on object location. To account for this aspect, we assessed segmentation accuracy using only the clicks generated by the 12 subjects the first time they played the game. The achieved performance is shown in column Clicks$_S$ of Table 1: it is possible to notice how the comparison between the click-based approach (Clicks$_S$) and eye-gaze based one was more balanced, thus indicating that object location prior is a key factor for accurate results.

We also investigated how the number of user feedback points (either clicks or eye fixations) affected the segmentation performance. Figure 3 shows how the F_1 measure changed w.r.t. points per frame. When few points were available, the difference between the two interaction modalities was small, while when the number of points available became consistent their performance diverged significantly. This reinforces our previous claim about the noisy nature of eye-gaze data especially when dealing with multiple objects; moreover, it confirms that when users are driven by a proper incentive to carry out a specific task, performance improves.

Additionally, it can be interesting to see how the proposed method, albeit more in line with the research on interactive video annotation, compares to state-of-the-art automated video object segmentation approaches. To do that, we used the Youtube-Objects dataset (largely employed as a benchmark for video object segmentation), and compared our approach (using game clicks as data points) with a selection of recent methods exploiting superpixels for the video object segmentation, namely, [9,10,18,19,28,32]. The results, in terms of average *Pascal Overlap Measure* (POM, i.e., intersection over union between output masks and ground truth segmentation masks) in percentage, are reported in Table 2, and show that our method outperforms automated video object segmentation methods. In general, this is not surprising, since it is common that interactive video annotation tools perform better than automated methods, but, on the contrary, they are hardly usable in case of large video datasets (e.g., Youtube-objects). While our method can be seen as an interactive video object segmentation approach, it enables multiple users to co-operate in large scale tasks (for the web-game, it might suffice to publish it on a social network and make people play to collect enough data) reducing the annotation/interaction burden, which usually lies on the shoulders of few people. Furthermore, the performance achieved in this work (72.8) was better than the ones in [26] (68.9) with much less users (12 vs. 63 players). This was due to the removal of several terms including the assessment of user quality or the assessment of superpixel similarity, and,

Table 1. F-measure scores obtained by the proposed method, using either eye-gaze data or user-click data. As for user-click we performed two evaluations: (a) exploiting clicks of first-time-play by users in order to eliminate the bias due to prior knowledge on object location (column Clicks$_S$), and (b) using all collected clicks (column Clicks$_M$).

Video	Gaze	Clicks$_S$	Clicks$_M$
animal_chase (VSB)	0.62	0.26	0.78
sled_dog_race (VSB)	0.52	0.53	0.76
tennis (VSB)	0.26	0.57	0.62
cheetah (SegT)	0.67	0.52	0.68
frog (SegT)	0.57	0.57	0.74
monkeydog (SegT)	0.43	0.40	0.64
camel01 (FBMS)	0.65	0.52	0.59
rabbits02 (FBMS)	0.70	0.72	0.89
rabbits04 (FBMS)	0.50	0.76	0.77
Average	0.55	0.54	0.72

Table 2. POM in percentage for the Youtube-Objects dataset

	[18]	[28]	[9]	[32]	[19]	[10]	Ours
Aeroplane	13.7	17.8	73.6	75.8	70.9	86.3	68.4
Bird	12.2	19.8	56.1	60.8	70.6	81.0	64.3
Boat	10.8	22.5	57.8	43.7	42.5	68.6	66.7
Car	23.7	38.3	33.9	71.1	65.2	69.4	72.5
Cat	18.6	23.6	30.5	46.5	52.1	58.9	61.4
Cow	16.3	26.8	41.8	54.6	44.5	68.6	77.2
Dog	18.0	23.7	36.8	55.5	65.3	61.8	76.4
Horse	11.5	14.0	44.3	54.9	53.5	54.0	87.0
Motorbike	10.6	12.5	48.9	42.4	44.2	60.9	80.3
Train	19.6	40.4	39.2	31.4	29.6	66.3	74.1
Average	15.5	23.9	46.3	53.7	53.8	67.6	72.8

provide indications that suitable changes to the segmentation method combined to increased motivation of subjects leads to better performance.

5　Conclusions

In this paper we presented a general interactive video object segmentation approach able to work with different user interaction modalities. We tested it on challenging video sequences by employing either eye gaze or user clicks as human feedback. The conclusions that can be drawn from performance analysis are: (1) task-driven user clicks allow for accurate segmentation performance; (2) collecting user clicks from multiple users is not enough to yield good performance, and prior knowledge on object location proved to be an influencing factor, and (3) eye-gaze user interaction allows for greatly reducing interaction times at the expenses of segmentation accuracy. In the future, we plan to perform a large-scale evaluation involving many more users as well as video sequences for a more accurate analysis of interaction behaviour in order to discovery which visual descriptors are mainly employed by users and incorporate such features into automated methods.

References

1. Achanta, R., Shaji, A., Smith, K., Lucchi, A., Fua, P., Susstrunk, S.: SLIC superpixels. EPFL Technical report 149300, p. 15, June 2010
2. Badrinarayanan, V., Galasso, F., Cipolla, R.: Label propagation in video sequences. In: 2010 IEEE Computer Society Conference on Computer Vision and Pattern Recognition, pp. 3265–3272 (2010)

3. Buscher, G., Dengel, A., van Elst, L.: Eye movements as implicit relevance feedback. In: CHI 2008 Extended Abstracts on Human Factors in Computing Systems, CHI EA 2008, pp. 2991–2996. ACM, New York (2008). https://doi.org/10.1145/1358628.1358796

4. Deng, J., Krause, J., Fei-Fei, L.: Fine-grained crowdsourcing for fine-grained recognition. In: CVPR 2013, pp. 580–587 (2013)

5. Druck, G., Settles, B., McCallum, A.: Active learning by labeling features. In: EMNLP 2009, pp. 81–90. Association for Computational Linguistics, Stroudsburg (2009). http://dl.acm.org/citation.cfm?id=1699510.1699522

6. Fathi, A., Balcan, M.F., Ren, X., Rehg, J.M.: Combining self training and active learning for video segmentation. In: Proceedings of the British Machine Vision Conference 2011, pp. 78.1–78.11 (2011). http://www.bmva.org/bmvc/2011/proceedings/paper78/index.html

7. Galasso, F., Nagaraja, N., Cardenas, T., Brox, T., Schiele, B.: A unified video segmentation benchmark: annotation, metrics and analysis. In: IEEE International Conference on Computer Vision (ICCV), December 2013. http://lmb.informatik.uni-freiburg.de/Publications/2013/NB13

8. Giordano, D., Murabito, F., Palazzo, S., Spampinato, C.: Superpixel-based video object segmentation using perceptual organization and location prior. In: Computer Vision and Pattern Recognition (2015)

9. Godec, M., Roth, P.M., Bischof, H.: Hough-based tracking of non-rigid objects. In: 2011 International Conference on Computer Vision, pp. 81–88, November 2011

10. Jain, S.D., Grauman, K.: Supervoxel-consistent foreground propagation in video. In: Fleet, D., Pajdla, T., Schiele, B., Tuytelaars, T. (eds.) ECCV 2014, Part IV. LNCS, vol. 8692, pp. 656–671. Springer, Cham (2014). https://doi.org/10.1007/978-3-319-10593-2_43

11. Kavasidis, I., Spampinato, C., Giordano, D.: Generation of ground truth for object detection while playing an online game: productive gaming or recreational working? In: 2013 IEEE Conference on Computer Vision and Pattern Recognition Workshops, pp. 694–699, June 2013

12. Lee, Y.J., Kim, J., Grauman, K.: Key-segments for video object segmentation. In: ICCV 2011, pp. 1995–2002 (2011). https://doi.org/10.1109/ICCV.2011.6126471

13. Lim, J., Han, B.: Generalized background subtraction using superpixels with label integrated motion estimation. In: Fleet, D., Pajdla, T., Schiele, B., Tuytelaars, T. (eds.) ECCV 2014, Part V. LNCS, vol. 8693, pp. 173–187. Springer, Cham (2014). https://doi.org/10.1007/978-3-319-10602-1_12

14. Liu, C., Adviser-Freeman, W., Adviser-Adelson, E.: Beyond pixels: exploring new representations and applications for motion analysis. In: Proceedings of the 10th European Conference on Computer Vision, Part III, pp. 28–42 (2009)

15. Maji, S.: Discovering a lexicon of parts and attributes. In: Fusiello, A., Murino, V., Cucchiara, R. (eds.) ECCV 2012. LNCS, vol. 7585, pp. 21–30. Springer, Heidelberg (2012). https://doi.org/10.1007/978-3-642-33885-4_3

16. Mohedano, E., Healy, G., McGuinness, K., Giró-i Nieto, X., O'Connor, N.E., Smeaton, A.F.: Object segmentation in images using eeg signals. In: ACM MM 2014, pp. 417–426. ACM, New York (2014). https://doi.org/10.1145/2647868.2654896

17. Nagaraja, N.S., Schmidt, F., Brox, T.: Video segmentation with just a few strokes. In: IEEE International Conference on Computer Vision (ICCV), December 2015

18. Ochs, P., Malik, J., Brox, T.: Segmentation of moving objects by long term video analysis. IEEE PAMI **36**(6), 1187–1200 (2014)

19. Papazoglou, A., Ferrari, V.: Fast object segmentation in unconstrained video. In: Proceedings of the IEEE International Conference on Computer Vision, pp. 1777–1784 (2013)

20. Parikh, D., Crandall, D., Grauman, K.: Discovering localized attributes for fine-grained recognition. In: 2012 IEEE Conference on Computer Vision and Pattern Recognition, pp. 3474–3481, June 2012

21. Parikh, D., Zitnick, C.L.: Human-debugging of machines. In: Neural Information Processing Systems, pp. 1–5 (2011)

22. Parkash, A., Parikh, D.: Attributes for classifier feedback. In: Fitzgibbon, A., Lazebnik, S., Perona, P., Sato, Y., Schmid, C. (eds.) ECCV 2012, Part III. LNCS, vol. 7574, pp. 354–368. Springer, Heidelberg (2012). https://doi.org/10.1007/978-3-642-33712-3_26

23. Peng, B., Zhang, L., Zhang, D., Yang, J.: Image segmentation by iterated region merging with localized graph cuts. Pattern Recogn. **44**, 2527–2538 (2011). http://www.sciencedirect.com/science/article/pii/S0031320311001282, semi-Supervised Learning for Visual Content Analysis and Understanding

24. Prest, A., Leistner, C., Civera, J., Schmid, C., Ferrari, V.: Learning object class detectors from weakly annotated video. In: 2012 IEEE Conference on Computer Vision and Pattern Recognition, pp. 3282–3289, June 2012

25. Salvador, A., Carlier, A., Giro-i Nieto, X., Marques, O., Charvillat, V.: Crowdsourced object segmentation with a game. In: Proceedings of the 2nd ACM International Workshop on Crowdsourcing for Multimedia - CrowdMM 2013, pp. 15–20 (2013)

26. Spampinato, C., Palazzo, S., Giordano, D.: Gamifying video object segmentation. IEEE Trans. Pattern Anal. Mach. Intell. **PP**(99), 1 (2016)

27. Spampinato, C., Palazzo, S., Murabito, F., Giordano, D.: Using the eyes to "see" the objects. In: Proceedings of the 23rd ACM International Conference on Multimedia, MM 2015, pp. 1231–1234. ACM, New York (2015). https://doi.org/10.1145/2733373.2806324

28. Tang, K., Sukthankar, R., Yagnik, J., Fei-Fei, L.: Discriminative segment annotation in weakly labeled video. In: Proceedings of International Conference on Computer Vision and Pattern Recognition (CVPR 2013) (2013)

29. Vijayanarasimhan, S., Grauman, K.: Large-scale live active learning: training object detectors with crawled data and crowds. Int. J. Comput. Vis. **108**(1-2), 97–114 (2014)

30. Von Ahn, L., Liu, R., Blum, M.: Peekaboom: a game for locating objects in images, pp. 55–64 (2006)

31. Walber, T., Scherp, A., Staab, S.: Can you see it? Two novel eye-tracking-based measures for assigning tags to image regions. In: Advances in Multimedia Modeling, vol. 7732, pp. 36–46 (2013)

32. Zhang, Y., Chen, X., Li, J., Wang, C., Xia, C.: Semantic object segmentation via detection in weakly labeled video. In: The IEEE Conference on Computer Vision and Pattern Recognition (CVPR), June 2015

"Don't Turn Off the Lights": Modelling of Human Light Interaction in Indoor Environments

Irtiza Hasan[1]([✉]), Theodore Tsesmelis[2], Alessio Del Bue[2], Fabio Galasso[3], and Marco Cristani[1]

[1] University of Verona, Verona, Italy
irtiza.hasan@univr.it
[2] Istituto Italiano di Tecnologia, Genoa, Italy
[3] Corporate Innovation OSRAM GmbH, Hamburg, Germany

Abstract. Human activity recognition and forecasting can be used as a primary cue for scene understanding. Acquiring details from the scene has vast applications in different fields such as computer vision, robotics and more recently smart lighting. This work brings together advanced research in computer vision and the most modern technology in lighting. The goal of this work is to eliminate the need for any switches for lighting, which means that each person in the office perceives the entire office as all lit, while lights, which are not visible by the person, are switched off by the system. This can be achieved by combining lighting with presence detection and smart light control.

Keywords: Scene understanding · Activity forecasting Activity recognition · Photometry

1 Introduction

A modern lighting system should automatically calibrate itself (determine the type and position of lights), assess its own status (which lights are on and how dimmed), and allow for the creation or preservation of lighting patterns, e.g. after the sunset. The lighting patterns should be adjusted in a way, that is optimal for people actions and locality. As most of our activities hold within a given light pattern [7] as illustrated in Fig. 1. Moreover, light influences our perception of space [8], for example we expect to see a certain illumination pattern in a musical concert etc. The essence of such a system would be to deploy an *invisible light switch*, where the change in illumination is not perceived by the user.

Furthermore, idea of a smart lighting system, is to deploy a dynamic illumination pattern for a given activity. In brief, *SCENEUNDERLIGHT* H2020-MSCA-ITN-2015 project encompasses both fundamental research in computer vision and innovation transfer in smart lighting with a goal being at researching and developing novel autonomous tools using advanced computer vision and

© Springer International Publishing AG 2017
S. Battiato et al. (Eds.): ICIAP 2017 International Workshops, LNCS 10590, pp. 143–151, 2017.
https://doi.org/10.1007/978-3-319-70742-6_13

machine learning approaches that seamlessly integrates into smart lighting systems for indoor environments.

SCENEUNDERLIGHT proposes a plan to create such an achievement, in light management systems, by enabling the understanding of the environment via long-term observation, that span days, weeks and even months, with a sensing device (i.e. RGB cameras or RGBD if including a depth sensor) for smart illumination and energy saving via an artificial intelligence (AI) processor (e.g. an algorithm to understand the scene and make decisions on lighting). More specifically in this Research and Development plan, top-view time-lapse images of the scene allow computer vision algorithms to understand it (1) To estimate the human activities from RGB and RGBD images: in particular, recognize which and where activities occur in the environment, using technologies of detection and tracking. (2) To forecast human activities, in order to predict what people are going to do and where they are going to move. Knowledge of scene is then used for light management. For example, switch off lights in areas which are not visible from the people currently acting within the scene. Activating/deactivating lights in relation to the predicted activities. This paper for the first time implements an invisible light switch: users have the feeling of all-lit, while their scene is only minimally lit, therefore providing a notable energy saving in the invisible.

Human activities can be characterized in several ways such as groups vs individual. As a proof of concept, we address activities that occur in indoor environments such as walking, working at the desk and discussing. Given our setup (top view camera), head orientation plays an important role as it identifies Visual Frustum of Attention (VFOA). VFOA approximates the volume of a scene where fixation of a person may occur. As head orientation captures attention [11], for example if I am looking at the a monitor most likely my activity has something to do with monitor. In this paper we demonstrate robust an dynamic modelling of VFOA for head orientation and scene understanding.

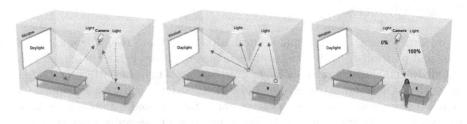

Fig. 1. Pipeline of an advanced lighting system. Left image, where the light sources are in camera view (calibration). Center image provides a visibility map (what they illuminate). Finally right image illustrates the adjustment of light sources based on people actions

2 State of the Art Review

Acquiring semantics from the scene is a fundamental requirement in several fields, ranging from computer vision to smart lighting. The project *SCENEUN-DERLIGHT* is aimed at modelling the relationship between light and human behavior. We provide a review of some state of the art methods focused on the modelling of light and behavior.

2.1 Lights and Behaviour

Relationship between human activities and lights is a widely studied topic in perceptual sciences [1,7,9]. Recently, it was illustrated by [25] that light intensifies people's perception. It triggers emotional system leading to intensified affective reactions. Light changes our perception of space [8], we associate different illumination patterns to different social gatherings (musical concert vs candle light dinner). People seem to share more details in bright light than darkness [5], as we human beings also rely on facial expressions which are only visible in light. Light provides sense of security [9], people adopted roads and streets in night due to the illumination [21]. Recently, studies targeting the office environments revealed a strong connection between people's productivity and the lights [19]. Eyeing the importance Eyeing the importance of lighting on humans, corresponding communities such as HCI [15] where interactive lighting deployed in city square provided a sense of "belongingness" to the residents. Furthermore, ubiquitous computing [10] and architectural design [14] also have investigated this topic to an extent.

2.2 Modelling Human Activities

Despite receiving a wide scale attention, the literature in computer vision seems to have ignored the modelling of light and behaviour. *SCENEUNDERLIGHT* for the first time models the relationship of light and human behavior via long term time-lapse observation of the scene by recognizing and forecasting activities in the scene. In this work, we propose the use of visual frustum of attention (VFOA) for scene understanding, activity recognition and activity forecasting. VFOA identifies the volume of a scene where fixation of a person may occur; It can be inferred from head pose estimation, and it is crucial in scenarios such as top-view office cameras and surveillance scenarios where precise gazing information cannot be retrieved.

Estimation of head pose is inherently a challenging task due to subtle differences between human poses. However, in the past several techniques ranging from low level image features to appearance based learning architectures were used to address the problem of head pose estimation. Previously, [12,24] used neural networks to estimate head pose. [4] adopted a randomized fern based approach to estimate head orientation. Only limited accuracy was achieved due to several reasons such as two images of the same person in different poses appeared more similar than two different people in same pose. Secondly, it was hard to compute low level image features in low resolution images. Recently, decision trees have been reported to achieve state of the art results [13]. However, they rely on local features and are prone to make errors when tested in real world crowded scenarios. We address the issue of having a head pose estimator that can work in unconstrained real world scenarios by utilizing the power of deep neural networks. In recent past, it has been used for pose estimation [22].

In this work, we plan to estimate VFOA with the help of an head pose estimator. We provide a review of the approaches that used VFOA in past in unconstrained scenarios. The earlier works that focus on estimating VFOA on low resolution images were [2,16,20], jointly with the pose of the person. VFOA has been used primarily for spotting social interactions: in [3] the head direction serves to infer a 3D visual frustum as approximation of the VFOA of a person. Given the VFOA and proximity information, interactions are estimated: the idea is that close-by people whose view frustum is intersecting are in some way interacting. The same idea has been explored, independently, in [17]. In [18], the VFOA was defined as a vector pointing to the focus of attention, thanks to an approximate estimation of the gazing direction at a low resolution; in that work the goal was to analyze the gazing behavior of people in front of a shop window. The projection of the VFOA on the floor was modeled as a Gaussian distribution of "samples of attention" ahead of a pedestrian in [6]: the higher the density, the stronger the probability that in that area the eyes' fixation would be present. More physiologically grounded was the modeling of [23]: in that work, the VFOA is characterized by a direction θ (which is the persons head orientation), an aperture $\alpha = 160°$ and a length l. The latter parameter corresponds to the variance of the Gaussian distribution centered around the location of a person. Even in this case, samples of attention were used to measure the probability of a fixation: a denser sampling was carried at locations closer to the person, decreasing in density in zones further away. The frustum is generated by drawing samples from the above Gaussian kernel and keeping only those that fall within the cone determined by the angle α. In [26], the aperture of the cone can be modulated in order to mimic more or less focused attention areas.

In all these approaches, VFOA has been employed to capture group formations. To the best of our knowledge, we propose here, for the first time, VFOA for use in a predictive model. In order to estimate VFOA, a robust Head Pose Estimator is required which can work well in un-constrained real life scenarios. To this end we propose a robust real time head pose estimator using convolutional neural networks. The preliminary results are encouraging, as we have not done any pre-processing of the input image.

Finally, the project *SCENEUNDERLIGHT* proposes to model the relationship between behaviour and light, by providing an invisible light switch. Where the main essence is to provide user's the feeling of "all-lit" while the scene is minimally lit. A step towards new generation type of lighting system.

3   Proposed Framework

Towards the understanding of the scene, we distinguish the scene structure material properties and the human-centric scene. The first regards the scene composition: its 3D structure, the objects materials, the light position and characterization (natural versus artificial) and their lighting patterns. The second regards the human activities and interactions, particularly the human-scene (walking, working at desk or reading, presenting at a board) and human-human interaction (where people meet, discuss, relax). These two aspects are tightly intertwined, since the structure of the scene allows and constrains human activities, but at the same time the human activities influence the scene structure. Consider for example a warehouse as the static scene: its structure continuously changes due to the different arrangement of the goods, the latter being a direct consequence of the human activities carried out in the environment. In other words, the structure of the scene and the human have to be considered as parts of a whole, accounting in addition for their continued temporal evolution. For this reason, it appears convenient to deal with the two topics within the same research framework, for the first time in the literature as illustrated in Fig. 2.

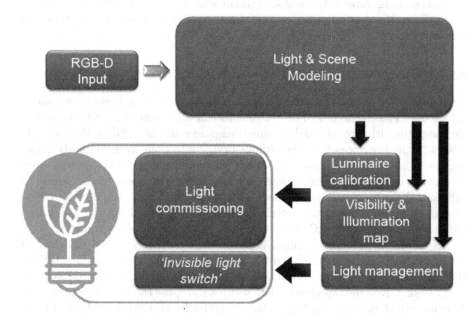

Fig. 2. Flowchart of the proposed system. An RGBD input image is used to model relationship between light and scene (human centric). The proposed system is capable of self calibration and finally implementing an invisible light switch, where the change in illumination is not perceived by the user.

3.1   Scene Composition Analysis

The structure of a scene consists of a number of material properties and their arrangement in the 3D space. This aspect is fundamental in order to understand the lighting propagation effects and the localization of the natural artificial sources. With the 3D scene structure, light propagation can be defined as an inverse problem called inverse lighting.

In this work, for the first time, inverse lighting is tackled in a real environment, typically indoor, that presents complex geometries and several types of lights (artificial and natural). Given the depth of the scene from a top-view RGBD sensor, the problem will result in the estimation of the photometric properties of the scene and objects material together with a coarse localization of the lights. In particular, we will rely on the fact that, given a large collection of images, inverse lighting becomes tractable. By leveraging a larger number of images depicting the same scene in time, it is possible to reduce the ambiguity of the problem by studying the evolving lighting conditions.

This information computed from the images will characterize the indoor scene by providing the estimation of the room light response, as a function of the different light sources and the different times during the day. This contributes to the final demonstrator with local scene estimates of how the current illumination differs from the one initially set, and how changing the lighting pattern can restore that.

3.2   Human Centric Scene Understanding

Further to the material properties, a scene is characterized by how humans interact with it. The research field of Ambient Intelligence (AmI) explicitly considers this, with the ultimate goal of designing transparent infrastructures, that actively adapts to the presence of people without prying into their lives. Similarly, lighting has to adapt to the specific activity of the human beings in the area in order to provide a light management system that follows the needs of the users. To this end, the project will design models and algorithms for estimating and forecasting the presence and the activity of humans, by exploiting the 3D+visual data (available from the RGBD images) and the inferred scene geometry.

As stated in previous sections, activities can be characterized into several categories such as individual vs group, etc. In this work we focus on activities that may occur in an office environment such as walking, discussing and working at the desk. Given the top view camera setup we propose the us a robust presence detector and dynamic modelling of human activities through VFOA. As VFOA identifies interest of people towards the scene, it can be used as a proxy for attention/gaze. Additionally this work for the first time proposes the use of head orientation in tracking. Given the fact that people usually walk in the direction they look at. Exploiting the information we can forecast future trajectories of humans in the scene. Activity analysis in a more robust fashion can be carried out using robust modelling of VFOA.

The goal is to discriminate among different human activities, intended as different trajectories and different elementary actions performed by the users (walking, writing at the PC, etc.). In this fashion, forecasting will be available, which will serve for implementing appropriate energy saving routines in the building (see next section). Once again, achieving such goals with RGBD data is a new challenge for the community: here, exploiting depth information could serve to ease the classification issue, that will be carried out using Social Affinity Maps.

3.3   The Invisible Light Switch

The idea behind the Invisible Light Switch is straightforward: the user controls and sets the illumination of the environment that he can see, while the proposed system acts on the part of the environment that the user cannot see, turning off the lights, thus ensuring a consistent energy saving. The study of the scene as discussed above serves this goal: knowing the 3D geometry of the scene and the map of inter-reflectance will allow to understand how the different light sources impact each point of the space; knowing where a user is located and what is his posture serves to infer what he can see and what he cannot, individuating potential areas where the light can be turned off. Being able to forecast his future activities will help understand (in advance) which lights should be turned on, avoiding the user to continuously act on the illumination system, and showing the user the illumination scenario that he wants to have.

4   Conclusion

The main aim of this research is to highlight the importance of smart lighting by implementing an *invisible light switch*. The key idea revolves around the fact knowledge of the static scene and light arrangement will allow the user to set a desired illumination pattern for the environment, which the system will maintain across daylight changes, e.g. augmenting the illumination level (given available light sources) when the sun sets. Secondly, detection, tracking and recognition of current and forecast human activities will allow an advanced occupancy detection, i.e. a control switch which turns lights on when the people are in the environment or about to enter it. Finally, this work joins research in smart lighting and computer vision towards the invisible light switch, which will bring both technologies together. The result light management system will be aware of the 3D geometry, light calibration, current and forecast activity maps. The user will be allowed to up an illumination pattern and move around in the environment (e.g. through office rooms or warehouse aisles). The system will maintain the lighting (given available light sources) for the user across the scene parts and across the daylight changes. Importantly, the system will turn lights off in areas not visible by the user, therefore providing energy saving in the invisible.

References

1. Adams, L., Zuckerman, D.: The effect of lighting conditions on personal space requirements. J. Gen. Psychol. **118**(4), 335–340 (1991)
2. Ba, S.O., Odobez, J.M.: A probabilistic framework for joint head tracking and pose estimation. In: IEEE International Conference on Pattern Recognition (ICPR) (2004)
3. Bazzani, L., Cristani, M., Tosato, D., Farenzena, M., Paggetti, G., Menegaz, G., Murino, V.: Social interactions by visual focus of attention in a three-dimensional environment. Expert Syst. **30**(2), 115–127 (2013)
4. Benfold, B., Reid, I.: Guiding visual surveillance by tracking human attention. In: British Machine Vision Conference (BMVC), pp. 1–11 (2009)
5. Carr, S.J., Dabbs Jr., J.M.: The effects of lighting, distance and intimacy of topic on verbal and visual behavior. Sociometry, pp. 592–600 (1974)
6. Cristani, M., Bazzani, L., Paggetti, G., Fossati, A., Tosato, D., Del Bue, A., Menegaz, G., Murino, V.: Social interaction discovery by statistical analysis of f-formations. In: British Machine Vision Conference (BMVC), pp. 23.1–23.12 (2011)
7. Flynn, J.E., Hendrick, C., Spencer, T., Martyniuk, O.: A guide to methodology procedures for measuring subjective impressions in lighting. J. Illuminating Eng. Soc. **8**(2), 95–110 (1979)
8. Galasiu, A.D., Veitch, J.A.: Occupant preferences and satisfaction with the luminous environment and control systems in daylit offices: a literature review. Energy Build. **38**(7), 728–742 (2006)
9. Gifford, R.: Light, decor, arousal, comfort and communication. J. Environ. Psychol. **8**(3), 177–189 (1988)
10. Gil-Castineira, F., Costa-Montenegro, E., Gonzalez-Castano, F., López-Bravo, C., Ojala, T., Bose, R.: Experiences inside the ubiquitous oulu smart city. Computer **44**(6), 48–55 (2011)
11. Goffman, E.: Behaviour in Public Places: Notes on the Social Order of Gatherings. Free Press, Glencoe (1963)
12. Gourier, N., Maisonnasse, J., Hall, D., Crowley, J.L.: Head pose estimation on low resolution images. In: Stiefelhagen, R., Garofolo, J. (eds.) CLEAR 2006. LNCS, vol. 4122, pp. 270–280. Springer, Heidelberg (2007). https://doi.org/10.1007/978-3-540-69568-4_24
13. Lee, D., Yang, M.H., Oh, S.: Fast and accurate head pose estimation via random projection forests. In: Proceedings of the IEEE International Conference on Computer Vision, pp. 1958–1966 (2015)
14. Magielse, R., Hengeveld, B.J., Frens, J.W.: Designing a light controller for a multi-user lighting environment (2013)
15. Poulsen, E.S., Morrison, A., Andersen, H.J., Jensen, O.B.: Responsive lighting: the city becomes alive. In: Proceedings of the 15th International Conference on Human-Computer Interaction with Mobile Devices and Services, pp. 217–226. ACM (2013)
16. Robertson, N., Reid, I.: Estimating gaze direction from low-resolution faces in video. In: European Conference on Computer Vision (ECCV) (2006)
17. Robertson, N.M., Reid, I.D.: Automatic reasoning about causal events in surveillance video. EURASIP J. Image Video Process. **1**, 1–19 (2011)
18. Smith, K., Ba, S.O., Odobez, J.M., Gatica-Perez, D.: Tracking the visual focus of attention for a varying number of wandering people. IEEE Trans. Pattern Anal. Mach. Intell. **30**(7), 1212–1229 (2008)

19. Smolders, K.C., de Kort, Y.A., Tenner, A.D., Kaiser, F.G.: Need for recovery in offices: behavior-based assessment. J. Environ. Psychol. **32**(2), 126–134 (2012)
20. Stiefelhagen, R., Finke, M., Yang, J., Waibel, A.: From gaze to focus of attention. In: Visual Information and Information Systems (1999)
21. Taylor, L.H., Socov, E.W.: The movement of people toward lights. J. Illuminating Eng. Soc. **3**(3), 237–241 (1974)
22. Toshev, A., Szegedy, C.: Deeppose: human pose estimation via deep neural networks. In: Proceedings of the IEEE Conference on Computer Vision and Pattern Recognition, pp. 1653–1660 (2014)
23. Vascon, S., Mequanint, E.Z., Cristani, M., Hung, H., Pelillo, M., Murino, V.: Detecting conversational groups in images and sequences: a robust game-theoretic approach. Comput. Vis. Image Underst. **143**, 11–24 (2016)
24. Voit, M., Nickel, K., Stiefelhagen, R.: A Bayesian approach for multi-view head pose estimation. In: 2006 IEEE International Conference on Multisensor Fusion and Integration for Intelligent Systems, pp. 31–34. IEEE (2006)
25. Xu, A.J., Labroo, A.: Incandescent affect: turning on the hot emotional system with bright light. ACR North American Advances (2013)
26. Zhang, L., Hung, H.: Beyond f-formations: determining social involvement in free standing conversing groups from static images. In: IEEE Conference on Computer Vision and Pattern Recognition (CVPR) (2016)

Automatic Affect Analysis and Synthesis (3AS)

An Affective BCI Driven by Self-induced Emotions for People with Severe Neurological Disorders

Giuseppe Placidi[1]([envelope]), Luigi Cinque[2], Paolo Di Giamberardino[3],
Daniela Iacoviello[3], and Matteo Spezialetti[1]

[1] Department of Life, Health and Environmental Sciences,
University of L'Aquila, L'Aquila, Italy
giuseppe.placidi@univaq.it
[2] Department of Computer Science, Sapienza University of Rome, Rome, Italy
[3] Department of Computer, Control and Management Engineering Antonio Ruberti,
Sapienza University of Rome, Rome, Italy

Abstract. Conditions of extreme neurological disability prevent any form of communication, even to show the emotional state. Brain Computer Interfaces (BCI) often use Electro-encephalography (EEG) measurements of the voluntary brain activity for driving a communication system. A BCI usage requires the activation of mental tasks. In the last few years, a new paradigm of activation has been used consisting in the autonomous brain activation through self-induced emotions, remembered on autobiographical basis. In the present paper, we describe the state of the art of an affective BCI system, a-BCI, based on self-induced emotions. It can be used by people with Severe Neurological Disorders (SND) for: alternative communication, emotion transmission.

Keywords: BCI · EEG · Emotions · Severe neurological disorders
Communication · Affective computing

1 Introduction

Conditions of Severe Neurological Disorders (SND) prevent people from expressing their thoughts, emotions and will and little remains of any voluntary motor function. The number of these patients is progressively increasing as a consequence of the growing population of adults who sustain traumatic brain injury, stroke, and other disabling diseases, combined with advances in cardiopulmonary resuscitation and cardiac life support. A BCI is a system that provides a communication and control tool towards the external environment that is independent of the traditional brain's pathways, such as muscles and nerves, and is based on the direct monitoring of the brain activity [1]. BCI systems are mostly based on event-related signals induced by external stimulations [2] and synchronized with them (some examples are the visual, auditory and tactile stimulations) or on signals produced by sensory-motor rhythms [3]. However, for many SND

© Springer International Publishing AG 2017
S. Battiato et al. (Eds.): ICIAP 2017 International Workshops, LNCS 10590, pp. 155–162, 2017.
https://doi.org/10.1007/978-3-319-70742-6_14

patients these activation protocols are precluded, being traditional BCIs completely ineffective, and there is currently no system that would allow to reveal their consciousness, to express their emotions, to communicate with the outside world and to take at least some simple, but crucial to their daily lives, decision (e.g. decide whether and when eat/drink). It has been demonstrated that in a good part of SND people emotional processing is preserved [4,5]. Recently, a prototype of a binary a-BCI, based on remembering just a single emotion (the disgust produced by remembering unpleasant odors) and on a relaxing state, has been designed and implemented at the University of L'Aquila [6], tested on healthy people [7] and on an MCS male subject, demonstrating that he was capable of taking some simple decisions [8]. In what follows we describe the details of the a-BCI, from the activation paradigm to the signal measurement and classification, ending with the proposed graphic user interface (GUI) used for synchronizing the user activation thoughts with the choices proposed by the GUI. Finally, we illustrate its future developments.

2   The a-BCI System as a Whole

The idea behind the a-BCI is to measure the human brain reaction to self-induced emotions, those reproduced autonomously by recalling in mind situations that generated real emotions, and to use them as commands of a BCI for helping SND people. But why emotions? (1) Emotional processing has been shown to be preserved in a significant portion of SND people [4,5]; (2) emotions could be an alternative paradigm where others failed [8]; (3) to allow the transmission of emotions towards the external world; (4) to allow the transformation of emotions in actions. Moreover, but not less important, self-induced emotions, recalled in

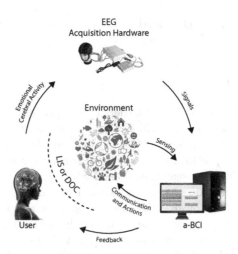

Fig. 1. Schematic representation of the proposed a-BCI.

mind as and when desired, represent an activation protocol which is not externally elicited, i.e. the user is completely free of using it autonomously, without additional stress. A scheme of the proposed a-BCI is reported in Fig. 1.

3   Signal Acquisition Hardware

Some of the possible interactions between the subject and the computer are measured by: pupil size oscillations, dry active electrode arrays, prosthesis and environment control, electrocardiogram (ECG) signals, magnetic resonance imaging (MRI), magnetoencephalography (MEG), near-infrared spectroscopy (NIRS) [9–16]. Among these, EEG [17] has been intensively used in BCI because of its low invasiveness, good temporal resolution and low cost. Regarding medical applications, BCI uses measurements of the voluntary brain activity for driving a communication system for SND people [1,18]. BCI may be invasive, semi-invasive and non-invasive. The invasiveness degree is often referred to the technique used for measuring brain signals: electrodes placed inside the brain are invasive. However, it could be also referred to the paradigm used for eliciting a brain response: the usage of an externally elicited response could be considered invasive, at least semi-invasive. Generally, a BCI user is in front of a computer screen and has to dress an EEG helmet, while he is responding to external stimulation or is performing an autonomous mental task. The GUI has the role of eliciting the stimulation and synchronizing the response of the user, in case of externally elicited stimulation, or simply the role of synchronizing the user activation with choices proposed by the graphic interface, in the case of autonomous mental task activation. The EEG system we discuss therein is completely non-invasive because it uses externally placed EEG electrodes (EnobioNE, an 8-channels, wireless, EEG equipment) positioned in the following locations of the 10-20 positioning systems: C3, C4, T7, T8, P3, P4, P7, P8 and, in the same time, it uses autonomous mental tasks.

4   Activation Task and Experimental Protocol

An emotion is a complex psychological state that involves a subjective experience, a physiological response, and a behavioral or expressive response [19,20]. Emotions have been described as discrete and consistent responses to events (external or internal) with significance for the organism [21]. Usually, all the emotions are originated by 8 basic emotions (anger, fear, sadness, disgust, surprise, curiosity, acceptance, and joy [22]): for example, disappointment is composed of surprise and sadness. A relative right frontal activation is associated with negative emotions, such as fear or disgust. A relatively greater left frontal activation is associated with positive emotions, such as joy or happiness. This lateralization can be exploited for a-BCI development. Emotions could be elicited by external stimulations [23], or could be really felt by the subject or could be self-induced by the subject by recalling in mind past experiences. External elicitation is really useful for understanding activation mechanisms related to emotions but are not really useful for BCI implementation; really felt emotions, though important for discovering the current mood state of the subject, are useless for BCI implementation; autonomously elicited emotions represent "switches" that are essential for driving a BCI. Recently, a self-induced activation task has been considered: the disgust generated by the memory of a bad smell [6]. It appears to be particularly interesting also for the subjects for which classical activation paradigms (such as sensory-motor) are ineffective. Disgust is a primordial, strong negative emotion. The signal of a self-induced, remembered, emotion presents a lower amplitude with respect to that generated by really felt emotion, but it is more localized both in space, because the mnemonic task requires concentration, and in frequency, because the remembered emotional task affects mainly the gamma band. Moreover, the disgust is an uncommon and unnatural feeling and it would unlikely happen during the BCI use, therefore it is a good candidate as a BCI command. However, besides disgust, also other basic emotions could be effectively used for driving an a-BCI. A first study and analysis has been performed by using trials collected inviting the subjects to think to a bad smell or in rest conditions [7, 24–27]. The experimental protocol consisted of a combination of two different stimuli: one produced by auto-induction of the disgust by remembering an unpleasant odor (identified as stimulus #1, or concentration); the other produced by relax (identified as stimulus #2, or relaxation). For data collection, each subject was sat in a comfortable armchair in a quiet and lit room. The experiment consisted in showing a random sequence of symbols "↓" or "+", each presented for 3.6 seconds on a computer screen. The subject was previously informed that when the symbol "↓" appeared on the computer screen, he had to concentrate on the disgust; whereas when the symbol + appeared, he had to relax. The stimulus had to be maintained until the symbol changed. During this time, the EEG signal, composing the current trial, was recorded. The order of presentation was random but the number of symbols "↓" was equal to the number of symbols "+" and their sum was always the same. 120 trials, 60 for each class, were recorded for all the subjects involved in the experiments. After the acquisition, the order of the collected trials were mixed (the outcomes of each trial were maintained) to avoid that signals allowing to a particular situation occurred during the experiment, maintained close each other, could affect the different phases of the classification algorithm. Anonymous symbols were used just to synchronize the task but not for eliciting any other mental state.

5   Classification Strategy

For classify the EEG signals from emotions, we mainly used an efficient classification method based on short-time Fourier transform [6]. Signals are filtered with a band-pass filter to maintain just the frequencies between 8 and 12 Hz (demonstrating cerebral activity due to concentration in the α band) and between 30 and 42 Hz (demonstrating disgusting activity in the γ band) [28]. Moreover, the only considered channels are P4, C4, T8 and P8, those mainly involved in remembering negative emotions, especially due to disgusting odors [29]. The strategy used to classify the signals consisted two phases,

Calibration and Classification (Fig. 2). The Calibration starts from a set of trials belonging to known classes. For each of them, a signal pre-processing step is applied. Considering a set C of channels, the Short-Time Fourier Transform is applied on each of them separately, in order to partitionate the signal in a set of q sub-trials, with an overlap of p samples between consecutive segments, and to obtain their frequency coefficients in the considered bands. Then, the mutual similarity between sub-trials is evaluated by means of r^2 computation [30]. The power spectra of the q sub-trials are compared: the s most similar are averaged together, the other are discarded. In addition, the obtained spectra of channels belonging to C are averaged together. The process serves to discard signal pieces mostly affected by noise. After the pre-processing step, an r^2 based selection and synthesis is performed again between each trial belonging to the same class. In this way, the information of a synthetized trial is obtained for both classes. At this point, r^2 is used to identify the frequencies where the differences, in r^2, between "activation" and "non-activation" trials were maxima. The maximum values of r^2 occurring inside each of the considered bands, and the absolute minimum of r^2, are also used to define the classification thresholds, $t\alpha$ and $t\gamma$ (see [6] for more details). The Classification phase analyzes a signal of an unknown class. First, the pre-processing phase used for the Calibration signals is applied. Then, the resulting spectra are compared with those synthetized in the Calibration phase for "activation" and "non-activation" stages. For better dealing with weak signals, such those deriving from remembered emotions, we also used machine learning approaches and their generalization for multiple emotions classifications [7, 26, 27].

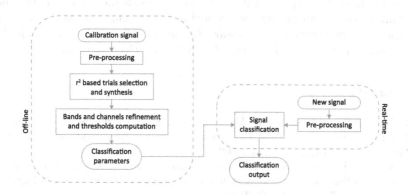

Fig. 2. Flow-chart of the used classification method.

6   The Graphic User Interface

Once the robust recognition of at least one emotion is achieved, it is integrated in a communication and control interface [31], a graphic user interface (GUI).

In [32], a modular framework for the design and the implementation of tabular graphic user interface was described. The proposed framework is intended to allow the implementation of the a-BCI by constructing a matrix of graphic symbols to be represented on a computer screen and a software that, cyclically, passes through the rows/columns of a matrix and remained on each of them for a fixed time interval (usually between 2 and 4 s). When the system enlightens the row containing the desired symbol, the user concentrates on a pre-determined mental task (the disgust) in order to select that row; elsewhere, the user has to relax. This is also repeated with the symbols associated with the chosen row. The GUI is hosted by a computer which collects the EEG signals from the user and performs a real-time signal analysis and classification: on the basis of the classification outcome, the a-BCI performs the corresponding action for allowing the GUI to present the communication message which is being composed or to activate the specific command associated to the chosen symbol. The resulting a-BCI has been used as a tool for evaluating consciousness in MCS subjects [8].

7 Conclusions and Future Developments

The state of the art of an a-BCI driven by remembered emotions has been presented and described. The proposed a-BCI has been used for ascertain the consciousness of persons in state of minimal consciousness, as an alternative communication tool for severely disabled people and could be used for transmitting emotions to the external world. The system has proven to operate in a binary mode but it would be useful to extend it toward a n-ary mode (n-1 emotions have to be used) for improving its performance. Both the GUI and the whole a-BCI are modular and can be used to deal also with multiple emotions. To this aim, specific "signatures" are necessary for allowing reciprocal discrimination. The research in this field will be useful also for affective computing.

References

1. Wolpaw, J.R., Birbaumer, N., McFarlandand, D.J., Pfurtscheller, G., Vaughan, T.M.: Braincomputer interfaces for communication and control. Clin. Neurophysiol. **113**(6), 767–791 (2002)
2. Farwell, L., Lawrence, A., Donchin, E.: Talking o the top of your head: toward a mental prosthesis utilizing event-related brain potentials. Electroencephalogr. Clin. Neurophysiol. **70**(6), 510–523 (1988)
3. Wolpaw, J.R., McFarland, D.J., Neat, G.W., Forneris, C.A.: An EEG-based brain-computer interface for cursor control. Electroencephalogr. Clin. Neurophysiol. **78**(3), 252–259 (1991)
4. Laureys, S., Perrin, F., Faymonville, M.E., Schnakers, C., Boly, M., Bartsch, V., Majerus, S., Moonen, G., Maquet, P.: Cerebral processing in the minimally conscious state. Neurology **63**, 916–918 (2004)
5. Heine, L., Castro, M., Martial, C., Tillmann, B., Laureys, S., Perrin, F.: Exploration of functional connectivity during preferred music stimulation in patients with disorders of consciousness. Front. Psychol. **6**, 1704 (2015)

6. Placidi, G., Avola, D., Petracca, A., Sgallari, F., Spezialetti, M.: Basis for the implementation of an EEG-based single-trial binary brain computer interface through the disgust produced by remembering unpleasant odors. Neurocomputing **160**, 308–318 (2015)
7. Iacoviello, D., Petracca, A., Spezialetti, M., Placidi, G.: A classification algorithm for electroencephalography signals by self-induced emotional stimuli. IEEE Trans. Cybern. **46**(12), 3171–3180 (2016)
8. Pistoia, F., Carolei, A., Iacoviello, D., Petracca, A., Sacco, S., Sar, M., Spezialetti, M., Placidi, G.: EEG-detected olfactory imagery to reveal covert consciousness in minimally conscious state. Brain Inj. **29**(13–14), 1729–1735 (2015)
9. Iacoviello, D., Lucchetti, M.: Parametric characterization of the form of the human pupil from blurred noisy images. Comput. Methods Programs Biomed. **77**, 39–48 (2005)
10. De Santis, A., Iacoviello, D.: Optimal segmentation of pupillometric images for estimating pupil shape parameters. Comput. Methods Programs Biomed. **84**, 174–187 (2006)
11. De Santis, A., Iacoviello, D.: Robust real time eye tracking for computer interface for disables people. Comput. Methods Programs Biomed. **96**, 1–11 (2009)
12. Placidi, G., Avola, D., Ferrari, M., Iacoviello, D., Petracca, A., Quaresima, V., Spezialetti, M.: A low-cost real time virtual system for postural stability assessment at home. Comput. Methods Programs Biomed. **117**(2), 322–333 (2014)
13. M. Ferrari, Bisconti, S. Spezialetti, M., Basso Moro, S., Di Palo, C., Placidi, G., Quaresima, V.: Prefrontal cortex activated bilaterally by a tilt board balance task: a functional near-infrared spectroscopy study in a semi-immersive virtual reality environment. Brain Topogr. **27**(3), 353–365 (2014)
14. Basso Moro, S., Bisconti, S., Muthalib, M., Spezialetti, M., Cutini, S., Ferrari, M., Placidi, G., Quaresima, V.: A semi-immersive virtual reality incremental swing balance task activates prefrontal cortex: a functional near-infrared spectroscopy study. Neuroimage **85**, 451–460 (2014)
15. Basso Moro, S., Carrieri, M., Avola, D., Brigadoi, S., Lancia, S., Petracca, A., Spezialetti, M., Ferrari, M., Placidi, G., Quaresima, V.: A novel semi-immersive virtual reality visuo-motor task activates ventrolateral prefrontal cortex: a functional near-infrared spectroscopy study. J. Neural Eng. **13**(3), 1–14 (2016)
16. Carrieri, M., Petracca, A., Lancia, S., Basso Moro, S., Brigadoi, S., Spezialetti, M., Ferrari, M., Placidi, G., Quaresima, V.: Prefrontal cortex activation upon a demanding virtual hand-controlled task: a new frontier for neuroergonomics. Front. Human Neurosci. **10**, 1–13 (2016)
17. Niedermeyer, E., Lopes da Silva, F.: Electroencephalography: Basic Principles, Clinical Applications, and Related Fields. Lippincott Williams & Wilkins, Philadelphia (2005)
18. Cincotti, F., Mattia, D., Aloise, F., Bufalari, S., Schalk, G., Oriolo, G., Cherubini, A., Marciani, M., Babiloni, F.: Non-invasive braincomputer interface system: towards its application as assistive technology. Brain Res. Bull. **75**, 796–803 (2008)
19. Hockenbury, D., Hockenbury, S.: Discovering Psychology. Macmillan Publishers, New York (2007)
20. Mauss, I.B., Robinson, M.D.: Measures of emotion: a review. Cogn. Emot. **23**(2), 209–237 (2009)
21. Fox, E.: Emotion Science: Cognitive and Neuroscientific Approaches to Understanding Human Emotions. Palgrave Macmillan, New York (2008)
22. Plutchik, R.: The nature of Emotions. American Scientist (2001)

23. Garcia-Molina, G., Tsoneva, T., Nijholt, A.: Emotional braincomputer interfaces. Int. J. Auton. Adapt. Commun. Syst. **6**(1), 9–25 (2013)
24. Placidi, G., Petracca, A., Spezialetti, M., Iacoviello, D.: Classification strategies for a single-trial binary brain computer interface based on remembering unpleasant odors. In: 37th Annual International Conference of the IEEE Engineering in Medicine and Biology Society (EMBC), pp. 7019–7022 (2015)
25. Iacoviello, D., Petracca, A., Spezialetti, M., Placidi, G.: A real-time classification algorithm for EEG-based BCI driven by self-induced emotions. Comput. Methods Programs Biomed. **122**, 293–303 (2015)
26. Iacoviello, D., Pagnani, N., Petracca, A., Spezialetti, M., Placidi, G.: A poll oriented classifier for affective brain computer interfaces. In: Proceedings of the 3rd International Congress on Neurotechnology, Electronics and Informatics, NEUROTECHNIX, Lisbon, pp. 978–989 (2015)
27. Placidi, G., Di Giamberardino, P., Petracca, A., Spezialetti, M., Iacoviello, D.: Classification of emotional signals from the DEAP dataset. In: Proceedings of the 4th International Congress on Neurotechnology, Electronics and Informatics, NEUROTECHNIX, Porto, pp. 15–21 (2016)
28. Coan, J., Allen, J.: Frontal EEG asymmetry as a moderator and mediator of emotion. Biol. Psychol. **67**(1–2), 7–50 (2004)
29. Henkin, R., Levy, L.: Lateralization of brain activation to imagination and smell of odors using functional magnetic resonance imaging (fMRI): left hemispheric localization of pleasant and right hemispheric localization of unpleasant odors. J. Comput. Assist. Tomogr. **25**(4), 493–514 (2001)
30. Draper, N., Smith, H.: Applied Regression Analysis. Wiley, New York (1998)
31. Avola, D., Spezialetti, M., Placidi, G.: Design of an efficient framework for fast prototyping of customized humancomputer interfaces and virtual environments for rehabilitation. Comput. Methods Programs Biomed. **110**(3), 490–502 (2013)
32. Placidi, G., Petracca, A., Spezialetti, M., Iacoviello, D.: A modular framework for EEG web based binary brain computer interfaces to recover communication abilities in impaired people. J. Med. Syst. **40**(34), 1–14 (2016)

Face Tracking and Respiratory Signal Analysis for the Detection of Sleep Apnea in Thermal Infrared Videos with Head Movement

Marcin Kopaczka[✉], Özcan Özkan, and Dorit Merhof

Institute of Imaging and Computer Vision, RWTH Aachen University,
Templergraben 55, 52074 Aachen, Germany
Marcin.kopaczka@lfb.rwth-aachen.de

Abstract. Infrared Thermography as imaging modality has gained increased attention over the last years. Its main advantages in human action monitoring are illumination invariance and its ability to monitor physiological parameters such as heart and respiratory rates. In our work, we present a novel approach for detecting respiratory-related data, in our case apnea events, from thermal infrared recordings. In contrast to already published methods where the subjects were required not to move, our approach uses state-of-the-art thermal face tracking technology to allow monitoring of subjects showing head movement, which is an important aspect for real-world applications. We implement different methods for apnea detection and face tracking and test them on videos of different subjects against a ground truth acquired with an established breathing rate monitoring system. Results show that our proposed approach allows robust apnea detection with moving subjects. Our methods allow using already presented or novel vital sign monitoring systems under conditions where the monitored persons are note required to keep their heads in a given position.

1 Introduction

Thermal Infrared or long-wave infrared (LWIR) thermography cameras detect electromagnetic waves with a wavelength between 7 and $14\,\mu$m. This is the energy window in which thermal radiation at room temperature is emitted, thereby allowing LWIR detectors to detect body heat without requiring an external light source, eliminating many problems connected to illumination variance. At the same time, thermal infrared is a relevant modality for human condition observation as many physiological parameters such as heart rate and breathing rate can be determined by analyzing the thermal infrared videos. However, while several authors have shown that vital signs can be derived from such video data, most of them have only presented results from lab studies where subject head movement was highly constrained, and pointed out that robust face tracking technology would be required in order to achieve applicability in unconstrained conditions. To this end, we present a comparison of different approaches for face tracking in thermal infrared images and show that they can be used to improve

S. Battiato et al. (Eds.): ICIAP 2017 International Workshops, LNCS 10590, pp. 163–170, 2017.
https://doi.org/10.1007/978-3-319-70742-6_15

robustness of algorithms for vital sign monitoring. Our chosen application is the detection of apnea events which has already been proven to work under constrained conditions.

2   Previous Work

There has been extensive previous work in the fields of sleep apnea detection, thermal infrared face tracking and thermal infrared vital sign extraction.

Obstructive sleep apnea is a common sleeping disorder that results in reduced blood oxygen levels and is mainly caused by obstruction of the upper airway [1]. Usually, sleep apnea is diagnosed using polysomnography, a method where different vial parameters such as EEG, EMG, EKG, air flow through mouth and nose and breathing movements are recorded during sleep and analyzed subsequenty [4]. A commonly used, versatile and efficient method that can also be part of a polysomnographic recording is a thoracic-abdominal band that allows to measure upper body circumference changes and thereby allows extraction of the breating movement [3].

Thermal imaging for medical purposes has been proven beneficial in different scenarios, for example for fever detection in airports [5], breast cancer detection [6] or inflammation [7]. A recent overview of different applications can be found in [2]. Contributions for the analysis and extraction of vital signs from facial images using thermal infrared recordings include methods for the monitoring of respiratory rate of newborns [9] and adults [8,10], heart rate [12,13] and more currently the thermal signatures of psychopsychological phenomena [14–16].

A common property of all literature listed above is that the presented approaches make only limited use of tracking technologies, in fact in most cases no tracking is applied at all. While this is sufficient for fundamental research or low-throughput measurements where the regions of interest (ROI) for thermal signature analysis can be updated manually on a frame-per-frame basis, any measurement that should allow head movement requires tracking. Only limited work has been published in the field of face and facial landmark tracking in thermal infrared images. Notably, [17] introduces a set of particle filters for tracking in thermal images, while the approach shown in [18] uses feature-based active appearance models for precise tracking of facial landmarks.

3   Materials and Methods

In this section we describe the tracking methods used to allow adapting ROI positions to head movements and the methods for apnea detection and respiratory rate measurement.

3.1   ROI Tracking

We implemented two state-of-the-art tracking mechanisms in order to allow tracking of facial regions:

- **TLD tracking** - TLD (Track, Learn, Detect) [19] is a general-purpose tracker making heavy use of online learning strategies. Constant updates of the target templates improve tracking accuracy over time, while a set of local and global correlation filters ensure robustness even for facial areas that strongly vary in appearance due to head movements. So far, TLD has not been applied to face tracking in thermal infrared images.
- **Feature-based active appearance models** - Feature-based active appearance models (AAMs) combine the well-established tracking approach of active appearance models with image feature descriptors for improved tracking robustness. They have been proven to show good performance in the tracking of faces in thermal infrared videos [18]. We used an AAM trained with a database of 2500 manually annotated thermal infrared images.

For TLD, the ROI for respiratory rate extraction was defined manually in the 1st frame of the video by drawing a box covering the nostrils. The tracker learned the ROI appearance and tracked it in the subsequent frames. For the feature-based AAM, the ROIs were defined automatically by using the two landmarks on the detected nostril positions and using them as centers of rectangular boxes with a width of 15 pixels. Figure 1 shows the results of both approaches on the same image.

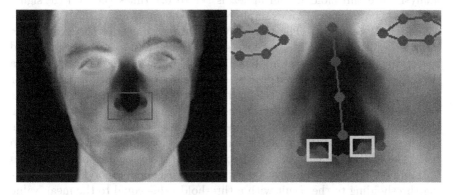

Fig. 1. ROI definition. Left: Manually defined bounding box for the static ROI and TLD tracking. Right: automatically defined ROIs computed from AAM tracking results.

3.2 Apnoe Detection

We developed and implemented different methods for apnea detection that all use the thermal signal extracted by computing the average or minimal temperature in the ROIs defined above. In a preprocessing step, all temporal temperature curves were filtered with a spectral lowpass defined using a Gaussian kernel with a width of 0.25s (7 frames at a frame rate of 30 fps) to reduce high-frequency noise. Subsequently, the following methods for apnea detection were applied:

- **Gradient Sum** - By assuming that regular breathing results in stronger signal change and thereby higher gradients, we computed the moving sum of the absolute temperature gradient curves over the past 4 s. Apnea events are considered as regions where the gradient value is below 0.6 times the average of the whole video sequence. An example of the output of the gradient analysis can be found in Fig. 2
- **Variance Analysis** - Similar to gradient analysis, the variance analysis method also relies on the fact that signal changes during apnea events occur less frequently than during regular breathing. For variance analysis, the temperature variance over the past 7 s is computed, subsequently all areas with a variance lower than 0.4 times the average variance of the analyzed video sequence are considered to be apnea events. Figure 3 shows the output of the variance analysis.
- **Spectral Analysis** - apnea events can be detected in the spectral domain as well. To this end, we analyze the temperature curve and subtract the average temperature of the past 1.3 s from each signal value to reduce low-frequency noise. Subsequently, Short-Time Fourier Transform with a window length of 10 s is applied to the filtered signal. We analyze the frequency window between 0.2 and 0.8 Hz over the last 5 s, as our preliminary studies have shown that the respiratory signal is dominant in this spectral range. When applying spectral analysis, the threshold for an apnea is set to 0.1 times the average signal energy of the sequence. An example result is shown in Fig. 4
- **Wavelet Transform** - The wavelet transform is similar to the Short-Time Fourier Transform since it also allows signal localization in both temporal and spectral space. The general applicability of the wavelet transform to apnea detection in thermal infrared images has already been shown in [11], in our work we introduce a slightly adapted and extended version that transforms the resulting wavelet into a set of one-dimensional values, thereby allowing the use of 1D signal processing methods as in the methods introduced above. In a first step, we use the method from [11], where we apply wavelet transform using the Mexican hat wavelet and compute 50 scales equidistantly between 0.21 and 0.75 Hz. Subsequently, we expand the original method by first applying thresholding to the result with a threshold value equal to the mean value of the wavelet coefficients. In order to extract a curve from the thresholded wavelet signal, we compute the sum of all coefficients for the past 5 s. The resulting curve has high similarity with the spectral curve shown in 4, and similar to the spectral analysis method introduced above we define an apnea event as areas where the extracted signal is lower than 0.1 times the average signal value.

4   Experiments and Results

To evaluate the implemented algorithms, we acquired thermal infrared recordings of 10 healthy subjects under laboratory conditions. The used camera provided a resolution of 1024×768 pixels with a thermal sensitivity of 0.03 K.

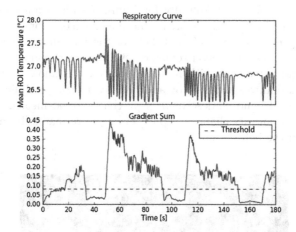

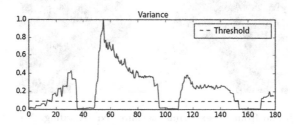

Fig. 2. Gradient analysis. Top: original temperature curve extracted from the ROI. Bottom: computed gradient sum.

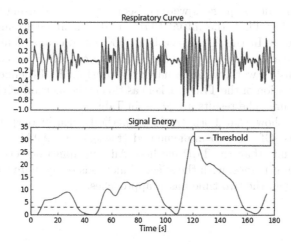

Fig. 3. Variance analysis results

Fig. 4. Spectral analysis results for a window length of 10 s.

Each participant was filmed frontally for 5 min, see Fig. 5 for a sample frame. The persons were instructed to breath normally except for simulated apnea events that started after 60, 150 and 240 s of the recording. Since apnea usually occurs during rest, the head remained still during the apnea. Between the events, free head movement with increasing speed was allowed. The reference for apnea estimation was acquired by additionally utilizing a clinically approved thoracic-abdominal band as described in [3] that allowed measurement of thorax circumference and its changes. Apnea events were manually marked in the output signal of the belt.

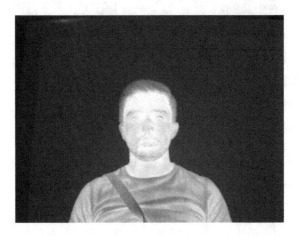

Fig. 5. Sample frame from an experimantal infrared recording. Note that a holding strap of the chest belt is visible in the recording as well.

All acquired video sequences were subsequently tracked using the TLD and AAM method. For TLD, the initial ROI was drawn manually and tracked in subsequent frames. In the AAM, the head position was also defined manually in the 1st frame and tracked by the algorithm afterwards. For comparison with previously published work, we also analyzed a constant ROI (defined as the ROI used for initialization of the TLD tracker) as this is the method of choice in most available literature. The results are given in Table 1.

The results show that both tracking methods clearly outperform a non-tracked analysis. Of the two implemented trackers, the AAM constantly provides better results than the TLD method. All four apnea detection algorithms show similar performance, with the spectral methods being more robust towards misdetections than the two time-based approaches.

Table 1. Apnoe detection results using different trackers and detectors.

Detector	Tracker	True Positive	False Positive	False Negative
Gradient Sum	Static	16	27	9
Gradient Sum	TLD	26	4	3
Gradient Sum	AAM	30	3	0
Variance Analysis	Static	17	33	6
Variance Analysis	TLD	25	25	3
Variance Analysis	AAM	29	9	1
Spectral Analysis	Static	18	23	3
Spectral Analysis	TLD	25	2	3
Spectral Analysis	AAM	30	2	0
Wavelet Transform	Static	20	14	6
Wavelet Transform	TLD	25	2	5
Wavelet Transform	AAM	29	1	1

5 Conclusion

In this work, we introduced different algorithms for the detection of sleep apnea in thermal infrared video sequences. To improve robustness of the detection methods, we also implemented two algorithms for face region tracking in thermal infrared recordings. Results show that the presented methods allow reliable apnea detection in thermal infrared recordings and that modern face tracking algorithms clearly improve the robustness of the apnea detection.

Future work should include a real-time implementation of the described algorithms and a validation of the proposed method in a clinical scenario.

References

1. Somers, V.K., White, D.P., Amin, R., Abraham, W.T., Costa, F., Culebras, A., Daniels, S., Floras, J.S., Hunt, C.E., Olson, L.J., et al.: Sleep apnea and cardiovascular disease. Circulation **118**(10), 1080–1111 (2008)
2. Lahiri, B.B., Bagavathiappan, S., Jayakumar, T., Philip, J.: Medical applications of infrared thermography: a review. Infrared Phys. Technol. **55**(4), 221–235 (2012)
3. Denissova, S.I., Yewondwossen, M.H., Andrew, J.W., Hale, M.E., Murphy, C.H., Purcell, S.R.: A gated deep inspiration breath-hold radiation therapy technique using a linear position transducer. J. Appl. Clin. Med. Phys. **6**(1), 61–70 (2005)
4. Bloch, K.E.: Polysomnography: a systematic review. Technol. Health Care **5**(4), 285–305 (1997)
5. Nguyen, A.V., Cohen, N.J., Lipman, H., Brown, C.M., Molinari, N.-A., Jackson, W.L., Kirking, H., Szymanowski, P., Wilson, T.W., Salhi, B.A., et al.: Comparison of 3 infrared thermal detection systems and self-report for mass fever screening. Emerg. Infect. Dis. **16**(11), 1710 (2010)

6. Arora, N., Martins, D., Ruggerio, D., Tousimis, E., Swistel, A.J., Osborne, M.P., Simmons, R.M.: Effectiveness of a noninvasive digital infrared thermal imaging system in the detection of breast cancer. Am. J. Surg. **196**(4), 523–526 (2008)
7. Lasanen, R., Piippo-Savolainen, E., Remes-Pakarinen, T., Kröger, L., Heikkilä, A., Julkunen, P., Karhu, J., Töyräs, J.: Thermal imaging in screening of joint inflammation and rheumatoid arthritis in children. Physiol. Meas. **36**(2), 273 (2015)
8. Pereira, C.B., Yu, X., Czaplik, M., Blazek, V., Venema, B., Leonhardt, S.: Estimation of breathing rate in thermal imaging videos: a pilot study on healthy human subjects. J. Clin. Monit. Comput. October 2016
9. Abbas, A.K., Heimann, K., Jergus, K., Orlikowsky, T., Leonhardt, S.: Neonatal non-contact respiratory monitoring based on real-time infrared thermography. Biomed. Eng. Online **10**(1), 93 (2011)
10. Fei, J., Pavlidis, I.: Thermistor at a distance: unobtrusive measurement of breathing. IEEE Trans. Biomed. Eng. **57**(4), 988–998 (2010)
11. Fei, J., Pavlidis, I., Murthy, J.: Thermal vision for sleep apnea monitoring. In: Yang, G.-Z., Hawkes, D., Rueckert, D., Noble, A., Taylor, C. (eds.) MICCAI 2009. LNCS, vol. 5762, pp. 1084–1091. Springer, Heidelberg (2009). https://doi.org/10.1007/978-3-642-04271-3_131
12. Gault, T.R., Farag, A.A.: A fully automatic method to extract the heart rate from thermal video. In: The IEEE Conference on Computer Vision and Pattern Recognition (CVPR) Workshops, June 2013
13. Jing, B., Li, H.: A novel thermal measurement for heart rate (2013)
14. Panasiti, M.S., Cardone, D., Pavone, E.F., Mancini, A., Merla, A., Aglioti, S.M.: Thermal signatures of voluntary deception in ecological conditions. Sci. Rep. **6** (2016)
15. Cardone, D., Merla, A.: New frontiers for applications of thermal infrared imaging devices: computational psychopshysiology in the neurosciences. Sensors **17**(5), 1042 (2017)
16. Paolini, D., Alparone, F.R., Cardone, D., van Beest, I., Merla, A.: The face of ostracism: The impact of the social categorization on the thermal facial responses of the target and the observer. Acta Psychol. **163**, 65–73 (2016)
17. Dowdall, J., Pavlidis, I.T., Tsiamyrtzis, P.: Coalitional tracking. Comput. Vis. Image Underst. **106**(2–3), 205–219 (2007)
18. Kopaczka, M., Acar, K., Merhof, D.: Robust facial landmark detection and face tracking in thermal infrared images using active appearance models. In: Proceedings of the 11th Joint Conference on Computer Vision, Imaging and Computer Graphics Theory and Applications (VISIGRAPP 2016), VISAPP, Rome, Italy, 27–29 February 2016, vol. 4, pp. 150–158 (2016)
19. Kalal, Z., Mikolajczyk, K., Matas, J.: Tracking-learning-detection. IEEE Trans. Pattern Anal. Mach. Intell. **34**(7), 1409–1422 (2012)

MOOGA Parameter Optimization for Onset Detection in EMG Signals

Mateusz Magda[1(✉)], Antonio Martinez-Alvarez[2],
and Sergio Cuenca-Asensi[2]

[1] Department of Computer Science and Management, Computer Science,
Wroclaw University of Technology, Wroclaw, Poland
mateusz.magda@pwr.edu.pl
[2] Department of Computer Technology, University of Alicante, Alicante, Spain

Abstract. Having a knowledge of muscle activity, one can draw conclusions related to human movement, health condition or even behaviour. Manual detection of a muscle activity based on the electromyographic (EMG) signals is a tedious and time-consuming task. Some applications require online indication what entails the need of automatic estimator. Popular and easily accessible method of measuring the signal on a skin surface is burdened with relatively large signal noise. It is only one of the problems that impedes the task of muscle activity onset detection. Statistically advanced automatic estimators depend on various parameters, two of which are usually left to be set by the user, what leaves space for inaccuracy. This paper presents a way of optimizing the results of onset detection algorithms by selecting the best tuple of parameters using a Multi Objective Optimization Genetic Algorithm (MOOGA). An exemplary threshold algorithm presented by Komi, supported by sliding test window solution and based on the signal variance has been trained and tested on a set of 120 signals recorded on Rectus Abdominis (RA). A well known second version of Nondominated Sorting Genetic Algorithm (NSGA-II) has been used in order to improve the quality of onset detection. Assessment criteria are the mean of the absolute value of error and the number of outliers ($|error| > 200$ ms). The mean error for automatically adjusted parameters was 15.94 ms, 370,26% lower than the same algorithm with parameters set manually (W = 100, h = 10).

1 Introduction

Information extracted from EMG signals is useful for the field of automatic affect analysis. An exemplary use of this technology for that purpose was presented by C. Rasch et al. in 2015 [1] where facial EMG was used together with eye tracking for product marketing. The realm of electromyographic (EMG) signal processing gained popularity thanks to the surface electromyography (sEMG) which allows for the noninvasive measurements. This technique has been applied to distinct areas like the remote control of electronic devices, exercise physiology, physical therapy [2], neurophysiological experiments or even athlete's and musician's workouts. The possibility of measuring the signal on a skin surface facilitated and popularized the measuring procedure but at the same time burdened the signal processing. Many factors including

S. Battiato et al. (Eds.): ICIAP 2017 International Workshops, LNCS 10590, pp. 171–180, 2017.
https://doi.org/10.1007/978-3-319-70742-6_16

the electrical conductivity of skin tissue [3] and fat layer caused the increased values of signal noise. Information that can be extracted from the signal depends strongly on the signal to noise ratio which varies dependently on many circumstances. Some of them are the type of recording device, electrodes used during the experiment, wires or wireless connectivity, skin preparation and finally, whether the recording was made on a skin surface or directly in the muscle using an electrode with needle.

For many applications it is necessary to obtain high accuracy of the muscle activity onset indication. Some of them, at the same time, demand high level of reliability. Especially those concerning human health or requiring to work in a real time. That imply the need for more advanced EMG signal processing algorithms. The vast majority of such solutions depend on several parameters, at least two of which are left to be adjusted by the end user. In general, that is the window size and some kind of a threshold value. Since it is too time consuming to manually select the optimal tuple, an automatic solution must be provided. Even though the authors usually provide some clues on how to set these parameters and what should be the optimal values, these propositions are set manually and tested only on their data. It creates space for inaccuracy and lack of reliability. This paper's contribution is describing the application of multi objective optimization genetic algorithm (MOOGA) into the EMG onset detection field. This way scientists can adjust parameters for their algorithms automatically. As an added value of MOOGA algorithm we achieve the multi-objectivity. It provides us with a Pareto front of optimal parameter tuples which can be later picked accordingly to the application area.

Section 2 describes essentials that need to be understood in order to profit from reading this paper. It explains primary concepts of EMG signal processing and MOOGA optimization in the context of muscle onset detection.

2 Background

Muscle activity onset detection basing on EMG signals consists in pointing the precise moment in which the electrical activity starts raising in voltage value. It is related to the moment of a muscle contraction. Basing on that information we can conclude about human movements, even their exact type and moment of the event [4].

In order to detect the onset of EMG automatically various algorithms were proposed in the academia. According to Staude et al. [5] there exists four basic ways of processing the signal: a single observation, a growing test window, a fixed test windows and a sliding test window. Since EMG signals differ in voltage values, shape and other characteristics automatic estimators require setting the internal parameters. The common minimal parameter set of onset detection algorithm is a tuple of w and h. W stands for size of a window frame, that is how many neighboring measurements shall be included in the calculations of statistical factors. H is a threshold, a value that once is exceeded the onset of a muscle is reported. It was originally set by Komi et al. to be 0.03 mV [6] for the single observation.

There exist another approaches to EMG onset detection like sequential analysis, mathematical signal modelling or adaptive linear detectors [7]. MOOGA optimization allows to suit not only two parameters, thus some sequential analysis methods [8] requiring to set more input parameters might be reconsidered to be applied into the field of EMG onset detection. However, in this paper we focus on a simple, slightly modified version of Komi threshold algorithm in order to test the usefulness of automatic parameter fitting and to be able to track the whole process.

2.1   The Problem of Parameter Selection

A vast majority of EMG onset detection methods has at least two parameters left to be adjusted by the user manually. Some, statistically advanced, have even more parameters [9] which strongly depend on the signal characteristics. In order to provide a robust solution, it is inevitable to adapt some kind of automatic parameter optimization. A solution of greedy search space gives the optimal solutions but for a continuous domain of parameters it has an infinite number of possible solutions to revise what makes it impossible. Even after restricting considered parameter values to a reasonable, finite set the execution is too time consuming and is very hard to be applied to this field. A relatively good idea is to deploy a heuristic solution based on the second version of Nondominated Sorting Genetic Algorithm (NSGA-II). It proved a satisfying performance when applied to the related field of Cortical Visual Neuroprosthesis [10]. As an output of this algorithm we achieve the Pareto front - a set of parameter tuples giving the globally best possible solutions [11].

2.2   MOOGA as a Solution for the Problem

The structure of MOOGA reminds of the genetic algorithm since it is built up on it [12] (Fig. 1). The process begins with the initialization stage in which parameters are set and population is created. In the evaluation stage all previously generated candidate solutions are assessed using fitness functions. Then comes the NSGA-II sorting which finds nondominated solutions. In order to do that the sorting algorithm picks globally best solutions according to the first criterion. In case of a draw it selects only those which are not dominated, that is not worse from the others according to the second criterion. The stopping condition checks if the algorithm came to the end. The process ends whenever we reach our goal, that is when a solution we found is better than or equal to the desired one or when it has reached the maximum iteration limit. If at least one of these conditions is satisfied the algorithm ends it task by outputting the final results and correlated parameter tuples which lead to them. If not, the algorithm goes to the stage related to the genetic algorithm. Gene representation of each candidate is determined and the best ones are selected. It creates a kind of a fusion of these solutions by going through the crossover stage. During this stage all genes are divided into parts and new solutions are created by combining them. At the end of this phase a selective mutation takes place; the algorithm takes a randomly picked cromosoma with a given probability and changes its value. Mutation stage provides a factor of randomness, in order to avoid getting stuck in one place of the subspace of possible solutions. After all these steps the candidates go again through the stage of evaluation using fitness function. They are sorted and basing on the stopping condition the decision is made whether to finish the whole process or go back to the cycle.

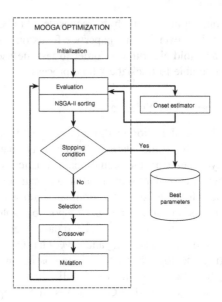

Fig. 1. Scheme of MOOGA algorithm adapted to onset detection

3   Case Study

In order to revise the capability of proposed parameter optimization method a basic muscle activity onset estimator has been prepared. It consists of two basic ideas. It is built up on a simple threshold algorithm proposed by Komi et al. [6]

$$emg(i) > h .\qquad(1)$$

which can be enhanced by using a sliding test window, making the solution more robust for a single voltage peaks.

$$Var\ (\ emg(i\ -\ w/2,\ i\ +\ w/2)) > h * iVar\ ,\ where:$$
$$i-\ index(w/2, 5000 - w/2),\ w-\ testing\ window\ size,\ iVar-\ initial\ variance$$
$$(2)$$

Thus, we decided to enhance it by a sliding test window mechanism and to replace the mean factor with more appropriate variance. We assumed that the first 100 samples of a signal do not contain the muscle activity and used it for adjusting to the specific case of each sequence. The final solution measures the variance of the first 100 samples, multiplies it by a threshold, which beside the size of a sliding test window is one of the input parameters, and compares achieved value with the variance of forthcoming sample windows. If the calculated value exceeds it a muscle activity is reported.

3.1   EMG Dataset

The electrical activity has been recorded by 6 surface electrodes placed on the Rectus Abdominis muscle. The exact description of data collection process has been described in details by Agnieszka Szpala [13] and Mateusz Magda [14]. For the purpose of this experiment 120 signals were selected. The dataset was divided into two equinumerous groups. The first has been used for adjusting the parameters and the second one - for testing. Below you can observe the format of data used in the experiment (Table 1).

Table 1. Testing dataset shape

Electrode 1	Electrode 2	...	Electrode 6	Onset
Recording 1	Recording 1	...	Recording 1	1st electrode onset
Recording 2	Recording 2	...	Recording 2	2nd electrode onset
Recording 3	Recording 3	...	Recording 3	3rd electrode onset
Recording 4	Recording 4	...	Recording 4	4th electrode onset
...	...	...	...	5th electrode onset
...	...	...	...	6th electrode onset

3.2   Parameter Fitting

The parameters have been selected automatically, according to the MOOGA NSGA-II algorithm described in the Sect. 2.2 above. The EMG estimator had to be adjusted in order to fit to the procedure. We made it by leaving only data, window size and threshold as an input. The output consists of the mean error and the number of the outliers. The upper and lower bounds of window size and threshold have been set respectively to (20–80) and (5–500). In such a form the estimator could be injected into the MOOGA loop. The whole process was limited in time to one hour of a single execution and in maximal number of generations which was set to 400. Remaining parameters relevant to the genetic algorithm were set as follows: population size –80, mutation factor –0.05, probability distribution - uniform. In the last execution of MOOGA algorithm the time constraint has been removed.

4   Results

Calculating the optimal parameter tuple as described in the above section we achieved the following results. Below we present visualized the space of revised parameter tuples, their results, Pareto front of solutions taken from the last population and the histogram of final errors. At the end of this section we include a Table 2 presenting its results. The process of browsing through all possible parameter tuples was supported by MOOGA algorithm using NSGAII as a sorting method and was executed on the learning part of the dataset. The revision of those parameters, i.e. the part related with final results has been conducted using the third point of the Pareto front and was executed on the testing part of the dataset. The middle point of the Pareto front meets the requirements for both criteria. It provides us with a solution which is both accurate and reliable, giving a considerably small number of outliers.

Table 2. Results

	Mean error	|Mean error|	% of outliers
3rd tuple of Pareto	15.94 ms	86.79 ms	3,57%

Figures 2 and 3 are enclosed for the illustration purpose and show the work of MOOGA algorithm. They both show data taken from randomly chosen, same population. Figure 2 shows the distribution of tested parameter tuples taken from the selected population. It represents one stage of browsing the space of possible solutions. We can observe that the space of solutions was browsed uniformly in a randomized way, without leaving unrevised territories. It is crucial to ensure the proper search space exploration, especially if it is considerably large. Leaving unrevised space exposes the risk of not finding the global optimum. Below we present the results for all individuals found in the previous stage. All candidates were evaluated and their values of fitness function are presented in Fig. 3. Each individual is represented with a mean error and the number of outliers. We can observe an initial stage of Pareto front created by the four bottom points of the figure. As it is the middle stage of MOOGA algorithm the population of solutions is spread all over the figure. In the final stages all solutions converge to the Pareto front.

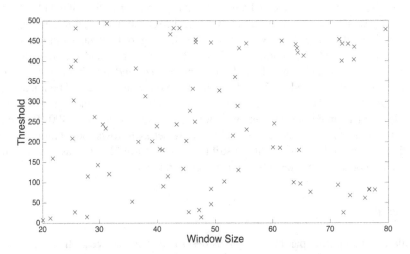

Fig. 2. Browsed set of parameters (one population)

The above Fig. 4 shows the final output of MOOGA algorithm, a Pareto front, i.e. the set of results for optimal parameter tuples. This figure shows the relation between the absolute value of mean error measured in milliseconds and the number of outliers. We can observe the necessity of a tradeoff between the accuracy and reliability that has to be made. The lower the mean error the higher the number of outliers. Some applications have a demand on a robust solution because false indications can cause hazardous situation like in case of artificial limbs or almost every real-time system. On

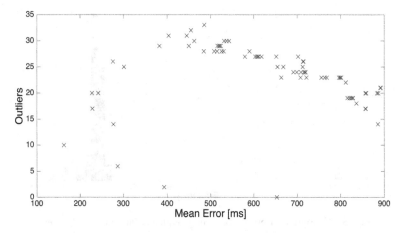

Fig. 3. Space of results for solutions found during MOOGA calculation

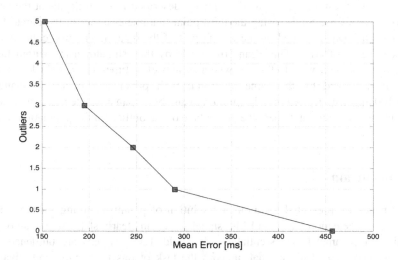

Fig. 4. Pareto front for threshold algorithm

the other side some may accept outliers in return for the highest possible accuracy as it is in case of physiological experiments in which every suspicious assessment can be revised by a specialist.

Histogram shown in the above Fig. 5 shows the final results, i.e. the error values achieved using parameters selected by MOOGA. This is the illustration of how the algorithm with automatically selected parameters performs on the testing part of the dataset. Looking at the histogram we can see that a vast majority of errors are constrained within the range of (–200 ms, 200 ms) what classifies them as non-outliers. The results are grouped around the value of 0 ms. There appear only 2 outliers which is less than 3,6% of the whole population.

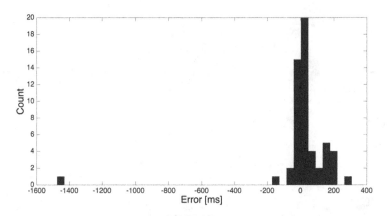

Fig. 5. Histogram of errors for testing sequence (automatic selection)

Table 2 shows the final results in a form of a summary. Results presented in it are the outcome of testing the prepared estimator, described more in details at the beginning of Sect. 3 Case Study, using the third point (parameter tuple) of the Pareto front. The algorithm was executed on the testing part of the dataset. The first column show the mean value of error. The mean error made by the estimator using automatically adjusted parameters was 15.94 ms, which is almost 4 times (370,26%) lower than 74.96 ms achieved by the same algorithm with parameters being set manually (W = 100, h = 10). In the second column we can observe an absolute value of the same error. In the third column appear the percentage of the outliers in the population of final results.

5   Conclusion

In this paper we presented an automatic solution of parameter fitting for the area of muscle onset detection based on EMG signals. We can clearly state that the automatic selection of parameters is essential for this field. EMG signals are burdened with relatively large signal noise what impedes the task of onset detection and advanced solutions must be provided in order to automatically detect the real onset of a muscle. MOOGA is a perfect solution for adjusting parameters of the onset detection algorithms. In order to test the proposed solution we chose the middle point of the Pareto front. However, we would like to point out, that accordingly to the needs, one may want to select different point from the Pareto front to meet the needs of particular application area. In this study case it revealed 4 times higher accuracy than the manual selection. Slow SNR (signal to noise) ratio is not the only obstacle in the process of extracting information from the signal. Depending on the place of the electrode placement crosstalks from surrounding muscles can also be the issue [15, 16]. It is extremely important to take it into account while measuring signal in the aggregation of various muscles, e.g. the forearm. Additionally, in case of trunk muscles cardiac crosstalks may appear in the recorded signal [17]. One must be aware of the above hindrances while processing the EMG signals.

For future improvement one can consider optimization by the recursive calculation of variance or appropriate statistical factor. Since MOOGA needs to evaluate the fitness thousands of times, it is inevitable to optimize the calculations within tested algorithm. Even though this solution proves good performance encountering global optima it is worth considering to allude the local optima like in two stage estimator [18].

References

1. Rasch, C., Louviere, J.J., Teichert, T.: Using facial EMG and eye tracking to study integral affect in discrete choice experiments. J. Choice Model. **14**, 32–47 (2015)
2. Merletti, R., Farina, D.: Surface Electromyography: Physiology, Engineering and Applications. Wiley, Hoboken (2016)
3. Tubbs, R.S., Rizk, E., Shoja, M.M., Loukas, M., Barbaro, N., Spinner, R.J.: Nerves and Nerve Injuries. Pain, Treatment, Injury, Disease and Future Directions, vol. 12. Academic Press, London (2015)
4. Angelov, P., Gegov, A., Jayne, C., Shen, Q. (Eds.): Advances in Computational Intelligence Systems: Contributions Presented at the 16th UK Workshop on Computational Intelligence, 7–9 September 2016. Springer, Lancaster, UK (2016)
5. Staude, G., Wolf, W.: Objective motor response onset detection in surface myoelectric signals. Med. Eng. Phys. **21**, 449–467 (1999)
6. Cavanagh, P.R., Komi, P.V.: Electromechanical delay in human skeletal muscle under concentric and eccentric contractions. Eur. J. Appl. Physiol. **42**, 159–163 (1979)
7. Bengacemi, H., Mesloub, A., Ouldali, A., Abed-Meraim, K.: Adaptive linear energy detector based on onset and offset electromyography activity detection. In: 2017 6th International Conference on Systems and Control (ICSC), pp. 409–413 (2017)
8. Tartakovsky, A., Nikiforov, I., Basseville, M.: Sequential Analysis: Hypothesis Testing and Changepoint Detection. CRC Press, Boca Raton (2014)
9. Staude, G., Flachenecker, C., Daumer, M., Wolf, W.: Onset detection in surface electromyographic signals: a systematic comparison of methods. EURASIP J. Adv. Signal Process. **2001**, 867853 (2001)
10. Martínez-Álvarez, A., Crespo-Cano, R., Díaz-Tahoces, A., Cuenca-Asensi, S., Ferrández Vicente, J.M., Fernández, E.: Automatic tuning of a retina model for a cortical visual neuroprosthesis using a multi-objective optimization genetic algorithm. Int. J. Neural Syst. **26**, 1650021 (2016)
11. He, Z.: Pareto-optimality is a criterion uniting efficiency and justice. In: 2011 IEEE 18th International Conference on Industrial Engineering and Engineering Management, pp. 406–408 (2011)
12. Deb, K., Agrawal, S., Pratap, A., Meyarivan, T.: A fast elitist non-dominated sorting genetic algorithm for multi-objective optimization: NSGA-II. In: Schoenauer, M., Deb, K., Rudolph, G., Yao, X., Lutton, E., Merelo, J.J., Schwefel, H.-P. (eds.) PPSN 2000. LNCS, vol. 1917, pp. 849–858. Springer, Heidelberg (2000). https://doi.org/10.1007/3-540-45356-3_83
13. Szpala, A., Rutkowska-Kucharska, A., Drapała, J., Brzostowski, K., Zawadzki, J.: Asymmetry of electromechanical delay (EMD) and torque in the muscles stabilizing spinal column. Acta Bioeng. Biomech. **12**, 11–18 (2010)
14. Magda, M.: EMG onset detection - a hidden factor. In: CBU International Conference Proceedings, vol. 4, pp. 873–878 (2016)

15. Mezzarane, R.A., Kohn, A.F.: A method to estimate EMG crosstalk between two muscles based on the silent period following an H-reflex. Med. Eng. Phys. **31**, 1331–1336 (2009)
16. Winter, D.A., Fuglevand, A.J., Archer, S.E.: Crosstalk in surface electromyography: Theoretical and practical estimates. J. Electromyogr. Kinesiol. **4**, 15–26 (1994)
17. Zhou, P., Zhang, X.: A novel technique for muscle onset detection using surface EMG signals without removal of ECG artifacts. Physiol. Meas. **35**, 45–54 (2014)
18. Drapała, J., Brzostowski, K., Szpala, A., Rutkowska-Kucharska, A.: Two stage EMG onset detection method. Arch. Control Sci. **22**, 427–440 (2013)

A Note on Modelling a Somatic Motor Space for Affective Facial Expressions

Alessandro D'Amelio[1], Vittorio Cuculo[1,2], Giuliano Grossi[1],
Raffaella Lanzarotti[1(✉)], and Jianyi Lin[3]

[1] PHuSe Lab - Dipartimento di Informatica, Università degli Studi di Milano,
Via Comelico 39/41, Milano, Italy
alessandro.damelio@studenti.unimi.it, vittorio.cuculo@unimi.it,
{grossi,lanzarotti}@di.unimi.it
[2] Dipartimento di Matematica, Università degli Studi di Milano,
Via Cesare Saldini 50, Milano, Italy
[3] Department of Mathematics, Khalifa University of Science and Technology,
Abu Dhabi, United Arab Emirates
jianyi.lin@kustar.ac.ae

Abstract. We discuss modelling issues related to the design of a somatic facial motor space. The variants proposed are conceived to be part of a larger system for dealing with simulation-based face emotion analysis along dual interactions.

Keywords: Emotion · Human-agent interaction · Simulation
Kalman filter · Probabilistic generative models

1 Introduction

In the course of actual interactions (human-human or human-agent), the unfolding of emotional episodes is likely to follow a different route than pursued by a large body of work in affective facial expression analysis where a computer vision "pipeline-based" approach is followed (feature extraction then recognition/classification [14]). Facial expressions are facial actions and are likely to draw on simulation mechanisms underlying action perception in general [16]. These rely on mirroring processes that ground the capability of own reproduction of the action in question "as if" a similar action were performed or a similar emotion experienced.

At the heart of the simulation-based framework is the modelling of a suitable visuomotor mapping of perceived facial cues to an internal somatic motor space, which, in turn, works side by side with core affect components via forward and backward connections [16]. Importantly, such internal motor space must be endowed with generative capabilities, so to support actual simulation (e.g. facial mimicry). In this note we discuss, from a probabilistic standpoint, some modelling issues that arise in this effort. A relevant one is the hierarchy of levels of predictive control (for an in-depth discussion see [11]).

© Springer International Publishing AG 2017
S. Battiato et al. (Eds.): ICIAP 2017 International Workshops, LNCS 10590, pp. 181–188, 2017.
https://doi.org/10.1007/978-3-319-70742-6_17

Not much effort has been spent in such direction. We build on [15], addressing a mapping from visual cues to a probabilistic core affect space within a simulation-based paradigm. However, in that case, only static images are considered, and most important, motor representation is not explicitly addressed. An even simpler variant is presented in [7]. Though not addressing the issue of motor simulation, Fan *et al.* [6] exploit the motor control sequence $\mathbf{m}(t)$ - derived from a 3D shape model as the observation input to a Kalman filter. The authors are mostly concerned with the classification of basic emotions, rather than building a continuous latent space of actions akin to support visuomotor learning and simulation.

2   Modelling Issues

We assume that the observer $\mathcal{O}$ perceives the facial action of the expresser $\mathcal{E}$ in terms of the visible cues, say $\mathbf{y}_{\mathcal{E}}$, captured by his visual system and maps such cues onto his own internal motor action representation (*visuomotor mapping* [9]). The observer's internal representation not only "stands for" the visual signalling generated by $\mathcal{E}$, but, in a simulation-based account of facial expression analysis, it must be apt to generate the internal facial dynamics for mirroring that of $\mathcal{E}$.

From a modelling perspective, the egocentric motor representation of the face of agent $\mathcal{I} \in \{\mathcal{E}, \mathcal{O}\}$ is accounted for by the state-space RV $\mathbf{w}(t) = \mathbf{w}(\mathbf{m}(t), \mathbf{s}_{\mathcal{I}})$.

Here, $\mathbf{s}_{\mathcal{I}}$ stands for a set of static parameters that control the biometric characteristics of each individual $\mathcal{I} \in \{\mathcal{E}, \mathcal{O}\}$; we assume that observer's parameters $\mathbf{s}_{\mathcal{O}}$ are given, while expresser's parameter $\mathbf{s}_{\mathcal{E}}$ are inferred by the observer at the onset of the interaction.

The action control is given by the motor parameters $\mathbf{m}(t)$ controlling the facial deformation due to muscle action. Motor control parameters $\mathbf{m}(t)$ tune the actual evolution of the internal facial dynamics $\mathbf{w}(t)$, but are in turn governed by a specific action which we represent as a trajectory in a latent action state-space, formalised via the time-varying hidden RV $\mathbf{h}(t)$. The latent facial action state-space dynamics is affect-driven, since in the context of affective interactions can be assumed to be "biased" by the dynamics of the core affect [13].

The generative stage can be written in the form of an ancestral sampling procedure on the Probabilistic Graphical Model (PGM) shown in Fig. 1a:

1. Sampling a time dependent action state from the latent affect-driven action space:

$$\widetilde{\mathbf{h}}(t+1) \sim P(\mathbf{h}(t+1) \mid \mathbf{h}(t)); \tag{1}$$

2. Sampling facial action control parameters conditioned on the current affect-state and on the inferred control parameters:

$$\widetilde{\mathbf{m}}(t+1) \sim P(\mathbf{m}(t+1) \mid \widetilde{\mathbf{h}}(t+1)), \tag{2}$$

3. Motor-state space dynamics towards visuomotor mapping

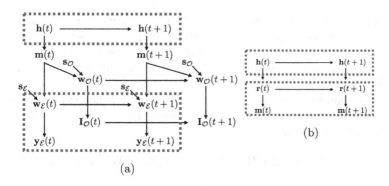

Fig. 1. Modelling issues at a glance. (a): the dynamic PGM representation of the model. The dashed boxes show the two levels of predictive control. (b): the Kalman-based predictive component summarised as a further level of control within the original PGM

(a) Use sampled control parameters, and sample a facial configuration of the expresser $\mathcal{E}$, by setting $\mathbf{w}_\mathcal{E}(t+1) = \mathbf{w}(\widetilde{\mathbf{m}}(t+1), \mathbf{s}_\mathcal{E})$:

$$\widetilde{\mathbf{w}}_\mathcal{E}(t+1) \sim P(\mathbf{w}_\mathcal{E}(t+1) \mid \mathbf{w}(t), \widetilde{\mathbf{m}}(t+1)) \tag{3}$$

(b) Sample facial landmarks in expresser visual space

$$\widetilde{\mathbf{y}}_\mathcal{E}(t+1) \sim P(\mathbf{y}_\mathcal{E}(t+1) \mid \widetilde{\mathbf{w}}_\mathcal{E}(t+1)) \tag{4}$$

If external simulation (actual facial mimicry) is enabled, the visible facial expression of the observer can be obtained by setting $\mathbf{w}(t+1) = \mathbf{w}_\mathcal{O}(\widetilde{\mathbf{m}}(t+1), \mathbf{s}_\mathcal{O})$. Then state is sampled analogously to Eq. 5 and facial mimicry generated via $\widetilde{\mathbf{I}}_\mathcal{O}(t+1) \sim P(\mathbf{I}_\mathcal{O}(t+1) \mid \mathbf{w}(t+1), \mathbf{I}_\mathcal{O}(t))$.

Note that such a generative model, focusing on the expresser's side, can be seen as a hierarchical predictive control model where the lowest level predicts the motor state and then generates an estimate of expresser's visual landmarks. At this level, novel predictions are governed by the error or discrepancy between the estimated landmarks and the observation of expresser's landmarks. Indeed, this level can be seen as an instance of model-based predictive coding that has been widely adopted in the video processing realm.

At the highest level, that is prediction, parameter estimation and error correction are implicitly obtained by relying on the action state-space dynamics, and on the optimization procedures in such latent space. This is the meaning of Eq. 2. This has some modelling compactness and efficiency advantages, whilst drawbacks could occur due to the fact that, in principle, the lower dimensionality action space (that is, in turn, related to core affect dynamics) might operate on a coarser time scale than that of motor parameter dynamics. In a more general setting one should consider parameter sampling based on the conditional distribution $P(\mathbf{m}(t+1) \mid \widehat{\mathbf{m}}(t), \widehat{\mathbf{h}}(t+1))$, where the dynamics is explicitly handled.

To suitably ground the discussion, the observer's internal motor space is formalised as a 3D *deformable shape model* consisting of a collection of N vertices represented by $\mathbf{w} = [\mathbf{w}_1 \cdots \mathbf{w}_N] \in \mathbb{R}^{3 \times N}$, where every 3-dimensional vector $\mathbf{w}_i = (X_i, Y_i, Z_i)^T$ corresponds to the i-th vertex in the model. The dynamical evolution of the motor state is captured in the model by the dependence of the vectors upon the time variable t, so that each vertex follows a curve $\mathbf{w}_i(t) = (X_i(t), Y_i(t), Z_i(t))^T$.

It can be shown that under Helmholtz's fundamental theorem for deformable bodies [8] and small rotations, prediction of face motion at vertex i can be written (assuming unitary time step) as:

$$\mathbf{w}_i(t+1) = \mathbf{w}_i(t) + \mathbf{R}(t)\mathbf{w}_i(t) + \mathbf{dW}_i^S \mathbf{s} + \mathbf{dW}_i^M \mathbf{m}(t) + \mathbf{t}(t). \qquad (5)$$

where the pose parameters $\boldsymbol{\theta}(t) = (\mathbf{R}(t), \mathbf{t}(t))$ represent the rotation matrix $\mathbf{R}(\omega) \in SO(3)$ with angular velocity vector $\omega = (\omega_x, \omega_y, \omega_z)$ and the translation vector, respectively, that is the global rigid motion constrained by cranial pose dynamics. As to the deformation term, $\mathbf{dW}_i^S \in \mathbb{R}^{3 \times N_s}$ and $\mathbf{dW}_i^M \in \mathbb{R}^{3 \times N_m}$ are respectively the matrices of Shape Unit (SU) and Action Unit Vector (AUV) deformation. Individual biometric control parameters $\mathbf{s}$ are considered fixed along the interaction, for both expresser and observer. Equation 5 applied to all vertices represents the motor state of the 3D face model evolving in time, i.e. the forward model.

The generation (estimate) of expresser's visual landmarks is obtained as the projection of the 3D vertices on the 2D image coordinate system, under weak perspective projection (given the small depth of the face [10]), namely $\widehat{\mathbf{y}}_{\mathcal{E},l} = \mathcal{T}\widetilde{\mathbf{w}}_{\mathcal{E},l}$ where l indexes the L vertices that are in correspondence with extracted facial landmarks. Under Gaussian assumption, parameter inference boils down to the negative log-likelihood minimisation problem, which gives the "observed" $\widehat{\mathbf{m}}(t)$ and where the error control is accounted for by term $\|\mathbf{y}_{\mathcal{E},l} - \widehat{\mathbf{y}}_{\mathcal{E},l}\|^2$.

As to the top control level, the latent action space can be specified by resorting to a dynamical variational Gaussian Process Latent Variable Model (DVGP-LVM, [4]). The variational $\mathcal{GP}$ provides an efficient nonlinear mapping. In such setting, Eqs. 1 and 2 are suitably implemented, and for a single parameter m_k, Eq. 2 becomes

$$m_k(t) = f_k(\mathbf{h}(t)) + \nu_\mathbf{h}(t), \quad \nu_\mathbf{h} \sim \mathcal{N}(0, \sigma_\mathbf{h}^2), \qquad (6)$$

where f_k is a latent mapping from the low dimensional action space to the k-th dimension of the parameter space of $\mathbf{m}$. The individual components of the latent function $\mathbf{h}$ are taken to be independent sample paths drawn from a Gaussian process with covariance function $k_h(t, t')$ and the components of $\mathbf{f}$ are independent draws from a Gaussian process with covariance function $k_f(\mathbf{h}(t), \mathbf{h}(t'))$, which determines the properties of the latent mapping.

To cope with limitations discussed above, we introduce a further control level (see Fig. 1b) where $\widetilde{\mathbf{m}}$ and related covariances, say Σ_{td}, serve as top-down bias. To such end we introduce a state variable $\mathbf{r}$ and design a prediction/correct scheme in the form of the Kalman filter shaped as proposed in [12].

In our case the ordinary Kalman filter assumes a predicted observation

$$\overline{\mathbf{m}}(t) = \mathbf{H}(t)\overline{\mathbf{r}}(t) + \boldsymbol{\zeta}(t), \qquad \boldsymbol{\zeta}(t) \sim \mathcal{N}(0, \Sigma_{bu}), \qquad (7)$$

with $\Sigma_{bu} = [\zeta(t)\zeta^T(t)]$ is the covariance of the "bottom up" noise ζ affecting observations $\overline{\mathbf{m}}$. Kalman filter dynamics can be written as a prediction step followed by a measurement or correction step. State prediction can be written as

$$\overline{\mathbf{r}}(t+1) = \mathbf{A}\widehat{\mathbf{r}}(t) + \boldsymbol{\eta}(t) \tag{8}$$

where $\boldsymbol{\eta}(t) \sim \mathcal{N}(\boldsymbol{\mu_r}(t), \Sigma_{\mathbf{r}}(t), \Sigma_{\mathbf{r}}(t) = E[(\boldsymbol{\eta}(t) - \boldsymbol{\mu_r}(t))(\boldsymbol{\eta}(t) - \boldsymbol{\mu_r}(t))^T]$. The evolution of $\overline{\mathbf{r}}$ goes together with covariance prediction $\mathbf{M}(t+1) = \mathbf{A}\mathbf{N}(t)\mathbf{A}^T + \Sigma_{\mathbf{r}}(t)$ and $\mathbf{N} = \mathbf{M}^{-1}(t) + \mathbf{H}^T\Sigma_{bu}^{-1}\mathbf{H}$ is a normalization matrix that maintains the covariance of the estimated state.

The update step corrects prediction by taking into account the measurement error

$$\widetilde{\mathbf{r}}(t+1) = \overline{\mathbf{r}}(t+1) + \mathcal{K}(t+1)(\widehat{\mathbf{m}}(t+1) - \overline{\mathbf{m}}(t+1)) \tag{9}$$

where $\mathbf{H}\overline{\mathbf{r}}(t+1)$ is the predicted measurement and $\mathcal{K}$ is the Kalman gain which is updated as $\mathcal{K}(t+1) = \mathbf{N}^{-1}\mathbf{H}^T\Sigma_{bu}^{-1}$.

The Kalman filter equation is obtained by combining Eqs. 8 and 9:

$$\widehat{\mathbf{r}}(t+1) = \mathbf{A}(\overline{\mathbf{r}}(t) + \mathcal{K}(t)(\widehat{\mathbf{m}}(t) - \overline{\mathbf{m}}(t))) + \boldsymbol{\eta}(t). \tag{10}$$

Set $\mathcal{K}_{bu} = \mathcal{K}$ $\mathbf{r}_{td} = \widetilde{\mathbf{m}}$ and define the top-down Kalman gain $\mathcal{K}_{td} = \mathbf{N}\Sigma_{td}$, Σ_{td} being the top-down covariance matrix provided by the upper-most level. Then the update step in Eq. 8 can be rewritten as

$$\widetilde{\mathbf{r}}(t+1) = \overline{\mathbf{r}}(t+1) + \mathcal{K}_{bu}(t+1)(\widehat{\mathbf{m}}(t+1) - \overline{\mathbf{m}}(t+1)) + \\ \mathcal{K}_{td}(t+1)(\widehat{\mathbf{r}}_{td}(t+1) - \overline{\mathbf{r}}(t+1)) - \mathbf{N}g(\overline{\mathbf{r}}(t+1)) \tag{11}$$

where the last term is a decay that penalizes overfitting of data and g an exponentially decreasing function. Eventually,

$$\widehat{\mathbf{r}}(t+1) = \mathbf{A}(\overline{\mathbf{r}}(t) + \mathcal{K}_{bu}(t)(\widehat{\mathbf{m}}(t) - \overline{\mathbf{m}}(t)) + \mathcal{K}_{td}(t+1)(\widehat{\mathbf{r}}_{td}(t) - \overline{\mathbf{r}}(t)) - \mathbf{N}g(\overline{\mathbf{r}}(t))) + \boldsymbol{\eta}(t). \tag{12}$$

3   Preliminary Results

We focus on the behaviour of the observer's visuomotor simulation component when the motor-state space is controlled either by "raw" or by Kalman filtered parameters. We also compare for completeness with parameters obtained by a Kalman smoother, though this is unsuitable for online processing.

In the simulations, expresser's landmarks $\mathbf{y}_\mathcal{E}$ are inferred via the Constrained Local Neural Field (CLNF) [2]; a viable alternative is in [17] (or its sparse variants, e.g. [3]).

For the motor space representation $\mathbf{w}$ and its deformations we exploit the 3D face model Candide-3 [1], which is a 3D wireframe model of approximately 113 vertices $\mathbf{w}_i$ and 184 triangles, that easily fits our needs. Indeed, Candide directly accounts for encoding the matrices of Shape Unit (SU) and Action Unit Vector (AUV) deformations parameters at vertices ($\mathbf{dW}_i^S$ and $\mathbf{dW}_i^M$) together with related control parameters **s** and **m**, respectively. AUVs determines a change in face geometry and implement a subset of the Ekman's Action Units of FACS [5]. The considered AUVs ($N_{AUV} = 11$) are $AUV_k, k = 0, 2, 3, 5, 6, 7, 8, 9, 10, 11, 14$. Observer's parameters s_O are derived offline, and expresser's parameters $s_{\mathcal{E}}$ inferred through the perceptual process at the very onset of the interaction.

As to Kalman based control, we consider the state variable as formed by position and velocity for all AUVs. Only the position vectors are eventually used to represent the motor action parameters. Parameter learning is performed via the EM algorithm. In the same framework, we also apply Kalman smoothing for comparison.

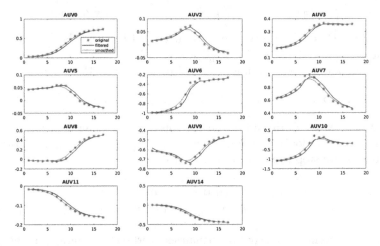

Fig. 2. Result of the Kalman filter (blue) and Kalman smoother (green) observations for each of the considered AUVs, related to the 'disgust' emotion. (Color figure online)

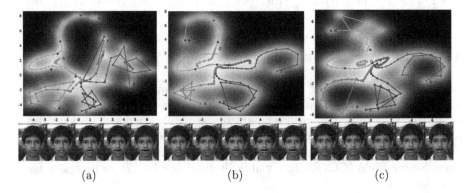

Fig. 3. Walking on the 'Happiness' trajectory. Top panels show the learned latent action spaces. To each red dot in top latent space corresponds facial synthesis (bottom panels). Latent space is learned by using raw motor parameters in a, Kalman filter state in b and Kalman smoother in c.

Due to limitations of space, we provide an excerpt of typical results so far achieved. Also, to provide clear clues to the reader these are related to motor trajectories of prototypical expressions (basic emotions), though the facial action space is a continuous manifold.

Figure 2 shows the result of the Kalman filter and smoother, as well as the original motor parameters from the prototypical "disgust" emotion of a subject from the Cohn-Kanade dataset.

Most important, is the latent action manifold as learned by adopting the different control schemes. One example is provided in Fig. 3, where basic emotion trajectories are shown within the GP-LVM latent space.

4   Conclusive Remarks

We have discussed modelling issues that arise in the design of a somatic facial motor space for affective interactions. We have considered different levels of hierarchical control for the generation and learning of motor control parameters tuning the unfolding of the facial expression. Preliminary results show that it is important to evaluate parameter dynamics not *per se* but related to the construction and the dynamics of the latent action space. On the example provided, and similar to other results, the Kalman level seems, in general, to better separate and constrain trajectories as produced along discrete expressions. This is consistent with the idea that basic expressions originate as prototypes that cluster and partition continuous manifolds [13]. As expected, the Kalman smoother achieves smoother results, however it is unsuitable to provide online control. On the other hand, the direct implicit control via the action space could gain some currency as to the parsimony of such representation.

We surmise that conclusive arguments on the choice between one or the other scheme need to take into account, beyond the latent action space, the continuous manifold of the core affect.

Acknowledgments. This research was carried out as part of the project "Interpreting emotions: a computational tool integrating facial expressions and biosignals based shape analysis and bayesian networks", supported by the Italian Government, managed by MIUR, financed by the *Future in Research* Fund.

References

1. Ahlberg, J.: CANDIDE-3 an updated parameterized face. Technical report. LiTH-ISY-R-2326, Linköping University, Department of Electrical Engineering, Linköping, Sweden (2010)
2. Baltrušaitis, T., Robinson, P., Morency, L.P.: Constrained local neural fields for robust facial landmark detection in the wild. In: Proceedings of the IEEE International Conference on Computer Vision Workshops, pp. 354–361 (2013)
3. Cuculo, V., Lanzarotti, R., Boccignone, G.: Using sparse coding for landmark localization in facial expressions. In: 5th European Workshop on Visual Information Processing (EUVIP), pp. 1–6, December 2014

4. Damianou, A.C., Titsias, M.K., Lawrence, N.D.: Variational inference for latent variables and uncertain inputs in Gaussian processes. J. Mach. Learn. Res. (JMLR) **17**(1), 1425–1486 (2016)
5. Ekman, P., Rosenberg, E.L.: What the Face Reveals: Basic and Applied Studies of Spontaneous Expression Using the Facial Action Coding System (FACS). Oxford University Press, New York (1997)
6. Fan, P., Gonzalez, I., Enescu, V., Sahli, H., Jiang, D.: Kalman filter-based facial emotional expression recognition. In: D'Mello, S., Graesser, A., Schuller, B., Martin, J.-C. (eds.) ACII 2011. LNCS, vol. 6974, pp. 497–506. Springer, Heidelberg (2011). https://doi.org/10.1007/978-3-642-24600-5_53
7. García, H.F., Álvarez, M.A., Orozco, Á.: Gaussian process dynamical models for emotion recognition. In: Bebis, G., Boyle, R., Parvin, B., Koracin, D., McMahan, R., Jerald, J., Zhang, H., Drucker, S.M., Kambhamettu, C., El Choubassi, M., Deng, Z., Carlson, M. (eds.) ISVC 2014. LNCS, vol. 8888, pp. 799–808. Springer, Cham (2014). https://doi.org/10.1007/978-3-319-14364-4_77
8. von Helmholtz, H.: Über integrale der hydrodynamischen gleichungen welche den wirbelbewegungen entsprechen. Crelles J. **55**, 25–55 (1858)
9. Lopes, M., Santos-Victor, J.: Visual learning by imitation with motor representations. IEEE Trans. Sys. Man Cybern. Part B Cybern. **35**(3), 438–449 (2005)
10. Orozco, J., Rudovic, O., Gonzlez, J., Pantic, M.: Hierarchical on-line appearance-based tracking for 3D head pose, eyebrows, lips, eyelids and irises. Image Vis. Comput. **31**(4), 322–340 (2013)
11. Pickering, M.J., Clark, A.: Getting ahead: forward models and their place in cognitive architecture. Trends Cogn. Sci. **18**(9), 451–456 (2014)
12. Rao, R.P., Ballard, D.H.: Dynamic model of visual recognition predicts neural response properties in the visual cortex. Neural Comput. **9**(4), 721–763 (1997)
13. Russell, J.A.: Core aect and the psychological construction of emotion. Psychol. Rev. **110**(1), 145 (2003)
14. Sariyanidi, E., Gunes, H., Cavallaro, A.: Automatic analysis of facial affect: a survey of registration, representation, and recognition. IEEE Trans. Patt. Anal. Mach. Intell. **37**(6), 1113–1133 (2015)
15. Vitale, J., Williams, M.A., Johnston, B., Boccignone, G.: Affective facial expression processing via simulation: a probabilistic model. Biologically Inspired Cogn. Architectures J. **10**, 30–41 (2014)
16. Wood, A., Rychlowska, M., Korb, S., Niedenthal, P.: Fashioning the face: sensorimotor simulation contributes to facial expression recognition. Trends Cogn. Sci. **20**(3), 227–240 (2016)
17. Zhu, X., Ramanan, D.: Face detection, pose estimation, and landmark localization in the wild. In: Proceedings of IEEE CVPR, pp. 2879–2886 (2012)

Taking the Hidden Route: Deep Mapping of Affect via 3D Neural Networks

Claudio Ceruti[1], Vittorio Cuculo[1,2], Alessandro D'Amelio[1], Giuliano Grossi[1], and Raffaella Lanzarotti[1(✉)]

[1] PHuSe Lab - Dipartimento di Informatica, Università degli Studi di Milano,
Via Comelico 39/41, Milano, Italy
{claudio.ceruti,vittorio.cuculo}@unimi.it,
alessandro.damelio@studenti.unimi.it,
{grossi,lanzarotti}@di.unimi.it
[2] Dipartimento di Matematica, Università degli Studi di Milano,
Via Cesare Saldini 50, Milano, Italy

Abstract. In this note we address the problem of providing a fast, automatic, and coarse processing of the early mapping from emotional facial expression stimuli to the basic continuous dimensions of the core affect representation of emotions, namely valence and arousal. Taking stock of results in affective neuroscience, such mapping is assumed to be the earliest stage of a complex unfolding of processes that eventually entail detailed perception and emotional reaction involving the proper body.

Thus, differently from the vast majority of approaches in the field of affective facial expression processing, we assume and design such a feedforward mechanism as a preliminary step to provide a suitable prior to the subsequent core affect dynamics, in which recognition is actually grounded. To this end we conceive and exploit a 3D spatiotemporal deep network as a suitable architecture to instantiate such early component, and experiments on the MAHNOB dataset prove the rationality of this approach.

Keywords: Deep neural networks · Continuous affect space

1 Introduction

Facial expression (FE) is the most effective modality for emotion display [8] and humans have developed specific skills to recognize even subtle expression changes [2]. FEs are generated by rapid (between 250 ms to 5 s) contraction of facial muscles. The accurate measure of FE could be delegated to the fEMG [7,19] or accomplished by computer vision techniques. In this vein, a plethora of approaches have been proposed ranging from local to holistic approaches, adopting deformation or motion-based models, being image or model-based (for an exhaustive discussion of FE methods see the survey [27]).

However, as a general comment on the large body of work that has been done in the field of affective FE detection/analysis, the vast majority of

© Springer International Publishing AG 2017
S. Battiato et al. (Eds.): ICIAP 2017 International Workshops, LNCS 10590, pp. 189–196, 2017.
https://doi.org/10.1007/978-3-319-70742-6_18

approaches mostly rely on the classic computer vision and pattern recognition "pipeline" [27], where visual feature extraction/reduction is followed by classification (discrete emotion recognition) or regression (continuous affect detection), e.g. [20].

In this note, we take a different perspective. As motivated in Sect. 2, our main concern is in providing a suitable account of the earliest stage of FE processing, where, upon stimulus onset, a fast, automatic trigger is fed into the continuous core affect state-space of valence and arousal. To such end, in this work we adopt a deep network architecture (Sect. 3). Recently, deep networks have proven their effectiveness in solving a variety of vision tasks. Also the FE task has been faced with deep networks [4,20]. Here, different from those works, we aim at achieving at the output of this automatic feed-forward step, a suitable prior in probabilistic terms, for the latent manifold that functionally models core-affect state-space [31].

This, in turn will initiate further processing that, eventually, will lead to emotion recognition/attribution. Remarkably, it has been shown that at the neurobiological level, processes that follow this "hidden", sub-cortical step, involve both visuomotor and visceromotor pathways that are likely to be used in simulation-based mechanisms for affective expression recognition [2,17,32].

2   Background and Motivations

FE analysis goes back to 1872, when Darwin demonstrated among other things the universality of facial and body expressions [10]. About one century later Ekman and Friesen [14] postulated six primary emotions that possess each a distinctive content together with a unique and universal facial expression. These prototypic emotional displays are also referred to as *basic emotions*. In more general terms, this is the bulk of the discrete theory of emotions. Pioneering work on automatic FE analysis goes back to Mase and Pentland [23]. Since then, in computer vision and markedly in the more recent affective computing field [24] a large body of work has been done in the framework of the discrete approach [11]. This success can be easily understood if one thinks of basic emotions as categorical constructs: then the attribution of emotion simply boils down to a classification problem over a set of suitable features (e.g., computational counterparts of Ekmans's Action Units -AUs [13]- in the case of FEs [27]).

There are however other competing theories to the discrete theory of emotions. The continuous, dimensional view parsimoniously proposes the two broad dimensions of valence (pleasure/displeasure) and arousal (sleepy/activated) of affect [25], as the core (core affect) of emotion representation and processing. This describes a kind of "kernel" neurophysiological state as the basis for grounding emotion episodes. Such view is supported by the fact that many kinds of emotion data can be mapped well into such a continuous two-dimensional space. Interestingly enough, the dimensional approach has received much more attention in affect evaluation via physiological, voice or music signals rather than FEs research [11], though, more recently, continuous representations are gaining currency [18]. Componential models of emotion [15,28] argue that the rich emotions that people experience unfold through a complex set of evaluations and coping mechanisms. Such "appraisal" theories invoke a larger vocabulary of features from which a correspondingly larger set of emotions can be constructed. In some respect, the computational models derived from appraisal theories have raised interest over the years in the classic Artificial intelligence (AI) community [11]. However the use of how to exploit this theoretical approach for automatic measurement of affect is an open research question since requiring, as discussed [18], complex, multicomponential and sophisticated measurements of change.

This long dispute by competing psychological theories might be eventually reconciled, as conjectured by Dubois and Adolphs: "*One could imagine constructing a more complex framework consisting of an underlying dimensionality of valence and arousal, a more fine-grained classification into six or so basic emotion categories, and a very fine-grained and more flexible attribution based on appraisal features*" [12].

Under such circumstances, it is best to take into account recent findings in affective neuroscience that might pave the way to a thorough and principled synthesis. Coming back to FE analysis, the unfolding of emotion attribution at the neurobiological level can be summarised as follows [1,2]. Upon the onset of an emotionally meaningful stimulus, observer's response undergoes the following stages: (1) fast early perceptual processing of highly salient stimuli (120 ms); (2) detailed perception and emotional reaction involving the body (170 ms); (3) retrieval of conceptual knowledge about the emotion signaled by the expresser's face (>300 ms).

At the core of all such stages lies the activity of the amygdala and the pre-frontal cortex. It has been argued [26] that functional interactions between the amygdala and pre-frontal cortex form a potential neural substrate for the encoding of the psychological dimensions of valence and arousal, thus of the core affect.

Most interesting for the work presented here is the first stage. Initial perception of the face modulates activity in subcortical structures as well as in early visual cortices. The subcortical structures, the superior colliculus and the pulvinar thalamus, are likely to be specialized for very fast, automatic, and coarse processing of the stimulus. In particular, coarse processing of the visual motion generated by dynamic facial expressions might be relevant. Crucially, information from the pulvinar feeds into early processing within amygdala. As to the cortical structures, it would include V1, V2, and other early visual cortices, via input from the lateral geniculate thalamus.

Early visual processing may be relatively specialized to extract information about highly salient stimuli and it may rely in large part on information based on specific features that are detected. These processes are likely to be fairly automatic and obligatory. Subsequently, it would be also supported by more anterior visual regions dedicated to face processing (e.g., superior temporal gyrus for what concerns mouth movement, eye movements, and changes in facial expression).

The amygdala participates in the recognition of emotional signals via at least the subcortical route (superior colliculus, pulvinar thalamus), and the cortical route via the visual neocortex. This is consistent with LeDoux dual-route proposal [9, 16, 21].

It has been shown that even subliminally presented facial expressions of fear activates the amygdala and such activation appears to depend on relatively passive or implicit processing of the emotion. Indeed, it is this fast automatic perceptual mapping from the early stimulus onset to basic "core affect components" that we are addressing in this note.

3 Architecture

To account for the early trigger to affective nuclei we propose to adopt an architecture inspired to the 3D convolutional network C3D presented in [30], allowing to learn spatiotemporal features. Since dealing with a more specific task than the usual video scene classification and using a small dataset, we opted for a shallower architecture than C3D to prevent overfitting. We choose three layers each composed by one 3D convolutional block, followed by *ReLU* nonlinearities, max pooling and layer normalization [3]. The last layer is a global average pooling block [22] followed by a linear fully connected layer and a *tanh* activation that outputs the estimates for valence and arousal. The network is fed by inputs composed by 16 consecutive frames, thus capturing spatiotemporal features. Groundtruth values of valence and arousal for these 16-frame volumes are obtained averaging the corresponding single-frame valence and arousal labels.

Table 1. Size of the 3D convolutional blocks for each layer

Layer	Convolutional filter size
1	$5 \times 5 \times 5 \times 3 \times 64$
2	$5 \times 5 \times 5 \times 64 \times 128$
3	$5 \times 5 \times 5 \times 128 \times 128$

4 Experimental Results

The training and test of the spatiotemporal convolutional network we proposed, has been setup considering the 23 most expressive videos of the MAHNOB dataset [5], and referring to the continuous valence/arousal labeling we produced exploiting a novel web-based annotation tool named DANTE (Dimensional ANnotation Tool for Emotions) [6]. 13 videos have been used for training and the remaining for test.

In Fig. 1 we report an example of both the manual annotations and the automatic regression values of valence on one of the tested video (vid9 in MAHNOB). We observe that the automatic values respect the trend of the ground truth, while the range of variability is slightly reduced.

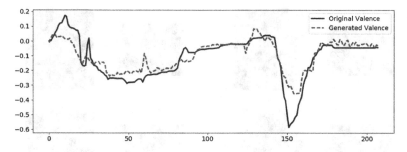

Fig. 1. An example of comparison between the ground truth (blue line) and the regressed value (red dashed line) on the Valence obtained by the trained convolutional network. (Color figure online)

As a quantitative and exhaustive evaluation of the regressor, we computed the root mean square error of the obtained emotional values, as reported in Table 2. The error is always contained, independently of the tested video, and this is reflected in the resulting low mean RMSE.

It is interesting to visualize network behavior. In Fig. 2 we show the input areas that are more informative for the regressor. We estimate these areas in a similar way as the *GRAD-Cam* method described in [29], using the mean of the feature maps of the last convolutional layer weighted by their backpropagated gradient. As we can observe the most informative areas concern the facial features, and in particular the eyes, but also, when the framing is larger, the body motion is captured and exploited to regress valence and arousal.

Table 2. Root Mean Square Error on the obtained values for each video and the mean value for the whole dataset.

Video	V1	V2	V3	V4	V5	V6	V7	V8	V9	V10	MEAN
RMSE	0.07	0.11	0.07	0.10	0.14	0.11	0.11	0.10	0.06	0.08	**0.08**

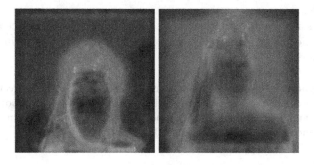

Fig. 2. Visualization of the last layer of the learnt convolutional network. Both the face and the body movements help the emotional state determination.

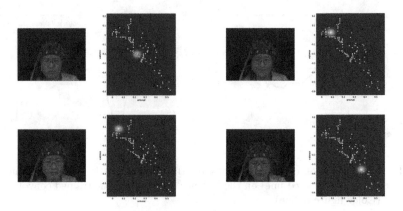

Fig. 3. Correspondences between the expresser and the "amygdala-like" activation.

Finally, in Fig. 3 we report the effect of the amygdala-like activation as a suitable prior for the latent manifold that has been learnt from valence-arousal labelling and that functionally models core-affect state-space. This very fast and automatic step it is likely to trigger the subsequent core affect representation of emotions.

5   Conclusions

We have presented a feed-forward mechanism providing a fast, automatic, and coarse processing of the earliest mapping from emotional facial expression stimuli to the core affect representation of emotions. Such mapping provides a suitable prior to the subsequent core affect dynamics, in which recognition is actually grounded.

To this end we designed a 3D spatiotemporal deep network as a suitable architecture to instantiate such early component. The network is quite shallow due to both the specificity of the task, and to the limited quantity of labeled data available.

The regression has produced satisfactory results on both valence and arousal dimensions, encouraging the integration of this preliminary step in a complete core affect model.

Acknowledgments. This research was carried out as part of the project "Interpreting emotions: a computational tool integrating facial expressions and biosignals based shape analysis and bayesian networks", supported by the Italian Government, managed by MIUR, financed by the *Future in Research* Fund.

References

1. Adolphs, R.: Neural systems for recognizing emotion. Curr. Opin. Neurobiol. **12**(2), 169–177 (2002)
2. Adolphs, R.: Recognizing emotion from facial expressions: psychological and neurological mechanisms. Behav. Cogn. Neurosci. Rev. **1**(1), 21–62 (2002)
3. Ba, J.L., Kiros, J.R., Hinton, G.E.: Layer normalization (2016). arXiv preprint: arXiv:1607.06450
4. Bargal, S.A., Barsoum, E., Canton-Ferrer, C., Zhang, C.: Emotion recognition in the wild from videos using images. In: Proceedings of the 18th ACM International Conference on Multimodal Interaction, ICMI 2016, Tokyo, Japan, pp. 433–436, 12–16 November 2016
5. Bilakhia, S., Petridis, S., Nijholt, A., Pantic, M.: The mahnob mimicry database: a database of naturalistic human interactions. Pattern Recogn. Lett. **66**, 52–61 (2015)
6. Boccignone, G., Conte, D., Cuculo, V., Lanzarotti, R.: Amhuse: A multimodal dataset for humour sensing. In: Proceedings of the 19th ACM International Conference on Multimodal Interaction, ICMI 2017, pp. 438–445. ACM, New York, NY, USA (2017)
7. Boccignone, G., Cuculo, V., Grossi, G., Lanzarotti, R., Migliaccio, R.: Virtual emg via facial video analysis. In: Battiato, S., Gallo, G., Schettini, R., Stanco, F. (eds.) ICIAP 2017, Part I. LNCS, vol. 10484, pp. 197–207. Springer International Publishing, Cham (2017)
8. Busso, C., Deng, Z., Yildirim, S., Bulut, M., Lee, C.M., Kazemzadeh, A., Lee, S., Neumann, U., Narayanan, S.: Analysis of emotion recognition using facial expressions, speech and multimodal information. In: Proceedings of the 6th International Conference on Multimodal Interfaces, ICMI 2004, pp. 205–211. ACM (2004)
9. Dalgleish, T.: The emotional brain. Nat. Rev. Neurosci. **5**(7), 583–589 (2004)
10. Darwin, C.: The Expression of the Emotions in Man and Animals. Oxford University Press, Oxford (1998)
11. D'mello, S.K., Kory, J.: A review and meta-analysis of multimodal affect detection systems. ACM Comput. Surv. (CSUR) **47**(3), 43 (2015)
12. Dubois, J., Adolphs, R.: Neuropsychology: how many emotions are there? Curr. Biol. **25**(15), R669–R672 (2015)
13. Ekman, P., Rosenberg, E.L.: What the Face Reveals: Basic and Applied Studies of Spontaneous Expression Using the Facial Action Coding System (FACS). Oxford University Press, Oxford (1997)
14. Ekman, P., Friesen, W.V.: Constants across cultures in the face and emotion. J. Pers. Soc. Psychol. **17**(2), 124 (1971)
15. Fontaine, J.R., Scherer, K.R., Roesch, E.B., Ellsworth, P.C.: The world of emotions is not two-dimensional. Psychol. Sci. **18**(12), 1050–1057 (2007)
16. Garrido, M.I., Barnes, G.R., Sahani, M., Dolan, R.J.: Functional evidence for a dual route to amygdala. Curr. Biol. **22**(2), 129–134 (2012)
17. Goldman, A.I., Sripada, C.S.: Simulationist models of face-based emotion recognition. Cognition **94**(3), 193–213 (2005)
18. Gunes, H., Schuller, B.: Categorical and dimensional affect analysis in continuous input: current trends and future directions. Image Vis. Comput. **31**(2), 120–136 (2013)
19. Hildebrandt, A., Recio, G., Sommer, W., Wilhelm, O., Ku, J.: Facial EMG responses to emotional expressions are related to emotion perception ability. PLoS ONE **9**(1), e84053 (2014)

20. Khorrami, P., Paine, T.L., Brady, K., Dagli, C.K., Huang, T.S.: How deep neural networks can improve emotion recognition on video data. In: 2016 IEEE International Conference on Image Processing, ICIP 2016, Phoenix, AZ, USA, pp. 619–623, 25–28 September 2016 (2016)

21. LeDoux, J.: The Emotional Brain: The Mysterious Underpinnings of Emotional Life. Simon and Schuster, New York (1998)

22. Lin, M., Chen, Q., Yan, S.: Network in network (2013). arXiv preprint: arXiv:1312.4400

23. Mase, K., Pentland, A.: Recognition of facial expression from optical flow. IEICE Trans. Inf. Syst. **74**, 3474–3483 (1991)

24. Picard, R.W.: Affective Computing. MIT Press, Cambridge (2000)

25. Russell, J.A.: Core affect and the psychological construction of emotion. Psychol. Rev. **110**(1), 145 (2003)

26. Salzman, C.D., Fusi, S.: Emotion, cognition, and mental state representation in amygdala and prefrontal cortex. Ann. Rev. Neurosci. **33**, 173–202 (2010)

27. Sariyanidi, E., Gunes, H., Cavallaro, A.: Automatic analysis of facial affect: a survey of registration, representation, and recognition. IEEE Trans. Pattern Anal. Mach. Intell. **37**(6), 1113–1133 (2015)

28. Scherer, K.R.: Emotion theories and concepts (psychological perspectives). In: Sander, D., Scherer, S.K.R. (eds.) Oxford Companion to Emotion and the Affective Sciences, pp. 145–149. Oxford University Press, Oxford (2009)

29. Selvaraju, R.R., Das, A., Vedantam, R., Cogswell, M., Parikh, D., Batra, D.: Grad-cam: why did you say that? Visual explanations from deep networks via gradient-based localization (2016). arXiv preprint: arXiv:1610.02391

30. Tran, D., Bourdev, L., Fergus, R., Torresani, L., Paluri, M.: Learning spatiotemporal features with 3d convolutional networks. In: Proceedings of the International Conference on Computer Vision, ICCV 2015 (2015)

31. Vitale, J., Williams, M.A., Johnston, B., Boccignone, G.: Affective facial expression processing via simulation: a probabilistic model. Biologically Inspired Cogn. Archit. J. **10**, 30–41 (2014)

32. Wood, A., Rychlowska, M., Korb, S., Niedenthal, P.: Fashioning the face: sensorimotor simulation contributes to facial expression recognition. Trends Cogn. Sci. **20**(3), 227–240 (2016)

Neonatal Facial Pain Assessment Combining Hand-Crafted and Deep Features

Luigi Celona[✉] and Luca Manoni

Department of Informatics, Systems and Communication,
University of Milano-Bicocca, viale Sarca, 336, 20126 Milano, Italy
luigi.celona@disco.unimib.it, l.manoni@campus.unimib.it

Abstract. In this paper we evaluate the combination of hand-crafted and deep learning-based features for neonatal pain assessment. To this end we consider two hand-crafted descriptors, i.e. Local Binary Patterns (LBP) and Histogram of Oriented Gradients (HOG), and features extracted from two pre-trained Convolutional Neural Networks (CNNs). Experimental results on the publicly available Infant Classification Of Pain Expressions (COPE) database show competitive results compared to previous methods.

Keywords: Neonatal pain assessment · Hand-crafted features
Convolutional Neural Networks · Transfer learning · Features reduction
Feature fusion

1 Introduction

Pain is defined as the unpleasant sensory emotional experience caused by trauma, disease or injury. Valid and reliable assessment of pain is essential for both clinical trials and effective pain management. However, pain is a subjective, multifaceted experience that varies between individuals due to: personality, age, gender, social class, past experience, individual coping strategies, culture and appraisal of current circumstances. The best source of information for inferring pain is to examine infant's facial expressions.

Automatic systems for the detection of neonatal pain are proposed. Some of the previous methods try to predict pain focusing on heart rate variability or infant cry vocalizations [16,21]. However, such systems are quite impractical as the neonates would need to be tethered to sensors. A more practical approach is to use cameras and develop machine vision systems that unobtrusively and constantly scan facial expressions [1,13]. Brahnam *et al.* [5] proposed the first method for infant pain detection and developed the Infant Classification Of Pain Expressions (COPE) database of neonatal facial images. Principal Component Analysis (PCA), Linear Discriminant Analysis (LDA), and Support Vector Machines (SVM) were applied for the classification of four noxious stimuli: transport from one crib to another, air puff on the nose, friction from cotton and

© Springer International Publishing AG 2017
S. Battiato et al. (Eds.): ICIAP 2017 International Workshops, LNCS 10590, pp. 197–204, 2017.
https://doi.org/10.1007/978-3-319-70742-6_19

alcohol rubbed on the lateral surface of the heel, and the puncture of a heel lance. However, in that paper experiments were conducted using a best-case scenario where samples of individual subjects were used both in testing and training sets. Brahnam *et al.* presented additional studies using the Infant COPE database [4,6,7]. These studies considered a more realistic scenario assuming that the classifiers would be trained on a set subjects and then applied to an unknown set of subjects. In [4], Brahnam *et al.* used raw pixel values of the grayscale image as feature vector, then they applied PCA for feature reduction and finally PCA, LDA SVMs and Neural Network Simultaneous Optimization Algorithm (NNSOA) were used to predict whether the neonatal face image contains a pain or nonpain expression. In [6], Brahnam *et al.* transformed raw pixel values of the gray-scale image using PCA or Discrete Cosine Transform (DCT). Then two methods were adopted for feature reduction: sorting by variance and Sequential Forward Floating Selection (SFFS); and four classifiers were evaluated: PCA, LDA, SVMs and NNSOA. Nanni *et al.* [18] compared several texture descriptors based on LBP in terms of AUC and proposed the ELongated Ternary Pattern (ELTP) and the Improved Local Ternary Pattern (ILTP) for infant pain classification. Recently, Mansor *et al.* [17] developed a system robust under different illumination levels. They achieved this results by altering illumination in original images, by estimating illumination thanks to the Multi Scale Retinex (MSR) algorithm for shadow removal, and finally by using LBP as features. Then Gaussian or Nearest Mean Classifier has been used as classifiers.

Feature fusion have been demonstrated to be very effective for various computer vision tasks. These methods generally involve the use of multiple handcrafted features, such as Local Binary Patterns (LBP) and Histogram of Oriented Gradients (HOG). However, features extracted from pre-trained Convolutional Neural Networks (CNNs) have recently been proven to be robust than the handcrafted features. This paper investigates the use of feature fusion for infant pain assessment. The experiments are conducted on the *infant Classification Of Pain Expression (COPE)* database which contains facial images of several neonates captured after distinct stimuli.

2   Infant Classification of Pain Database

The Infant COPE (Classification Of Pain Expressions) database [4–6] is the only public available database for infants pain detection. It contains a total of 204 color facial images of 26 Caucasian neonates (13 boys and 13 girls) ranging in age from 18 h to 3 days. The facial expressions of the newborns were photographed in one session while the infants were experiencing four distinct stimuli in the following sequence:

1. **Rest/Cry** - After being transported from one crib to another
2. **Air puff** - Exposition to a puff of air emitted from a squeezable plastic camera lens cleaner
3. **Friction** - Friction on the heel using cotton wool soaked in alcohol
4. **Pain** - Puncture of a heel lance

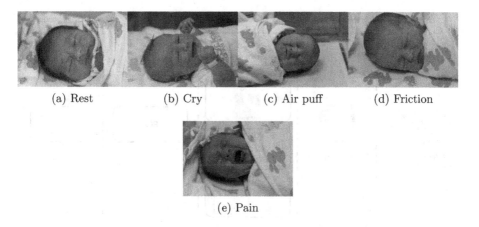

(a) Rest   (b) Cry   (c) Air puff   (d) Friction

(e) Pain

Fig. 1. Sample images from the COPE database.

Among the 204 images in the database, 67 are rest, 18 are cry, 23 are air puff, 36 are friction, and 60 are pain. Figure 1 shows some samples from the COPE database.

For the pain assessment problem, all images of the stimuli are divided into two categories: nonpain and pain. The set of nonpain images combines rest, cry, air puff and friction stimuli, and consists of 140 images. The set of pain images being a collection of the remaining 60 images.

3   The Proposed Method

The main steps of the proposed method for the facial neonatal pain assessment are shown in Fig. 2. Given an image: (1) we detect and align the original facial image using an affine transformation; (2) we extract both hand-crafted and deep features; (3) we apply Principal Component Analysis (PCA) as feature reduction algorithm and concatenate features for feature fusion; (4) finally, we train a linear Support Vector Machine (SVM) using fused features. What follows in this section is a detailed description of the previous steps.

3.1   Pre-processing

In the pre-processing step, we use a state-of-the-art algorithm for face detection and landmarks estimation [14]. The detected faces are rotated and aligned thanks to an affine transformation based on five landmarks, i.e. eyes corners, nose tip and mouth corners. Facial images are then obtained by cropping and scaling the transformed images to 224×224 pixels.

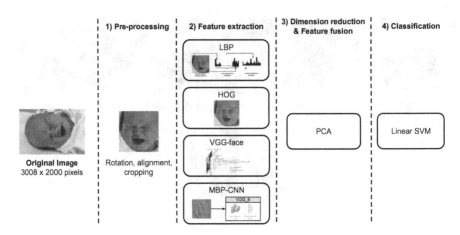

Fig. 2. Pipeline of the proposed method.

3.2 Feature Extraction

Hand-crafted features based methods achieved state-of-the-art performance on many machine vision tasks, such as object classification, object detection, texture classification and visual search in past few years [2,8–11].

Local Binary Patterns (LBP) [19] is a powerful local texture operator with a low computational complexity, and low sensitivity to changes in illumination. The LBP operator is computed by thresholding the value of the neighbors of each pixel with the value of the pixel itself. More in detail, it consists in the binary difference between the gray value of a pixel x and the gray values of its P neighborhood placed on a circle of radius of R. In this work we use a *uniform* LBP setting $P = 8$ and $R = 1$, resulting in a histogram of 59-bins. To better capture local texture, we divide the face into 25 (5×5) non-overlapping regions to extract LBP histograms. The LBP features extracted from each sub-region are concatenated into a single, spatially enhanced feature histogram. Furthermore we retain the color information by computing LBP histograms for each color channel and then by concatenating them. Thus, the resulting feature vector has length of 4,425 (59 bins $\times$ 25 regions $\times$ 3 channels).

Histogram of Oriented Gradients (HOG) [12] counts the occurrence of gradient orientation in local regions of an image. In this paper we use 2×2 blocks of 8×8 pixel cells with an overlap of half the block and histograms of 9 bins evenly spread from 0 to 180 degrees. The dimensions of such HOG descriptor on a 224×224 gray-scale image is 26,244 (729 regions $\times$ 4 blocks $\times$ 9 bins).

Transfer learning strategies by using CNN as feature extractor have proven to be more powerful than hand-crafted features on several application, e.g. object recognition and detection. They are based on the fact that a CNN pre-trained on a large dataset could be exploited for another task by reusing the learnt parameters of the source task [22]. Specifically, we feed the pre-trained CNN with a sample and then we use activation of a desired layer as features. In this paper, we consider the features extracted from the *VGG face* [20] and from the *Mapped LBP+CNN* (MBPCNN) [15]. VGG face consists in a VGG-16 network architecture trained for the recognition among 2,622 celebrities. Instead, MBPCNN involves the use of mapped LBP features as input of a VGG_S network architecture for emotion recognition in the wild. For both CNNs we obtain the feature vector by removing the final last two fully connected layers and the softmax layer. The length of the feature vector is 4,096.

3.3 Feature Reduction and Fusion

In this step each feature vector is reduced to 175-dimension via Principal Component Analysis (PCA) and L2-normalized. Finally, we perform a feature fusion by a linear concatenation of the reduced features. The result is a single feature vector with length equal to $175 \times L$, where L is the number of considered feature vectors.

3.4 Classification

Support Vector Machine (SVM) with linear kernel is used for pain/nonpain classification. The regularization parameter C is determined using a grid search.

4 Experimental Setup

We evaluate the proposed method on the infant COPE database. The evaluation protocol we used consists in dividing the images by subject: the testing set contains images of a given subject and all the other subjects used for the training. This procedure has been repeated for each one of the 26 subjects of the COPE

Table 1. Results on the COPE database in terms of average accuracy over the 26 subjects.

Features	PCA	Accuracy (%)
LBP		77.52
HOG		81.75
VGG face		82.42
MBPCNN		81.53
HOG+LBP		82.80
HOG+LBP	✓	81.98
VGG face+MBPCNN		82.56
VGG face+MBPCNN	✓	**83.78**
HOG+LBP+VGG face+MBPCNN		81.96
HOG+LBP+VGG face+MBPCNN	✓	82.95

database. Table 1 reports the results for all of the experiments. The performance measure adopted in the experiments is the average accuracy over the 26 subjects.

We investigate the performances obtained considering a single feature at time. Specifically, we run a set of experiments using: LBP features extracted from a RGB image divided into sub-regions; HOG computed on gray-scale image; features extracted from the pre-trained VGG face; and features extracted from the pre-trained MBPCNN. According to the results it is possible to see that we achieve the best performance thanks to the 4096-dimension features extracted using the pre-trained VGG face. The average accuracy is equal to 82.42%.

In another set of experiments we fuse the pair of hand-crafted features (i.e. LBP+HOG) and the pair of deep features (i.e. VGG face and MBPCNN). More in detail, we run an experiment fusing LBP and HOG features by simply concatenating the two feature vectors and obtaining a vector of length 30,669. For this experiment the resulting accuracy is 82.80%. In the second experiment we first reduce the dimensionality of both feature vectors to 175 and then we concatenate the two vectors obtaining a vector of 350 features. The resulting average accuracy is equal to 81.98%. For the remaining two experiments we fuse the 4096-dimension feature vectors extracted from the VGG face and MBPCNN: in the first case we only concatenate the two feature vectors and obtain an accuracy of 82.56%; in the second case, at first each feature vector is reduced to 175 dimensions and then they are concatenated into a 350-dimension feature vector. This last experiment obtains the best average accuracy of 83.78%. Figure 3 depicts some misclassified faces obtained in the aforementioned experiment: Fig. 3a reports faces labeled as nonpain in the COPE database, but classified as pain; instead Fig. 3b shows some examples of faces labeled as pain, but

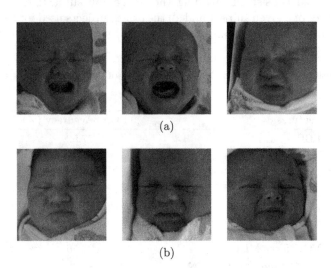

Fig. 3. Some misclassified samples: (a) Faces labeled as nonpain in the COPE database that the proposed method classifies as pain, (b) Faces labeled as pain in the COPE database that the proposed method classifies as nonpain.

classified as nonpain by our approach. From these images it is possible to see that some classification errors are due to incorrect labels in the dataset.

The last set of experiments consists in fusing all the considered features. For the first experiment we concatenate features and obtain a 38861-dimension feature vector. Instead, for the second experiment we apply PCA on each feature vector and then concatenate the four 175-dimension feature vectors. These experiments obtain an accuracy respectively of 81.96% and 82.95%.

To the best of our knowledge the best performance on pain assessment using the COPE database is obtained by Brahnam et al. [4]. For the sake of comparison we have reimplemented their method obtaining an average accuracy equal to 78.94%.

5   Conclusion

In this work we proposed a pipeline for pain assessment in newborn face images. The proposed method involves the fusion of both hand-crafted and deep features. More in detail, faces are detected using a face detector and then aligned using an affine transformation. LBP and HOG have been considered as hand-crafted features, pre-trained VGG face and MBPCNN have been used for deep feature extraction. Experimental results on the COPE database show the effectiveness of the proposed solution. As a future work, we plan to investigate other features and more powerful mechanisms [1,3] for feature selection and fusion.

References

1. Bianco, S., Celona, L., Schettini, R.: Robust smile detection using convolutional neural networks. J. Electron. Imaging 25(6), 063002 (2016)
2. Bianco, S., Mazzini, D., Pau, D.P., Schettini, R.: Local detectors and compact descriptors for visual search: a quantitative comparison. Digital Sig. Process. 44, 1–13 (2015)
3. Bianco, S., Schettini, R.: Adaptive color constancy using faces. IEEE Trans. Pattern Anal. Mach. Intell. 36(8), 1505–1518 (2014)
4. Brahnam, S., Chuang, C.F., Sexton, R.S., Shih, F.Y.: Machine assessment of neonatal facial expressions of acute pain. Decis. Support Syst. 43(4), 1242–1254 (2007)
5. Brahnam, S., Chuang, C.F., Shih, F.Y., Slack, M.R.: Machine recognition and representation of neonatal facial displays of acute pain. Artif. Intell. Med. 36(3), 211–222 (2006)
6. Brahnam, S., Nanni, L., Sexton, R.: Introduction to neonatal facial pain detection using common and advanced face classification techniques. In: Yoshida, H., Jain, A., Ichalkaranje, A., Jain, L.C., Ichalkaranje, N. (eds.) Advanced Computational Intelligence Paradigms in Healthcare-1, pp. 225–253. Springer, Heidelberg (2007)
7. Brahnam, S., Nanni, L., Sexton, R.S.: Neonatal facial pain detection using NNSOA and LSVM. In: IPCV, pp. 352–357 (2008)
8. Cusano, C., Napoletano, P., Schettini, R.: Illuminant invariant descriptors for color texture classification. In: Tominaga, S., Schettini, R., Trémeau, A. (eds.) CCIW 2013. LNCS, vol. 7786, pp. 239–249. Springer, Heidelberg (2013). https://doi.org/10.1007/978-3-642-36700-7_19

9. Cusano, C., Napoletano, P., Schettini, R.: Intensity and color descriptors for texture classification. Proc. SPIE **8661**, 866113 (2013)
10. Cusano, C., Napoletano, P., Schettini, R.: Combining local binary patterns and local color contrast for texture classification under varying illumination. JOSA A **31**(7), 1453–1461 (2014)
11. Cusano, C., Napoletano, P., Schettini, R.: Local angular patterns for color texture classification. In: Murino, V., Puppo, E., Sona, D., Cristani, M., Sansone, C. (eds.) ICIAP 2015. LNCS, vol. 9281, pp. 111–118. Springer, Cham (2015). https://doi.org/10.1007/978-3-319-23222-5_14
12. Dalal, N., Triggs, B.: Histograms of oriented gradients for human detection. In: IEEE Computer Society Conference on Computer Vision and Pattern Recognition, CVPR 2005, vol. 1, pp. 886–893. IEEE (2005)
13. Florea, C., Florea, L., Butnaru, R., Bandrabur, A., Vertan, C.: Pain intensity estimation by a self-taught selection of histograms of topographical features. Image Vis. Comput. **56**, 13–27 (2016)
14. King, D.E.: Dlib-ml: a machine learning toolkit. J. Mach. Learn. Res. **10**, 1755–1758 (2009)
15. Levi, G., Hassner, T.: Emotion recognition in the wild via convolutional neural networks and mapped binary patterns. In: Proceedings of ACM International Conference on Multimodal Interaction (ICMI), November 2015
16. Lindh, V., Wiklund, U., Håkansson, S.: Heel lancing in term new-born infants: an evaluation of pain by frequency domain analysis of heart rate variability. Pain **80**(1), 143–148 (1999)
17. Mansor, M.N., Rejab, M.N.: A computational model of the infant pain impressions with Gaussian and nearest mean classifier. In: 2013 IEEE International Conference on Control System, Computing and Engineering (ICCSCE), pp. 249–253. IEEE (2013)
18. Nanni, L., Brahnam, S., Lumini, A.: A local approach based on a local binary patterns variant texture descriptor for classifying pain states. Expert Syst. Appl. **37**(12), 7888–7894 (2010)
19. Ojala, T., Pietikainen, M., Maenpaa, T.: Multiresolution gray-scale and rotation invariant texture classification with local binary patterns. IEEE Trans. Pattern Anal. Mach. Intell. **24**(7), 971–987 (2002)
20. Parkhi, O.M., Vedaldi, A., Zisserman, A.: Deep face recognition. In: British Machine Vision Conference (2015)
21. Petroni, M., Malowany, A.S., Johnston, C.C., Stevens, B.J.: Identification of pain from infant cry vocalizations using artificial neural networks (ANNs). In: SPIE's 1995 Symposium on OE/Aerospace Sensing and Dual Use Photonics, pp. 729–738. International Society for Optics and Photonics (1995)
22. Razavian, A.S., Azizpour, H., Sullivan, J., Carlsson, S.: CNN features off-the-shelf: an astounding baseline for recognition. In: Proceedings of the IEEE Conference on Computer Vision and Pattern Recognition Workshops, pp. 806–813 (2014)

Background Learning for Detection and Tracking from RGBD Videos (RGBD)

People Detection and Tracking from an RGB-D Camera in Top-View Configuration: Review of Challenges and Applications

Daniele Liciotti, Marina Paolanti$^{(\boxtimes)}$, Emanuele Frontoni, and Primo Zingaretti

Dipartimento di Ingegneria dell'Informazione, Università Politecnica delle Marche,
Via Brecce Bianche, 60131 Ancona, Italy
{d.liciotti,m.paolanti}@pm.univpm.it, {e.frontoni,p.zingaretti}@univpm.it

Abstract. This paper presents a literature review on the use of RGB-D camera for people detection and tracking. Our aim is to use this state-of-the-art report to demonstrate the potential of top-view configuration for people detection and tracking applications in several sub-domains, to outline key limitations and to indicate areas of technology, where solutions for remaining challenges may be found. The survey examines the success of RGB-D cameras because of their affordability and for the additional rough depth information coupled with visual images that provide. These cameras in configuration top-view have already been successfully applied in the several fields to univocally identify people and to analyse behaviours and interactions. From this report, it emerges that detecting and tracking people can be a valuable source of information for many fields and purposes.

Keywords: Top-View · RGB-D camera · Tracking · Detection

1 Introduction

Detecting and tracking people is an important and fundamental component for many interactive and intelligent systems. The problem remains largely open due to several serious challenges, such as occlusion, change of appearance, complex and dynamic background [26]. Popular sensors for this task are RGB-D cameras because of their availability, reliability and affordability. Studies have demonstrated the great value (both in accuracy and efficiency) of depth camera in coping with severe occlusions among humans and complex background. The appearance of devices, such as Microsoft's Kinect and Asus's Xtion Pro Live Sensors motivates a revolution in computer vision and vision related research. The combination of high-resolution depth and visual information opens up new challenges and opportunities for activity recognition and people tracking for many application fields that ranges from retail to Ambient Assisted Living (AAL). Reliable depth maps can provide valuable additional information to significantly improve tracking and detection results.

© Springer International Publishing AG 2017
S. Battiato et al. (Eds.): ICIAP 2017 International Workshops, LNCS 10590, pp. 207–218, 2017.
https://doi.org/10.1007/978-3-319-70742-6_20

The task of detecting and tracking people in such image and sequences has proven very challenging although sustained research over many years has created a range of smart methods. Techniques involve extracting spatially global features and using statistical learning with local features and boosting, such as EOH [10], HOG [7] and edgelet [37]. Other challenges such as high variation in human poses, self-occlusions and cross-occlusions make the problem even more complicated.

To counter these challenges, several research papers adopt the top-view configuration because it eases the task and makes simple to extract different trajectory features. This setup also introduces robustness, due to the lack of occlusions among individuals. Figure 1 depicts a people counting system from top-view configuration with an RGB-D camera.

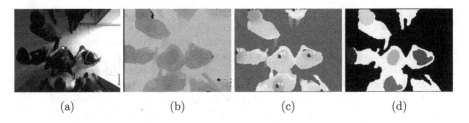

(a)   (b)   (c)   (d)

Fig. 1. People counting system from top-view configuration with RGB-D camera. (Color figure online)

The objective of this survey is to provide a comprehensive overview of the recent developments of people detection and tracking with RGB-D technologies from the perspective of top-view, mainly published in the computer vision and machine intelligence communities. The criteria for topic selection arises from our previous experience with approaches with RGB-D cameras installed in a top-view configuration. More specifically, the review includes person tracking and recognition, human activity analysis, hand gesture recognition, and fall detection in different fields. The broad diversity of topics clearly shows the potential impact of top-view configuration in computer vision. We also summarize main paths that most approaches follow and point out their contributions. We categorize and compare the reviewed approaches from multiple perspectives, including information modality, representation coding, structure and transition, and feature engineering methodology, and analyse the pros and cons of each category.

The rest of the paper is organized as follows: Sect. 2 is an overview of the research status on algorithms and approaches adopted with RGB-D sensors installed in a top-view configuration; Sect. 3 introduces the main research fields in which these sensors are installed and employed, such as Security and Video Analytics (Subsect. 3.1), Intelligent Retail Environment (Subsect. 3.2) and Activities of Daily Living (ADLs) (Subsect. 3.3); final section presents the conclusions and our considerations (Sect. 4).

2   Top-View Configuration: Algorithms and Approaches

Many vision techniques and algorithms for person detection and tracking have been proposed during the last years and these greatly restrict the generality of the approach in real-world settings. In this section, we survey current methods, covering both early and recent literature related to algorithms and techniques applied for tracking and detecting humans from top view RGB-D data. In particular, we review the approaches related to segmentation using background subtraction, Water Filling and Statistical algorithms.

Kouno et al. in [17] describe an image-based person identification task focusing on an image from an overhead camera. The process is based on the background subtraction approach. They apply four features to the identification method, i.e. estimated body height, estimated body dimensions, estimated body size and depth histogram.

In [38], the authors propose a system for passengers counting in buses based on stereovision. The processing chain corresponding to this counting system involves different steps dedicated to the detection, segmentation, tracking and counting. In fact, they have segmented the height maps for highlighting the passengers heads at different levels (i.e. adults, teenagers, children). The result is binary images that contain information related to the heads, called "kernels". The extraction part attributes a number of parameters to the kernel such as, size of the kernel, shape, average greylevel, average height level. Then, with the kernel information, a tracking procedure is applied to analyse the trajectories of the kernels.

The top-view camera setting is also adopted in [25]. In this paper, each depth image in a sequence is segmented into K layers as the computer tomography (CT) slides where the depth spacing between two adjacent layers is set to be a fixed value, distance and the number K is an a priori chosen parameter. After that, the region of each slide can be found based on the classic contour finding algorithm. Dynamic time warping algorithm is also applied to address the different sequence length problem. Finally, a SVM classifier is trained to classify the activities.

In another work the authors with methods of low-level segmentation and tracking develop a system that maps the customers in the store, detects the interactions with products on the shelves and the movement of groups of people within the store [24].

Microsoft Kinect depth sensor is employed in [12] in an "on-ceiling" configuration based on the analysis of depth frames. The elements acquired in the depth scene are recognized by a segmentation algorithm, which analyses the raw depth data directly provided by the sensor. The system extracts the elements, and implements a solution to classify all the blobs in the scene. Anthropometric relationships and features are used to recognize human subjects among the blobs. Once a person is detected, he is followed by a tracking algorithm between different frames.

Dittrich et al. [9] present an approach for low-level body part segmentation based on RGB-D data. The RGB-D sensor is installed at the ceiling and observed a shared workspace for human-robot collaboration in the industrial domain.

The object classes are the distinct human body parts: Head, Upper Body, Upper and Lower Arm, Hand, Legs and the background rejection. For the generation of data for the classifier training, they use a synthetic representation of the human body in a virtual environment, where synthetic sensors generate depth data.

A variant of classical segmentation is the one proposed by Tseng in [36]. In this paper, they present a real-time indoor surveillance system which installs multiple depth cameras from vertical top-view to track humans. The system with a framework tries to solve the traditional challenge of surveillance through tracking of multiple persons, such as severe occlusion, similar appearance, illumination changes, and outline deformation. The background subtraction of the stitched top-view image has been performed to extract the foreground objects in the cluttered environment. The detection scheme involves different phases such as the graph-based segmentation, the head hemiellipsoid model, and the geodesic distance map. Furthermore, the shape feature based on diffusion distance has been designed to verify the human tracking hypotheses within particle filter.

An improvement of the classical segmentation techniques is the algorithm proposed by Kepski et al. [15]. The first step of the algorithm is nearest neighbor interpolation to fill the holes in the depth map and to get the map with meaningful values for all pixels. Then, the median filter with a 5×5 window on the depth array is executed to make the data smooth. The algorithm also extracts the floor and removes their corresponding pixels from the depth map. Given the extracted person in the last depth frame, the region growing is performed to delineate the person in the current frame. To confirm the presence of the tracked subject as well as to give head location a Support Vector Machine (SVM) based person finder is used. On the basis of the persons centroid the pan-tilt head rotates the camera to keep the head in the central part of the depth map. Finally, a cascade classifier consisting of lying pose detector and dynamic transition detector is carried out.

An additional paper that describes a method for people counting in public transportation with a segmentation approach is [28]. Kinect sensor mounted vertically has been employed to acquire an images database of 1–5 persons, with and without body poses of holding a handrail. However, in this case the image is processed in blocks in order to find potential local maxima, which are subsequently verified to find head candidates. Finally, non-head objects have been filtered out, based on the ratio of pixels with similar and near-zero value, in the neighbourhood of the maxima.

The approach in [3] investigated a real time people tracking system able to work even under severe low-lighting conditions. The system relies on a novel active sensor that provides brightness and depth images based on a Time of Flight (TOF) technology. This is performed by means of a simple background subtraction procedure based on a pixelwise parametric statistical model. The tracking algorithm is efficient, being based on geometrical constraints and invariants. Experiments are performed under changing lighting conditions and involving multiple people closely interacting with each other.

The same technique is the one applied in [39]. In this paper, the method is composed by two behaviour estimators. The first one is based on height of hand with depth information the second instead on SVM with depth and PSA (Pixel State Analysis) based features and these estimators are used by cascading them.

A method to detect human body parts in depth images based on an active learning strategy is proposed in [4]. The approach is evaluated on two different scenarios: the detection of human heads of people lying in a bed and the detection of human heads from a ceiling camera. The proposal is to reduce both the training processing time and the image labelling efforts, combining an online decision tree learning procedure that is able to train the model incrementally and a data sampling strategy that selects relevant samples for labelling The data are grouped into clusters using as features the depth pixel values, with an algorithm such as k-means.

Tian et al., in [35] have adopted the median filtering to noise removal, because it could well filter the depth image noise obtained by Kinect, and at the same time could protect edge information well. A human detection method using HOG features, that are local descriptors, of head and shoulder based on depth map and detecting moving objects in particular scene is used. SVM classifier has isolated regions of interest (features of head and shoulder) to achieve real-time detection of objects (pedestrian).

A method for human detection and tracking in depth images captured by a top-view camera system is presented in [32]. They have introduced feature descriptor to train a head-shoulder detector using a discriminative class scheme. A separate processing step has ensured that only a minimal but sufficient number of head-shoulder candidates is evaluated. A final tracking step reliably propagated detections in time and provides stable tracking results. The quality of the method has allowed to recognise many challenging situations with humans tailgating and piggybacking.

An interesting binary segmentation approach is the one proposed by Wu et al. [37] that have used a Gaussian Mixture Models algorithm and reduced depth-sensing noise from the camera and background subtraction. Moreover, the authors have smoothed the foreground depth map using a 5 by 5 median filter. The real-time segmentation of a tracked person and their body parts has been the first phase of the EagleSense tracking pipeline.

In [13] the authors described and evaluated a vision-based technique for tracking many people with a network of stereo camera sensors. They have modelled the stereo depth estimation error as Gaussian and track the features using a Kalman filter. The feature tracking component starts by identifying good features to track using the Harris corner detector. It has tracked the left and right image features independently in the time domain using Lucas-Kanade-Tomasi (LKT) feature tracking. The approach has been evaluated using the MOTA-MOTP multi-target tracking performance metrics on real data sets with up to 6 people and on challenging simulations of crowds of up to 25 people with uniform appearance. This technique uses a separate particle filter to track each person and thus a data association step is required to assign 3D feature measurements to individual trackers.

Migniot in papers such as [30,31] has addressed the problem of the tracking of 3D human body pose from depth image sequences given by a Xtion Pro-Live camera. Human body poses have been estimated through model fitting using dense correspondences between depth data and an articulated human model. Two trackers using particle filter have been presented.

A computer vision algorithm adopted by many researchers in case of RGB-D cameras placed in top-view configuration is Water filling.

Zhang et al. [40] have built a system with vertical Kinect sensor for people counting, where the depth information is used to remove the effect of the appearance variation. Since the head is closer to the Kinect sensor than other parts of the body, people counting task found the suitable local minimum regions. The unsupervised water filling method finds these regions with the property of robustness, locality and scale-invariance.

Even in [1] and in [6], the authors have presented a water filling people counting algorithm using depth images acquired from a Kinect camera that is installed vertically, i.e., pointing toward the floor. The algorithm in [1] is referred to as Field seeding algorithm. The people head blobs are detected from the binary images generated with regard to the threshold values derived from the local minimum values. In [6] the approach called as people tracking increases the performance of the people counting system.

3   Top-View Configuration: Challenges and Opportunities in Research Fields

The main motivating factors for the installation of RGB-D cameras in top-view configuration are brought back to some related applications that we describe in this section. Firstly, the reliable and occlusion free counting of persons that is crucial to many applications. Most previous works can only count moving people from a single camera, which cannot count still people or can fail badly when there is a crowd and occlusions are very frequent. In this survey, we have focused on the works with RGB-D cameras in top-view configuration in three fields of research: Security and Video Analytics, Intelligent Retail Environment and ADLs.

3.1   Security and Video Analytics

The applications developed in this field are related to safety and security in crowded environments, people flow analysis and access control as well as counting. Actual tracking accuracy of top-view cameras over-performs all other point of view in crowded environments with accuracies up to 99%. When there are special security applications or the system is working in usually crowded scenarios the proposed architecture and point of view is the only suitable.

In [5], the authors have focused on the development of an embedded smart camera network dedicated to track and count people in public spaces. In the network, each node is capable of sensing, tracking and counting people while communicating with the adjacent nodes of the network. Each node uses a 3D-sensing camera positioned in a downward-view. This system has performed background modelling during the calibration process, using a fast and lightweight segmentation algorithm.

A vision based method for counting the number of persons which cross a virtual line is presented in [8]. The method analyses the video stream acquired by a camera mounted in a zenithal position with respect to the counting line, allowing to determine the number of people that cross the virtual line and providing the crossing direction for each person. This approach was designed to achieve high accuracy and computational efficiency. An extensive evaluation of the method has been carried out taking into account the factors that may impact on the counting performance and, in particular, the acquisition technology (traditional RGB camera and depth sensor), the installation scenario (indoor and outdoor), the density of the people flow (isolated people and groups of persons), the acquisition frame rate, and the image resolution. They also analysed the combination of the outputs obtained from the RGB and depth sensors as a way to improve the counting performance.

Another work for people counting is done in [11]. An algorithm by multimodal joint information processing for crowd counting is developed. In this method, the authors have used colour and depth information together with an ordinary depth camera (e.g. Microsoft Kinect). Firstly, they have detected each head of the passing or still person in the surveillance region with adaptive modulation ability to varying scenes on depth information. Then, they have tracked and counted each detected head on colour information.

In order to guarantee security in e.g. critical infrastructure a pipeline is presented in [34]. It verifies that only a single, authorized subject can enter a secured area. Verification scenarios are carried out by using a set of RGB-D images. Features, invariant to rotation and pose are used and classified by different metrics to be applied in real-time.

The combination of the people counting problem with re-identification and trajectory analysis is faced in [14]. They have extracted useful information using depth cameras. The re-identification task is studied by [27]. The authors have introduced a study on the use of different features exclusively obtained from depth images captured with top-view RGB-D cameras. TVPR is the dataset for person re-identification with an RGB-D camera in a top-view configuration. The registrations are made in an indoor scenario, where people pass under the camera installed on the ceiling [23].

3.2   Intelligent Retail Environment

An important scope is the interactions detection between people and environment with the many applications for the field of Intelligent retail environment and intelligent shelf such as Shopper Analytics [18]. The aim of this paper is to present a low cost integrated system consisting of a RGB-D camera and a software able to monitor shoppers. The camera installed in above the shelf detects the presence of people and univocally identifies them. Through the depth frames, the system detects the interactions of the shoppers with the products on the shelf and determines if a product is picked up or if the product is taken and then put back and finally, if there is not contact with the products.

The same authors, in [20] have described the monitoring of consumer behaviours. The autonomous and low cost system employed is based on a software infrastructure connected to a video sensor network, with a set of computer vision algorithms, embedded in the distributed RGB-D cameras.

GroupTogether is another system that explores cross-device interaction using two sociological constructs [29]. It supports fluid, minimally disruptive techniques for co-located collaboration by leveraging the proxemics of people as well as the proxemics of devices.

Migniot et al. have explored the problem of people tracking with a robust and reliable markerless camera tracking system for outdoor augmented reality using only a mobile handheld camera. The method was particularly efficient for partially known 3D scenes where only an incomplete 3D model of the outdoor environment was available [31].

3.3   Activities of Daily Living (ADLs)

Another research field with RGB-D camera top-view is ADLs. In this field the application range goes from high reliability fall detection to occlusion free Human Behaviour Analysis (HBA) at home for elders in AAL environments. All these applications have relevant outcomes form the current research with the ability to identify users while performing tracking, interaction analysis or HBA. Furthermore all these scenario can gather data using low cost sensors and processing units, ensuring scalability. Finally the proposed architecture can be certified on a EU basis Privacy by Design approach.

An example is the system for real-time human tracking and predefined human gestures detection using depth data acquired from Kinect sensor installed right above the detection region described in [2]. The tracking part is based on fitting an articulated human body model to obtained data using particle filter framework and specifically defined constraints which originate in physiological properties of the human body. The gesture recognition part has used the timed automaton conforming to the human body poses and regarding tolerances of the joints positions and time constraints.

For advanced analysis of human behaviours Liciotti et al. in [19] have developed a highly-integrated system. The video framework exploits vertical RGB-D sensors for people tracking, interaction analysis and users activities detection in domestic scenarios. The depth information has been used to remove the affect of the appearance variation and to evaluate users activities inside the home and in front of the fixtures. In addition, group interactions have been monitored and analysed. The audio framework has recognised voice commands by continuously monitoring the acoustic home environment.

As previously stated, another important issue to monitor and evaluate during the people tracking is the fall detection [12,15,16,22]. The solution implemented in these papers with RGB-D camera in a top-view configuration are suitable and affordable for this aim.

An automated RGB-D video analysis system that recognises human ADLs activities, related to classical daily actions is described in [21]. The main goal is to predict the probability of an analysed subject action. Thus, abnormal behaviour can be detected. The activity detection and recognition is performed using an affordable RGB-D camera. Action sequence recognition is then handled using a discriminative Hidden Markov Model (HMM).

4 Conclusion and Considerations

In this paper, our aim has been to use this state-of-the-art report to demonstrate the potential of top-view configuration for detection and tracking applications in several sub-domains, to outline key limitations and to indicate areas of technology where solutions for remaining challenges may be found. The success of RGB-D cameras can be closely linked to their affordability and for the additional rough depth information coupled with visual images that provide. These cameras have already been successfully applied in the several field to univocally identify people and to analyse behaviours and interactions. The choice of the RGB-D camera in a top view configuration is due to its greater suitability compared with a front view configuration, usually adopted for gesture recognition or even for video gaming. The top-view configuration reduces the problem of occlusions and has the advantage of being privacy preserving, because a persons face is not recorded by the camera. Starting from this, further investigation could be devoted to explore approaches more accurate and effective such as Convolutional Neural Networks or U-Net [33].

References

1. Agusta, B.A.Y., Mittrapiyanuruk, P., Kaewtrakulpong, P.: Field seeding algorithm for people counting using kinect depth image. Indian J. Sci. Technol. 9(48) (2016)
2. Bednarık, J., Herman, D.: Human gesture recognition using top view depth data obtained from kinect sensor (2015)
3. Bevilacqua, A., Di Stefano, L., Azzari, P.: People tracking using a time-of-flight depth sensor. In: IEEE International Conference on Video and Signal Based Surveillance, AVSS 2006, pp. 89–89. IEEE (2006)
4. Bonnin, A., Borràs, R., Vitrià, J.: A cluster-based strategy for active learning of rgb-d object detectors. In: 2011 IEEE International Conference on Computer Vision Workshops (ICCV Workshops), pp. 1215–1220. IEEE (2011)
5. Burbano, A., Bouaziz, S., Vasiliu, M.: 3D-sensing distributed embedded system for people tracking and counting. In: 2015 International Conference on Computational Science and Computational Intelligence (CSCI), pp. 470–475. IEEE (2015)
6. Coşkun, A., Kara, A., Parlaktuna, M., Ozkan, M., Parlaktuna, O.: People counting system by using kinect sensor. In: 2015 International Symposium on Innovations in Intelligent SysTems and Applications (INISTA), pp. 1–7. IEEE (2015)

7. Dalal, N., Triggs, B.: Histograms of oriented gradients for human detection. In: IEEE Computer Society Conference on Computer Vision and Pattern Recognition, CVPR 2005, vol. 1, pp. 886–893. IEEE (2005)
8. Del Pizzo, L., Foggia, P., Greco, A., Percannella, G., Vento, M.: Counting people by RGB or depth overhead cameras. Pattern Recogn. Lett. **81**, 41–50 (2016)
9. Dittrich, F., Woern, H., Sharma, V., Yayilgan, S.: Pixelwise object class segmentation based on synthetic data using an optimized training strategy. In: 2014 First International Conference on Networks & Soft Computing (ICNSC), pp. 388–394. IEEE (2014)
10. Felzenszwalb, P.F.: Learning models for object recognition. In: Proceedings of the 2001 IEEE Computer Society Conference on Computer Vision and Pattern Recognition, CVPR 2001, vol. 1, pp. I–1056. IEEE (2001)
11. Fu, H., Ma, H., Xiao, H.: Scene-adaptive accurate and fast vertical crowd counting via joint using depth and color information. Multimedia Tools Appl. **73**(1), 273 (2014)
12. Gasparrini, S., Cippitelli, E., Spinsante, S., Gambi, E.: A depth-based fall detection system using a kinect® sensor. Sensors **14**(2), 2756–2775 (2014)
13. Heath, K., Guibas, L.: Multi-person tracking from sparse 3D trajectories in a camera sensor network. In: Second ACM/IEEE International Conference on Distributed Smart Cameras, ICDSC 2008, pp. 1–9. IEEE (2008)
14. Hernandez, D., Castrillon, M., Lorenzo, J.: People counting with re-identification using depth cameras (2011)
15. Kepski, M., Kwolek, B.: Detecting human falls with 3-axis accelerometer and depth sensor. In: 2014 36th Annual International Conference of the IEEE Engineering in Medicine and Biology Society (EMBC), pp. 770–773. IEEE (2014)
16. Kepski, M., Kwolek, B.: Fall detection using ceiling-mounted 3D depth camera. In: 2014 International Conference on Computer Vision Theory and Applications (VISAPP), vol. 2, pp. 640–647. IEEE (2014)
17. Kouno, D., Shimada, K., Endo, T.: Person identification using top-view image with depth information. In: 2012 13th ACIS International Conference on Software Engineering, Artificial Intelligence, Networking and Parallel & Distributed Computing (SNPD), pp. 140–145. IEEE (2012)
18. Liciotti, D., Contigiani, M., Frontoni, E., Mancini, A., Zingaretti, P., Placidi, V.: Shopper analytics: a customer activity recognition system using a distributed RGB-D camera network. In: Distante, C., Battiato, S., Cavallaro, A. (eds.) VAAM 2014. LNCS, vol. 8811, pp. 146–157. Springer, Cham (2014). https://doi.org/10.1007/978-3-319-12811-5_11
19. Liciotti, D., Ferroni, G., Frontoni, E., Squartini, S., Principi, E., Bonfigli, R., Zingaretti, P., Piazza, F.: Advanced integration of multimedia assistive technologies: a prospective outlook. In: 2014 IEEE/ASME 10th International Conference on Mechatronic and Embedded Systems and Applications (MESA), pp. 1–6. IEEE (2014)
20. Liciotti, D., Frontoni, E., Mancini, A., Zingaretti, P.: Pervasive system for consumer behaviour analysis in retail environments. In: Nasrollahi, K., Distante, C., Hua, G., Cavallaro, A., Moeslund, T.B., Battiato, S., Ji, Q. (eds.) FFER/VAAM -2016. LNCS, vol. 10165, pp. 12–23. Springer, Cham (2017). https://doi.org/10.1007/978-3-319-56687-0_2
21. Liciotti, D., Frontoni, E., Zingaretti, P., Bellotto, N., Duckett, T.: Hmm-based activity recognition with a ceiling RGB-D camera. In: Proceedings of the 6th International Conference on Pattern Recognition Applications and Methods, pp. 567–574 (2017)

22. Liciotti, D., Massi, G., Frontoni, E., Mancini, A., Zingaretti, P.: Human activity analysis for in-home fall risk assessment. In: 2015 IEEE International Conference on Communication Workshop (ICCW), pp. 284–289. IEEE (2015)
23. Liciotti, D., Paolanti, M., Frontoni, E., Mancini, A., Zingaretti, P.: Person re-identification dataset with RGB-D camera in a top-view configuration. In: Nasrollahi, K., Distante, C., Hua, G., Cavallaro, A., Moeslund, T.B., Battiato, S., Ji, Q. (eds.) FFER/VAAM -2016. LNCS, vol. 10165, pp. 1–11. Springer, Cham (2017). https://doi.org/10.1007/978-3-319-56687-0_1
24. Liciotti, D., Zingaretti, P., Placidi, V.: An automatic analysis of shoppers behaviour using a distributed RGB-D cameras system. In: 2014 IEEE/ASME 10th International Conference on Mechatronic and Embedded Systems and Applications (MESA), pp. 1–6. IEEE (2014)
25. Lin, S.-C., Liu, A.-S., Hsu, T.-W., Fu, L.-C.: Representative body points on top-view depth sequences for daily activity recognition. In: 2015 IEEE International Conference on Systems, Man, and Cybernetics (SMC), pp. 2968–2973. IEEE (2015)
26. Liu, J., Liu, Y., Zhang, G., Zhu, P., Chen, Y.Q.: Detecting and tracking people in real time with RGB-D camera. Pattern Recogn. Lett. **53**, 16–23 (2015)
27. Lorenzo-Navarro, J., Castrillón-Santana, M., Hernández-Sosa, D.: An study on re-identification in RGB-D imagery. In: Bravo, J., Hervás, R., Rodríguez, M. (eds.) IWAAL 2012. LNCS, vol. 7657, pp. 200–207. Springer, Heidelberg (2012). https://doi.org/10.1007/978-3-642-35395-6_28
28. Malawski, F.: Top-view people counting in public transportation using kinect. Challenges Mod. Technol. **5** (2014)
29. Marquardt, N., Hinckley, K., Greenberg, S.: Cross-device interaction via micro-mobility and f-formations. In: Proceedings of the 25th Annual ACM Symposium on User Interface Software and Technology, pp. 13–22. ACM (2012)
30. Migniot, C., Ababsa, F.: Hybrid 3D–2D human tracking in a top view. J. Real-Time Image Proc. **11**(4), 769–784 (2016)
31. Migniot, C., Ababsa, F.: 3D Human Tracking in a Top View Using Depth Information Recorded by the Xtion Pro-Live Camera. In: Bebis, G., Boyle, R., Parvin, B., Koracin, D., Li, B., Porikli, F., Zordan, V., Klosowski, J., Coquillart, S., Luo, X., Chen, M., Gotz, D. (eds.) ISVC 2013. LNCS, vol. 8034, pp. 603–612. Springer, Heidelberg (2013). https://doi.org/10.1007/978-3-642-41939-3_59
32. Rauter, M.: Reliable human detection and tracking in top-view depth images. In: Proceedings of the IEEE Conference on Computer Vision and Pattern Recognition Workshops, pp. 529–534 (2013)
33. Ronneberger, O., Fischer, P., Brox, T.: U-net: convolutional networks for biomedical image segmentation. arXiv preprint arXiv:1505.04597 (2015)
34. Siegmund, D., Wainakh, A., Braun, A.: Verification of single-person access in a mantrap portal using RGB-D images. In: XII Workshop de Visao Computacional (WVC) (2016)
35. Tian, Q., Zhou, B., Zhao, W.-H., Wei, Y., Fei, W.-W.: Human detection using hog features of head and shoulder based on depth map. JSW **8**(9), 2223–2230 (2013)
36. Tseng, T.-E., Liu, A.-S., Hsiao, P.-H., Huang, C.-M., Fu, L.-C.: Real-time people detection and tracking for indoor surveillance using multiple top-view depth cameras. In: 2014 IEEE/RSJ International Conference on Intelligent Robots and Systems (IROS 2014), pp. 4077–4082. IEEE (2014)
37. Wu, B., Nevatia, R.: Detection and tracking of multiple, partially occluded humans by bayesian combination of edgelet based part detectors. Int. J. Comput. Vision **75**(2), 247–266 (2007)

38. Yahiaoui, T., Meurie, C., Khoudour, L., Cabestaing, F.: A people counting system based on dense and close stereovision. In: Image and Signal Processing, pp. 59–66 (2008)
39. Yamamoto, J., Inoue, K., Yoshioka, M.: Investigation of customer behavior analysis based on top-view depth camera. In: 2017 IEEE Winter Applications of Computer Vision Workshops (WACVW), pp. 67–74. IEEE (2017)
40. Zhang, X., Yan, J., Feng, S., Lei, Z., Yi, D., Li, S.Z.: Water filling: unsupervised people counting via vertical kinect sensor. In: 2012 IEEE Ninth International Conference on Advanced Video and Signal-Based Surveillance (AVSS), pp. 215–220. IEEE (2012)

A Benchmarking Framework for Background Subtraction in RGBD Videos

Massimo Camplani[1], Lucia Maddalena[2](✉), Gabriel Moyá Alcover[3],
Alfredo Petrosino[4], and Luis Salgado[5,6]

[1] University of Bristol, Bristol, UK
[2] National Research Council, Naples, Italy
lucia.maddalena@cnr.it
[3] Universitat de les Illes Balears, Palma, Spain
[4] University of Naples Parthenope, Naples, Italy
[5] Universidad Politécnica de Madrid, Madrid, Spain
[6] Universidad Autónoma de Madrid, Madrid, Spain

Abstract. The complementary nature of color and depth synchronized information acquired by low cost RGBD sensors poses new challenges and design opportunities in several applications and research areas. Here, we focus on background subtraction for moving object detection, which is the building block for many computer vision applications, being the first relevant step for subsequent recognition, classification, and activity analysis tasks. The aim of this paper is to describe a novel benchmarking framework that we set up and made publicly available in order to evaluate and compare scene background modeling methods for moving object detection on RGBD videos. The proposed framework involves the largest RGBD video dataset ever made for this specific purpose. The 33 videos span seven categories, selected to include diverse scene background modeling challenges for moving object detection. Seven evaluation metrics, chosen among the most widely used, are adopted to evaluate the results against a wide set of pixel-wise ground truths. Moreover, we present a preliminary analysis of results, devoted to assess to what extent the various background modeling challenges pose troubles to background subtraction methods exploiting color and depth information.

Keywords: Background subtraction · Color and depth data · RGBD

1 Introduction

The advent of low cost RGBD sensors such as Microsoft Kinect or Asus Xtion Pro is completely changing the computer vision world, as they are being successfully used in several applications and research areas. Many of these applications, such as gaming or human computer interaction systems, rely on the efficiency of learning a scene background model for detecting and tracking moving objects, to be further processed and analyzed. Depth data is particularly attractive and suitable for applications based on moving objects detection, since

© Springer International Publishing AG 2017
S. Battiato et al. (Eds.): ICIAP 2017 International Workshops, LNCS 10590, pp. 219–229, 2017.
https://doi.org/10.1007/978-3-319-70742-6_21

they are not affected by several problems representative of color-based imagery. However, depth data suffer from other problems, such as depth camouflage or depth sensor noisy measurements, which limit the efficiency of depth-only based background modeling approaches. The complementary nature of color and depth synchronized information acquired by RGBD sensors poses new challenges and design opportunities. New strategies are required that explore the effectiveness of the combination of depth- and color-based features, or their joint incorporation into well known moving object detection and tracking frameworks.

In order to evaluate and compare scene background modelling methods for moving object detection on RGBD videos, we assembled and made available the SBM-RGBD dataset[1]. It provides all facilities (data, ground truths, and evaluation scripts) for the SBM-RGBD Challenge, organized in conjunction with the Workshop on Background Learning for Detection and Tracking from RGBD Videos, 2017. The dataset and the results of the SBM-RGBD Challenge, which are described in the following sections, will remain available also after the competition, as reference for future methods.

2   Video Categories

The SBM-RGBD dataset provides a wide set of synchronized color and depth sequences acquired by the Microsoft Kinect. The dataset consists of 33 videos (about 15000 frames) representative of typical indoor visual data captured in video surveillance and smart environment scenarios, selected to cover a wide range of scene background modeling challenges for moving object detection. The videos come from our personal collections as well as from existing public datasets, including the GSM dataset, described in Moyá-Alcover et al. [13], MULTIVISION, described in Fernandez-Sanchez et al. [5], the Princeton Tracking Benchmark, described by Song and Xiao [14], the RGB-D object detection dataset, described by Camplani and Salgado [3], and the UR Fall Detection Dataset, described by Kwolek and Kepski [7].

The videos have 640×480 spatial resolution and their length varies from 70 to 1400 frames. Depth images are recorded at either 16 or 8 bits. They are already synchronized and registered with the corresponding color images by projecting the depth map onto the color image, allowing a color-depth pixel correspondence. For each sequence, pixels that have no color-depth correspondence (due to the difference in the color and depth cameras centers) are indicated in black in a binary Region-of-Interest (ROI) image (see Fig. 2-(c)) and are excluded by the evaluation (see Sect. 4).

The videos span seven categories, selected to include diverse scene background modelling challenges for moving object detection. These well known challenges can be related only to the RGB channels (RGB), only to the depth channel (D), or can be related to all the channels (RGB+D):

---

[1] http://rgbd2017.na.icar.cnr.it/SBM-RGBDdataset.html.

1. **Bootstrapping** (RGB+D): Videos including foreground objects in all their frames. The challenge is to learn a model of the scene background (to be adopted for background subtraction) even when the usual assumption of having a set of training frames empty of foreground objects fails.
   This category includes five videos, in most of which the background is never shown in some scene regions, being always occupied by foreground people.
2. **Color Camouflage** (RGB): Videos including foreground objects whose color is very close to that of the background, making hard a correct segmentation based only on color.
   This category consists of four videos where foreground objects are moved in front of similarly colored background (e.g., a white box in front of other white boxes or a rolling furniture moving in front of other furniture of the same color).
3. **Depth Camouflage** (D): Videos including foreground objects very close in depth to the background. Indeed, in these cases the sensor gives the same depth data values for foreground and background, making hard a correct segmentation based only on depth.
   The category consists of four videos where people move their hands or other objects very close to the background.
4. **Illumination Changes** (RGB): Videos containing strong and mild illumination changes. The challenge here is to adapt the color background model to illumination changes in order to achieve an accurate foreground detection.
   Four videos are included into this category, where the illumination varies due to the covering of the light source or to unstable illumination acquisition.
5. **Intermittent Motion** (RGB+D): Videos with scenarios known for causing ghosting artifacts in the detected motion, i.e., abandoned foreground objects or removed foreground objects. The challenge here is to detect foreground objects even if they stop moving (abandoned object) or if they were initially stationary and then start moving (removed object).
   This category consists of six videos including abandoned and removed objects. Two videos are obtained by reversing the original temporal order of the frames (so that an object that is abandoned in the original sequence results as removed in the reversed sequence).
6. **Out of Sensor Range** (D): Videos including foreground or background objects that are too close to/far from the sensor. Indeed, in these cases the sensor is unable to measure depth, due to its minimum and maximum depth specifications, resulting in *invalid* depth values.
   Five videos are included into this category, where several invalid depth values are due to foreground objects whose distance from the sensor is out of the admissible sensor range.
7. **Shadows** (RGB+D): Videos showing shadows caused by foreground objects. Indeed, foreground objects block the active light emitted by the sensor from reaching the background. This causes the casting on the background of shadows, that apparently behave as moving objects. RGBD sensors exhibit two different types of shadows: visible-light shadows in the RGB channels or IR shadows in the depth channel.

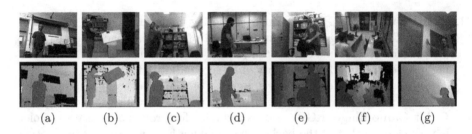

Fig. 1. Examples of videos from all the categories: (a) Bootstrapping, (b) Color-Camouflage, (c) DepthCamouflage, (d) IlluminationChanges, (e) IntermittentMotion, (f) OutOfRange, (g) Shadows.

The category consists of five videos including more or less strong shadows.

Examples of videos from all the categories are reported in Fig. 1.

3   Ground Truths

To enable a precise quantitative comparison of various algorithms for moving object detection from RGBD videos, all the videos come with pixel-wise ground truth foreground segmentations for each video. A foreground region is intended as anything that does not belong to the background, including abandoned objects and still persons, but excluding light reflections, shadows, etc. The ground truth images, some of which created using the GroundTruther software kindly made available by the organizers of changedetection.net, contain four labels (see Fig. 2-(d)), namely:

- 0: Background
- 85: Outside ROI
- 170: Unknown motion
- 255: Foreground

Areas around moving objects are labeled as *unknown motion*, due to semi-transparency and motion blur that do not allow a precise foreground/background classification. Therefore, these areas, as those not included into the ROI, are excluded by the evaluation.

While our evaluation is made across all the ground truths for all the videos, only a subset of the available ground truths is made publicly available for testing, in order to reduce the possibility of overtuning method parameters.

4   Metrics

The SBM-RGBD dataset comes also with tools to compute performance metrics for moving object detection from RGBD videos, and thus identify algorithms that are robust across various challenges. Let TP, FP, FN, and TN indicate,

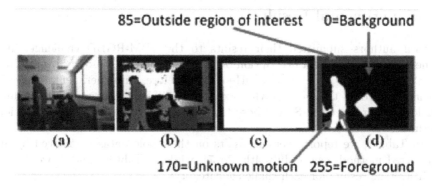

Fig. 2. Sequence ChairBox: (a) color and (b) depth images; (c) ROI; (d) ground truth.

for each video, the total number of True Positive, False Positive, False Negative, and True Negative pixels, respectively. The seven adopted metrics, widely adopted in the literature for evaluating the results of moving object detection (e.g., [6]), are

1. Recall
$$Rec = \frac{TP}{TP + FN}$$

2. Specificity
$$Sp = \frac{TN}{TN + FP}$$

3. False Positive Rate
$$FPR = \frac{FP}{FP + TN}$$

4. False Negative Rate
$$FNR = \frac{FN}{TP + FN}$$

5. Percentage of Wrong Classifications
$$PWC = 100 * \frac{FN + FP}{TP + FN + FP + TN}$$

6. Precision
$$Prec = \frac{TP}{TP + FP}$$

7. F-Measure
$$F_1 = \frac{2 * Prec * Rec}{Prec + Rec}$$

The Matlab scripts to compute all performance metrics have been adapted by the scripts available from changedetection.net.

5   Experimental Results

Several authors submitted their results to the SBM-RGBD challenge, and some of them provided a description of their method: RGBD-SOBS and RGB-SOBS [11], SCAD [12], and cwisardH+ [4]. Therefore, our experimental analysis is mainly devoted to assess to what extent the different background modelling challenges introduced in Sect. 2 pose troubles to these background subtraction methods.

In Table 1, we report average results on the whole dataset achieved by all submitted methods (as of July 4th, 2017), while in Tables 2 and 3, we report their average results for each challenge category[2].

Table 1. Average results on the whole SBM-RGBD dataset.

Method Name	Rec	Sp	FPR	FNR	PWC	$Prec$	F_1
RGBD-SOBS [11]	0.8391	0.9958	0.0042	0.0895	1.0828	0.8796	0.8557
RGB-SOBS [11]	0.7707	0.9708	0.0292	0.1578	5.4010	0.7247	0.7068
SRPCA [2]	0.7786	0.9739	0.0261	0.1499	3.1911	0.7474	0.7472
AvgM-D	0.7065	0.9869	0.0131	0.2221	2.8848	0.7498	0.7157
Kim	0.8493	0.9947	0.0053	0.0793	1.0292	0.8764	0.8606
SCAD [12]	0.8847	0.9932	0.0068	0.0439	0.9088	0.8698	0.8757
cwisardH+ [4]	0.7622	0.9817	0.0183	0.1664	2.8806	0.7556	0.7470

Bootstrapping can be a problem, especially for selective background subtraction methods (e.g., [9]), i.e. those that update the background model using only background information. Indeed, once a foreground object is erroneously included into the background model (e.g., due to inappropriate background initialization or to inaccurate segmentation of foreground objects), it will hardly be removed by the model, continuing to produce false negative results. The problem is even harder if some parts of the background are never shown during the sequences, as it happens in most of the videos of the Bootstrapping category. Indeed, in these cases, also the best performing background initialization methods [1] fail, as illustrated in Fig. 3, and only alternative techniques (e.g., inpainting) can be adopted to recover missing data [10]. Nonetheless, depth information seems to be beneficial for affording the challenge, as reported in Table 2, where accurate results are achieved by most of the methods that exploit depth information.

As expected, all the methods that exploit depth information achieve high accuracy in case of *color camouflage*. An evident example of the benefits induced by depth information for this category is given by the F-measure value achieved

---

[2] All the results are available at http://rgbd2017.na.icar.cnr.it/SBM-RGBDchallenge Results.html.

Table 2. Average results for each category of the SBM-RGBD dataset (Part 1).

Method Name	Rec	Sp	FPR	FNR	PWC	Prec	F_1
Bootstrapping							
RGBD-SOBS	0.8842	0.9925	0.0075	0.1158	2.3270	0.9080	0.8917
RGB-SOBS	0.8023	0.9814	0.0186	0.1977	4.4221	0.8165	0.8007
SRPCA	0.7284	0.9914	0.0086	0.2716	3.7409	0.9164	0.8098
AvgM-D	0.4587	0.9861	0.0139	0.5413	7.1960	0.6941	0.5350
Kim	0.8805	0.9965	0.0035	0.1195	1.5227	0.9566	0.9169
SCAD	0.8997	0.9940	0.0060	0.1003	1.8015	0.9319	0.9134
cwisardH+	0.5727	0.9616	0.0384	0.4273	8.1381	0.5787	0.5669
ColorCamouflage							
RGBD-SOBS	0.9563	0.9927	0.0073	0.0437	1.2161	0.9434	0.9488
RGB-SOBS	0.4310	0.9767	0.0233	0.5690	16.0404	0.8018	0.4864
SRPCA	0.8476	0.9389	0.0611	0.1524	4.3124	0.8367	0.8329
AvgM-D	0.9001	0.9793	0.0207	0.0999	2.0719	0.8096	0.8508
Kim	0.9737	0.9927	0.0073	0.0263	0.7389	0.9754	0.9745
SCAD	0.9875	0.9904	0.0096	0.0125	0.7037	0.9677	0.9775
cwisardH+	0.9533	0.9849	0.0151	0.0467	1.1931	0.9502	0.9510
DepthCamouflage							
RGBD-SOBS	0.8401	0.9985	0.0015	0.1599	0.9778	0.9682	0.8936
RGB-SOBS	0.9725	0.9856	0.0144	0.0275	1.5809	0.8354	0.8935
SRPCA	0.8679	0.9778	0.0222	0.1321	2.9944	0.7850	0.8083
AvgM-D	0.8368	0.9922	0.0078	0.1632	1.6943	0.8860	0.8538
Kim	0.8702	0.9968	0.0032	0.1298	0.9820	0.9433	0.9009
SCAD	0.9841	0.9963	0.0037	0.0159	0.4432	0.9447	0.9638
cwisardH+	0.6821	0.9949	0.0051	0.3179	2.4049	0.9016	0.7648
IlluminationChanges							
RGBD-SOBS	0.4514	0.9955	0.0045	0.0486	0.9321	0.4737	0.4597
RGB-SOBS	0.4366	0.9715	0.0285	0.0634	3.5022	0.4759	0.4527
SRPCA	0.4795	0.9816	0.0184	0.0205	1.9171	0.4159	0.4454
AvgM-D	0.3392	0.9858	0.0142	0.1608	3.0717	0.4188	0.3569
Kim	0.4479	0.9935	0.0065	0.0521	1.1395	0.4587	0.4499
SCAD	0.4699	0.9927	0.0073	0.0301	0.9715	0.4567	0.4610
cwisardH+	0.4707	0.9914	0.0086	0.0293	1.0754	0.4504	0.4581
IntermittentMotion							
RGBD-SOBS	0.8921	0.9970	0.0030	0.1079	0.8648	0.9544	0.9202
RGB-SOBS	0.9265	0.9028	0.0972	0.0735	9.3877	0.4054	0.5397
SRPCA	0.8893	0.9629	0.0371	0.1107	3.7026	0.7208	0.7735
AvgM-D	0.8976	0.9912	0.0088	0.1024	1.4603	0.9115	0.9027
Kim	0.9418	0.9938	0.0062	0.0582	0.9213	0.9385	0.9390
SCAD	0.9563	0.9914	0.0086	0.0437	0.8616	0.9243	0.9375
cwisardH+	0.8086	0.9558	0.0442	0.1914	5.0851	0.5984	0.6633

Table 3. Average results for each category of the SBM-RGBD dataset (Part 2).

Method Name	Rec	Sp	FPR	FNR	PWC	Prec	F_1
OutOfRange							
RGBD-SOBS	0.9170	0.9975	0.0025	0.0830	0.5613	0.9362	0.9260
RGB-SOBS	0.8902	0.9896	0.0104	0.1098	1.3610	0.8237	0.8527
SRPCA	0.8785	0.9878	0.0122	0.1215	1.6100	0.7443	0.8011
AvgM-D	0.6319	0.9860	0.0140	0.3681	2.7663	0.6360	0.6325
Kim	0.9040	0.9961	0.0039	0.0960	0.8228	0.9216	0.9120
SCAD	0.9286	0.9965	0.0035	0.0714	0.5711	0.9357	0.9309
cwisardH+	0.8959	0.9956	0.0044	0.1041	0.8731	0.9038	0.8987
Shadows							
RGBD-SOBS	0.9323	0.9970	0.0030	0.0677	0.7001	0.9733	0.9500
RGB-SOBS	0.9359	0.9881	0.0119	0.0641	1.5128	0.9140	0.9218
SRPCA	0.7592	0.9768	0.0232	0.2408	4.0602	0.8128	0.7591
AvgM-D	0.8812	0.9876	0.0124	0.1188	1.9330	0.8927	0.8784
Kim	0.9270	0.9934	0.0066	0.0730	1.0771	0.9404	0.9314
SCAD	0.9665	0.9910	0.0090	0.0335	1.0093	0.9276	0.9458
cwisardH+	0.9518	0.9877	0.0123	0.0482	1.3942	0.9062	0.9264

by the RGBD-SOBS method, that doubles the value achieved by the same method but without considering depth (RGB-SOBS). A similar reasoning can be applied to the *illumination changes* challenge. However, we point out that, in this case, the analysis should be based on Specificity, FPR, FNR, and PWC, rather than on the other three metrics. Indeed, two of the four videos of this category have no foreground objects throughout the whole duration, their rationale being the willingness of not detecting false positives under varying illumination conditions. This leads to have no positive cases in all ground truths and, consequently, to undefined values of Precision, Recall, and F-measure (in the experiments, values for these undefined cases are set to zero).

Depth can be beneficial also for detecting and properly handling cases of *intermittent motion*. Indeed, foreground objects can be easily identified based on their depth, that is lower than that of the background, even when they remain stationary for long time periods. Methods that explicitly exploit this characteristic (e.g., RGBD-SOBS and SCAD) succeed in handling cases of removed and abandoned objects, achieving high accuracy.

Overall, *shadows* do not seem to pose a strong challenge to most of the methods. Indeed, depth shadows due to moving objects cause some undefined depth values, generally close to the object contours, but these can be handled based on motion. Color shadows can be handled either exploiting depth information, that is insensitive to this challenge, or through color shadow detection techniques (e.g., as in RGB-SOBS and SCAD), when only color information is taken into

Fig. 3. Background image for sequence adl24cam0 (where the center area of the room is always covered by the man) computed using: (a) temporal median filter and (b) LabGen [8].

account. Instead, they are still a challenge when the sole grey level intensity is considered (e.g., as in SRPCA).

Out of range and *Depth camouflage* are among the most challenging issues, at least when information on color is disregarded or not properly combined with depth. Indeed, even though accuracy of most of the methods is moderately high, several false negatives are produced, as shown in Fig. 4 for depth camouflage.

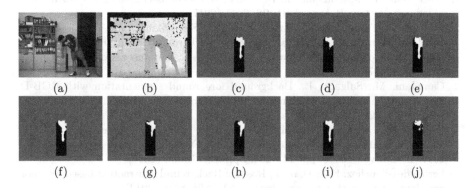

Fig. 4. Sequence DCamSeq2 (DepthCamouflage): (a) image no. 534, corresponding (b) depth image, and (c) ground truth; segmentation masks achieved by: (d) RGBD-SOBS, (e) RGB-SOBS, (f) SRPCA, (g) AvgM-D, (h) Kim, (i) SCAD, (j) CwisardH+.

6   Conclusions and Perspectives

The paper describes a novel benchmarking framework that we set up and made publicly available in order to evaluate and compare scene background modeling methods for moving object detection on RGBD videos. The SBM-RGBD dataset is the largest RGBD video collection ever made available for this specific purpose. The 33 videos span seven categories, selected to include diverse scene background modeling challenges for moving object detection. Seven evaluation metrics, chosen among the most widely used, are adopted to evaluate the results against a wide set of pixel-wise ground truths. A preliminary analysis of results achieved by several methods investigates to what extent the various background modeling challenges pose troubles to background subtraction methods that exploit color and depth information. The proposed framework will serve as a reference for future methods aiming at overcoming these challenges.

Acknowledgments. We would like to thank all the authors who submitted their results to the SBM-RGBD Challenge, which will serve as reference for future generation methods. L. Maddalena wishes to acknowledge the GNCS (Gruppo Nazionale di Calcolo Scientifico) and the INTEROMICS Flagship Project funded by MIUR, Italy. A. Petrosino wishes to acknowledge Project VIRTUALOG Horizon 2020-PON 2014/2020. L. Salgado wishes to acknowledge projects TEC2013-48453 (MR-UHDTV) and TEC2016-75981 (IVME) funded by the Ministerio de Economa, Industria y Competitividad (AEI/FEDER) of the Spanish Government.

References

1. Bouwmans, T., Maddalena, L., Petrosino, A.: Scene background initialization: a taxonomy. Pattern Recogn. Lett. **96**, 3–11 (2017)
2. Bouwmans, T., Sobral, A., Javed, S., Jung, S.K., Zahzah, E.-H.: Decomposition into low-rank plus additive matrices for background/foreground separation: a review for a comparative evaluation with a large-scale dataset. Comput. Sci. Rev. **23**, 1–71 (2017)
3. Camplani, M., Salgado, L.: Background foreground segmentation with RGB-D Kinect data: an efficient combination of classifiers. J. Vis. Commun. Image Represent. **25**(1), 122–136 (2014)
4. De Gregorio, M., Giordano, M.: CwisarDH$^+$: Background Detection in RGBD Videos by Learning. In: Battiato, S., Gallo, G., Farinella, G., Leo, M. (eds.) ICIAP 2017. LNCS, vol. 10590, pp. 242–253. Springer, Cham (2017)
5. Fernandez-Sanchez, E.J., Diaz, J., Ros, E.: Background subtraction based on color and depth using active sensors. Sensors **13**, 8895–8915 (2013)
6. Goyette, N., Jodoin, P.M., Porikli, F., Konrad, J., Ishwar, P.: Changedetection.net: a new change detection benchmark dataset. In: IEEE Computer Society Conference on Computer Vision and Pattern Recognition Workshops (CVPRW), 2012, pp. 1–8, June 2012
7. Kwolek, B., Kepski, M.: Human fall detection on embedded platform using depth maps and wireless accelerometer. Comput. Methods Programs Biomed. **117**(3), 489–501 (2014)
8. Laugraud, B., Piérard, S., Braham, M., Van Droogenbroeck, M.: Simple median-based method for stationary background generation using background subtraction algorithms. In: Murino, V., Puppo, E., Sona, D., Cristani, M., Sansone, C. (eds.) ICIAP 2015. LNCS, vol. 9281, pp. 477–484. Springer, Cham (2015). https://doi.org/10.1007/978-3-319-23222-5_58

9. Maddalena, L., Petrosino, A.: A self-organizing approach to background subtraction for visual surveillance applications. IEEE Trans. Image Process. **17**(7), 1168–1177 (2008)
10. Maddalena, L., Petrosino, A.: Background model initialization for static cameras. In: Bouwmans, T., Porikli, F., Hoferlin, B., Vacavant, A. (eds.) Background Modeling and Foreground Detection for Video Surveillance, pp. 3-1-3-16. Chapman & Hall/CRC (2014)
11. Maddalena, L., Petrosino, A.: Exploiting color and depth for background subtraction. In: Battiato, S., Gallo, G., Farinella, G., Leo, M. (eds.) ICIAP 2017. LNCS, vol. 10590, pp. 254–265. Springer, Cham (2017)
12. Minematsu, T., Shimada, A., Uchiyama, H., Taniguchi, R.: Simple combination of appearance and depth for foreground segmentation. In: Battiato, S., Gallo, G., Farinella, G., Leo, M. (eds.) ICIAP 2017. LNCS, vol. 10590, pp. 266–277. Springer, Cham (2017)
13. Moyá-Alcover, G., Elgammal, A., Jaume-i-Capó, A., Varona, J.: Modeling depth for nonparametric foreground segmentation using RGBD devices. Pattern Recogn. Lett. **96**, 76–85 (2017)
14. Song, S., Xiao, J.: Tracking revisited using RGBD camera: unified benchmark and baselines. In: Proceedings of the 2013 IEEE International Conference on Computer Vision, ICCV 2013, pp. 233–240. IEEE Computer Society (2013)

Moving Object Detection on RGB-D Videos Using Graph Regularized Spatiotemporal RPCA

Sajid Javed[1], Thierry Bouwmans[2], Maryam Sultana[1], and Soon Ki Jung[1(✉)]

[1] School of Computer Science and Engineering, Kyungpook National University,
80 Daehak-ro, Buk-gu, Daegu 702-701, Republic of Korea
{sajid,maryam}@vr.knu.ac.kr, skjung@knu.ac.kr
[2] Laboratoire MIA (Mathematiques, Image et Applications),
Université de La Rochelle, 17000 La Rochelle, France
thierry.bouwmans@univ-lr.fr

Abstract. Moving object detection is the fundamental step for various computer vision tasks. Many existing methods are still limited in accurately detecting the moving objects because of complex background scenes such as illumination condition, color saturation, and shadows etc. RPCA models have shown potential for moving object detection, where input data matrix is decomposed into a low-rank matrix representing the background image and a sparse component identifying moving objects. However, RPCA methods are not ideal for real-time processing because of the batch processing issues. These methods also show a performance degradation without encoding spatiotemporal and depth information. To address these problems, we investigate the performance of online Spatiotemporal RPCA (SRPCA) algorithm [1] for moving object detection using RGB-D videos. SRPCA is a graph regularized algorithm which preserves the low-rank spatiotemporal information in the form of dual spectral graphs. This graph regularized information is then encoded into the objective function which is solved using online optimization. Experiments show competitive results as compared to four state-of-the-art subspace learning methods.

1 Introduction

The segmentation of moving objects from video sequence is the first step in surveillance video analysis [2] and higher level computer vision and image processing tasks, such as anomaly detection [3], salient object detection [4], image rain streak removals [5], video inpainting [6], and visual object tracking [7]. This preprocessing step consists of disentangling moving objects known as foreground from the static or dynamic scene called background component. Moving object detection becomes more challenging when the video sequences include strong and mild illumination changes, foreground objects that are very close in color to the background, and foreground or background objects that are too close to/far from the sensor [8]. Moreover, sequences containing foreground objects in all their frames called bootstrapping, shadows caused by foreground objects, and

© Springer International Publishing AG 2017
S. Battiato et al. (Eds.): ICIAP 2017 International Workshops, LNCS 10590, pp. 230–241, 2017.
https://doi.org/10.1007/978-3-319-70742-6_22

sequences with scenarios known for causing ghosting artifacts in the detected motion, i.e., abandoned foreground objects or removed foreground objects, have remained challenging scenarios [9,10].

Many methods have been reported to cope with the aforementioned problems in the literature [9,11–20]. Moving object segmentation from these videos is still a challenging problem [8,9,21,22]. Subspace learning methods, such as Robust Principal Component Analysis (RPCA) [23], have gained significant attention in the past few years for background-foreground separation [21,22]. In [23], J. Wright *et al.* presented the theory of RPCA for the extraction of redundant and grossly corrupted information from input data matrix. Background-Foreground modeling is considered as a matrix decomposition problem in [23,24] as:

$$\min_{\mathbf{B},\mathbf{F}} ||\mathbf{B}||_* + \lambda||\mathbf{F}||_1, \text{ such that}, \mathbf{X} = \mathbf{B} + \mathbf{F}, \tag{1}$$

where $\mathbf{X} = [\mathbf{x}_1, \mathbf{x}_2, ..., \mathbf{x}_n] \in \mathbb{R}^{p \times n}$ is the input video sequence of n frames, and each $\mathbf{x}_i \in \mathbb{R}^p$ denotes i-th frame with p pixels. RPCA-based matrix decomposition model defined by (1) assumes that the sequence $\mathbf{X}$ can be represented as a combination of highly redundant information part (e.g., visually consistent background regions) and a grossly corrupted sparse component (e.g., distinctive foreground object regions). The redundant information part usually lies in a low dimensional feature subspace, which can be approximated by a low-rank feature matrix called background component $\mathbf{B}$. In contrast, the foreground component $\mathbf{F}$ deviating from the low-rank subspace can be viewed as noise or errors, which are represented by a sparse sensory matrix. It is shown in [24] that if the singular vectors of $\mathbf{B}$ component satisfy some incoherent conditions, $\mathbf{B}$ is low-rank and $\mathbf{F}$ is sufficiently sparse, then $\mathbf{B}$ and $\mathbf{F}$ can be recovered with high probability by solving the convex optimization method proposed in [24].

In (1), $||\mathbf{B}||_*$ denotes the nuclear norm (sum of the singular values of $\mathbf{B}$), $||\mathbf{F}||_1$ is the l_1-norm (sum of the absolute values of all the entries in $\mathbf{F}$), and $\lambda = 1/\sqrt{\max(p, n)}$. RPCA and its extensions have been successfully applied for background-foreground detection [14–16,19]. Interested readers can explore more details in [21,22].

One major shortcoming of RPCA is that it can only handle two dimensional input data matrix. Hence, the spatial information is lost and causes performance degradation because of re-structuring each frame into 1-D vector. Second, majority of the RPCA models work under batch processing, that is, in order to solve (1), one has to store all video frames in a memory before optimization. Such a batch processing fashion is not ideal for real-time processing. Third, previous state-of-the-art RPCA models [14,19,21] process only color or intensity information as a result the performance also degrades because of lack of additional features.

To address these problems, this paper presents the evaluation of online *Spatiotemporal RPCA* (SRPCA) algorithm [1] for moving object detection on RGB-D video sequences. SRPCA algorithm consists of three main stages: (i) detection of dynamic images to create an input dynamic sequence by discarding motionless video frames, (ii) computation of spatiotemporal graph Laplacians, and

(iii) application of RPCA to incorporate the preceding two steps for the separation of background and foreground components. We evaluate the performance of SRPCA algorithm on a new SBM-RGBD designed for moving object detection. We test SRPCA algorithm on each video of SBM-RGBD by using only intensity, RGB, and depth features. Experimental evaluations show that the performance of SRPCA algorithm is significantly better than existing methods by employing intensity features. Depth information assists to improve the detection performance in the presence of color saturation problem however the depth features are very noisy in SBM-RGBD. Therefore, the performance of SRPCA algorithm degraded by fusing RGB-D features.

The rest of this paper is organized as follows. In Sect. 2, the related work is reviewed. Section 3 describes the SRPCA algorithm in detail. Experimental results are discussed in Sect. 4, and finally the conclusion and some future directions are shown in Sect. 5.

2   Related Work

Over the past few decades, numerous research works have been carried out on background subtraction also known as foreground detection [21,22] as well as background initialization [1,13]. In background subtraction, emphasize is to improve the accuracy of foreground detection. While the task of estimating a foreground-free image is called background modeling. Many surveys are also contributed to these topics [21,22]. In this paper we propose a novel algorithm for background modeling which is inspired from subspace learning methods. Therefore, in this section we mainly focus on background-foreground separation methods based on subspace learning.

Wright *et al.* [23] presented the first proposal of RPCA to handle the outliers in data. Candeś *et al.* [24] used RPCA for background-foreground separation. RPCA-based approaches for background-foreground separation are not ideal for surveillance applications mainly because these approaches suffer from high computational complexity. The traditional RPCA implementations processed data in batches. Many studies have been reported in literature to make the batch methods faster [1,19]. However batch methods are not real-time and mostly work offline. Some online methods have also been reported to handle this problem while global optimality is still the challenging issue in these approaches [1,21].

Many authors have contributed interesting works in the direction of enhancing only foreground detection[1]. For this purpose, a number of constraints have been suggested [11,19,20]. For example, Cao *et al.* [11] improved the performance of foreground detection by proposing total variation regularized RPCA method. Zhao *et al.* [19] proposed a markov random field constraint on the foreground matrix to eliminate noise and small background movements. Though the segmentation performance improved, but foreground regions tend to be over-smoothed [16] because of neighboring pixels smoothing constraints. Unfortunately, research

---

[1] http://wordpress-jodoin.dmi.usherb.ca/results2014/.

has not been focused improving low-rank background modeling[2] [22]. Therefore, there is need to design robust algorithm to recover background component in the challenging scenarios of real-life [25].

3   The SRPCA Algorithm [1]

The online *Spatiotemporal RPCA* (SRPCA) algorithm consists of several components. Initially, a dense optical flow is computed between each pair of consecutive video frames and motion-compensated binary mask $\mathbf{M}$ is generated. This motion mask is utilized to remove the motionless video frames from sequence $\mathbf{X}$ and to prepare a set of dynamic frames $\mathbf{D} \in \mathbb{R}^{p \times c}$ (where c is the number of dynamic frames), which only consists of those video clips that show dynamic scenes either because of the foreground or background variations. Then, two graphs are constructed to encode the spatiotemporal invariance of the scene background. Both of these graphs lie on two manifolds and ensure spatiotemporal smoothness. These two embedded manifolds, one among the video frames and the second among the spatial locations, are then incorporated in a unified iterative optimization scheme. The objective function is solved using matrix factorization based on alternating minimization strategy. Most of the existing methods [14,19] use batch processing while the proposed SRPCA algorithm is made computationally efficient by using iterative processing approach. In the following, we describe each step of the proposed SRPCA algorithm in detail.

3.1   Objective Function Formulation

Given a sequence $\mathbf{D}$, SRPCA algorithm decomposes it into the sum of background and foreground components by minimizing the loss function defined by (1). For ease of optimization, we use the maximum norm [26] on the matrix $\mathbf{B}$ to relax the matrix rank. Model (1) becomes

$$\min_{\mathbf{B},\mathbf{F}} ||\mathbf{B}||^2_{max} + \lambda||\mathbf{F}||_1, \text{ such that}, \mathbf{D} = \mathbf{B} + \mathbf{F}. \tag{2}$$

We incorporate temporal smoothness constraint into (2) by encoding pairwise similarities among the video frames. We also enforce the spatial graph regularization into (2) to incorporate the spatial smoothness among the background pixels. With these constraints, the proposed SRPCA model is then re-formulated as:

$$\min_{\mathbf{B},\mathbf{F}} ||\mathbf{B}||^2_{max} + \lambda||\mathbf{F}||_1 + \gamma_1 \text{tr}(\mathbf{B}^\top \Phi_s \mathbf{B}) + \gamma_2 \text{tr}(\mathbf{B}^\top \Phi_t \mathbf{B}), \text{ such that}, \mathbf{D} = \mathbf{B} + \mathbf{F}, \tag{3}$$

where $\Phi_t \in \mathbb{R}^{c \times c}$ is the Laplacian matrix of a temporal graph computed among the video frames. This is the first data manifold information that can be leveraged in the form of discrete graph. Similarly, $\Phi_s \in \mathbb{R}^{p \times p}$ is the Laplacian of a spatial graph computed among the spatial locations of sequence $\mathbf{D}$. The regularization terms $\text{tr}(\mathbf{B}^\top \Phi_s \mathbf{B})$ and $\text{tr}(\mathbf{B}^\top \Phi_t \mathbf{B})$ in (3) are known as spatiotemporal

---

[2] http://pione.dinf.usherbrooke.ca/results/.

graph regularization of background model. These terms encode a weighted penalization on the Laplacian basis.

Incorporation of spatiotemporal graph constraints on matrix $\mathbf{B}$ enhances the robustness of the component $\mathbf{F}$ against noise and dynamic pixels. As a result, spatiotemporally coherent foreground mask can be obtained. The parameters γ_1 and γ_2 assign relative importance to each of the terms while optimizing (3). Before optimizing (3), we first compute the matrix $\mathbf{D}$ and graph Laplacian matrices as described in the following sections.

3.2   Removing Motionless Video Frames

We remove motionless video frames by computing the dense optical flow [27] between two consecutive frames $\mathbf{x}_i$ and $\mathbf{x}_{i-1}$ at times t and t-1, respectively. This pre-processing step assists SRPCA algorithm to avoid overwhelming outliers appear in the intermittent foreground object motion sequences. To prepare matrix $\mathbf{D}$, it is empirically observed that the flow field is very small for motionless frames and slowly moving objects, i.e., when the pixel value does not deviate between two consecutive frames. Hence, the nth frame in $\mathbf{X}$ is considered to be redundant or motionless, if all entries are 1 in the corresponding n^{th} column of motion mask; otherwise, if some parts of the entries are 0, then the frame is considered as dynamic and it is augmented in matrix $\mathbf{D} = [\mathbf{d}_1, \mathbf{d}_2, ..., \mathbf{d}_c] \in \mathbb{R}^{p \times c}$. More details can be found in [1].

3.3   Spatiotemporal Regularization

Let $\mathbf{G}_t = (\mathbf{V}_t, \mathbf{E}_t, \mathbf{A}_t)$ be the temporal graph with vertex $\mathbf{V}_t$ as the frames of matrix $\mathbf{D}$, the set of pairwise edges $\mathbf{E}_t$ between $\mathbf{V}_t$, and the adjacency matrix $\mathbf{A}_t$, which encodes the weights and connectivity of the graph.

The frames connected with similar pixel values most likely are part of $\mathbf{B}$. Therefore a segmentation that is temporally consistent with $\mathbf{B}$ can be obtained. For this purpose we find similarity between every two frames in the temporal direction. The graph $\mathbf{G}_t$ is then built using s-nearest neighbor strategy [28]. The first step consists of searching the closest neighbors for all the samples using Euclidean distances, where each node is connected to its s nearest neighbors. Let Δ be the matrix that contains all pairwise distances, $\Delta_{i,j}$ is the Euclidean distance between $(\mathbf{d}_i , \mathbf{d}_j) \in \mathbf{D}$ as $\Delta_{i,j} = \sqrt{||\mathbf{d}_i - \mathbf{d}_j||_2^2}$. Then, the adjacency matrix $\mathbf{A}_t$ for the $\mathbf{G}_t$ can be computed using

$$\mathbf{A}_t(i,j) = exp\left(-\frac{\Delta_{i,j} - \omega_{min}}{\sigma^2}\right), \tag{4}$$

where ω_{min} is the minimum non-zero distance in Δ, and σ^2 is the smoothing factor in $\mathbf{G}_t$, which can be set equal to the average distance of the s-nearest neighbors. In general, if $\mathbf{d}_i$ is in the s-nearest neighbors of $\mathbf{d}_j$ then there is a link between two nodes $\{\mathbf{d}_i, \mathbf{d}_j\}$ and $\mathbf{A}_t(i,j)$ is > 0; otherwise, $\mathbf{A}_t(i,j) = 0$. Maximum value of $\mathbf{A}_t(i,j)$ will be 1. Finally, the normalized temporal graph

Laplacian matrix that characterizes graph $\mathbf{G}_t$ is computed as $\Phi_t = \mathbf{W}^{-1/2}(\mathbf{W} - \mathbf{A})\mathbf{W}^{-1/2} = \mathbf{I} - \mathbf{W}^{-1/2}\mathbf{A}\mathbf{W}^{-1/2}$, where $\mathbf{I}$ is the identity matrix and $\mathbf{W}$ is the degree matrix defined as $\mathbf{W} = diag(w_i)$, where $w_i = \sum_j \mathbf{A}_t(i, j)$. For ease of notation we ensure the size of Φ_t to be $p \times p$. In case the number of frames c are larger than p, we select $p < c$ frames randomly to compute Φ_t. If c is less than p padding is performed to ensure the size of Φ_t to be $p \times p$.

Similarly, the spatial graph $\mathbf{G}_s = (\mathbf{V}_s, \mathbf{E}_s, \mathbf{A}_s)$ can be constructed with the set $\mathbf{V}_s$ as the rows of matrix $\mathbf{D}$. The pairwise relationship between the pixels is information that could alternatively be exploited to refine matrix $\mathbf{B}$ for the spatially consistent background modeling. For the construction of Laplacian of spatial graph, $\Phi_s \in \mathbb{R}^{p \times p}$, we enforce smoothness on the patch level of matrix $\mathbf{D}$ rather than on the pixel level, because comparing patches of the image allows one to use the local information of the image.

3.4 Solution for Objective Function

One of the main deficiency of model (3) is that it requires the computation of full (or partial) SVD of matrix $\mathbf{B}$ in every iteration, which could become prohibitively expensive when the dimensions are large. We overcome this problem by first adopting a proxy for the max-norm of rank of matrix $\mathbf{B}$ defined in [26] as:

$$\|\mathbf{B}\|_{max} = \min_{\mathbf{U} \in \mathbb{R}^{p \times r}, \mathbf{V} \in \mathbb{R}^{r \times c}} \frac{1}{2}(\|\mathbf{U}\|_{2,\infty} \cdot \|\mathbf{V}\|_{2,\infty}), \text{ such that, } \mathbf{B} = \mathbf{UV}. \quad (5)$$

where $\mathbf{U}$ is termed the spatial basis, and $\mathbf{V}$ represents the temporal coefficients of $\mathbf{U}$ in r-dimensional linear space, and r is a rank that is upper bounded by the rank of $\mathbf{B}$. The product $\mathbf{UV}$ is known as the approximation $\mathbf{B}$ of matrix $\mathbf{D}$. Taking this into account (5) can be substituted into (3) by considering that $\|\mathbf{V}\|_{2,\infty}^2 = 1$ [26] as:

$$\min_{\mathbf{U} \in \mathbb{R}^{p \times r} \mathbf{V} \in \mathbb{R}^{r \times c}} \|\mathbf{D} - \mathbf{UV}\|_F^2 + \frac{1}{2}\|\mathbf{U}\|_{2,\infty}^2 + \gamma_1 tr(\mathbf{V}^\top\mathbf{U}^\top \Phi_s \mathbf{UV}) + \gamma_2 tr(\mathbf{V}^\top\mathbf{U}^\top \Phi_t \mathbf{UV}). \quad (6)$$

Model (6) is based on batch processing optimization in which all video frames have to be available in a memory prior to any processing. SRPCA is targeted to derive an iterative solution of (6) over spatiotemporal graph regularizations which only processes one frame per time instance. To do so, the iterative solution of (6) is formulated as:

$$\min_{\mathbf{U} \in \mathbb{R}^{p \times r}, \mathbf{v}_t} \sum_{t=1}^c \left(\|\mathbf{m}_t \circ (\mathbf{d}_t - \mathbf{Uv}_t)\|_2^2 + \gamma_1(\mathbf{v}_t^\top \mathbf{U}^\top \Phi_s \mathbf{Uv}_t) + \gamma_2(\mathbf{v}_t^\top \mathbf{U}^\top \Phi_t \mathbf{Uv}_t) \right) + \frac{\lambda_1}{2}\|\mathbf{U}\|_{2,\infty}^2. \quad (7)$$

which can be solved via alternating minimization strategy, in which the cost function is minimized with respect to each individual optimization variable, whereas the other functions remain fixed. The detailed solution for solving (7) can be found in [1]. Figure 1 presents the visual results obtained by SRPCA algorithm.

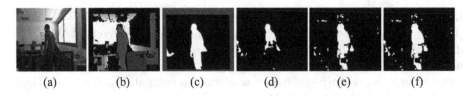

(a)   (b)   (c)   (d)   (e)   (f)

Fig. 1. Results of the proposed SRPCA algorithm on *ChairBox* sequence taken from 'Illumination Changes' category of RGBD dataset [25]. From left to right: (a) Input image, (b) Depth image, (c) Ground truth, (d) SRPCA results using RGB color features, (e) SRPCA results using depth features, and (f) SRPCA results using RGBD color features.

4   Experimental Evaluations

We evaluated the SRPCA algorithm on new challenging SBM-RGBD dataset [25]. SRPCA algorithm is compared with four current state-of-the-art subspace learning methods 2P-RPCA [14], DECOLOR [19], 3TD [17], and BS-GFL [20]. The implementation of all these methods is publicly available on authors websites. SRPCA algorithm requires the following parameters, $\lambda_1 = 1/\sqrt{\max(p, n)}$ [24], γ_1 and γ_2 are set to 10 (see Fig. 2 for more details). For the construction of $\mathbf{G}_s$ on image patches, we used patch size of 5×5 pixels. The number of nearest neighbors s is set to 10 for both graphs. We used the FLANN [28] libraries for more efficient computation of the graphs. Better tuned values of these parameters may generate better results, however, we have emphasized on generalization of the proposed algorithm over unseen datasets.

The SBM-RGBD dataset consists of 33 diverse video sequences with 7 different categories (see Fig. 3). The SBM-RGBD dataset comprises of complex scenes in which the goal is to show that the integration of depth features enhance the performance of moving object detection. This is because depth may be less effected in the presence of shadows and color saturation problem. The visual results over seven selected sequences (one sequence per category) with corresponding ground truth images are illustrated in Fig. 3. Figure 3 shows that the estimated mask of moving objects is close to the ground truth images.

We also quantitatively compared SRPCA algorithm results with existing methods. For this purpose, we computed a well-known $\mathbf{F}_1$ score as an accuracy measure. The goal is to maximize the $\mathbf{F}_1$ measure for more accurate moving object detection. Table 1 presents the comparison of the SRPCA algorithm with other methods using only intensity features. Table 2 presents the comparison of the SRPCA algorithm with other methods using intensity, RGB, depth, and RGBD features. SRPCA model defined in (7) processes each individual channel independently and then fuses the RGB and RGB-D results. On the average, the SRPCA algorithm achieved 0.75, 0.71, and 0.72 $\mathbf{F}_1$ score which is significantly higher than existing best performing method 2PRPCA which obtained 0.62 and 0.65.

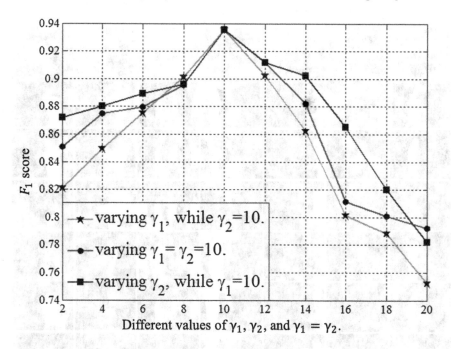

Fig. 2. Variations in F_1 score using different values of γ_1 and γ_2. Experiment performed on 'genSeq1' sequence of SBM-RGBD dataset [25]. The best results are obtained by using $\gamma_1 = \gamma_2 = 10$.

For 'Illumination Changes' category, only SRPCA and 2PRCPA produced good results (see Table 1). While remaining methods such as DECOLOR and BS-GFL etc. perform well with some small discrepancies. This is because the nuclear norm they are based on constraints the low-rank background model to capture the background appearance. The additional spatio-temporal constraints encoded in SRPCA assisted to achieve good results.

The 'Color Camouflage' and 'Depth Camouflage' are more challenging sequences than 'Illumination Changes' category. In these videos, the moving objects are very close in color and depth to the background component. Table 1 shows that the SRPCA obtained, on the average, the higher F_1 score. In these cases, the existing methods performed poor discrimination between background and foreground segments. Overwhelming outliers of color saturated foreground objects were incorporated into the estimated background. In contrast, the spatio-temporal constraints in SRPCA efficiently handled these outliers and estimated outlier-free low-rank component.

In 'Intermittent Motion' category, some foreground objects remained motionless and then started moving created outliers in the background model. SRPCA considered the motionless frames as redundant and removed them. All of the existing methods failed to cope with incorporated outliers because of motionless foreground objects. Only SRPCA algorithm effectively handled these outliers in

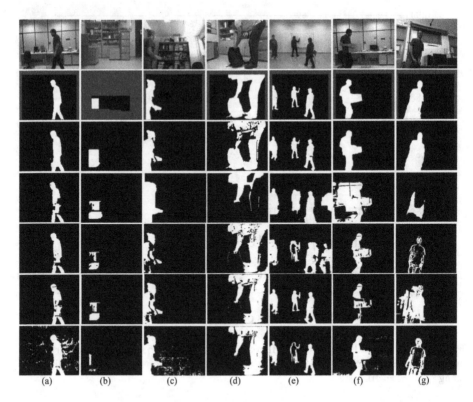

Fig. 3. Visual results of the SRPCA algorithm [1] in comparison with four state-of-the-art subspace learning methods on the SBM-RGBD dataset [25] using intensity features. From left to Right: (a) sequence 'genSeq1' from category 'Illumination Changes', (b) 'colorCam1y' from 'Color Camouflage', (c) 'Despatx_ds' from 'Depth Camouflage', (d) 'movedBackground2' from 'Intermittent Motion', (e) 'MultiPeople2' from 'Out of Sensor Range', (f) 'genSeq2' from 'Shadows', and (g) 'Bootstrapping_ds' from 'Bootstrapping'. From top to bottom: seven input images, ground truth images, the results obtained by SRPCA algorithm, DECOLOR [19], 2PRPCA [14], 3TD [17], and BS-GFL [20].

Table 1. Comparison of average F_1 measure score on SBM-RGBD dataset [25]. See Fig. 3 for visual comparisons with other methods. Note that the F_1 score is computed using only intensity features. The first and second best performing methods are shown in red and blue colors.

Methods	Illumination changes	Color camouflage	Depth camouflage	Intermittent motion	Out of sensor range	Shadows	Bootstrapping	Average
DECOLOR	0.48	0.70	0.72	0.46	0.58	**0.62**	**0.76**	0.61
2PRPCA	0.38	**0.74**	0.68	**0.51**	**0.74**	0.61	0.69	**0.62**
3TD	0.20	0.66	0.62	0.38	0.66	0.59	0.71	0.54
BS-GFL	0.29	0.73	**0.75**	0.40	0.71	0.58	0.57	0.57
SRPCA	**0.44**	0.85	0.81	0.77	0.80	0.77	0.81	0.75

the final estimation of background. The proposed SRPCA algorithm exhibited best performance ($\mathbf{F}_1 = 0.77$).

For 'Out of Sensor Range' sequences, most of the methods performed poor estimation of moving objects except 2P-RPCA. In this case, SRPCA have shown significantly better performance than existing methods. In all of these sequences, the performance of the moving object detection is improved by incorporating spatio-temporal constraints. For sequences that belong to the 'Shadows' category, the proposed SRPCA algorithm exhibited significant improvements ($\mathbf{F}_1 = 0.77$) over current methods. The current methods have shown degraded performance of $\mathbf{F}_1 < 0.70$. For complex dynamics in 'Bootstrapping' category, all methods have shown relatively poor performance. This is because of the absence of foreground-free images. The SRPCA algorithm performed significantly better than others by obtaining $\mathbf{F}_1 = 0.81$, while all the others obtained 0.76, 0.69, 0.71, and 0.57, respectively. Overall, the subspace learning methods are sensitive against noisy or missing information in depth features. Therefore, fusing RGB and depth information could not perform better discrimination of background-foreground segment as compare to intensity features.

Execution time of all algorithms was compared on a machine with 3:0 GHz Intel core i5 processor and 4 GB RAM. For fair comparison with the above mentioned approaches, the time is recorded in seconds. It takes about 40s to process a 90 video frames of intensity channel with resolution of [480 × 640]. While, DECOLOR [19] takes 760s, 2PRPCA [14] takes 300s, and BS-GFL [20] takes about 603s, respectively.

Table 2. Comparison of average $\mathbf{F}_1$ measure score on SBM-RGBD dataset [25]. The $\mathbf{F}_1$ score is computed using intensity, RGB, Depth, and RGB+Depth (RGBD) features. The first and second best performing methods are shown in red and blue colors.

Methods	Intensity features	Depth features	RGB features	RGBD features
DECOLOR	0.61	0.20	0.56	0.63
2PRPCA	**0.62**	**0.29**	**0.65**	**0.65**
3TD	0.54	0.31	0.57	0.59
BS-GFL	0.57	0.21	0.63	0.60
SRPCA	0.75	0.24	0.71	0.72

5   Conclusion

In this paper, we evaluated the performance of SRPCA algorithm on SBM-RGBD using color, intensity, and depth features for moving object detection. SRPCA is semi-online algorithm which processes one video frame per time instance. Experimental evaluations showed that the SRPCA performed better than other state of the art subspace learning methods using intensity features. Depth is an important clue for segmentation of moving object detection in the presence of scenes containing shadows, lighting condition, and color camouflage. Since, this rich information is less effected in these scenarios. In the future, we will design an efficient fusion strategy to combine the depth and color information for more accurate moving object detection system. We will first recover the death images from missing data and then we will fuse them with intensity or color information.

Acknowledgments. This work was supported by the National Research Foundation of Korea funded by the Korean Government (NRF-20170915).

References

1. Javed, S., Mahmood, A., Bouwmans, T., Jung, S.K.: Spatiotemporal low-rank modeling for complex scene background initialization. IEEE T-CSVT **PP**, 1 (2016)
2. Wang, S., Yang, J., Zhao, Y., Cai, A., Li, S.Z.: A surveillance video analysis and storage scheme for scalable synopsis browsing. In: IEEE ICCV-Workshops, pp. 1947–1954 (2011)
3. Chandola, V., Banerjee, A., Kumar, V.: Anomaly detection: a survey. ACM CSUR **41**, 15 (2009)
4. Peng, H., Li, B., Ling, H., Hu, W., Xiong, W., Maybank, S.J.: Salient object detection via structured matrix decomposition. IEEE T-PAMI **39**, 818–832 (2017)
5. Kang, L.W., Lin, C.W., Fu, Y.H.: Automatic single-image-based rain streaks removal via image decomposition. IEEE T-IP **21**, 1742–1755 (2012)
6. Newson, A., Almansa, A., Fradet, M., Gousseau, Y., Pérez, P.: Video inpainting of complex scenes. SIAM J-IS **7**, 1993–2019 (2014)
7. Yilmaz, A., Javed, O., Shah, M.: Object tracking: a survey. ACM CSUR **38**, 13 (2006)
8. Bouwmans, T., El Baf, F., Vachon, B.: Background modeling using mixture of gaussians for foreground detection-a survey. RPCS **1**, 219–237 (2008)
9. Bouwmans, T., Maddalena, L., Petrosino, A.: Scene background initialization: a taxonomy. PRL (2017)
10. Joddoin, P.M., Maddalena, L., Petrosino, A.: Scene background modeling.net. In: IEEE ICPR (2016)
11. Cao, X., Yang, L., Guo, X.: Total variation regularized RPCA for irregularly moving object detection under dynamic background. IEEE T-Cybern. **46**, 1014–1027 (2016)
12. Chen, M., Wei, X., Yang, Q., Li, Q., Wang, G., Yang, M.H.: Spatiotemporal GMM for background subtraction with superpixel hierarchy. IEEE T-PAMI **PP**, 1 (2017)
13. Diego, O., Juan, C.S.M., Jose, M.M.: Rejection based multipath reconstruction for background estimation in video sequences with stationary objects. CVIU **147**, 23–37 (2016)
14. Gao, Z., Cheong, L.F., Wang, Y.X.: Block-sparse RPCA for salient motion detection. IEEE T-PAMI **36**, 1975–1987 (2014)
15. Javed, S., Ho Oh, S., Sobral, A., Bouwmans, T., Ki Jung, S.: Background subtraction via superpixel-based online matrix decomposition with structured foreground constraints. In: IEEE ICCVW (2015)
16. Liu, X., Zhao, G., Yao, J., Qi, C.: Background subtraction based on low-rank and structured sparse decomposition. IEEE T-IP **24**, 2502–2514 (2015)

17. Oreifej, O., Li, X., Shah, M.: Simultaneous video stabilization and moving object detection in turbulence. IEEE T-PAMI **35**, 450–462 (2013)
18. Stagliano, A., Noceti, N., Verri, A., Odone, F.: Online space-variant background modeling with sparse coding. IEEE T-IP **24**, 2415–2428 (2015)
19. Zhou, X., Yang, C., Yu, W.: Moving object detection by detecting contiguous outliers in the low-rank representation. IEEE T-PAMI **35**, 597–610 (2013)
20. Xin, B., Tian, Y., Wang, Y., Gao, W.: Background subtraction via generalized fused lasso foreground modeling. In: IEEE CVPR (2015)
21. Bouwmans, T., Zahzah, E.H.: Robust PCA via principal component pursuit: a review for a comparative evaluation in video surveillance. CVIU **122**, 22–34 (2014)
22. Bouwmans, T., Sobral, A., Javed, S., Jung, S.K., Zahzah, E.H.: Decomposition into Low-rank plus additive matrices for background/foreground separation: a review for a comparative evaluation with a large-scale dataset. CSR **23**, 1–71 (2016)
23. Wright, J., Ganesh, A., Rao, S., Peng, Y., Ma, Y.: Robust principal component analysis: exact recovery of corrupted low-rank matrices via convex optimization. In: NIPS (2009)
24. Candès, E.J., Li, X., Ma, Y., Wright, J.: Robust principal component analysis? JACM **58**, 11 (2011)
25. Camplani, M., Maddalena, L., Moy Alcover, G., Petrosino, A., Salgado, L.: A benchmarking framework for background subtraction in RGBD videos. In: Battiato, S., Gallo, G., Farinella, G., Leo, M. (eds.) ICIAP 2017. LNCS, vol. 10590, pp. 219–229. Springer, Cham (2017)
26. Lee, J.D., Recht, B., Srebro, N., Tropp, J., Salakhutdinov, R.R.: Practical large-scale optimization for max-norm regularization. In: NIPS, pp. 1297–1305 (2010)
27. Liu, C., et al.: Beyond pixels: exploring new representations and applications for motion analysis. Ph.D. thesis. MIT (2009)
28. Muja, M., Lowe, D.G.: Scalable nearest neighbor algorithms for high dimensional data. IEEE T-PAMI **36**, 2227–2240 (2014)

CwisarDH$^+$: Background Detection in RGBD Videos by Learning of Weightless Neural Networks

Massimo De Gregorio[1] and Maurizio Giordano[2(✉)]

[1] Istituto di Scienze Applicate e Sistemi Intelligenti "E. Caianiello" (ISASI - CNR), Via Campi Flegrei, 34, 80078 Pozzuoli, Naples, Italy
massimo.degregorio@cnr.it
[2] Istituto di Calcolo e Reti ad Alte Prestazioni (ICAR - CNR), Via Pietro Castellino, 111, 80131 Naples, Italy
maurizio.giordano@cnr.it

Abstract. This work is a continuation of our past experiences in investigating learning and classification capabilities of weightless neural networks (WNNs) for background modeling and object motion detection in videos. In the current work, we adapted and modified a previous method, called CwisarDH, to the domain of RGBD videos. In the proposed approach two main strategies were adopted. First, by decoupling the RGB color information from the pixel depth information, the two video streams are synchronously but separately (under different neural configurations) modeled by WNNs at each pixel. Depending on the video temporal ROI, a preliminary set of frames is used solely for network training. In the detection phase, classification is interleaved with re-training on current colors whenever pixels are detected as belonging to the background. Secondly, the independent outputs of the two video processing are combined by an OR operator and post-processed by erosion/dilation filters. With this simple approach, we obtained an efficient background modeling in RGBD videos, as we were confident of this considering the good results gathered by CwisarDH in the ChangeDetection.net 2014 challenge.

1 Introduction

Today background and object motion detection in videos can take advantage of the excellent ability and flexibility to capture RGBD images provided by recent sensing technologies, such as Microsoft Kinect [17] and Asus Xtion Pro.

In the complex task of learning a background model of a scene for the detection and tracking of moving objects in videos in several domains (not only limited to gaming and HCI scenarios), depth images have the advantage of not suffering from typical problems of RGB images, such as illumination changes/motion, shadowing and color camouflage. On the other hand, depth images suffer other problems, such as depth-camouflage or depth sensor noisy measurements, which bound the efficiency of depth-only based background modeling approaches.

© Springer International Publishing AG 2017
S. Battiato et al. (Eds.): ICIAP 2017 International Workshops, LNCS 10590, pp. 242–253, 2017.
https://doi.org/10.1007/978-3-319-70742-6_23

Although in recent years some approaches to background modeling of video scenes exploiting both RGB and depth data provided by RGBD sensors have been proposed, there is still a lack of research on methods in this field. This situation is exhibited in the recent review articles [4,7] in which few works use depth data. Some examples are: the mixture of Gaussians (MoG) algorithm [16], which models the background by a combination of four-dimensional Gaussian distributions per pixel; the Vibe algorithm [3], which combines with logical operations two independent models to obtain foreground masks, then processed with morphological filters; in [6] per-pixel statistical classifiers (Bayesian Networks and mixture Gaussians models) based on depth and color data are fused with a weighted average combiner; in [12] depth information is used to enhance the performance of a codebook based background subtraction method.

In literature, the majority of methods approaching background modeling in videos as a learning/classification problem of artificial neural networks falls in the class of weighted neural network systems [10,11]. As far as we know, there is only one system not authored by us and described in [15] which exploits learning/classification capabilities of a weightless neural network (WNN) architecture to address the problem of estimating the background of video scenes with the goal of automatically counting people in indoor scenes.

In this work we propose an adaptation of a previous method, called CwisArDH [8], to the domain of RGBD videos. Like the previous system it derives from, the proposed method relies on a weightless neural network, named WiSARD [1], chosen as modeling technology for both color and depth data in the domain of RGBD videos. While in several related works depth information is used as an additional component of the 3-dimensional RGB vector, in the current approach we decouple the RGB value from the pixel depth, such that the two videos (i.e., the RGB video and the Depth video) are synchronously but separately processed by respectively two pixel-wise WNNs: one network plays the role of background modeler for the RGB color of the pixel, while the other produces a background model of the pixel depth. By "separate modeling" we mean that the two modelers act under different neural settings and, at each frame, the decision of updating the pixel model may occur in none, only one or both modelers, depending on the specific learning history acquired up to that time.

In addition, the proposed system architecture is very simple and based on the following assumptions: (1) pixel-based processing without the need of neighborhood information; (2) straightforward use of two different WNNs to respectively model the pixel RGB color and depth; (3) an OR combination of segmentation results produced by the system on the two video streams. The proposed method has been applied to the recent SBM-RGBD video dataset [5]. The dataset consists of 33 videos representing typical indoor scenes in video surveillance and smart environment scenarios, selected to cover a wide range of scene background modeling challenges for moving object detection.

The paper is so organized: Sect. 2 describes the adopted weightless neural architecture; Sect. 3 discusses the proposed method for background detection that uses color and depth information in RGBD videos; Sect. 4 discusses the experimental setup and results of our method applied to the SBM-RGBD video dataset; Sect. 5 summarizes concluding remarks and future perspectives.

2   The Weightless Neural Model

WiSARD[1] belongs to the family of Weightless Neural Systems [1], and it adopts a RAM-based model of neuron by which learned information about a data domain is stored into RAM contents instead of computed weights of neuron connections. A RAM neuron receives an n-bit input that is interpreted as a unique address (stimulus) of a RAM cell, and used to access it either in writing (learning) or reading (classification) mode. WiSARD is formed by as many discriminators[2] as the number of classes of patterns to be recognized.

Figure 1 describes a WiSARD *discriminator* composed by m RAMs ($m = 4$) with input lines connected to the retina by means of a biunivocal pseudo–random mapping as a set of uncorrelated n–tuples ($n = 3$). The discriminator is trained with representative data of a specific class. In order to use the network as a discriminator, one has to set all RAM memory locations to '0' and choose a training set formed by binary patterns of ($m \times n$) bits. For each training pattern, a '1' is stored in the memory location of each RAM addressed by this input pattern. Once the training of patterns is completed, RAM memory contents will be set to a certain number of '0's and '1's. The information stored by RAM nodes during the training phase is used to deal with previous unseen patterns. When one of these is given as input, RAM memory contents addressed by the input pattern are read and summed by the summing device Σ. The number r thus obtained, which is called the *discriminator response*, is equal to the number of RAMs that output '1'. Intermediate values of r express a kind of "similarity measure" of the input pattern with respect to the patterns in the training set. The summing

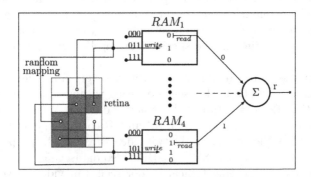

Fig. 1. A WiSARD discriminator

---

[1]   **Wilkes, Stonham and Aleksander Recognition Device.**
[2]   Also known as *multi-discriminator system*.

device enables this network of RAM nodes to exhibit – just like other ANN models based on synaptic weights – generalization and noise tolerance [2].

3 The CWISARDH$^+$ Approach to Background Detection

3.1 Architecture

CWISARDH$^+$ system architecture is depicted in Fig. 2. From the picture it is clear how the two video streams, i.e. the RGB video and the pixel-depth video are separately processed. The ROI mask is applied to both RGB and depth frames to restrict background learning and detection to the fixed region of interest.

At each pixel location of both RGB and depth frames, a WiSARD discriminator is created with the role of learning and classifying, during the timeline, changing values of that pixel as belonging (or not) to the background. To this end, two WiSARDs are configured with proper parameters, respectively to play the role of RGB modeler and Depth modeler for that pixel (see the two CWISARDH modules of Fig. 3). Indeed, RGB pixels are 3-channels integer values in the range 0–255, while pixel depth data are 1-channel integers in the range 0–65535. In order to model a variety of 256^3 different colors, a large $n_{rgb} \times z_{rgb}$ configuration is needed to guarantee a sufficient number of RAMs to represent with high resolution the current RGB value in its discretized binary encoding.

Lower numbers of RAMs are in general needed to represent depth values. Indeed, in our approach depth values are normalized to the range of depths that are assumed between the minimal and maximum used depths in the current scene.[3] Therefore, depth values span the potential range 0–65535 only in indoor scenes with long corridors or large halls. In indoor scenes of rooms or offices, the used depth ranges are smaller, thus resulting in lower requirements in terms of WiSARD nodes (RAMs) to cover the input. As a result, the corresponding

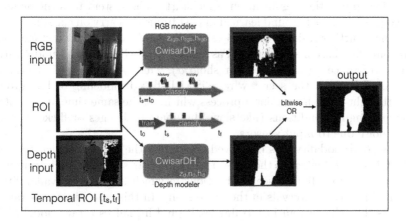

Fig. 2. CWISARDH$^+$ system architecture and modes

---

[3] Missing (or undefined) depth data are set to the maximum in the chosen range.

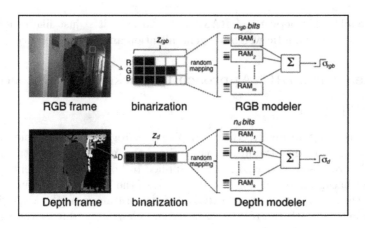

Fig. 3. CwisaRDH$^+$ input encoding

CwisaRDH module can be initialized with a smaller $n_d \times z_d$ configuration which is enough to represent with high resolution the current depth range.

3.2 Operating Modes

CwisaRDH$^+$ has been designed to operate in two modes: with and without pre-training. The first modality applies when the input RGBD video has a temporal ROI $[t_s, t_f]$ with detection timing starting after a time interval from the beginning of the video (that is, $t_s > t_0$). In this case, the dataset organizers assume implicitly that foreground objects are not present in the first time interval $[t_0, t_s]$. This information is exploited by our system starting working in training mode for all pixels and at each frame in the time interval $[t_0, t_s]$. Once the pre-training interval is expired, the classification stage starts. The system uses the acquired knowledge of pixel background learned in past frames to carry on classification on new frames. Further training on pixel values during the classification stage is carried on only for those pixels detected as "close" to the background model within a certain tolerance (classification threshold σ). This typical way of functioning in CwisaRDH [8] is the secret why WiSARD-based modeling of background can be thought as an incremental process which, at the same time, adapts itself to scene changing conditions (like slow illumination changes or flickering) and absorbs noise due to input sensors.

The second modality was conceived to address the cases in which the temporal ROI is $[t_0, t_f]$ whereas the detection timing starts at the very beginning of the video, corresponding to scene situations in which there is no availability of foreground-free time intervals in the video scene. In this case, since pre-training is not possible, the system just trains itself (and initializes a raw model of the background) using only the very first frames. This is possible thanks to the WiSARD learning mechanism: in successive frames, like in the previous mode, successful classification of pixels values as background are used to further train

```
Input: RGB or Depth video
Output: outvideo (B&W video with detected moving objects)
1   while getting a new frame from video  do
2       if frame belogs to trainset  then
3           foreach pixel in frame  do
4               train the pixel discriminator with its value encoding (RGB or Depth);
5               set pixel as bg in outframe;

6       else
7           foreach pixel in frame  do
8               use pixel encoding (RGB or Depth) to get response from pixel discriminator;
9               if response > σ  then
10                  empty pixel history buffer;
11                  train the pixel discriminator with pixel value encoding;
12                  set pixel as bg in outframe;
13              else
14                  if pixel history buffer is full then
15                      re-train pixel discriminator with pixel values in the pixel history buffer;
16                      empty pixel history buffer;
17                  else
18                      store pixel value encoding in pixel history buffer;
19                  set pixel as fg in outframe;
```

Algorithm 1. CwisarDH algorithm

and reinforce the model. Nevertheless, we have to cope with foreground objects which might be static in first frames, while moving later on: without any additional modification, the system would have detected as foreground the part of the scene background occluded by the delayed movement of objects (ghost effects). To cope with these effects the pixel values history buffer is used to this aim: the system resets the pixel model and reconstructs it from scratch using the more recent pixel values as soon as the pixel has assumed enough different values to fill the fixed-length buffer. The details of the pixel value history buffer are better described in the Algorithm 1. The presented pseudocode applies both to RGB and Depth videos.

3.3   RGB and Depth Modelers

Each CwisarDH module outputs a binary image representing the frame background/foreground detection. The two outputs are first post-processed by applying an erosion filter followed by a dilation filter. The so filtered outputs are combined by a binary OR and the result is the final output of the system.

Algorithm 1 describes the CwisarDH method pseudocode. In order to feed the discriminators with the right input, CwisarDH creates one discriminator for each pixel of the video frame. The RGB color or the pixel depth is represented by a binary (black & white) image, where the rows represent data components (three channels of RGB and one channel for depth) and the columns represent values of each data component (see Fig. 3). The CwisarDH optimal parameters depend on the application domain. As an example, in case of dynamic background scenarios, like shimmering water or waving trees, the CwisarDH can better face the problem with threshold values around 80%.

After the training phase, CWISARDH classifies the pixel as belonging to the background only if the corresponding discriminator response is greater than the fixed threshold σ, otherwise the pixel is considered belonging to the foreground. The system takes the correctly classified pixels to further train the associated discriminator: the online training is a peculiar characteristic of weightless systems. In this way, CWISARDH adapts itself both to dynamic backgrounds and to gradual changes in light.

CWISARDH extends the previous method CwisarD [9] by introducing a pixel classification history support: a h–sized buffer is associated to each pixel to store pixel colors continuously classified as foreground in h successive frames. When the buffer is full, the color history is used to reset and then to train the associated discriminator on buffered data (see Algorithm 1). On the contrary, each time the pixel is classified as background the history is emptied.

The history buffer support was introduced to improve performance especially to face with both the case of intermittent objects, like (des)appearing of objects that change status from background to foreground in the scene, and the case of sudden changes in light, shape and colors of background regions (like in *IlluminationChanges* category).

3.4 Implementation

CWISARDH$^+$ is implemented[4] in C++ and uses the OpenCV library [13] for image pre/post–processing and visualization. CWISARDH$^+$ software is characterized by a high degree of potential parallelism, since pixel–based computation in a frame has neither data nor control dependency on other pixel computations in the same frame. In fact, one WiSARD discriminator is associated to each pixel and trained by pixel values gathered in successive frame of the timeline. For this reason we implemented an OpenMP [14] C++ version of CWISARDH$^+$ to better exploit parallelism on a multicore CPUs. On a 720×480 RGBD video and under the parameter settings used in the experiments, CWISARDH$^+$ runs at 8 fps in training and at 2 fps in classification on a 4 GHz Intel Core i7.

4   CWISARDH$^+$ Results

The method CWISARDH$^+$ has been executed on all video categories in the same configuration: $z_{rgb} = 256$, $z_d = 64$, $n_{rgb} = 8$, $n_d = 4$, $\sigma_{rgb} = 0.70$, $\sigma_d = 0.70$. Note that this configuration was fixed after several experiments in which we varied all modeler parameters and we measured raw estimates of performance based on the limited number of groundtruth images published by SBM-RGBD challenge organizers. We are aware this configuration cannot be considered the optimal one and we are confident that longer experimentation will bring to a more efficient configuration with respect to the overall performance.

---

[4] The software is publicly available for download and testing on GitHub at: https://github.com/giordamaug/CwisarDHplus.

Pixel value history buffer size was in both modelers fixed to 50 items. Notice that history buffer usage to retrain the network is enabled only in case of temporal ROIs with $t_s = t_0$, like in the case of *Bootstrapping* video category. For all the other categories, $t_s > t_0$ so that the time interval $\Delta t = t_s - t_0$ is used to pre-train modelers, while the use of reinitialization and retraining on pixel values stored in the buffer is disabled for the entire timeline. In all situations training on current pixel values occurs everytime the current pixel value is classified as background based on the past knowledge.

Snapshots of the system outputs are reported in Fig. 4. Table 1 reports system results on all videos in the SBM-RGBD dataset. Table 2 reports estimates of background models obtained by CwisarDH$^+$ either using only RGB images (C) or only Depth images (D), or an OR-combination of the two (C+D). Note that the results of C+D models are different from those reported in Table 1, since the latter were calculated on groundtruth images which are fewer than those used by SBM-RGBD challenge organizers for method evaluation. In the average, we experienced that the D models provide better recalls, since our learning mechanism is highly sensitive to changes in depth images, thus resulting both in higher TP and lower FN rates as well, thus increasing the recalls. TN rates of D models are similar to those obtained in C models. On the other hand,

Fig. 4. CwisarDH$^+$ outputs on SBM-RGBD dataset

Table 1. CWISARDH$^+$ results on SBM-RGBD dataset

Videoname	Recall	Specif.	FPR	FNR	PWC	Prec.	F-meas.
Bootstrapping							
BootStrapping_ds	0.9426	0.9875	0.0125	0.0574	1.6659	0.8845	0.9126
adl24cam0	0.3310	0.9579	0.0421	0.6690	8.0174	0.3366	0.3338
bear_front	0.4344	0.9349	0.0651	0.5656	19.6902	0.7045	0.5374
fall01cam0	0.6510	0.9739	0.0261	0.3490	4.4015	0.5949	0.6217
fall20cam0	0.5044	0.9540	0.0460	0.4956	6.9155	0.3732	0.4290
AVG	0.5727	0.9616	0.0384	0.4273	8.1381	0.5787	0.5669
ColorCamouflage							
Cespatx_ds	0.9826	0.9992	0.0008	0.0174	0.1163	0.9615	0.9719
Hallway	0.8379	0.9962	0.0038	0.1621	1.2094	0.9235	0.8786
colorCam1	0.9938	0.9908	0.0092	0.0062	0.8509	0.9690	0.9812
colorCam2	0.9988	0.9535	0.0465	0.0012	2.5959	0.9469	0.9722
AVG	0.9533	0.9849	0.0151	0.0467	1.1931	0.9502	0.9510
DepthCamouflage							
DCamSeq1	0.7005	0.9973	0.0027	0.2995	1.9267	0.9389	0.8024
DCamSeq2	0.4279	0.9962	0.0038	0.5721	2.8621	0.8391	0.5668
Despatx_ds	0.9839	0.9942	0.0058	0.0161	0.6787	0.9449	0.9640
Wall	0.6162	0.9920	0.0080	0.3838	4.1520	0.8836	0.7261
AVG	0.6821	0.9949	0.0051	0.3179	2.4049	0.9016	0.7648
IlluminationChanges							
ChairB	0.8831	0.9966	0.0034	0.1169	1.5766	0.9694	0.9242
Ls_ds	0.0000	0.9999	0.0001	0.0000	0.0108	0.0000	0.0000
TimeOf	0.0000	0.9983	0.0017	0.0000	0.1718	0.0000	0.0000
genSeq	0.9997	0.9710	0.0290	0.0003	2.5425	0.8323	0.9083
AVG	0.4707	0.9914	0.0086	0.0293	1.0754	0.4504	0.4581
IntermittentMotion							
Shelves	0.7475	0.9984	0.0016	0.2525	0.6503	0.9038	0.8182
Sleeping_ds	0.9307	0.9117	0.0883	0.0693	8.4413	0.7281	0.8170
abandoned1	0.9795	0.9823	0.0177	0.0205	1.7793	0.5865	0.7337
abandoned2	0.9988	0.9877	0.0123	0.0012	1.0981	0.9179	0.9566
movedBackground1	0.9314	0.9702	0.0298	0.0686	3.0378	0.3192	0.4754
movedBackground2	0.2640	0.8847	0.1153	0.7360	15.5038	0.1352	0.1789
AVG	0.8086	0.9558	0.0442	0.1914	5.0851	0.5984	0.6633

Table 1. *(Continued)*

Videoname	Recall	Specif.	FPR	FNR	PWC	Prec.	F-meas.
OutOfRange							
MultiPeople1	0.9206	0.9930	0.0070	0.0794	1.2660	0.9179	0.9192
MultiPeople2	0.9014	0.9964	0.0036	0.0986	1.1326	0.9572	0.9285
TopViewLab1	0.9462	0.9958	0.0042	0.0538	0.5833	0.8863	0.9153
TopViewLab2	0.9506	0.9956	0.0044	0.0494	0.6157	0.8958	0.9224
TopViewLab3	0.7608	0.9974	0.0026	0.2392	0.7681	0.8619	0.8082
AVG	0.8959	0.9956	0.0044	0.1041	0.8731	0.9038	0.8987
Shadows							
Shadoww_ds	0.9795	0.9953	0.0047	0.0205	0.5702	0.9300	0.9541
fall01cam1	0.7870	0.9947	0.0053	0.2130	1.8362	0.9092	0.8437
genSeq2	0.9979	0.9869	0.0131	0.0021	1.1832	0.9056	0.9495
shadows1	0.9980	0.9830	0.0170	0.0020	1.4885	0.9055	0.9495
shadows2	0.9969	0.9786	0.0214	0.0031	1.8931	0.8806	0.9352
AVG	0.9518	0.9877	0.0123	0.0482	1.3942	0.9062	0.9264
Overall							
AVG	0.7622	0.9817	0.0183	0.1664	2.8806	0.7556	0.7470

Table 2. Contributions of Color and Depth models to CWISARDH$^+$ final results

Videoname	Model	TP	FP	FN	TN	Recall	Specif.	Prec.	F-meas.
BootStrapping_ds	C+D	163498	37081	13355	2678953	0.9245	0.9863	0.8151	0.8664
	C	104530	11889	72323	2704145	0.5911	0.9956	0.8979	0.7129
	D	161979	36670	14874	2679364	0.9159	0.9865	0.8154	0.8627
Cespatx_ds	C+D	194286	10005	4832	2333570	0.9757	0.9957	0.9510	0.9632
	C	62015	3397	137103	2340178	0.3114	0.9986	0.9481	0.4689
	D	193143	9529	5975	2334046	0.9700	0.9959	0.9530	0.9614
Despatx_ds	C+D	262003	20984	5750	2776857	0.9785	0.9925	0.9258	0.9515
	C	80076	5793	187677	2792048	0.2991	0.9979	0.9325	0.4529
	D	259635	19308	8118	2778533	0.9697	0.9931	0.9308	0.9498
ChairBox	C+D	1315792	107582	238401	12534539	0.8466	0.9915	0.9244	0.8838
	C	642668	52566	911525	12589555	0.4135	0.9958	0.9244	0.5714
	D	1234349	88625	319844	12553496	0.7942	0.9930	0.9330	0.8580
movedBackground1	C+D	253733	557468	23222	17950778	0.9162	0.9699	0.3128	0.4664
	C	195960	132747	80995	18375499	0.7076	0.9928	0.5962	0.6471
	D	187642	538175	89313	17970071	0.6775	0.9709	0.2585	0.3742
MultiPeople1	C+D	647639	114656	111586	9016614	0.8530	0.9874	0.8496	0.8513
	C	395383	63630	363842	9067640	0.5208	0.9930	0.8614	0.6491
	D	579274	94232	179951	9037038	0.7630	0.9897	0.8601	0.8086
Shadows_ds	C+D	143026	5573	1179	2154732	0.9918	0.9974	0.9625	0.9769
	C	19711	47	124494	2160258	0.1367	1.0000	0.9976	0.2404
	D	142432	5554	1773	2154751	0.9877	0.9974	0.9625	0.9749

depth images are also prone to provide more FPs in moving detection, thus resulting in worst precisions with respect to C models. Although C and D models seem to be complementary with respect to recall and precision performances, by OR-combining outputs the C+D models inherits recalls and F-measures of D models, but also the lower precision of C models, while specificity remains almost unchanged. These considerations hold in the majority of our experiments, with the exception of same cases (like *movedBackground1*) in which the C model gets better recall and precision due to the lower FP rates.

CwISARDH$^+$ gives good results on videos belonging to *IlluminationChanges* and satisfactory results on *OutOfRange* and *Shadows* videos but, unfortunately not very good results on *Bootstrapping* and *IntermittentMotion* videos. This is due to the fact that the system needs a set of foreground-free frames to start classifying (this is not the case of *Bootstrapping* videos), and after an interval of time (h frames), it includes in the background model the intermittent objects.

5   Conclusions

Pixel depth information, provided by low-costs RGBD cameras such as Microsoft Kinect, has demonstrated in recent years to be a very useful sensor data for the development of efficient background subtraction algorithms. Indeed, effects of illumination changes, shadows, and color camouflage can be significantly reduced with the use of depth information. On the other hand, depth data exhibit several problems such as depth camouflage and depth noise which effect object silhouettes efficient recognition.

Starting from the experiences of CwISARDH [8] in the ChangeDetection.net 2014 challenge, in this work we proposed and extension of it, called CwISARDH$^+$. This new method exploits both pixel color and depth information in the domain of RGBD videos. CwISARDH$^+$ is composed of two independent background modelers, one for RGB colors and the other for depth values of video frame pixels. Each modeler uses, for each pixel location, a weightless neural network to build up and constantly adapt an estimation of the background value of the pixel (color or depth).

In its preliminary design, the system combines by logical OR the outputs of the two background estimation processes. We are aware that the OR-combination of outputs, on one hand compensates true positives prediction defects of one of the two modelers, as well as, on contrary, it also results in false negatives and false positives predictions of one modeler to affect the final results. Nevertheless, with this naive approach of fusing RGB and depth information we gained good and promising results on the recent SBM-RGBD dataset. In the future more sophisticated and case-driven heuristics for modelers outputs combination will be investigated.

References

1. Aleksander, I., Thomas, W.V., Bowden, P.A.: WiSARD a radical step forward in image recognition. Sens. Rev. **4**, 120–124 (1984)
2. Aleksander, I., Morton, H.: An Introduction to Neural Computing. Chapman & Hall, London (1990)
3. Barnich, O., Droogenbroeck, M.V.: Vibe: a universal background subtraction algorithm for video sequences. IEEE Trans. Image Process. **20**(6), 1709–1724 (2011)
4. Bouwmans, T.: Recent advanced statistical background modeling for foreground detection: a systematic survey. Recent Patents Comput. Sci. **4**(3), 147–176 (2011)
5. Camplani, M., Maddalena, L., Moy Alcover, G., Petrosino, A., Salgado, L.: A benchmarking framework for background subtraction in RGBD videos. In: Battiato, S., Gallo, G., Farinella, G., Leo, M. (eds.) ICIAP 2017. LNCS, vol. 10590, pp. 219–229. Springer, Cham (2017)
6. Camplani, M., Salgado, L.: Background foreground segmentation with RGB-D kinect data: an efficient combination of classifiers. J. Vis. Commun. Image Represent. **25**(1), 122–136 (2014)
7. Cristani, M., Farenzena, M., Bloisi, D., Murino, V.: Background subtraction for automated multisensor surveillance: a comprehensive review. EURASIP J. Adv. Sig. Process. **2010**(1), 343057 (2010)
8. De Gregorio, M., Giordano, M.: Change detection with weightless neural networks. In: 2014 IEEE Conference on Computer Vision and Pattern Recognition Workshops, pp. 409–413, June 2014
9. De Gregorio, M., Giordano, M.: A WiSARD-based approach to CDnet. In: Proceedings of 1st BRICS Countries Congress (BRICS-CCI) (2013)
10. Ghosh, S., Roy, M., Ghosh, A.: Semi-supervised change detection using modified self-organizing feature map neural network. Appl. Soft Comput. **15**, 1–20 (2014)
11. Maddalena, L., Petrosino, A.: The SOBS algorithm: what are the limits? In: CVPR Workshops, pp. 21–26 (2012)
12. Murgia, J., Meurie, C., Ruichek, Y.: An improved colorimetric invariants and RGB-depth-based codebook model for background subtraction using Kinect. In: Gelbukh, A., Espinoza, F.C., Galicia-Haro, S.N. (eds.) MICAI 2014. LNCS (LNAI), vol. 8856, pp. 380–392. Springer, Cham (2014). https://doi.org/10.1007/978-3-319-13647-9_35
13. OpenCV: Open source computer vision. http://www.opencv.org
14. OpenMP: The OpenMP api specification for parallel programming. http://www.openmp.org
15. Schofield, A., Mehta, P., Stonham, T.: A system for counting people in video images using neural networks to identify the background scene. Pattern Recogn. **29**(8), 1421–1428 (1996)
16. Stauffer, C., Grimson, W.: Adaptive background mixture models for real-time tracking. In: Proceedings of IEEE Conference on Computer Vision and Pattern Recognition, pp. 246–252 (1999)
17. Zhang, Z.: Microsoft Kinect sensor and its effect. IEEE MultiMedia **19**(2), 4–10 (2012)

Exploiting Color and Depth for Background Subtraction

Lucia Maddalena[1(✉)] and Alfredo Petrosino[2]

[1] National Research Council, Naples, Italy
lucia.maddalena@cnr.it
[2] University of Naples Parthenope, Naples, Italy

Abstract. Background subtraction from color and depth data is a fundamental task for indoor video surveillance applications that use data acquired by RGBD sensors. This paper proposes a method based on two background models for color and depth information, exploiting a self-organizing neural background model previously adopted for RGB videos. The resulting color and depth detection masks are combined, not only to achieve the final results, but also to better guide the selective model update procedure. The experimental evaluation on the SBM-RGBD dataset shows that the exploitation of depth information allows to achieve much higher performance than just using color, accurately handling color and depth background maintenance challenges.

Keywords: Background subtraction · Color and depth data · RGBD

1 Introduction

Low cost RGBD sensors are being successfully used in several indoor video surveillance applications. Many of them rely on a scene background model learned from data for detecting moving objects, to be further processed and analyzed.

Background subtraction from color video data is a widely studied problem, as witnessed by several recent surveys [1,6,19,21]. Main challenges include *illumination changes* (where the background model should adapt to strong and mild illumination changes), *color camouflage* (where foreground objects having color very close to the background are hardly segmented), *shadows* caused by foreground objects occluding the visible light, *bootstrapping* (where the background model should be properly set up even in the absence of a training set free of foreground moving objects), and the so-called *intermittent motion*, referring to videos with scenarios known for causing "ghosting" artifacts in the detected motion, i.e., foreground objects that should be detected even if they stop moving (abandoned object) or if they were initially stationary and then start moving (removed object).

Depth data is particularly attractive for background subtraction, since it is not affected by illumination changes or color camouflage; thus some background modeling approaches based only on depth have been proposed [9,20].

© Springer International Publishing AG 2017
S. Battiato et al. (Eds.): ICIAP 2017 International Workshops, LNCS 10590, pp. 254–265, 2017.
https://doi.org/10.1007/978-3-319-70742-6_24

However, depth data suffers from other types of problems, such as *depth camouflage* (where foreground objects having depth very close to the background are hardly segmented), and *out of sensor range* (where the sensor produces *invalid* depth values for foreground or background objects that are too close to/far from it). Moreover, depth data shares with color data other challenges, including intermittent motion, bootstrapping, and shadows caused by foreground objects occluding the IR light coming from the emitter.

Many recent methods try to exploit the complementary nature of color and depth information acquired with RGBD sensors. Generally, these methods either extend to RGBD data well-known background models originally designed for color data [8,12] or model the scene background (and sometimes also the foreground) based on color and depth independently and then combine the results, on the basis of different criteria [5,10,13,15]

The method proposed in this paper belongs to the latter class of methods. Two background models are constructed for color and depth information, exploiting a self-organizing neural background model previously adopted for RGB videos [18]. The resulting color and depth detection masks are then combined to achieve the final detection masks, also used to better guide the selective model update procedure.

2 RGBD-SOBS Algorithm

The proposed algorithm for background subtraction using RGBD video data exploits the background model constructed and maintained in the SC-SOBS algorithm [18], originally designed for RGB data. It is based on the idea of building a neural background model of the image sequence by learning in a self-organizing manner image sequence variations, seen as trajectories of pixels in time. Two separated models are constructed for color and depth data, and their resulting background subtraction masks are suitably combined in order to update the models and to achieve the final result. In the following, we provide a self-contained description of the color and depth models, referring to [18] for further details on the original neural model, and of the combination criterion.

2.1 The Color Model

Given the color image sequence $\{I_1, \ldots, I_T\}$, at each time instant t we build and update a neuronal map for each pixel $\mathbf{p}$, consisting of $n \times n$ weight vectors $cm_t^{i,j}(\mathbf{p}), i,j = 0, \ldots, n-1$, which will be called the *color model* for pixel $\mathbf{p}$ and will be indicated as $CM_t(\mathbf{p})$:

$$CM_t(\mathbf{p}) = \left\{ cm_t^{i,j}(\mathbf{p}), \ i,j = 0, \ldots, n-1 \right\}. \tag{1}$$

If every sequence image has size $N \times P$, the complete set of models $CM_t(\mathbf{p})$ for all pixels $\mathbf{p}$ of the t-th sequence image I_t is organized as a 2D neuronal map CB_t

of size $(n \times N) \times (n \times P)$, where the weight vectors $cm_t^{i,j}(\mathbf{p})$ for the generic pixel $\mathbf{p} = (x, y)$ are at neuronal map position $(n \times x + i, n \times y + j)$, $i, j = 0, \ldots, n-1$:

$$CB_t(n \times x + i, n \times y + j) = cm_t^{i,j}(\mathbf{p}), \ i, j = 0, \ldots, n-1. \tag{2}$$

Although redundant, notations CM_t and CB_t introduced in Eqs. (1) and (2) will both be adopted. Indeed, the color model $CM_t(\mathbf{p})$ will be adopted in order to indicate the whole set of color weight vectors for each single pixel $\mathbf{p}$ at time t, helping to focus on the pixelwise representation of the background model. On the other side, the neuronal map CB_t will be adopted in order to refer to the whole color background model for an image sequence at time t, to highlight spatial relationships among weight vectors of adjacent pixels (see Eq. (7)).

Differently from [18], for *color model initialization*, we construct a color image CE that is an estimate of the color scene background. Then, for each pixel $\mathbf{p}$, the corresponding weight vectors of the color model $CM_0(\mathbf{p})$ are initialized with the pixel color value $CE(\mathbf{p})$:

$$cm_0^{i,j}(\mathbf{p}) = CE(\mathbf{p}), \quad i, j = 0, \ldots, n-1. \tag{3}$$

Among the several state-of-the-art background estimation methods [2] for constructing CE, in the experiments we have chosen the LabGen algorithm [14], which is one of the best performing on the SBMnet dataset[1]. Specifically, LabGen was run over the first L initial color frames, where $L = 100$.

At each time step t, *color background subtraction* sis achieved by comparing each pixel $\mathbf{p}$ of the t-th sequence frame I_t with the current pixel color model $CM_{t-1}(\mathbf{p})$, to determine the weight vector $BM_t^C(\mathbf{p})$ that best matches it:

$$d(BM_t^C(\mathbf{p}), I_t(\mathbf{p})) = \min_{i,j=0,\ldots,n-1} d(cm_{t-1}^{i,j}(\mathbf{p}), I_t(\mathbf{p})), \tag{4}$$

For the experiments reported in Sect. 3, the metric $d(\cdot, \cdot)$ is chosen as the Euclidean distance in the HSV color hexcone as in [18]. The color background subtraction mask for pixel $\mathbf{p}$ is then computed as

$$M_t^C(\mathbf{p}) = \begin{cases} 1 & \text{if } NCF_t(\mathbf{p}) \leq 0.5 \\ 0 & \text{otherwise} \end{cases}, \tag{5}$$

where the *Neighborhood Coherence Factor* is defined as $NCF_t(\mathbf{p}) = |\Omega_\mathbf{p}|/|N_\mathbf{p}|$ [7]. Here $|\cdot|$ refers to the set cardinality, $N_\mathbf{p} = \{\mathbf{q}: |\mathbf{p} - \mathbf{q}| \leq h\}$ is a 2D spatial neighborhood of $\mathbf{p}$ having width $(2h + 1) \in \mathbb{N}$ (in the experiments $h = 2$), and

$$\Omega_\mathbf{p} = \{\mathbf{q} \in N_\mathbf{p}: (d(BM_t^C(\mathbf{q}), I_t(\mathbf{p})) \leq \varepsilon^C) \vee (shadow(BM_t^C(\mathbf{q}), I_t(\mathbf{p})))\}. \tag{6}$$

$\Omega_\mathbf{p}$ is the set of pixels $\mathbf{q}$ belonging to $N_\mathbf{p}$ that either have in their background model a best match that is close enough to their value $I_t(\mathbf{q})$ or are shadows of the background. ε^C is a color threshold enabling the distinction between foreground and background pixels, while $shadow(\cdot)$ is a function implementing the shadow

---

[1] http://SceneBackgroundModeling.net.

detection mechanism adopted in [16]. It has been shown that the introduction of spatial coherence enhances robustness of the background subtraction algorithm against false detections [17].

An *update of the color neuronal map* is performed in order to adapt the color background model to scene modifications. At each time step t, the weight vectors of CB_{t-1} in a neighborhood of the best matching weight vector $BM_t^C(\mathbf{p})$ are updated according to weighted running average. In details, if $BM_t^C(\mathbf{p})$ is found at position $\bar{\mathbf{p}}$ in CB_{t-1}, then weight vectors of CB_{t-1} are updated according to

$$CB_t(\mathbf{q}) = (1 - \alpha_t^C(\mathbf{p}))CB_{t-1}(\mathbf{q}) + \alpha_t^C(\mathbf{p})I_t(\mathbf{p}) \quad \forall \mathbf{q} \in N_{\bar{\mathbf{p}}}, \tag{7}$$

where $N_{\bar{\mathbf{p}}} = \{\mathbf{q} : |\bar{\mathbf{p}} - \mathbf{q}| \leq k\}$ is a 2D spatial neighborhood of $\bar{\mathbf{p}}$ having width $(2k+1) \in \mathbb{N}$ (in the reported experiments $k = 1$). Moreover,

$$\alpha_t^C(\mathbf{p}) = \gamma \cdot G(\mathbf{q} - \bar{\mathbf{p}}) \cdot (1 - M_t(\mathbf{p})), \tag{8}$$

where γ represents the learning rate, $G(\cdot) = \mathcal{N}(\cdot; \mathbf{0}, \sigma^2 I)$ is a 2D Gaussian low-pass filter with zero mean and $\sigma^2 I$ variance (in the reported experiments $\sigma^2 = 0.75$). The $\alpha_t^C(\mathbf{p})$ values in Eq. (8) are weights that allow us to smoothly take into account the spatial relationship between current pixel $\mathbf{p}$ (through its best matching weight vector found at position $\bar{\mathbf{p}}$) and its neighboring pixels in I_t (through weight vectors at position $\mathbf{q} \in N_{\bar{\mathbf{p}}}$), thus preserving topological properties of the input in the neural network update (close inputs correspond to close outputs). In [18], $M_t(\mathbf{p})$ is the background subtraction mask value $M_t^C(\mathbf{p})$ for pixel $\mathbf{p}$, computed as in Eq. (5).

In the usual case that a set of K initial sequence frames is available for training, the above described initialization and update procedures on the first K sequence frames are adopted for training the neural network background model, to be used for detection and update in all subsequent sequence frames. What differentiates the training and the online phases in the proposed algorithm is the background subtraction mask $M_t(\mathbf{p})$ adopted in Eq. (8), besides the choice of parameters in Eqs. (6) and (8). Indeed, during the online phase, $M_t(\mathbf{p})$ is the combined mask value for pixel $\mathbf{p}$ (see Sect. 2.3):

$$M_t(\mathbf{p}) = \begin{cases} M_t^C(\mathbf{p}) & \text{if } 1 \leq t \leq K \\ M_t^{Comb}(\mathbf{p}) & \text{if } t > K \end{cases}, \tag{9}$$

in order to exploit depth information for the update of the color background model. The threshold ε^C in Eq. (6) is chosen as $\varepsilon^C = \varepsilon_1^C$ during training and $\varepsilon^C = \varepsilon_2^C$ during the online phase, with $\varepsilon_2^C \leq \varepsilon_1^C$, in order to include several observed pixel color variations during training and to obtain a more accurate color background model during the online phase (in the experiments, $\varepsilon_1^C = 0.1$ and $\varepsilon_2^C = 0.008$). The learning rate γ in Eq. (8) is set as $\gamma = \gamma_1 - t(\gamma_1 - \gamma_2)/K$ during training and as $\gamma = \gamma_2$ during the online phase, where γ_1 and γ_2 are predefined constants such that $\gamma_2 \leq \gamma_1$, in order to ensure neural network convergence during the training phase and to adapt to scene variability during the online phase. In order to have in (7) values for $\alpha_t^C(\mathbf{p})$ that belong to $[0,1]$, we set $\gamma_1 = c_1/ \max\limits_{\mathbf{q} \in N_{\overline{\mathbf{p}}}} G(\mathbf{q} - \overline{\mathbf{p}})$ and $\gamma_2 = c_2/ \max\limits_{\mathbf{q} \in N_{\overline{\mathbf{p}}}} G(\mathbf{q} - \overline{\mathbf{p}})$, with c_1 and c_2 constants such that $0 \leq c_2 \leq c_1 \leq 1$ (in the experiments, $c_1 = 0.1$ and $c_2 = 0.05$). For a deeper explanation of the mathematical ground behind the choice of color model parameters, the interested reader is referred to [18].

2.2 The Depth Model

The neural model adopted for depth information is analogous to the one adopted for color information. Differences are mainly due to the special treatment of invalid values inherent in the depth information acquisition phase.

Given the depth image sequence $\{D_1, \ldots, D_T\}$, at each time instant t we build and update a depth neuronal map for each pixel $\mathbf{p}$. It consists of $n \times n$ weight vectors $dm_t^{i,j}(\mathbf{p}), i, j = 0, \ldots, n\text{-}1$, which will be called the *depth model* for pixel $\mathbf{p}$ and will be indicated as $DM_t(\mathbf{p})$:

$$DM_t(\mathbf{p}) = \left\{ dm_t^{i,j}(\mathbf{p}), \; i, j = 0, \ldots, n - 1 \right\}. \tag{10}$$

Analogously to the case of the color model, the complete set of models $DM_t(\mathbf{p})$ for all pixels $\mathbf{p}$ of the t-th depth frame D_t is organized as a 2D neuronal map DB_t of size $(n \times N) \times (n \times P)$.

For *depth model initialization*, an estimate DE of the depth scene background is constructed based on the observation that the scene background is generally further away from the camera as compared to the foreground. Therefore, DE is obtained by accumulating, for each pixel, the highest depth value held in the first L depth frames. Then, for each pixel $\mathbf{p}$, the corresponding weight vectors of the depth model $DM_0(\mathbf{p})$ are initialized with the pixel depth value $DE(\mathbf{p})$:

$$dm_0^{i,j}(\mathbf{p}) = DE(\mathbf{p}), \quad i, j = 0, \ldots, n - 1. \tag{11}$$

At each time step t, *depth background subtraction* is achieved by comparing each pixel $\mathbf{p}$ of the t-th depth frame D_t having valid value with the current pixel depth model $DM_{t-1}(\mathbf{p})$, to determine the closest weight vector $BM_t^D(\mathbf{p})$:

$$|BM_t^D(\mathbf{p}) - D_t(\mathbf{p})| = \min_{i,j=0,\ldots,n-1} |dm_{t-1}^{i,j}(\mathbf{p}) - D_t(\mathbf{p})|. \tag{12}$$

The depth background subtraction mask for pixel $\mathbf{p}$ is then computed as

$$M_t^D(\mathbf{p}) = \begin{cases} 2 & \text{if } (D_t(\mathbf{p}) \; invalid) \\ 0 & \text{if } (D_t(\mathbf{p}) \; valid) \wedge (BM_t^D(\mathbf{p}) - D_t(\mathbf{p}) \leq \varepsilon^D), \\ 1 & \text{otherwise} \end{cases} \tag{13}$$

where $\wedge$ denotes the logical AND operator and ε^D is a predefined threshold. In the experiments, depth values are normalized in $[0,1]$ and ε^D is chosen as $\varepsilon_1^D = 0.1$ during training and $\varepsilon_2^D = 0.00075$ for 16bit depth images and 0.005 for 8bit depth images in the online phase. According to Eq. (13), incoming pixels having invalid depth value are signaled in the depth detection mask (being assigned the value 2), so as to be suitably treated in the mask combination step (see Sect. 2.3). Moreover, all pixels that have depth value greater than all weight vectors of their depth model are considered as background pixels (being assigned the value 0). This is in line with the observation that the scene background is generally further away from the camera as compared to the foreground, already exploited in the depth model initialization step.

Depth neuronal map update is also performed in order to adapt the depth background model to scene modifications. At each time step t and for each pixel $\mathbf{p}$ having valid depth value $D_t(\mathbf{p})$, the weight vectors of DB_{t-1} in a neighborhood of a valid best matching weight vector $BM_t^D(\mathbf{p})$, found at position $\overline{\mathbf{p}}$ in DB_{t-1}, are updated according to

$$DB_t(\mathbf{q}) = (1 - \alpha_t^D(\mathbf{p}))DB_{t-1}(\mathbf{q}) + \alpha_t^D(\mathbf{p})D_t(\mathbf{p}) \quad \forall \mathbf{q} \in N_{\overline{\mathbf{p}}}, \qquad (14)$$

where $\alpha_t^D(\mathbf{p}) = \gamma \cdot G(\mathbf{q} - \overline{\mathbf{p}}) \cdot (1 - M_t^D(\mathbf{p}))$, and the remaining notations are defined as those for Eqs. (7) and (8).

Moreover, during training, valid depth values for pixels that in previous frames had invalid values are included into the depth model. Specifically, weight vectors for generic pixel $\mathbf{p} = (x, y)$ that are still invalid at time t, $1 \leq t \leq K$, are initialized with valid depth values $D_t(\mathbf{p})$

$$DB_t(n{\times}x+i, n{\times}y+j) = dm_t^{i,j}(\mathbf{p}) = D_t(\mathbf{p}), \quad i,j = 0,\ldots,n-1, 1 \leq t \leq K. \quad (15)$$

This leads to learning a more complete depth background model during training. The process is not applied during the online phase, in order to avoid to include into the depth model new valid values that might belong to foreground objects.

2.3 Combining Color and Depth Masks

During online learning, color mask M_t^C and depth mask M_t^D are combined in order to produce a combined mask M_t^{Comb}, that is adopted to selectively update the color model (see Eq. (9)). In case of invalid depth values (signaled by $M_t^D(\mathbf{p})=2$ in Eq. (13)), only color mask values are considered; otherwise, depth values are considered. In order to reduce the adverse effect of noisy depth values around the object contours, signaled by setting $M_t^D(\mathbf{p}) = 3$, color mask values are considered instead in these areas. Thus, the combined mask is computed as

$$M_t^{Comb}(\mathbf{p}) = \begin{cases} M_t^C(\mathbf{p}) & \text{if} \quad M_t^D(\mathbf{p}) > 1 \\ M_t^D(\mathbf{p}) & \text{if} \quad otherwise \end{cases} . \qquad (16)$$

An example is provided in Fig. 1. Similarly to [10], the object contours are obtained as $dil(\overline{M}_t^D) \wedge M_t^D$, where $dil(\cdot)$ is the morphological dilation operator with a $3{\times}3$ structuring element and $\overline{M}_t^D$ denotes the complement of M_t^D.

2.4 The Algorithm

The above described procedure for each pixel can be sketched as the RGBD-SOBS algorithm reported in Fig. 2.

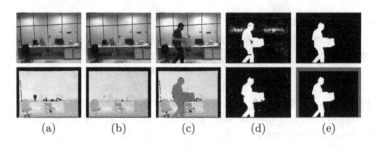

$$\text{(a)} \qquad \text{(b)} \qquad \text{(c)} \qquad \text{(d)} \qquad \text{(e)}$$

Fig. 1. Sequence genseq2 of the SBM-RGBD dataset: (a) color and depth images I_1 and D_1; (b) color and depth background estimates CE and DE; (c) color and depth images I_{159} and D_{159}; (d) color and depth detection masks M^C_{159} and M^D_{159}; (e) combined mask M^{Comb}_{159} and ground truth mask GT_{159}. (Color figure online)

RGBD-SOBS Algorithm

Input: color value $I_t(\mathbf{p})$ in frame I_t, $t = 1, \ldots, T$;
      depth value $D_t(\mathbf{p})$ in frame D_t, $t = 1, \ldots, T$;
Output: detection mask value $M^{Comb}_t(\mathbf{p})$ at time t, $t = 1, \ldots, T$;
      color neuronal map CB_t at time t, $t = 1, \ldots, T$;
      depth neuronal map DB_t at time t, $t = 1, \ldots, T$.

1. Initialize color model $CM_0(\mathbf{p})$ as in Eq. (3)
2. Initialize depth model $DM_0(\mathbf{p})$ as in Eq. (11)
3. **for** $t = 1, K$ /*Training phase*/
4.   Compute the color mask value $M^C_t(\mathbf{p})$ as in Eq. (5)
5.   Compute the depth mask value $M^D_t(\mathbf{p})$ as in Eq. (13)
6.   Update the color neuronal map CB_t as in Eq. (7) using mask M^C_t
7.   Update the depth neuronal map DB_t as in Eqs. (14) and (15) using mask M^D_t
8. **endfor**
9. **for** $t = K + 1, T$ /*Online phase*/
10.   Compute the color mask value $M^C_t(\mathbf{p})$ as in Eq. (5)
11.   Compute the depth mask value $M^D_t(\mathbf{p})$ as in Eq. (13)
12.   Compute the combined mask value $M^{Comb}_t(\mathbf{p})$ as in Eq. (16)
13.   Update the color neuronal map CB_t as in Eq. (7) using mask M^{Comb}_t
14.   Update the depth neuronal map DB_t as in Eq. (14) using mask M^D_t
15. **endfor**

Fig. 2. RGBD-SOBS algorithm for pixel $\mathbf{p}$.

3 Experimental Results

Experimental results have been carried out on the SBM-RGBD dataset [3,4], consisting of 33 RGBD videos acquired by the Microsoft Kinect, spanning 7 categories that include diverse scene background modelling challenges (see Sect. 1): Illumination Changes (IC), Color Camouflage (CC), Depth Camouflage (DC), Intermittent Motion (IM), Out of sensor Range (OR), Shadows (Sh), and Bootstrapping (Bo).

Table 1. Parameter values adopted for evaluating the RGBD-SOBS algorithm.

n	L	h	ε_1^C	ε_2^C	k	σ^2	c_1	c_2	ε_1^D	ε_2^D (16bit)	ε_2^D (8bit)
3	100	2	0.1	0.008	1	0.75	0.1	0.05	0.1	0.00075	0.005

Parameter values for the RGBD-SOBS algorithm common to all the SBM-RGBD videos are summarized in Table 1. In practice, all default SC-SOBS parameter values [18], well established on CDnet.net [11], have been chosen for the color model, and an analysis analogous to the one reported in [16] has been carried out for choosing the initialization and depth model parameters.

Accuracy is evaluated in terms of seven well-known metrics [3]: Recall (Rec), Specificity (Sp), False Positive Rate (FPR), False Negative Rate (FNR), Percentage of Wrong Classifications (PWC), Precision ($Prec$), and F-Measure (F_1).

Average performance metrics[2] achieved by the proposed RGBD-SOBS algorithm are reported in Table 2 for all the categories of the SBM-RGBD dataset, showing that, on average, RGBD-SOBS performs quite well. Moreover, comparisons with the RGB-SOBS results (obtained by RGBD-SOBS using only color

Table 2. Average performance results of RGBD-SOBS and RGB-SOBS in each category of the SBM-RGBD dataset. In boldface the best results for each metric.

Cat.	Method	Rec	Sp	FPR	FNR	PWC	$Prec$	F_1
Bo	RGBD-SOBS	**0.8842**	**0.9925**	**0.0075**	**0.1158**	**2.3270**	**0.9080**	**0.8917**
"	RGB-SOBS	0.8023	0.9814	0.0186	0.1977	4.4221	0.8165	0.8007
CC	RGBD-SOBS	**0.9563**	**0.9927**	**0.0073**	**0.0437**	**1.2161**	**0.9434**	**0.9488**
"	RGB-SOBS	0.4310	0.9767	0.0233	0.5690	16.0404	0.8018	0.4864
DC	RGBD-SOBS	0.8401	**0.9985**	**0.0015**	0.1599	**0.9778**	**0.9682**	**0.8936**
"	RGB-SOBS	**0.9725**	0.9856	0.0144	**0.0275**	1.5809	0.8354	0.8935
IC	RGBD-SOBS	**0.4514**	**0.9955**	**0.0045**	0.0486	**0.9321**	0.4737	**0.4597**
"	RGB-SOBS	0.4366	0.9715	0.0285	**0.0634**	3.5022	**0.4759**	0.4527
IM	RGBD-SOBS	0.8921	**0.9970**	**0.0030**	0.1079	**0.8648**	**0.9544**	**0.9202**
"	RGB-SOBS	**0.9265**	0.9028	0.0972	**0.0735**	9.3877	0.4054	0.5397
OR	RGBD-SOBS	**0.9170**	**0.9975**	**0.0025**	**0.0830**	0.5613	**0.9362**	**0.9260**
"	RGB-SOBS	0.8902	0.9896	0.0104	0.1098	1.3610	0.8237	0.8527
Sh	RGBD-SOBS	0.9323	**0.9970**	**0.0030**	0.0677	**0.7001**	**0.9733**	**0.9500**
"	RGB-SOBS	**0.9359**	0.9881	0.0119	**0.0641**	1.5140	0.9140	0.9218
Avg.	RGBD-SOBS	**0.8391**	**0.9958**	**0.0042**	**0.0895**	**1.0828**	**0.8796**	**0.8557**
"	RGB-SOBS	0.7707	0.9708	0.0292	0.1578	5.4012	0.7247	0.7068

---

[2] Performance values on each video of the SBM-RGBD dataset are available at http://www.na.icar.cnr.it/~maddalena.l/MODLab/RGBD-SOBS/results.html.

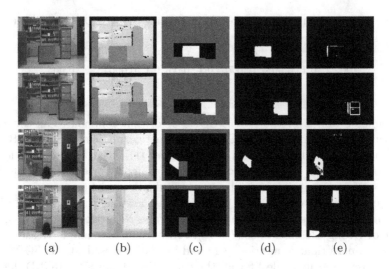

(a)   (b)   (c)   (d)   (e)

Fig. 3. Sequence colorCam1 (CC, 1st and 2nd row) and abandoned1 (IM, 3rd and 4th row): (a) color images; (b) depth images; (c) ground truth masks; masks computed by (d) RGBD-SOBS and (e) RGB-SOBS. (Color figure online)

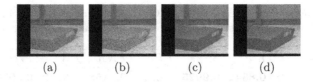

(a)   (b)   (c)   (d)

Fig. 4. Sequence abandoned1: detail of color background models for RGBD-SOBS at frames (a) 161 and (b) 185; and for RGB-SOBS at frames (c) 161 and (d) 185. (Color figure online)

information) clearly show that the exploitation of depth information helps in achieving much higher performance. This is particularly true for disambiguating color camouflage, as exemplified in the first two rows of Fig. 3. Great improvement is also achieved for the Intermittent Motion category, where depth information can be easily exploited to detect both abandoned and removed objects and, thus, can help driving the update of the color model in a much more consistent way (see Fig. 3, third and fourth rows). Indeed, since selectivity prevents the model update in foreground areas, a correct classification of the removed foreground (e.g., the box that originally was on the floor, as shown in Fig. 4), is essential for achieving an accurate background model and, consequently, accurate detection results.

Other well-known challenges, such as bootstrapping, illumination changes, and shadows, are partly well handled also by RGB-SOBS (see Fig. 5). It should be observed that, although performance results are on average comparable for the Depth Camouflage category, sometimes the strategy for combining color and depth masks (see Sect. 2.3) can lead to results worse that using only color

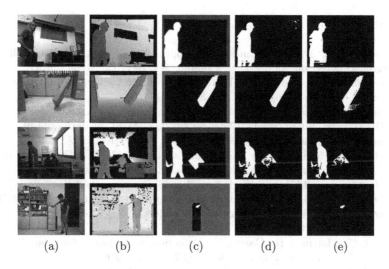

Fig. 5. Sequences BootStrapping_ds (Bo, 1st row), shadows2 (Sh, 2nd row), and Chair-Box (IC, 3rd row), DCamSeq2 (DC, 4th row): (a) color images; (b) depth images; (c) ground truth masks; masks computed by (d) RGBD-SOBS and (e) RGB-SOBS. (Color figure online)

information, as shown in the last row of Fig. 5, suggesting that further work is still needed for accurately handling this challenge.

4   Conclusions and Perspectives

The paper proposes the RGBD-SOBS algorithm for detecting moving objects in RGBD video sequences. Two background models are constructed for color and depth information, exploiting a self-organizing neural background model previously adopted for RGB videos. The resulting color and depth detection masks are combined, not only to achieve the final results, but also to better guide the selective model update procedure. The evaluation of the algorithm on the SBM-RGBD dataset shows that the exploitation of depth information helps in achieving much higher performance than just using color. This is true not only for sequences showing color camouflage, but also for those including many other color and depth background maintenance challenges (e.g., intermittent motion, bootstrapping, and out of sensor range data). Further work will be devoted to specifically handling the depth camouflage challenge, for which only fair results are achieved by the proposed method.

Acknowledgments. L. Maddalena wishes to acknowledge the GNCS (Gruppo Nazionale di Calcolo Scientifico) and the INTEROMICS Flagship Project funded by MIUR, Italy. A. Petrosino acknowledges Project VIRTUALOG Horizon 2020-PON 2014/2020.

References

1. Bouwmans, T.: Traditional and recent approaches in background modeling for foreground detection: an overview. Comput. Sci. Rev. **11**, 31–66 (2014)
2. Bouwmans, T., Maddalena, L., Petrosino, A.: Scene background initialization: a taxonomy. Pattern Recogn. Lett. **96**, 3–11 (2017)
3. Camplani, M., Maddalena, L., Alcover, G.M., Petrosino, A., Salgado, L.: SBM-RGBD Dataset. http://rgbd2017.na.icar.cnr.it/SBM-RGBDdataset.html
4. Camplani, M., Maddalena, L., Moyà Alcover, G., Petrosino, A., Salgado, L.: A benchmarking framework for background subtraction in RGBD videos. In: Battiato, S., Gallo, G., Farinella, G., Leo, M. (eds.) New Trends in Image Analysis and Processing-ICIAP 2017 Workshops. LNCS. Springer, Heidelberg (2017)
5. Camplani, M., Salgado, L.: Background foreground segmentation with RGB-D Kinect data: an efficient combination of classifiers. J. Vis. Commun. Image Represent. **25**(1), 122–136 (2014)
6. Cuevas, C., Martínez, R., García, N.: Detection of stationary foreground objects: a survey. Comput. Vis. Image Underst. **152**, 41–57 (2016)
7. Ding, J., Ma, R., Chen, S.: A scale-based connected coherence tree algorithm for image segmentation. IEEE Trans. Image Process. **17**(2), 204–216 (2008)
8. Fernandez-Sanchez, E.J., Rubio, L., Diaz, J., Ros, E.: Background subtraction model based on color and depth cues. Mach. Vis. Appl. **25**(5), 1211–1225 (2014)
9. Frick, A., Kellner, F., Bartczak, B., Koch, R.: Generation of 3D-TV LDV-content with time-of-flight camera. In: 3DTV Conference: The True Vision - Capture, Transmission and Display of 3D Video, pp. 1–4, May 2009
10. Gallego, J., Pardás, M.: Region based foreground segmentation combining color and depth sensors via logarithmic opinion pool decision. J. Vis. Commun. Image Represent. **25**(1), 184–194 (2014)
11. Goyette, N., Jodoin, P.M., Porikli, F., Konrad, J., Ishwar, P.: Changedetection.net: a new change detection benchmark dataset. In: 2012 IEEE Computer Society Conference on Computer Vision and Pattern Recognition Workshops (CVPRW), pp. 1–8, June 2012
12. Harville, M., Gordon, G., Woodfill, J.: Foreground segmentation using adaptive mixture models in color and depth. In: Proceedings of IEEE Workshop on Detection and Recognition of Events in Video, pp. 3–11 (2001)
13. Huang, J., Wu, H., Gong, Y., Gao, D.: Random sampling-based background subtraction with adaptive multi-cue fusion in RGBD videos. In: International Congress on Image and Signal Processing, BioMedical Engineering and Informatics, pp. 30–35 (2016)
14. Laugraud, B., Piérard, S., Braham, M., Van Droogenbroeck, M.: Simple median-based method for stationary background generation using background subtraction algorithms. In: Murino, V., Puppo, E., Sona, D., Cristani, M., Sansone, C. (eds.) ICIAP 2015. LNCS, vol. 9281, pp. 477–484. Springer, Cham (2015). https://doi.org/10.1007/978-3-319-23222-5_58
15. Liang, Z., Liu, X., Liu, H., Chen, W.: A refinement framework for background subtraction based on color and depth data. In: 2016 IEEE International Conference on Image Processing (ICIP), pp. 271–275, September 2016
16. Maddalena, L., Petrosino, A.: A self-organizing approach to background subtraction for visual surveillance applications. IEEE Trans. Image Process. **17**(7), 1168–1177 (2008)

17. Maddalena, L., Petrosino, A.: A fuzzy spatial coherence-based approach to background/foreground separation for moving object detection. Neural Comput. Appl. **19**, 179–186 (2010)
18. Maddalena, L., Petrosino, A.: The SOBS algorithm: what are the limits? In: IEEE Computer Society Conference on Computer Vision and Pattern Recognition Workshops (CVPRW), pp. 21–26, June 2012
19. Shah, M., Deng, J.D., Woodford, B.J.: Video background modeling: recent approaches, issues and our proposed techniques. Mach. Vis. Appl. **25**(5), 1105–1119 (2014)
20. Stormer, A., Hofmann, M., Rigoll, G.: Depth gradient based segmentation of overlapping foreground objects in range images. In: International Conference on Information Fusion, pp. 1–4, July 2010
21. Xu, Y., Dong, J., Zhang, B., Xu, D.: Background modeling methods in video analysis: a review and comparative evaluation. CAAI Trans. Intell. Tech. **1**(1), 43–60 (2016)

Simple Combination of Appearance and Depth for Foreground Segmentation

Tsubasa Minematsu$^{(\boxtimes)}$, Atsushi Shimada, Hideaki Uchiyama,
and Rin-ichiro Taniguchi

Kyushu University, Fukuoka, Japan
{minematsu,atsushi,uchiyama,rin}@limu.ait.kyushu-u.ac.jp

Abstract. In foreground segmentation, the depth information is robust to problems of the appearance information such as illumination changes and color camouflage; however, the depth information is not always measured and suffers from depth camouflage. In order to compensate for the disadvantages of the two pieces of information, we define an energy function based on the two likelihoods of depth and appearance backgrounds and minimize the energy using graph cuts to obtain a foreground mask. The two likelihoods are obtained using background subtraction. We use the farthest depth as the depth background in the background subtraction according to the depth information. The appearance background is defined as the appearance with a large likelihood of the depth background to eliminate appearances of foreground objects. In the computation of the likelihood of the appearance background, we also use the likelihood of the depth background for reducing false positives owing to illumination changes. In our experiment, we confirm that our method is sufficiently accurate for indoor environments using the SBM-RGBD 2017 dataset.

Keywords: Background subtraction · RGB-D camera
Depth camouflage · Color camouflage

1 Introduction

Recently, RGB-D cameras have become affordable and easily available, e.g., Microsoft's Kinect and Intel's RealSense. In foreground segmentation based on a background subtraction strategy, the depth information has some benefits for the problems of the appearance information, such as illumination changes and color camouflage caused when the colors of foreground objects are very close to the background color, because the depth information is independent of appearance information such as color and texture features. However, the depth information has some disadvantages such as the limitation of the measurement range and problems of depth camouflage such as color camouflage.

The depth and appearance information are combined in order to compensate for the disadvantages of the two pieces of information. Gordon et al. [1] combined two binary segmentations detected based on the depth and appearance

S. Battiato et al. (Eds.): ICIAP 2017 International Workshops, LNCS 10590, pp. 266–277, 2017.
https://doi.org/10.1007/978-3-319-70742-6_25

information independently. Some researchers proposed multidimensional background models using the appearance and depth information. Moyà-Alcover et al. [2] proposed a multidimensional statistical background model based on the appearance and depth information using kernel density estimation. Fernandez-Sanchez et al. [3] proposed the combination of depth and RGB information for the codebook background subtraction model. The other researchers adaptively weighted the depth and appearance cues to select more reliable cues for the foreground segmentation. Schiller and Koch [4] proposed a reliability measure based on the variance in the depth and weighted the depth and RGB cues based on the reliability measure. Camplani and Salgado [5] used the global edge-closeness probability. At a pixel close to the edges, the authors considered that the appearance information is more reliable for the foreground segmentation.

In this paper, we propose a simple combination of the appearance and depth information (SCAD) in order to compensate for the disadvantages of the two pieces of information. Our method is inspired by [1]. We compute the two likelihoods of the background based on the appearance and depth information. Each background likelihood is computed based on a background subtraction strategy. Subsequently, we define an energy function based on the two likelihoods of the background and minimize the energy to obtain a foreground mask. In our experiment, we confirm that our simple combination exhibits satisfactory performance for indoor environments using the SBM-RGBD 2017 dataset [6].

2   Simple Combination of Appearance and Depth

We propose a batch algorithm using two likelihoods of depth and appearance backgrounds in order to compensate for problems such as color camouflage and depth camouflage. We minimize the energy function based on the two likelihoods by using graph cuts [7] in order to obtain a foreground mask. The two likelihoods are obtained based on background subtraction strategies. We apply the farthest depth for the depth background. The likelihood of the depth background is computed based on depth-based background subtraction. The appearance background image is defined as the appearance with a large likelihood of the depth background to eliminate the appearances of foreground objects. The likelihood of the appearance background is computed based on texture-based and RGB-based background subtraction. In order to reduce false positives owing to illumination changes, we roughly detect foreground objects by using texture-based background subtraction. Subsequently, RGB-based background subtraction is performed in order to improve the results of texture-based background subtraction. The likelihood of the depth background is used for the decision of the pixels to which RGB-based background subtraction is applied. Moreover, we detect changes in illumination by using the hue, saturation, and value (HSV) color space.

2.1   Background Subtraction Using Depth

We perform background subtraction at each pixel $x = (x, y)$ and obtain the likelihood of the depth background $p^t(x)$ at frame t as follows:

$$p^t(x) = \frac{1.0 + \exp(-k)}{1.0 + \exp(D_d^t(x) - k)} \tag{1}$$

$$D_d^t(x) = \frac{|B_d(x) - I_d^t(x)|}{\sigma_{d_x}}, \tag{2}$$

where I_d^t is the depth image at frame t, $B_d(x)$ is the depth background image, and σ_{d_x} is the deviation from $B_d(x)$. Furthermore, k is a parameter that controls the increment of p^t according to the increment of $D_d^t(x)$.

We assume that background objects do not move because indoor environments do not have dynamic backgrounds such as waving trees. Therefore, we consider the farthest depth as the depth background. We select the farthest depth value as $B_d(x)$. In this study, we used all the target frames for obtaining $B_d(x)$. In order to obtain σ_{d_x}, we select depth values similar to $B_d(x)$ for eliminating depth values from the foreground objects. The number of selected depth values is 25 % of the number of frames. We limit the range of the deviation to avoid a significantly large/small value. The lower-bound is $\max(1.0, 0.1\mu)$ and the upper-bound is 1.1μ. Further, μ is the mean of σ_{d_x}. Dilation is performed for the deviation image in order to smoothen the deviation.

The depth values are not always measured at each pixel. When we cannot measure depth values, we perform background subtraction based on the status and trend of depth observation at each pixel. The status of depth observation has two states: md, which indicates measurement depth, and nmd, which indicates non-measurement depth. We classify the trend of depth observation into three classes: the constant nmd, rippling nmd, and constant md. The constant md indicates that we can measure the depth value stably; whereas, the constant nmd indicates that we cannot measure the depth value stably. The rippling nmd indicates that the status of depth observation changes from nmd to md frequently. We count the number of instances of nmd ($\#nmd$) and the switching from nmd to md (($\#switch$) at each pixel using all the target frames. We classify the trend of depth observation as follows:

$$td(x) = \begin{cases} \text{constant nmd} & \#nmd > 0.5N \wedge \#switch < 0.1N \\ \text{rippling nmd} & \#switch > 0.1N \\ \text{constant md} & \text{otherwise} \end{cases}, \tag{3}$$

where N is the number of frames.

We modify the likelihood of the depth background $p^t(x)$ as $p_d^t(x)$ based on the status and trend of depth observation.

$$p_d^t(x) = \begin{cases} p^t(x), & I_d^t(x) = \text{md} \wedge \\ & td(x) = \text{rippling nmd or constant md} \\ 1.0, & I_d^t(x) = \text{nmd} \wedge \\ & td(x) = \text{rippling nmd or constant nmd} \\ \dfrac{1}{2dt+1} \displaystyle\sum_{i=t-dt}^{t+dt} p^i(x), & \text{otherwise} \end{cases} \quad (4)$$

where dt is the range of neighboring frames used for calculating the average p^t. We used $dt = 2$ in this study. We consider that a pixel x with the trend of rippling nmd has two background depth values: $B_d(x)$ and non-measurement depth value. Therefore, we compute $p^t(x)$ in the case of md and return 1.0 in the case of nmd when $td(x)$ is the rippling nmd. When the status of depth observation is md and $td(x)$ is the constant nmd, we average $p^t(x)$ in the neighboring frames because we cannot determine whether the depth value originates from the foreground objects or sudden depth noises. In this case, we set 0.5 to $p^t(x)$ at frame t. When the status of depth observation is nmd and $td(x)$ is the constant md, we also average p^t to obtain $p_d^t(x)$.

2.2 Background Subtraction Using Appearance

It is efficient to use the appearance information for reducing false negatives owing to the depth camouflage problem. Appearance-based background subtraction mainly suffers from illumination changes in indoor environments. Many researchers proposed robust strategies of appearance-based background subtraction for illumination changes [8]. In our method, we use two approaches for illumination changes.

First, we detect foreground objects using texture-based background subtraction for reducing false positives from global illumination changes. We use a scale invariant local ternary pattern (SILTP) [9] as a texture-based feature and visual background extractor (ViBe) [10] as a background subtraction strategy. In the foreground detection of ViBe, we use Hamming distance instead of L2 distance. For the initialization of ViBe, we make an RGB background image $B_a(x)$. We use $p_d^t(x)$ in order to eliminate RGB values from the foreground objects as follows:

$$B_a(x) = \frac{1}{\sum_{t \in \{i|p_d^i(x)>0.75\}} p_d^t(x)} \sum_{t \in \{i|p_d^i(x)>0.75\}} p_d^t(x) I_a^t(x), \quad (5)$$

where I_a^t is the RGB image at frame t.

Second, we perform RGB-based background subtraction around the pixels detected by the texture-based background subtraction because the results of the texture-based background subtraction are mainly foreground boundaries as shown in Fig. 1a. However, the final results may suffer from false positives from illumination changes if we uniformly apply RGB-based background subtraction to the neighboring pixels. We select the neighboring pixels to which

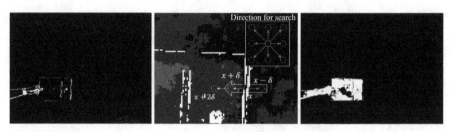

(a) Result of texture-based background subtraction

(b) Decision procedure of pixels to which RGB-based background subtraction is applied

(c) Result of RGB-based background subtraction

Fig. 1. Appearance-based background subtraction. In (a), texture-based background subtraction detects foreground boundaries. (b) illustrates p_d^t of the upper-right region of the object in (a). p_d^t has larger values in darker regions. White pixels indicate the result of texture-based background subtraction, and RGB-based background subtraction is performed in the yellow solid/dotted circles. The white arrow indicates the direction of gradient descents based on p_d^t. We consider that there are gradient descents based on p_d^t at the boundaries between foreground objects and background regions. Therefore, we perform RGB-based background subtraction in this direction. (c) shows the result of RGB-based background subtraction. (Color figure online)

RGB-based background subtraction is applied based on the likelihood of the depth background p_d^t. Figure 1b shows the procedure of the decision. We compare $p_d^t(\boldsymbol{x})$ at a pixel $\boldsymbol{x}$ with $p_d^t(\boldsymbol{x} + \delta)$ and $p_d^t(\boldsymbol{x} - \delta)$ at the two neighboring pixels as shown in Fig. 1b. We consider that there are gradient descents based on $p_d^t(\boldsymbol{x})$ at the boundaries between the foreground objects and background regions. If $p_d^t(\boldsymbol{x}) - p_d^t(\boldsymbol{x} + \delta) > th_g \wedge |p_d^t(\boldsymbol{x}) - p_d^t(\boldsymbol{x} - \delta)| < th_g$ or $p_d^t(\boldsymbol{x}-\delta)-p_d^t(\boldsymbol{x}) > th_g \wedge |p_d^t(\boldsymbol{x})-p_d^t(\boldsymbol{x}+\delta)| < th_g$ are satisfied, we perform RGB-based background subtraction for 5×5 neighboring pixels at $\boldsymbol{x} + \delta$. We also perform RGB-based background subtraction for $\boldsymbol{x}+i\delta$ if $|p_d^t(\boldsymbol{x}+i\delta)-p_d^t(\boldsymbol{x}+\delta)| < th_g$ until $i = 4$ because the regions where the likelihood of the depth background are similar to $p_d^t(\boldsymbol{x} + \delta)$ also likely to be foreground objects. In this study, we compare eight neighboring pixels as shown in Fig. 1b.

We compute RGB-based background subtraction as follows:

$$p_a^t(\boldsymbol{x}) = \frac{1.0 + \exp(-k)}{1.0 + \exp(D_a^t(\boldsymbol{x}) - k)} ic(\boldsymbol{x}) + (1.0 - ic(\boldsymbol{x})) \tag{6}$$

$$D_a^t(\boldsymbol{x}) = \frac{|B_a(\boldsymbol{x}) - I_a^t(\boldsymbol{x})|^2}{\sigma_a}, \tag{7}$$

where σ_a is a parameter that controls the similarity between $B_a(\boldsymbol{x})$ and $I_a^t(\boldsymbol{x})$, and $ic(\boldsymbol{x})$ is the penalty term for illumination changes.

The texture-based approach is robust to global illumination changes; however, this approach often causes false positives in the case of local illumination changes such as shadows. Similar to [11], we perform the detection of illumination changes in the HSV color space.

$$ic(\boldsymbol{x}) = \begin{cases} 0.0 & \begin{aligned} &(\cos(B_H(\boldsymbol{x}) - I_H(\boldsymbol{x})) > th_H \wedge |B_S(\boldsymbol{x}) - I_S(\boldsymbol{x})| < th_S \\ &\wedge B_V(\boldsymbol{x})I_V(\boldsymbol{x}) > 0.1) \vee \\ &(B_S(\boldsymbol{x}) + I_S(\boldsymbol{x}) < th_S \wedge |B_V(\boldsymbol{x}) - I_V(\boldsymbol{x})| < th_V) \end{aligned} \\ 1.0 & otherwise \end{cases}, \quad (8)$$

where $I_{H,S,V}$ and $B_{H,S,V}$ indicate hue, saturation, and brightness of I_a^t and B_a in the HSV color space, respectively. Further, $th_{H,S,V}$ represents chosen parameters. This condition has two parts. The former part indicates the similarity of hue and saturation between I_a^t and B_a in an environment with sufficient light. The latter part indicates the similarity of brightness between I_a^t and B_a in dark regions. We remove the condition based on hue because hue is not stable in dark regions.

2.3   Combination of Depth and Appearance Information

We combine $p_d^t(\boldsymbol{x})$ and $p_a^t(\boldsymbol{x})$ using a graph-based approach for obtaining a foreground mask L^t at frame t. We define the energy function as follows:

$$E(L^t) = \sum_{\boldsymbol{x}} f(L^t(\boldsymbol{x})) + \alpha \sum_{(\boldsymbol{x}_i, \boldsymbol{x}_j) \in \xi} g(L^t(\boldsymbol{x}_i), L^t(\boldsymbol{x}_j)), \quad (9)$$

where $L^t(\boldsymbol{x}) = \{1.0 \equiv FG, 0.0 \equiv BG\}$ and ξ is a set of connected pixel pairs in an eight-connected 2D grid graph; $f(L^t(\boldsymbol{x}))$ evaluates the likelihood of the foreground and background; $g(L^t(\boldsymbol{x}_i), L^t(\boldsymbol{x}_j))$ represents the relationship between neighboring pixels using the depth and the appearance information; α is a parameter defined by the user. We minimize $E(L^t)$ using graph cuts [7] in order to obtain the optimal L^t.

We compute $f(L^t(\boldsymbol{x}))$ as follows:

$$f(L^t(\boldsymbol{x})) = \begin{cases} fg & L^t(\boldsymbol{x}) = 0.0 \\ 1.0 - fg & L^t(\boldsymbol{x}) = 1.0 \end{cases} \quad (10)$$

$$fg = \frac{2.0}{1.0 + \exp(-\sigma_f(1.0 - p_d^t(\boldsymbol{x}) + 1.0 - p_a^t(\boldsymbol{x})))} - 1.0, \quad (11)$$

where σ_f emphasizes the likelihood of the foreground. Figure 2 shows p_d^t, p_a^t, and fg. In Fig. 2d, the likelihood that his arm is in the foreground is enhanced owing to p_a^t.

We compute $g(L^t(\boldsymbol{x}_i), L^t(\boldsymbol{x}_j))$ as follows:

$$g(L^t(\boldsymbol{x}_i), L^t(\boldsymbol{x}_j)) = \begin{cases} g_d + g_a & L^t(\boldsymbol{x}_i) \neq L^t(\boldsymbol{x}_j) \\ 0 & L^t(\boldsymbol{x}_i) = L^t(\boldsymbol{x}_j) \end{cases} \quad (12)$$

$$g_d = \exp(-\frac{|I_d^t(\boldsymbol{x}_i) - I_d^t(\boldsymbol{x}_j)|^2}{\sigma_{ds}^2}) \quad (13)$$

$$g_a = \exp(-\frac{|I_a^t(\boldsymbol{x}_i) - I_a^t(\boldsymbol{x}_j)|^2}{\sigma_{as}^2}), \quad (14)$$

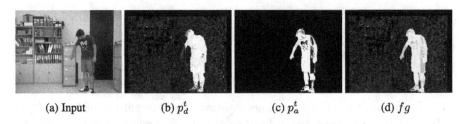

(a) Input   (b) p_d^t (c) p_a^t (d) fg

Fig. 2. Combination of p_d^t and p_a^t. Depth-based background subtraction suffers from depth camouflage in his arm as shown in (b). In (d), the likelihood that the man is in the foreground is enhanced thanks to the combination of p_d^t and p_a^t.

where σ_{ds} and σ_{as} are parameters that control the similarity of the depth and RGB values. If neighboring pixels have similar depth and RGB values, the labels of the neighboring pixels are likely to be the same owing to the term g, which reduces false positives using the spatial similarity of the depth and appearance information.

3   Dataset and Parameter Settings

We used an open access dataset provided by SBM-RGBD 2017 [6]. The following seven video categories are available.

1. **Illumination Changes** (4 videos) owing to light switches or automatic camera brightness changes.
2. **Color Camouflage** (4 videos) containing foreground objects with color very close to that of the background.
3. **Depth Camouflage** (4 videos) containing foreground objects with depth very close to that of the background.
4. **Intermittent Motion** (6 videos) with foreground objects which cause "ghosting" artifacts in the detected motion.
5. **Out of Sensor Range** (5 videos) with non-measurement depth region resulting from being too close to or far from the sensor.
6. **Shadows** (5 videos) caused by foreground objects.
7. **Bootstrapping** (5 videos) with foreground objects in all the frames.

We evaluated the performance of our method using seven metrics: recall, specificity, false positive rate (FPR), false negative rate (FNR), percentage of wrong classifications (PWC), precision, and FMeasure. We used the parameters described in Table 1. These parameters were fixed for all the scenes. For further details of the parameters for SILTP and ViBe, please refer to [9, 10].

Our method was implemented in C++ and executed using a single thread. The performance measurements were carried out on 3.70 GHz Intel Xeon processor with main memory of 32.0 GB. The average computational time was 1.95 fps. Notably, our method is a batch algorithm.

Table 1. Parameter settings.

Parameters for p_d^t and p_a^t		ViBe Parameters		Graph cuts Parameters	
k	2.5	N	20	α	0.25
σ_a	160	R	6 ·	σ_f	2
$|\delta|$	8	#min	2	σ_{ds}	1024
th_g	0.1	SILTP Parameters		σ_{as}	20
th_H	0.75	N	8		
th_S	0.2	R	3		
th_V	0.3	τ	0.1		

4   Experimental Results

Table 2 presents the results of quantitative evaluation. We confirmed that our method (SCAD) exhibits satisfactory performance in indoor environments. Notably, FMeasure, precision, and recall in Illumination Changes are lower because two videos of the category do not contain foreground objects.

Table 2. Averaged quantitative evaluation results.

Name	Recall	Specificity	FPR	FNR	PWC	Precision	FMeasure
Bootstrapping	0.900	0.994	0.006	0.100	1.801	0.932	0.913
Color Camouflage	0.988	0.990	0.010	0.012	0.704	0.968	0.977
Depth Camouflage	0.984	0.996	0.004	0.016	0.443	0.945	0.964
Illumination Changes	0.470	0.993	0.007	0.030	0.971	0.457	0.461
Intermittent Motion	0.956	0.991	0.009	0.044	0.862	0.924	0.937
Out Of Range	0.929	0.997	0.003	0.071	0.571	0.936	0.931
Shadows	0.967	0.991	0.009	0.033	1.009	0.928	0.946
Overall	0.885	0.993	0.007	0.044	0.909	0.870	0.876

Figures 3 and 4 show the examples of input images, results of SCAD, p_d^t, and p_a^t. We observed that SCAD detected foreground objects in Depth Camouflage and Color Camouflage as shown in Fig. 3. In Fig. 3, the appearance-based background subtraction is not efficient for colorCam2 according to p_a^t and the depth-based background subtraction is not efficient for DCamSeq2 according to p_d^t. However, SCAD reduces false negatives by combining p_d^t and p_a^t. Moreover, SCAD suppressed false positives owing to the influence of noise on p_d^t by using graph cuts.

In the category of bootstrapping, we observed that SCAD did not detect a part of the foreground objects as shown in Fig. 4. SCAD failed to enable the

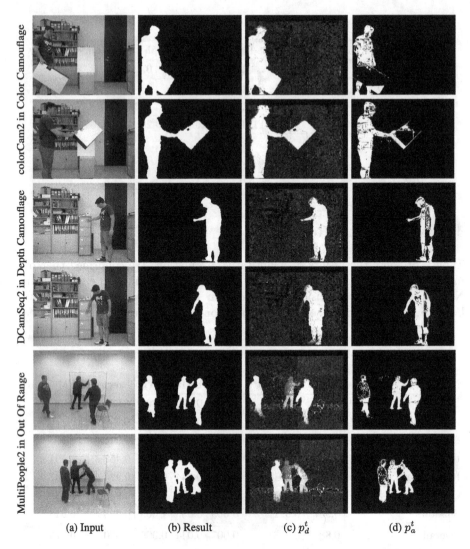

Fig. 3. Results of identification of foreground and background using SCAD for Color Camouflage, Depth Camouflage, and Out Of Range.

background images to eliminate foreground objects because these objects stay at the same position in all the frames.

SCAD has a drawback owing to the combination of depth and appearance information. In the category of Illumination Changes, we observed some false positives. The false positives were caused by false detection of texture-based background subtraction when the room became darker and the observed RGB image is noisy. The texture-based background subtraction does not function well because the method detects noise as local changes. Moreover, SCAD classified

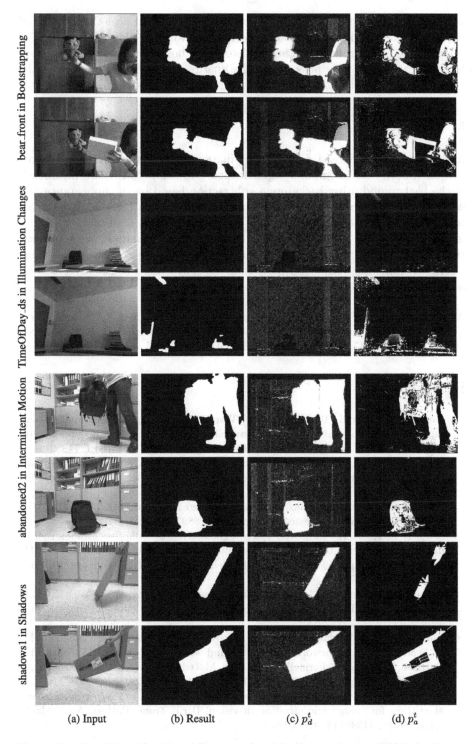

Fig. 4. Results of identification of foreground and background using SCAD for Bootstrapping, Illumination Changes, Intermittent Motion, and Shadows.

weak shadows as the background; however, strong shadows near the foreground object were detected as foreground objects as shown in shadows1 of Fig. 4. The texture-based background subtraction detects the boundaries of strong shadows. In these categories, false positives in the final results of SCAD depend on the errors from texture-based background subtraction.

5   Conclusion

In this paper, we proposed a simple combination of appearance and depth information (SCAD) for foreground segmentation. We compute the two likelihoods of the background using background subtraction based on the appearance and depth information. Subsequently, we optimize the energy function based on the two likelihoods of the background using graph cuts in order to obtain foreground masks. We used the SBM-RGBD 2017 dataset in our evaluation. We confirmed that SCAD was effective for indoor environments. In future work, we will convert SCAD to online methods. We expect that the conversion will be easy based on a sequential updating strategy.

Acknowledgment. This work was partially supported by JSPS KAKENHI Grant Number JP16J02614 and JP15K12066. We acknowledge the SBM-RGB dataset web page http://rgbd2017.na.icar.cnr.it/SBM-RGBDdataset.html.

References

1. Gordon, G., Darrell, T., Harville, M., Woodfill, J.: Background estimation and removal based on range and color. In: IEEE Computer Society Conference on Computer Vision and Pattern Recognition, vol. 2, pp. 459–464. IEEE (1999)
2. Moyà-Alcover, G., Elgammal, A., Jaume-i Capó, A., Varona, J.: Modeling depth for nonparametric foreground segmentation using RGBD devices. Pattern Recognit. Lett. (2016)
3. Fernandez-Sanchez, E.J., Diaz, J., Ros, E.: Background subtraction based on color and depth using active sensors. Sensors **13**(7), 8895–8915 (2013)
4. Schiller, I., Koch, R.: Improved video segmentation by adaptive combination of depth keying and mixture-of-gaussians. In: Heyden, A., Kahl, F. (eds.) SCIA 2011. LNCS, vol. 6688, pp. 59–68. Springer, Heidelberg (2011). https://doi.org/10.1007/978-3-642-21227-7_6
5. Camplani, M., Salgado, L.: Background foreground segmentation with RGB-D kinect data: an efficient combination of classifiers. J. Vis. Commun. Image Represent. **25**(1), 122–136 (2014)
6. Camplani, M., Maddalena, L., Moy Alcover, G., Petrosino, A., Salgado, L.: A benchmarking framework for background subtraction in RGBD videos. In: Battiato, S., Gallo, G., Farinella, G.M., Leo, M. (eds.) New Trends in Image Analysis and Processing-ICIAP 2017 Workshops, LNCS, vol. 10590. Springer (2017)
7. Boykov, Y., Kolmogorov, V.: An experimental comparison of min-cut/max-flow algorithms for energy minimization in vision. IEEE Trans. Pattern Anal. Mach. Intell. **26**(9), 1124–1137 (2004)

8. Bouwmans, T.: Traditional and recent approaches in background modeling for foreground detection: an overview. Comput. Sci. Rev. **11**, 31–66 (2014)
9. Liao, S., Zhao, G., Kellokumpu, V., Pietikäinen, M., Li, S.Z.: Modeling pixel process with scale invariant local patterns for background subtraction in complex scenes. In: 2010 IEEE Conference on Computer Vision and Pattern Recognition (CVPR), pp. 1301–1306. IEEE (2010)
10. Barnich, O., Van Droogenbroeck, M.: Vibe: a powerful random technique to estimate the background in video sequences. In: IEEE International Conference on Acoustics, Speech and Signal Processing, ICASSP 2009, pp. 945–948. IEEE (2009)
11. Cucchiara, R., Grana, C., Neri, G., Piccardi, M., Prati, A.: The Sakbot system for moving object detection and tracking. In: Remagnino, P., Jones, G.A., Paragios, N., Regazzoni, C.S. (eds.) Video-Based Surveillance Systems, pp. 145–157. Springer, Boston (2002), https://doi.org/10.1007/978-1-4615-0913-4_12

Natural Human-Computer Interaction and Ecological Perception in Immersive Virtual and Augmented Reality (NIVAR)

Going to a Virtual Supermarket: Comparison of Different Techniques for Interacting in a Serious Game for the Assessment of the Cognitive Status

Alice E. Martis, Chiara Bassano, Fabio Solari, and Manuela Chessa(✉)

Department of Informatics, Bioengineering, Robotics and System Engineering - DIBRIS, University of Genoa, Genoa, Italy
{fabio.solari,manuela.chessa}@unige.it

Abstract. An increasing number of people suffers from cognitive impairments, also related to aging. Several approaches are used to evaluate the mental status of people affected by cognitive diseases, and there is a growing interest toward approaches that allow a quantitative and personalized evaluation of such impairments. Such approaches comprise serious games and VR-based cognitive assessment systems. Nevertheless, few works attempt to understand how people interact in such systems, and which human-computer interaction modalities are to be preferred when targeting impaired people. The aim of this work is to quantitative and qualitative compare two solutions to play in a virtual supermarket (a PC and a tablet-based solution). The obtained results can be used as a starting point to design VR-based serious games to be used instead of questionnaire-based approaches, thus improving both clinical evaluation performances and patients' motivation.

Keywords: Human-computer interaction · Serious games
Neuropsychological assessment · Virtual reality
VR-based cognitive assessment

1 Introduction

The constant increase of the average age of people has determined a higher incidence of neurodegenerative pathologies related with aging. One of this is dementia, a disease which compromises the abilities of attention, concentration, memory, reasoning, calculation, logic, and orientation, with repercussions not only on the individual but also on his/her family. Until some decades ago, dementia was considered a condition without return but, with the progress of research on central nervous system and in the neuropsychological field, there has been a greater understanding of this pathology, a better differentiation of its forms and, consequently, a therapeutic approach. For this reason, it is essential to use effective screening tools to provide early diagnosis [1,2].

At present, the most widely used and validated test is the Mini-Mental State Examination (MMSE) that allows to evaluate cognitive functions and their modifications over time [3]. It consists of eleven questions referring to seven different

© Springer International Publishing AG 2017
S. Battiato et al. (Eds.): ICIAP 2017 International Workshops, LNCS 10590, pp. 281–289, 2017.
https://doi.org/10.1007/978-3-319-70742-6_26

cognitive areas (orientation, registration, attention and calculation, recall, language and praxis), it is easily administered by the physician and it takes about 10 min to be executed. However, it also has some limitations: it shows poor sensitivity to detect mild/early dementia and individual performance can be influenced by the presence of hearing and visual impairment or by poor education [4,5].

In the last few years, efforts have been made to develop additional tools for the assessment of cognitive functions through the use of Virtual Reality (VR) in order to find a valid alternative to pencil-and-paper tests. In fact, VR allows to reproduce complex situations of daily living where psychopathological reactions and cognitive functions of patients can be more reliably evaluated than laboratory situations. In addition, through VR, it is possible to reproduce environmental and social situations that can stimulate the subject in a similar way to the corresponding context [6], allowing to modulate the intensity and duration of the experience according to the program's needs and the needs of the subject. For these reasons VR-based cognitive assessment represents a tool with a great ecological validity [7,8], meant as the ability to actually measure what it is supposed to [9].

To date, there are many serious games that use both non-immersive and immersive VR to simulate daily activities and that are able to evaluate the cognitive status of elderly people. Regarding non-immersive VR, we must mention the works of Zucchella et al. [10] and Vourvopulos et al. [11]. In the first one, authors have created a first-person game for touch screen platforms. It is set in a virtual apartment in which the subject must perform 5 tasks, each of them evaluating a different cognitive function. The second research presents a game set in a virtual city in which the user can move through the use of a joystick to reach places of interest (pharmacy, supermarket, bank and post office) and perform the required tasks. Regarding immersive VR, we can mention the study of Parsons et al. [12], which consists of a virtual supermarket where the user wears a head-mounted display and interacts with the objects of the scene directly with his/her own hand thanks to markers placed in a wearable glove. Another important work is the one conducted by Tarnanas et al. [8,13], in which a fire evacuation is simulated. The subject can move using a treadmill and can interact with objects using the Leap Motion[1], a hand tracker device.

Following the state of the art tendencies, the work presented in this paper aims to propose an alternative to pencil-and-paper traditional tests with a greater ecological validity. We have created a simple virtual supermarket and we have developed it for two different platforms, tablet and pc. The main difference between the two devices is the interaction modality: in one case users have to tap and scroll on the screen; whereas in the other case they use a standard mouse. Our primary aim is to assess whether the different type of human-computer interaction can affect the performance of subjects, using both subjective and objective evaluation parameters. Therefore, we want to determine which device can better perform an analysis of the cognitive status of the elderly.

---

[1] https://www.leapmotion.com.

2 Materials and Methods

2.1 Platforms

For our study, we have developed two different versions of the same game: the first one runs on a 13,3-inch MacBook Pro with a 2,5 GHz Intel Core i5 processor and Intel HD Graphics 4000 1536 MB graphics processor; while the second one runs on a 10,1-inch Samsung Tab 4 with a 1,2 GHz Quad-Core processor and Android 5.0.2 operating system.

The game was created with *Unity 3D*[2], a cross-platform game engine for the development of 2D and 3D videogames for desktop, web and mobile devices. Most of the items in the game were made with *SketchUp*[3], a 3D modeling software commonly used to design very realistic 3D objects or to download them from a free library (3D Warehouse) and export them in a Unity-compatible format.

2.2 Participants

The game was tested on 32 volunteer healthy subjects with an age range of 21–78 years (mean 39.8 ± 18.8). We divided the participants into two groups: *Under60* group (22 people in an actual age range of 21–49 and average age 28.1 ± 6.4) and *Over60* group (10 people in an age range of 60–78 and average age 65.7 ± 6.6). Neither people in the *Under60* group nor in the *Over60* group were affected by any degenerative or cognitive disease.

All the participants were asked to try the game with both devices and to report which one they preferred to use and why. The first device they had to try has been randomly chosen. Therefore, half of the participants started with the tablet and the other half with the computer.

2.3 Experimental Procedure

The serious game consists of a virtual supermarket with two shelves and a fruit counter as shown in Fig. 1. The subject has to perform two tasks. The first one consists in buying all the items (in our experiments 10) on a shopping list, the items are randomly chosen when the game starts, but a control ensures that they are all different. The second task consists in paying the exact total amount.

Each experiment consists of:

– a Training with the demo scene;
– a First Trial with a device randomly chosen between pc and tablet;
– a Second Trial with the other device.

The Second Trial usually began immediately after the end of the first one. After each trial the subject was asked to write down all the bought items. The question was first asked at the end of the First Trial, so the subject, initially, did not know that he/she had to memorize the list.

---

[2] https://unity3d.com.
[3] http://www.sketchup.com.

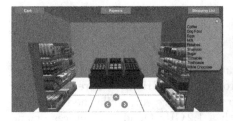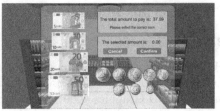

Fig. 1. A view of the Shopping Task scene (left) and of the Payment Task scene (right)

2.4   Game Design

We designed the game in order to keep the interface as simple as possible. The user cannot freely navigate the scene but he/she has to turn the camera toward the selected shelf using the arrows at the bottom of the screen. Only when he/she is in front of the desired shelf, he/she can interact with the items on it, for example by clicking or tapping on one of them a pop-up window with the product name is displayed and the player is asked if he/she wants to add that article to the cart or not.

The game is composed by three scenes, a menu, a demo scene and the main scene. The menu allows the subject to choose whether to try the demo scene or to go directly to the game. This way the demo scene can be skipped if the user is performing the Second Trial. The demo scene is a simplified version of the main scene and its aim is to explain the game to the player and to allow him/her to learn how to interact with objects and buttons. We have used it in a trial session before each experiment.

Shopping Task. Once the demo is completed, the main scene is loaded. The subject has to type the ID assigned to him/her in an input field and to press the *Start!* button. At this point the game begins and a shopping list appears in the upper right corner of the screen (Fig. 1, left). The player has to buy only the things displayed on the shopping list, if he/she does not recognize an object he/she can click on it and its name appears, then he/she can choose whether or not to put it in the cart.

The subject can interact with the scene through several buttons:

- *Cart* (top left corner): by pressing it a dropdown list with all the selected items appears and the user can choose to delete a product from the cart simply clicking on its name;
- *Shopping List* (top right corner): which shows or hides the shopping list;
- *Payment* (top center): which enables the payment screen and disables the shopping scene.

When the player presses on *Payment* button, a pop-up appears asking him/her if he/she wants to proceed with the payment, as once accepted, he/she will not be allowed to go back to the supermarket view.

Payment Task. In this task the subject is asked to pay the precise sum displayed, clicking on Euro bills and coins (Fig. 1, right). He/She can reset the selected amount, in case of error, or confirm the payment by pressing respectively the *Cancel* and the *Confirm* buttons.

2.5   Evaluated Parameters

The performance of the subjects has been evaluated through several parameters. For both tasks we measured the execution time and computed a score. The ShoppingScore (*SS*) takes into account the number of the bought items that are (*CI*) and are not (*WI*) in the list and also the number of items deleted from the cart (*DI*). *SS* can vary between 0 and 10 and it is obtained thanks to the following equation:

$$SS = CI - \alpha * WI - \beta * DI \tag{1}$$

Different weights (α and β) are associated with different errors: if player selects an incorrect item it is a mistake, but if he/she realizes it and corrects it he/she will be less penalized. The PaymentScore (*PS*) is set to 0 if the payed amount is incorrect and 10 if it is correct, otherwise it is computed, taking into account the number of times the player has reset the total, which is considered an error (*E*), as:

$$PS = 10 - 0.5 * E \tag{2}$$

In both cases, a low score can be related to an impairment in solving the task, and a high score means that the user completed it easily. Another evaluated parameter is the number of remembered items, at the end of the game the subject was asked to write down all the items he/she remember he/she had bought.

Finally, at the end of the test, participants were asked to express a preference, between interaction with pc and with tablet, and to explain the reason of their choice.

3   Results

In order to evaluate which device could be more suitable for our purpose, we made three different types of analysis: the first one was the comparison of parameters measured with the tablet version and the pc version of the game; the second one consisted in comparing the performances obtained in the First and the Second Trial, regardless the device type; in the last analysis we compared the performances of the *Under60* group versus the *Over60* group, taking into account both the type of device and the difference between First and Second Trial. We also evaluated the statistical significance of the compared data groups by performing a *two-sample t-test* for all of the three cases, in order to assess if differences in results were actually linked to different conditions or not.

Table 1 summarizes the average of the parameters considered in the first and the second analysis. Comparing tablet and pc performances it can be noticed that there are not significant differences neither for the execution times nor for the scores of both tasks. Regarding the comparison between First and Second Trial, times and scores do not significantly differ one from another. Execution times do not decrease in the Second Trial as we would be expected, but as the standard deviations are very high this may be due to an internal variability of the data. Furthermore, the average number of remembered items does not considerably vary during the Second Trial despite subjects were aware of having to memorize the shopping list. Many subjects complained that first time they had to write down the list, their bad results were due to the fact that they did not know they had to remember items in the list; while the second time they got confused and risked to write items from the first list. So results are not directly related to concentration but to subjective short term memory capability.

Table 1. Mean and standard deviation of evaluated parameters obtained dividing participants in two different conditions: results obtained with the tablet and the pc; results obtained in the First and Second Trial.

	Tablet	Pc	First Trial	Second Trial
Shop.Score/10	9.6 ± 0.9	9.6 ± 0.6	9.5 ± 1.0	9.8 ± 0.5
Paym.Score/10	9.9 ± 0.2	9.9 ± 0.1	9.9 ± 0.2	9.9 ± 0.1
Shop.Time [sec]	185.5 ± 114.7	191.4 ± 136.9	196.8 ± 132.1	180.0 ± 119.8
Paym.Time [sec]	18.8 ± 10.3	20.8 ± 16.1	20.8 ± 13.2	18.8 ± 13.8
Rememb.Items/10	-	-	8.6 ± 1.4	8.4 ± 1.5

Significant differences were found between the performances of *Over60* and *Under60* groups regarding the mean execution time of both tasks (see Fig. 2): as expected, *Under60* group times are much lower ($p < 0.05$ in both cases). Considering each group separately, we can notice that in the younger group results with the two devices in both tasks are comparable, while in the elderly group performances may look slightly better (but not significantly) in the case of the tablet. Also variability is lower in the case of *Under60* group, maybe because more subjects were considered, or because they are more confident with technologies, on average. However, considering all the data, average scores of both tasks (see equations (1) and (2)) are particularly high for both groups: 9.2±1.2 and 9.8±0.4 are the shopping scores respectively of *Over60* and *Under60* group; 9.9 ± 0.3 and 9.9 ± 0.1 are the payment scores respectively of *Over60* and *Under60* group.

Figure 3 shows execution times (3(a) and (b)) and number of remembered items (3(c)) regarding the First and the Second Trial for both age groups. Average shopping time slightly decreases for *Over60* group (347.6 ± 147.6 First vs 319.3 ± 120.5 Second) as well as for *Under60* group (128.3 ± 26.2 First vs 116.7 ± 38.6 Second), but the difference is not significant probably because of

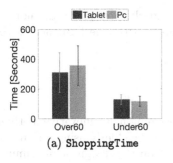
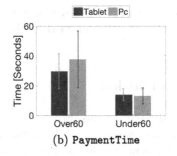

(a) ShoppingTime

(b) PaymentTime

Fig. 2. Comparison of the times required to complete the shopping (a) and the payment (b) task. Comparison between *Over60* and *Under60* groups and between tablet and pc.

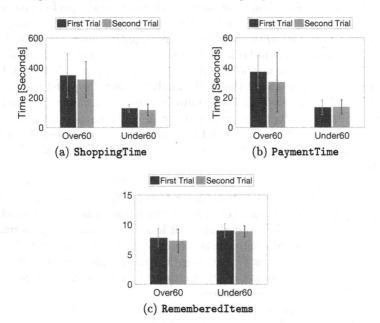

(a) ShoppingTime

(b) PaymentTime

(c) RememberedItems

Fig. 3. Comparison of the times required to complete the shopping (a) and the payment (b) task and of the number of remembered items (c). Comparison between *Over60* and *Under60* groups and between First and Second Trial.

the high variability of data. The average number of remembered items in the First and Second Trial remains quite constant inside the two groups, but it is significantly higher ($p < 0.05$) in the *Under60* group with respect to the *Over60* group (7.8 ± 1.5 vs 7.3 ± 1.9 for *Over60*, 9.0 ± 1.1 vs 8.9 ± 0.9 for *Under60*).

The last evaluated aspect has been the preferences of the subjects for one device over the other. In general, the 50% of participants said they preferred to use the pc because the screen was larger and the objects were more visible, the 30% of them preferred the tablet for the more intuitive interface and the last 20% enjoyed both devices. In the case of elderly, preferences did not match the objective data, indeed they obtained slightly better performances with the tablet.

4   Conclusion

Our work fits with the current research on designing new innovative methodologies for the assessment of the cognitive status of the elderly using serious games approach. Unlike other works, our focus is not on the design of the simulation environment itself but on the evaluation of the best human-computer interface to be used. Indeed, we developed a simple virtual supermarket and exported it into two devices, a tablet and a pc, in order to compare the performances with the two types of interaction (touch screen and mouse). The game was tested on 32 volunteer healthy subjects without any cognitive disorder, each of them was asked to try the game in both modalities. The performances of the subjects were evaluated by measuring the execution times of the proposed tasks and computing a score for each one of them. We analyzed and compared the acquired data in three different ways: first we compared the performance obtained with the tablet and the pc, then we compared the results obtained in the First and Second Trial and finally we compared the performance of the elderly (*Over60* group) over the young people (*Under60* group), based on the device used and the trial.

From the analysis of the results, no significant differences have been arisen between tablet and pc or between First and Second Trial. This could be due to the high variability of data, heterogeneity in the dataset and limited number of participants. Regarding the latest analysis, it has emerged that the performances of young people were significantly better than those of the elderly, both in terms of execution times and scores. Considering only the results of the elderly group, however, there are small but not significant differences between the performances obtained with the two different devices.

For these reasons we can state that the type of interaction does not significantly affect the performance of the subjects. Both devices, therefore, are potentially valid for developing a serious game for assessing cognitive functions of the elderly. However, the game could be implemented on both platforms and the choice of the device could be left to the patients according to their preferences.

The presented study is a preliminary work that could be used as a starting point for many future works. First of all, it is our strong interest the improvement of the layout and of the usability of the game in the two platforms and the implementation of the game even in an Immersive Virtual Reality in order to obtain a more natural experience and interaction. We have also planned to collaborate with doctors in order to acquire data from cognitive impaired people and old-age people. The cooperation with the medical staff will provide us a better understanding of the problem of assessment of people cognitive status, so we will be able to develop new features for our application in order to create an *ad hoc* tool for doctors. Finally, a comparison and correlation with the score given by the MMSE will be required to understand whether such a game can be used to assess the cognitive status of people.

References

1. Prince, M., Bryce, R., Ferri, C.: World Alzheimer Report 2011: The benefits of early diagnosis and intervention. http://www.alz.co.uk/research/WorldAlzheimer Report2011.pdf. Accessed 20 June 2017
2. Fox, C., Lafortune, L., Boustani, M., Brayne, C.: The pros and cons of early diagnosis in dementia. Br. J. Gen. Pract. **63**(612), e510–e512 (2013)
3. Folstein, M.F., Folstein, F.E., McHugh, P.R.: Mini-Mental State: a practical method for grading the cognitive state of patients for the clinician. J. Psychiatr. Res. **12**, 189–198 (1975)
4. Wind, A., Schellevis, F.G., Van Staveren, G.E., van Eijk, J.T.M.: Limitations of the Mini-Mental State Examination in diagnosing dementia in general practice. Int. J. Geriatr. Psychiatry **12**(1), 101–108 (1997)
5. Kurlowicz, L., Wallace, M.: The Mini-Mental State Examination (MMSE). J. Gerontological Nurs. **25**(5), 8–9 (1999)
6. Rizzo, A.A., Schultheis, M., Kerns, K.A., Mateer, C.: Analysis of assets for virtual reality applications in neuropsychology. Technol. Cogn. Rehabil. **14**, 207–239 (2004)
7. Spooner, D.M., Pachan, N.A.: Ecological validity in neuropsychological assessment: a case for greater consideration in research with neurologically intact populations. Arch. Clin. Neuropsychol. **21**(4), 327–337 (2006)
8. Tarnanas, I., Schlee, W., Tsolaki, M., Müri, R., Mosimann, U., Nef, T.: Ecological validity of virtual reality daily living activities screening for early dementia: longitudinal study. JMIR Serious Games **1**, 1–14 (2014)
9. Bronfenbrenner, U.: The Ecology of Human Development. Harvard University Press, Cambridge (2009)
10. Zucchella, C., Sinforiani, E., Tassorelli, C., Cavallini, E., Tost-Pardell, D., Grau, S., Nappi, G.: Serious games for screening pre-dementia conditions: From virtuality to reality? A pilot project. Funct. Neurol. **29**, 153–158 (2014)
11. Vourvopoulos, A., Faria, A.L., Ponnam, K., Bermúdez i Badia, S.: RehabCity: design and validation of a cognitive assessment and rehabilitation tool through gamified simulations of activities of daily living. In: Advances in Computer Entertainment Technology Conference (2014)
12. Parsons, T.D, McPherson, S., Interrante, V.: Enhancing neurocognitive assessment using immersive virtual reality. In: 1st Workshop on Virtual and Augmented Assistive Technology (VAAT), 2013, pp. 27–34. IEEE (2013)
13. Tarnanas, I., Tsolaki, M., Nef, T., Müri, R., Mosimann, U.: Can a novel computerized cognitive screening test provide additional information for early detection of Alzheimer's disease? Alzheimer's Dement. **10**(6), 790–798 (2014)

Interaction in an Immersive Collaborative Virtual Reality Environment: A Comparison Between Leap Motion and HTC Controllers

Elisa Gusai, Chiara Bassano, Fabio Solari, and Manuela Chessa[✉]

Department of Informatics, Bioengineering, Robotics and System Engineering - DIBRIS, University of Genoa, Genoa, Italy
chiara.bassano@dibris.unige.it, {fabio.solari,manuela.chessa}@unige.it

Abstract. The spread of immersive virtual reality technologies, e.g. low-cost head-mounted-displays, has opened the way to the development of collaborative and interactive virtual environments, which can be exploited to obtain effective exergames. One open issue is how to obtain a natural interaction within these environments. This paper presents a prototype of collaborative environment, where users, immersed into virtual reality, can manipulate objects by using the HTC Vive controllers or the Leap Motion. We investigate which interaction modality is better by taking into account both objective measurements (e.g. the number of positioning errors) and qualitative observations.

Keywords: Human-computer interaction · VR-based exergames HTC vive · Leap motion · Immersive VR

1 Introduction

The spread of virtual reality (VR) technologies and innovative devices has contributed to the expansion of their application domains much further than the ones that could be defined as traditional fields of interest. VR allows to isolate the user from real world and teleport her/him in a virtual environment in which the only limit is imagination. Immersivity and an intuitive interface have certainly contributed to increase the interest in this computer technology, so, even if virtual reality is still a prerogative in sectors such as military industry and simulation, it is starting to play an important role also in the game and entertainment sectors. Moreover, researchers have understood its huge potential and are investigating the use of VR in many others different fields: from the design of serious games, which combine entertainment with educational purpose [1], to support surgeons in diagnosis, operation planning and minimal invasive surgery and in rehabilitation contexts [2,3]; from products design, assembly and prototyping process to cultural heritage applications such as virtual museums [4] or historic sites modeling [5,6]. It is now evident how virtual reality is becoming a significant part of consumer everyday life. Thinking of VR mainly as a way

© Springer International Publishing AG 2017
S. Battiato et al. (Eds.): ICIAP 2017 International Workshops, LNCS 10590, pp. 290–300, 2017.
https://doi.org/10.1007/978-3-319-70742-6_27

to isolate people from real world and provide an individual experience, however, would be wrong. Indeed, another sector that has particularly benefited of VR is certainly the one of *Collaborative Virtual Environments* (CVE). Several studies have proved that, when multiple subjects who have to carry out a common task share the same work space, this cooperation can bring a series of great advantages [7,8]. While the concept of CVE is quite clear, the actual creation of this cooperative work space remains an open problem and a research topic.

This paper mainly focuses on the interaction between user and virtual objects and our contribution consists in the evaluation of the intuitiveness and naturalness of the human-computer interaction. We have designed a simple exergame in which the player is asked to grab and move objects. We use the HTC Vive Head-Mounted Display (HMD) to visualize the scene and two different modalities to interact with it: one modality uses the controllers that HTC Vive itself provides; the other modality uses the Leap Motion, a low-cost hand tracker meant to provide a natural interaction in VR. Our aim is to identify which one between the two devices represents the best solution to be employed within the field of a manipulation task, both in terms of performances in accomplishing the task and in terms of the quality of the experience of the involved subjects.

2   Related Works

Recently, several studies took in examination different aspects of CVEs in several domains of application. One of the greatest results has been obtained by the comparison of the CAVE system's performances and the HMD's ones in a collaborative task of abstract data visualization [9]. Three different aspects have been taken into account: functionality, esteem of collaboration degree and evaluation of the quality of the experience lived by the users. Under all these points of view it has came out that the employment of a low cost technology like HMD, can provide results as accurate as those obtainable through a system such us the CAVE, also offering the advantage of being more versatile and easy to handle. Beyond the purely technical aspects, when studying CVE, researchers have to take into account another important factor related to the type and degree of collaboration between the users that the system is able to support [10]. When speaking of CVEs, it is necessary to take into account the role [11] of each user in the task, as well as the factors influencing the behavior of the subject in terms of what he is allowed to do or not, and consequently the strategy he adopted in order to pursue the final aim. Of course, this has an impact also on the task's structure and on the type of reciprocal interactions the participants can establish. In fact the situation is quite different if all the participants are equally free to act or have some restrictions. In a similar context it is indispensable to preliminary make a point on the users, especially in terms of their cultural background and degree of expertise toward the task they have to perform. This particular aspect associated with CVE can be dealt through a particular approach, drawing a parallel with the interactions between users and those that rule the dynamics human-robot [12]. From that point of view it is possible to define a kind of interactive hierarchy which starts from the so called *tele-operation* strategy, in which the supervisor has to completely control the machine (or another user's actions, in case of human - human interactions). The autonomy's degree gets higher and higher as we go up from the bottom to the top of the chain of command; each one of them corresponds to a different level of *tele-assistance* strategies and results in a totally autonomous modality of work [13]. To choose the best interactive strategy to adopt it is necessary to take into account the precise task to carry out and the specific required performances. The particular type of approach employed, in fact, influences the results of the work: if in a certain context the priority is to complete the task as quickly as possible despite the precision, the best choice might be reducing supervision of the expert-user on his partner's actions; on the contrary, when accuracy is preferred with respect to the execution speed, a greater control over the actions of the beginner might require, therefore giving him a less autonomy. Finally, it is also important to define a series of customized metrics in order to effectively measure all the parameters necessary to evaluate the performances and the quality of users' experience inside VR [14,15].

3   Materials and Methods

3.1   Hardware Components

The collaborative task we have defined requires the use of the following devices: a Head-Mounted Display, connected to a computer (running a 64 bit Windows10 operating system, with an Intel(R) Core(TM) i7 2.67 GHz processor, 8 GB RAM and a NVIDIA GeForce GTX680 graphic card), a pair of controllers designed for interactive VR or the Leap Motion[1]. The HMD we used is the HTC Vive[2] developed by HTC and Valve Corporation; it belongs to the class of *'room scale'* virtual reality technology. The HTC headset includes two wireless controllers and two 'lighthouse' basestations, that are able to track the head-mounted display and the controllers position in a certain area, 4.6 by 4.6 m, defined through a calibration process. The HMD consists of two screens, one per eye, with a resolution of 1080×1200 and provides a refresh rate of 90 Hz and a field of view of about $110°$.

Manipulation and interaction with the virtual objects in the scene was provided by two different devices: in particular, we carried out two distinct series of experiments in which the users were able to interact with the scene using the HTC's controllers and the Leap Motion respectively. HTC Vive supplies two wireless and ergonomic controllers that allows an easy handle with just a hand (Fig. 1(a)). They have a great number of passive sensors that guarantees an extremely accurate tracking contributing to obtain an incredibly stable system. The Leap Motion (Fig. 1(b)), instead, is a hand tracker: it has been fixed on the HTC Vive with a special support placed in the frontal part of the HMD at the center. Thanks to this particular configuration it is possible to easily track and represent hands in VR. It is worth noting that in our experiments we use only

---

[1] https://www.leapmotion.com/.
[2] https://www.vive.com/eu/.

one HTC controller. This does not affect performances, since to accomplish the task only one controller is necessary.

(a)   (b)

Fig. 1. The input devices used to interact with objects in the immersive VR environment: (a) the HTC Vive controllers and (b) the Leap Motion controller.

3.2 Software Components

The immersive VR has been developed mostly by using *Unity 3D* 5.5.1[3]. Concerning the virtual objects, we employed Blender 2.78[4], an open source computer-graphics software widely used for creating and manipulating 3D objects. Before exporting the *fbx* models obtained from Blender on Unity, it was necessary to use *Autodesk Netfabb* 2017.3[5]. Finally we downloaded some already done 3D models from *SketchUp*[6].

3.3 Subjects

30 people, 15 males and 15 females, aged between 20 and 49 years (mean 27 ± 6.6), took part in this experiment and constitute the control group, composed by healthy subjects. Only few of the participants had already had past experiences in VR, while the majority of them had never got in touch with it, even if they had heard about it. Thereafter their experience or their confidence in virtual reality is very different. All the subjects took part in the study voluntarily and nobody perceived any kind of reward.

3.4 Collaborative Task

Since our aim is to test how people interact in an immersive VR system, in order to understand which solution is preferred by the users, we propose a very simple collaborative task: this way the obtained performances actually reflect the interaction mode rather than the complexity of the task itself. It requires the

---

[3] https://unity3d.com/.

[4] https://www.blender.org/.

[5] https://www.autodesk.com/products/netfabb/overview.

[6] http://www.sketchup.com/it.

presence of two users who play extremely different roles: one of them, the *main user*, has to place 12 three-dimensional objects, different in color and shape, inside the corresponding holes (Fig. 2(a)), while the other one, the *supervisor*, supports his companion's actions and helps her/him to achieve the requested target. The task structure is completely asymmetrical because the two users work through different interfaces. The *main user* employs the HMD and acts inside an extremely immersive virtual environment. In order to guarantee safety conditions during the task accomplishment, the HMD users had to play in a restricted area of the lab, corresponding to the HTC Vive calibration area. He/she can interact with virtual objects using two different modalities: HTC controllers and Leap Motion. In the first case, items are grabbed just pushing a button on the controller and dropped when the button is released; in the second case, the player can interact with objects using his own hand and natural reaching, grasping and releasing gestures. The *supervisor*, instead, uses a simple desktop application (Fig. 2(b)), she/he is able to see *main user*'s actions from a fixed point of view on the scene and can help her/him replacing single objects thrown out of the game area in their original positions, deleting some of them in order to simplify the individualization and positioning of a piece, or selecting a hole to indicate the position into which a certain piece has to be insert. The *main user* is not able to see *supervisor* user-interface, so she/he can just see a clean blackboard as shown in the images below.

(a)	(b)

Fig. 2. (a) *Main user* point of view during the execution of the task. (b) *Supervisor* point of view during the execution of the task.

Regarding the application structure, it consists of three different scenes: a start menu, in which it is possible to insert the user's ID, and to select the interaction mode; a demo scene consisting in a virtual office room, where the player is free to move, explore the game area and to interact with objects according to the selected interaction mode; the main scenario, similar to the demo, in which, on the desk, there are 12 objects and a base with holes in which to put them. A blue cage, visible in the second and first scene, mark the boundaries of the calibrated game area and defines a space inside which the user can move safely (Fig. 3).

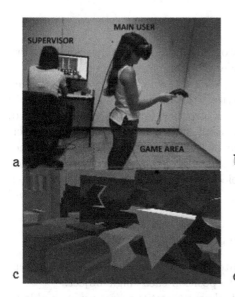

Fig. 3. Experiment setup. The *main user* wears the HTC Vive and can freely and safely move in the game area and interact with the virtual objects using the controller (a) o the Leap Motion (b). The *supervisor* sits in front of the desktop and observes main user's actions ready to intervene in case of need. Interaction with the virtual objects using the HTC controller (c) and the Leap Motion (d).

3.5   Experimental Procedure

The experiment has been carried out with 30 subjects as *main user*. The *supervisor* was always the same person. The experimental setup included two trials for each volunteer. Firstly, we asked the players to submit the Simulator Sickness Questionnaire (SSQ) [16], a 16 questions' questionnaire specifically used in the literature to evaluate the user physical status before the exposure to the virtual environment (pre-exposure). Then the users had to perform the task according to the selected interaction mode. The task ended when all the 12 objects were correctly positioned. After completing the first trial, the subjects had to submit the post-exposure SSQ; those answers have been used to evaluate users' status following the first exposure and preceding the second exposure to the VR. The second trial was executed with the interaction device complementary to the one used during the previous task. Subsequently, the users had to submit the post-exposure SSQ in order to evaluate their physical conditions at the end of the experiment. Finally, all the volunteers were asked which interaction mode they preferred. To reduce the statistical variability half of the participants carried out the first task using the Leap Motion and half using the controllers. To avoid learning the position of all the objects on the desk has been modified in the two trials.

3.6 Metrics

To evaluate the performances with the two different devices we have analyzed two distinct classes of parameters: the number of errors and the times necessary to correctly position the virtual objects. We defined a score for every task, assigning one point to each object correctly inserted (the baseline score starts from 12 points) and subtracting a certain number of points for each error committed. We associated a different coefficient to each kind of error according to their severity. The final score (S) is the result of the difference between the number of objects correctly positioned (12) and the sum of the number of repositioned (RP) and deleted (DP) piecies, and of selections (SP) and reset (R) actions, each one multiplied for its own coefficient ($c_1 \ldots c_4$, empirically evaluated), as shown in the following formula:

$$S = 12 - (RP * c_1 + DP * c_2 + SP * c_3 + R * c_4)$$

Through the time analysis, we computed the total time necessary to complete the task and the average time required to position each single object.

Furthermore, using the *Simulation Sickness Questionnaires* we were able to analyze the participants' *status* before and after each exposure to virtual reality in order to assess if the experience inside a virtual environment, even if brief, had physical effects on the users or not.

4 Results

The metrics defined to evaluate the task performances have been used to obtain an analysis on three levels: firstly we compared the performances obtained with the HTC controllers and with the Leap Motion; then we made a general comparison between the results relative to the first and the second trial, without considering the employed interaction device; in the end, we made a 'crossed' comparison to link the data relative to the first and the second trial taking into account the interaction mode used in both cases. Note that in all the experiments the only kind of help that the *main users* needed was the repositioning of objects; therefore, we decided to make an independent analysis on the number of repositioned elements in addition to those related to the score, the completion time and the single object's average time. In each analysis the statistical significance of the differences between data was estimate by making a *t-test* analysis.

The comparison between the performances of the two interaction devices highlights that all the considered parameters are significantly lower for the HTC controller. The median value related to the number of repositioned elements is equal to 0 in case of the HTC controller and to 2 in case of the Leap Motion, while the average value is 0.3 versus 3.4 (Fig. 4(a)). The score varies from a mean of 11.8 points in the HTC controller trials to 10.3 in the Leap Motion trials (Fig. 4(b)).

The average completion time is 68.5 s for the controller and it is 92.5 s lower compared to the one obtained with the Leap Motion, which is 161.1 s (Fig. 5(a)).

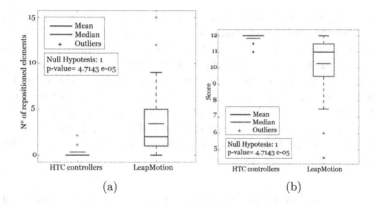

Fig. 4. Mean, median and standard deviation of (a) repositioned elements and (b) the final score for HTC controller and Leap Motion trials. p-value shows statistical significance.

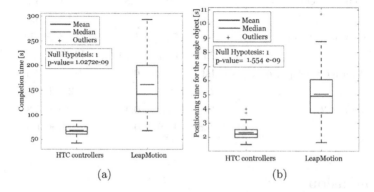

Fig. 5. Mean, median and standard deviation of (a) completion times and (b) positioning times for the single object for HTC controller and Leap Motion trials. p-value shows statistical significance.

Similarly the average positioning times for the single object are equal to 2.3 s and 5.0 s for the HTC controller and the Leap Motion, respectively (Fig. 5(b)). All these results are statistically significant.

The analysis performed on the data relative to the first and second trials shows no statistically significant differences for any of the considered parameters. Those results seem to indicate that no learning process happened between two consecutive trials. Nevertheless, this can be explained taking into account that the two series of trial have been execute with distinct interaction mode; therefore the users had to learn how to use each kind of device. The crossed comparison which considers both the order and the modality of the execution, underlines that there is not a learning pattern between first and second trials (Table 1). But comparing the performances of the first and second tasks performed using the same interaction mode, all the considered variables have a little lower value in the second trial case for both devices, though the differences are not statistically significant as explained before. The crossed analysis shows the better performances related to the first trial with the HTC controller. Similarly, the results relative to the second trial are significantly lower for the HTC controller. Finally, the SSQ analysis highlights no difference between the data acquired before and after the task execution thus indicating that the virtual environment does not cause sickness to the user. The open discussion shows how 73% of the users has preferred the HTC controller and only the 13% of them the Leap Motion device.

Table 1. Cross comparison of mean and standard deviation for each considered parameter between HTC controllers and Leap Motion relative to the first and second tasks.

Parameters	Trials	HTC controllers	Leap motion
Replaced elements	1st	0.4 ± 0.8	4.1 ± 3.7
	2nd	0.3 ± 0.6	2.8 ± 3.9
Completion time [s]	1st	73.9 ± 10.4	180.7 ± 67.9
	2nd	63.7 ± 10.9	141.1 ± 65.8
Average time per object [s]	1st	1.2 ± 0.7	2.7 ± 3.3
	2nd	1.3 ± 1.2	2.3 ± 65.8
Score/12	1st	11.8 ± 0.4	10 ± 1.8
	2nd	11.9 ± 0.3	10.6 ± 1.9

5   Conclusion

In this study, we specifically address human-computer interaction in a collaborative virtual environment, in particular comparing the Leap Motion and the HTC controller. We have developed an asymmetrical collaborative task in which one of the two involved users works inside a highly immersive 3D virtual environment and is supported in achieving his/her task by a partner who interacts with the virtual scene through a pc. The research purpose is to assess how the task's performances and the quality of the users experience inside the CVE vary according to the specific interaction device employed: the HTC Vive controller or the Leap Motion. The data analysis has included the evaluation of specific parameters related to the particular task, the measures of the users' physical conditions before and after the exposure to the virtual reality using the *Simulator Sickness Questionnaire* and the assessment of the participants quality experience inside the CVE based on the answers that they supplied during the open debate at the end of the experiment. The results we obtained highlight a statistically significant difference between the performances related to the two devices in favor to the HTC controller, in term of the number of repositioned elements, task completion time, single object average time and score. Comparing the first and second trial no relevant differences has arose, which means that the user has to learn from time to time how to interact with virtual objects through different devices. Nevertheless, the comparison between first and second trial carried out through the same device underlines that in the second case performances increase. The SSQ analysis shows that the VR exposure has not significant effects on the physical conditions of the users: this might be due also to the short time the task required to be completed. Based on the debated answers we state that the majority of the participants has been more comfortable using the HTC controller, probably because of the greater simplicity of interaction with the objects and the better stability of the system. This results was confirmed by quantitative analysis. Only 13% of the users has preferred working with the Leap Motion because of the greater natural interaction with the objects, despite obtaining worse performances; the remaining 13% liked both HTC controller and Leap Motion.

In conclusion we can declare that the system HMD - Controller offers the best performances thanks to its greater stability and accuracy; those characteristics guarantee a simpler handling providing a better experience for the user. The Leap Motion allows the user to interact with the objects in a more natural way compared to the controller, but it fails on stability and accuracy and its performances are extremely variables from subject to subject. In the future we are planning to fix some of the stability and accuracy problems related to the use of the Leap Motion and make further investigations on the manipulation of the objects in VR with HTC controllers and Leap Motion.

References

1. Monahan, T., McArdle, G., Bertolotto, M.: Virtual Reality for Collaborative e-Learning. Elsiever (2006)
2. Bouchard, S., Renaud, P., Robillard, G., St-Jacques, J.: Applications of virtual reality in clinical psychology: illustrations with the treatment of anxiety disorders. In: IEEE International Workshop 2002 HAVE Haptic Virtual Environments and Their Applications (2002)
3. Mclay, R.N., Wood, D.P., Murphy, J., Wiederhold, B.K.: A randomized, controlled trial of virtual reality-graded exposure therapy for post-traumatic stress disorder in active duty service members with combat-related post-traumatic stress disorder. Cyberpsychology Behav. Soc. Netw. 14(4), 223–229 (2011)
4. Chessa, M., Garibotti, M., Rossi, V., Novellino, A., Solari, F.: A virtual holographic display case for museum installations. In: 2015 7th International Conference on Intelligent Technologies for Interactive Entertainment (INTETAIN), pp. 69–73. IEEE (2015)
5. Li, N., Nittala, A.S., Sharlin, E., Sousa, M.C.: Shvil: collaborative augmented reality land navigation. In: Proceedings of the Extended Abstracts of the 32nd Annual ACM Conference on Human Factors in Computing Systems, pp. 1291–1296. ACM (2014)
6. Shia, Y., Dub, J., Lavyc, S., Zhaod, D.: A multiuser shared virtual environment for facility management. In: International Conference on Sustainable Design, Engineering and Construction (2016)

7. Churchill, E.F., Snowdon, D.: Collaborative virtual environments: an introductory review of issues and systems. Virtual Reality **3**(1), 3–15 (1998)
8. Okada, K.: Collaboration support in the information sharing space. IPSJ Mag. **48**(2), 123–125 (2007)
9. Cordeil, M., Dwyer, T., Klein, K., Laha, B., Mariott, K., Thomas, B.H.: Investigation of interactive strategies used in undertaking collaborative tasks. IEEE Trans. Vis. Comput. Graph. **23**, 441–450 (2017)
10. Sarmeinto, W.J., Maciel, A., Nedel, L., Collazos, C.A.: Measuring the collaboration degree in immersive 3D collaborative virtual environments. In: IEEE VR International Workshop on Collaborative Virtual Environment (3D CVE) (2014)
11. Claude, G., Gouranton, V., Arnaldi, B.: Roles in collaborative virtual environments for training. In: IEEE VR International Workshop on Collaborative Virtual Environment (3D CVE) (2017)
12. Lo, K., Zeng, T., Hu, Y.: Investigation of interactive strategies used in undertaking collaborative tasks. Appl. Sci. **7**(4), 318 (2017)
13. Sheridan, T.B.: Telerobotics, Automation, and Human Supervisory Control. MIT Press, Cambridge (1992)
14. Erfanian, A., Hu, Y.: Multi-user efficacy of collaborative virtual environments. In: IEEE 20th International Conference on Computer Supported Cooperative Work in Design (2016)
15. Geszten, D., Hmornik, B.P., Hercegfi, K.: User experience in a collaborative 3D virtual environment. In: IEEE 6th International Conference on Cognitive Infocommunications (2015)
16. Kennedy, R.S., Lane, N.E., Berbaum, K.S., Lilienthal, M.G.: Simulator sickness questionnaire: an enanched method for quantifying simulator sickness. Int. J. Aviat. Psychol. **3**, 203–220 (1993)

Ecological Validity of Virtual Reality:
Three Use Cases

Alexis Paljic[(✉)]

MINES ParisTech, PSL-Research University, Centre for Robotics, Paris, France
alexis.paljic@mines-paristech.fr

Abstract. This paper is a discussion on the question of ecological validity of virtual reality in the light of three studies that we have done in previous works. These works are chosen as a basis for the discussion because they are all designed to assess validity using one method: the comparison of user perception and behavior between real and virtual environments. The first study explores visual perception of complex materials, the second studies the role of visual feedback on user gestures and object manipulation, the third is a study of virtual reality as a tool for assessing the acceptability of human robot collaboration in a car factory. We discuss our methodology, the limits of validity of VR in our three use cases and suggest future developments in VR to provide design tools for more valid VR environments.

Keywords: Virtual reality · Ecological valididy
Comparative approach · Real vs. Virtual comparison
Perception of complex materials · Manipulation gestures
Human Robot cooperation

1 Introduction

Ecological validity of Virtual Reality is a central question when VR is used as a predictive tool. This is typically the case in the context of industrial product design, where human in the loop simulations of products is part of the design process, to avoid the cost of real prototypes. It is also the case in therapy applications where VR is used to assess human behavior. Indeed in such predictive uses, the proximity of human response within the virtual environment to the equivalent real situation is necessary.

We here define our use of two terms in this paper, *Immersion*, and *Ecological Validity*. We will use the term *immersion* as encompassing two things: (1) sensori-motor interfaces i.e. what a virtual reality system provides from the technical point of view to address visual, haptic, audidory or other modalities (2) the cognitive interfaces, describing the way activities are performed in the virtual environment. We consider as *ecological validity* the fact that the user's behavioral response is realistic.

In the specific case of VR as a predictive tool, the role of the designer of the VR simulation is to choose the immersion for each use case and human activity

© Springer International Publishing AG 2017
S. Battiato et al. (Eds.): ICIAP 2017 International Workshops, LNCS 10590, pp. 301–310, 2017.
https://doi.org/10.1007/978-3-319-70742-6_28

that he or she wants to simulate, with the objective of maximizing the ecological validity.

The research field of ecological validity in VR is very large since sensori-motor and cognitive resources are different for each activity, and may be even so between different users. Thus each activity requires an adaptation of the levels of immersion VR and an assessment of its validity.

We can consider that ecological validity in VR is a specific case of a more general question, that is the relation between immersion and presence. The specificity of ecological validity in VR being that the definition of presence that is considered is "response as if real", one of the definitions proposed by Slater [14].

On the general problem, which is the relation between immersion and presence, there is a large number of user studies in VR that focus on the role of specific level of immersion, visual, haptic, auditory, on activities in virtual reality. Part of those activities are not considered in relation to an equivalent real activity, and thus cannot be considered as within the ecological validity scope of research. As examples, research on immersion in VR to help scientific data visualization (fluid dynamics, molecular visualization), or studies on levels of immersion for application control using menus, are not representative of real activities. There are activities that cannot be performed in real life. Some activities in VR are of ecological nature such as navigation or object manipulation, but there is not a large amount of literature that actually objectively looks at how close those are to the real thing. The VR Knowledge database[1] is a curated repository of research findings in the field of virtual reality, and is potentially very useful to the research community. It aims at bringing together research results on the relation between levels of immersion, and performance metrics on various tasks in VR. The ecological validity, as defined in this paper is not directly considered though.

Some works have considered comparing behavioral metrics, between a virtual activity and its real counterpart, to assess ecological validity. Various tasks have been considered. We would be tempted here to present a list sorted by a (tentative) level of complexity of tasks. However sorting tasks by complexity is a difficult and open problem. We will just list a series of tasks, and will start with the ones that require only a perceptive component, requiring no active and conscious reaction by the user, then considering more interactive ones[2]. Note that this list is not exhaustive, and is meant to show the variety of tasks being considered in the literature. There have been real/virtual comparisons on Visual Perception of Distances [12], Heights [13], or perception of materials [6]. On more interactive tasks, we can note: the hoop and wire game [1], playing with Lego Bricks [3], peg insertion [21], aiming movements [9], reaching [17]. We could consider that the next tasks require a supplemementary level of cognitive involvement: navigation and spatial knowledge [10], car driving [11], wheelchair driving [4]. As a last

---

[1] http://knowledgebase.cs.vt.edu/.

[2] Although this also can be discussed: tasks that appear to be of only of perceptive nature, are likely to include human actions, even non conscious, as Varela et al. suggest in their work on Enaction [16].

group we propose works that tackle activities that have an emotional or social component: collaboratively solving puzzle with other people [2], social behavior in small groups [15], or cooperation with robots [20].

This list is not exhaustive at all, as this paper's focus is not to do a review of the literature on ecological validity. The intent of the author is to present different ways of tackling the question. I will do so by reporting on three studies that were previously done by the author and his colleagues [6–8,18–20] that are at located at 3 different points in the continuum of tasks proposed in the previous paragraph: perception only, perception and action, emotional and/or interaction with other entities.

2   Complex Material Observation

In the domains of Cinema or video Games, an esthetically driven, or simply plausible visual appearance of objects can be acceptable. It not the case for the use of VR for the design of visual appearance of materials, where object's visual aspects needs to be physically realistic. The industrial need is a virtual material design workshop, in which the user virtually specifies a material composition, then he is able to visualize its resulting visual aspect in a VR environment. In this virtual material workshop, we determine the composition of a future real material whose appearance is supposedly predicted by the virtual one. The realistic nature of the image is thus paramount. In order to set up such a workshop, a research project[3] is built on a 4 step methodology: (1) optical measures to characterize the composition of the chosen material samples, (2) light-matter interaction models, (3) Rendering in a VR system, (4) Perceptive validations with the human in the loop by comparing real and virtual samples. The results of this research are described, for the case of homogeneous coloured materials in Medina et al.'s works [18,19] and as for complex materials (such as car paints with effects) in [6,7].

The first step in order to obtain a realistic appearance in VR is to ensure a proper calibration of the display chain (including display and stereoscopic glasses characteristics), given that the rendering models and engine provide the spectrum of the light being emitted by the virtual materials. We have set up such a process, in the case of homogeneous materials [18,19] (Fig. 1).

We will focus in this paper on another material type, which is complex materials with visual effects, such as car paints which have metallic flakes embedded in the base coat and produce sparkling effects. Statistical models describing such materials have been set up in the project [5], based on optical measurements. The models create virtual microstructures, that are fed into a rendering engine (see Fig. 2). To sum up the general results for that case, the above methodology allowed to show two results. Firstly, the use of stereoscopy decreases perception thresholds of specific properties of the material (size and density of aluminium particles) [7]. Secondly, we have validated that our VR visualization system

---

[3] See acknowledgements.

allows to make a correspondence, for a given visual aspect, between the descriptive metrics of the virtual material to the ones of the real material, through user perceptive studies [6].

Both these results have a consequence on ecological validity of VR for the observation of materials: (1) we show that stereoscopy has an impact on perception thresholds and that we are able to quantify it. This quantification can be used as a guideline for the design of VR systems for ecological validity as is can drive immersion choices (given a threshold need, should we use stereo or not?). (2) we show that ecological validity can be achieved in VR at the level of material composition. In the experimental setup, a simple stereoscopic display was used, without dynamic perspective (no head tracking).

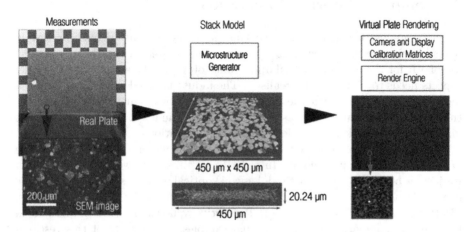

Fig. 1. In order to simulate car paints that have metallic flakes embedded in the base coat and produce sparkling effects, statistical models describing such materials have been set up [5], based on optical measurements. The models create virtual microstructures, that are fed into a rendering engine for stereoscopic visualization.

3   Gestures in Object Manipulation

Gestures that are performed in a virtual reality system are likely to be different than gestures from everyday life tasks. The quality of virtual reality systems can modify the way gestures are performed. As examples, we can point out the visual latency of the system, being the delay between movement capture and the resulting visual feedback on the avatar of one's hand. High latencies are known to decrease performance. The number of degrees of freedom that are captured, between a simple hand pose measurement, or a full hand joints configuration acquisition using gloves or vision based cameras, achieve very different levels of ecology of prehension. The use of props, reproducing the shape of the manipulated object can improve user experience and gesture validity.

Here the question we asked ourselves is how much can we play (reduce, distort) with visual feedback and still get stable, close to normal results?

We looked into the role of visual feedback and visual appearance of objects on manipulation gestures in VR. In a previous work [8] we have studied the role of visual feedback and visual appearance of objects on manipulation gestures (gestures performed while manipulating objects).

A variety of feedbacks where implemented, on a box opening task. The user performed the gesture to open the box, and depending on the progression of his gesture (depending on its position along a prerecorded gesture) a visual feedback on the opening of the box was provided. The visual feedbacks (see Fig. 2) where ranging from boolean (box would visually open only at the end of the gesture), textual (a percentage of the opening was displayed), discrete (only a few steps were displayed), normal, enhanced (with a >1 gain between motion capture and visual displacement) and non coupled (or open loop: meaning that an automatic animation of the box would start at contact user movements having no effect on it).

Fig. 2. Study of gesture feedback: on a box opening task, the gesture is measured and several visual feedbacks are proposed to the user (from left to right: boolean, textual, steps, normal, enhanced, openloop) and compared in terms of gesture completion and proximity to an initially recorded natural gesture

We compared descriptors of gestures between an initially recorded natural gesture (done with no feedback constraints), and the gestures performed with the feedbacks. Results showed firstly that the non coupled feedback is immediately recognized as such, and gesture descriptors greatly differ from initial gesture (small movements, shorter time). Mechanical work and completion time are also different for all feedbacks. Finally the subjective preferences of users went to enhanced feedback, and diminish with for lower levels of information. In a second experiment, we studied the role of affordances on gesture memorization. We have shown that affordances, which is the visual appearance of objects that shows how it is operated, increase user recall of gestures.

The outcome of this study was mainly to set up a method to explore immersion and its effects: a systematic approach of gradually simplifying feedback in order to determine what is necessary in the stimuli in virtual environments to perform valid/representative actions.

4   Human Robot Cooperation

The introduction of robots as coworking or collaborative units with humans would help reducing physical strain for difficult tasks. However it opens a lot of questions on their social and practical acceptability. We looked into the validity of virtual reality as a tool to assess the acceptability, from the human point of view, to work with a robot. To do so, we set up two use cases in both a real setup and a virtual environment (CAVE), and compared what is representative in VR and what is not [20]. The two use cases were, Human Robot (HR) Copresence and HR Cooperation. Both are studied in the context of car parts mounting tasks in a factory. In the case of HR Copresence, a worker and a robot are working side by side on mounting parts of a car door (see Figs. 3 and 4). The studied variables were environment type (Real/Virtual) and the distance between the operator and the robot (Close, Far).

Fig. 3. Human Robot copresence study. Real environment.

Fig. 4. Human Robot copresence study. Virtual environment.

In the case of HR Cooperation the worker and the robot are facing each other, and the robot can give various parts to the worker (see Figs. 5 and 6). Here the variables that were studied were environment type (Real/Virtual) and different levels of assistance of the robot. In the copresence scenario users preference (questionnaires) went to the 'far' condition, and this result was consistent between real and virtual environments. A increase in heart rate was found when the robot was close, in both real and virtual conditions. Finally, a skin conductance raise (that may be representative of user stress) when the robot was close, in the real conditions, was not found in the virtual condition. In the cooperation scenario, the main result is again that the questionnaires get close responses between real and virtual conditions (acceptability, perceived security, usability). And we observe the same trends on physiological measures as for the copresence use case. We can hypothesize that more complete feedbacks (such as *haptics* providing contact information with the environment, or auditory feedback for factory or simulated robot sounds) may increase ecological validity, but these require specific studies.

Fig. 5. Human Robot cooperation study. Real environment.

Fig. 6. Human Robot cooperation study. Virtual environment

5   Discussion

Virtual reality shows ecological validity for each of the tasks that we have studied. However, this validity is only proven to a certain extent. Some of the descriptors of human behavior do not match between VR and real (physiological measures for example). The results that we have presented, on comparing behavior descriptors between same activities performed in real and virtual situations, are specific to the use cases an considered tasks. Especially, for each use case, many additional studies can and should be performed to assess the influence of other levels of immersion. We propose below a few examples of characteristics of immersion that could change user response towards higher ecological validity.

1. *Material Observation*: Resolution of displays, gamut of displays, high dynamic range displays, use of head tracking and dynamic perspective.
2. *Gestures in Object Manipulation*: Use of finger tracking, Use of physics engine, Haptic feedback.
3. *Human Robot Cooperation*: Hapic Feedback, Auditory Feedback.

Here, we argue that the three use cases that we have presented have also a methodological interest. They showed that, for each use case, we can make real/virtual comparisons at very different levels: global subjective appearance of materials, or, at a totally different level, validate underlying physics models. For the Gestures case, two different methods were used. The first is spatial and temporal gesure comparison. For the second, we have tried to develop a method that not only seeks to assertain real/virtual coherence, but also to find out what is the minimal relevant information in the feedback. We did so by stripping down feedback with the goal of finding the minimal information that is needed to have a valid gesture. In this case, the method showed that the maximum info is needed, it is the opinion of the author that this method can be used in different contexts. Finally, for HR copresence and cooperation: we have used subjective questionnaires (Acceptability, Security) or more objective physiological measures[4].

---

[4] Although physiological measures require careful use because of practical reasons: sensors on the skin can move, and add strong variability in data.

An important question that is open is how can designers of VR systems re-use such results? Indeed, if one has to set up an activity that is *close* to ones that appear in the real/virtual comparison literature, a transposition of the results should lead her or him to choose similar levels of immersion. Here the difficulty resides in deciding what *close* means. For example, in our material observation use case, we have proven ecological validity for a specific type of metallic flakes. Do these results hold if we change average flake size, or flake shape, or size/shape of the sample on which the material is presented? And what to do if the use case one is setting up does not appear at all in the literature? No guidelines at all in that case. A dream tool answering the question of reusability would be a dictionary of core activities, and the associated immersion needed for ecological validity. Those core activities, simple in nature, would be the building blocks of any more complex activity. Thus the dictionary would provide building blocks to infer immersion for any given task. Today this dream tool is purely conceptual.

6   Conclusion

We have shown that in our three use cases, ecological validity can be proven through a real/virtual comparison method. They work for some of descriptors: questionnaires, movement measures, visual perception of specific properties, and for some not, such as physiological measures. Virtual reality communities have to continue exploring the question of ecological validity and adding up results for the reuse in future designs. But it is a long work. VR and Cognitives Sciences have started to interact, and share their results on the role of immersion on presence. Would this be the beginning of a dictionary of (micro level) tasks that could be combineable to describe any (macro level) task? In that case a dream tool adding up immersion for ecological validity at the micro level, to construct the immersion at a macro level would be a little bit closer to a reality.

Acknowledgments. A part of this work (material perception) was funded by French National Research Agency project funded LIMA (Light Interaction Matter Aspect, 2012–2016) under grant number ANR2011RMNP01401. The work on Human Robot cooperation was funded by PSA Group through a research Chair (Chaire Robotique et Realite Virtuelle).

References

1. Arnold, P., Farrell, M.J., Pettifer, S., West, A.J.: Performance of a skilled motor task in virtual and real environments. Ergonomics **45**(5), 348–361 (2002)
2. Axelsson, A.S., Abelin, A., Heldal, I., Schroeder, R., Wideström, J.: Cubes in the cube: a comparison of a puzzle-solving task in a virtual and a real environment. Cyberpsychol. Behav. **4**(2), 279–286 (2001). The Impact of the Internet, Multimedia and Virtual Reality on Behavior and Society
3. Baradaran, H., Stuerzlinger, W.: A comparison of real and virtual 3D construction tools with novice users. In: CGVR, vol. 6, pp. 10–15 (2006)

4. Cooper, R.A., Spaeth, D.M., Jones, D.K., Boninger, M.L., Fitzgerald, S.G., Guo, S.: Comparison of virtual and real electric powered wheelchair driving using a position sensing joystick and an isometric joystick. Med. Eng. Phys. **24**(10), 703–708 (2002)
5. Couka, E., Willot, F., Jeulin, D.: A mixed Boolean and deposit model for the modeling of metal pigments in paint layers. Image Anal. Stereology **34**(2), 125–134 (2015)
6. Da Graça, F.E., Paljic, A., Diaz, E.: Evaluating stereoscopic visualization for predictive rendering. In: 23rd WSCG International Conference in Central Europe on Computer Graphics, Visualization and Computer Vision, Plzen, Czech Republic, June 2015
7. Da Graça, F.E., Paljic, A., Lafon-Pham, D., Callet, P.: Stereoscopy for visual simulation of materials of complex appearance. In: Stereoscopic Displays and Applications XXV, San Francisco, United States, pp. 9011–9030, February 2014
8. Jégo, J.-F., Paljic, A., Fuchs, P.: User-defined gestural interaction: a study on gesture memorization. In: IEEE 3D User Interfaces, 3DUI 2013, Orlando, FL, United States, 8 p., March 2013
9. Liu, L., van Liere, R., Nieuwenhuizen, C., Martens, J.-B.: Comparing aimed movements in the real world and in virtual reality. In: IEEE Virtual Reality Conference, VR 2009, pp. 219–222. IEEE (2009)
10. Mania, K., Troscianko, T., Hawkes, R., Chalmers, A.: Fidelity metrics for virtual environment simulations based on spatial memory awareness states. Presence Teleoperators Virtual Environ. **12**(3), 296–310 (2003)
11. Milleville-Pennel, I., Charron, C.: Driving for real or on a fixed-base simulator: is it so different? An explorative study. Presence **24**(1), 74–91 (2015)
12. Renner, R.S., Velichkovsky, B.M., Helmert, J.R.: The perception of egocentric distances in virtual environments - a review. ACM Comput. Surv. **46**(2), 23:1–23:40 (2013)
13. Simeonov, P.I., Hsiao, H., Dotson, B.W., Ammons, D.E.: Height effects in real and virtual environments. Hum. Factors **47**(2), 430–438 (2005)
14. Slater, M.: A note on presence terminology. Presence Connect **3**(3), 1–5 (2003)
15. Slater, M., Sadagic, A., Usoh, M., Schroeder, R.: Small-group behavior in a virtual and real environment: a comparative study. Presence Teleoperators Virtual Environ. **9**(1), 37–51 (2000)
16. Varela, F., Thompson, E., Rosch, E., et al.: L'Inscription corporelle del l'esprit, Paris, Seuil (1993)
17. Viau, A., Feldman, A.G., McFadyen, B.J., Levin, M.F.: Reaching in reality and virtual reality: a comparison of movement kinematics in healthy subjects and in adults with hemiparesis. J. NeuroEng. Rehabil. **1**(1), 11 (2004)
18. Victor, M., Paljic, A., Lafon-Pham, D.: A study of image exposure for the stereoscopic visualization of sparkling materials. In: IS&T/STIE Electronic Imaging 2015. International Society for Optics and Photonics, San Francisco, February 2015
19. Victor, M., Lafon-Pham, D., Paljic, A., Diaz, E.: Physically based image synthesis of materials: a methodology towards the visual comparison of physical vs. virtual samples. In: Colour and Visual Computing Symposium, Gjovik, Norway, August 2015

20. Weistroffer, V., Paljic, A., Fuchs, P., Hugues, O., Chodacki, J.-P., Ligot, P., Morais, A.: Assessing the acceptability of human-robot co-presence on assembly lines: a comparison between actual situations and their virtual reality counterparts. In: 2014 RO-MAN: The 23rd IEEE International Symposium on Robot and Human Interactive Communication, Edinburgh, United Kingdom, pp. 377–384. IEEE, August 2014
21. Yoshikawa, T., Kawai, M., Yoshimoto, K.: Toward observation of human assembly skill using virtual task space. In: Siciliano, B., Dario, P. (eds.) Experimental Robotics VIII. STAR, vol. 5, pp. 540–549. Springer, Heidelberg (2003). https://doi.org/10.1007/3-540-36268-1_49

Biometrics As-a-Service: Cloud-Based Technology, Systems and Applications (IWBAAS)

Biometric Traits in Multi-secret Digital Steganography

Katarzyna Koptyra and Marek R. Ogiela[⊠]

Faculty of Electrical Engineering, Automatics, Computer Science and
Biomedical Engineering, AGH University of Science and Technology, 30
Mickiewicza Ave., 30-059 Krakow, Poland
{kkoptyra,mogiela}@agh.edu.pl

Abstract. This paper discusses the usage of biometrics in multi-secret steganography as one of three levels of information protection. Each secret is related to an individual key, which is fully or partially derived from personal trait. The chosen container is fuzzy vault cryptosystem that works well with biometric features and allows to reveal secrets independently of each other. Presented idea may be used in single-user system in which one person stores a number of secrets or in multi-user cloud-based systems. The additional topics covered in this study are pros and cons of diverse types of biometric data with regard to information protection and also security issues of biometrics application in general.

Keywords: Biometrics · Multi-secret steganography · Information hiding
Fuzzy vault

1 Introduction

There are usually three methods of controlling access to an important resource. These are: something you know, something you have and something you are. To prevent unauthorized access, one can use a combination of depicted measures or at least one of them. Each method provides different type of protection and has its own advantages and disadvantages.

Something you know is the most common category which reaches passwords, passphrases, PINs and similar codes. People are used to this form of access control in their daily lives, it is cheap, easy to implement and does not need any external device. However, users are required to remember a number of codes which sometimes may be problematic and lead to security risks, e.g. using the same password in many places or noting it on a piece of paper. Additionally each person is responsible for their own protection as weak passphrases are vulnerable to be guessed. On the other hand, passwords are not assigned to the user forever and can easily be changed in case of leakage. Therefore security codes are good and wide spread, but need some precautions.

Something you have is another class of methods based on a physical device, most often in the form of a card or a key fob. This object can either be passive (with fixed secret code, like RFID [1]) or active (that generates multiple codes, like token).

© Springer International Publishing AG 2017
S. Battiato et al. (Eds.): ICIAP 2017 International Workshops, LNCS 10590, pp. 313–319, 2017.
https://doi.org/10.1007/978-3-319-70742-6_29

Some devices are equipped with more advanced solutions, for instance challenge-response mode. To grant access to the system, the user does not need to remember anything. Instead, he or she is obligated to have the device, which serves as a key. Thus this type of access control can be regarded as convenient for some people, but a few threats should also be noted. The user may lose access to the system if the device is lost or stolen. So it is easier for adversary to intentionally block authorized person than in case of password.

Something you are is the last group which uses personal traits to identify user. This includes various biometric features, like fingerprints, voice, iris, face shape, DNA, vein pattern etc. The main advantage of this method is that it does not require carrying any additional device nor remembering any secret code. In short-term biometric features are constant, they may change gradually with regard to age and weight. There is very low probability of biometrics match between two people excluding very close family relationships. The problem with this type of access control is that each measurement is a little imprecise and has some discrepancies comparing to a reference object. For that reason methods that use biometric traits have to compensate those inaccuracies. What is more, every system which relies only on biometrics exposes user to risk of privacy and identity theft [2]. Personal traits cannot be easily changed and some of them are not very difficult to obtain, for example fingerprints or voice sample. The user may lose access to their data in case of accident or serious illness, but those situations are rare. Normally biometric features change very little in long-time period.

In practice we can not only see solutions based on one approach, but also multi-factor authentications. Systems that use many methods at the same time are more secure, but less user-friendly and may be annoying for users. The major advantage of combining different approaches is the fact that even if some pieces of information are compromised, the adversary is still not able to grant access to the system. Nevertheless, to increase the level of security, one needs to reduce usability, which is not always acceptable.

This paper focuses on biometric features in multi-secret steganography. Personal traits will serve to encode and decode hidden secrets by being used in key derivation process. This task requires obtained data to be in form of a number or set of numbers. What is more, a few biometric observations of the same person are slightly different, but the output key should nonetheless be able to decode the secret. Thus we need a method which can deal with these issues. An algorithm that meets above require-ments is described in Sect. 2. Section 3 presents a few biometrics that may be used in multi-secret steganography together with their strong and weak points. Section 4 summarizes entire discussion and draws some conclusions.

2 Hiding Many Secrets with Biometric Features

Multi-secret steganography [3] is a branch of information hiding in which many secrets are embedded in a single container. The user should be able to decode each information in a lossless way, which means that secrets cannot overwrite each other. Additionally, to use biometric features, the algorithm ought to have the ability to work on imprecise data. These demands are fulfilled by multi-secret fuzzy vault [4], a cryptosystem which is presented below.

Fuzzy vault is a construction consisted of great amount of points. A few of them are genuine and store important information. The rest is only a chaff destined to hide real secrets between a noise. In this cryptosystem we can distinguish two phases: vault creation and secret reconstruction.

The aim of the first phase is to produce a vault with hidden secrets. To do this, we need the secrets itself (numbers) and also associated to them secret keys (unordered sets of numbers). The keys are required to be disjunctive. Then for every secret we create a polynomial that encodes this secret in its coefficients. In next step each polynomial is evaluated on the elements of related key. In this way all genuine points are generated. Algorithm 1 presents this part of vault creation.

Algorithm 1. Creating genuine points

> Input: secrets $k_1, \ldots, k_N$; disjunctive keys $A_1, \ldots, A_N$
> Output: sets of genuine points $P_1, \ldots, P_N$
>
> 1.   for i = 1, ..., N:
> 2.   Create polynomial p_i which encodes secret k_i in its coefficients
> 3.   Create empty set P_i
> 4.   for j = 0, ..., length(A_i):
> 5.   add $(A_i[j], p_i(A_i[j]))$ to P_i
> 6.   return $P_1, \ldots, P_N$

Eventually, the important data need to be hidden between a noise. Thus the final stage is chaff points generation. They may be scattered randomly, but have to fulfill following two demands. Firstly, false points cannot lie on any of the polynomials. Secondly, x coordinates of chaff points and genuine points have to be different (or not too close to each other). After the great amount of noise is created, the vault is ready. The whole process is depicted in Fig. 1. There are also different approaches to chaff points generation, for instance method based on circle packing [5].

When the vault is constructed, it is possible to start recovering embedded secrets. Each secret information is linked to individual key, which is in form of unordered set. Therefore the proper key is needed to filter correct points from the whole collection. Then selected points are used to reconstruct the polynomial, from which the secret is decoded. This procedure is presented in Fig. 2.

As mentioned previously, every secret is encoded in its individual polynomial. The degree of each polynomial is chosen at the beginning and does not change later. This is very important parameter that determines minimal length of secret key (which is equal degree+1). However, the keys can be longer as with more points we are also able to reconstruct the formula. Moreover, if the key is redundant, some of its parts may be invalid and the secret is still recoverable. This means that the key used to extract secret information is not required to be exactly the same like the original key used in vault creation. It is enough to them to overlap substantially, which gives us error-tolerance. In consequence we can use incomplete or imprecise data, that is exactly which is needed for biometric purposes.

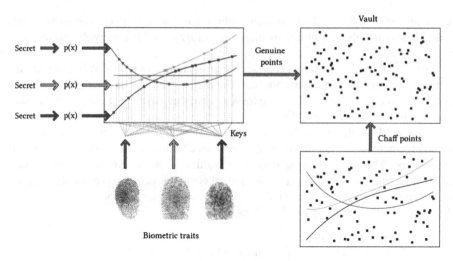

Fig. 1. Vault creation process.

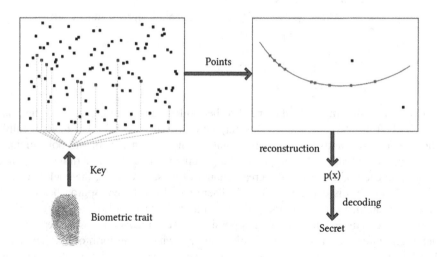

Fig. 2. Secret extraction process.

Biometric features may be applied in steganographic algorithms as keys or key fragments. This necessitates traits that can be expressed as set of numbers (for example fingerprints) or as numbers (like iris). Biometrics from former group give keys directly as they are already in required format. The latter features should be joined into one set to create full key. This means that the key can be derived fully or partially from some personal trait. It is also possible to combine this approach with other methods of information protection. One fragment of the key may be originated from biometric feature, another based on the passphrase and the last one can be stored on external device.

Presented idea of applying personal traits in multi-secret steganography is suitable not only for systems in which one person stores many secrets in single container. It works well with systems destined for many participants in which each user has own secret, thus there is an opportunity of using it in cloud. It should be noted that flexibility of described solution allows to select the most appropriate method of key generation.

3 Applicability of Various Biometric Features in Multi-secret Steganography

There are many traits which can be applied in multi-secret steganography. Below we present and characterize a few of them.

Fingerprints are subject of research since many years and are well studied. They can be acquired in fast, safe and non-invasive manner for the user. Additionally, scanning devices are cheap and easy to use. Each finger has its own pattern, thus it is possible to encode ten pieces of information in this way. Moreover, fingerprints do not change with age and weight. However, every person leave them in many places by simply touching a surface, so it is possible to obtain one's biometric data even after long time. There are known cases of deceiving the scanner with artificial finger and granting access to the system [6].

Voice sample is a trait which is very easy and cheap to obtain, as it only requires a microphone. The recording process may take a few seconds, but it is non-invasive and safe. This biometric feature gives the possibility of combining authentication and authorization at the same time (match of person and a secret phrase). On the other hand, the user may not be correctly identified if his voice is modified as a result of illness. What is more, the system may be attacked with use of samples which were recorder earlier.

Iris are feature which can be an option with moderate budget. The scanning is fast and safe for the user. This trait may be analyzed with use of color or grayscale images, therefore we are also flexible in device selection. Iris have individual characteristics and are harder to copy than fingerprints. The next advantage is that each of two eyes may be used to encode different information.

Face shape can be analyzed on the basis of camera image or 3D scan. Depending of applied hardware, it can be either cheap or expensive. The whole procedure is fast and safe for the user. Face shape may somewhat change as a result of losing or gaining weight. If the recognition is based on single image, it is possible to break into the system by presenting a photograph. Additionally, most cameras are sensitive to changes in illumination and a skin tone. On the other hand, deceiving 3D scanner is much more complicated.

Vein pattern is very characteristic trait. For biometric purposes usually blood vessels in hand are used as a feature. This is because that body part contains many small vessels which are highly individual. The examination is not invasive, but requires specialized and expensive equipment. What is more, it is difficult to get one's vein pattern, thus granting access to some resource in an unauthorized way is not a simple task. It should also be noted that there is a possibility of encoding two different secrets with both hands.

Bone shape is a feature which can vary between people, especially in case of hands or frontal sinus. It can express many individual characteristics, like previous fractures or disorders, for example rheumatoid arthritis and osteoarthritis [7]. It rarely changes, mainly as a result of disease or accident. To make such imaging, an interesting body part should be x-rayed. This type of examination cannot be made very often, because it impacts strongly on user's health. Also, the equipment is expensive and needs additional antiradiation shields or walls. From security point of view this feature is very hard to forge [8].

DNA is the most detailed feature which contains the largest amount of information. It is highly unique, although can be identical in monozygotic twins. The sample of DNA can be easily obtained, but the sole examination is complex and very expensive. Genetic code of the user may be recognized regardless of their age or weight. Collecting one's DNA in an unauthorized way is possible for example from a glass or used tissue.

4   Conclusions

This paper presents application of biometric features in multi-secret steganography. It describes an algorithm which is able to work on imprecise data and also the method of using personal traits in secret encoding and decoding. The advantages of that approach are that it allows to reconstruct all secrets independently from each other and that it can be combined with other measures of information protection. Additionally presented idea is suitable for multi-user cloud systems, but also for system in which one user has many secrets.

The conclusions of this study are as follows. Biometric features may be used as keys in steganography and there is a number of traits from which we can choose. However, as they cannot be easily changed, there is a risk of obtaining one's feature in an unauthorized way. For that reason personal traits are not recommended to solely secure really important information. They can and they should be used in cooperation with different techniques of access control.

Biometric systems are usually comfortable for users because they do not impose carrying physical device nor remembering a password. But this convenience cannot overshadow security aspects of biometrics, which are really important and should always be taken into consideration.

Acknowledgments. This work was supported by the AGH University of Science and Technology research Grant No. 15.11.120.868.

References

1. Valero, E., Adán, A.: Integration of RFID with other technologies in construction. Measurement **94**, 614–620 (2016)
2. Lee, V.: Biometrics and identity fraud. Biometric Technol. Today **16**(2), 7–11 (2008)

3. Ogiela, M.R., Koptyra, K.: False and multi-secret steganography in digital images. Soft Comput. **19**(11), 3331–3339 (2015)
4. Koptyra, K., Ogiela, M.R.: Fuzzy vault schemes in multi-secret digital steganography. In: 10th International Conference on Broadband and Wireless Computing, Communication and Applications, BWCCA 2015, Krakow, Poland, pp. 183–186 (2015)
5. Hani, M.K., Marsono, M.N., Bakhteri, R.: Biometric encryption based on a fuzzy vault scheme with a fast chaff generation algorithm. Future Gener. Comp. Syst. **29**(3), 800–810 (2013)
6. Espinoza, M., Champod, C., Margot, P.: Vulnerabilities of fingerprint reader to fake fingerprints attacks. Forensic Sci. Int. **204**(1), 41–49 (2011)
7. Sumarahinsih, A., Kalim, H., Yueniwati, Y.P.W., Naba, A.: Image segmentation: determination of joint space area inhand radiographs. ARPN J. Eng. Appl. Sci. **11**(3), 1931–1935 (2016)
8 Castiglione, A. (et al.): On secure data management in health-care environment. In: Seventh International Conference on Innovative Mobile and Internet Services in Ubiquitous Computing, IMIS 2013, pp. 666–671. Taichung, Taiwan (2013)

Efficacy of Typing Pattern Analysis in Identifying Soft Biometric Information and Its Impact in User Recognition

Soumen Roy[1(✉)], Utpal Roy[2], and D.D. Sinha[1]

[1] Department of Computer Science and Engineering, University of Calcutta,
92 APC Road, Calcutta 700 009, India
soumen.roy_2007@yahoo.co.in,
devadatta.sinha@gmail.com
[2] Department of Computer and System Sciences, Visva-Bharati,
Santiniketan 731235, India
roy.utpal@gmail.com

Abstract. Identifying soft biometric traits such as gender, age group, handedness, hand(s) used, typing skill and emotional states from typing pattern and the inclusion of these traits as additional features in user recognitionis a recent research area in order to improve the performance of keystroke dynamics technique. Knowledge-based user authentication with the combination of keystroke dynamics as biometric characteristics relates the issues to user authentication/identification in cloud computing based applications. Our approach is the one way, where the performance of the keystroke dynamics biometricin user recognition can be improved by using soft biometric traits that provides some additional information about the user which can be extracted from the typing pattern on a computer keyboard or touch screen phone. These soft biometric traits have low discriminating power but can be used to enhance the performance of user recognition in accuracy and time efficiency. In this paper, we are interested in using this technique in thestatic keystroke dynamics user authentication system. It has been observed that the age group (18−30/30 +or < 18/18+), gender (male/female), handedness (left-handed/right-handed), hand(s) used (one hand/both hands), typing skill (touch/others) and emotional states (Anger/Excitation) can be extracted from the way of typing on a computer keyboard for single predefined text. This soft biometric information from typing pattern as extra features decreases the Equal Error Rate (EER). We have used two leading machine learning approaches: Support Vector Machine with Radial Basis Function (SVM-RBF) and Fuzzy-Rough Nearest Neighbour with Vaguely Quantified Rough Set (FRNN-VQRS) on multiple publicly available authentic and recognized keystroke dynamics datasets. Our approach on CMU keystroke dynamics datasetsindicates the impact of soft biometric traits.

Keywords: Keystroke dynamics · Soft biometric · Machine learning
Fuzzy Rough NN (FRNN) · Vaguely Quantified Rough Set (VQRS)
LibSVM · Anomaly detector

© Springer International Publishing AG 2017
S. Battiato et al. (Eds.): ICIAP 2017 International Workshops, LNCS 10590, pp. 320–330, 2017.
https://doi.org/10.1007/978-3-319-70742-6_30

1 Introduction

Cloud computing based technology such as e-mail services, social network services, storage services, application services, web hosting services, TV services and more; we are probably using it in each day.As of now, knowledge-based user authentication/verification methods have been applied in cloud based technology. Building a more secure solution is needed due to the risk associated with this technique such as shoulder surfing attack, dictionary attack, brute-force attack. Keystroke dynamics with the combination of knowledge based authentication as a security solution could be used in practice. Since keystroke dynamics is a method where people can be identified through their way of typing. It has been established that habitual typing pattern is a behavioral biometric trait in biometric science relates the issues in user identification/authentication. Nevertheless, being nonintrusive and cost effective, keystroke dynamics is a strong alternative to other biometric modalities that can be easily integrated into any existing knowledge-based user authentication system with minor alternation. Obtained accuracies in previous studies are impressive but not acceptable in practice due to the high rate of Failure to Enroll Rate (FER) or intra-class variation. The performances of behavioral biometrics are not impressive in accuracy than morphological biometric modalities. It is very hard to achieve the acceptable accuracy. As per European Standards, access control system mandates the False Acceptance Rate is 1% and Miss Rate is 0.001% [1]. In behavioral biometric characteristics, keystroke dynamics is in trouble due to high rate of intra-class variations (problems in aging, mental state while typing, hand injury, tiredness, ...) or data acquisition methods (cross device validation, timing resolution of the system, features selection, keyboard position, hand(s) used, ...) which increase the error rate in keystroke dynamics user authentication technique.

Recent keystroke dynamics studies found that personal traits such as age, gender, dominant hand, hand(s) used, emotional state, and typing skill can be explained through the typing pattern on a computer keyboard [6]. Few studies found only age and gender can be explained through the behavior on the touch screen. The science behind this technique is users' physical structure, hand weight, fingertips size, neurophysiological and neuropsychological factors reflect on the keyboard which discriminates the typing pattern.

These personal traits affect the typing characteristics and consequently affect the classification performance. For instance, touch size area of the child user might less than the touch type of the adult user. Same as the length of the fingers of the female users might higher than fingers of male users. The right-handed user might type digraph consisting keys from the right side of the keyboard more quickly than type digraph consisting keys from the left side. Typing digraph from a key from the left side and another is from the right side of the keyboard then typing pattern might differ among the users used one hand or both hands. If the user is distracted or frustrated by the unnatural behavior of computer then user's typing pattern change massively. These are the soft biometric features affect the typing characteristics consequently with the classification performance. Type of text, length, clock resolution of the system, the number of running software(s) and type, keyboard type and size with different layout also affect the performance. Therefore, the experimental results are impressive in the lab-based environment to be used in web-based applications but the performance of keystroke dynamics is not 100% accurate in practice. To improve the performance, inclusions of personal traits such as age, gender, handedness, hand(s) used and typing skill are the new direction of keystroke dynamics research. Predicting of such traits is the new research direction not only to increase the keystroke dynamics user recognition performance; it has separate advantages in social network sites to E-Business. The performance in identifying the personal traits is more important. Otherwise, classification performance might be decreased instead.

Some study has been conducted to improve the performance of predicting personal traits to be used this technique in real life applications with the web-based environment. Some study went step to identify the traits of the users based on typing pattern on a computer keyboard but not provided sufficient evidence to be used it on a touchscreen smartphone which is the most common and popular electronic gadgets. Social networking is becoming more popular to keep touch with the large and diverse body of people and groups. Nowadays, users of social network under age group below 18 are rapidly increasing. They easily reach out the contents which are not supposed to access or not suited for them. They share their personal information with strangers. Most of them have included a large number of strangers in their friend list. Social networking administrators delete thousands of profiles for people who do not meet the age group requirement and who behave unnaturally on site. But no potential method has been applied to identify the age group and gender automatically based on the user's typing pattern on a computer keyboard and touch screen smartphone instead of taking the age and gender information based on trust. Not only the age, it can be used to detect fraudulent claims of handedness and typing skill.

The journey of keystroke dynamics has been started in 1980. Throughout these three decades more than 500 papers have been published in the form of a journal, conference proceeding, and thesis, still, the accuracy of this technique is not reached its goal. More research work has to be done so this technique can achieve its goal and can be used in practice. Ancillary information can significantly improve the recognition performance of biometric systems.

The studies in theliterature are summarized in Table 1 have been conducted in thelab-based environment. They use AZERTY and/or QWERTY keyboard as asensing device. Text patterns of different studies are varied. Some of the texts are short, where some of thetexts are long. Some of thetexts are simply common words, where some of thetexts are logically complex. Some of the studies used 5 fold cross validation test option, where some of the studies used training-testing ratio test option in performance evaluation. The number of examples used in the previous studies is different, some of them maintained the session in data acquisition. It is clear from Table 1 that studies conducted on different datasets to meet the aim of extracting the personal traits based on typing pattern instead of improving the evaluation performed in identifying traits.

Machine learning technique as a classification method is common in all the listed studies in Table 1. Selection of appropriate method is an important issue in keystroke dynamics domain, where the performance of one method in accuracy jumps from 65% to 90%. In our study, we have applied FRNN with VQRS. The performance of our approach is very impressive, consistent, and significantly better than the previously

Table 1. Success achieved by researchers to recognize the soft biometric traits on keystroke dynamics datasets

Study	Soft biometric traits	Categorization of classes	Obtained results	Instances	Test options	Classifiers	Simulators	Text Patterns	Sensing devices
Epp et al. [3]	Emotional states	Anger and excitation	84% accuracy	1129	10 fold cross validation	C4.5	Weka [4]	Randomly selected piece of text from Alice's Adventures in Wonderland	Standard keyboard
Giot et al. [5]	Gender	Male and female	91% accuracy	7555	5 fold cross validation	SVM (RBF)	Python script	"greyc laboratory"	AZERTY keyboards
Syed-Idrus et al. [6]	Gender	Male and female	65%-90% accuracy	2200	50% training ratio	SVM (RBF)	Python script	"leonardodicaprio", "the rolling stones", "Michael schumacher", "red hot chilli peppers", "united states of america"	AZERTY and QWERTY keyboard
Syed-Idrus et al. [6]	Hand(s) used	One hand and two hands	90% accuracy						
Syed-Idrus et al. [6]	Age group	<30 and ≥ 30 < 32 and ≥ 32	65%-82% accuracy						
Syed-Idrus et al. [6]	Handedness	Left handed and right handed	70%-90% accuracy						
Uzun et al. [7]	Age group	≤ 18 and 18+	<10% EER	500	5 fold cross validation	LDA, SVM (Linear, SVM (RBF) etc.	MATLAB	".tie5Roanl", "MercanOtu", ". tie5RoanlMercan Otu"	QWERTY keyboard

used leading machine learning method SVM. In this study, we compare our approach with SVM with RBF.

The main objective of this study is to develop a model allowing identify the proper gender, age group, handedness, and typing skill of users through the typing pattern on keyboard and touching screen for a predefined text and improve the accuracy by using this soft biometric information as extra features in keystroke dynamics user authentication technique.

Our objective and contribution of this paper are listed below:

- This study provides an efficient approach to recognizing ancillary information through typing pattern. The performance is comparable with other approaches in the literature.
- Evaluate the performance of leading machine learning approaches to determine the soft biometric information.
- Evaluate and compare the performancesof 9 leading anomaly detectors using and without using soft biometric approach.

We have used authentic and shared CMU keystroke dynamics dataset [8] along with dataset collected through anAndroidhandheld device [9]. The details of the datasets are described in Table 1.

2 Static and Shared Keystroke Dynamics Datasets

Many datasets on keystroke dynamics have been created in the last 30 years but some of them are available on the Internet or we can download on request. Details of the publicly available datasets are summarized in Table 2.

Soft biometric information is not included in all the datasets. Datasets created by Killourhy et al. [2], Idrus et al. [7], Yuzun et al. [5] and El-Abed et al. [11] provided soft biometric information with keystroke dynamics datasets which will be the most suitable datasets for our experiment. We have given some names on each dataset

Table 2. Details of static and shared datasets on keystroke dynamics through keyboard

Study	Considered text	Number of subjects	Session	Repetition	Total sample	Feature subsets	Sensing device
Uzun et al. [7]	".tie5Roanl", "MercanOtu", ". tie5RoanlMercan Otu"	100	1	5	500 500 500	KD, DD, UD	QWERTY keyboard
El-Abed et al. [7]	"rhu.university"	51	3	15-20	951	DD, DU, UD, UU	Nokia Lumia 920
Antal et al. [10]	".tie5Roanl", "kicsikutyatarka", "Kktsf2!2014"	54	2	>30	3303 3323 3308	DU, DD, UD, Pressure, Velocity, Total time, Accelerations, Total Distance etc.	Nexus 7 tablet, Mobil LG Optimus L7 II P710
Loy et al. [11]	"try4-mbs"	100	10	1	10000	Latency and Pressure	A special pressure sensitive keyboard
Giot et al. [5]	"greyc laboratory"	100/133	12	4	4800	DD, UU, UD, DU	AZERTY keyboard
Roth et al. [12]	First paragraph of "A Tale of Two Cities" by Charles Dickens, Half page email	45/50	2	4	90 audio files	di-graph time from keystroke Sound	QWERTY keyboard
Killourhy et al. [8]	".tie5Roanl"	51	8	50	20400	KD, DD,UD	QWERTY keyboard
Jugurta et al. [13]	"chocolate", "zebra", "banana", "taxi", "computadorcalcula"	10, 8 , 4, 15	2	5	100, 80, 140, 150	DD	standard 101/102 keys, Brazilian layout - similar to the EUA layout
Bello et al. [14]	15 Spanish sentences and 15 Unix commands	58	1	1	282020 key events	Di-graph	Uncontrolled environment
Syed-Idrus et al. [15]	"leonardodicaprio", "the rolling stones", "Michael schumacher", "red hot chilli peppers" "united states of america"	110	2	10 for each hand (s) used classes	2200, 2200, 2200, 2200, 2200	UU, DU, UD, KD	AZERTY and QWERTY keyboard
Giot et al. [16]	Login information and password	118	3	1	9087 genuine samples, 10043 imposter samples, and 9346 imposed samples	UU, DD, UD, KD, total time	Uncontrolled

Table 3. Details of static and shared datasets used in this study

Dataset name	Study	Considered text	Gender	Age group	Handedness	Skill	Hand(s) used
Dataset A	Killourhy et al. [2]	".tie5Roanl"	M = 38 F = 27	<30 = 38 30 +=27	L = 9 R = 56	T = 37 O = 28	–
Dataset B	Killourhy et al. [2]	"4121937162"	M = 25 F = 13	<30 = 23 30 +=15	L = 4 R = 38	T = 20 O = 18	–
Dataset C	Killourhy et al. [2]	"hester"	M = 21 F = 21	<30 = 24 30 +=18	L = 5 R = 33	T = 23 O = 19	–
Dataset D	Idrus et al. [6]	"leonardodiscaprio"	F = 78 M = 32	<30 = 51 ≥ 30 = 59	L = 12 R = 98	–	One hand = 110 Both hands = 110
Dataset E	Idrus et al. [6]	"the rolling stons"	F = 78 M = 32	<30 = 51 ≥ 30 = 59	L = 12 R = 98	–	One hand = 110 Both hands = 110
Dataset F	Idrus et al. [6]	"Michael schumaclur"	F = 78 M = 32	<30 = 51 ≥ 30 = 59	L = 12 R = 98	–	One hand = 110 Both hands = 110
Dataset G	Idrus et al. [6]	"red hot chilliperpers"	F = 78 M = 32	<30 = 51 ≥ 30 = 59	L = 12 R = 98	–	One hand = 110 Both hands = 110
Dataset H	Idrus et al. [6]	"united states of america"	F = 78 M = 32	<30 = 51 ≥ 30 = 59	L = 12 R = 98	–	One hand = 110 Both hands = 110
Dataset I	El-Abed et al. [9]	"rhu.university"	M = 26 F = 25	<18 = 11 19 +=40	–	–	–
Dataset J	Uzun et al. [7]	".tie5Roanl"	–	≤ 18 = 51 18 +=49	–	–	–
Dataset K	Uzun et al. [7]	"MercanOtu"	–	≤ 18 = 51 18 +=49	–	–	–
Dataset L	Uzun et al. [7]	".tie5RoanlMercan Otu"	–	≤ 18 = 51 18 +=49	–	–	–

depending on considered text type and data acquisition method in this paper so we can easily identify each dataset throughout this paper. Details are in Table 3.

M, F, L, R, T, and O represent Male, Female, Left-hander, Right-hander, Touch and another type respectively.

3   Research Methodology

The proposed methodology is described in the following subsections. The first objective is to identify personal traits based on typing pattern on different datasets collected in adifferent environment and improve the keystroke dynamics recognition performance with theinclusion of these personality traits as additional features. In order to solve this problem, we have followed following steps.

We used the following equations to extract the features from the selected dataset. Where some of the features are not presented in the dataset. We recalculated all the 8 features by the following equations:

The timing features of the keystroke dynamics are as follows:

$$\text{Key\_Duration(KD)} = R_i - P_i \tag{1}$$

$$\text{UpUp Key Latency (UU)} = R_{i+1} - R_i \tag{2}$$

$$\text{DownDown Key Latency (DD)} = P_{i+1} - P_i \tag{3}$$

$$\text{UpDown Key Latency (UD)} = P_{i+1} - R_i \tag{4}$$

$$\text{DownUp Key Latency (DU)} = R_{i+1} - P_i \tag{5}$$

$$\text{TotalTime Key Latency (t)} = R_n - P_1 \tag{6}$$

$$\text{Tri} - \text{graph Latency (T)} = R_{i+2} - P_i \tag{7}$$

$$\text{Four} - \text{graph Latency (F)} = R_{i+3} - P_i \tag{8}$$

Here P and R represent the pressed and released time of each i'th key event. We used a different combination of features to find the best choice of feature subset. Generally speaking, we have not applied any filtered or wrapper approach to select the features. We normalized all the datasets within the range [−1, +1] in order to speed up the process. We have used two leading machine learning approaches: SVM and FRNN. Fuzzy-rough nearest neighbor (FRNN) [17] classification algorithm is an alternative to Sarkar's fuzzy-rough ownership function (FRNN-O) approach [18].

Some anomaly detection algorithms have been applied to keystroke dynamics pattern with the inclusion of personal traits manually. The results show that inclusion of personal traits increases the performance of the keystroke dynamics user recognition system.

4   Experimental Results

Two leading machine learning algorithms have been applied to each dataset and accuracy with 10 fold cross validation has been listed in Tables 4, 5, 6, 7, 8 and 9 to predict the soft biometric information. As per obtained results, FRNN with VQRS is proved to be the suitable learning methods in both desktop and Android environments. Accuracies were recorded by Weka 3.7.4 simulator with default parameter values.

Table 4. Accuracy with standard deviation in identifying gender on different datasets

Classification algorithms	Accuracy (%)								
	Dataset A	Dataset B	Dataset C	Dataset D	Dataset E	Dataset F	Dataset G	Dataset H	Dataset H
LibSVM	82.67(0.21)	76.30(0.69)	86.87(0.46)	72.12(0.79)	74.60(0.43)	71.28(0.46)	76.07(1.25)	76.14(0.66)	75.52(1.10)
FRNN-VQRS	94.97(0.12)	87.29(0.48)	93.97(0.31)	80.92(1.03)	86.54(0.79)	83.29(0.86)	86.44(1.13)	90.17(1.23)	83.87(1.42)

Table 5. Accuracy with standard deviation in identifying age group (< 30/30 +) on different datasets

Classification algorithms	Accuracy (%)							
	Dataset A	Dataset B	Dataset C	Dataset D	Dataset E	Dataset F	Dataset G	Dataset H
LibSVM	81.97(0.32)	73.57(0.42)	83.49(0.46)	62.03(1.43)	63.58(1.45)	60.08(1.74)	65.87(1.19)	64.82(1.12)
FRNN-VQRS	94.93(0.17)	87.23(0.46)	93.90(0.41)	75.97(0.91)	81.95(1.09)	79.05(0.84)	84.90(1.01)	88.61(0.97)

Table 6. Accuracy with standard deviation in identifying age group (< 18/18 +) on different datasets

Classification algorithms	Accuracy (%)			
	Dataset I	Dataset J	Dataset K	Dataset L
LibSVM	82.00(1.56)	88.60(1.77)	88.11(1.97)	90.4(1.98)
FRNN-VQRS	87.99(1.00)	88.32(4.13)	93.22(3.43)	94.68(3.00)

Table 7. Accuracy with standard deviation in identifying handedness on different datasets

Classification algorithms	Accuracy (%)							
	Dataset A	Dataset B	Dataset C	Dataset D	Dataset E	Dataset F	Dataset G	Dataset H
LibSVM	91.61(0.16)	92.46(0.22)	94.85(0.27)	96.93(0.59)	97.05(0.29)	95.97(0.37)	95.65(0.79)	96.55(0.72)
FRNN-VQRS	97.77(0.07)	94.99(0.20)	97.12(0.19)	98.90(0.26)	98.85(0.18)	98.11(0.43)	98.11(0.37)	98.44(0.57)

Table 8. Accuracy with standard deviation in identifying typing skill (touch/others) on different datasets

Classification algorithms	Accuracy (%)		
	Dataset A	Dataset B	Dataset C
LibSVM	83.72(0.30)	76.91(0.54)	87.03(0.30)
FRNN-VQRS	95.19(0.16)	88.63(0.27)	93.94(0.17)

Table 9. Accuracy with standard deviation in identifying hand(s) used on different datasets

Classification algorithms	Accuracy (%)				
	Dataset D	Dataset E	Dataset F	Dataset G	Dataset H
LibSVM	96.93(0.59)	97.05(0.29)	95.97(0.37)	95.65(0.79)	96.55(0.72)
FRNN-VQRS	98.90(0.26)	98.85(0.18)	98.11(0.43)	98.11(0.37)	98.44(0.57)

Tables 10, 11 and 12 represent the performance of 9 anomaly detectors described in [8] after considering soft biometric information. We observed that instead of using the only gender multiple soft biometrics information decreases the EER significantly. Here, we take the median of samples. In keystroke dynamics, domain median proximity is better than mean.

Table 10. Comparative analysis of anomaly detectors with inclusion of personal traits by using performance metric Equal Error Rate (EER) in % on Dataset A

Classifiers	Including all features	Including age, gender, and handedness	Including age and gender	Including age group	Including gender	Including handedness	Including typing skill	Only typing pattern
Canberra	12.28	13.33	13.85	15.19	15.24	16.16	15.18	16.81
Chebyshev	2.8	4.41	5.27	7.94	7.9	9.65	7.9	11.3
Czekanowski	2.8	4.39	5.26	7.87	8.05	9.61	7.99	12.08
Lorentzian	**2.53**	**4.07**	**4.82**	**7.39**	**7.38**	**9.16**	**7.48**	**10.69**
Minkowski	4.44	6.84	8.18	12.02	11.98	14.42	11.74	17.18
Sorensen	2.8	4.39	5.26	7.84	8.01	9.6	7.96	11.92
Euclidean	3.85	6	7.15	10.55	10.39	12.46	10.26	14.71
Manhattan	2.8	4.41	5.27	7.94	7.9	9.65	7.9	11.3
SVM	3.59	5.2	6.24	9.04	9.12	11.1	9.37	10.64

Table 11. Comparative analysis of anomaly detectorswith inclusion of personal traitsby using performance metric Equal Error Rate (EER) in % on Dataset B

Classifiers	Including all features	Including age, gender, and handedness	Including age and gender	Including age group	Including gender	Including handedness	Including typing skill	Only typing pattern
Canberra	4.43	5.74	6.23	7.62	8.13	9.36	7.75	10.03
Chebyshev	2.87	4.32	4.91	7.58	7.82	10.16	7.38	11.56
Czekanowski	2.87	4.34	4.86	7.65	8.05	10.2	7.8	12.48
Lorentzian	**2.73**	**4.1**	**4.6**	**7.33**	**7.47**	**9.87**	**7.06**	**11.2**
Minkowski	3.73	5.69	6.53	9.77	9.65	12.8	9.4	14.36
Sorensen	2.87	4.34	4.86	7.65	8.05	10.2	7.8	12.48
Euclidean	3.31	5.21	5.93	9.01	9.02	11.81	8.59	13.3
Manhattan	2.87	4.32	4.91	7.58	7.82	10.16	7.38	11.56
SVM	3.35	5.07	5.76	8.95	9.22	11.27	8.74	11.88

Table 12. Comparative analysis of anomaly detectorswith inclusion of personal traitsby using performance metric Equal Error Rate (EER) in % on Dataset C

Classifiers	Including all features	Including age, gender, and handedness	Including age and gender	Including age group	Including gender	Including handedness	Including typing skill	Only typing pattern
Canberra	22.08	23.73	24.29	26.27	26.54	27.67	26.19	28.16
Chebyshev	4.59	6.77	7.68	10.06	10.35	11.43	10.15	12.79
Czekanowski	4.56	6.75	7.43	9.81	10.06	11.36	10.05	13.24
Lorentzian	**4.41**	**6.6**	**7.53**	**9.76**	**10.21**	**11.34**	**10**	**12.69**
Minkowski	6.09	9.32	10.51	14.45	13.97	16.33	13.49	17.89
Sorensen	4.54	6.75	7.28	9.58	9.72	11.31	9.95	12.3
Euclidean	5.51	8.21	9.29	12.27	12.14	13.79	11.66	15.16
Manhattan	4.59	6.77	7.68	10.06	10.35	11.43	10.15	12.79
SVM	4.55	6.45	7.12	9.09	9.56	10.44	8.95	11.9

5   Conclusion

It is possible to predict the gender, age group, handedness, hand(s) used, and typing skill of the user through the way of typing as it is evident from our experiment with impressive results. It can be used to recognize the gender and age group prediction since keystroke dynamics is a common measurable activity to be used in web-based applications. The activities on the keyboard and touch screen are behavioral biometric characteristics and it could be used to predict the gender and age group to deal with the problem of fake accounts and would enable to create a more loyal and authentic social networking sites. This may facilitate social network sites a fake free, genuine and more loyal user base. Automatically identifying and the inclusion of such traits also can be used as additional soft biometric information to reduce the error rate in the keystroke dynamics user recognition system. This technique also could help E-Commerce site to reach out to the right client. Similarly, this could avoid adverse products more efficiently based on the gender and age group. This technique also can be very useful in a web-based environment for auto profiling of the users. The results also show that age group below 18 can be identify based on typing pattern which can be used to protect the kids from Internet threats.

We have used two leading machine learning methods to predict personal traits on multiple publicly available authentic datasets. Our proposed approaches FRNN-VQRS, a new approach to FRNN achieved impressive results significantly better than previously used SVM with RBF to determine the personality traits in desktop and Android environments. This is a very positive outcome in keystroke dynamics system for a single predefined text which can be used as soft biometric additional features in user identification/authentication technique which decrease the EER 10.69 to 2.53 on CMU keystroke dynamics dataset. This is the modest as well as an efficient approach towards the keystroke dynamics user authentication system which could be used in cloud computing based techniques.

References

1. CENELEC: Alarm systems - Access control systems for use in security applications – Part 1, in System requirements, EN 50133-1 edition (1996)
2. Killourthy, K.: A Scientific Understanding of Keystroke Dynamics, Doctoral Thesis, School of Computer Science Computer Science Department CarnegieMellon University Pittsburgh, PA 15213 (2012)
3. Epp, C., Lippold, M., Mandryk, R.L.: Identifying emotional states using keystroke dynamics. In: Proceedings of SIGCHI Conference on Human Factors Computer System, pp. 715–724 (2011)
4. Frank, E., Hall, M.A., Witten, I.H.: The Weka Workbench Data Mining Practical Machine Learning Tools and Techniques, 4th ed. (1999)
5. Giot, R., Rosenberger, C.: A new soft biometric approach for keystroke dynamics based on gender recognition. Int. J. Inf. Technol. Manag. Spec. Issue Adv. Trends Biometrics **11**, 1–16 (2012)
6. Idrus, S.Z.S., Cherrier, E., Rosenberger, C., Bours, P.: Soft biometrics for keystroke dynamics. In: Kamel, M., Campilho, A. (eds.) ICIAR 2013. LNCS, vol. 7950, pp. 11–18. Springer, Heidelberg (2013). https://doi.org/10.1007/978-3-642-39094-4_2
7. Uzun, Y., Bicakci, K., Uzunay, Y.: Could we distinguish child users from adults using keystroke dynamics? (2014)

8. Killourhy, K.S., Maxion, R.A.: Comparing anomaly-detection algorithms for keystroke dynamics. In: Proceedings of the International Conference on Dependable Systems and Networks, pp. 125–134 (2009)
9. El-Abed, M., Dafer, M., El Khayat, R.: RHU keystroke: a mobile-based benchmark for keystroke dynamics systems. In: 2014 International Carnahan Conference on Security Technology, pp. 1–4 (2014)
10. Antal, M., Szabo, L.Z.: An evaluation of one-class and two-class classification algorithms for keystroke dynamics authentication on mobile devices. In: Proceedings - 2015 20th International Conference Control System Comput. Science CSCS 2015, pp. 343–350 (2015)
11. Loy, C.C., Lim, C.P., Lai, W.K.: Pressure-based typing biometrics user authentication using the fuzzy ARTMAP neural network. In: International Conference on Neural Information Processing (ICONIP) (2005)
12. Roth, J., Liu, X., Ross, A., Metaxas, D.: Biometric authentication via keystroke sound. In: 2013 International Conference biometrics, pp. 1–8 (2013)
13. Montalvão, J., Freire, E.O., Bezerra, M.A., Garcia, R.: Contributions to empirical analysis of keystroke dynamics in passwords. Pattern Recogn. Lett. 52, 80–86 (2015)
14. Bello, L., Bertacchini, M.: Collection and publication of a fixed text keystroke dynamics dataset. In: CACIC 2010 - XVI Congreso ARGENTINO CIENCIAS LA Computer, pp. 822–831 (2010)
15. Idrus, S.Z.S., Cherrier, E., Rosenberger, C., Bours, P.: Soft biometrics database: a benchmark for keystroke dynamics biometric systems. In: 2013 International Conference of the Biometrics Special Interest Group (BIOSIG), pp. 1–8, September 2013
16. Giot, R., El-Abed, M., Rosenberger, C.: Web-based benchmark for keystroke dynamics biometric systems: a statistical analysis. In: Intelligent Information hiding and multimedia signal Processing, pp. 11–15 (2012)
17. Jensen, R., Cornelis, C.: Fuzzy rough nearest neighbour classification and prediction. Theor. Comput. Sci. 412(42), 5871–5884 (2011)
18. Sarkar, M.: Fuzzy-rough nearest neighbor algorithms in classification. Fuzzy Sets Syst. 158 (19), 2134–2152 (2007)

Leveraging Continuous Multi-modal Authentication for Access Control in Mobile Cloud Environments

Gianni Fenu$^{(\boxtimes)}$ and Mirko Marras

Department of Mathematics and Computer Science, University of Cagliari,
V. Ospedale 72, 09124 Cagliari, Italy
{fenu,mirko.marras}@unica.it

Abstract. Mobile cloud computing integrates cloud computing into mobile environments, allowing users to use data, infrastructure, platforms, and applications on the cloud from their mobile devices. However, accessing and exploiting cloud-based resources and services is associated with numerous security implications (e.g. authentication and authorization) which represent the major barriers making individuals and organizations hesitant to migrate data or processing to the cloud. Using biometric techniques is increasingly emerging to secure such users' assets. In this paper, we propose a bi-modal continuous authentication approach integrating face and touch biometrics into mobile cloud environments, going beyond traditional one-off authentication. The system reacts to sliding windows of recent user's actions to dynamically update the trust in genuineness for the current user. For each biometric trait, it calculates the similarity scores resulting from the comparison between probes and templates, then they are fused together. If the fusion score is above a given threshold, the system rewards the current user; otherwise, they are penalized. In case the trust in the current user drops below a predefined threshold, the system raises an alarm. Experimental results indicate the advantage offered by our approach on performance of continuous authentication systems, providing a good security-usability tradeoff to mobile cloud environments.

Keywords: Mobile cloud computing · Mobile biometrics
Biometric access control · Multi-Modal authentication
Continuous authentication

1 Introduction

Mobile devices (e.g. smartphone and tablet) are increasingly becoming an essential part of everyday life, playing the role of the most convenient communication tool with no constraints in time and place. In parallel, various challenges in terms of the resource use and the communication workload are preventing the improvement of the service quality they can offer. Mobile Cloud Computing (MCC) integrates cloud computing into mobile environments in order to provide high-quality services to mobile users and overcome such emerging issues [1]. MCC is widely recognized as the next generation computing disruption, enabling mobile users to exploit infrastructure (e.g. servers and

© Springer International Publishing AG 2017
S. Battiato et al. (Eds.): ICIAP 2017 International Workshops, LNCS 10590, pp. 331–342, 2017.
https://doi.org/10.1007/978-3-319-70742-6_31

networks), platforms (e.g. services and operating systems), and software (e.g. applications) made available on-demand by cloud providers (e.g. Google and Microsoft).

However, accessing and exploiting cloud-based resources and applications is associated with numerous security and privacy implications (e.g. user authentication and authorization) which represent the major barriers making individuals and organizations hesitant to migrate data or processing to the cloud [2]. For instance, a stolen mobile device could be abused to download sensitive data from the cloud, if a mobile user is registered with a cloud service provider. Using techniques to control the access to data and applications becomes essential to secure users' assets hosted by cloud providers [3].

Existing access control methods based on passwords and smartcards tend to suffer from the lack of authenticity and non-repudiation. By contrast, biometrics are becoming an attractive feature for cloud providers in order to provide novel security features and service models to their clients [4]. In user authentication, both physical and behavioral characteristics promise to be stronger than passwords. Human peculiarities cannot be easily stolen, forgotten, nor guessed. Emerging biometric systems are mainly required to (i) have a high level of accuracy to be secure and practical for widespread adoption in the cloud, (ii) operate continuously to avoid impostor users using the system after the genuine user logs in, and (iii) protect biometric samples to preserve users' privacy. Meeting the requirements is essential for the successful adoption of biometric systems.

In this paper, we specifically focus on the first two requirements and propose a multi-modal biometric approach in order to authenticate users continuously and transparently in mobile cloud environments. In our investigated scenario, the fusion system uses two standalone biometrics (i.e. face and touch) and calculates the score-level fusion of the corresponding matching scores. However, due to the natural variation in behavior and the heterogeneous conditions in operation, a user can deviate from the normal condition on a minority of situations as well as impostor users can appear as genuine for certain periods. The concept of trust in genuiness of the user models this variation. The system computes the similarity scores resulting from the comparison between probes and templates, then they are fused together. If the fusion score is above a given threshold, the system rewards the current user; otherwise, they are penalized. The global system trust in the user is updated accordingly. If it is above a given threshold, then the user continues the normal activities; otherwise, the user is locked out. Experiments on a publicly-available dataset were carried out to validate the methodology. The results show the potential of our approach to strength the security provided for MCC environments.

The rest of this paper is organized as follows. Section 2 introduces a brief overview of the related work, Sect. 3 describe the proposed approach, Sect. 4 presents experiments and results, and Sect. 5 provides conclusions and insights for future work.

2 Related Work

2.1 Access Control in Cloud Environments

Cloud services relies heavily on authentication methods based on passwords and/or personal identification numbers. Biometrics are an attractive feature to overcome various problems and emerge as a practical alternative to password authentication [5].

In biometric systems running on the cloud, one of the most challenging problems is preserving user's privacy and maintaining the confidentiality of users' biometric data during transfer or storing. Unlike passwords and tokens, biometric traits cannot be canceled and reissued (i.e. if a user's fingerprint is compromised it cannot be changed and the user cannot use it in the future). Moreover, unsecured biometric templates are vulnerable to biometric dilemma threat [6], where an impostor accesses a biometric template in a less secure biometric system and uses it to gain access to a high secure system. Hence, biometric authentication systems must consider the security of users' biometric data. Some schemes apply biometric authentication in the cloud without taking user's template protection into account. For instance, Cloud Iris Verification System (CIVS) [7] applies iris authentication for authenticating users of the cloud software as a service. CIVS stores iris patterns on the cloud without protection. Other approaches apply biometric authentication in the cloud with template protection mechanisms (e.g. Revocable Bio-tokens [8]). Biometric template protection mechanisms are surveyed by [9].

In general, biometric systems in cloud environments tend also to suffer from low matching accuracy and tradeoffs between FAR (False Acceptance Rate) and TAR (True Acceptance Rate). In general, whenever the FAR is set to a low level, the TAR falls down too. Moreover, the low FAR can be vulnerable to doppelganger threat [6], where a set of biometric data (i.e. stolen biometric database) can be applied to get access to a system by leveraging the FAR. It follows that biometric authentication should have a high TAR and very low FAR to be a secure and practical. For instance, the authors in [10] used keystroke authentication scheme for the cloud environment. Nevertheless it enhances the matching computation time, the authentication accuracy does not ensure high security (FAR = 1.65%, FRR = 2.75%). In fact, even though this FAR can be seen as practical rate, it can be exploited due to the biometric doppelganger attack [6].

In general, impostors can take advantage of the mentioned drawbacks to access data and applications improperly since existing biometric systems in cloud environments appear to authenticate users only at login time. By contrast, continuous authentication promises to verify users' identity throughout the session, strengthening the ability of the system of locking out impostors even when the recognition ability on an individual sample is not high. Moreover, they leverage behavioral biometrics which are not easily to be stolen and replicated since they depend on users' action in the context of the given session and application. This makes harder improper access even when impostors have a copy of the biometric trait. Furthermore, the fusion of behavioral biometrics and physical biometrics (e.g. face) can be exploited to improve overall recognition capabilities.

2.2 Continuous Biometric Authentication on Mobile Device

In recent years, biometrics and security research communities have developed techniques and methodologies for continuous implicit user authentication by mobile devices [11]. We show a set of academic and commercial examples, both uni and multi-modal.

Continuous biometric systems usually require real-time processing capabilities and optimization methods already explored in various domains such as finance [12] and computer networks [13]. First, biometric modalities such as gait, face, typing, or voice are continuously measured by the built-in sensors integrated into a mobile device (e.g. camera, touch screen, accelerometer, orientation sensor). Then, the system determines whether these biometric traits correspond to a genuine user. If the features correspond to a genuine user, the biometric system continues to process new incoming data [14].

Touch dynamics is one of the most commonly used continuous authentication methods for mobile devices using touchscreen input as a data source. The way users swipe their fingers on touchscreen of mobile devices is used to continuously authenticate users while they perform basic operations [15]. For instance, [16, 17] studied whether a classifier can continuously authenticate users based on the way they interact with the touchscreen of a smartphone. They proposed a set of behavioral touch features that can be extracted from raw touchscreen logs. Other continuous authentication systems monitor user's identity based on face recognition. In [18], it was designed a method for detecting partially cropped and occluded faces captured using a smartphone's front-facing camera for continuous authentication. The key idea is to detect facial segments in frames and cluster the results to obtain the region which is most likely to contain a face. Then, it was used for verification. In [19], a face-based continuous authentication system operates in an unobtrusive manner, fusing mobile device face capture with gyroscope, accelerometer, and magnetometer to correct face image orientation. Several studies have used contextual information to enhance the performance of continuous authentication such as investigating how the position in which the smartphone is held affects user authentication. For instance, the authors in [20] proposed a set of behavioral features useful to capture micro-movement and orientation dynamics resulting from how a user grasps, holds, and taps on smartphones. Behavior modelling as developed in [21] enabled cross-device authentication based on how users perform actions.

It has been observed that some of the limitations of unimodal continuous authentication systems can be addressed by deploying multi-modal systems that essentially integrate the evidence presented by multiple sources of information. For instance, [22] introduced a transparent authentication framework utilizing a combination of behavioural biometrics: keystroke dynamics and voice recognition. Similarly, [23] examined the combination of keystroke dynamics, behavioural profiling and linguistic profiling. In [24], the authors proposed a multi-biometric system based on the observation that the instinctive gesture of responding to a phone call can be used to capture two different biometrics, namely ear and arm gesture, which are complementary due to their physical and behavioral nature. Literature in this field demonstrates that human authentication based on multi-modal biometrics is becoming an emerging trend, and one of the most important reasons to combine different modalities is to improve recognition accuracy.

3 The Proposed System

The proposed approach is built on top of a modular architecture. Each component performs a task in the typical operational cascade of a biometric system. The implementation of single modules has been properly analyzed to ensure both the effectiveness and the efficiency of the overall system. It follows that this increases the number of functionalities provided with no degradation in the tradeoff between security and usability. Such feature is essential for biometric systems, especially when they operate continuously to authenticate users based on what they do.

The underlying architecture depicted in Fig. 1 includes two independent biometric authentication modules: face authentication module and touch authentication module. The input of each module is the data captured by the corresponding sensor on the mobile device, while the output is a matching score for each one of them. Each module performs score normalization separately on the obtained scores from each of these two biometric modules. Matching scores lie in the range [0,1], where 0 means totally different, while 1 means the same. Then, these scores are fused together by the Trust Manager to obtain the final matching score used to decide whether the test subject is genuine and update the trust level accordingly.

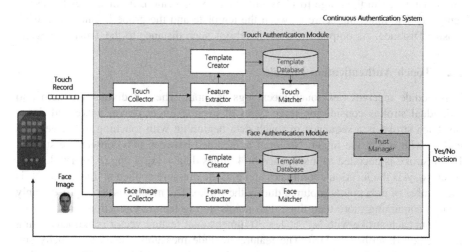

Fig. 1. Overall architecture of the proposed multi-modal system.

3.1 Face Authentication Module

Nowadays, mobile devices provide routines and drivers to access on-board cameras. Using them, it is easy to acquire users' face images coming from a continuous clip.

The module receives an image as input. It implements the FaceNet algorithm [25] for the localization of the relevant subregion of the image containing the face. FaceNet has been proven to work well when face samples are collected in the wild, including partial visibility, illumination changes, occlusion and wide variation in poses and facial expressions. To accomplish this task, a FaceNet-based model is pre-trained on

CASIA-Webface dataset[1]. The face region is cropped and aligned. Then, the module detects the key points of interest on the face. More precisely, it tries to localize and label the left eyebrow, the right eyebrow, the left eye, the right eye, the nose and the mouth. The implemented landmark detector is based on the ensemble of regression trees trained to estimate the facial landmark positions directly from the pixel intensities as proposed in [26]. Each landmark is cropped and stored separately. An image correction routine is used to normalize illumination on both the face image and the landmark images.

Five different types of features are extracted as follows: (i) the pre-processed face is converted to grayscale, rescaled and vectorized as uni-dimensional vector; (ii) from the 64×64 rescaled grayscale image, Local Binary Pattern (LBP) features as uni-dimensional vector are extracted for a cell size of 8×8 pixels; (iii) bounding boxes of the landmarks are computed for each face part from the pre-processed grayscale image. The eye-based, nose and mouth bounding boxes are resized to 16×20, 28×17 and 22×46 pixels respectively, then vectorized to a uni-dimensional vector; (iv) LBP features are obtained from the resized bounding boxes with a size of 12×12 pixels; (v) FaceNet embeddings resulting from the whole face and individual landmarks are extracted.

The above features are concatenated to form a unique feature vector whose values are transformed in the range [0,1] by min-max normalization. It constitutes the user's template. The matching score between the template and the probe is calculated using Cosine Distance. As output, the module returns such distance to the Trust Manager.

3.2 Touch Authentication Module

The module receives raw touchscreen logs as input. Then, it divides up them into individual strokes considering three types of events: finger down, move and finger up. Each stroke is a sequence of touch data beginning with touching the screen and ending with lifting the finger. No input is recorded between two consecutive strokes. Every stroke is encoded as a sequence of 4-tuples data = (x_i, y_i, p_i, t_i) for $i \in 1,...,N_c$ where x_i, y_i is the location coordinates and p_i is the pressure applied at time t_i, and N_c is the number of data points captured during the stroke. The module is set to process only strokes containing more than three data points during feature extraction.

From each stroke with $N_c \geq 4$, a 30-dimensional feature vector is extracted using the method described in [16]. The features include measures related to velocity and acceleration both between internal-stroke points and first and last stroke points. Past research has proven that these stroke features exhibit a larger variance across different users than for a single user. The template is represented by an ensemble of three classifiers properly trained with genuine data and impostor data coming from the dataset in [16], following the one-vs-all protocol. More precisely, the three classifiers are the AdaBoost classifier, RandomForest classifier and Stochastic Gradient Descent classifier with a log loss function and L2 penalty. During verification, the ensemble classifier predicts the overall matching score based on the maximum argument of the

---

[1] http://www.cbsr.ia.ac.cn/english/CASIA-WebFace-Database.html.

sums of the predicted probabilities from each classifier, which is recommended for an ensemble of well-calibrated classifiers. The matching score is normalized in the range [0,1] by min-max normalization. As output, the module return such value to the Trust Manager.

3.3 Trust Manager Module

The module receives two distances as matching scores coming from the Touch Authentication module and the Face Authentication module, as input. It can operate in two different modalities: *standard continuous mode* and *trusted continuous mode*. The first one includes the fusion of the matching scores using a weighted sum. If the fusion score is above a given threshold the user continues the activities, otherwise an alarm is raised.

However, due to the natural variation in behavior and the heterogeneous conditions in operation, a user can deviate from the normal condition on a minority of situations as well as impostor users can appear as genuine for certain periods. Hence, the second mode of operation includes the concept of trust in genuiness of the user. If a specific action is performed in accordance with the normal behavior of a genuine user, then the system's trust in the genuineness of this user will increase. If there is a large deviation between the behaviour of the genuine user and the current user, the trust of the system will decrease. A small deviation from the behavior of the current user, when compared to the template, leads to a small decrease in trust, while a large deviation to a larger decrease. The fusion score is computed by merging the scores from the independent biometric systems as performed in standard continuous mode. But, if the score is high enough, the system will reward the current user, otherwise the user is penalized. If the system trust drops below a pre-defined threshold T, the system locks itself. The penalty/reward and the current system trust are calculated dynamically using the formulas provided in [27]. As parameters for those formulas, the module sets $A = 0.54$, $B = 0.005$, $C = D=2$, $T = 50$. The upper limit of the system trust is 100 to ensure an imposter cannot benefit from the high trust obtained by the genuine user, before they access the system.

4 Experimental Evaluation

4.1 Dataset

To evaluate the applicability of our proposed approach, we used the highly-challenging UMDAA-02 [28] multi-modal database. It consists of data recorded by built-in cameras and touchscreen sensors during activities performed on smartphones.

It includes a set of over 33,000 images captured by smartphone cameras and recorded during all the sessions of 43 users at 7-s intervals for the first 60 s of interaction during each session. The number of images varies between 300 to 2,700 per user, while the number of sessions varies between 25 and 750, providing a wide range of images for each user and session. They include faces with partial visibility, illumination changes, occlusion and variation in poses and facial expressions.

From the same set of users during the same tasks, raw touch events were also recorded. The number of strokes varies around 3,500 per user, while the number of strokes per user for each session is around 196. The maximum number of data points in a stroke ranges between 4 and 3,000. These features demonstrate this database meets our goal.

4.2   Evaluation Protocol

We carried out extensive experiments in two different settings based on the mode of operation of the Trust Manager (i.e. standard continuous mode and trusted continuous mode) in order to evaluate the effectiveness of the proposed continuous biometric approach. For each setting, we firstly consider the biometric modules separately. During face verification, the combination of N consecutive face images is computed by averaging the matching scores to reinforce the recognition during each iteration. In the same way, M consecutive strokes are used to calculate the matching score for touch authentication. Then, we combined the biometrics by averaging the scores obtained by matching N face images and M touch strokes. M and N varies during the experiments.

In standard continuous mode, we calculated the False Recognition Rate (FRR) by matching the user's template against the remaining samples of the same user. If the matching h against g is performed, the symmetric one (i.e. g against h) is not executed to avoid correlation. Then, we computed the False Acceptance Rate (FAR) by matching the template of each user against all the samples of the other subjects. Finally, the Equal Error Rate (EER) is calculated starting from FAR and FRR values.

In trusted continuous mode, we replicated the evaluation protocol in [27] based on the computation of the Average Number of Imposter Actions (ANIA) and the Average Number of Genuine Actions (ANGA) as evaluation metrics. These indicators reveal how much imposters can do before they are locked out and how much genuine users can do before they are locked out of the system. Each user can be classified into one of the following categories: the genuine user is never locked out and all impostors are detected (+/+); the genuine user is not locked out, but some impostors are not detected ($\pm$); the genuine user is locked out, but all the impostors are detected ($\mp$); the genuine user is locked out, while some of the impostors are not detected (–/–).

4.3   Experimental Results

Standard Continuous Mode. The EERs obtained using different values of M and N for touch and face respectively are reported in Fig. 2. The values of M range from 2 to 14. N is set to M/2 to achieve a good tradeoff between security and usability.

From these results, we see for single-trait biometric verification, face matcher achieved the lowest performance comparing to touch and fusion matchers. This is reasonable, since the face images collected into the database contain a vast variety of challenging conditions regarding illumination, head pose, facial expression, and age difference. All these factors contribute negatively to the verification process. Meanwhile, the multi-modal fusion always obtained higher performance than single-trait

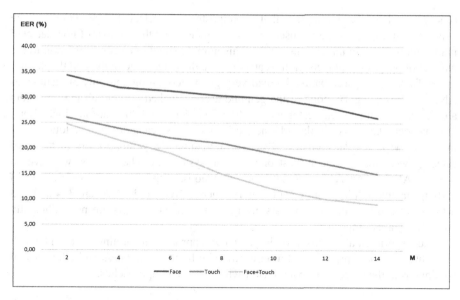

Fig. 2. The performance of the proposed bi-modal approach in standard continuous mode.

approaches. As proposed in this work, integrating these two modalities into the fusion system and averaging their contribution results in a performance improvement. In addition to it, we observed that the lowest EER values achieved in the benchmark results carried out on the UMDAA database for uni-modal traits are EER = 18.44% and EER = 22.10%, using N = 30 face images and M = 16 touchscreen strokes respectively. With our approach, we achieved EER = 9.61% combining only M = 14 touch strokes and N = 14 face images. This demonstrated that the bi-modal fusion can improve both effectiveness and efficiency.

Trusted Continuous Mode. Table 1 shows the results achieved by our approach fusing face and touch biometrics. We report results for M = 2 and N = 1 to hold a good trade-off between usability and security while maintaining efficiency. The guidelines followed to report the performance are provided by [27]. The column "# Users" defines the number of users for each category. The ANGA indicates the average number of genuine actions before genuine users are locked out. If the genuine users are not locked out, no ANGA is reported. The column ANIA displays the average number of impostor

Table 1. The performance of our bi-modal approach in trusted continuous mode (M = 2, N = 1).

Category	#Users	ANGA	ANIA	#NDI
+/+	16	–	30	–
+/–	7	–	42	27 (9%)
–/+	18	680	26	–
–/–	3	344	113	3 (2%)

actions based on the assumption that all impostors are detected. The actions of the non-detected impostors are not used in this calculation, but the number of non-detected impostors is given in the column #NDI. This number should be seen in relation to the number of biometric subjects in that category (see the percentage in the #NDI column).

In Table 1, 16 participants obtained very good recognition and only 30 actions as ANIA. In this category, none of the genuine users is locked out and all the impostors are detected. In the second category, we find 7 participants which are not locked out. The average ANIA is similar (42 actions) to the first category and a total of 27 imposters were not detected (i.e. 9%). The remaining 18 genuine users in the third category were locked out at least once by the system. For these users, we have an average ANGA and ANIA of 680 and 26 actions, respectively. There are only 3 participants that fall into the worst category where ANGA and ANIA are 344 and 113 actions respectively and 3 imposters are not detected. Such users are not sufficiently protected against impostors.

The experimental results promise that our approach integrating face and touch biometrics can be a practical solution to improve both effectiveness and efficiency of continuous authentication in comparison with uni-modal approaches.

5   Conclusions

In this paper, we presented an approach for integrating face recognition together with touch behavior recognition to increase the overall performance of a continuous multi-modal authentication system in mobile cloud environments, going beyond traditional one-off authentication. The system reacts to users' actions and dynamically update the trust in genuiness for the user. Experimental results show promising performance which indicates the advantage offered by our system and makes it suitable for mobile cloud applications requiring a good security-usability tradeoff.

In next steps, we will investigate approaches to improve recognition scores returned by individual biometric systems, adding novel types of feature as an example. Larger datasets where to test our approach will be considered. Furthermore, we will study other penalty-reward equations in order to dynamically update the trust level. We also plan to employ Big Data architectures to support large-scale fast computations and leverage the cloud's unbounded computational resources and attractive properties of flexibility, scalability, and cost reduction to enhance the overall performance of our approach.

Acknowledgements. Mirko Marras acknowledge Sardinia Regional Government for the financial support of his PhD scholarship (P.O.R. Sardegna F.S.E. Operational Programme of the Autonomous Region of Sardinia, European Social Fund 2014-2020 - Axis III Education and Training, Thematic Goal 10, Priority of Investment 10ii, Specific Goal 10.5).

References

1. Dinh, H.T., Lee, C., Niyato, D., Wang, P.: A survey of mobile cloud computing: architecture, applications, and approaches. Wirel. Commun. Mobile Comput. **13**(18), 1587–1611 (2013). Wiley
2. Coppolino, L., D'Antonio, S., Mazzeo, G., Romano, L.: Cloud security: Emerging threats and current solutions. Comput. Electr. Eng. **59**, 126–140 (2017). Elsevier
3. Onankunju, B.K.: Access control in cloud computing. Int. J. Sci. Res. Publ. **3**(9), 1 (2013). IGI Global
4. Alizadeh, M., Abolfazli, S., Zamani, M., Baharun, S., Sakurai, K.: Authentication in mobile cloud computing. J. Netw. Comput. Appl. **61**, 59–80 (2016)
5. Ali, M., Khan, S.U., Vasilakos, A.V.: Security in cloud computing: opportunities and challenges. Inf. Sci. **305**, 357–383 (2015). Elsevier
6. Scheirer, W., Bishop, B., Boult, T.: Beyond PKI: the biocryptographic key infrastructure. In: Workshop on Information Forensics and Security (WIFS), pp. 1–6. IEEE (2010)
7. Ruiu, P., Caragnano, G., Masala, G.L., Grosso, E.: Accessing cloud services through biometrics authentication. In: 10th International Conference on Complex, Intelligent, and Software Intensive Systems (CISIS), pp. 38–43. IEEE (2016)
8. Scheirer, W.J., Boult, T.E.: Bipartite biotokens: definition, implementation, and analysis. In: Tistarelli, M., Nixon, Mark S. (eds.) ICB 2009. LNCS, vol. 5558, pp. 775–785. Springer, Heidelberg (2009). https://doi.org/10.1007/978-3-642-01793-3_79
9. Jain, A.K., Nandakumar, K., Nagar, A.: Biometric template security. EURASIP J. Adv. Signal Process. **113** (2008). ACM
10. Zhu, H.H., He, Q.H., Tang, H., Cao, W.H.: Voiceprint-biometric template design and authentication based on cloud computing security. In: International Conference on Cloud and Service Computing (CSC), pp. 302–308. IEEE (2011)
11. Alotaibi, S., Furnell, S., & Clarke, N.: Transparent authentication systems for mobile device security: A review. In: 2015 10th International Conference for Internet Technology and Secured Transactions (ICITST), pp. 406–413. IEEE (2015)
12. Aymerich, F.M., Fenu, G., Surcis, S.: A real time financial system based on grid and cloud computing. In: Proceedings of ACM Symposium on Applied Computing, pp. 1219–1220 (2009)
13. Fenu, G., Nitti, M.: Strategies to carry and forward packets in VANET. In: Cherifi, H., Zain, J.M., El-Qawasmeh, E. (eds.) DICTAP 2011. CCIS, vol. 166, pp. 662–674. Springer, Heidelberg (2011). https://doi.org/10.1007/978-3-642-21984-9_54
14. Patel, V.M., Chellappa, R., Chandra, D., Barbello, B.: Continuous user authentication on mobile devices: recent progress and remaining challenges. IEEE Signal Process. Mag. **33**(4), 49–61 (2016)
15. Jiang, L., Meng, W.: Smartphone user authentication using touch dynamics in the big data era: challenges and opportunities. In: Jiang, R., Al-maadeed, S., Bouridane, A., Crookes, P., Beghdadi, A. (eds.) Biometric Security and Privacy. Signal Processing for Security Technologies, pp. 163–178, Springer, Cham (2017)
16. Frank, M., Biedert, R., Ma, E., Martinovic, I., Song, D.: Touchalytics: On the applicability of touchscreen input as a behavioral biometric for continuous authentication. IEEE Trans. Inf. Forensics Secur. **8**(1), 136–148 (2013)
17. Van Nguyen, T., Sae-Bae, N., Memon, N.: DRAW-A-PIN: authentication using finger-drawn PIN on touch devices. Comput. Secur. **66**, 115–128 (2017). Elsevier

18. Mahbub, U., Patel, V.M., Chandra, D., Barbello, B., Chellappa, R.: Partial face detection for continuous authentication. In: IEEE International Conference on Image Processing (ICIP), pp. 2991–2995. IEEE (2016)
19. Crouse, D., Han, H., Chandra, D., Barbello, B., Jain, A.K.: Continuous authentication of mobile user: fusion of face image and inertial measurement unit data. In: International Conference on Biometrics (ICB), pp. 135–142. IEEE (2015)
20. Buriro, A., Crispo, B., Zhauniarovich, Y.: Please hold on: unobtrusive user authentication using smartphone's built-in sensors. In: International Conference on Identity, Security and Behavior Analysis (ISBA), pp. 1–8. IEEE (2017)
21. Wang, X., Yu, T., Mengshoel, O., Tague, P.: Towards continuous and passive authentication across mobile devices: an empirical study. In: Proceedings of the 10th ACM Conference on Security and Privacy in Wireless and Mobile Networks, pp. 35–45. ACM (2017)
22. Crawford, H., Renaud, K., Storer, T.: A framework for continuous, transparent mobile device authentication. Comput. Secur. **39**, 127–136 (2013). Elsevier
23. Fridman, L., Weber, S., Greenstadt, R., Kam, M.: Active authentication on mobile devices via stylometry, application usage, web browsing, and GPS. IEEE Syst. J. (2016)
24. Abate, A.F., Nappi, M., Ricciardi, S.: I-Am: implicitly authenticate me person authentication on mobile devices through ear shape and arm gesture. IEEE Trans. Syst. Man Cybern. Syst. **74** (2017). IEEE
25. Schroff, F., Kalenichenko, D., Philbin, J.: Facenet: a unified embedding for face recognition and clustering. In: Proceedings of the IEEE Conference on Computer Vision and Pattern Recognition, pp. 815–823. IEEE (2015)
26. Kazemi, V., Sullivan, J.: One millisecond face alignment with an ensemble of regression trees. In: IEEE Conference on Computer Vision and Pattern Recognition. IEEE (2014)
27. Bours, P., Mondal, S.: Performance evaluation of continuous authentication systems. IET Biometrics **4**(4), 220–226 (2015). IEEE
28. Mahbub, U., Sarkar, S., Patel, V.M., Chellappa, R.: Active user authentication for smartphones: a challenge data set and benchmark results. In: International Conference on Biometrics Theory, Applications and Systems, pp. 1–8. IEEE (2016)

Distributed Anti-Plagiarism Checker for Biomedical Images Based on Sensor Noise

Andrea Bruno[1]([✉]), Giuseppe Cattaneo[1], Umberto Ferraro Petrillo[2],
Fabio Narducci[3], and Gianluca Roscigno[1]

[1] Dipartimento di Informatica, Università degli Studi di Salerno,
84084 Fisciano, SA, Italy
{andbruno,cattaneo,giroscigno}@unisa.it
[2] Dipartimento di Scienze Statistiche,
Università degli Studi di Roma "Sapienza", Roma, Italy
umberto.ferraro@uniroma1.it
[3] Università degli Studi del Molise, Isernia, Italy
fabio.narducci@unimol.it

Abstract. The increasing number of scientific papers reporting false or stolen data calls for the needs of new tools able to automatically detect plagiarism or unfaithful ownerships. This problem is particularly actual for the health sciences, as the number of biomedical images that are stolen or manipulated and, then, published in scientific papers is becoming higher and higher [1].

In this paper we present an automatic anti-plagiarism checker that relies on the concept of *Pixel Non-Uniformity* (PNU) noise. This is the characteristic noise left by source sensors of devices like digital cameras, electron microscopes or *Magnetic Resonance Imaging* (MRI) to define a sort of fingerprint for these devices. The intended use of our system requires two steps. In a first step and on a voluntary base, the researchers register to the system their imaging devices by providing a training set of images. These will be used to extract the device fingerprint called *Reference Pattern* (RP).

In a second step, the system will periodically scan a set of known scientific digital libraries (most publishers offer on-line access to their papers) downloading the new papers and extracting all the images herein contained. The output produced by a specialized filter on such images will enable the system to compare the *Residual Noise* (RN) with all the enrolled device patterns, allowing the identification of the device that captured the image.

Given the huge amount of papers and images to process, our system has been implemented as a distributed application running on top of the Spark cluster engine.

Keywords: Biomedical images · Plagiarism · PNU noise · Sensor noise

1 Introduction

The problem of image plagiarisms in biomedical scientific paper has been steadily increasing in the last years. A recent study [1] estimated that approximately 1

© Springer International Publishing AG 2017
S. Battiato et al. (Eds.): ICIAP 2017 International Workshops, LNCS 10590, pp. 343–352, 2017.
https://doi.org/10.1007/978-3-319-70742-6_32

published article over 25 contains *problematic images*. The same studies has shown that on a total of 20,621 research papers from 40 different journals, 782 (∼3.8%) were found to include inappropriate image duplications. Indeed, in the biomedical scientific field the falsification of the results can lead to societal injuries, like in the case of the now-retracted study on the relation between vaccines and autism, that is still contributing to lower the vaccination rates.

The availability of an automated system that is able to check if the image in a paper that is presumed to come from a *Scanning Electron Microscope* (SEM) but has been stolen from somewhere else or manipulated to alter it, can discourage an author from carrying on this kind of fraud and for the publisher to detect them before the article is published.

We notice that there are currently several anti-plagiarism systems for checking the textual of a scientific paper, i.e. iThenticate [8]. Instead, no system is currently available for detecting SEM images plagiarisms.

In this article, we show the feasibility of an automated system that allows the owner of a biomedical imaging device to identify all the images that have been taken with that device and fraudulently published in some other papers. For this purpose we use the well-known and strongly-tested technique by *Fridrich et al.* [7]. In that paper, the authors showed that every *Charge-Coupled Device* (CCD) camera sensor has his unique sensor noise generated by the imperfection in the production of the sensor itself.

With the same system is also possible to identify forgery in images that are performed on images taken from a known source [2].

Organization of the paper: In Sect. 2 we will analyze the state of the art about currently available fraud-detection systems for scientific papers. In particular in Sect. 2.1 we will give a brief introduction about *Source Camera Identification* (SCI) problem and its more popular solution, i.e., *Fridrich et al.* algorithm [7]. In Sect. 3 we will extensively discuss about the particular problem of SCI for electron microscopy. In Sects. 4 and 5 we will introduce the structure of our proposed system, and finally, in Sect. 6 we will provide some conclusions for our work and outline the possible future directions.

2   State of the Art

The problem of image plagiarism and forgery in biomedical scientific papers is very actual. In 2016 the author of [1] analysed the trend in the last 20 year showing that the number of fraud in scientific data is growing constantly, and that roughly the 4% of the published articles contains *problematic images* (i.e. duplicated or forged images). Fanelli in 2009 [6] made a deep analysis on survey data and calculated that 1.9% of researchers have confessed a modification, falsification, or fabrication of data. In 2013 *Steen et al.* [10] showed that there is an high increase in the number of retracted works and in the number of case of plagiarism in the last year that is not directly related with the increased number of publications. Such an elevated number of retracted papers has also an high financial costs. For instance, the authors in [11] estimated that such a cost is about \$58 millions in the period ranging from 1992 to 2012 in the US.

2.1 Source Camera Identification

Fridrich et al. showed in [7] that any digital camera sensor based on Charge-Coupled Device (CCD) has his unique noise that depends on the imperfection during the manufacturing process of the sensor. This noise is left on any image shot using that sensor and cannot be eliminated. The idea they carried out was to use this noise as a fingerprint for identifying the source camera used to shot a picture under scrutiny.

Formally, their technique allows to establish if an input image I has been taken by a camera (or device) C using the Pixel Non-Uniformity (PNU) noise present in I. This noise can be estimated on an image I using a PNU denoising filter F_{PNU} and is called *Residual Noise* (RN). The RN can be estimated this way:

$$RN_I = I - F_{PNU}(I). \tag{1}$$

Having a way to estimate the RN the process by *Fridrich et al.* can be described in three steps.

Step 1: Enrollment. This step aims at calculating the *Reference Pattern* (RP) for the device C, i.e., its fingerprint. The RP is obtained as an approximation by averaging a set of RNs extracted from a set of images taken using C. Formally, given a device C and a set $\{RN_1^C, \ldots, RN_m^C\}$ of RNs from images taken by C, RP_C can be calculated as:

$$RP_C = \frac{\sum_{i=1}^{m} RN_i^C}{m}. \tag{2}$$

Step 2: Training. In this step a set of acceptance threshold associated each of the cameras (i.e., RPs) under scrutiny must be calculated. This is done by using a set of training images.

Formally, let T be a training image and RN_T the residual noise extracted from T, RP_C is correlated with RN_T using the Bravais-Pearson correlation index as defined in the following formula:

$$corr(RN_T, RP_C) = \frac{(RN_T - \overline{RN_T})(RP_C - \overline{RP_C})}{\|RN_T - \overline{RN_T}\|(RP_C - \overline{RP_C}\|}. \tag{3}$$

The result is a value in the range $[-1, 1]$, where higher values implies an higher confidence that T comes from camera C. Using this correlation the threshold t_C for camera C is calculated using the Neyman-Pearson method. The resulting thresholds are chosen in order to minimize the *False Rejection Rate* (FRR) for images taken by using C, given an upper bound on the *False Acceptance Rate* (FAR) for images taken by using a different camera than C (see [7] for details).

Step 3: Detection. In this step we used the residual noise RN_I extracted from an image under scrutiny I to identify the camera used to acquire it. Formally, if the correlation between the RN_I of an image I and the RP_C of a camera C is greater than corresponding acceptance threshold, then I is marked as taken with that camera.

Formally:

$$I \in C? = \begin{cases} YES, & \text{if } corr(RN_I, RP_C) \geq t_C \\ NO, & \text{otherwise} \end{cases} \tag{4}$$

3   Source Camera Identification Applied to Electron Microscope

While there is a vast literature about the source identification problem applied to consumer digital cameras [3–5], there is almost no contribution for the analogous problem applied to digital microscopes.

In order to understand the problem is necessary a little introduction of the SEM sensors. For the sake of simplicity, we describe the main components of an Electron Microscope (i.e., Scanning Electron Microscope (SEM), see Fig. 1) [9]. Simplifying the process, in a SEM an electron gun emits an electron beam that hits the specimen and it is deflected to a small sensor that register the intensity of the deflected electron beam and convert it into an image sent to a monitor or digitally stored on a computer.

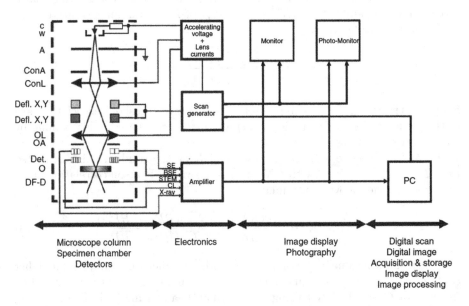

Fig. 1. Schematic drawing of a conventional SEM [9].

Because of the difference between the CCD Sensor and a SEM sensor, we need to experimentally verify if the PNU noise can be used even with SEM as device fingerprint.

For this reason we built a test-bed dataset composed by:

- 652 images taken from a Zeiss EVO MA10 SEM device (100 used for training and 552 used for testing);
- 67 images taken from a Zeiss Merlin SEM device.

Then we applied the process described in Sect. 2.1 to calculate the RP for the Zeiss EVO MA10 using the 100 training images from this device in dataset. In this way, we obtained the RP shown in Fig. 2.

Fig. 2. Particular of reference pattern for electron microscope Zeiss EVO MA10

Finally, we calculated the reference noise for all the remaining images from Zeiss EVO MA10 and the images from the Zeiss Merlin, after calculating the correlation, we obtained the result in Fig. 3.

As shown in Fig. 3, there is a visible separation between the correlation values for the image taken from the same microscope used for calculating the RP and the correlation values of the images coming from the other microscope. This separation is so large that is possible to define a threshold with a naked eye, in fact, there is 10 as difference factor between the minimum value of the correlation for the image taken from the first microscope, that is 0.0213, and the maximum from the second one, that is 0.0029, as reported in Table 1.

As a result from this experiment, we can assume that the technique by *Fridrich et al.* could work also on images taken using a SEM.

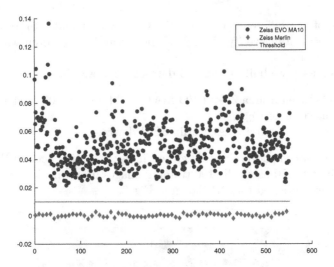

Fig. 3. Scatter plot of the correlation values between the reference pattern of the device Zeiss EVO MA10 and the residual noises of the images of device Zeiss EVO MA10 and Zeiss Merlin.

Table 1. Minimum, maximum and average correlation values between the reference pattern of the device Zeiss EVO MA10 and the residual noises of the images of device Zeiss EVO MA10 and Zeiss Merlin.

	Zeiss EVO MA10	Zeiss Merlin
Min correlation value	0.0213	−0.0022
Max correlation value	0.1364	0.0029
Average correlation value	0.0493	$4.3381e^{-4}$

4   The Methodology in Practice

In Sect. 3 we have proven that the technique by *Fridrich et al.* can be extended to the different digital sensors like SEM ones to extract their own noise, namely the PNU noise. This allows to link images to the imaging device used to acquire them by means of this noise. This is useful when there is the suspect that the image was not original from the author.

Now we provide more details about the system design that allows to automatically discover image plagiarisms by scanning al the scientific article in registered on-line publishing platform and comparing the residual noise existing in all the images contained therein with the reference pattern of a set of imaging devices.

The architecture of our system (see Fig. 4) is organized in 3 modules:

1. **Reference Pattern Module:** it is in charge to collect the training images voluntarily uploaded by the owner of a SEM and used to calculate the *RPs* and relatives thresholds.

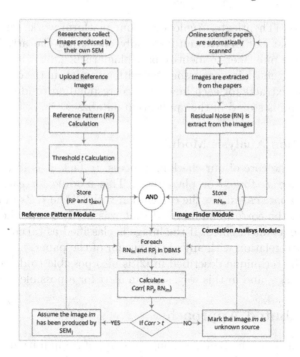

Fig. 4. Flowchart of the proposed antiplagiarism checker

2. **Image Finder Module:** it is in charge to scan the registered online publishing platform to collect all the image taken from a paper and extract for each one the corresponding Residual Noise RN.
3. **Correlation Analysis Module:** it is in charge to calculate the correlation value between each RN and each RP with the purpose to associate each image with the corresponding SEM. If no matching RP is present, the image is classified as unknown.

4.1 Reference Pattern Module

The authors, laboratory or institution that owns a SEM are interested in maintain the intellectual properties of their works, so they can register on the platform and upload two set of images (i.e., enrollment and training) taken from their device D that will be used respectively to calculate the RP_D and t_D for their device as seen in Sect. 2.1. The module then will compute RP_D and t_D, and it stores them in the application database so that can be accessed by the other module in the application, i.e., by the correlation module.

4.2 Image Finder Module

When a paper is submitted for publication, often it will be scanned for antiplagiarism system to check if the text in the paper was copied from other article in literature, i.e., iThenticate. Analogously our platform works on images, with the difference that our system automatically checks all the articles stored in registered on-line publisher to identify past plagiarism.

The platform gets all images associated with an article in the on-line publisher platform and it extracts for each image the corresponding residual noise. Then, the residual noise is stored in the application database.

4.3   Correlation Analysis Module

This module is the core of our checking process. In fact, it is in charge of classifying the image as forged or plagiarized. This module for each RN in the application database calculates the correlation with all the RPs in the database in order to find the corresponding SEM that was used to take the image or to mark the image as unclassified. If the image is classified as taken with SEM for which there is no relation with any of the author of the paper, an alert is raised.

Applying the technique described in [2] is also possible to detect the forged region of the image, and in this way, send an alert for a possible scientific fraud.

5   A Distributed Approach

The problem we are facing requires a huge amount of computational resources as we need to compute all the possible correlation values between the RN of each single image under scrutiny and the RP of each known imaging device. Obviously, such a task cannot be carried out using in a feasible amount of time using a single computer. Instead, we propose the adoption of a distributed approach able to deliver a scalable, fault-tolerant and efficient solution to the problem using a cloud computing approach. Our solution is an evolution of the one proposed in [4,5] that was based on the usage of the Apache Hadoop distributed computing framework.

One of the main advantages of our solution is that it has been developed using Apache Spark, because this distributed framework also supports a streaming data processing. This is a unified engine for distributed data processing proposed in [12]. It uses a programming model similar to MapReduce used in Apache Hadoop but extends it with a data-sharing abstraction called *Resilient Distributed Datasets* (RDDs) Using these features, Spark can run a wide range of distributed workloads that previously required separate engines like SQL, machine learning and streaming.

This generality brings several benefits. For example, the application development process is simplified by the presence of an unified API. In addition, Spark is more efficient than Hadoop in the iterative execution of several processing tasks because, differently from Hadoop, it can run several functions in a distributed way over the data stored in a RDD without using the disk as a temporary buffer (provided that the available main memory is enough).

Currently we are developing a working prototype of this distributed approach. A first working proof of concet was made on the platform Apache Hadoop and a new porting on Apache Spark is currentlly in advanced state of development.

6   Conclusion and Future Works

In this paper we dealt with the increasing problem of fraud in biomedical scientific images by introducing a distributed anti-plagiarism and anti-forgery system for the massive checking of these images. This phenomenon has an high financial cost as reported in Sect. 2.

We believe that introducing a platform for anti-plagiarism and anti-forgery checker can discourage an author from carrying on this kind of fraud. Our system builds on the SCI technique proposed by *Fridrich et al.* in [7], by applying it to the special case of digital images taken using Scanning Electron Microscopes (SEM).

First of all, we experimentally proved that this technique can be applied also to the SEM sensors even if they are different from CCD sensors used by digital cameras. For this purpose we created a dataset of SEM images to feed our implementation of the by *Fridrich et al.* technique properly tuned for this kind of sensors.

Achieved this goal, we described the three components of our system: one to collect the training and testing images submitted by the owner of device (i.e., digital cameras or SEM) that calculates the RP for these devices, another one that scans the online repositories of biomedical scientific papers to collect images of published articles and, finally, a correlation module responsible to clusterize the image linking them with the correct generator device.

This technique applied to the large number of article and device require a lot of computation costs, so we proposed a distributed approach based on Apache Spark to cope with a huge number of papers. A prototype of this system in currently in advanced phase of development and testing.

As future works, in order to automatically extract images from online papers, we are currently investigating on the properties hold by images extracted directly from the paper in PDF format. In fact, it is necessary to verify the conditions under which these kind of images could preserve the source PNU noise, i.e., which impact is produced by external factors like compression or any further transformations.

Another interesting evolution of the system is the creation of a "ballistic image database". Like in this scenario we can store the residual noise of each unclassified image to estimate the possibility that another image in the database is taken from the same source even if we do not know this source.

References

1. Bik, E.M., Casadevall, A., Fang, F.C.: The prevalence of inappropriate image duplication in biomedical research publications. MBio **7**(3), e00809–16 (2016)
2. Cattaneo, G., Ferraro Petrillo, U., Roscigno, G., De Fusco, C.: A PNU-based technique to detect forged regions in digital images. In: Battiato, S., Blanc-Talon, J., Gallo, G., Philips, W., Popescu, D., Scheunders, P. (eds.) ACIVS 2015. LNCS, vol. 9386, pp. 486–498. Springer, Cham (2015). https://doi.org/10.1007/978-3-319-25903-1_42

3. Cattaneo, G., Roscigno, G., Bruno, A.: Using PNU-based techniques to detect alien frames in videos. In: Blanc-Talon, J., Distante, C., Philips, W., Popescu, D., Scheunders, P. (eds.) ACIVS 2016. LNCS, vol. 10016, pp. 735–746. Springer, Cham (2016). https://doi.org/10.1007/978-3-319-48680-2_64

4. Cattaneo, G., Ferraro Petrillo, U., Nappi, M., Narducci, F., Roscigno, G.: An efficient implementation of the algorithm by Lukáš et al. on Hadoop. In: Au, M.H.A., Castiglione, A., Choo, K.-K.R., Palmieri, F., Li, K.-C. (eds.) GPC 2017. LNCS, vol. 10232, pp. 475–489. Springer, Cham (2017). https://doi.org/10.1007/978-3-319-57186-7_35

5. Cattaneo, G., Roscigno, G., Petrillo, U.F.: A scalable approach to source camera identification over Hadoop. In: 2014 IEEE 28th International Conference on Advanced Information Networking and Applications (AINA), pp. 366–373. IEEE (2014)

6. Fanelli, D.: How many scientists fabricate and falsify research? A systematic review and meta-analysis of survey data. PLoS ONE 4(5), e5738 (2009)

7. Fridrich, J., Lukáš, J., Goljan, M.: Digital camera identification from sensor noise. IEEE Trans. Inf. Secur. Forensics 1(2), 205–214 (2006)

8. iThenticate: Plagiarism detection software—ithenticate. http://www.ithenticate.com/

9. Reichelt, R.: Scanning electron microscopy. In: Science of microscopy, pp. 133–272. Springer (2007)

10. Steen, R.G., Casadevall, A., Fang, F.C.: Why has the number of scientific retractions increased? PLoS ONE 8(7), e68397 (2013)

11. Stern, A.M., Casadevall, A., Steen, R.G., Fang, F.C.: Financial costs and personal consequences of research misconduct resulting in retracted publications. Elife 3, e02956 (2014)

12. Zaharia, M., Xin, R.S., Wendell, P., Das, T., Armbrust, M., Dave, A., Meng, X., Rosen, J., Venkataraman, S., Franklin, M.J., et al.: Apache spark: a unified engine for big data processing. Commun. ACM 59(11), 56–65 (2016)

Exploring the Feasibility to Authenticate Users of Web and Cloud Services Using a Brain-Computer Interface (BCI)

Michael Philip Orenda[1], Lalit Garg[1,2(✉)] ⓘ, and Gaurav Garg[3] ⓘ

[1] University of Liverpool, Liverpool, UK
lalit.garg@um.edu.mt
[2] Computer Information Systems, University of Malta, Msida, Malta
[3] Intelligent Systems Research Centre, University of Ulster, Coleraine, UK

Abstract. Business has come to a point whereby there is a substantial reliance on computing devices. People using machines need to be identified by who they are and not what they know or have. Real identity is the individual. Biometrics is the way to go if this is to be achieved. The biometric is a statistical measurement of biological data; be it physical, chemical or electric. Brain Computer Interface (BCI) is a maturing technology, becoming more affordable, easier to use and integrate with computing devices. With the increasing need of the internet based services (web and cloud services), it has become paramount for identification technologies to get close to natural means of identification, and biometrics offers this mechanism because it is a genuine identity of an individual. Therefore, this work aims to explore the feasibility that computer systems can use brain signals as a biometric method for authentication for web and cloud services users through a brain-computer interface (BCI). Though the main aim of this study is not to create a perfect solution, yet use the prototype as a suggestion to spur and provoke identification mechanisms to catch on in this direction. This study has been validated using the electroencephalography (EEG) scans using the Emotiv's 5-channel EEG headset and recording devices and the survey of the 52 volunteers participated in the study. As the same brain signals authentication can be used for all services irrespective of service or provider, therefore, it can be an ideal candidate for the Biometrics-as-a-Service (BaaS). The brain scan can be stored once at the BaaS provider and would be used by all service providers for all services. It can also be combined with other authentication methods to have multi-factor authentication (MFA) for improved security.

Keywords: Biometrics · Identification · Authentication · Web services
Cloud services · Brain computer interface (BCI)
Electroencephalography (EEG) · Biometrics-as-a-Service (BaaS)

1 Introduction

Humans are social beings. In this social society, each one has a need or demand and may be a supply to others. In social interactions, which have also grown to business interactions, there is need to identify each entity. The fundamental ways of identifying each

S. Battiato et al. (Eds.): ICIAP 2017 International Workshops, LNCS 10590, pp. 353–363, 2017.
https://doi.org/10.1007/978-3-319-70742-6_33

other are by sight, voice, and feel for those with disabilities. For, those with no sight disability, the face of the other human is the basic and natural way to identify the person. A human face has many features which make it almost unique (Prakash and Rogers 2015, p. 309–p. 310; Shyam and Singh 2016, p. 2; Dospinescu and Popa 2016, p. 20–p. 21). We know people by their faces, physique and voice, and through this way of identification, we interact appropriately. Business is the interaction between human beings. Identification, even in business interactions is key for appropriate interactions and in today's business, computers have become an integral part and for this reason, computers also need to have a mechanism for identifying entities. Biometrics is a statistical measurement of the physiological and behavioural aspects of an individual. It is paramount for identification mechanisms to get as close to natural means of identification and biometrics offers this mechanism because it is the true identity of an individual. Here, the hypothesis considered to prove is "Neural signals through a Brain Computer Interface (BCI), when matured enough can be effectively used for Identity Management."

With the ever increasing usage of the web and cloud services by humans, authentication and identity become a challenge and growing need. In this study, a prototype system is implemented to explore the feasibility that computer systems can use brain signals as a biometric method for authentication for web and cloud services users through a brain-computer interface (BCI). As the same brain signals authentication can be used for all services irrespective of service or provider, therefore, it can be an ideal candidate for the Biometrics-as-a-Service (BaaS). The brain scan can be stored once at the BaaS provider and would be used by all service providers for all services. It can also be combined with other authentication methods to have multi-factor authentication (MFA) for improved security.

Therefore, the scope of this study is to explore the feasibility of using brain signals as a way of authentication. The study does not intend to create an immediate working solution, but a suggested means of authentication using a Brain Computer Interface integrated into a web or cloud application. Web and cloud users' anticipations, optimism towards using neural signals are also surveyed in this study.

1.1 Downsides of the Popular Authentication Methods

Username & password combination is the most commonly used and most easily implemented authentication and authorization technique used in web applications. However, there are disadvantages to this technique. One disadvantage to this technique is that it depends on the user's cognitive ability, hence it is the security stored in the individual's brain. Many business services; financial services, insurance services, government services, retailers, wholesalers, etc. are increasingly using the internet (web and cloud) and computing devices to trade and offer services online, where all type of user data is now being made accessible on-the-go through the cloud networking. It would mean that for each of these services offered online (through web or cloud), a person would, therefore, need to have more than one set of authentication credentials. It implies that a user should recall all the usernames and passwords for each online service (web or cloud) offered to which they have subscribed to and an increasing number of devices that connect online. (Nasirinejad and Yazdi 2012; Conklin et al. 2004).

It is like having a big bunch keys for different doors in multiple locations. Here, knowing which key unlocks which door and losing a key will not be a desirable experience.

A second drawback is that each institution offering web or cloud services has its own security policies. These differences in security policy enforcement, force users to use different credentials for each web and cloud service. Some of these policies include the number of characters, type of characters and expiry periods of the credentials. (Nasirinejad and Yazdi 2012)

Another drawback is that passwords are vulnerable to dictionary attacks. If anyone guesses the correct password or uses brute force to dig up the password, they can easily masquerade as the authorised user (Thorpe et al. 2005, p. 3)

Though the fingerprints as biometric-based authentication are becoming very popular nowadays, however, the main downside of using fingerprints is the fact that these can be stolen. It comes as a surprise that stolen fingerprint data is more than estimated by the U.S. Office of Personnel Management (Kerner 2015; Constantin 2015). One cannot change fingerprints; therefore, when stolen, nothing can be done about it because an individual cannot change his/her fingerprints. It is essential that authentication systems should allow changing authentication data in case of compromise (Thorpe et al. 2005, p. 4)

BCI technologies are not yet matured enough for a wide acceptance. However, this disadvantage will be swept away as more interest in this area of research would yield breakthroughs. O'Gorman (1996, p. 61–p. 62) also foresees that the future of biometrics could be bright given the fact that the prices and sizes of biometric devices are reducing.

1.2 Why EEG Signals?

There have been a lot of research for non-invasive observation of brain activity. In a non-invasive method, no surgery is required to place equipment for monitoring brain and neural activities in the body. These methods include functional Magnetic Resonance Imaging (fMRI), Positron Emission Tomography (PET), Transcranial Magnetic Stimulation (TMS), Near Infrared Spectroscopy (NIRS), and Electroencephalograph (EEG) or Magnetoencephalography (MEG).

The fMRI device measures by detecting oxygen supplied blood to the brain. Brain's Neural activities are observed through bloodstream fluctuations, thus generating an fMRI activity map (Garg et al. 2013). PET beams positrons, an anti-electron of the same mass but opposite charge, to facilitate viewing of bio-chemical reactions. CT-scans use X-Ray technology with 360° rotational system to get 3D images. This technology involves radiation and should not be used frequently. NIRS is similar to fMRI but less expensive and portable. It measures brain activities using hemodynamic (Blood Oxygenation Level) response of neurons (Garg et al. 2013).

EEG is an electrophysiological signal measuring device, which measures electric activities of neurons in real-time. Voltage pulses are detected by the electrodes placed on the scalp. These recorded signals provide information about activities in the brain. (Katona and Kovari 2015). In essence, the EEG is recording and measurement of voltage fluctuations of the brain and with each brain being unique; there is a high possibility that these voltages can be used for identification (Yang 2015, p. 10; Campisi et al. 2012). It is consequently proven that an individual can be identified using EEG signals and, additionally, EEG signals from individuals apart from identity can be used to carry out various ICT, robotic and other electronic functions (Palaniappan 2008; Yoon Jae et al. 2015).

The EEG recorded brain waves can be divided into three frequency bands; slow, moderate and fast which are categorized as; delta (<4 Hz), theta(4–7 Hz), alpha (8-15 Hz), beta(16–31 Hz) and gamma (>32 Hz) (Schultz 2012).

An advantage of EEG worth mentioning is that it does not exclude people with disabilities. Unlike the fingerprint solution to authentication when stolen, EEG authentication data can always be changed while identity is still retained. This can be done by choosing different type of cognitive activity, few of them may be left-hand push, right hand pull, right-leg up action etc. and other combinations. and recording the corresponding EEG/electrophysiological signal in the database for matching and authorization purpose at later stage. Also, these recordings are unique to every individual.

fMRI and PET produce high resolution images. However, these images are large in size and thus expensive and slow to process. They are primarily used for medical examinations. TMS could raise some controversy because the effect of depolarization is not known. EEG devices being relatively inexpensive and portable have become more available in the market, which will bring into play more innovations from many researchers, businesses and developers beyond medical use. (Katona and Kovari 2015) There are many uses of EEG device, especially in the gaming and toy industries, where action and control are detected from brain signals.

2 Methodology

A biometric fingerprint reader is used to capture fingerprints for use in authentication. Likewise, the fact that there is already an interface that is developed to send neural signals from the brain to a computer system, the Brain Computer Interface (BCI) can be used to capture brain signals that may well be used for authorization and authentication amongst other uses. It is logical to create systems that use EEG as there is an interest to research more in the area of EEG. (Al-Hudhud 2014).

In theory and practice, authenticating web and cloud services users using brain signals should not be a complex undertaking. Research carried out by Novak and Švogor (2016) indicates the use and growth of Component-based systems or designs (CBD) for web and cloud services. Computer systems are components working together to achieve certain objectives. These components are both hardware and software components. CBD simplifies innovations and allows for independent improvements and reuse of each component (Sommerville 2011, p. 452–p. 478). Using components help us apply the design pattern and principle of separation of concerns (SoC) that makes it possible for independent research and improvements on each component. It means that research on EEG hardware and EEG software can independently continue. Improvement of current computer hardware, and software (browsers, thin client and desktop software), and programming languages can also independently improve to include EEG effortlessness.

The prototype, along these lines, is a three-tier architecture with each tier having subcomponents. The main subcomponent of this feasibility study is the BCI which resides at the client-side of the architecture.

2.1 System Architecture and Components

The prototype system is made up of server side and client side devices as well as software. The server side is essentially a computer that has a web server, application server and database server. Client side consists of a computer that has a web browser such as Mozilla's Firefox Browser which, when browsing the web application will pull the client-side script and prompt a download of a plugin from Emotiv. The client side also includes the Emotive Insight, a Brain-Computer Interface device from Emotiv. All components, except the components specific to the Emotiv Insight, are common components. Figure 1 illustrates the components and architecture of the prototype.

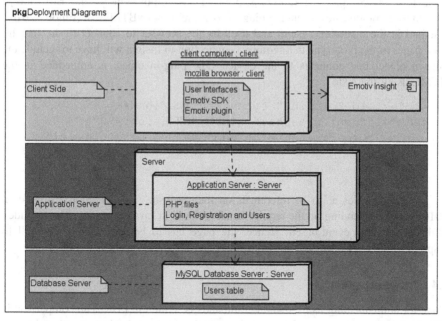

Fig. 1. System Architecture & Components

2.2 Emotive Insight Brainwear

Emotive Insight Brianwear (say Insight hereafter), as shown in Fig. 2, is a five channel EEG headset that records brainwaves and make those brain signals available for further

Fig. 2. Emotiv Insight Brainwear (Emotiv 2 2016)

processing. Insight connects to a wide variety of computing devices; computers, tablets and phones with support for the common operating systems; Windows, Linux, MAC OSX, Android and IOS via Bluetooth. The five signal channels are AF3, AF4, T7, T8 and Pz. (Emotiv 2016)

2.3   Emotiv Plugin and SDK

The Emotiv software development kit (SDK) used for this project consists of mainly these four JavaScript files; EdkDll.js, EmoState.js, EmoEngine.js and ElsCloud.js. This SDK communicates through a plug-in software, EmotivBTLE.msi (Emotiv 2016), installed in the operating system and used by the browser to connect to the Insight. Web pages in the prototype that require a connection to Insight will have to include the plug-in object that connects to the device. The plug-in object is embedded in the HTML using the code

```
<object id="plugin0" type="application/x-
emotivlifesciencesbtle" width="0" height="0">
        <param name="onload" value="pluginLoaded" />
</object>
```

Emotiv provides a list of references on their website (Cpanel.emotivinsight.com 2016) which, depending on the requirements are used in JavaScript files. The provided SDK is primarily event-based. Hence, the page has to be programmed as well to respond to the events originating from users and the events from Insight.

2.4   Implementation

Code for authenticating using mental commands is written in PHP. The comparison is not clear-cut as with a normal password comparison from a database compared to the provided one. Emotive insight records the electrical activity of brain and saves it in the comma separated value (*.csv) format. Emotiv Insight data is comma delimited with some values repeating (see Table 1). The code takes the highest repeated value from Emotive Insight data in the database and compares to the highest repeated value provided by the user through the login page.

Table 1. Illustration of the user database including part of Emotiv Insight recorded EEG data

Column	Data
usr_id	21
username	Michael
firstname	Michael
lastname	Orenda
email	michael.orenda@online.liverpool.ac.uk
EEG of 'neutral' state brain	<... ... ... "4174.358872", "4174.358872", "4174.358872", "3848.717855", "3868.205034", "3865.128111", "3861.025547", "3861.025547", "3856.410162", "3850.769137", "3850.256316", "3860.512726", "3864.61529", "3851.281957", "3845.640932", "3860.512726", "3857.435803", "3854.35888", "3872.307598", "3963.589647", "3941.025545", "3957.948621", "3982.564005", "3973.333236", "3948.717852", "3954.871698", "3970.769134", "3961.025544"... ... ... >
EEG of 'push' command	<... ... ... >
EEG of 'pull' command	<... ... ... >
EEG of 'up' command	<... ... ... >
EEG of 'down' command	<... ... ... >
EEG of 'left' command	<... ... ... >
EEG of 'right' command	<... ... ... >

The registration and login at the user interfaces (page) do not have the usual submit button. Fields are event-based, hence the user of the client-side scripting (JavaScript). With a click being an event for the mental command fields, each click triggers an event that connects to Emotiv Insight which also responds. Emotiv Insight responses are also events that are captured and necessary action taken. All successful actions trigger a database transaction, to either save data if the page is registration page or authenticate if the page is the login page.

2.5   Web Page for Biometric Authentication Using Brain Signals

Connection Testing Webpage.
It is a webpage that is used to ensure that there is a connection to Insight headset. Emotiv provided the page, and there are no changes done to this webpage.

Registration and Login Page.
It is a page created to allow users to record their mental commands into the system (see Fig. 3(a).). The page has some changes but relies on the samples obtained from Emotiv as examples. The page has input fields where a user can enter their username, first name, last name and email. The other fields are event based fields, whereby the user clicks on the mental command which he/she wants to train. It is paramount to train the neutral state of the brain first. Successful and accepted recordings are saved into the database using Ajax. There is no submit button, the acceptance of the recording is the event equal to 'submit' in this set-up.

The login page is similar to the registration page. It only differs because the user will only enter a username and select the mental command he/she wish to login with (see Fig. 3(b).).

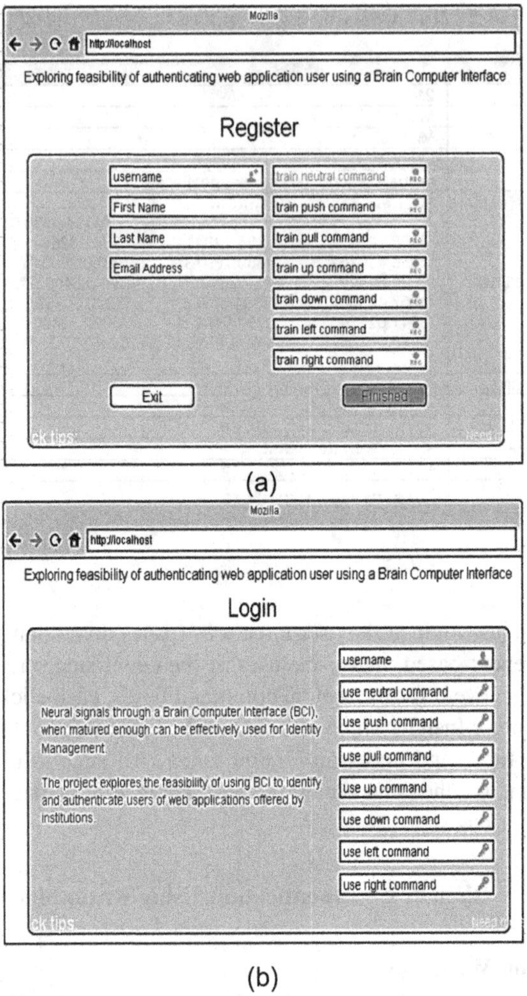

(a)

(b)

Fig. 3. (a) Registration Page and (b) Login Page

2.6   Application Server and Database

The application server consists of Apache v2.4 and PHP v5.4. For installation of these servers, Xampp and WAMP both were tested to get the complexity of the configurations out of the way. Xampp and WAMP both configure Apache to run PHP scripts which are used at the back end, more importantly, to communicate with the database server and holds the authentication algorithm.

The system uses MySQL database v5.6. Only one schema with one table used for authentication. In this, all the columns are considered as described on the login page. Though, other columns are optional and can be changed to some other complex brain-based command, except usr_id and username columns, which also have the UNIQUE constraint to them.

2.7   Evaluation Survey Design

A questionnaire is aimed at getting information and opinion from users. The target sample size of 52 is drawn from banks, health insurance, government, private investigation and ICT companies. The banks include the two largest banks in the region, Equity Bank, Kenya Commercial Bank and another bank CFC Stanbic and any other that will randomly accept. Health and Insurance include again the largest players in the region; Jubilee and CIC insurance. From government, targeted participants are from Kenya Revenue Authority and National Transport and Safety Authority. ICT companies included Oracle Kenya, Institute of Software Technologies, and Software Technologies Ltd. All these organisations serve millions of Kenyans thus evaluation is designed to get opinions from the wide variety of users.

A survey is done after the completion of the implementation of the prototype. The target sample size is 52 who answered the questionnaire after voluntarily interacting with the prototype. The questionnaire is designed to explore the opinion and anticipation of participants about the feasibility of using brain signals as a way of authenticating users of web or cloud services and receiving government services online and opinions about the methods and technologies used for authentication.

3   Results and Evaluation

The hypothesis tests positive if the users affirm the fact that they believe it better and will be possible to use neural signals especially brain signals for authentication.

Based on those above though rudimentary BCI prototype and survey results, it can be considered feasible to use brain signals for authentication of web and cloud based applications. The findings of the survey are better represented in a straightforward way rather than the complex percentage among the user opinion. Most of the respondents after just seeing the BCI despite knowing the difficulties, agreed that brain signals should be one of the authentication methods in the future.

Authentication Preferences and Feasibility of Using Brain Signals.
Users of this system were asked if the available authentication technologies are matured what authentication method would be their preference, 88% of the participants with ± 9% confidence interval (c.i.) at 95% confidence level (c.l.) preferred biometrics. And 58% of these (i.e., 51% of all participants with ± 14% c.i. at 95% c.l. specify brain signals (cf. Fig. 4.). Over 80% of the participants (with ± 11% c.i. at 95% c.l. affirmed that biometrics is the true identity of an individual.

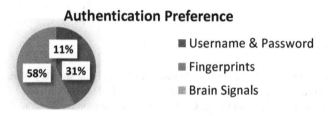

Fig. 4. Authentication Preference

Limitations of Using Brain Signals for Authentication.
Regardless of the preference for BCI-based authentication as has been experienced by the users during the registration process, it is not easy thinking for 8 s without wavering into other thoughts. Thinking left, push, pull, top, down or right is not as easy as said. Another limitation is 'slow to use'. The device must be worn on the head, and one must ensure that there are signals being acquired. It means that it cannot be spontaneously used.

4 Conclusion

The BCI system prototype in the project is based on the Emotiv's device, SDK and plugin (Emotiv 2016; Emotiv 2 2016; Cpanel.emotivinsight.com 2016). However, it is not worth making recommendations based on Emotiv proprietary products, but use it as a pointer to make recommendations for standardisation that would lead easy and wide usage of biometrics especially neural signals for authentication and identity management. Businesses need to identify the entities receiving their web or cloud based services or products. This basic reality of identifying entities, put to work in devices using biometrics, would prove to be a great and necessary business exploit; it could be a significant application that is required virtually in most of the electronic devices which require authentication.

This study can be further developed to perfection for use not only in internet based usage but also to other required authentication purposes in all kinds of wearable electronic gadgets which have even wider and deeper reach to users. Security systems such as opening doors and approving transactions may also be put into the context of this. Also, as we do not require the complete brain scan for the authentication, but a part of it is sufficient, the complete brain scan data can be stored in a cloud, and a part can randomly be selected for the authentication each time. During the authentication, only the selected part of the brain signal will be collected from the user and authentication process would take place in the cloud or server. If the service requires authentication process to be completed on the client side, only the selected part of the brain scan can be accessed from the cloud by the client application. It will help ensure enhanced security, faster authentication and protecting brain scans from being copied by the eavesdroppers and con-artists. Further, as the same brain signals authentication can be used for all services irrespective of service or provider, therefore, it can be an ideal candidate for the BaaS. The brain scan can be stored once at the BaaS provider and would be used by all service providers for all services. It can also be combined with other authentication methods to have multi-factor authentication (MFA) for improved security.

References

Al-Hudhud, G., Alzamel, M., Alattas, E., Alwabil, A.: Using brain signals patterns for biometric identity verification systems. Comput. Hum. Behav. **31**, 224–229 (2014)

Campisi, P., La Rocca, D., Scarano, G.: EEG for automatic person recognition. Computer **45**(7), 87–89 (2012)

Conklin, A., Dietrich, G., Walz, D.: Password-based authentication: a system perspective. In: Proceedings of the 37th Annual Hawaii International Conference on System Sciences, p. 10 (2004)

Constantin, L.: US govt's OPM underestimated the number of stolen fingerprints by 4.5 million, Cio (13284045), p. 1 (2015)

Cpanel.emotivinsight.com.: API Reference, https://cpanel.emotivinsight.com/BTLE-/api.htm. Accessed 24 Sep 2016

Dospinescu, O., Popa, I.: Face detection and face recognition in android mobile applications. Informatica Economica **20**(1), 20–28 (2016). Business Source Complete

Emotiv.: About Emotiv, http://emotiv.com/about-emotiv/. Accessed 25 June 2016

Emotiv 2.: Image of Emotive Insight Brainwear, https://i1.wp.com/www.emotiv.com/wp-content/uploads/2016/04/emotiv-insight-square-w.jpg. Accessed 26 Sep 2016

Garg, G., Prasad, G., Coyle, D.: Gaussian Mixture Model-based noise reduction in resting state fMRI data. J. Neurosci. Methods **215**(1), 71–77 (2013)

Kerner, S.M.: OPM says far more fingerprint data stolen than first reported. Eweek, 1 (2015). Business Source Complete

Katona, J., Kovari, A.: EEG-based computer control interface for brain-machine interaction. Int. J. Online Eng. **11**(6), 43–48 (2015). Computers & Applied Sciences Complete

Nasirinejad, M., Yazdi, A.: SASy username and password management on the cloud. In: Proceedings 2012 International Conference on Cyber Security, Cyber Warfare and Digital Forensic, CyberSec 2012, pp. 242–246 (2012)

Novak, M., Švogor, I.: Current usage of component based principles for developing web applications with frameworks: a literature review. Interdisc. Description Complex Syst. **14**(2), 253–276 (2016)

O'Gorman, L.: Fingerprint verification. In: Jain, A.K., Bolle, R., Pankanti, S. (eds.) Biometrics, pp. 43–64. Springer, Boston (1996)

Palaniappan, R.: Two-stage biometric authentication method using thought activity brain waves. Int. J. Neural Syst. **18**(01), 59–66 (2008)

Prakash, A., Rogers, W.: Why some humanoid faces are perceived more positively than others: effects of human-likeness and task. Int. J. Soc. Robot. **7**(2), 309–331 (2015). PsycINFO

Schultz, T.L.: Technical tips: mri compatible eeg electrodes: advantages, disadvantages, and financial feasibility in a clinical setting. Neurodiagnostic J. **52**(1), 69–81 (2012)

Shyam, R., Singh, Y.: Multialgorithmic frameworks for human face recognition. J. Electr. Comput. Eng., 1–9 (2016). Academic Search Complete

Sommerville, I.: Software Engineering, pp. 452–478. Pearson, Boston (2011)

Thorpe, J., Van Oorschot, P., Somayaji, A.: Pass-thoughts. In: Proceedings of the 2005 Workshop on New Security Paradigms - NSPW 2005 (2005)

Yang, S.: The use of EEG signals for biometric person recognition, Doctoral dissertation, University of Kent (2015)

Yoon Jae, K., Sung Woo, P., Hong Gi, Y., Moon Suk, B., June Sic, K., Chun Kee, C., Sungwan, K.: A study on a robot arm driven by three-dimensional trajectories predicted from non-invasive neural signals. Biomed. Eng. Online **14**(1), 1–19 (2015)

A Smart Peephole on the Cloud

Maria De Marsico$^{(\boxtimes)}$, Eugenio Nemmi, Bardh Prenkaj, and Gabriele Saturni

Sapienza University of Rome, Rome, Italy
demarsico@di.uniroma1.it, eugenio.nemmi@uniroma1.it,
prenkaj.1602894@studenti.uniroma1.it, gabriele.saturni@gmail.com

Abstract. This paper does not present a novel technique for biometric recognition, but rather a novel way to use it. The proposal is to exploit cloud computing in order to support everyday applications. These are not necessarily bound to security, but span a wide range of possible useful tasks. This work presents a smart peephole able to recognize the person at the door, possibly automatically allowing entrance according to rules decided by the home keeper. The novelty is that very little processing is carried out locally, and biometrics is implemented as a service. The system relies on Microsoft Cognitive Services, a suite of remote services included in Microsoft Azure platform. The single user has to install nothing but a camera with a sound capture facility in correspondence to the peephole, and a lightweight software. A movement detector module triggers the capture/recognition activity. The captured audio and video samples are sent to the service. Most processing and recognition are carried out via the remote suite, and a final result is sent back to possibly trigger a response action. The present prototype includes face, speech and emotion recognition. It does not completely cover all system aspects. The aim is to demonstrate the feasibility of the approach.

Keywords: Biometrics · Microsoft cognitive services · Cloud computing

1 Introduction

Nowadays, more and more sophisticated devices and software applications have to address both traditional as well as new challenges. These arise with the increasing use of digital resources and information. Having to cope with enormous quantity of daily data a person downloads, uploads and reads, private personal data and information are exposed to potential, usually hidden threats. The possible weaknesses of password-based and token-based approaches led to the genesis and continuous development of biometric security systems [3]. In principle, any human trait (DNA, face, retina, palm, iris, fingerprints, ears, etc.) which differs from one person to another, is universally available and measurable, and permanent over time, can be used as a personal identification key [2]. A biometric system collects, processes and records this kind of data (enrollment) in order to verify the identity or identify a person at a later time (recognition).

© Springer International Publishing AG 2017
S. Battiato et al. (Eds.): ICIAP 2017 International Workshops, LNCS 10590, pp. 364–374, 2017.
https://doi.org/10.1007/978-3-319-70742-6_34

Biometrics technology finds application in many diverse fields, which are divided by access control type, either physical or logical. When the size of data or the size of possible users increases, both processing and storage resources may become an issue. This is the joining point between biometrics and cloud computing. When the single user cannot afford maintaining locally the needed resources, it is possible to rely on a smart remote distribution and deployment of storage, resources, and processing tools, which is the basic mechanism underlying cloud technology. In general, more and more kinds of resources can be remotely provided as a service. Microsoft Cognitive Services (MCS) is used here as an example platform to demonstrate the feasibility of biometrics as a service.

Smart Peephole can be deployed as a house security system. As the name suggests, it has the capability to observe incoming objects (humans, animals and so on) at the house doorstep. It carries out the basic function of a classic door peephole; however, rather than the person looking through the peephole, the system will take the decision whether to open the door, thus accepting the object in front of the door, or to remain in a closed state, rejecting the objects entrance. The system is composed of four main modules, implementing different biometric recognition tasks and combining their results, which will be described in detail in the following sections. These modules rely on MCS, and are combined together to make up a robust control mechanism, able to discriminate between members of the allowed group of people (*members*), and *intruders*.

Peephole module is responsible of detecting movements and to recognize whether, at the moment a movement is detected, there is a face in front of the peephole.

Face detection module can both register a family member (or other allowed subject) to the system by uploading a number of photos of that person's face and facial expressions, and identify the person later by matching the incoming face image with the gallery set (enrolled faces).

Speech verification module uses a microphone to record a person' s voice and upload it to the system; when a user desires to enter the house, he/she has to speak in through an appropriate microphone to be recognized as a member of the allowed group.

Emotion detection module aims at catching the mood of the person in front of the peephole, by extracting and analyzing features from facial expression.

The rest of the paper continues as follows. Section 2 presents the general ideas underlying this biometric security system, and its key requirements. Also, it discusses the decisions taken to implement efficiently the system and to guarantee a high responsiveness to the user. Microsoft Cognitive Services are also briefly introduced. Section 3 describes *Smart Peephole* system and its design. Section 4 synthesizes the system performance, and finally Sect. 5 draws conclusions and briefly summarizes future developments.

2 System Requirements and Implementation Choices

2.1 The Functions of *Smart Peephole* and the remote choice

The aim of *Smart Peephole* is to realize an intelligent peephole for the recognition of family members or house mates, such as extended family members or family friends. The purpose of this project is to create a smart system able to grant access to the house in a secure and easy way and, possibly, to eliminate the need for a key to open the house door. This is achieved by a combination of biometric measurements. As a particular security system, *Smart Peephole* should address the three principles of data security: Confidentiality, Integrity and Availability (CIA triad [14]). A detailed discussion about related topics is out of the scope of this paper, and also implementation of possible countermeasures was out of the scope of the present design.

Smart Peephole has to recognize subjects belonging to two groups: *members* and *intruders*. *Members* are persons that are registered by an administrator, who will install the equipment and set up the system. The *intruders*, on the other hand, are all other persons that are not in the members set. *Smart Peephole* recognizes persons via face and voice recognition. As any biometric system, it includes two phases:

(1) In the first phase, or the *enrollment* phase, a person is registered by memorizing an arbitrary number (typically twenty) of photos into the system and by recording his/her voice. The system searches for face-like silhouettes in the stored photos: if a photo does not contain a face, the system responds with a rejection of that photo, thus the user has to send another picture of his/her face. The sound quality is verified too: if there is noise in the background, the user is required to resend another clearer voice recording. For security matters, a person is required to insert a secret password just in case that the first two barriers will be broken by an impostor. At the end of this procedure, the person will result enrolled and can be recognized correctly during the identification phase.

(2) The second phase, or the *identification* phase, requires for a person to stand in front of the camera in order to capture a face picture. If the picture matches with one of the set of photos in the system memory, then the user is prompted to speak to an appropriate microphone; when this is completed, the system checks whether the audio recorded corresponds to the same person's voice whose audio lies in the systems. If these two verification steps lead to a positive result then the person is allowed to enter the house classifying the person as a *member*; otherwise if one of these two steps does not end leading to a "true result", then the person is required to provide his/her secret password memorized at enrollment time. If the password provided is wrong, then the person is refused to enter the house and is classified as an *intruder*.

The face recognition task could have relied on a vast variety of methods, including the popular Local Binary Pattern (LBP) with its variations ([1,11]).

In the same way, voice recognition could have been implemented as suggested in
[7] where feature extraction relies on an algorithm based on Mel Frequency Cepstral Coefficients (MFCC), widely exploited for voice processing, while Dynamic
Time Warping(DTW) is used to measure the similarity between two time series
which may vary in time or speed. Starting from the wheel when building an
application is nowadays substituted by the massive use of library functions made
available in many contexts. As for image processing, it is sufficient mentioning
OpenCV [6]. The functions provided can be integrated seamlessly within one
owns' code. The next step is to rely on complete frameworks, where functions
are executed by a completely detached module according to a black-box model,
where only interfaces or API are exposed. When the detached module is a remote
one, it is possible to consider this at large as an example of programming by
services or cloud computing. The advantage is the ready availability of a rich
set of pre-coded functions, which are possibly updated and optimized in a way
transparent to the final user (in this case, the programmer of an application).
Given that APIs stay unchanged, the algorithms and their implementations may
change without affecting the existing software.

Along the preceding line, *Smart Peephole* was implemented by choosing
suited API procedure calls from Microsoft Cognitive Services (MCS). Such services are part of Microsoft Azure[1] [9], a collection of cloud computing integrated
services that can be used by developers to create, deploy, and manage applications across a network. Azure can be distributed by connecting the cloud environment and the local environment through consistent hybrid cloud capabilities
and using open source technologies to achieve maximum portability. While it
was born as a solution for enterprise settings [10], it can also be used on a
smaller scale for consumer applications like the one presented here. API method
calls were really efficient and demonstrated a high responsiveness during the
testing phase, thus leading us to exploit them to build *Smart Peephole*. In particular, the application exploits MCS Faces API, which identifies and recognizes
faces, Speech Recognition API, which recognizes voice, and an additional module that interfaces with Emotion API. The last mentioned module was added
to interact with the person standing at the doorstep in a "more human way".
This is obtained by catching up with the person's mood and deciding whether
it is worth to improve it if his/her emotions are negative (anger, sadness, fear,
disgust, contempt), or to favor it if his/her emotions are positive (happiness,
neutral, surprise). All of the core biometric functions planned for the application now are reduced only to API function calls that execute on highly efficient
machines requiring a minimal temporal cost. In fact, the temporal costs are
mostly reduced to the transmission of the algorithmic request to the server and
the arrival of the response: an error code or the answer related to request. The
reverse of the medal for this service (in practice Biometrics As A Service) is the
cost due for full functionality and storage capacity. However, this is often the
case for commercial cloud-distributed resources. Moreover, given the commercial

---

[1] https://azure.microsoft.com/it-it/.

nature of the services, the algorithmic details are not available. In any case, they are out of the scope of this work.

2.2 Microsoft Cognitive Services

Microsoft Cognitive Services work across devices and platforms such as iOS, Android and Windows, keep improving and are easy to set up. The framework contains a lot of APIs to facilitate programmers dealing with difficult problems by exploiting remote calls in a remote access machine. The APIs used for the implementation of *Smart Peephole* are: Face API, Speech Recognition API and Emotion API which we describe in the following.

Face API - The Face API has two main functions: face detection with attributes and face recognition. The first function detects up to 64 human faces in the same image with high precision location. The input can be specified by a file name or by a valid URL. The face rectangle (left, top, width and height) indicating the face location in the image is returned along with each detected face. Optionally, the face detection function extracts a series of face related characteristics such as pose, gender, age, head position, facial hair and glasses. Four face recognition functions are provided: face verification, finding similar faces, face grouping, and person identification. At present *Smart Peephole* exploits the Face Identification function. It can be used to match a probe subject against a people database (a *person group*) which must be created in advance and can be edited over time. Each group may contain up to one thousand person objects. Each person can have one or more faces registered. Later on, identification can be carried out against the created *person group*. If the probe face is identified as a person object in the group, the person object with be returned.

Speech Recognition API - A voice has unique characteristics that can be used to identify a person, just as in the case of a fingerprint. Using voice for access control and authentication scenarios has emerged as a tool that can be used to offer a level up in security, that also simplifies the authentication experience for customers. MCS offer Speaker Recognition following two modalities: speaker verification and speaker identification. *Smart Peephole* only exploits the Speaker Verification API. It can be used to automatically verify and authenticate users using their voice or speech. The implemented approach is text dependent, i.e. the user is asked to pronounce a predetermined text. The Speaker Verification is divided into two submodules as follows:

(1) Enrollment - each enrolling speaker has to choose a specific pass phrase to use during both enrollment and verification phases. Thus, the speaker's voice is recorded saying a specific phrase, then a number of features are extracted that will be used to recognize the subject to match by the chosen phrase. The extracted voice features for the chosen phrase form a unique signature.

(2) Verification - an input spoken phrase is compared against an enrollment voice signature and phrase in order to verify whether or not they are from the same person, and if this person is saying the correct phrase. In *Smart Peephole*

voice and text verification is used in cascade after face identification, so that only the template of the identified person is verified by speech.

Emotion API - The Emotion API takes a facial expression in an image as an input, and returns the confidence across a set of emotions for each face in the image, as well as bounding boxes for such faces, using the Face API. If the application has already called the Face API, it can submit the face rectangle as an optional input. The emotions detected are the following: anger, contempt, disgust, fear, happiness, neutral, sadness, surprise.

The emotions are understood to be cross-culturally and universally communicated with particular facial expressions, even if with a different level of sharpness. The Emotion API uses world class machine learning techniques to provide the results. In interpreting them, the emotion detected should be interpreted as the one with the highest normalized score. Users may choose to set a higher confidence threshold within their application depending on their needs. The Emotion API works also with videos. However, this functionality is out of the scope of *Smart Peephole* and consequently of this paper.

3 Architecture of *Smart Peephole*

The `Peephole Module` is the core of the proposed application, which interacts with every other module, exploiting their features to the maximum extent in order to achieve system requirements. Among its functions, it is worth mentioning movement detection, from which a recognition action is triggered. The module uses Dense Optical Flow (DOPTFlow) based on Gunner Farnebäck's algorithm [4] that computes the optical flow for all the points in the frame. In this way, setting a threshold chosen empirically, it is possible to infer when a person is in front of the peephole. Optical flow is the pattern of apparent motion of image objects between two consecutive frames caused by the movement of objects or camera. It is a 2D vector field where each vector is a displacement vector showing the movement of points from the first frame to the second one. The optical flow is always calculated from the previous frame to the current one, making the algorithm resistant to the light changes during the day. Figure 1 shows an example of the movement caught by the vectors during the execution of the DOPTFlow algorithm. If the `Peephole Module` recognizes some movement, face detection is triggered, using the popular Viola-Jones algorithm [13] implemented in OpenCV. It is worth noticing that this task is carried out locally, in order to improve performance and avoid a bottleneck to the MCS Servers to compute face detection and most likely respond with a negative result. To improve the overall efficiency, if a face is detected, eyes are searched for. This helps decreasing false positives and executing a call to the API only if the system is confident enough to have retrieved a face-like contour.

The `Face Recognition Module` exploits the Face Identify function from MCS. It identifies unknown faces from a person group. For each face in the set of detected faces, it will compute similarities between the query face and all the faces in the enrolled person group, and will return candidate person(s) for

Fig. 1. An example of result from DOPTFlow algorithm.

face(s) ranked by similarity confidence. The algorithm allows more than one face to be identified independently at the same request, but no more than 10 faces. Identification works well for frontal faces and near-frontal faces, but, given the application context, this is not a true limitation. As a matter of fact, people that in front of a peephole do not maintain such pose are likely to be trying to avoid recognition, and therefore they could be automatically marked as *intruders*.

The **Speech Recognition Module** uses two main methods, Speech Enrollment and Speech Verification, whose functions rely on Verification Profile - Create Enrollment and Speaker Recognition - Verification APIs, respectively. The enrollment supported by Speaker Recognition - Create Enrollment API is text-dependent: the speaker needs to choose a specific phrase to use in both enrollment and verification. The list of possible phrases is found by making another API call to the function Verification Phrase - List All Supported Verification Phrases. The service requires at least three enrollment captures for each speaker before the profile can be used in verification scenarios. It is also recommended to use the same device in both enrollment and verification. The audio length should be at least 1 s and no longer than 15 s.

The Speaker Recognition - Verification has the same technical requirements for the audio file format and length. During verification, a *confidence* level is returned associated with the verification result. Usually, a *Low* or *Normal* confidence level could mean that the person is not speaking with the same timbre of voice or the device he/she is using to authenticate is not working properly.

In *Smart Peephole* application, the **Emotion Recognition Module** processes the face images resulting from the previous detection step. According to the response, the execution flow of the system could vary producing a different action for each different response code. At present, playing of a different song while entering the door is associated to each emotion. The main problem encountered during the implementation is the ambiguous way the humans show their emotion, according to the level of expression. For example, fear can be misunderstood with sadness, happiness with neutrality, anger with disgust and so on. Hence, sometimes the module might produce false positives. A related problem is that users may have to accentuate their facial expressions to allow recognizing the emotion flawlessly an unambiguously.

4   Experimental Results

This section presents experiments for two out of three modules: Face and Emotion Recognition.

4.1   Experiments on Face Recognition

For the face recognition module two different experiments were carried out in order to confront them with each other. The first one was based on a subset of the LFW (Labeled Faces in the Wild)[2] dataset [5] consisting of 55 persons (where 5 persons are genuine and the rest are considered as impostors) each of them with a single photo (of course the test photo of the genuine persons is different from the photos used to register them in the system). The second experiment dealt with testing the aforementioned module with high quality pictures coming from the same device. This last dataset, referred to as HD-MCS[3], includes 3 pictures of 15 different persons with 3 different head positions (straight, half-left and half-right). Two of these persons are considered as genuine users and, thus, are registered in the system. The others are used to estimate the expected threshold using False Acceptance (FAR) and False Rejection (FRR) curves.

Figure 2 shows The FRR/FAR plot for the subset of LFW. Equal Error Rate (EER) of 0.02 is achieved with a threshold of 0.61. It is worth noticing that the reduced LFW set includes problematic pairs of subjects, e.g., pictures of the Olsen twins (Mary Kate was considered as a genuine user and Ashley as an impostor).

Figure 3 shows an optimal EER of 0.0 achieved with a threshold of 0.5. It is possible to observe that the photo quality does not impact enormously on the setting of the recognition threshold (0.61 in the first experiment and 0.5 in this experiment) but the achieved accuracy does.

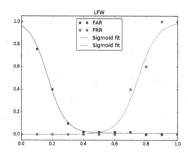

Fig. 2. Result for LFW subset.

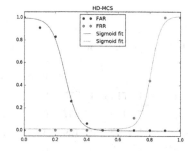

Fig. 3. Results for HD-MCS.

---

[2] http://vis-www.cs.umass.edu/lfw/#download.
[3] The pictures are taken with MacBook Pro 13 Retina 2016.

4.2   Experiments on Emotion Recognition

The Karolinska Directed Emotional Faces (KDEF)[4] [8] is a set of 4900 pictures of human facial expressions of emotion. The dataset was collected in 1998 at Karolinska Institutet, Department of Clinical Neuroscience, Section of Psychology, Stockholm, Sweden. Participants were 70 amateur actors, 35 females and 35 males, between 20 and 30 years of age. No beards, mustaches, earrings or eyeglasses, and preferably no visible makeup was allowed during photo session. Each subject reproduced 7 natural but strong and clear expressions: neutral, happy, angry, afraid, disgusted, sad, surprised. Face images were captured at 5 different angles: $-90, -45, 0, +45, +90$ degrees, i.e., full left profile, half-left profile, straight, half-right profile, full right profile, in two sessions.

The original KDEF dataset contains also images of full right and full left faces, however, because the proposed system only recognizes straight, half-left and half-right face positions, the original dataset was reduced to contain only straight, half-left/ right pictures. In this manner, the test dataset contains 140 photos for each of the 7 emotions (leaving out the contempt emotion). Contempt was not considered because it is not included in the set of the six basic emotions of anger, disgust, fear, sadness, happiness and surprise, but is rather considered a mix of anger and disgust [12]. The following Tables 1, 2, and 3 summarize the results of each orientation of face in the pictures, half-left, half-right and frontal, respectively, for the 7 emotions. The results reported on the tables are represented in percentages, where the columns represent the emotion detected by the system and the rows represent the true emotion of the face image. The last column of the table represents the percentage of photos rejected by the system. Tables 1 and 2 show that the number of possibly unclassified expressions is about the same in the two half profile poses. All tables show that Anger, Disgust and Fear are the most problematic expressions. Table 3 (frontal pose) also includes the results corresponding to the emotion of contempt. It was introduced because the system sometimes fails in recognizing contempt instead of anger or fear.

Table 1. Confusion matrix for emotion recognition in images were face is half-left.

	Anger	Disgust	Fear	Sadness	Happiness	Surprise	Neutral	Error
Anger	10.7143	4.2857	0	3.5714	0	0	81.4286	0
Disgust	7.1426	57.8571	0	16.4286	2.8571	0	14.2857	**1.4286**
Fear	1.4287	2.1429	3.5714	15	7.1429	36.4286	34.2857	0
Sadness	0	0	0	63.5714	1.4286	0	34.4286	0
Happiness	0	0	0	0	100	0	0	**0**
Surprise	0	0	0	0	0.7143	85	14.2857	0
Neutral	0	0	0	0	0	0	99.2857	**0.7143**

---

[4] http://www.emotionlab.se/resources/kdef.

Table 2. Confusion matrix for emotion recognition in images were face is half-right.

	Anger	Disgust	Fear	Sadness	Happiness	Surprise	Neutral	Error
Anger	17.1429	2.1429	0	0.7143	0.7143	0.7143	78.5714	0
Disgust	13.5714	53.5714	0	13.5714	2.1429	0	17.1429	0
Fear	1.4286	2.1429	2.8571	13.5714	4.2857	36.4286	39.2857	0
Sadness	0	0	0	51.4285	0.7142	0	47.8571	0
Happiness	0	0	0	0	99.2857	0	0.7143	0
Surprise	0	0	0	0	0.7143	78.5714	20	0
Neutral	0	0	0	0	0	0	99.2857	**0.71423**

Table 3. Confusion matrix for emotion recognition in images were face is frontal.

	Anger	Disgust	Contempt	Fear	Sadness	Happiness	Surprise	Neutral	Error
Anger	55	2.1429	2.8571	0.7143	2.8571	0	0.7143	35.7143	0
Disgust	7.8571	71.4286	0	0	14.2857	2.1429	0	4.2857	0
Fear	1.4286	0.7143	2.1429	17.142	20.7143	4.2857	42.8571	10.7143	0
Sadness	0	0	0	0	86.4286	0.7143	0.7143	12.1429	0
Happiness	0	0	0	0	0	100	0	0	0
Surprise	0	0	0	0	0	0.7143	95.7143	3.5714	0
Neutral	0	0	0	0	0	0	0	100	0

The fact that the emotion of anger is swapped by the contempt one is not surprising. On the other hand, confusing fear with contempt implies a critical error in the emotion detection system.

5 Conclusions

This paper has presented *Smart Peephole*, a biometrics security system based on cloud services (biometrics as a service), that has the capability to observe incoming subjects at the house doorstep. It plays the role of a classic door peephole taking decisions to open or not the door for a certain person. The system is composed of four main modules: Peephole module, Face detection module, Speech verification module, and Emotion detection module, that rely on APIs provided by Microsoft Cognitive Services. The tests carried out for this project highlight that the system has optimal capability of distinguishing enrolled persons from the so called intruders. Accuracy is optimal upon recognition of a frontal or near-frontal person picture, which is a normal situation given the kind of application. Regarding the future works, we would like to integrate *Smart Peephole* into an overall smart ambient project, to construct a smart environment system which increases the house awareness with respect to the habits of its inhabitants. This would imply the implementation of a smart algorithm that, upon recognizing a certain person, remembers the recognized person' s habits and manners around the house and tries, with respect to these habits, to make him/her feel as comfortable as possible, trying at the same time to diminish energy consumption.

References

1. Ahonen, T., Hadid, A., Pietikainen, M.: Face description with local binary patterns: application to face recognition. IEEE Trans. Pattern Anal. Mach. Intell. **28**(12), 2037–2041 (2006)
2. Jain, A.K., Ross, A., Prabhakar, S.: An introduction to biometric recognition. IEEE Trans. Circ. Syst. Video Technol. **14**(1), 4–20 (2004)
3. Clarke, R.: Human identification in information systems: management challenges and public policy issues. Inf. Technol. People **7**(4), 6–37 (1994)
4. Farnebäck, G.: Two-frame motion estimation based on polynomial expansion. In: Proceedings of the 13th Scandinavian Conference on Image Analysis (2003)
5. Huang, G.B., Ramesh, M., Berg, T., Learned-Miller, E.: Labeled faces in the wild: A database for studying face recognition in unconstrained environments. Technical Report 07–49, University of Massachusetts, Amherst (2007)
6. Kaehler, A., Bradski, G.: Learning OpenCV 3: Computer Vision in C++ with the OpenCV Library. O'Reilly Media Inc., Sebastopol (2016)
7. Muda, L., Begam, M., Elamvazuthi, I.: Voice recognition algorithms using Mel Frequency Cepstral Coefficient (MFCC) and Dynamic Time Warping (DTW) techniques. J. Comput. **2**(3) (2010)
8. Lundqvist, D., Flykt, A.,Ohman, A.: The karolinska directed emotional faces (KDEF). CD ROM from Department of Clinical Neuroscience, Psychology section, Karolinska Institutet (1998)
9. Microsoft: Truly consistent hybrid cloud with microsoft azure. Website (2017), https://azure.microsoft.com/mediahandler/les/resourceles/bf2fe090-ec7c-4463-92e7-92501d86dd28/Truly%20Consistent%20Hybrid%20Cloud%20with%20Microsoft%20Azure.pdf
10. Nickel, J.: Mastering Identity and Access Management with Microsoft Azure. Packt Publishing Ltd., Birmingham (2016)
11. Ojala, T., Pietikäinen, M., Mäenpää, T.: Multiresolution gray-scale and rotation invariant texture classification with local binary patterns. IEEE Trans. Pattern Anal. Mach. Intell. **24**(7), 971–987 (2002)
12. TenHouten, W.D.: A General Theory of Emotions and Social Life. Routledge, London (2006)
13. Viola, P., Jones, M.: Rapid object detection using a boosted cascade of simple features. In: Proceedings of IEEE Conference on Computer Vision and Pattern Recognition - CVPR 2001, pp. 511–518 (2001)
14. Stallings, W., Brown, L.: Computer Security: Principles and Practice, 3rd edn. Pearson Education, London (2015)

WhoAreYou (WAY): A Mobile CUDA Powered Picture ID Card Recognition System

Raffaele Montella, Alfredo Petrosino$^{(\boxtimes)}$, and Vincenzo Santopietro

Department of Science and Technology, University of Naples Parthenope,
Naples, Italy
petrosino@uniparthenope.it

Abstract. The paper reports a novel cloud based approach for image matching between high-resolution images of faces and low resolution images of ID Cards. We design our application matching the mobile cloud computing design guidelines with the use of CUDA kernel invocation from regular mobile devices (devices that naively don't support CUDA GPGPUs) as a novel contribution. Face matching is performed by the OpenFace deep neural network, which evaluates pre-processed images in cloud, whilst pre-processing is done on mobile device. To test our system, we built an image dataset of 30 subject caputeres in 10 different poses, denoised to reduce any traces of stamps or watermark on the ID cards, mixed to the well known ORL and LFW datasets.

Keywords: Cloud computing · Neural network · Deep learning
Face matching

1 Introduction

This paper proposes a cloud based solution to automatic face matching between low resolution photos on ID Cards and high-resolution face photos. This solution could be applied to every possible scenario where an identification is required. The are several aspects that may affect performances, that may be due to the person that is going to be identified, due to the documents or to the acquisition system, like hair-style changes, since the photo on ID Cards is shot way before the identification step (*aging*), stamps or watermarks on the ID Card and other aspects introduced by the acquisition system like the resolution of the device used to scan the ID Card. As instance, in Fig. 1, we can clearly see some of the aspects we discussed about, for example the poor conservation of the ID Card on the right that led to the erosion of the photo.

The contribution of the present paper is thus twofold. We design our application matching the mobile cloud computing design guidelines with the use of CUDA kernel invocation from regular mobile devices (devices that naively don't support CUDA GPGPUs) to allow fase detection be a service to provide to user who usually adopts mobile devices. Also, we describe a novel benchmarking framework that we set up in order to evaluate and compare face detection based

© Springer International Publishing AG 2017
S. Battiato et al. (Eds.): ICIAP 2017 International Workshops, LNCS 10590, pp. 375–382, 2017.
https://doi.org/10.1007/978-3-319-70742-6_35

Fig. 1. Two ID Cards obtained in different cities.

on matching for recognizing person identity by his/her face compared with ID Card. The results are devoted to assess to what extent typical aspects in face matching challenges pose troubles to common, like EigenFaces and LBPH, and novel, like deep neural OpenFace, methods.

The paper is organized in four sections. Section 2 describes the system, while Sect. 3 describes the algorithms adopted for benchmarking. Section 4 reports results and discusses some critical issues. Sections 5 draws some conclusions and future developments.

2   Design and Architecture

The capabilities of mobile devices have been improving very quickly in terms of computing power, storage, feature support, and developed applications [4]. We design our application matching the mobile cloud computing design guidelines with the use of CUDA kernel invocation from regular mobile devices (devices that naively don't support CUDA GPGPUs) as a novel contribution. To make it possible we use GVirtuS4j [9] a pure Java framework enabling Android devices to CUDA remote invocation calls using the GVirtuS Linux back-end [8]. The developer prototypes the kernels on a CUDA enabled regular x86_64 machine. Then the compiled kernels are embedded in the application project and invoked using GVirtuS4j. The actual GPU used by the mobile phone could be hosted on cloud or on premises: it works in both cases. Nevertheless for a real working ID Card face recognition application the scalability and the availability is one of the main design requirements. We used the Amazon Web Services because offering an advanced Infrastructure as a Service deployment, affordable GPGPU equipped virtual machine instances, a complete API for programmatical interaction with the cloud and, last but not the least, a good level of service uptime.

The Figure 2 represents system big picture.

When the application is deployed in the wild, the user scan the ID-Card picture using the WAY app. The app performs all the preparation steps using the CUDA kernels invoked remotely in order to extract the face features. Then a

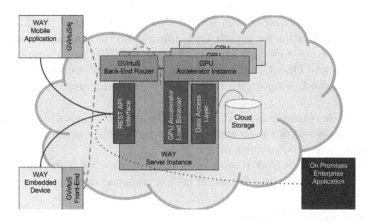

Fig. 2. The architectural schema of the Amazon Web Service deployment. Dotted lines represent GVirtuS CUDA remote invocations performed by mobile or embedded devices. Filled lines are regular REST requests/responses performed by client applications or remote enterprise infrastructures.

REST service is invoked for the main recognition step. The result is returned by the service. The both stages could be computationally intensive, battery eager, and privacy demanding. With the proposed system we overcome the three pits:

- Compute-intensive operations: the GVirtuS load balancer distributes CUDA remote kernel invocations on different GPGPU enabled instances in respect of computation load and costs;
- Battery-consuming task: the computation is offload tightly for CUDA invocation and loseley for feature recognition with the main target of energy usage drainage mitigation.
- Privacy-enforcing: there is no ID-Card picture related image transfer among the WAY app and the recognition engine: the app invokes the CUDA kernel remotely in order to extract the pattern's features. The app leverages on a remote REST web service to get data about the recognized picture.

GVirtuS (back-end) and GVirtuS4j (front-end) implement a split driver based virtualization and remoting. While other similar software components for GPGPU vitalization are strongly CUDA oriented, GVirtuS is completely plug-in based: both front-end/back-end and the communicator could be enhanced implementing new capabilities.

The GPU virtualization architecture is based on a split-driver model [3] (also known as driver paravirtualization), involves sharing a physical GPU. Hardware management is left to a privileged domain. A front-end driver runs in the unprivileged VM and forwards calls to the back-end driver in the privileged domain [5]. The back-end driver then takes care of sharing resources among virtual machines. This approach requires special drivers for the guest VM. The split driver model is currently the only GPU virtualization technique that effectively allows sharing the same GPU hardware between several VMs simultaneously [7]. This framework offers virtualization for generic GPU libraries on traditional x86 computers. At the current state, GVirtuS supports leading GPGPU programming models such as CUDA and OpenCL. It also enables platform independence from all the underlying involved technologies (i.e. hypervisor, communicator, and target of virtualization).

The GPU Accelerator Load Balancer component is responsible for GPGPU enabled instances metrics measurement and related policy enforcement in order to honour the expected performances.

The GVirtuS Back-End Router component ensure the coherence between GPGPU enabled clients and the cloud hosted back-end instances.

2.1 The Toolkit Libraries

In order to extend the set of CUDA functions supported by GvirtuS, it necessary to define three main components for each library that are responsible for the communication between the guest and host machine:

- Front-end Layer
- Back-end Layer
- Function Handler

The first one contains the definitions of the wrapper functions called by the client, with the same signature as the library ones, where the name of the requested routine and the addresses of the input parameters, variables and host/device pointers, are encapsulated in a buffer that is sent to the back-end through a communicator. For each CUDA toolkit library the back-end layer stores a function handler that declares, for each function of the toolkit library, a handler function used to execute the requested routine properly. Once the buffer is received by the back-end, the handler retrieves the input parameters, executes the requested routine and if needed sends a buffer containing the output variables and host/device pointers back to the client. With the described technique we implemented cuFFT, cuBLAS, cuRAND e cuDNN libraries we used for the algorithm implementation.

3   Face Matching

In this section we are going to describe the algorithms used and their performances, focusing on the approach based on deep learning.

3.1 Eigenfaces

Given an image of a face that has to be recognized, the algorithm [12] compares the input image with other images of known subjects. The most meaninfgul features are called eigenfaces, since they represent the eigenvectors of the features-space. We can recognize a face by comparing the sum of the eigenvectors of an unknown face and the sum of the eigevectors of a known face. This approach may fail often if the background is rich of details or the size of the face changes.

3.2 LBPH

Local Binary Patterns (LBP) [1] is a highly used operator in computer vision. This approach is robust when there are light changes, since it uses local features. LBP is based on a non-parametric operator defined as a binary string (descriptor of p), which given a pixel p in position (x, y), estimates the structure of the neighborhood of p. Let's consider a 3×3 window, as shown in Fig. 3, each bit of the string is 1 if the value of the pixel of the corresponding pixel in neighborhood is less than the central pixel. Furthermore, the LBP operator has been extended (Extended Local Binary Patterns) in order to handle windows of arbitrary size.

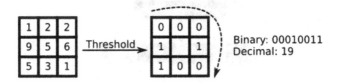

Fig. 3. LBP operator example

3.3 OpenFace

OpenFace [2] is a Python and Torch implementation of face recognition with deep neural networks [11]. OpenFace is based on the logic flow shown in Fig. 4 to compute low-dimensional representations for the faces in the image. The face detection procedure returns a list of bounding boxes, but there's the problem that a face could not be looking right into the camera. OpenFace handles this situations by applying a 2D affine transformation, which also crops the face so the image is 96×96 pixels. This image in then processed by the neural network estimates the normalized probability for each user of our database.

4 Evaluation

We have conducted four tests in order to evaluate the performances of the approaches mentioned before for face recognition between the photo extracted from the ID Card and a high-resolution photo. We used:

1. ID Card photos and high-resolution photos of 30 subjects (FRs)
2. ORL Database
3. LFW database

In order to create the dataset the first dataset used for performance evaluation, we used a 13 megapixels camera to take high-resolution images of faces and a Brother MFC 1910W to scan the ID Cards. High-resolution face photos have been taken at a distance of 150 cm in a closed environment with white background. We collected data from 30 subjects, whose age goes from 25 up to 45. These data can be arranged in three subsets:

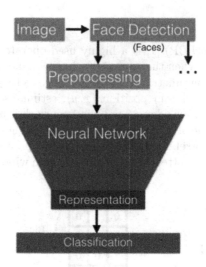

Fig. 4. Face recognition with Neural Networks, as shown in [2]

- **Face subset** (Fs), which contains high-resolution face images
- **ID Card Face subset** (IDCFs), which contains the photos on the scanned ID Cards
- **Face Recognition subset** (FRs), which contains the pre-processed images from the Fs and IDCFs.

The ORL [10] dataset of faces, now claimed AT&T "The Database of Faces", includes ten different images of each of 40 distinct subjects. For some subjects, the images were taken at different times, varying the lighting, facial expressions (open/closed eyes, smiling/not smiling) and facial details (glasses/no glasses). All the images were taken against a dark homogeneous background with the subjects in an upright, frontal position (with tolerance for some side movement).

Labeled Faces in the Wild [6] is a database of face photographs designed for studying the problem of unconstrained face recognition. The data set contains more than 13,000 images of faces collected from the web. Each face has been labeled with the name of the person pictured. 1680 of the people pictured have two or more distinct photos in the data set.

For each test we performed the training of the faces included in the FRs, a substet of identities from ORL and FLW databases. Then the face recognition procedure is executed over the face extracted from an ID Card. For each test we changed the number of identities that composes the training set, setting it to 10,25,50,100. Since we only have 30 identities that are linked to an ID Card, we performed 30 test of identification. We performed tests on a remote machine with an Intel Core i5-3320m CPU and a Nvidia Geforce 920m. Figure 5 show that the OpenFace solution is of course the most accurate.

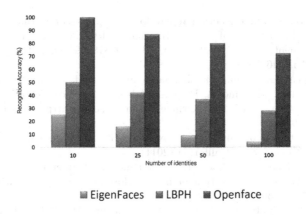

Fig. 5. Algorithms' accuracy

5   Conclusions and Future Works

The exponential growth of computer hardware performance is leading to faster matching. A system like WAY uses a video stream which is already being captured in most of the places in which security is important, like airports, banks etc. As future work we could use the proposed system with company badges too and not just with ID Cards, capturing employees entrance end exit times. This kind of application is not affected by aging and light changes, since the training photos of the employees can be updated regularly and the camera is set in the always in the same place.

Acknowledgement. This research has been funded by the European Commission under the Horizon 2020 program through Grant Agreement No 644312, corresponding to the "Heterogeneous Secure Multi-level Remote Acceleration Service for Low-Power Integrated Systems and Devices" (RAPID) project.

References

1. Ahonen, T., Hadid, A., Pietikainen, M.: Face description with local binary patterns: Application to face recognition. IEEE Trans. Pattern Anal. Mach. Intell. **28**(12), 2037–2041 (2006)
2. Amos, B., Ludwiczuk, B., Satyanarayanan, M.: Open-face: a general-purpose face recognition library with mobile applications. Technical report CMU-CS-16-118, CMU School of Computer Science (2016)
3. Armand, F., Gien, M.: A practical look at micro-kernels and virtual machine monitors. In: Proceedings of the 6th IEEE Conference on Consumer Communications and Networking Conference, CCNC 2009, pp. 395–401. IEEE Press, Las Vegas (2009). ISBN:978-1-4244-2308-8, http://dl.acm.org/citation.cfm?id=1700527.1700644
4. Bahl, P., et al.: Advancing the state of mobile cloud computing. In: Proceedings of the Third ACM Workshop on Mobile Cloud Computing and Services, pp. 21–28. ACM (2012)

5. Dunlap, G.W., et al.: Execution replay for multiprocessor virtual machines. In: VEE 2008 - Proceedings of the 4th International Conference on Virtual Execution Environments, pp. 121–130 (2008). ISBN: 9781595937964. https://doi.org/10.1145/1346256.1346273

6. Learned-Miller, E., et al.: Labeled faces in the wild: a survey. In: Kawulok, M., Emre Celebi, M., Smolka, B. (eds.) Advances in Face Detection and Facial Image Analysis, pp. 189–248. Springer, Cham (2016). https://doi.org/10.1007/978-3-319-25958-1_8

7. Li, W.: GPU-based computation of Voxelized Minkowski Sums with Applications. PhD thesis. University of California (2011)

8. Montella, R., Giunta, G., Laccetti, G.: Virtualizing high-end GPGPUs on ARM clusters for the next generation of high performance cloud computing. Cluster Comput. 17(1), 139–152 (2014)

9. Montella, R., Giunta, G., Laccetti, G., Lapegna, M., Palmieri, C., Ferraro, C., Pelliccia, V.: Virtualizing CUDA enabled GPGPUs on ARM clusters. In: Wyrzykowski, R., Deelman, E., Dongarra, J., Karczewski, K., Kitowski, J., Wiatr, K. (eds.) PPAM 2015. LNCS, vol. 9574, pp. 3–14. Springer, Cham (2016). https://doi.org/10.1007/978-3-319-32152-3_1

10. Samaria, F.S., Harter, A.C.: Parameterisation of a stochastic model for human face identication. In: Proceedings of 1994 IEEE Workshop on Applications of Computer Vision, pp. 138–142 (1994). https://doi.org/10.1109/ACV.1994.341300

11. Schro, F., Kalenichenko, D., Philbin, J.: FaceNet: a unied embedding for face recognition and clustering. In: The IEEE Conference on Computer Vision and Pattern Recognition (CVPR) (2015)

12. Turk, M., Pentland, A.: Eigenfaces for Recognition. J. Cognit. Neurosci. 3(1), 71–86 (1991). ISSN: 0898–929X

Multimedia Assisted Dietary Management (MADiMa)

Personalized Dietary Self-Management Using Mobile Vision-Based Assistance

Georg Waltner[1]([✉]), Michael Schwarz[2], Stefan Ladstätter[2], Anna Weber[2],
Patrick Luley[2], Meinrad Lindschinger[3], Irene Schmid[3], Walter Scheitz[4],
Horst Bischof[1], and Lucas Paletta[2]

[1] Graz University of Technology, Graz, Austria
waltner@icg.tugraz.at
[2] Joanneum Research Forschungsgesellschaft mbH, Graz, Austria
[3] Institute for Nutritional and Metabolic Diseases, Lassnitzhöhe, Austria
[4] FH Joanneum University of Applied Sciences, Graz, Austria

Abstract. Daily appropriate decision making on nutrition requires application of knowledge where it matters, and being adjusted to the individual requirements. We present a highly personalized mobile application that assists the user in appropriate food choices during grocery shopping, while simultaneously incorporating a personalized dietary recommender system. The application can be used in video based augmented reality mode, where a computer vision algorithm recognizes presented food items and thus replaces tedious search within the food database. The recognition system employs a shallow Convolutional Neural Network (CNN) based classifier running at 10 fps. An innovative user study demonstrates the high usability and user experience of the application. The vision classifier is evaluated on a newly introduced reference image database containing 81 grocery foods (vegetables, fruits).

1 Introduction

Today's population lives in a fast-paced society with challenging work environments, a multitude of free time activities available and increasingly less knowledge about food origins and nutritional value. Intelligent dietary self-management systems can save time, improve personal nutrition and such lead to a healthier living and decreased stress. In recent programs like the *Food Scanner Prize* of the European Commission (EC), institutions and authorities expend much effort into developing systems that reduce food-related problems.

Such systems should comply with four general demands. First, it should be a portable solution packed into a small mobile device. Second, it must be simple to use without prior knowledge in nutrition concerns and with basic computer skills. Third, the applied system should work fast and reliable. Finally, it should be able to provide valuable feedback to users regarding their health and lifestyle, resulting in better decision making.

We propose a system that aims to comprise all requirements and is intended to be used by nutrition-aware persons. Our system is developed as a portable,

© Springer International Publishing AG 2017
S. Battiato et al. (Eds.): ICIAP 2017 International Workshops, LNCS 10590, pp. 385–393, 2017.
https://doi.org/10.1007/978-3-319-70742-6_36

easy to use system running on a smart phone. It enables situated dietary information assistance and simplifies food choices with the aim to improve the user's overall health and well-being. Our proposed system has two core components (Fig. 1). First, we have implemented a mobile application that integrates personalized dietary concerns into a recommendation system used during grocery shopping. This diet has been developed by medical experts in the field of nutrition and metabolism [18]. The user can take a survey for a customized grocery basket and additionally enter information about her personal condition, which is used for calculating personal energy expenditure. Second, we have developed a fast lightweight computer vision component that enables the user to retrieve information from the food database by pointing the device to grocery items for automatic recognition, instead of tediously entering information by hand. The image recognition system runs with high accuracy on a big set of different grocery food classes. It facilitates information retrieval, providing added benefit to the user.

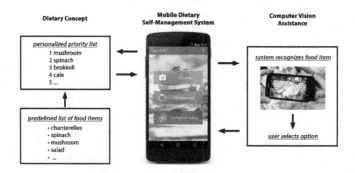

Fig. 1. System overview. The dietary self-management system consists of two core elements: a personalized list of recommended groceries and computer vision based assistance for information retrieval.

2   Related Work

Dietary Mobile Applications. Mobile health and wellness is a rapidly expanding market, with daily emergence of innovative dietary management apps. For example, *LoseIt*[1] aids the user in loosing weight by setting daily calorie limits and monitoring food intake. It also features a recognition system which is coupled to a database of dishes where the user must select the appropriate one. In contrast, our system is designed to aid already during the food selection process in grocery stores and targets a more general audience that wants to better its eating behaviour. *ShopWell*[2] rates scanned foods and provides appropriate recommendations according to a personalized profile. The scanning works

---

[1] https://www.loseit.com.
[2] http://www.shopwell.com.

for barcodes only, which is also available in our application besides automated video recognition. Several EC research programs fund the investigation of dietary management, such as, for the care of elderly. *CordonGris*[3] manages relevant data for a healthy diet recommendation, coming from different sources: activity sensors, food composition tables, retailers' or service providers' information. *HELICOPTER*[4] exploits ambient-assisted living techniques and provides older adults and their informal caregivers with support, motivation and guidance in pursuing a healthy and safe lifestyle, including decision making on nutrition in grocery shopping. *ChefMySelf*[5] is a customizable open and extensible eco-system built around an automatic cooking solution to support elderly in preparing healthy meals.

Food Recognition Systems. Most research in computer vision based methods targets the recognition of meals as well as extracting the components of plated food. First food recognition systems have already been introduced in the late 90s, "Veggie Vision" [2] eases the checkout process at supermarkets. The topic regained attention recently with published food datasets for comparison of methods, e.g., PFID [5], UNICT-FD889/1200 [7,8], Food-101 [3], UECFOOD-100/256 [14,21]. Until the recent rise of CNN based methods [13], that automatically learn optimal feature representations from thousands of images, researchers mostly combined handcrafted color and texture descriptors with SVM classifiers or other kernel methods. In [12], a CNN recognizes the 10 most frequent food items in the FoodLog [17] image collection and is able to distinguish food from non-food items. In [15,16] a CNN is finetuned on 1000 food related classes from the ImageNet database [6]. Recent wider [19] and deeper [11] CNNs boosted the results at the cost of high computational requirements. Compared to our method, that is running at 10 fps on standard smart phones, most afore-mentioned classification approaches are intractable to handle on mobile devices.

Dietary Self-Management Systems. Few available applications combine dietary mobile systems with automated food recognition. In [20], a mobile recipe recommender recognizes ingredients and retrieves recipes online. A mobile application proposed in [1] supports type 1 diabetes patients in counting carbohydrates and provides insulin dose advice. "Snap-n-Eat" [27] identifies food and portion size for calorie count estimation by incorporating contextual features (restaurant locations, user profiles). None of the above aids the user as early as in the food selection stage, but only when meals are already prepared. Some also rely on an internet connection while our system is entirely running on device. Compared to [26], this work uses a lightweight CNN instead of a Random Forest classifier which allows to recognize more than double the classes. Personalization has also been lifted to a new level, comprising personalized energy expenditure

---

[3] http://cordongris.eu.

[4] http://www.aal-europe.eu/projects/helicopter.

[5] http://www.chefmyself.eu.

calculation and target weight advice. Usability is evaluated via an innovative user study.

3   Personalized Dietary Self-Management System

The proposed system enables dietary self-management on a mobile device. It includes integrated nutrition assistance based on an augmented reality recommender component. This recommender assistant provides an intuitive interface and is supported by video based food recognition. A user specific profile is assessed by a dietary questionnaire on first use. Afterwards, upon selection of food items, either from automated video recognition or from manual user selection, tailored nutritional advice is given to the user depending on her profile.

3.1   Dietary Concept for Self-Management

The dietary concept behind the recommender system is based on a personalized dietary concept with the idea of removing stringent rules (e.g. calorie counting, physical activity demands). Instead of forcing the patient to give up all possibly bad eating habits at once, the diet slowly changes nutrition habits to lose (gain) weight. Considering that every person has its own requirements concerning nutrition and every fruit or vegetable has its own composition of micronutrients, a correct food combination is indispensable to fulfill one's individual demand of essential nutrients. The utilized diet incorporates this by defining several groups according to lifestyle, job, age, gender and the intensity of personal exercise. The groups are connected to different stress types and include nutrition recommendations, upon individual baskets of commodities that are composed based on investigation of a large medical dataset of 17,000 entries in [18]. Our mobile application incorporates these baskets and provides situated feedback on the user's food choices during grocery shopping, where decision making for mid and long-term lasting food choice is actually taking place. This aims at a lasting change in eating behaviour for increased mental and physical performance according to the *functional eating diet* [26]. The app automatically classifies presented food and upon commodity selection the user gets recommendations triggered by her individual profile and is presented detailed nutrition information. This includes micronutrients with corresponding health claims as well as further food recommendations matching the user profile.

3.2   Personalization

Personalization of the self-management system is based on two main factors. First, the assignment of the user to a certain nutrition group (see [26]) and, second, customized energy expenditure calculation. The questionnaire for user to group assignment consists of multiple rating scale questions from whom the user type can be calculated, e.g. "Do you often feel stressed?" with possible answers between "1, not at all" to "4, very often". We will now describe how the personalized energy expenditure is calculated, as it is influenced by the height, age, body type and physical activity level (PAL) of a person.

To account for different body types (slim, normal, muscular) and gender differences, the body structure of a person is incorporated through a weighting term δ, that ranges from 0.945 (slim) to 1.055 (muscular) for men and 0.900 to 1.000 for women respectively. A personalized target weight w_p is calculated by multiplication of the body weight w with δ: $w_p = w * \delta$. The energy demand E as defined by [10] is adopted to the newly calculated weight with $E^{\male} = 66.473 + (5.003 * l * 100) + (13.752 * w_p) - (6.755 * \alpha)$ for men and $E^{\female} = 655.096 + (1.85 * l * 100) + (9.563 * w_p) - (4.676 * \alpha)$ for women, where l is the height and α is the age of the person. Finally, PAL are considered through a factor γ_{PAL}. They reflect the energy demand in dependence of physical activity and are such very suitable for personalized energy expenditure calculation. PAL factors range from $\gamma_{PAL} = 1.2$ for elderly people without any physical activity to $\gamma_{PAL} = 3.3$ for construction workers spending 20+ hours on sport. The final personalized daily energy expenditure is calculated as $E_p = E * \gamma_{PAL}$.

3.3 Mobile Recognition System

We improve the usability of the recommender system and automatically classify food items with Convolutional Neural Networks (CNN). The user taps on an item, confirms the classification result and is displayed the desired information instead of cumbersome manual search. Our motivation is to get a fast, scalable classifier and we implement a shallow CNN network, running within our Android based mobile application at 10 fps. We design our CNN to have minimum complexity while performing at good accuracy.

4 Experimental Results

We evaluate our system with respect to usability through a user study and measure the performance of the recognition system on a novel grocery database.

4.1 Usability

For the purpose of user-centered optimisation of the novel computer vision based interface design, an innovative interaction and usability analysis was performed with 16 persons, $M = 26.3$ years of age. We used eye tracking to evaluate the automated nutrition information feedback interface component and evaluated the user experience in the frame of using the complete app. Eye tracking as a method to evaluate novel interface designs has been established, for example, using fixation durations on objects in the user interface: depending on the context, high numbers of fixations indicate less efficient search strategies, long fixation durations indicate difficulties of the user with the perception of the display [9]. Test persons were equipped with SMI^{TM} eye tracking glasses, the viewing behavior was video captured, and fixations on the display were localised

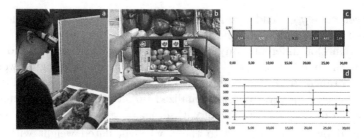

Fig. 2. Innovative interaction and usability analysis: (a) mobile eye tracking glasses (b) automated gaze localisation and analysis of seven stages of interaction from (c) stage duration and (d) corresponding fixation analysis.

[23]. From the investigation of the *Seven Stages of (Inter-)Action* [22] and corresponding fixation analysis interaction design was updated and optimised towards a SUS usability score [4] of 80% and user experience evaluation (UEQ [25]) of 72% ($\pm$5%, 90% confidence interval; [24]) which represent high scores considering the early stage of development. See Fig. 2 for illustrations.

4.2   Recognition System

We evaluate our method on a newly recorded dataset, which we term *FruitVeg-81*[6]. The database contains 15630 images of 81 raw fruit and vegetable classes. The proposed CNN processes images with a size of 56×56 pixels and consists of three convolutional layers: the first two are of size $5 \times 5 \times 32$, the third layer is $5 \times 5 \times 64$. We apply pooling with size 3 and stride 2 after each layer. After the third convolutional layer we add a 1024-dimensional fully connected layer with dropout and a soft-max classification layer with 81 units for food classification and 82 units when integrating a garbage class. We subtract the training set mean and train the network in minibatches of size 128, the training set is shuffled in the beginning of the training procedure. As it is unlikely to reach 100% accuracy in practical use, we give the users several choices for selecting the correct food item and reflect this in our experiments by reporting the *top*-1 to *top*-5.

Baseline. As Baseline, we evaluate all models on the 81 classes using leave-one-out cross-validation. We augment the training data with mirroring, cropping, rotating and color shifting. During test time we use mirroring and random crops.

Non-food Class. For our real-world application it is important to reduce false positives, e.g. on food items missing in the visual database. When the application recognizes non food items, appropriate feedback is displayed on the screen. We

---

[6] https://www.tugraz.at/institute/icg/research/team-bischof/lrs/downloads/fruitveg81/.

extract around 200 random images from 500 non-food categories of the ImageNet Challenge [6] and use those to add another category to the CNN. Due to the high variance within this non-food class, we choose the amount of images for training to be 10 times the average number of images per food category. For testing, we use the average number of per class test images.

Results are listed in Table 1, it can be seen that the image quality of the mobile phones differs. On average a top-5 accuracy of around 90% shows the good performance of the trained network. As we add one more class to the system the accuracy decreases, however the resulting decrease of the *top*-1 mean accuracy is stronger than expected. This is presumably due to the very heterogeneous structure and different domain of the non-food samples, which is hard to model with the limited number of parameters. On the other hand the *top*-5 accuracy is stable, which is a desired behavior for our application.

Table 1. Results for baseline and integration of a non-food class. The mean *top-k* accuracy ranges from 69.77% to 90.19% for the baseline and from 60.47% to 90.41% for non-food integration (best *top*-1 accuracy is 76.14% and 71.74%). With non-food integration the *top*-1 mean accuracy drops by roughly 9%, while the *top*-5 mean accuracy remains the same.

Model	Baseline					Non-food				
	Top-1	Top-2	Top-3	Top-4	Top-5	Top-1	Top-2	Top-3	Top-4	Top-5
Samsung Galaxy S3	72.99	84.34	88.93	92.27	94.58	64.45	80.72	87.55	91.15	93.39
Samsung Galaxy S5	76.14	86.66	90.82	92.46	93.82	71.74	84.30	89.11	92.69	94.52
HTC	71.99	84.06	87.86	89.77	91.03	60.17	77.89	84.49	89.00	91.77
HTC One	65.28	76.95	82.84	85.65	88.40	52.30	71.32	80.41	85.50	88.14
Motorola G	62.43	73.72	78.22	81.00	82.94	53.70	68.54	75.17	79.98	84.21
Avg	69.77	81.15	85.72	88.23	90.16	60.47	76.53	83.35	87.66	90.41

5 Conclusion

We have presented a innovative mobile application with a recommender engine and a fast recognition system running at 10 fps as core elements. The recommender engine supports users in decision making during grocery shopping and helps to improve health conditions backed on scientific findings. The recognition system is robustly recognizing food and non-food items. Along with this publication we make our grocery dataset *FruitVeg-81* available for the public, with the intention to be used by scientific researchers around the globe for improvement of their nutrition related computer systems.

Acknowledgments. This work was supported by the Austrian Research Promotion Agency (FFG) under the project MANGO (Mobile Augmented Reality for Nutrition Guidance and Food Awareness), No. 836488.

References

1. Anthimopoulos, M., Dehais, J., Diem, P., Mougiakakou, S.: Segmentation and recognition of multi-food meal images for carbohydrate counting. In: Proceedings of the BIBE, pp. 1–4 (2013)
2. Bolle, R.M., Connell, J.H., Haas, N., Mohan, R., Taubin, G.: VeggieVision: a produce recognition system. In: Proceedings of the IEEE Winter Conference on Applications of Computer Vision, pp. 244–251 (1996)
3. Bossard, L., Guillaumin, M., Van Gool, L.: Food-101 - mining discriminative components with random forests. In: Proceedings of the ECCV, pp. 446–461 (2014)
4. Brooke, J.: SUS-A quick and dirty usability scale. Usability Eval. Ind. **189**(194), 4–7 (1996)
5. Chen, M., Dhingra, K., Wu, W., Yang, L., Sukthankar, R., Yang, J.: PFID: Pittsburgh fast-food image dataset. In: Proceedings of the ICIP, pp. 289–292 (2009)
6. Deng, J., Dong, W., Socher, R., Li, L.J., Li, K., Fei-Fei, L.: ImageNet: a large-scale hierarchical image database. In: Proceedings of the CVPR (2009)
7. Farinella, G.M., Allegra, D., Stanco, F.: A Benchmark dataset to study the representation of food images. In: Agapito, L., Bronstein, M.M., Rother, C. (eds.) ECCV 2014. LNCS, vol. 8927, pp. 584–599. Springer, Cham (2015). https://doi.org/10.1007/978-3-319-16199-0_41
8. Farinella, G.M., Moltisanti, M., Battiato, S.: Classifying food images represented as bag of textons. Comput. Biol. Med. **77(C)**, 23–39 (2016)
9. Goldberg, J.H., Kotval, X.P.: Computer interface evaluation using eye movements: methods and constructs. Int. J. Ind. Ergon. **24**(6), 631–645 (1999)
10. Harris, J.A., Benedict, F.G.: A biometric study of human basal metabolism. PNAS **4**(12), 370–373 (1918)
11. Hassannejad, H., Matrella, G., Ciampolini, P., De Munari, I., Mordonini, M., Cagnoni, S.: Food image recognition using very deep convolutional networks. In: Proceedings of the MADiMa, pp. 41–49 (2016)
12. Kagaya, H., Aizawa, K., Ogawa, M.: Food detection and recognition using convolutional neural network. In: Proceedings of the ACM MM, pp. 1085–1088 (2014)
13. Karpathy, A., Toderici, G., Shetty, S., Leung, T., Sukthankar, R., Fei-Fei, L.: Large-scale video classification with convolutional neural networks. In: Proceedings of the CVPR, pp. 1725–1732 (2014)
14. Kawano, Y., Yanai, K.: Automatic expansion of a food image dataset leveraging existing categories with domain adaptation. In: Agapito, L., Bronstein, M.M., Rother, C. (eds.) ECCV 2014. LNCS, vol. 8927, pp. 3–17. Springer, Cham (2015). https://doi.org/10.1007/978-3-319-16199-0_1
15. Kawano, Y., Yanai, K.: Food image recognition using deep convolutional features pre-trained with food-related categories. In: Proceedings of the MBDA Workshop (2014)
16. Kawano, Y., Yanai, K.: Food image recognition with deep convolutional features. In: Proceedings of the UbiComp Adjunct, pp. 589–593 (2014)
17. Kitamura, K., Yamasaki, T., Aizawa, K.: Food log by analyzing food images. In: Proceedings of the ICM, pp. 999–1000. ACM (2008)
18. Lindschinger, M., Nadlinger, K., Adelwöhrer, N., Holweg, K., Wögerbauer, M., Birkmayer, J., Smolle, K.H., Wonisch, W.: Oxidative stress: potential of distinct peroxide determination systems. Clin. Chem. Lab. Med. **42**(8), 907–914 (2004)
19. Martinel, N., Foresti, G.L., Micheloni, C.: Wide-Slice Residual Networks for Food Recognition, arXiv preprint arXiv:1612.06543 (2016)

20. Maruyama, T., Kawano, Y., Yanai, K.: Real-time mobile recipe recommendation system using food ingredient recognition. In: Proceedings of the IMMPD, pp. 27–34 (2012)
21. Matsuda, Y., Hoashi, H., Yanai, K.: Recognition Of multiple-food images by detecting candidate regions. In: Proceedings of the IEEE International Conference on Multimedia and Expo, pp. 25–30 (2012)
22. Norman, D.A., Draper, S.W.: User Centered System Design: New Perspectives on Human-Computer Interaction. L. Erlbaum Associates Inc., Hillsdale, NJ 3 (1986)
23. Paletta, L., Neuschmied, H., Schwarz, M., Lodron, G., Pszeida, M., Ladstätter, S., Luley, P.: Smartphone eye tracking toolbox: accurate gaze recovery on mobile displays. In: Proceeding of the Symposium on Eye Tracking Research and Applications, pp. 367–368. ACM (2014)
24. Rexeis, V.: Usability Benchmark und Aktivitäts-Analyse mit Eye Tracking von Mobile Augmented Reality unterstützten Ernährungsempfehlungen. Master's thesis, Graz University of Technology (2015)
25. Schrepp, M., Olschner, S., Schubert, U.: User Experience Questionnaire Benchmark: Praxiserfahrungen zum Einsatz im Business-Umfeld (2013)
26. Waltner, G., Schwarz, M., Ladstätter, S., Weber, A., Luley, P., Bischof, H., Lindschinger, M., Schmid, I., Paletta, L.: MANGO - mobile augmented reality with functional eating guidance and food awareness. In: Murino, V., Puppo, E., Sona, D., Cristani, M., Sansone, C. (eds.) ICIAP 2015. LNCS, vol. 9281, pp. 425–432. Springer, Cham (2015). https://doi.org/10.1007/978-3-319-23222-5_52
27. Zhang, W., Yu, Q., Siddiquie, B., Divakaran, A., Sawhney, H.: Snap-n-Eat: food recognition and nutrition estimation on a smartphone. JDST **9**(3), 525–533 (2015)

Food Ingredients Recognition Through Multi-label Learning

Marc Bolaños[1,2(✉)], Aina Ferrà[1], and Petia Radeva[1,2]

[1] Universitat de Barcelona, Barcelona, Spain
{marc.bolanos,aferrama10.alumnes,petia.ivanova}@ub.edu
[2] Computer Vision Center, Bellaterra, Spain

Abstract. Automatically constructing a food diary that tracks the ingredients consumed can help people follow a healthy diet. We tackle the problem of food ingredients recognition as a multi-label learning problem. We propose a method for adapting a highly performing state of the art CNN in order to act as a multi-label predictor for learning recipes in terms of their list of ingredients. We prove that our model is able to, given a picture, predict its list of ingredients, even if the recipe corresponding to the picture has never been seen by the model. We make public two new datasets suitable for this purpose. Furthermore, we prove that a model trained with a high variability of recipes and ingredients is able to generalize better on new data, and visualize how it specializes each of its neurons to different ingredients.

1 Introduction

People's awareness about their nutrition habits is increasing either because they suffer from some kind of food intolerance; they have mild or severe weight problems; or they are simply interested in keeping a healthy diet. This increasing awareness is also being reflected in the technological world. Several applications exist for manually keeping track of what we eat, but they rarely offer any automatic mechanism for easing the tracking of the nutrition habits [2]. Tools for automatic food and ingredient recognition could heavily alleviate the problem.

Since the reborn of Convolutional Neural Networks (CNNs), several works have been proposed to ease the creation of nutrition diaries. The most widely spread approach is food recognition [8]. These proposals allow to recognize the type of food present in an image and, consequently, could allow to approximately guess the ingredients contained and the overall nutritional composition. The main problem of these approaches is that no dataset covers the high amount of existent types of dishes worldwide (more than 8,000 according to Wikipedia).

On the other hand, a clear solution for this problem can be achieved if we formulate the task as an ingredients recognition problem instead [6]. Although tens of thousands of types of dishes exist, in fact they are composed of a much smaller number of ingredients, which at the same time define the nutritional composition of the food. If we formulate the problem from the ingredients recognition perspective, we must consider the difficulty of distinguishing the presence

S. Battiato et al. (Eds.): ICIAP 2017 International Workshops, LNCS 10590, pp. 394–402, 2017.
https://doi.org/10.1007/978-3-319-70742-6_37

of certain ingredients in cooked dishes. Their visual appearance can greatly vary from one dish to another (e.g. the appearance of the ingredient 'apple' in an 'apple pie', an 'apple juice' or a 'fresh apple'), and in some cases they can even be invisible at sight without the proper knowledge of the true composition of the dish. An additional benefit of approaching the problem from the ingredients recognition perspective is that, unlike in food recognition, it has the potential to predict valid outputs on data that has never been seen by the system.

In this paper, we explore the problem of food ingredients recognition from a multi-label perspective by proposing a model based on CNNs that allows to discover the ingredients present in an image even if they are not visible to the naked eye. We present two new datasets for tackling the problem and prove that our method is capable of generalizing to new data that has never been seen by the system. Our contributions are four-fold. (1) Propose a model for food ingredients recognition; (2) Prove that by using a varied dataset of images and their associated ingredients, the generalization capabilities of the model on never seen data can be greatly boosted; (3) Delve into the inner layers of the model for analysing the ingredients specialization of the neurons; and (4) Release two datasets for ingredients recognition.

This paper is organized as follows: in Sect. 2, we review the state of the art; in Sect. 3, explain our methodology; in Sect. 4, we present our proposed datasets, show and analyse the results of the experiments performed, as well as interpret the predictions; and in Sect. 5, we draw some conclusions.

2 Related Work

Food analysis. Several works have been published on applications related to automatic food analysis. Some of them proposed food detection models [1] in order to distinguish when there is food present in a given image. Others focused on developing food recognition algorithms, either using conventional hand-crafted features, or powerful deep learning models [8]. Others have applied food segmentation [11]; use multi-modal data (i.e. images and recipe texts) for recipe recognition [15]; tags from social networks for food characteristics perception [9]; food localization and recognition in the wild for egocentric vision analysis [3], etc.

Multi-Label learning. Multi-label learning [13] consists in predicting more than one output category for each input sample. Thus, the problem of food ingredients recognition can be treated as a multi-label learning problem. Several works [14] argued that, when working with CNNs, they have to be reformulated for dealing with multi-label learning problems. Some multi-label learning works have already been proposed for restaurant classification. So far, only one paper [6] has been proposed related to ingredients recognition. Their dataset, composed of 172 food types, was manually labelled considering visible ingredients only, which limits it to find 3 ingredients on average. Furthermore, they propose a double-output model for simultaneous food type recognition and multi-label ingredients recognition. Although, the use of the food type for optimizing the model limits

its capability of generalization only to seen recipes and food types. This fact becomes an important handicap in a real-world scenario when dealing with new recipes. As we demonstrate in Sects. 4.3 and 4.4, unlike [6], our model is able to: (1) recognize the ingredients appearing in unseen recipes (see Fig. 1b); (2) learn abstract representations of the ingredients directly from food appearance (see Fig. 2); and (3) infer invisible ingredients.

Interpreting learning through visualization. Applying visualization techniques is an important aspect in order to interpret what has been learned by our model. The authors in [17] have focused on proposing new ways of performing this visualization. At the same time, they have proven that CNNs have the ability to learn high level representations of the data and even hidden interrelated information, which can help us when dealing with ingredients that are apparently invisible in the image.

3   Methodology

Deep multi-ingredients recognition. Most of the top performing CNN architectures have been originally proposed and intended for the problem of object recognition. At the same time, they have been proven to be directly applicable to other related classification tasks and have served as powerful pre-trained models for achieving state of the art results. In our case, we compared either using the InceptionV3 [12] or the ResNet50 [7] as the basic architectures for our model. We pre-trained it on the data from the ILSVRC challenge [10] and modified the last layer for applying a multi-label classification over the N possible output ingredients. When dealing with classification problems, CNNs typically use the softmax activation in the last layer. The softmax function allows to obtain a probability distribution for the input sample x over all possible outputs and thus, predicts the most probable outcome, $\hat{y}_x = \arg\max_{y_i} P(y_i|x)$.

The softmax activation is usually combined with the categorical cross-entropy loss function L_c during model optimization, which penalizes the model when the optimal output value is far away from 1:

$$L_c = -\sum_x \log(P(\hat{y}_x|x)). \tag{1}$$

In our model, we are dealing with ingredients recognition in a multi-label framework. Therefore, the model must predict for each sample x a set of outputs represented as a binary vector $\hat{Y}_x = \{\hat{y}_x^1, ..., \hat{y}_x^N\}$, where N is the number of output labels and each $\hat{y}_x^i$ is either 1 or 0 depending if it is present or not in sample x. For this reason, instead of softmax, we use a sigmoid activation function:

$$P(y_i|x) = \frac{1}{1 - \exp^{-f(x)_i}} \tag{2}$$

which allows to have multiple highly activated outputs. For considering the binary representation of $\hat{Y}_x$, we chose the binary cross-entropy function L_b [5]:

$$L_b = -\sum_x \sum_i^N (\hat{y}_x^i \cdot log(P(y_i|x)) + (1 - \hat{y}_x^i) \cdot log(1 - P(y_i|x))) \qquad (3)$$

which during backpropagation rewards the model when the output values are close to the target vector $\hat{Y}_x$ (i.e. either close to 1 for positive labels or close to 0 for negative labels).

4   Results

In this section, we describe the two datasets proposed for the problem of food ingredients recognition. Later we describe our experimental setup and at the end, we present the final results obtained both for ingredients recognition on known classes as well as recognition results for generalization on samples never seen by the model.

4.1   Datasets

In this section we describe the datasets proposed for food ingredients recognition and the already public datasets used.

Food101 [4] is one of the most widely extended datasets for food recognition. It consists of 101,000 images equally divided in 101 food types.

Ingredients101[1] is a dataset for ingredients recognition that we constructed and make public in this article. It consists of the list of most common ingredients for each of the 101 types of food contained in the Food101 dataset, making a total of 446 unique ingredients (9 per recipe on average). The dataset was divided in training, validation and test splits making sure that the 101 food types were balanced. We make public the lists of ingredients together with the train/val/test split applied to the images from the Food101 dataset.

Recipes5k[2] is a dataset for ingredients recognition with 4,826 unique recipes composed of an image and the corresponding list of ingredients. It contains a total of 3,213 unique ingredients (10 per recipe on average). Each recipe is an alternative way to prepare one of the 101 food types in Food101. Hence, it captures at the same time the intra-class variability and inter-class similarity of cooking recipes. The nearly 50 alternative recipes belonging to each of the 101 classes were divided in train, val and test splits in a balanced way. We make also public this dataset together with the splits division. A problem when dealing with the 3,213 raw ingredients is that many of them are sub-classes (e.g. 'sliced tomato' or 'tomato sauce') of more general versions of themselves (e.g. 'tomato').

---

[1] http://www.ub.edu/cvub/ingredients101/.

[2] http://www.ub.edu/cvub/recipes5k/.

Thus, we propose a simplified version by applying a simple removal of overly-descriptive particles[3] (e.g. 'sliced' or 'sauce'), resulting in 1,013 ingredients used for additional evaluation (see Sect. 4.3).

We must note the difference between our proposed datasets and the one from [6]. While we consider any present ingredient in a recipe either visible or not, the work in [6] only labelled manually the visible ingredients in certain foods. Hence, a comparison between both works is infeasible.

4.2 Experimental Setup

Our model was implemented in Keras[4], using Theano as backend. Next, we detail the different configurations and tests performed. **Random prediction:** (baseline) a set of K labels are generated uniformly distributed among all possible outputs. K depends on the average number of labels per recipe in the corresponding dataset. **InceptionV3 + Ingredients101**: InceptionV3 model pre-trained on ImageNet and adapted for multi-label learning. **ResNet50 + Ingredients101**: ResNet50 model pre-trained on ImageNet and adapted for multi-label learning. **InceptionV3 + Recipes5k**: InceptionV3 model pre-trained on InceptionV3 + Ingredients101. **ResNet50 + Recipes5k**: ResNet50 model pre-trained on ResNet50 + Ingredients101.

4.3 Experimental Results

In Table 1, we show the ingredient recognition results on the Ingredients101 dataset. In Fig. 1a some qualitative results are shown. Both the numerical results and the qualitative examples prove the high performance of the models in most of the cases. Note that although a multi-label classification is being applied, considering that all the samples from a food class share the same set of ingredients, the model is indirectly learning the inherent food classes. Furthermore, looking at the results on the Recipes5k dataset in Table 2 (top), we can see that the very same model obtains reasonable results even considering that it was

Table 1. Ingredients recognition results obtained on the dataset Ingredients101. Prec stands for *Precision*, Rec for *Recall* and F_1 for F_1 *score*. All measures reported in %. The best test results are highlighted in boldface.

	Validation			Test		
	Prec	Rec	F_1	Prec	Rec	F_1
Random prediction	2.05	2.01	2.03	2.06	2.01	2.04
InceptionV3 + Ingredients101	80.86	72.12	76.24	83.51	**76.87**	80.06
ResNet50 + Ingredients101	84.80	67.62	75.24	**88.11**	73.45	**80.11**

---

[3] https://github.com/altosaar/food2vec.
[4] www.keras.io.

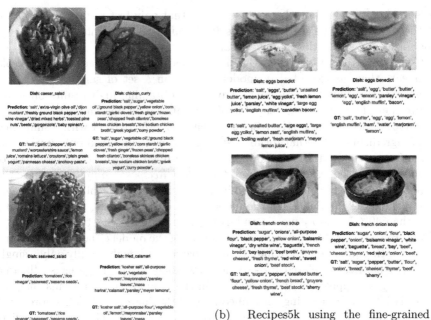

(a) Ingredients101 samples.

(b) Recipes5k using the fine-grained 3,213 ingredients (left), and using the 1,013 simplified ingredients (right).

Fig. 1. Our method's results. TPs in green, FPs in red and FNs in orange. (Color figure online)

Table 2. Ingredients recognition results on Recipes5k (top) and on Recipes5k simplified (bottom). Prec stands for *Precision*, Rec for *Recall* and F_1 for F_1 *score*. All measures reported in %. Best test results are highlighted in boldface.

	Validation			Test		
	Prec	Rec	F_1	Prec	Rec	F_1
Random prediction	0.33	0.32	0.33	0.54	0.53	0.53
InceptionV3 + Ingredients101				23.80	18.24	20.66
ResNet50 + Ingredients101				26.28	16.85	20.54
InceptionV3 + Recipes5k	36.18	20.69	26.32	35.47	**21.00**	**26.38**
ResNet50 + Recipes5k	38.41	19.67	26.02	**38.93**	19.57	26.05
Random prediction	6.27	6.29	6.28	6.14	6.24	6.19
InceptionV3 + Ingredients101				44.01	34.04	38.39
ResNet50 + Ingredients101				47.53	30.91	37.46
InceptionV3 + Recipes5k	56.77	31.40	40.44	55.37	31.52	40.18
ResNet50 + Recipes5k	56.73	28.07	37.56	**58.55**	28.49	38.33
InceptionV3 + Recipes5k simplified	53.91	42.13	47.30	53.43	**42.77**	**47.51**

not specifically trained on that dataset. Note that only test results are reported for the models trained on Ingredients101 because we only intend to show its generalization capabilities on new data.

Comparing the results with the models specifically trained on Recipes5k, it appears that, as expected, a model trained on a set of samples with high variability of output labels is more capable of obtaining high results on never seen recipes. Thus, it is more capable of generalizing on unseen data.

Table 2 (bottom) shows the results on the Recipes5k dataset with a simplified list of ingredients. Note that for all tests, the list was simplified only during the evaluation procedure for maintaining the fine-grained recognition capabilities of the model, with the exception of *Inception V3 + Recipes5k simplified*, where the simplified set was also used for training. The simplification of the ingredients list enhances the capabilities of the model when comparing the results, reaching more than 40% in the F_1 metric and 47.5% also training with them.

Figure 1b shows a comparison of the output of the model either using the fine-grained or the simplified list of ingredients. Overall, although usually only a single type of semantically related fine-grained ingredients (e.g. 'large eggs', 'beaten eggs' or 'eggs') appears at the same time in the ground truth, it seems that the model is inherently learning an embedding of the ingredients. Therefore, it is able to understand that some fine-grained ingredients are related and predicts them at once in the fine-grained version (see waffles example).

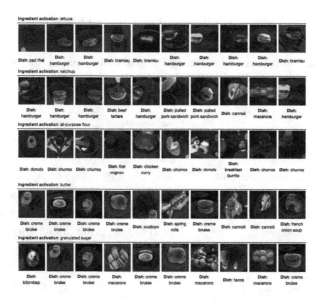

Fig. 2. Visualization of neuron activations. Each row is associated to a specific neuron from the network. The images with top activation are shown as well as the top ingredient activation they have in common. The name of their respective food class is only for visualization purposes and is displayed in green if the recipe contains the top ingredient. Otherwise, it is shown in red. (Color figure online)

4.4   Neuron Representation of Ingredients

When training a CNN model, it is important to understand what it is able to learn and interpret from the data. To this purpose, we visualized the activations of certain neurons of the network in order to interpret what is it able to learn.

Figure 2 shows the results of this visualization. As we can see, it appears that certain neurons of the network are specialized to distinguish specific ingredients. For example, most images of the 1st and 2nd rows illustrate that the characteristic shape of a hamburger implies that it will probably contain the ingredients 'lettuce' and 'ketchup'. Also, looking at the 'granulated sugar' row, we can see that the model learns to interpret the characteristic shape of *creme brulee* and *macarons* as containing sugar, although it is not specifically seen in the image.

5   Conclusions and Future Work

Analysing both the quantitative and qualitative results, we can conclude that the proposed model and the two datasets published offer very promising results for the multi-label problem of food ingredients recognition. Our proposal allows to obtain great generalization results on unseen recipes and sets the basis for applying further, more detailed food analysis methods. As future work, we will create a hierarchical structure [16] relationship of the existent ingredients and extend the model to utilize this information.

References

1. Aguilar, E., Bolaños, M., Radeva, P.: Exploring food detection using CNNs. In: Proceedings of the 16th International Conference on Computer Aided Systems Theory, pp. 242–243. Springer (2017)
2. Aizawa, K., Ogawa, M.: FoodLog: multimedia tool for healthcare applications. IEEE MultiMedia **22**(2), 4–8 (2015)
3. Bolaños, M., Radeva, P.: Simultaneous food localization and recognition. In: Proceedings of the 23rd International Conference on Pattern Recognition (ICPR) (2016)
4. Bossard, L., Guillaumin, M., Van Gool, L.: Food-101 – mining discriminative components with random forests. In: Fleet, D., Pajdla, T., Schiele, B., Tuytelaars, T. (eds.) ECCV 2014. LNCS, vol. 8694, pp. 446–461. Springer, Cham (2014). https:// doi.org/10.1007/978-3-319-10599-4_29
5. Buja, A., Stuetzle, W., Shen, Y.: Loss functions for binary class probability estimation and classification: structure and applications. Working draft, November 2005
6. Chen, J., Ngo, C.-W.: Deep-based ingredient recognition for cooking recipe retrieval. In: Proceedings of the 2016 ACM on Multimedia Conference, pp. 32–41. ACM (2016)
7. He, K., Zhang, X., Ren, S., Sun, J.: Deep residual learning for image recognition. In: Proceedings of the IEEE Conference on Computer Vision and Pattern Recognition, pp. 770–778 (2016)

8. Martinel, N., Foresti, G.L., Micheloni, C.: Wide-slice residual networks for food recognition. arXiv preprint arXiv:1612.06543 (2016)

9. Ofli, F., Aytar, Y., Weber, I., al Hammouri, R., Torralba, A.: Is saki# delicious? the food perception gap on instagram and its relation to health. arXiv preprint arXiv:1702.06318 (2017)

10. Russakovsky, O., Deng, J., Hao, S., Krause, J., Satheesh, S., Ma, S., Huang, Z., Karpathy, A., Khosla, A., Bernstein, M., et al.: Imagenet large scale visual recognition challenge. Int. J. Comput. Vis. **115**(3), 211–252 (2015)

11. Shimoda, W., Yanai, K.: CNN-based food image segmentation without pixel-wise annotation. In: Murino, V., Puppo, E., Sona, D., Cristani, M., Sansone, C. (eds.) ICIAP 2015. LNCS, vol. 9281, pp. 449–457. Springer, Cham (2015). https://doi.org/10.1007/978-3-319-23222-5_55

12. Szegedy, C., Vanhoucke, V., Ioffe, S., Shlens, J., Wojna, Z.: Rethinking the inception architecture for computer vision. In: Proceedings of the IEEE Conference on Computer Vision and Pattern Recognition, pp. 2818–2826 (2016)

13. Tsoumakas, G., Katakis, I.: Multi-label classification: an overview. Int. J. Data Warehouse. Min. **3**(3), 1–13 (2006)

14. Wang, J., Yang, Y., Mao, J., Huang, Z., Huang, C., Xu, W.: CNN-RNN: a unified framework for multi-label image classification. In: Proceedings of the IEEE Conference on Computer Vision and Pattern Recognition, pp. 2285–2294 (2016)

15. Wang, X., Kumar, D., Thome, N., Cord, M., Precioso, F.: Recipe recognition with large multimodal food dataset. In: 2015 IEEE International Conference on Multimedia and Expo Workshops (ICMEW), pp. 1–6. IEEE (2015)

16. Wu, H., Merler, M., Uceda-Sosa, R., Smith, J.R.: Learning to make better mistakes: semantics-aware visual food recognition. In: Proceedings of the 2016 ACM on Multimedia Conference, pp. 172–176. ACM (2016)

17. Yosinski, J., Clune, J., Nguyen, A., Fuchs, T., Lipson, H.: Understanding neural networks through deep visualization. arXiv preprint arXiv:1506.06579 (2015)

Building Parsimonious SVM Models for Chewing Detection and Adapting Them to the User

Iason Karakostas, Vasileios Papapanagiotou$^{(\boxtimes)}$, and Anastasios Delopoulos

Multimedia Understanding Group, Department of Electrical
and Computer Engineering, Aristotle University of Thessaloniki, Thessaloniki, Greece
iasonekv@auth.gr, vassilis@mug.ee.auth.gr, adelo@eng.auth.gr
https://mug.ee.auth.gr

Abstract. Monitoring of eating activity is a well-established yet challenging problem. Various sensors have been proposed in the literature, including in-ear microphones, strain sensors, and photoplethysmography. Most of these approaches use detection algorithms that include machine learning; however, a universal, non user-specific model is usually trained from an available dataset for the final system. In this paper, we present a chewing detection system that can adapt to each user independently using active learning (AL) with minimal intrusiveness. The system captures audio from a commercial bone-conduction microphone connected to an Android smart-phone. We employ a state-of-the-art feature extraction algorithm and extend the Support Vector Machine (SVM) classification stage using AL. The effectiveness of the adaptable classification model can quickly converge to that achieved when using the entire available training set. We further use AL to create SVM models with a small number of support vectors, thus reducing the computational requirements, without significantly sacrificing effectiveness. To support our arguments, we have recorded a dataset from eight participants, each performing once or twice a standard protocol that includes consuming various types of food, as well as non-eating activities such as silent and noisy environments and conversation. Results show accuracy of 0.85 and F1 score of 0.83 in the best case for the user-specific models.

Keywords: Active learning · Dietary monitoring
Chewing detection · Wearable sensors

1 Introduction

Automatically monitoring eating activity has received significant attention in the research community; a variety of novel sensors and detection algorithms have been proposed that monitor eating activity based on detecting chewing or swallowing. Microphones are often used, placed either near the throat in order to detect swallowing sounds [8], or in-ear to detect chewing sounds [1,5]. More recent approaches rely on strain sensors to capture muscle activity [8,9] and

© Springer International Publishing AG 2017
S. Battiato et al. (Eds.): ICIAP 2017 International Workshops, LNCS 10590, pp. 403–410, 2017.
https://doi.org/10.1007/978-3-319-70742-6_38

detect chewing. Other types of proposed sensors include custom build or modified proximity sensors placed on the wrists and head of the subject that detect hand movement transferring food from plate to mouth [3], or use commercial smart-watches to detect food-intake cycles [4].

Some systems take advantage of multiple sensor signals. In [7], a custom built sensor which consists of an open-air in-ear microphone, a photoplethysmography sensor, and an acceleromenter is proposed; the detection algorithm calculates, among other features, the fractal dimension of the microphone signal as proposed in [6]. Authors report accuracy of 0.938 and F1 score of 0.761. In [10], a system with two off-the-shelf in-ear bone-conduction microphones is proposed. Through spectrum analysis and k-NN classification the system can differentiate between eating, speaking and drinking activities, with average intra-subject accuracy of 0.8 and average inter-subject accuracy of 0.7.

Most of the proposed algorithms incorporate machine learning, usually the Support Vector Machine (SVM), and more recently convolutional neural networks [5]. Thus, they require sufficient data to train an effective classification model; this model can then be deployed in the final system, and is used unaltered during its life-span. However, not every person eats and chews in exactly the same manner; thus, it is reasonable for a system to be able to adapt to each different user to increase its effectiveness overall. In this paper, we propose such a user adaptable chewing detection system based on an off-the-self bone conduction in-ear microphone with an integrated speaker and an Android smart-phone. We employ the same audio features of [7] to detect eating events, and extend it with active learning (AL) for the SVM classification step in two-fold. First, we propose a non-interactive strategy to create a parsimonious SVM model that includes few support vectors (SVs) and is thus easy to compute and retrain on smart phones, and show that the effectiveness of the parsimonious model quickly converges to that of an equivalent SVM model. Second, we propose a feedback-request (interactive) method with low user intrusiveness for the deployed version of our system that enables per user-adaptation of the deployed model in order to increase effectiveness. The rest of this paper is organised as follows. Section 2 presents the bone-conduction microphone, the captured signals, and the extracted features. Section 3 presents the SVM-based chewing classification and AL. In Sect. 4 the experimental dataset is presented along with the evaluation results of the system. Finally, Sect. 5 concludes the paper.

2 Chewing Sensor and Signals

The chewing detection hardware consists of an off-the-shelf bone-conduction microphone connected via wire to the headphone jack of an Android smart-phone (Fig. 1b). The microphone (Invisio M3h) exhibits a sensitivity of -32 dB around the 1 kHz frequency band. We sample audio at 4 kHz which is the lowest sampling frequency allowed by the Android operating system, in order to reduce the computational burden without sacrificing effectiveness [6]. The microphone is housed in an ear-bud which is placed inside the outer ear canal (Fig. 1).

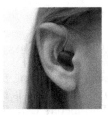

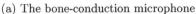

(a) The bone-conduction microphone   (b) The complete system

Fig. 1. The microphone placement, and the complete detection system.

We have opted for a bone-conduction microphone since it can naturally elimi-nate external (non-user generated) sounds very well, since sound is captured by measuring the vibration transmitted through user's bones, not air pressure.

The microphone captures body-generated sounds such as voice and chew-ing sounds. A pre-processing step applies a high-pass FIR filter with a cut-off frequency of 20 Hz in order to remove low frequency content, which does not include chewing-related information. Subsequently, we extract overlapping win-dows every 160 samples (sampling interval of $T_f = 25$ Hz) and compute a fea-ture vector $\mathbf{f}[n]$ (where n is the time-index corresponding to nT_f sec). The set of extracted features are described in detail in [7] and in this work are aug-mented with the signal's variance, resulting in 16 features in total. The time-domain features (fractal dimension, moments) are computed on windows of 0.1 s (400 samples), while the spectral features on windows of 0.2 s (800 samples). Before computing the features, each window is normalised by subtracting its mean and dividing it by its standard deviation (with the exception of variance). Figure 2 shows the histograms of fractal dimension (2a) and log of variance (2b) for the chewing and non-chewing classes. Both features are quite discriminative individually; combining all the extracted features can better distinguish chewing from non-chewing windows. More details about each feature can be found in [7].

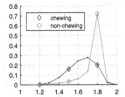   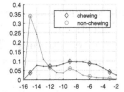

(a) Fractal dimension histogram   (b) Log of variance histogram

Fig. 2. Histograms of the fractal dimension (a) and log of variance (b) for the chewing and non-chewing classes.

3   Classification and Active Learning

In order to classify each feature vector $\mathbf{f}[n]$ into chewing (positive class) or non-chewing (negative class) we employ the SVM classifier with RBF kernel. Initially, each feature is smoothed in the time domain using a Hamming filter of 3.72 s. The SVM scores are computed as $s[n] = \mathbf{w} \cdot \mathbf{f}[n] + b$ where $\mathbf{w}$ is the separating hyper-plane normal vector, and b is the offset. Parameters C of SVM and γ of RBF are chosen based on preliminary experiments described in Sect. 4.1.

AL is a method of improving a classifier's effectiveness [11] by enhancing the training set in "rounds". In each round, the current classification model is applied on a pool of available feature vectors; some few feature vectors are selected from the pool and the user is requested to provide feedback (the correct label) for these feature vectors. As a result, it is not necessary to annotate the entire pool. In this work, we propose to use AL in two distinct tasks: (a) a parsimonious AL training (PALT) approach without any user feedback to build a reduced complexity classifier (small number of SVs), and (b) an inter-active learning adaptation (IALA) strategy to adapt a pre-trained model to the user's eating style and improve effectiveness.

3.1   PALT

Given a training set $\mathcal{T} = \{(\mathbf{f}[i], y[i]) : i = 0, 1, \ldots, N - 1\}$, one can directly train an SVM model $\mathcal{M}$. PALT uses AL to create a model with much fewer SVs without sacrificing the model's discriminative power. First, a few items of $\mathcal{T}$ are selected and form the initial training set $\mathcal{T}_0$, and an SVM model $\mathcal{M}_0$ is trained on it. The model is applied on the remaining data $\mathcal{P}_0 = \mathcal{T} - \mathcal{T}_0$ and $s[i]$ is computed for each item of $\mathcal{P}_0$. We then select the l positive misclassifications ($s[i] > 0$ and $y[i] = -1$) that are closest to the separating hyperplane, and similarly the l negative misclassifications ($s[i] < 0$ and $y[i] = +1$) closest to the separating hyperplane, since such vectors are more likely to become SVs. Let $\mathcal{U}_0$ be the set of the selected $2l$ misclassifications. For the next round, we create the new training set as $\mathcal{T}_1 = \mathcal{T}_0 \cup \mathcal{U}_0$; a new SVM model $\mathcal{M}_1$ is trained on $\mathcal{T}_1$, and then applied to $\mathcal{P}_1 = \mathcal{P}_0 - \mathcal{U}_0$. A new AL round can take place, and this process can continue until there are no more misclassifications or the model is "large" or "effective enough", depending on the requirements for computational complexity and effectiveness. Thus, PALT collects the vectors that are more likely to become SVs and affect the separating hyperplane orientation the most.

In our case, we start with a $\mathcal{T}_0$ that contains 20 positive and 20 negative feature vectors, selected randomly from $\mathcal{T}$. An initial training set of 40 vectors is very small and allows us to observe the effect of augmenting the training set. At each AL round, we add only one positive and one negative misclassification ($l = 1$). We repeat this process for 800 rounds, so our final model is $\mathcal{M}_{800}$. In Sect. 4.1 we compare $\mathcal{M}_{800}$ to the model $\mathcal{M}$ obtained by training directly on the entire $\mathcal{T}$.

3.2   IALA

This method aims at adapting a pre-trained SVM model to a single user based on inter-active feedback requests for ambiguous time intervals. The pre-trained model can be that of a straight-forward SVM training, or the result of the PALT approach proposed in Sect. 3.1. Note that PALT cannot be directly applied in this scenario for two reasons. First, it requires a large dataset to work on, and thus precious storage space of smart phones. Second, for every feature vector that feedback is required, the user would have to recall past eating activity, however evidence shows that people tend to under-report eating [2]. This would compromise the feedback quality, rendering PALT useless.

IALA is based on two thresholds, a time threshold t_{thr} and an SVM score threshold s_{thr}, and detecting in real-time ambiguous intervals; the user is then immediately asked if she/he is eating. Let $f[n]$ by the stream of feature vectors and $s[n]$ their SVM scores based on the current model $\mathcal{M}_c$, trained on $\mathcal{T}_c$. The most recent $f[n]$ along with their $s[n]$ are buffered in memory, so that they cover the last t_{thr} seconds. If the SVM score is closer to the separating hyperplane than s_{thr} for all of the buffered vectors, the user is immediately asked if she/he is eating. The requirement for t_{thr} eliminates false alarms, and prevents the system from overwhelming the user with feedback requests and $\mathcal{T}_c$ with new vectors. From the buffered feature vectors, the q closest to the hyperplane are added in $\mathcal{T}_c$ with the label the user provides, and a new model is trained. Through the experiments we have set $t_{thr} = 1\,\text{s}$, $s_{thr} = 0.2$, and $q = 6$, as we have observed that windows of $1\,\text{s}$ where $s[n]$ remains $s_{thr} = 0.25$ do not occur too often, so that the user is not constantly asked for feedback.

4   Experimental Evaluation

To evaluate our proposed system, we have collected a dataset of audio recordings using the bone-conduction microphone and a dedicated Android application that allows easy time-stamping. The experimentation protocol followed by each participant includes chewing activities with 7 different food types, as well as common non-chewing activities (e.g. walking, talking, and listening to music) both in silent and noisy setups. The dataset includes recordings from 8 participants (6 males and 2 females with mean age 30.6 and 28.2 years). The total duration of the recordings is 90 min (6.5 min per protocol). Six participants recorded the protocol twice, and the other two only once; the other two were unavailable at the day of the second recordings. Ground truth labels were assigned based on the time-stamps as well as audio and visual inspection of the captured signals; positive class was assigned on entire eating sessions (e.g. the entire time during which an apple is consumed is marked as positive). Prior probability is 0.45 corresponding to 40 min of eating time and 50 min of non-eating time.

4.1   PALT Evaluation Results

We first perform a baseline k-fold cross validation (CV) experiment on the entire dataset as an estimation of intra-subject effectiveness. Feature vectors

Table 1. Evaluation results of cross-validation (CV) and leave-one-subject-out (LOSO) experiments for baseline and PALT SVM models on the entire dataset.

	Precision	Recall	F1 score	Accuracy	SVs
CV baseline	0.89	0.89	0.89	0.90	33,552
CV PALT@100	0.83	0.89	0.86	0.87	232
CV PALT@800	0.85	0.90	0.87	0.88	1,633
LOSO baseline	0.84	0.81	0.81	0.83	31,152
LOSO PALT@100	0.82	0.79	0.79	0.83	233
LOSO PALT@800	0.81	0.82	0.80	0.83	1,632

are randomly partitioned into k folds. For each fold, an SVM model is trained on the other $k - 1$ folds and is used to predict the labels of the fold. We set $k = 14$ so that the number of feature vectors of each fold is approximately equal to the length of the experimental protocol. The evaluation is performed per feature vector. Before each training, each feature is linearly normalised to $[0, 1]$, and the same transformations are applied to the evaluation set. Precision, recall, F1 score, accuracy, and number of SVs are shown as "CV baseline" of Table 1. To evaluate PALT, we repeat the CV experiment and at each iteration we start with an initial training set T_0 of 40 feature vectors (20 positive and 20 negative). We run PALT for 800 rounds. Rows "CV PALT@m" of Table 1 show the results after $m = 100$ and $m = 800$ rounds.

To evaluate our approach for inter-subject effectiveness we repeat the experiments in leave-one-subject-out (LOSO) fashion. Similar to CV, the dataset is partitioned to folds where each fold now contains data from a single participant. Thus, 8 partitions are created. Row "LOSO baseline" of Table 1 shows the results, and rows "LOSO PALT@m" show the results after $m = 100$ and $m = 800$ rounds of PALT. Figure 3a shows the mean (per subject) accuracy for the LOSO PALT experiments across all 800 rounds. LOSO baseline accuracy is also shown for comparison. The thinner lines show ± 1 standard deviation.

During the LOSO baseline experiment, we further partitioned the available training data of each iteration randomly, in a 70%–30% ratio for hyper-parameter search. However, we have found that for 7 out of the 8 participants, the optimal values are $C = 1$ for the SVM, and $\gamma = 10 \cdot D^{-1}$ for the RBF kernel, where $D = 16$ is the number of features. We have thus selected these values for all of our experiments.

Baseline models outperform PALT, however the difference in effectiveness is rather small. For CV, PALT after 800 rounds is only 2 percentage units lower in F1 score and accuracy, while for LOSO, PALT achieves the same accuracy 0.83 and only one percentage unit less in F1 score. However, PALT models include approximately 30 times less SVs compared to baseline.

Table 2. Evaluation results of leave-one-subject-out (LOSO) experiments for IALA, using the baseline and PALT to create the initial model.

	Precision	Recall	F1 score	Accuracy	SVs
$LOSO_6$ baseline	0.84	0.82	0.81	0.82	25,043
$LOSO_6$ PALT	0.87	0.66	0.72	0.82	1,633
$LOSO_6$ baseline + IALA	0.84	0.83	0.82	0.83	25,038
$LOSO_6$ PALT + IALA	0.88	0.80	0.83	0.85	1,652

4.2 IALA Evaluation Results

To evaluate IALA we perform additional experiments on the six participants that recorded the protocol twice. The prior probability in this subset is 0.46. The LOSO baseline and PALT experiments are repeated on the six participants subset. We then use one of the protocol recordings to simulate the stream of feature vectors, and the second protocol to evaluate effectiveness. Results before and after running IALA are shown in Table 2. IALA improves baseline accuracy from 0.82 to 0.83, and PALT accuracy from 0.82 to 0.85. PALT F1 score is improved from 0.72 to 0.83, however this huge improvement is caused by the low recall (and thus F1) of the PALT models; the PALT + IALA F1 score of 0.83 is higher than the baseline 0.81. These results are quite encouraging given the short duration of the protocol used for simulating streaming mode (roughly (6 min). In addition, inter-subject variance of accuracy (see Fig. 3b) decreases as SVM models are adapted per-subject, indicating robust convergence to more effective models. The highest effectiveness among all LOSO experiments is achieved by the combination of PALT and IALA.

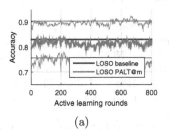

(a)

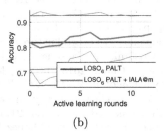

(b)

Fig. 3. Accuracy across active learning rounds vs. baseline. (a) LOSO baseline vs. LOSO PALT. (b) $LOSO_6$ PALT vs. $LOSO_6$ PALT + IALA.

5 Conclusions

This paper presents a chewing detection system based on audio signals from an off-the-shelf bone-conduction microphone connected to an Android smart-phone.

The system uses AL for two tasks; to create and deploy a classification model with fewer SVs that requires reduced computational resources, and to enable per-user adaptation of the deployed model requiring minimal and real-time user feedback. Validation on an experimental dataset recorded in lab conditions shows inter-subject accuracy of 0.85 using user-adapted models and parsimonious initial SVM models. Future work includes evaluation the proposed system on a larger dataset under free-living conditions.

Acknowledgements. The work leading to these results has received funding from the European Communitys Health, demographic change and well-being Programme under Grant Agreement No. 727688, 01/12/2016 - 30/11/2020.

References

1. Amft, O., Stäger, M., Lukowicz, P., Tröster, G.: Analysis of chewing sounds for dietary monitoring. In: Beigl, M., Intille, S., Rekimoto, J., Tokuda, H. (eds.) UbiComp 2005. LNCS, vol. 3660, pp. 56–72. Springer, Heidelberg (2005). https://doi.org/10.1007/11551201_4
2. Archer, E., Hand, G.A., Blair, S.N.: Validity of us nutritional surveillance: national health and nutrition examination survey caloric energy intake data, 1971–2010. PloS ONE **8**(10), e76632 (2013)
3. Fontana, J.M., Farooq, M., Sazonov, E.: Automatic ingestion monitor: a novel wearable device for monitoring of ingestive behavior. IEEE Trans. Biomed. Eng. **61**(6), 1772–1779 (2014)
4. Kyritsis, K., Tatli, C.L., Diou, C., Delopoulos, A.: Automated analysis of in meal eating behavior using a commercial wristband IMU sensor. In: 2017 39th Annual International Conference of the IEEE Engineering in Medicine and Biology Society (EMBC) (July 2017, to appear online)
5. Papapanagiotou, V., Diou, C., Delopoulos, A.: Chewing detection from an in-ear microphone using convolutional neural networks. In: 2017 39th Annual International Conference of the IEEE Engineering in Medicine and Biology Society (EMBC) (July 2017, to appear online)
6. Papapanagiotou, V., Diou, C., Lingchuan, Z., van den Boer, J., Mars, M., Delopoulos, A.: Fractal nature of chewing sounds. In: Murino, V., Puppo, E., Sona, D., Cristani, M., Sansone, C. (eds.) ICIAP 2015. LNCS, vol. 9281, pp. 401–408. Springer, Cham (2015). https://doi.org/10.1007/978-3-319-23222-5_49
7. Papapanagiotou, V., Diou, C., Zhou, L., van den Boer, J., Mars, M., Delopoulos, A.: A novel chewing detection system based on PPG, audio and accelerometry. IEEE J. Biomed. Health Inf. **21**, 607–618 (2016)
8. Sazonov, E., Schuckers, S., Lopez-Meyer, P., Makeyev, O., Sazonova, N., Melanson, E.L., Neuman, M.: Non-invasive monitoring of chewing and swallowing for objective quantification of ingestive behavior. Physiol. Meas. **29**(5), 525 (2008)
9. Sazonov, E.S., Fontana, J.M.: A sensor system for automatic detection of food intake through non-invasive monitoring of chewing. IEEE Sens. J. **12**(5), 1340–1348 (2012)
10. Shuzo, M., Komori, S., Takashima, T., Lopez, G., Tatsuta, S., Yanagimoto, S., Warisawa, S., Delaunay, J.J., Yamada, I.: Wearable eating habit sensing system using internal body sound. J. Adv. Mech. Des. Syst. Manuf. **4**(1), 158–166 (2010)
11. Tong, S., Koller, D.: Support vector machine active learning with applications to text classification. J. Mach. Learn. Res. **2**, 45–66 (2001)

Food Intake Detection from Inertial Sensors Using LSTM Networks

Konstantinos Kyritsis[✉], Christos Diou, and Anastasios Delopoulos

Information Processing Laboratory, Multimedia Understanding Group,
Aristotle University of Thessaloniki, Thessaloniki, Greece
{kokirits,diou}@mug.ee.auth.gr, adelo@eng.auth.gr
https://mug.ee.auth.gr/

Abstract. Unobtrusive analysis of eating behavior based on Inertial Measurement Unit (IMU) sensors (e.g. accelerometer) is a topic that has attracted the interest of both the industry and the research community over the past years. This work presents a method for detecting food intake moments that occur during a meal session using the accelerometer and gyroscope signals of an off-the-shelf smartwatch. We propose a two step approach. First, we model the hand micro-movements that take place while eating using an array of binary Support Vector Machines (SVMs); then the detection of intake moments is achieved by processing the sequence of SVM score vectors by a Long Short Term Memory (LSTM) network. Evaluation is performed on a publicly available dataset with 10 subjects, where the proposed method outperforms similar approaches by achieving an F1 score of 0.892.

Keywords: Food intake · Eating monitoring · Wearable sensors · LSTM

1 Introduction

Recent reports[1] from the World Health Organization (WHO) point out the global epidemic status that obesity has reached by doubling the affected population worldwide since 1980. In particular, overweight and obesity are two of the most prevalent *preventable* causes of death, alongside smoking tobacco and sexually transmitted diseases, and are responsible for over 2.5 million deaths per annum since 2001 [11]. Thus, the ability to unobtrusively monitor eating behavior plays a key role in the study and treatment of obesity.

Several devices have been introduced specifically for measuring meal eating behavior, e.g. by weight scale [8] or based on sound [9]. In this paper, we are interested in detecting eating moments *during the course of a meal* using general purpose IMU sensors. This enables us to automatically measure in-meal eating behavior in terms of number of bites, bite frequency and bite frequency acceleration or deceleration, thus approximating the food intake curve of [8].

---

[1] http://who.int/mediacentre/factsheets/fs311/en/.

© Springer International Publishing AG 2017
S. Battiato et al. (Eds.): ICIAP 2017 International Workshops, LNCS 10590, pp. 411–418, 2017.
https://doi.org/10.1007/978-3-319-70742-6_39

Several approaches use multiple sensors to achieve high detection accuracy. In particular, the work of [1] involve the usage of multiple body-mounted accelerometers with the goal of detecting eating related gestures, whereas the authors of [6] combine a number of audio and motion sensors in order to detect bites and estimate intake weight. The main drawback of these methods, however, is the low usability compared to using a single, commercially available device.

Less obtrusive approaches exist, that employ the IMU sensors of a single smartwatch. Specifically, the authors of [12] propose the dissection of a feeding gesture into two sub-feeding movements, namely food-to-mouth and back-to-rest. Following the authors' proposed gesture recognition scheme, a clustering approach is used to detect the final eating moments, resulting in 0.757 F1 score on a laboratory controlled dataset. The work of [10] makes use of the sequential dependency between a small number of gestures leading to a bite of food. Moreover, the authors propose the usage of Hidden Markov Models (HMM) to capture the temporal evolution of eating. The results show the high performance of the proposed approach in manually segmented sequences in a large dataset. However, no results on non-segmented sequences are presented. A gyroscope-based approach is introduced in [2]. The authors make use of a characteristic wrist roll pattern that is exhibited during a meal to detect biting moments.

In our previous work [4], we showed how classification of hand movements into five meal-related gestures, followed by two discrete HMMs, can be used to characterize a food intake cycle. In this paper, we improve on this approach, by modeling hand micro-movements as an SVM score vector and by subsequently using an LSTM network to classify each sequence as an intake or non-intake cycle. Experimental results on our publicly available *Food Intake Cycle*[2] (FIC) dataset show the effectiveness of this method.

Following the introduction, Sect. 2 introduces the terminology and presents the steps of the method towards the detection of food intake cycles. Information about the dataset is presented in Sect. 3, whereas Sect. 4 presents the conducted experiments and their results. Finally, Sect. 5 concludes the paper.

2   Proposed Approach

The work presented in this paper aims at identifying *food intake cycles* during a meal session. Each food intake cycle consists of a series of hand *micro-movements*. The relation between meal session, food intake cycle and micro-movement is depicted in Fig. 1.

In its ideal form, a food intake cycle starts by manipulating a utensil to pick up food from a plate, continues with an upwards movement of the hand operating the utensil towards the mouth, followed by inserting the food in the mouth and concluding with a downwards motion of the hand away from the mouth. However, in real meals we observe repetitions of certain hand movements, unrecognized hand movements, or no hand movement at all. In the same context, the term

---

[2] https://mug.ee.auth.gr/intake-cycle-detection/.

micro-movement is used to describe a hand movement of limited duration that is related with the food intake cycle. A typical micro-movement example is the upwards movement of the hand operating the utensil from the plate towards the mouth. The micro-movements that we used in this study originate from the FIC dataset and are presented in Table 1.

Table 1. Table listing the selected micro-movements

Micro-movement	Description
Pick food	Hand manipulates a utensil to pick food from a plate
Upwards	Hand moves upwards, towards the mouth area
Downwards	Hand moves downwards, away from the mouth area
Mouth	Hand inserts food in mouth
No movement	Hand exhibits no movement
Other movement	Every other hand movement

The proposed method uses the acceleration and gyroscope signals of a smartwatch with the purpose of detecting food intake moments within a meal session. An array of binary (one-versus-one) SVMs is used to represent the initial signals as micro-movement score vectors; whereas an LSTM network is used to classify sequences of micro-movement score vectors as intake or non-intake cycles. An overview of the proposed system architecture is presented in Fig. 2.

2.1 Data Pre-processing

Initially, the synchronized 3D accelerometer $(a_x[n], a_y[n], a_z[n])$ and gyroscope $(g_x[n], g_y[n], g_z[n])$ sensor streams of a meal session are individually smoothed by a 5th order median filter. Furthermore, since the accelerometer sensor captures both the acceleration caused by the hand's movement as well as the acceleration due to the earth's gravitational field, the next step is to remove the gravity from the acceleration signal. To this end, we use the method proposed by [5]. More specifically, the gyroscope samples are used to estimate the rotation of the smartwatch with respect to a reference frame. We use the first sample as the reference frame (i.e. the position of the smartwatch when recording starts). Then, by assuming that the smartwatch is initially still, gravity can be removed by subtracting the first acceleration sample from the rotated sequence.

2.2 Feature Extraction

Given the pre-processed accelerometer and gyroscope streams feature extraction is performed by extracting frames of length w_l and step w_s corresponding to 0.2 and 0.1 s respectively. Let $\boldsymbol{w}_{a_x}^i$ be the i-th extracted frame from $a_x[n]$ channel of the accelerometer signal. For each $\boldsymbol{w}_{a_x}^i$ a number of both time and

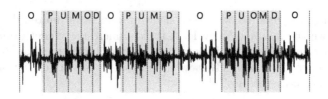

Fig. 1. Segmentation of a meal session (solid line) into intake cycles (shaded area) and micro-movements (dotted line).

frequency domain features are calculated, including (i) the number of zero crossings, (ii) the mean, (iii) the standard deviation, (iv) the variance, (v) the maximum value and minimum value, (vi) the range of values, (vii) the normalized energy and (viii) the first $\frac{w_l}{2} + 1$ Discrete Fourier Transform coefficients. These features are also extracted for the rest of the accelerometer and gyroscope channels. Furthermore, the simple moving average is also calculated by $SMA_a^i = \frac{1}{w_l} \sum_{j=k}^{w_l+k} |w_{a_x}^i[j]| + |w_{a_y}^i[j]| + |w_{a_z}^i[j]|$ for the acceleration stream and in a similar manner for the gyroscope. The result of feature extraction is the representation of the $a_x[n]$, $a_y[n]$, $a_z[n]$, $g_x[n]$, $g_y[n]$ and $g_z[n]$ time series as a series of L-dimensional feature vectors f_i.

2.3 Modeling the Micro-movements

From the list of micro-movements of Table 1, we observed that class O exhibits high inner class variance, since it is used to represent every hand movement other than P, U, D, M and N. As a result, all extracted features belonging in the O class are excluded from the learning procedure. The micro-movement learning process is achieved by employing an array of one-versus-one SVM classifiers with the Radial Basis Function (RBF) kernel. Given the features belonging in the five classes of interest, a total of ten one-versus-one classifiers are trained. In addition, since some micro-movements are inherently longer in duration than others (e.g. P and N) all classes are weighted according to their prior probabilities. Finally, prior to training, all features are linearly scaled in $[0, 1]$. Given the trained SVM models, each feature f_i extracted as in Sect. 2.2 is converted into a 10-dimensional vector s_i composed of the pair-wise prediction scores of the 10 one-versus-one SVM classifiers.

2.4 Learning the Food Intake Sequences

We designed an LSTM network with the purpose of classifying sequences of s_i as intake or non-intake cycles. The LSTM network is an extension of the Recurrent Neural Network (RNN) specifically designed to solve the long term dependency and vanishing gradient problems, thus giving it the ability to effectively model large intra-dependent sequences such as micro-movement sequences. In contrast with Markov models where the current state depends solely on the previous state in time, LSTM networks use a combination of input, output and forget gates

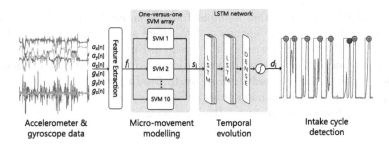

Fig. 2. Overview of the proposed system.

to retain information over a long period; thus, model more efficiently intake sequences that differ greatly from the *ideal* intake sequence due to the insertion of non intake-related micro-movements between intake-related micro-movements.

The proposed network's architecture consists of two consecutive LSTM layers with 128 hidden cells each, followed by a fully connected output layer with a single neuron. For the activation function of the recurrent steps we used the hard sigmoid defined as $\sigma(x) = \max(0, \min(1, x\,0.2 + 0.5))$, while for the output layer we used the sigmoid function. In a compact notation, the network can be written as $L(128) - L(128) - D(1)$, where $L(k_1)$ represents an LSTM layer with k_1 hidden cells and $D(k_2)$ a fully connected layer with k_2 neurons. The reason for using two LSTM layers stems from the work of Karpathy *et al.* [3], where the authors have shown that using a depth of at least two recurrent layers is beneficial when learning sequences.

Both intake and non-intake sequences are introduced to the network during training. Given the true label corresponding to each s_i, a sequence of $s_i, i = 1, 2, \ldots, n_j$ is considered an intake cycle if it starts with P (the first P in a sequence of P labels), ends with D (the last D in a sequence of D labels) and contains at least an M micro-movement. On the other hand, the remaining sequences that appear between consecutive intake cycles, are considered as non-intake cycles. We then represent each intake and non-intake sequence by their appropriate $n_j \times 10$ SVM score matrix. Since the input sequence of each LSTM layer is required to have a constant length, each sequence was pre-padded with zeros to a size $n' \times 10$, where $n' = \max\{n_j : j = 1, 2, 3 \ldots\}$. Thus, the input is long enough to contain every intake or non-intake sequence in the corpus. We used binary cross-entropy loss with the RMSprop optimizer (with 10^{-3} learning rate) that has demonstrated high effectiveness in a recurrent network topology [7]. Finally, the network is trained using an batch size M equal to 32 for 5 epochs.

2.5   Food Intake Cycle Detection

Given the trained LSTM network and a sequence of s_i that represents a meal session, intake cycle detection is performed by extracting 3 s frames from the sequence of s_i with a step of 0.2 s. The extracted frames are then pre-padded with zeros to the target size $n' \times 10$ and given as input to the LSTM network. The network output $d[m]$ (i.e. the output of the sigmoid function) represents the normalized probability that an input frame is an intake cycle. Subsequently, by replacing with zeros the elements of the $d[m]$ series that are lower than a threshold T_d, the filtered series $d'[m]$ is created. Finally, food intake cycles are detected by performing a local maximum search in $d'[m]$, with the minimum distance between two successive peaks set to 3 s. In particular, the timestamp corresponding to each local maximum (i.e. intake cycle) is the timestamp of the middle of the frame that produced the local maximum.

3   Dataset

In this study we used our publicly available FIC dataset. The FIC dataset consists of recordings from 10 subjects performing one meal session each, with an average duration of 13.2 min, in the restaurant of Aristotle University of Thessaloniki. The accelerometer and gyroscope streams originate from the Microsoft Band 2 smartwatch and are provided at a sample rate of approximately 62 Hz. The ground truth is provided at a micro-movement level based on analysis of video sequences captured during each subject's meal session. No specific instructions were given to the participating subjects other than clapping their hands once in the beginning and once in the end of the session for video/smartwatch synchronization purposes. Thus, the participants were able to engage in activities such as talking to other individuals in their proximity, during the recording. Table 2 provides additional information regarding the appearances of micro-movements in the dataset. Additionally, the average food intake cycle duration (from P to D) and the average distance between two consecutive food intakes were 5.39 (±3.86) and 11.22 (±8.79) s, respectively.

Table 2. Details of the exhibited micro-movements in the food intake cycle dataset

Label	Instances	Total duration (sec)	Mean (± std) duration (sec)
P	727	1613.43	2.21 (± 1.71)
U	700	678.28	0.96 (± 0.58)
D	694	518.37	0.74 (± 0.57)
M	695	311.96	0.44 (± 0.17)
N	161	965.67	5.99 (± 5.71)
O	742	3837.92	5.17 (± 7.42)

4   Experiments and Results

Given the true start and end moments of the i-th food intake cycle, t_s^i and t_e^i respectively, as well as t_d^j the moment of the j-th detected intake cycle in the same meal session, performance metrics were calculated by the following evaluation scheme. If for a given true intake cycle i, t_d^j is outside $[t_s^i, t_e^i]$ for any detected intake cycle j, then it counted as a false negative. Otherwise it counted as a true positive. However, every other occurrence of detected intake cycle in the same $[t_s^i, t_e^i]$ interval counted as a false positive. Finally, if a detected intake cycle didn't belong in $[t_s^i, t_e^i]$ for any i, then it also counted as a false positive.

We used Leave One Subject Out (LOSO) cross validation for both training steps of the pipeline. As a result, for the evaluation of a single subject in the corpus, we trained ten SVM arrays, and one LSTM network. Since the LSTM is trained in a stochastic fashion, we repeated the LSTM training process for ten times, resulting in a total of 100 SVM arrays and 100 LSTM networks for the entire corpus. Experimentation with a small subset of the corpus led us to the selection of the C and γ parameters of the SVM to be equal to 100 and 0.1 respectively. Similarly, the threshold parameter T_d was set to 0.89 by picking the value that achieved the highest F1 score.

We used precision and recall for evaluation. The approaches of [2,4] were also implemented and evaluated against the same dataset. Parameter selection for those approaches was performed according to the authors' suggestions. Figure 3 depicts the precision-recall curves for all approaches, while Table 3 provides numerical results for the top F1 score. The decimals in the TP and FN columns arise from the averaging over the ten LSTM training repetitions.

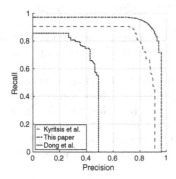

Fig. 3. Precision recall curves for the proposed approach (blue dash-dot line), the approach by [4] (red dash line) and by [2] (black dotted line). (Color figure online)

Table 3. Evaluation results.

Method	TP	FP	FN	Prec	Rec	F1
Proposed approach	623.7	89	60.3	0.875	0.911	0.892
Approach by [4]	603	193	81	0.757	0.881	0.814
Approach by [2]	508	683	176	0.426	0.742	0.541

5   Conclusions

We presented a method for detecting food intake cycles during a meal, using an off-the-shelf smartwatch. Results on a 10-subject publicly available corpus indicate that the combination of multiple micro-movement SVMs and an LSTM network for score sequence classification is highly effective and outperforms similar approaches found in the literature.

Acknowledgments. The work leading to these results has received funding from the European Community's Health, demographic change and well-being Programme under Grant Agreement No. 727688 (http://bigoprogram.eu), 01/12/2016–30/11/2020. We gratefully acknowledge the support of NVIDIA Corporation with the donation of the Tesla K40 GPU used for this research.

References

1. Amft, O., Junker, H., Troster, G.: Detection of eating and drinking arm gestures using inertial body-worn sensors. In: Ninth IEEE International Symposium on Wearable Computers, pp. 160–163 (2005)
2. Dong, Y., Hoover, A., Scisco, J., Muth, E.: A new method for measuring meal intake in humans via automated wrist motion tracking. Appl. Psychophysiol. Biofeedback **37**(3), 205–215 (2012)
3. Karpathy, A., Johnson, J., Li, F.: Visualizing and understanding recurrent networks. CoRR abs/1506.02078 (2015). http://arXiv.org/abs/1506.02078
4. Kyritsis, K., Tatli, C.L., Diou, C., Delopoulos, A.: Automated analysis of in meal eating behavior using a commercial wristband IMU sensor. In: 2017 39th Annual International Conference of the IEEE Engineering in Medicine and Biology Society (EMBC) (2017)
5. Madgwick, S.O.H., Harrison, A.J.L., Vaidyanathan, R.: Estimation of IMU and MARG orientation using a gradient descent algorithm. In: 2011 IEEE International Conference on Rehabilitation Robotics, pp. 1–7 (2011)
6. Mirtchouk, M., Merck, C., Kleinberg, S.: Automated estimation of food type and amount consumed from body-worn audio and motion sensors. In: Proceedings of the 2016 ACM International Joint Conference on Pervasive and Ubiquitous Computing, pp. 451–462 (2016)
7. Ordez, F.J., Roggen, D.: Deep convolutional and LSTM recurrent neural networks for multimodal wearable activity recognition. Sensors **16**(1), 115 (2016)
8. Papapanagiotou, V., Diou, C., Langlet, B., Ioakimidis, I., Delopoulos, A.: A parametric probabilistic context-free grammar for food intake analysis based on continuous meal weight measurements. In: 2015 37th Annual International Conference of the IEEE Engineering in Medicine and Biology Society (EMBC) (2015)
9. Papapanagiotou, V., Diou, C., Zhou, L., van den Boer, J., Mars, M., Delopoulos, A.: A novel chewing detection system based on PPG, audio, and accelerometry. IEEE J. Biomedical Health Inf. **21**(3), 607–618 (2017)
10. Ramos-Garcia, R.I., et al.: Improving the recognition of eating gestures using intergesture sequential dependencies. IEEE J. Biomed. Health Inf. **19**(3), 825–831 (2015)
11. World Health Organization: Global health risks: mortality and burden of disease attributable to selected major risks. World Health Organization (2009)
12. Zhang, S., et al.: Food watch: detecting and characterizing eating episodes through feeding gestures. In: Proceedings of the 11th EAI International Conference on Body Area Networks, pp. 91–96 (2016)

Understanding Food Images to Recommend Utensils During Meals

F. Ragusa, A. Furnari[(✉)], and G.M. Farinella

Department of Mathematics and Computer Science, Image Processing Laboratory,
University of Catania, Catania, Italy
francescoragusa@outlook.com, {furnari,gfarinella}@dmi.unict.it

Abstract. Understanding food images can be useful to enable different technologies aimed at improving the quality of life of the society. We focus on the problem of analyzing food images to recognize the utensils to be used to consume the meal depicted in the image. The proposed investigation has both a practical and a theoretical relevance, since (1) it can contribute to the design of intelligent systems able to assist people with mental disabilities and (2) it allows to assess if high level concepts related to food (e.g., how to eat food) can be inferred from visual analysis. We augment the FD1200 dataset with labels related to utensils and perform experiments considering AlexNet features coupled with a multi-class SVM classifier. Results show that, even such a simple classification pipeline can achieve promising results.

Keywords: Image understanding · Food analysis
Assistive technologies

1 Introduction and Motivations

Analysis and understanding of food images is a challenging Computer Vision task which has gathered much interest of the research community due to its potential impact on the quality of life of modern society [1]. In this context, the main problems considered by the community are related to the discrimination of food images vs other images [11,15,16], the detection/localization of food in images [17,23], the recognition and classification of the food depicted in an image [19–21], the segmentation of food images to distinguish the different parts and ingredients [18,22,25], the estimation of the volume and nutrients contained in a food plate detected in an image [24,26,27]. A big issue in this application domain is the availability of public datasets, as well as the lack of common procedures for testing and evaluation of the different tasks. Despite some food datasets exist [1,28], their size and variability is still limited to properly feed modern supervised learning approaches currently employed to solve different computer vision tasks [29].

In recent years, considering the advancement in the fields of Computer Vision and Machine Learning, the research community is making a great effort in

© Springer International Publishing AG 2017
S. Battiato et al. (Eds.): ICIAP 2017 International Workshops, LNCS 10590, pp. 419–425, 2017.
https://doi.org/10.1007/978-3-319-70742-6_40

designing and investigating intelligent systems able to help people in their daily activities [2]. Different studies have been proposed to design robotic personal assistants [4,5], advanced wearable vision systems to help people to augment their memory [6–8], as well as to monitor daily activities in order and improve quality of life [9,10]. The main motivation behind these studies is to help society by exploiting the advancements of computer and engineering science. In this regard, this paper builds on the following question: can we train a computer vision system to recognize the eating utensils to be used during a meal in order to help patients with dementia diseases in reminding how to eat food?

Eating is an important aspect of life. It is important to satisfy hunger, to stimulate our senses, to share moment with others, but, most importantly, to acquire the needed nutrients to live and be in good health. While the recognition of which utensils to use when eating a meal might seem to be straightforward, it is not so simple for people affected by dementia disease, such as Alzheimer. When the disease start to become severe, patients can experience problems in using utensils during a meal because of loose memory and other mental disabilities. The ability to correctly recognize which utensils to use during a meal is one of the aspect that is analyzed to monitor the functional abilities of dementia patients [3]. Patients often do not remember how to use eating utensils, and in late stages of the disease, food which can be eaten with fingers is usually adopted by caregivers to help patients.

Figure 1 illustrates the investigated problem: given a food image, the computer vision engine should be able to predict which utensils are to be used to consume the meal. We would like to note that the proposed investigation is of interest both from an application and a theoretical standpoint. On one hand, the proposed system can be used for practical purposes. For instance, it could be exploited in a wearable device or in a robotic personal assistant to provide suggestions to patients during meals, a task usually performed by the caregivers in real life. On the other hand, we find interesting to investigate up to what extent visual features can be used to infer higher level concepts such as utensils to be used for meal consumption.

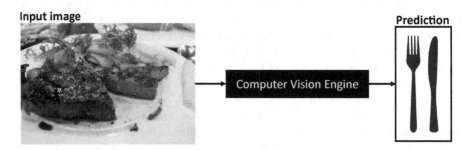

Fig. 1. The investigated problem.

To benchmark the problem, we consider the UNICT-FD1200 dataset [1]. To perform the experiments, each image of the dataset has been labeled according to five different classes related to the utensils to be used for meal consumption: *Chopsticks, Fork, Fork and Knife, Hands* and *Spoon*. We investigate an approach based on the combination of features extracted using the AlexNet CNN architecture proposed in [12] and a Support Vector Machine to perform classification [14]. This simple pipeline has obtained a classification accuracy of 86.27%.

The paper is organized as following. Section 2 summarizes the representation and classification components adopted to address the considered problem. Section 3 details the experimental settings and discusses the results. Conclusions are given in Sect. 4.

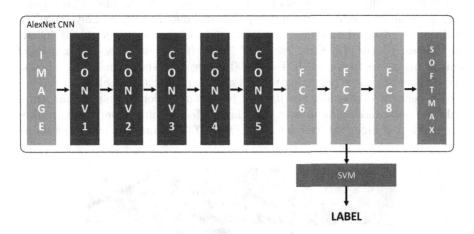

Fig. 2. The considered approach based on features extracted using the AlexNet CNN architecture and an SVM classifier.

2   Food Image Representation and Classification

In our experiments, we considered an image representation based on deep features. In particular, we use the AlexNet deep learning architecture proposed in [12]. The model has been pre-trained to categorize images from ImageNet into 1000 different object classes. The AlexNet architecture has 8 layers, plus a Softmax module at the end of the network. In our experiments, we used the activations of the fully connected seventh layer (FC7) as features. We choose to extract features form the FC7 layer since such activations are believed to have a high semantic relevance but are more general than the 1000 features of the FC8 layer which are to be considered as class-related scores. Classification is performed using a multiclass SVM classifier [14] with an RBF (Radial Basis Function) kernel. See Fig. 2 for a diagram of the approach.

The SVM has been trained on a balanced set of images with equal amounts of images for each of the considered class, i.e., *Chopsticks, Fork, Fork and Knife, Hands and Spoon.* Hyper-parameters (e.g., cost C and γ in the RBF kernel) are optimized using cross-validation.

3   Experimental Settings and Results

We consider the UNICT-FD1200 [1] for our experiments. The dataset contains 4754 images of 1200 distinct dishes of food plates characterized by different nationalities (e.g., English, Japanese, Indian, Italian, Thai, etc.). Each dish has been acquired with a smartphone several times to introduce geometric and photometric variability in the dataset (such as Flash vs. No Flash, different rotations, multiple scale, different points of view). To carry out the proposed investigation, each image of the dataset has been manually labeled considering the following classes: *Chopsticks, Fork, Fork and Knife, Hands* and *Spoon.* Examples of images belonging to the UNICT-FD1200 dataset are shown in Fig. 3, whereas the number of images belonging to each class is reported in Table 1.

To perform evaluation, the dataset has been randomly divided into three balanced non-overlapping subsets. The three different splits allow to obtain three independent training set/test set pairs. Once FC7 features are extracted for all

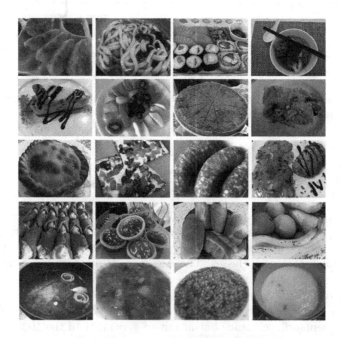

Fig. 3. Example of images belonging to the UNICT-FD1200 dataset. Each row correspond to a specific class: (1) Chopsticks, (2) Fork, (3) Fork and Knife, (4) Hands, (5) Spoon

Table 1. Per-class number of images in the UNICT-FD1200 dataset.

Class	Number of images
Chopsticks	248
Fork	1468
Fork and Knife	2048
Hands	699
Spoon	291

images in the dataset, the SVM classifier is trained and tested considering the three different split. Accuracy values over the three runs are hence averaged to assess overall performance. The proposed method is implemented using the Caffe library [13] to extract FC7 features form a pre-trained AlexNet model [12] and LibSVM [14] to implement the multi-class classifier.

Table 2 summarizes the results and reports the performances of the classifier in the different runs. In Table 3 the confusion matrix with respect to the five considered classes is reported. The approach obtains good results for the *Fork and Knife* class, probably because in the dataset there are more images than in the other classes. The method has difficulties in recognizing images belonging to the *Chopsticks* class (e.g., noodle plates), which are confused in those in which a fork utensil is used during meals.

Table 2. Accuracy of our classification model.

Run 1	Run 2	Run 3	Average
87.24	85.06	86.50	86.27

Table 3. Confusion Matrix. Rows report real classes, while columns report predicted ones.

Classes	Chopsticks	Fork	Fork and Knife	Hands	Spoon
Chopsticks	**60.87%**	6.52%	28.26%	2.17%	2.17%
Fork	0%	**86.47%**	11.88%	0.82%	0.82
Fork and Knife	0.27%	17%	**92.88%**	2.19%	0%
Hands	0.84%	2.52%	14.28%	**82.35%**	0%
Spoon	1.78%	7.14%	17.85%	1.78%	**72.43%**

4   Conclusions

We have considered the problem of recognizing utensils to be used during meal consumption. The investigation is both of practical interest (e.g., to design systems to assist people with mental disabilities) and theoretical interest (i.e., to assess whether higher level concept related to how to eat food can be obtained from visual features). To address the problem, we augment the FD1200 dataset introducing labels related to utensils to be used to consume the food detected in the images. Experiments show that even a simple pipeline based on AlexNet features and an SVM classifiers can be leveraged to perform classification despite it can be considered only as a baseline approach to be improved.

References

1. Farinella, G.M., Allegra, D., Moltisanti, M., Stanco, F., Battiato, S.: Retrieval and classification of food images. Comput. Biol. Med. **77**, 2339 (2016)
2. Leo, M., Medioni, G., Trivedi, M., Kanade, T., Farinella, G.M.: Computer vision for assistive technologies. Comput. Vis. Image Underst. **154**, 1–15 (2017)
3. Razani, J., Wong, J.T., Dafaeeboini, N., et al.: Predicting everyday functional abilities of dementia patients with the mini mental state exam. J. Geriatr. Psychiatry Neurol. **22**(1), 62–70 (2009)
4. Vincze, M., Bajones, M., Suchi, M., Wolf, D., Weiss, A., Fischinger, D., da la Puente, P.: Learning and detecting objects with a mobile robot to assist older adults in their homes. In: Hua, G., Jégou, H. (eds.) ECCV 2016. LNCS, vol. 9914, pp. 316–330. Springer, Cham (2016). https://doi.org/10.1007/978-3-319-48881-3_22
5. Yamazaki, K., Ueda, R., Nozawa, S., Kojima, M., Okada, K., Matsumoto, K., Ishikawa, M., Shimoyama, I., Inaba, M.: Home-assistant robot for an aging society. Proc. IEEE, Centennial Year, Special Issue, Quality Life Technol. **100**(8), 2429–2441 (2012)
6. Kanade, T., Hebert, M.: First-person vision. Proc. IEEE **100**(8), 2442–2453 (2012)
7. Damen, D., Leelasawassuk, T., Mayol-Cuevas, W.: You-Do, I-Learn: egocentric unsupervised discovery of objects and their modes of interaction towards video-based guidance. Comput. Vis. Image Underst. (CVIU) **149**, 98–112 (2016)
8. Soran, B., Farhadi, A., Shapiro, L.: Generating notifications for missing actions: don't forget to turn the lights off! In: IEEE International Conference on Computer Vision (2015)
9. Furnari, A., Farinella, G.M., Battiato, S.: Recognizing personal locations from egocentric videos. IEEE Trans. Human-Mach. Syst. **47**, 6–18 (2017)
10. Ortis, A., Farinella, G.M., Damico, D., Addesso, L., Torrisi, G., Battiato, S.: Organizing egocentric videos for daily living monitoring. In: Lifelogging Tools and Applications in Conjunction with ACM Multimedia, Amsterdam (2016)
11. Ragusa, F., Tomaselli, V., Furnari, A., Battiato, S., Farinella, G.M.: Food vs non-food classification. In: 2nd International Workshop on Multimedia Assisted Dietary Management (MADiMa) in Conjunction with ACM Multimedia, Amsterdam (2016)
12. Krizhevsky, A., Sutskever, I., Hinton, G.E.: Imagenet classication with deep convolutional neural networks. In: Advances in Neural Information Processing Systems (2012)
13. Berkeley Vision and Learning Center (BVLC). Cae, http://caffe.berkeleyvision.org/
14. Chih-Chung, C., Chih-Jen, L.: Libsvm: a library for support vector machines (2001)
15. Singla, A., Yuan, L., Ebrahimi, T.: Food/non-food image classification and food categorization using pre-trained GoogLeNet model. In: Proceedings of the 2nd International Workshop on Multimedia Assisted Dietary Management (2016)

16. Farinella, G.M., Allegra, D., Stanco, F., Battiato, S.: On the exploitation of one class classification to distinguish food vs non-food images. In: Murino, V., Puppo, E., Sona, D., Cristani, M., Sansone, C. (eds.) ICIAP 2015. LNCS, vol. 9281, pp. 375–383. Springer, Cham (2015). https://doi.org/10.1007/978-3-319-23222-5_46

17. Kagaya, H., Aizawa, K., Ogawa, M.: Food detection and recognition using convolutional neural network. In: ACM International Conference on Multimedia, pp. 1085–1088 (2014)

18. Shimoda, W., Yanai, K.: Foodness proposal for multiple food detection by training of single food images. In: International Workshop on Multimedia Assisted Dietary Management, pp. 13–21 (2016)

19. Merler, M., Wu, H., Uceda-Sosa, R., Nguyen, Q.B., Smith, J.R.: Snap, eat, RepEat: a food recognition engine for dietary logging. In: Proceedings of the 2nd International Workshop on Multimedia Assisted Dietary Management, pp. 31–40 (2016)

20. Farinella, G.M., Moltisanti, M., Battiato, S.: Classifying food images represented as bag of Textons. In: IEEE International Conference on Image Processing (ICIP), Paris, pp. 5212–5216 (2014)

21. Martinel, N., Piciarelli, C., Micheloni, C.: A supervised extreme learning committee for food recognition journal article. Comput. Vis. Image Underst. **148**, 67–86 (2016)

22. Dehais, J., Anthimopoulos, M., Mougiakakou, S.: Food image segmentation for dietary assessment. In: International Workshop on Multimedia Assisted Dietary Management, pp. 23–28 (2016)

23. Shimoda, W., Yanai, K.: CNN-based food image segmentation without pixel-wise annotation. In: Murino, V., Puppo, E., Sona, D., Cristani, M., Sansone, C. (eds.) ICIAP 2015. LNCS, vol. 9281, pp. 449–457. Springer, Cham (2015). https://doi.org/10.1007/978-3-319-23222-5_55

24. Ciocca, G., Napoletano, P., Schettini, R.: Food recognition and leftover estimation for daily diet monitoring. In: Murino, V., Puppo, E., Sona, D., Cristani, M., Sansone, C. (eds.) ICIAP 2015. LNCS, vol. 9281, pp. 334–341. Springer, Cham (2015). https://doi.org/10.1007/978-3-319-23222-5_41

25. Ciocca, G., Napoletano, P., Schettini, R.: Food recognition: a new dataset, experiments and results. IEEE J. Biomed. Health Inf. **21**(3), 588–598 (2017)

26. Myers, A., Johnston, N., Rathod, V., Korattikara, A., Gorban, A., Silberman, N., Guadarrama, S., Papandreou, G., Huang, J., Murphy, K.: Im2Calories: towards an automated mobile vision food diary. In: IEEE International Conference on Computer Vision, pp. 1233–1241 (2015)

27. Beijbom, O., Joshi, N., Morris, D., Saponas, S., Khullar, S.: Menu-match: restaurant-specific food logging from images. In: IEEE Winter Conference on Applications of Computer Vision, pp. 844–851 (2015)

28. Bossard, L., Guillaumin, M., Van Gool, L.: Food-101 – mining discriminative components with random forests. In: Fleet, D., Pajdla, T., Schiele, B., Tuytelaars, T. (eds.) ECCV 2014. LNCS, vol. 8694, pp. 446–461. Springer, Cham (2014). https://doi.org/10.1007/978-3-319-10599-4_29

29. LeCun, Y., Bengio, Y., Hinton, G.: Deep learning. Nature **521**(7553), 436–444 (2015)

Learning CNN-based Features for Retrieval of Food Images

Gianluigi Ciocca, Paolo Napoletano[(✉)], and Raimondo Schettini

DISCo (Dipartimento di Informatica, Sistemistica e Comunicazione),
Università degli Studi di Milano-Bicocca, Viale Sarca 336, 20126 Milano, Italy
{ciocca,napoletano,schettini}@disco.unimib.it

Abstract. Recently a huge amount of work has been done in order
to develop Convolutional Neural Networks (CNNs) for supervised food
recognition. These CNNs are trained to classify a predefined set of food
classes within a specific food dataset. CNN-based features have been
largely experimented for many image retrieval domains and to a lesser
extent to the food domain. In this paper, we investigate the use of CNN-
based features for food retrieval by taking advantage of existing food
datasets. To this end, we have built the Food524DB, the largest publicly available food dataset with 524 food classes and 247,636 images by
merging food classes from existing datasets in the state of the art. We
have then used this dataset to fine tune a Residual Network, ResNet-50,
which has demonstrated to be very effective for image recognition. The
last fully connected layer is finally used as feature vector for food image
indexing and retrieval. Experimental results are reported on the UNICT-
FD1200 dataset that has been specifically design for food retrieval.

Keywords: Food retrieval · Food dataset · Food recognition
CNN-based features

1 Introduction

Recently, food recognition received a considerable amount of attention due to
the importance of monitoring food consumption for a balanced and healthy
diet. To this end, computer vision techniques can help to build systems to
automatically recognize diverse foods and to estimate the food quantity. Many
works exist in the literature that exploit hand-crafted visual features for
food recognition and quantity estimation both for desktop as well as mobile
applications [1, 3, 17, 27, 28].

With the advent of practical techniques for training large convolutional
neural networks, hand-crafted features are being reconsidered in favor of learned
ones [30]. Features learned by deep convolutional neural networks (CNNs) have
been recognized to be more robust and expressive than hand-crafted ones. They
have been successfully used in different computer vision tasks such as object
detection, pattern recognition and image understanding. It is not surprising that

© Springer International Publishing AG 2017
S. Battiato et al. (Eds.): ICIAP 2017 International Workshops, LNCS 10590, pp. 426–434, 2017.
https://doi.org/10.1007/978-3-319-70742-6_41

a number of studies have investigated the use of deep neural networks for food recognition as well. Table 1 shows the most notable works on food recognition using deep learning techniques along with the datasets on which they have been evaluated their performances in terms of Top-1 and Top-5 classification accuracy.

Table 1. Performances of food recognition methods using deep learning techniques.

Reference	Network	Dataset	Top-1 (%)	Top-5 (%)
Kawano et al. [22]	DeepFoodCam	UECFOOD-100	72.26	92.00
		UECFOOD-256	63.77	85.82
Yanai et al. [32]	DCNN-FOOD(ft)	UECFOOD-100	78.48	94.85
		UECFOOD-256	67.57	88.97
		Food-101	70.41	-
Liu et al. [23]	DeepFood	UECFOOD-100	76.30	94.60
		UECFOOD-256	54.70	81.50
		Food-101	77.40	93.70
Hassannejad et al. [15]	Inception V3	UECFOOD-100	81.45	97.27
		UECFOOD-256	76.17	92.58
		Food-101	88.28	96.88
Martinel et al. [25]	WISeR	UECFOOD-100	89.58	99.23
		UECFOOD-256	83.15	95.45
		Food-101	90.27	98.71
Chen et al. [6]	MultiTaskDCNN	UECFOOD-100	82.12	97.29
		VIREO	82.05	95.88

A Convolutional Neural Network technique requires a large dataset to build a classification model. To overcome this, often previously pre-trained models on a different dataset are fine tuned using a small sized dataset specific for the current classification task. Since the larger and heterogeneous the dataset is, the more the network can be used to learn powerful models, for the food retrieval task, we have decided to create a very large food dataset starting from existing ones. We have analyzed the public datasets and merged some of them depending on their availability and characteristics thus creating the largest food dataset available in the literature with 524 food classes and 247,636 images. The lowest number of images for a given class is 100 while the largest is about 1,700. We exploit this dataset for learning robust features for food retrieval using a Residual Network. Our intuition is that, having this dataset more food classes than the ones used in previous works, the network should be more powerful, generalizes better and thus the extracted features should be more expressive.

Table 2. List of food datasets used in the literature. S: Single instance food images. M: Multi-instance food images.

Name	Year	#Images	#Classes	Type	Reference
Food50	2009	5,000	50	S	[20]
PFID	2009	1,098[a]	61[a]	S	[7]
TADA	2009	50/256	-	S, M	[24]
Food85[b]	2010	8,500	85	S	[18]
Chen	2012	5,000	50	S	[8]
UECFOOD-100	2012	9,060	100	S, M	[26]
Food-101	2014	101,000	101	S	[5]
UECFOOD-256[c]	2014	31,395	256	S, M	[21]
UNICT-FD889	2014	3,583	889	S	[14]
Diabetes	2014	4,868	11	S	[2]
UMPCFood-101[d]	2015	90,993	101	S	[31]
UNIMIB2015	2015	$1,000 \times 2$	15	M	[9]
UNICT-FD1200[e]	2016	4,754	1,200	S	[13]
UNIMIB2016	2016	1,027	73	M	[10]
VIREO	2016	110,241	172	S	[6]
Food524DB	2017	247,636	524	S	-

[a] Numbers refer to the baseline dataset.
[b] Includes Food50.
[c] Includes UECFOOD-100.
[d] Includes same classes of Food-101.
[e] Includes UNICT-FD889.

2   CNN-based Features for Food Retrieval

Domain adaptation, also known as transfer learning or fine tuning, is a machine learning procedure designed to adapt a classification model trained on a set of data to work on a different set of data. The importance and the usefulness of a domain adaptation process has been largely discussed in the food recognition literature [4,11,12,22,23,25,32]. Taking inspiration from these works, in this paper we fine-tuned a CNN architecture using a large, heterogeneous, food dataset, namely the Food524DB. The rational behind the creation of the Food524DB is that building a robust food recognition algorithm requires a large image dataset of different food instances.

2.1   The Food524DB Food Dataset

Table 2 summarizes the characteristic of the food datasets that can be found in the literature. For each dataset, we have reported its size, the number of food classes and the type of images it contains: either single, i.e. each image depict a single food category, or multi, i.e. the images can contain multiple food classes.

We decided to consider only datasets publicly available, with many food classes, and, most importantly, where each food category is represented by at least 100 images. After having analyzed the available datasets, we finally selected Food50, Food-101, UECFOOD-256, and VIREO. Since UECFOOD-256 contains multi-food instance images, we extracted from these images each food region using the bounding boxes provided in the ground truth. The combined dataset is thus composed of 247,636 images grouped in 579 food classes making this dataset the largest and most comprehensive food dataset available nad that can be used for training food classifiers. Some food classes are present in more than one of the four datasets. For example both the UECFOOD-256 and Food-101 contain the "apple_pie" category; UECFOOD-256 contains the "beef noodle" category while the VIREO dataset contains the "Beef noodles" category. In order to remove these redundancies we applied a category merging procedure based on the category names. After this procedure, the number of food classes in our dataset that we named Food524DB is reduced to 524 as reported in the last row of Table 2.

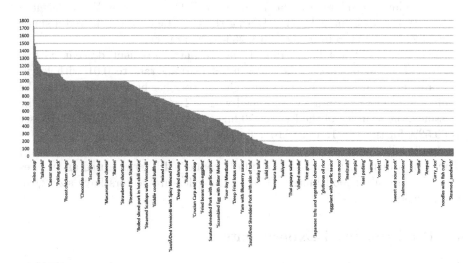

Fig. 1. Distribution of the cardinalities of the Food524DB food classes. Names are shown one every ten.

The sizes of the 524 food classes are reported in Fig. 1. The smallest food category contains 100 images; 241 classes have size between 100 and 199 images, 58 classes have size between 200 and 499 images, 113 have size between 500 and 999 images, and 112 have more than 1,000 images. The top-5 largest classes are: "Miso Soup" with 1,728 images; "Rice" with 1,499 images; "Spaghetti alla Bolognese" with 1,462 images; "Hamburger" with 1,333 images; and "Fried Rice" with 1,269 images. The Food524db is publicly available at http://www.ivl.disco. unimib.it/activities/food524db/.

2.2   CNN-based Food Features

The CNN-based features proposed in this paper have been obtained by exploiting a deep residual architecture. Residual architectures are based on the idea that each layer of the network learns residual functions with reference to the layer inputs instead of learning unreferenced functions. Such architectures demonstrated to be easier to optimize and to gain accuracy by considerably increasing the depth [16].

Our network architecture is based on the ResNet-50 which represents a good trade-off between depth and performance. ResNet-50 demonstrated to be very effective on the ILSVRC 2015 (ImageNet Large Scale Visual Recognition Challenge) validation set with a top 1- recognition accuracy of about 80% [16]. We did not train the ResNet-50 from the scratch on Food524DB because the number of images for each class is not enough. As in previous work on this topic [22,25], we started from a pre-trained ResNet-50 on ILSVRC2012 scene image classification dataset [29]. The Food524DB dataset has been split in 80% of training data and 20% of test data. During the fine-tuning stage each image has been resized to 256×256 and a random crop has been taken of 224×224 size. We augmented data with the horizontal flipping. During the test stage we considered a single central 224×224 crop from the 256×256-resized image.

The ResNet-50 has been trained via stochastic gradient descent with a mini-batch of 16 images. We set the initial learning rate to 0.01 with learning rate update at every 5 K iterations. The network has been trained within the Caffe [19] framework on a PC equipped with a Tesla NVIDIA K40 GPU. The classification accuracy of the ResNet-50 fine-tuned with the Food524DB dataset is 69.52% for the Top-1, and 89.61% for the Top-5.

In the following experiments, the ResNet-50 is then used as feature extractor. The activations of the neurons in the fully connected layer are used as features for the retrieval of food images. The resulting feature vectors have size 2,048 components.

3   Food Retrieval Experiments

We have evaluated the classification performances of our network on the UNICT-FD1200 dataset, chosen because it was specifically designed for food retrieval. The UNICT-FD1200 dataset is composed by 4,754 images and 1,200 distinct dishes of food of different nationalities. We followed the evaluation procedures described in the original paper [13]. Specifically, the food dataset is divided into a training set of 1,200 images and in a test set with the remaining ones. The three training/test splits provided by the authors of the dataset are considered. The overall retrieval performances are measured as the average on the three splits.

The retrieval performances are measured using the $P(n)$ quality metric and the mean Average Precision (mAP). The $P(n)$ is based on the top n criterion: $P(n) = Q_n/Q$, where Q is the number of queries (test images) and Q_n the number of correct queries among the first n retrieved images [13]. For the retrieval

task, the images in the training set are considered as database images, while
the images in the test set are the queries. Moreover, for each query there is one
correct image to be retrieved. We also report the Top-1 recognition accuracy.

Table 3 shows the retrieval results obtained on the UNICT-FD1200 dataset.
We compare the performances of the features extracted with the fine-tuned network, "Activations ResNet-50 (Food524DB)" against those obtained with the
original network, "Activation ResNet-50 (ImageNet)", and against the hand-
crafted features used in [13]. As it can be seen the using the fine tuned network
outperform all the other methods in the classification task as well as in the
retrieval task. As expected the learned features greatly outperforms the hand-
crafted ones. The fine tuning of the ResNet-50 improves the retrieval results of
3% for the Top-1 and of 2.4% for the mAP. Figure 2 shows the $P(n)$ curves of
the methods in Table 3. It can be appreciated how the CNN-based features are
able to effectively retrieve the relevant images in the first position.

Table 3. Classification and retrieval results on the UNICT-FD1200 dataset.

Representation	Top-1 (%)	mAP (%)
Bag of SIFT 12000 [13]	21.81	29.14
Textons (MR8) - RGB - Global [13]	71.55	77.00
Textons (Schmidt) - Lab - Global [13]	87.44	90.06
Activations ResNet-50 (ImageNet)	91.84	94.15
Activations ResNet-50 (Food524DB)	**94.96**	**96.56**

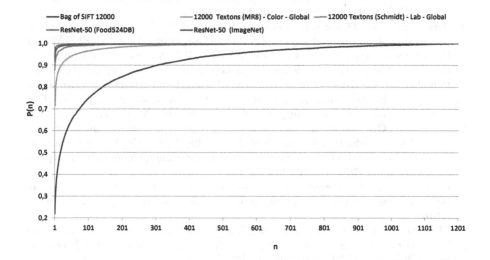

Fig. 2. P(n) curves of the methods in Table 3.

4 Conclusions

In this paper we investigated the use of CNN-based features for food retrieval. In order to accomplish this task we have created the Food524DB dataset by merging food classes from existing datasets in the state of the art. To date, Food524DB is the largest publicly available food dataset with 524 food classes and 247,636 images. The proposed CNN-based features have been obtained from a Residual Network (ResNet-50) fine tuned on Food524DB. The evaluation have been carried out on the UNICT-FD1200 dataset, that is a specific food retrieval dataset with 1,200 classes. Results demonstrated the powerful of the proposed CNN-based features with respect to CNN-based features extracted from the same network architecture trained on scene images and with respect to the state of the art features evaluated on the same dataset.

Acknowledgements. We gratefully acknowledge the support of NVIDIA Corporation with the donation of the Tesla K40 GPU used for this research.

References

1. Akpro Hippocrate, E.A., Suwa, H., Arakawa, Y., Yasumoto, K.: Food weight estimation using smartphone and cutlery. In: Proceedings of the First Workshop on IoT-enabled Healthcare and Wellness Technologies and Systems, IoT of Health 2016, pp. 9–14. ACM (2016)
2. Anthimopoulos, M.M., Gianola, L., Scarnato, L., Diem, P., Mougiakakou, S.G.: A food recognition system for diabetic patients based on an optimized bag-of-features model. IEEE J. Biomed. Health Inf. **18**(4), 1261–1271 (2014)
3. Bettadapura, V., Thomaz, E., Parnami, A., Abowd, G., Essa, I.: Leveraging context to support automated food recognition in restaurants. In: 2015 IEEE Winter Conference on Applications of Computer Vision (WACV), pp. 580–587 (2015)
4. Bianco, S., Ciocca, G., Napoletano, P., Schettini, R., Margherita, R., Marini, G., Pantaleo, G.: Cooking action recognition with iVAT: an interactive video annotation tool. In: Petrosino, A. (ed.) ICIAP 2013. LNCS, vol. 8157, pp. 631–641. Springer, Heidelberg (2013). https://doi.org/10.1007/978-3-642-41184-7_64
5. Bossard, L., Guillaumin, M., Van Gool, L.: Food-101 – mining discriminative components with random forests. In: Fleet, D., Pajdla, T., Schiele, B., Tuytelaars, T. (eds.) ECCV 2014. LNCS, vol. 8694, pp. 446–461. Springer, Cham (2014). https://doi.org/10.1007/978-3-319-10599-4_29
6. Chen, J., Ngo, C.W.: Deep-based ingredient recognition for cooking recipe retrieval. In: Proceedings of the 2016 ACM on Multimedia Conference, pp. 32–41. ACM (2016)
7. Chen, M., Dhingra, K., Wu, W., Yang, L., Sukthankar, R., Yang, J.: PFID: pittsburgh fast-food image dataset. In: 2009 16th IEEE International Conference on Image Processing (ICIP), pp. 289–292. IEEE (2009)
8. Chen, M.Y., Yang, Y.H., Ho, C.J., Wang, S.H., Liu, S.M., Chang, E., Yeh, C.H., Ouhyoung, M.: Automatic chinese food identification and quantity estimation. In: SIGGRAPH Asia 2012 Technical Briefs, p. 29. ACM (2012)

9. Ciocca, G., Napoletano, P., Schettini, R.: Food recognition and leftover estimation for daily diet monitoring. In: Murino, V., Puppo, E., Sona, D., Cristani, M., Sansone, C. (eds.) ICIAP 2015. LNCS, vol. 9281, pp. 334–341. Springer, Cham (2015). https://doi.org/10.1007/978-3-319-23222-5_41

10. Ciocca, G., Napoletano, P., Schettini, R.: Food recognition: a new dataset, experiments and results. IEEE J. Biomed. Health Inf. 21(3), 588–598 (2017)

11. Cusano, C., Napoletano, P., Schettini, R.: Intensity and color descriptors for texture classification. In: IS&T/SPIE Electronic Imaging, p. 866113. International Society for Optics and Photonics (2013)

12. Cusano, C., Napoletano, P., Schettini, R.: Combining local binary patterns and local color contrast for texture classification under varying illumination. JOSA A 31(7), 1453–1461 (2014)

13. Farinella, G.M., Allegra, D., Moltisanti, M., Stanco, F., Battiato, S.: Retrieval and classification of food images. Comput. Biol. Med. 77, 23–39 (2016)

14. Farinella, G.M., Allegra, D., Stanco, F.: A benchmark dataset to study the representation of food images. In: Agapito, L., Bronstein, M.M., Rother, C. (eds.) ECCV 2014. LNCS, vol. 8927, pp. 584–599. Springer, Cham (2015). https://doi.org/10.1007/978-3-319-16199-0_41

15. Hassannejad, H., Matrella, G., Ciampolini, P., De Munari, I., Mordonini, M., Cagnoni, S.: Food image recognition using very deep convolutional networks. In: Proceedings of the 2nd International Workshop on Multimedia Assisted Dietary Management, MADiMa 2016, pp. 41–49. ACM (2016)

16. He, K., Zhang, X., Ren, S., Sun, J.: Deep residual learning for image recognition. In: Proceedings of the IEEE Conference on Computer Vision and Pattern Recognition, pp. 770–778 (2016)

17. He, Y., Xu, C., Khanna, N., Boushey, C., Delp, E.: Analysis of food images: features and classification. In: 2014 IEEE International Conference on Image Processing (ICIP), pp. 2744–2748 (2014)

18. Hoashi, H., Joutou, T., Yanai, K.: Image recognition of 85 food categories by feature fusion. In: IEEE International Symposium on Multimedia (ISM) 2010, pp. 296–301. IEEE (2010)

19. Jia, Y., Shelhamer, E., Donahue, J., Karayev, S., Long, J., Girshick, R., Guadarrama, S., Darrell, T.: Caffe: convolutional architecture for fast feature embedding. arXiv preprint arXiv:1408.5093 (2014)

20. Joutou, T., Yanai, K.: A food image recognition system with multiple kernel learning. In: 2009 16th IEEE International Conference on Image Processing (ICIP), pp. 285–288. IEEE (2009)

21. Kawano, Y., Yanai, K.: Automatic expansion of a food image dataset leveraging existing categories with domain adaptation. In: Agapito, L., Bronstein, M.M., Rother, C. (eds.) ECCV 2014. LNCS, vol. 8927, pp. 3–17. Springer, Cham (2015). https://doi.org/10.1007/978-3-319-16199-0_1

22. Kawano, Y., Yanai, K.: Food image recognition with deep convolutional features. In: Proceedings of the 2014 ACM International Joint Conference on Pervasive and Ubiquitous Computing, UbiComp 2014 Adjunct, pp. 589–593 (2014)

23. Liu, C., Cao, Y., Luo, Y., Chen, G., Vokkarane, V., Ma, Y.: DeepFood: deep learning-based food image recognition for computer-aided dietary assessment. In: Chang, C.K., Chiari, L., Cao, Y., Jin, H., Mokhtari, M., Aloulou, H. (eds.) ICOST 2016. LNCS, vol. 9677, pp. 37–48. Springer, Cham (2016). https://doi.org/10.1007/978-3-319-39601-9_4

24. Mariappan, A., Bosch, M., Zhu, F., Boushey, C.J., Kerr, D.A., Ebert, D.S., Delp, E.J.: Personal dietary assessment using mobile devices, vol. 7246, pp. 72460Z-1–72460Z-12 (2009)
25. Martinel, N., Foresti, G.L., Micheloni, C.: Wide-slice residual networks for food recognition. arXiv preprint arXiv:1612.06543 (2016)
26. Matsuda, Y., Hoashi, H., Yanai, K.: Recognition of multiple-food images by detecting candidate regions. In: 2012 IEEE International Conference on Multimedia and Expo (ICME), pp. 25–30 (2012)
27. Nguyen, D.T., Zong, Z., Ogunbona, P.O., Probst, Y., Li, W.: Food image classification using local appearance and global structural information. Neurocomputing **140**, 242–251 (2014)
28. Pouladzadeh, P., Kuhad, P., Peddi, S.V.B., Yassine, A., Shirmohammadi, S.: Food calorie measurement using deep learning neural network. In: IEEE International Instrumentation and Measurement Technology Conference, pp. 1–6 (2016)
29. Russakovsky, O., Deng, J., Su, H., Krause, J., Satheesh, S., Ma, S., Huang, Z., Karpathy, A., Khosla, A., Bernstein, M., Berg, A.C., Fei-Fei, L.: ImageNet large scale visual recognition challenge. Int. J. Comput. Vis. (IJCV) **115**(3), 211–252 (2015)
30. Sharif Razavian, A., Azizpour, H., Sullivan, J., Carlsson, S.: CNN features off-the-shelf: an astounding baseline for recognition. In: Proceedings of the IEEE conference on computer vision and pattern recognition workshops, pp. 806–813 (2014)
31. Wang, X., Kumar, D., Thome, N., Cord, M., Precioso, F.: Recipe recognition with large multimodal food dataset. In: 2015 IEEE International Conference on Multimedia and Expo Workshops (ICMEW), pp. 1–6. IEEE (2015)
32. Yanai, K., Kawano, Y.: Food image recognition using deep convolutional network with pre-training and fine-tuning. In: 2015 IEEE International Conference on Multimedia Expo Workshops (ICMEW), pp. 1–6 (2015)

On Comparing Color Spaces for Food Segmentation

Sinem Aslan[✉], Gianluigi Ciocca, and Raimondo Schettini

Department of Informatics, Systems and Communication,
University of Milano-Bicocca, Milano, Italy
{sinem.aslan,ciocca,schettini}@disco.unimib.it

Abstract. Accurate segmentation of food regions is important for both food recognition and quantity estimation and any error would degrade the accuracy of the food dietary assessment system. Main goal of this work is to investigate the performance of a number of color encoding schemes and color spaces for food segmentation exploiting the JSEG algorithm. Our main outcome is that significant improvements in segmentation can be achieved with a proper color space selection and by learning the proper setting of the segmentation parameters from a training set.

Keywords: Automatic food segmentation · Color spaces · JSEG

1 Introduction

Measuring nutrition intake and food calorie in daily diets is important to not only treat and control food-related health problems, but also for people who want to be aware of their nutrition habits to maintain a healthy weight. Recent developments at vision-based measurement [1–3] has gained significant attention from community dealing with dietary assessment, since the process is quietly simplified for the users, i.e., they simply take the photo of their food with a mobile device and calorie calculation is achieved automatically in the pipeline of processes employing computer vision techniques.

A general pipeline of calorie calculation by vision-based measurement consists of four stages [1]: (i) Preprocessing for image enhancement; (ii) Food segmentation to determine the food regions inside dishes; (iii) Food recognition where representative features are extracted on the segmented regions and fed into a classifier; (iv) Calorie measurement where the mass of the food is estimated and corresponding calories are computed using existing nutrition tables. In this paper, we have focused on the second stage, i.e. food region segmentation that greatly influence the accuracy of the subsequent stages.

Plenty of papers for food segmentation has been published and a number of outstanding ones are presented in Table 1. The literature works on food segmentation have employed a variety of segmentation schemes, e.g., thresholding, active contours, JSEG, normalized cuts, mean shift, etc., by utilizing a different

© Springer International Publishing AG 2017
S. Battiato et al. (Eds.): ICIAP 2017 International Workshops, LNCS 10590, pp. 435–443, 2017.
https://doi.org/10.1007/978-3-319-70742-6_42

color space, e.g., gray-scale, CIELUV, CIELAB. Moreover, performance of these algorithms have been evaluated on different food image datasets. In this work, we aim to make a comparative evaluation of different color encoding schemes and color spaces for food region segmentation on the same dataset and by using the same segmentation scheme.

The color encoding schemes and color spaces [4,5] that we have considered are Y′IQ, Y′CbCr, Y′PbPr, Y′DbDr, CIEXYZ, CIELAB and CIELUV, $O_1O_2O_3$, rgb (normalized RGB), and $I_1I_2I_3$. Y′IQ, Y′CbCr, Y′PbPr, and Y′DbDr are the luma and chroma encoding systems that separates the sRGB into one luminance and two chrominance components. Taking advantage of human vision's sensitivity to changes on the luminance component, these systems are useful for compression applications. CIEXYZ, CIELAB and CIELUV colorimetric spaces are device independent, i.e., they do not depend on the parameter settings of the devices but represent the colors based on response of an ideal standard observer to wavelengths of light. CIELAB and CIELUV are perceptionally uniform, i.e., the Euclidean distance between two colors in CIELAB and CIELUV is strongly correlated to the distance perceived in human vision. rgb is invariant to surface orientation, illumination direction and intensity [4]. O_1 and O_2 components of the opponent color space $O_1O_2O_3$ are independent of highlights, but sensitive to surface orientation, illumination direction and illumination intensity, while O_3 has no invariant property [4]. Color information is separated into three approximately othogonal components at $I_1I_2I_3$ and it is reported as useful for segmentation in [5].

Table 1. Literature works on food region segmentation

Publication	Color space	Segmentation scheme
Shroff et al. [6]	Gray-scale	Adaptive thresholding
He et al. [7]	Gray-scale	Active contours, normalized cuts, and local variation performed on the detected foreground
Zhu et al. [8]	Gray-scale	Normalized cuts performed on the foreground region, that is tuned regarding to the resulted food recognition performance
Anthimopoulos et al. [1]	CIELAB	Mean-shift performed on the plate region which is detected by RANSAC
Bettadapura et al. [2]	CIELAB and gray-scale	Hierarchical segmentation with the GPS-based location heuristics providing assumptions for segmentation
Ciocca et al. [3]	CIELUV	JSEG on the detected food regions
Matsuda et al. [9]	CIELUV and gray-scale	Regions that are segmented by Deformable Part Model, a circle detector and JSEG are integrated according to the score of classification accuracy they provide

We have chosen the well-known JSEG automatic color segmentation algorithm [10] to integrate the computations in different color spaces. JSEG has been successfully used in many literature works and the published source code [11] yields modifications on the method conveniently.

The experiments are done on automatically cropped images of UNIMIB2016 food dataset [3] which includes a wide range of food types with both bounding box and polygon annotations.

2   JSEG

JSEG [10], illustrated in Fig. 1, accomplishes segmentation in two main stages, i.e., *color quantization* and *spatial segmentation*. In the first stage, the colors of images are coarsely quantized into several representing classes to obtain a class-map where each pixel is labeled with its corresponding color class label. It is suggested in [10] to use the color quantization algorithm developed by Deng et al. [12] which conforms to human perception sensitivity. According to this method [12], the images are initially smoothed by *Peer Group Filtering* (*PGF*) which avoids to blur the edges. Then, using the local statistics provided by PGF, the color quantization algorithm with the implementation steps as follows is performed: (1) Assign weights to pixels in a way that noisy regions are weighted less and smoothed regions are weighted more; (2) Estimate the initial number of clusters by considering the smoothness of the entire image, i.e., the less smooth the image is, the higher number of initial clusters is; (3) Determine the initial clusters by splitting initialization algorithm [12] and implement vector quantization by modified Generalized Lloyd Algorithm (GLA) which incorporates the weights that were computed at the first step; (4) Perform an agglomerative clustering algorithm [13] to merge the close clusters until the minimum distance between two centroids satisfies a preset threshold T_Q. The novelty of the algorithm in [12] lies at the weighting scheme employed at the first step which yields GLA to shift the centroids towards points with higher weights, i.e., smoother regions.

In the second stage of JSEG, a homogeneity measurement, called as *J-value*, is computed by using the obtained color class-map in a local window around each pixel. High and low J-values indicate possible region boundaries and centers, respectively. Computed J-values for all pixels form a gray-scale pseudo-image called as *J-Image* and computing J-values in N different window sizes results with J-images in N number of scales. Small and larger sized windows provide to

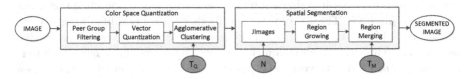

Fig. 1. Schematic of the JSEG algorithm. The ellipses in yellow represent the algorithm's parameteres. (Color figure online)

localize color edges and detect texture boundaries, respectively, and it is useful to employ multiple scales of J-Images in the segmentation process in order to facilitate from both information. What is next is, the resulted multi scale J-Images are used by a region growing scheme in an iterative way to accomplish the initial segmentation which essentially constitutes to the over segmentation of the input image. In order to obtain the final segmentation, over segmented regions are merged by the agglomerative method [13] that was already employed at the color quantization algorithm. The most similar neighbour region pairs are merged until the minimum Euclidean distance between two histogram features satisfies a preset threshold T_M.

JSEG and the employed color quantization scheme process images in the CIELUV color space. Three parameters are set by users in the whole process, i.e., color quantization threshold (T_Q), number of scales of J-Images (N), and region merge threshold (T_M). These parameters directly influence the segmentation results. Low values of both the color quantization threshold T_Q and region merge threshold T_M encourage over segmentation. Finer details are segmented with higher values of N and vice versa.

3   Experimental Setup

Food Dataset. We have used UNIMIB-2016 dataset [3] since it includes a wide variety of food types, i.e. 1,027 tray images including 73 food categories; in addition to the bounding box annotations, the published polygon annotations provide evaluation with more precise ground truth compared to existing datasets; and it is sufficiently challenging for segmentation. The main challenges can be listed as (i) white colored placemats and plates complicates to segment the food regions in the same color, e.g., *riso in bianco* and *pasta pesto besciamella e cornetti* (see Fig. 2a), (ii) includes multiple food segmentation problem, since side and main dishes are served in the same plate (see Fig. 2b); (iii) images are acquired in an uncontrolled environment by a hand-held smart phone and includes illumination (see Fig. 2c).

Differently from [3], we assume that the photos of food regions on a tray were shot individually in this paper. In order to obtain such material, we cropped the tray images into subimages by exploiting the published bounding box annotations as a subimage would include the Region of Interest (ROI), i.e., food region. Each sub-image is cropped from a custom space $d_h/2$ and $d_v/2$ from the borders of the bounding box, where d_h and d_v are the distances (in pixels) from center to horizontal and vertical borders of the bounding box. We desire to crop main and side foods together in a single subimage and with a new bounding box annotation covering both. Thus, we co-cropped foods if their bounding boxes overlap in the ratio of 95%. Using this simple heuristic we obtain the new dataset that includes 2,679 images and with a quick check we eliminated 50 images which were not cropped at all due to very close positions of the foods on the trays. A new challenge as a result of automatic cropping is the "noise" objects around ROI (See Fig. 2d). The dataset of cropped UNIMIB-2016 images and their polygon and bounding box annotations will be published.

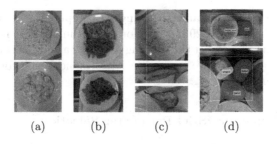

(a)   (b)   (c)   (d)

Fig. 2. Challenges of UNIMIB2016 dataset (automatically cropped images).

Parameter Setting Schemes for JSEG. The JSEG default values suggested in the published implementation [11] are $T_Q = 250$, $T_M = 0.4$, and although the parameter N can be set by the user, it is suggested in [10,11] to use the automatic setting in JSEG which specifies N according to the input image size. It is mentioned in [10] that JSEG works well on a large set of images, i.e., 2500 images, with the mentioned fixed values of the parameters without any requirement for tuning. However, transforming the input images to other color spaces requires to update the fixed value of T_Q while N and T_M would not get affected from this operation. Thus, we have used the default values of $T_M = 0.4$ and N(automatic) [11] at the experiments, and we define another termination criterion for color quantization which is independent to underlying color space. The new criterion considers the *resulting number of clusters* after merging operation instead of minimum distance between quantized colors.

We have followed two approaches for setting of T_C: *(i) Fixed scheme of parameter setting.* We fix the T_C to the value which yields segmentation performance be most close to (or slightly better than) the performance obtained with the default parameter setting, i.e., $T_Q = 250$, for images in CIELUV color space [11]. *(ii) Optimized scheme of parameter setting.* We learn the value of T_C from a training set for each color space individually.

4   Results

We have resized the images as their smallest length would be 128 and 256 pixels to investigate performance at different image sizes. In order to assess the quality of the segmentation, we applied the evaluation benchmarks suggested in [14]. Specifically, we compute *boundary-based* measurements Precision (P), Recall (R) and Fscore (F) and *region-based* measurements, i.e., covering (of ground truth by segmentation), Probabilistic Rand Index (PRI), and the Variation of Information (VI). Differently from [14], we have one ground truth data and one scale of segmentation (since we do not perform hierarchical segmentation) for each image. P, R, F and segment covering are aggregated scores on the whole dataset, i.e., fractions are computed after aggregating statistics from all images, whereas PRI and VI are the averaged scores over number of images [14].

For the fixed scheme of parameter setting, we compute the performance scores on the whole dataset, i.e., 2,629 images. For the optimized scheme, we randomly sample 200 images to construct the training set and learning the optimal parameter value on the training set, we present the performance results on the remaining 2,429 testing set images.

4.1   Fixed Scheme for JSEG Parameter Selection

At the first stage of the fixing scheme, we have segmented 2,629 images in CIELUV color space by $T_Q = 250$ setting as suggested in [11], and with a number of T_C settings, i.e., $T_C = \{2, 3, 4, 5, 6, 7, 8, 9, 10\}$. We have obtained the performance results in Table 2. In this experiment, we evaluate the quality of segmentation with respect to the average of boundary and region based Fscores, i.e. $(F_{boundary} + F_{region})/2$, in order to include contribution of both region and boundary-based assessment. We observe in Table 2 that in comparison with $T_Q = 250$ setting, the closest and slightly better performance is obtained with $T_C = 4$.

Table 2. Performance results, in terms of $(F_{boundary} + F_{region})/2$, that are obtained with default setting of T_Q and different settings of T_C.

Image size at shortest side	$T_Q = 250$	$T_C = 2$	$T_C = 3$	$T_C = 4$	$T_C = 5$	$T_C = 6$	$T_C = 7$	$T_C = 8$	$T_C = 9$	$T_C = 10$
128 pix.	**0.49**	0.62	0.55	**0.51**	0.47	0.43	0.40	0.38	0.35	0.33
256 pix.	**0.45**	0.61	0.53	**0.48**	0.43	0.35	0.39	0.33	0.30	0.28

In the second stage, we fix $T_C = 4$, and segment the images in other color spaces. The obtained performance results are given in Table 3. It is observed that the highest boundary based Fscore is obtained with CIELUV, which is followed by Y'DbDr and rgb in both image sizes. Moreover, covering score of Y'DbDr is 3% and 2% better than CIELUV and rgb respectively in both image sizes. PRI and VOI scores are also compatible with this observation. Among all CIEXYZ is the worst in all experiments.

4.2   Optimized Scheme for JSEG Parameter Selection

We have measured the score of $(F_{boundary} + F_{region})/2$ with each $T_C \in \{2, 3, 4, 5, 6, 7, 8, 9, 10\}$ setting on training images, and the best performed setting is employed in segmentation of the testing images. We present the performance results with optimal T_C setting for each color space in Table 4. We also include the performance that we obtained with the published implementation of JSEG that works in CIELUV with fixed $T_Q = 250$ setting [10,11].

Table 3. Performance results obtained by JSEG with fixed $T_C = 4$ setting varying the color spaces.

Color space	128 Pix.						256 pix.					
	Boundary-based			Region-based			Boundary-based			Region-based		
	P	R	F	Covering	PRI	VOI	P	R	F	Covering	PRI	VOI
Y'CbCr	0.27	0.45	0.33	0.57	0.65	1.82	0.20	0.51	0.29	0.54	0.63	2.14
Y'DbDr	**0.34**	0.48	**0.40**	**0.69**	**0.73**	**1.34**	**0.28**	0.55	0.37	**0.67**	**0.72**	**1.55**
Y'IQ	0.28	0.43	0.34	0.62	0.68	1.66	0.21	0.50	0.30	0.59	0.66	1.96
Y'PbPr	0.28	0.44	0.34	0.62	0.68	1.64	0.21	0.51	0.30	0.58	0.66	1.97
CIELAB	0.23	0.37	0.29	0.54	0.63	1.88	0.18	0.44	0.25	0.52	0.62	2.17
CIELUV	0.33	0.50	**0.40**	0.66	0.71	1.46	**0.28**	0.56	**0.38**	0.64	0.70	1.63
CIEXYZ	0.20	0.38	0.26	0.43	0.56	2.35	0.16	0.48	0.24	0.41	0.55	2.73
rgb	0.33	0.48	0.39	0.67	0.72	1.41	0.27	0.54	0.37	0.65	0.71	1.59
$O_1O_2O_3$	0.21	0.40	0.28	0.46	0.58	2.25	0.17	0.48	0.25	0.42	0.56	2.64
$I_1I_2I_3$	0.20	0.39	0.27	0.44	0.57	2.33	0.16	0.47	0.23	0.40	0.55	2.76

Table 4. Performance results obtained by the optimal value of T_C learned on the training set for each color space. [*]Benchmark using $T_Q = 250$

Color space	128 Pix.						256 pix.					
	Boundary-based			Region-based			Boundary-based			Region-based		
	P	R	F	Covering	PRI	VOI	P	R	F	Covering	PRI	VOI
Y'CbCr	0.30	0.32	0.31	0.66	0.70	1.26	0.24	0.34	0.28	0.65	0.68	1.39
Y'DbDr	0.49	0.37	0.42	0.79	0.81	0.79	0.45	0.40	0.42	0.78	0.81	0.82
Y'IQ	0.34	0.32	0.33	0.70	0.71	1.12	0.28	0.35	0.31	0.69	0.72	1.22
Y'PbPr	0.34	0.32	0.33	0.70	0.73	1.11	0.28	0.35	0.31	0.69	0.72	1.21
CIELAB	0.25	0.33	0.28	0.59	0.66	1.60	0.21	0.28	0.24	0.61	0.65	1.47
CIELUV	0.47	0.42	**0.45**	0.79	0.82	0.84	0.43	0.45	0.44	0.79	0.81	0.88
CIEXYZ	0.27	0.32	0.30	0.63	0.67	1.41	0.22	0.34	0.27	0.62	0.67	1.52
rgb	**0.52**	0.40	**0.45**	**0.82**	**0.84**	**0.71**	**0.49**	0.43	**0.46**	**0.81**	**0.83**	**0.74**
$O_1O_2O_3$	0.27	0.32	0.29	0.63	0.67	1.42	0.22	0.34	0.27	0.62	0.67	1.52
$I_1I_2I_3$	0.26	0.32	0.29	0.63	0.67	1.44	0.21	0.34	0.26	0.61	0.66	1.56
CIELUV[*]	0.32	**0.51**	0.39	0.64	0.70	1.57	0.26	**0.58**	0.36	0.60	0.68	1.85

We list our observations as follows: (*i*) *Comparison of color spaces:* rgb and CIELUV gives the same best boundary-based Fscore at the smaller sized images while rgb is 2% better than CIELUV for larger sized images. rgb outperforms others in all region-based scores. Y'DbDr follows them both in boundary and region based scores. The worst performances are obtained for CIELAB and $I_1I_2I_3$; (*ii*) *Comparison with Table* 3: Optimizing T_C improved boundary-based performance for most of the color spaces, e.g., ~6%, ~5%, and ~2% improvement in Fscore is obtained for rgb, CIELUV and Y'DbDr, respectively, for smaller sized images, and even more for larger size images. Besides, performance at

Y′CbCr, YIQ, Y′PbPr and CIELAB slightly (∼1%) degrades with optimized T_C at smaller sized images, but same for all at larger sized images. Optimizing T_C improved region-based scores significantly for all color spaces, e.g., around 15%, 16%, 10% and 20% improvement in covering score is achieved for rgb, CIELUV, Y′DbDr and CIELAB at both image sizes, respectively; (*iii*) *Comparison with benchmark:* Default JSEG implementation with fixed $T_Q = 250$ at CIELUV gives better boundary-based recall, however since their precision is not good enough optimized scheme outperforms benchmark in the rates of ∼6% and ∼10% at boundary-based Fscore for small and larger sized images, respectively. Improvement in region-based performance is even more remarkable, i.e., in the rates of ∼20%.

5 Conclusion

In this paper we studied the segmentation algorithm of the processing pipeline for food dietary assessment. We focused on color space selection food segmentation. More precisely, an extensive comparative evaluation of ten color encoding scheme and spaces is made by using the well-known JSEG segmentation algorithm. We have also investigated the optimal parameter setting for JSEG to work in different color spaces. Experimental results show that representations in Y′DbDr and rgb is to be preferred for food segmentation.

References

1. Anthimopoulos, M., Dehais, J., Diem, P., Mougiakakou, S.: Segmentation and recognition of multi-food meal images for carbohydrate counting. In: Proceedings of the IEEE 13th International Conference on Bioinformatics and Bioengineering (BIBE 2013), pp. 1–4 (2013)
2. Bettadapura, V., Thomaz, E., Parnami, A., Abowd, G.D., Essa, I.: Leveraging context to support automated food recognition in restaurants. In: Proceedings of the IEEE Winter Conference on Applications of Computer Vision (WACV 2015), pp. 580–587 (2015)
3. Ciocca, G., Napoletano, P., Schettini, R.: Food recognition: a new dataset, experiments, and results. IEEE J. Biomed. Health Inform. **21**(3), 588–598 (2017)
4. Lee, D., Plataniotis, K.N.: A taxonomy of color constancy and invariance algorithm. In: Celebi, M.E., Smolka, B. (eds.) Advances in Low-Level Color Image Processing. LNCVB, vol. 11, pp. 55–94. Springer, Dordrecht (2014). https://doi.org/10.1007/978-94-007-7584-8_3
5. Ohta, Y.I., Kanade, T., Sakai, T.: Color information for region segmentation. Comput. Graph. Image Process. **13**(3), 222–241 (1980)
6. Shroff, G., Smailagic, A., Siewiorek, D.P.: Wearable context-aware food recognition for calorie monitoring. In: Proceedings of the 12th IEEE International Symposium on Wearable Computers (ISWC 2008), pp. 119–120 (2008)
7. He, Y., Khanna, N., Boushey, C., Delp, E.: Image segmentation for image-based dietary assessment: a comparative study. In: Proceedings of the IEEE International Symposium on Signals, Circuits and Systems (ISSCS 2013), pp. 1–4 (2013)

8. Zhu, F., Bosch, M., Khanna, N., Boushey, C.J., Delp, E.J.: Multiple hypotheses image segmentation and classification with application to dietary assessment. IEEE J. Biomed. Health Inform. **19**(1), 377–388 (2015)
9. Matsuda, Y., Hoashi, H., Yanai, K.: Recognition of multiple-food images by detecting candidate regions. In: Proceedings of the IEEE International Conference on Multimedia and Expo (ICME 2012), pp. 25–30 (2012)
10. Deng, Y., Manjunath, B.: Unsupervised segmentation of color-texture regions in images and video. IEEE Trans. Pattern Anal. Mach. Intell. **23**(8), 800–810 (2001)
11. Deng, Y., Manjunath, B.: JSEG Project. http://old.vision.ece.ucsb.edu/segmentation/jseg/software/ (1999). Accessed 27 June 2017
12. Deng, Y., Kenney, C., Moore, M.S., Manjunath, B.: Peer group filtering and perceptual color image quantization. In: Proceedings of the IEEE International Symposium on Circuits and Systems, (ISCAS 1999), Vol. 4, pp. 21–24. IEEE (1999)
13. Duda, R.O., Hart, P.E., Stork, D.G., et al.: Pattern classification, vol. 2. Wiley, New York (1973)
14. Arbelaez, P., Maire, M., Fowlkes, C., Malik, J.: Contour detection and hierarchical image segmentation. IEEE Trans. Patt. Anal. Mach. Intell. **33**(5), 898–916 (2011)

Pocket Dietitian: Automated Healthy Dish Recommendations by Location

Nitish Nag$^{(\boxtimes)}$, Vaibhav Pandey, Abhisaar Sharma, Jonathan Lam,
Runyi Wang, and Ramesh Jain

University of California, Irvine, USA
nagn@uci.edu

Abstract. A root cause of chronic disease is a lack of timely informed decision power in everyday lifestyle choices, such as in diets. Users are unable to clearly delineate and demand healthy food in a quantitative manner. To scale the benefit of health nutrition coaching in broad real-world scenarios, we need a technological solution that is constantly able to interpret nutrition information. We ingest nutritional facts about products to efficiently calculate which items are healthiest. We deliver these results to users based on their location context. Our ranking algorithm outperforms major nutrition score metrics, and is more consistent than human dietitians in real world scenarios. Most importantly, our system gives the user a rapid way to connect with healthy food in their vicinity, reducing the barriers to a healthy diet.

Keywords: Cybernetics · Precision medicine · Disease prevention
Context awareness · Mobile health · Personalized · Nutrition
Expert systems

1 Introduction

Health is essentially a product of our genome and lifestyle [12]. Dietary choices are a major component of lifestyle and can have great impact on an individual's long term health outcomes.

US federal nutrition guidelines (Fig. 1) are hard to translate into everyday life decisions. Although the knowledge exists, it is not in an actionable form. For example, typically patients with diabetes who are supervised by nutrition experts meet once every three months. Even if a nutritionist is available to guide a client, they don't usually have all information related to the appropriate nutrition in immediate context of the individual.

Real-time *multimedia* technologies will play a major role in powering recommendations to solve health issues. Leading medical professionals have advocated for a deeper integration of technology into health care [12]. Patients make better lifestyle choices that would combat diabetes if given guidance [11]. Ultimately, transforming data and knowledge to actionable lifestyle choices is the

© Springer International Publishing AG 2017
S. Battiato et al. (Eds.): ICIAP 2017 International Workshops, LNCS 10590, pp. 444–452, 2017.
https://doi.org/10.1007/978-3-319-70742-6_43

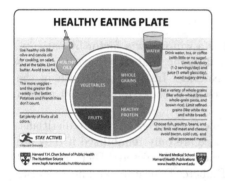

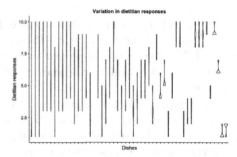

Fig. 1. Recommendations from health experts as shown here from the Harvard Medical School are compiled from consensus nutrition experts. Yet these recommendations are hard to translate into everyday life decisions for the public population, especially in the context of eating out.

Fig. 2. For 50 dishes given on the x-axis, each dish was given a score of 1–10, 1 being the most unhealthy, and 10 being very healthy. Amongst 7 professional dietitians, the variance for a given dish was highly unpredictable, with only 19 items having less than a 30% range.

most promising, effective, and attainable method to improve human health. We have developed a system that can place a dietitian level of decision support for finding food within a location aware automated smartphone application.

Of all the food consumers eat, now more than half comes from eating out, with the future trend toward increasing food purchases made out. Assisting everyday lifestyle management must be inexpensive, scalable, and increase health transparency of consumer purchasing. This is especially important to reach all ends of the socioeconomic spectrum [9]. Companies like Amazon use quantitative measures like reviews or filters to help customers easily find what they are looking for at the correct granularity of the product. The essential question we want to answer for every consumer is: "How will this product affect my health?". At the moment, labels on products falsely claim how "healthy" a product is, but consumers do not trust companies to give them an honest depiction of their product. We aim to develop a third party platform that can independently judge the health metrics given product specifications.

Recommendations via expert knowledge are the key to unlock healthy diets for the world. Multimedia work in this field has primarily focused on giving the user figures and statistics of past data. Tracking diet is a very useful feature, but lacks the capability of giving actionable suggestions to improve health. The core problem at hand we are attempting to solve is real time needs-resource matching. Recommendations are essential to modern content and product consumption. Ultimately this system effortlessly connects a tasty and healthy meal to the consumer, which is the key to driving behavior change for healthier lifestyles.

2 Related Work

Better lifestyle management is appreciated as a win-win-win factor by patients, providers, and insurance entities. Programs like the Diabetes Prevention Program (DPP) have been approved by the National Institute of Health in the United States for health insurance reimbursement codes for over 100 million patients.

Socioeconomic factors prevent most people from access to private dietitians. Furthermore, even those with health insurance are only reimbursed if they are at high risk or diseased, which is too late. Practicing Registered Dietitians, PhD researchers with diabetes clients, Certified Diabetes Educators, and nutritionists all spend significant amounts of time trying to help recommend what their clients should eat. These providers spend most of their interaction time with clients also trying to understand their dietary habits. This can be streamlined through intelligent diet tracking from transactions that take place from the recommendations and image understanding, potentially reducing visit times by 30–45%. There have been large research efforts by nutrition experts to try and grade the quality of food. Qualitative approaches include the Healthy Eating Index and the Diet Quality Index are semi-quantitative [5]. From these methods, nutritionists have vocalized the need to translate expert recommendations into a usable platform for simple consumption by users [7]. Given a certain budget, finding the best nutrition has also been explored [2]. Quantitative approaches of most scoring mechanisms show weak associations with actual disease outcomes [1,14]. Efforts in modeling expert knowledge has just used linear correlations with a small panel of nutritionists [8]. Because nutrition facts are readily available for all major restaurant chains and for packaged items, algorithms that use this information are most promising for immediate consumer use. The North American derived Nutrient Rich Foods Index 6.3 (NRF) [4], French derived SAIN/LIM method [15], and British FSA [6] all are based more heavily on available nutrition facts. Evaluation of online recipes using these previous methods have shown that users are unaware of the healthiness of the food [13]. Popular food mobile apps, like Yelp.com amongst others, allow the user to search for their restaurants in their vicinity but the user has to spend considerable effort to find a dish they prefer which satisfies their preferences. One app, named HealthyOut, allows users to filter items with certain allergens (which do not follow standard USDA guidelines) and calories caps [10]. Delivery platforms are in hot demand with systems like DeliveryHero.com amongst others attract users through convenience. Most importantly, health and allergy information is never taken into consideration most existing platforms.

3 System Architecture

Our basic architecture applies the algorithms we have developed to the meals available in a given vicinity surrounding a user. The person vector is defined by their location and the entity vector is defined based on the nutritional analysis of each dish.

The first major component includes the **data filter** to ensure quality recommendations. Data quality is checked by numeric checks on ingredients and nutritional values. The filters are: 1. **Calories** filter ensures that the caloric value provided matches the nutritional value (carbohydrates, fat and alcohol) available with the dish. 2. **Carbohydrates** filter ensures that the total carbohydrates reported matches with different sources of carbs (such as sugar, fiber and starch). 3. **Fat** filter ensures that reported total fat with the meal matches with different sources of fat (such as saturated fat, trans fat etc.). 4. **Red meat filter** ensures that if a dish contains red meat then the quantity of saturated fat reported is not zero.

The second major component **simulates the expert knowledge**. We assign a personalized health score (1–100 with 100 being healthiest) to every dish and food item based on their nutritional content and the caloric needs of the user that are located near the user. This score evaluates the items in a much more relevant manner for consumers to make their dietary choices, which has been called for previously as the Nutrient Density Score [3]. There are standardized algorithms available for measuring the nutrient density in the food items but none have been used in a user friendly manner. We are incorporating the expert knowledge of the dietitians via this algorithm and providing instant guidance around the clock to our users. We call our algorithmic scoring system Environment and Life Integreated eXpert Individualized Recommendation System (ELIXIR) (Algorithm 1), which uses expert tuned weights (Table 1). The weights were tuned with a nutrition expert manually adjusting the weights till the rank list of the items represented an accurate depiction of what the human nutritionist would suggest. The algorithm considers 3 different categories of macro nutrients: recommended base and additional nutrients, and restricted base nutrients. In simple terms, the algorithm places healthy components of the nutrition in the numerator, and unhealthy sections in the denominator. The ratio of these two components is then scaled from 1–100 for a user friendly experience.

The last component of the **user interface** involves a smart phone application for a logged in user (Fig. 3). This information is then used to show them the best available meals (based on their requirements) in the vicinity in form of a map view and a list view. The user also has the ability to search for a particular type of dish (eg. pizza) or a particular restaurant. The application would recommend the healthiest dish related to the search query in the user local vicinity.

4 Dataset

We have used two independent datasets for our experiments. First is the USDA food composition database, which is publicly available at USDA.gov. The USDA food composition database contains nutritional values for 158,552 food items and the appropriate food group. Second, we created a geo-tagged nutritional dataset for restaurant dishes. This was done by scraping the restaurant menus using Google Places API to search for restaurants in the California region. The data set contains dishes with nutrition facts from 596 food chain menus from Google.

Table 1. Weights and Daily Values

Nutrients	Weight	Daily value
Calories	1.00	2000 cal
Protein	1.00	50 g
Sugar	1.10	50 g
Total Fat	1.10	60 g
Saturated Fat	1.70	20 g
Carbohydrate	1.00	300 g
Fiber	1.50	25 g
Sodium	1.00	2400 mg
Cholesterol	1.20	300 mg
Vit A	1.00	5000 IU
Vit C	1.00	60 mg
Calcium	1.00	1000 mg
Iron	1.00	18 mg
Trans Fat	0.91	NA
Complex Carb	0.10	NA

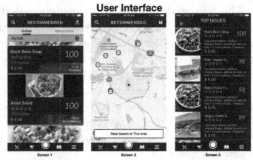

Fig. 3. User interface demonstration through mobile application. Screen 1 demonstrates how the healthiest dishes are automatically populated. S2 shows the map context of the user with locations of all the healthy dishes. S3 curates the healthiest dishes at the restaurant.

We match the locations of restaurants to the respective dishes to create 10 million geo-tagged dish/nutrition dataset of California, USA. Figure 4 illustrates data quality after filtering. The health score for each dish was calculated using Algorithm 1. The distribution of these dishes across the ELIXIR spectrum is shown in Fig. 5. The database distribution in Fig. 5 does not contain duplicate dishes.

Algorithm 1. ELIXIR

1: **procedure** ELIXIR–SCORE(weights, DailyValues, Mult)

2:     $RecBN = (Protein, Fiber)$

3:     $RecAN = (VitA, VitC, Ca, Fe)$

4:     $RestBN = (Cal, Chol, Na, SatFat, TotFat, Sugar)$

5:     $RecBase = \sum\limits_{i \in RecBase} weights[i] * \frac{dish[i]}{DailyValues[i]}$

6:     $RecBase = RecBase + weights[Fiber] * \frac{dish[Fiber]}{dish[Carb]} + weights[ComplexCarb] * \frac{(dish[Carb]-dish[Fiber]-dish[Sugar])}{dish[Carb]}$

7:     $RecAdd = \sum\limits_{i \in RecAN} weights[i] * \frac{dish[i]}{DailyValues[i]}$

8:     $RestBase = \sum\limits_{i \in RestBN} weights[i] * \frac{dish[i]}{DailyValues[i]}$

9:     $RestBase = RestBase + weights[Carb] * \frac{dish[Sugar]}{dish[Carb])} + weights[SatFat] * \frac{dish[SatFat]}{dish[TotalFat]} + weights[TransFat] * dish[TransFat]$

10:     $BaseElixir = \frac{(RecBase+Mult*RecAdd)}{((1+Mult)*(RestBase))}$

11:     **return** $BaseElixir$

12: **end procedure**

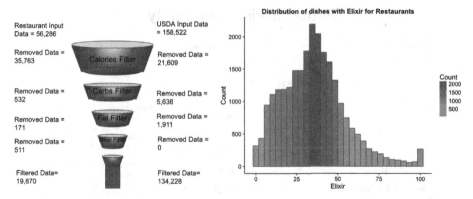

Fig. 4. Data of menu and dish items filtered for high quality.

Fig. 5. Dish database histogram along their ELIXIR scores.

5   Experiments and Results

The recommendation problem for food is inherently more difficult than the search problem. To illustrate the scale, a 20 km radius centered in Los Angeles, CA includes 32,000 restaurants, each having nearly 70 menu items on an average. These 2.24 million menu items must be ranked to maximize person's nutritional and culinary expectations. This is beyond the capacity of human dietitians. Disregarding this problem, we explored how much variance expert dietitians would have in their recommendations. Seven clinical dietitians were given a list of 50 meals with nutrition facts and images of the dishes to rank with a score of 1–10, 1 being the most unhealthy, and 10 being very healthy. Figure 2 shows that for most dishes, there is a large range of opinions on how healthy dishes are. Even though dietitians were given the nutrition facts, the range demonstrates how human evaluators are not quantitatively precise in their recommendations. We have compared the proposed algorithm (ELIXIR) against existing nutritional ranking algorithms (FSA, SAIN, NRF) by calculating mean scores for different food groups present in the USDA dataset. The values are plotted against Energy density (calories per 100g) in Fig. 6 Given the consensus knowledge about nutrition in Fig. 1, we show in Fig. 6, we can clearly separate healthy and unhealthy items on the USDA database of 158,522 items, which other global algorithms are unable to accomplish. This is one piece of confirmation that ELIXIR algorithm can encapsulate expert knowledge. We then evaluate restaurant food items that are geo-tagged in the user system with ELIXIR When comparing the average ratings by expert dietitians for the top 50 recommendations via each global algorithm, ELIXIR has a clear advantage. ELIXIR scored an average of 8.9 out of 10, SAIN average at 8.2, FSA at 7.1, and NRF at 6.9. We use top 50 recommendations because this is primarily recommendation system, where top results are the most relevant from the user's perspective as they are unlikely to browse through all the available options.

Food Scoring Capability

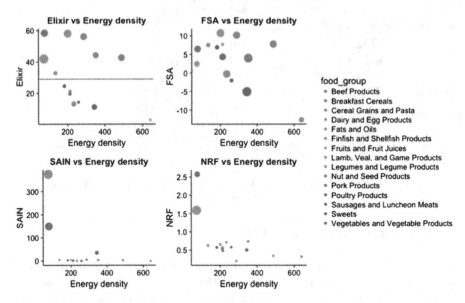

Fig. 6. The ELIXIR algorithm is able to clearly separate the healthy food groups from the unhealthy items, as shown with the red line (at approximately an ELIXIR score of 30). Healthy food groups are defined by guidelines from Fig. 1 and the American Heart and American Diabetes Associations. This clear separation of healthy food groups from unhealthy food groups is not possible with current scoring algorithms that use nutrition facts. Energy Density is given as calories per 100 grams of food. The y-axis is the arbitrary ranking score for each algorithm. Circle size represents variance within food group.

6   Future Work

Camera Based Logging for Non-Purchased Items: This constitutes about half of the individual's diet. Thus using the smart phone camera to capture the food items to auto-populate a health diary is essential for diet evaluation.

Adaptive weights and Daily Values: The algorithm presented in the paper can be viewed as the inner most layer in a health based personalized food ranking system, i.e. the algorithm is to be used to provide a quantitative measure of how a given food item would affect the person's health given their context and health status. The layers above this are responsible for adjusting the weights and daily nutritional values for the person based on data such as activity and diet history with environmental factors such as temperature and altitude.

Determining portion sizes: A meal may consist of different food items in varying portions such that the overall meal may still be healthy even if there are a few unhealthy items (e.g. chocolate cake slice for dessert). Determining ideal portion sizes is out of scope for this paper and is a topic for future research that incorporates total diet tracking and recommendations.

Knowledge Base of Taste/Cuisine: Most people do not eat healthy food if it tastes bad. In order to enable people to make healthy lifestyle choices, we need to make sure that the recommendations are aligned with the user preferences while maintaining their health goals/status.

User Filtering System: Filtering items at an ingredient level can help unique allergy needs. Food-drug interactions can also be captured through this method.

7   Conclusions

Our goal is to rapidly connect people to the healthy food. Expert recommendations with context increases probability of positive health actions. Traditional advertising, popularity based, or importance based rank listing systems will change with health based recommendations. Food providers are motivated to supply products that are inherently healthy to have a high rank result. The most important concept in this paper is how expert knowledge and health multimedia fusion will fuel the recommendation engines of the future.

References

1. Asghari, G., Azizi, F.: A systematic review of diet quality indices in relation to obesity. Br. J. Nutr., 1–11 (2017)
2. Darmon, N., Darmon, M., Maillot, M., Drewnowski, A.: A nutrient density standard for vegetables and fruits: nutrients per calorie and nutrients per unit cost. J. Am. Diet. Assoc. **105**(12), 1881–1887 (2005)
3. Drewnowski, A.: Concept of a nutritious food: toward a nutrient density score. Am. J. Clin. Nutr. **82**(4), 721–32 (2005)
4. Fulgoni, V.L., Keast, D.R., Drewnowski, A.: Development and validation of the nutrient-rich foods index: a tool to measure nutritional quality of foods. J. Nutr. **139**(8), 1549–1554 (2009)
5. Guenther, P.M., Kirkpatrick, S.I., Reedy, J., Krebs-Smith, S.M., Buckman, D.W., Dodd, K.W., Casavale, K.O., Carroll, R.J.: The healthy eating index-2010 is a valid and reliable measure of diet quality according to the 2010 dietary guidelines for americans. J. Nutr. **144**(3), 399–407 (2014)
6. Julia, C., Méjean, C., Touvier, M., Pneau, S., Lassale, C., Ducrot, P., Hercberg, S., Kesse-Guyot, E.: Validation of the FSA nutrient profiling system dietary index in French adults, findings from SUVIMAX study. Eur. J. Nutr. **55**(5), 1901–1910 (2016)
7. Kennedy, E.: Putting the pyramid into action: the healthy eating index and food quality score. Asia Pac. J. Clin. Nutr. **17**(Suppl 1), 70–4 (2008)
8. Martin, J.M., Beshears, J., Milkman, K.L., Bazerman, M.H., Sutherland, L.A.: Modeling expert opinions on food healthfulness: a nutrition metric. J. Am. Diet. Assoc. **109**(6), 1088–1091 (2009)
9. Monsivais, P., Aggarwal, A., Drewnowski, A.: Are socio-economic disparities in diet quality explained by diet cost? J. Epidemiol. Community Health **66**(6), 530–535 (2012)

10. Rise Labs Inc., HealthyOut Mobile App (2015)
11. Sherifali, D., Viscardi, V., Bai, J.-W., Ali, R.M.U.: Evaluating the effect of a dia-
    betes health coach in individuals with type 2 diabetes. Can. J. Diab. **40**(1), 84–94
    (2016)
12. Topol, E.J.: The Creative Destruction of Medicine: How the Digital Revolution
    will Create Better Health Care. Basic Books, New York (2012)
13. Trattner, C., Elsweiler, D., Howard, S.: Estimating the healthiness of internet
    recipes: a cross-sectional study. Front. Pub. Health **5**, 16 (2017)
14. Waijers, P.M.C.M., Feskens, E.J.M., Ocké, M.C.: A critical review of predefined
    diet quality scores. Br. J. Nutr. **97**(2), 219–231 (2007)
15. World Health Organization. Nutrient profiling: Report of a WHO/IASO technical
    meeting, pp. 1–18, October 2010

Comparison of Two Approaches for Direct Food Calorie Estimation

Takumi Ege and Keiji Yanai[(✉)]

Department of Informatics, The University of Electro-Communications,
Tokyo 1-5-1 Chofugaoka, Chofu-shi, Tokyo 182-8585, Japan
yanai@cs.uec.ac.jp

Abstract. In this paper, we compare CNN-based estimation and search-based estimation for image-based food calorie estimation. As the up-to-date direct food calorie estimation methods, we proposed a CNN-based calorie regression in [5], while Miyazaki et al. [9] proposed an image-search-based estimation method. The dataset used in the CNN-based direct estimation [5] contained 4877 images of 15 kinds of food classes, while the dataset used in the search-based work [9] consisted of 6522 images without any category information. In addition, in [9], hand-crafted features are used such as BoF and color histogram. The problems are that both the datasets are small and as far as we know there are no work to clearly compare CNN-based and search-based with the same dataset. In this work, we construct a calorie-annotated 68,774 food image dataset, and compare CNN-based estimation [5] and search-based estimation [9] with the same datasets. For the search-based estimation, we use CNN features instead of hand-crafted features used in [9].

Keywords: food recognition · image-based food calorie estimation CNN

1 Introduction

In recent years, because of a rise in health thinking on eating, many mobile applications for recording everyday meals have been released so far. Some of them employ food image recognition which can estimate not only food names but also food calories. However, since these applications often require users to enter information such as food categories and size or volume, there are problems that it is troublesome and subjective evaluation. To solve these problems, automatic recognition of food photos on mobile devices is effective [1,4,6,10,11,15]. However, in most of the cases, estimated calories are just associated with estimated food categories, or a relative size compared to the standard size of each food category which is usually indicated by a user manually. Currently, no applications which can estimate food calories automatically exist. Although most of the image recognition tasks including food category recognition have great progress of due to CNN-based image recognition methods [2,7,16], fully-automatic food calorie estimation from a food photo has still remained as an unsolved problem.

© Springer International Publishing AG 2017
S. Battiato et al. (Eds.): ICIAP 2017 International Workshops, LNCS 10590, pp. 453–461, 2017.
https://doi.org/10.1007/978-3-319-70742-6_44

Regarding food calorie estimation, a lot of approaches have been proposed so far. The major approach is to estimate calories based on the estimated food category and its size or volume [3,4,6,10–12]. Since food calories strongly depend on food categories and volumes, this approach is effective and important. In this approach, since it is costly to create a food image dataset with pixel-wise annotation for segmentation, the number of the foods the calories of which can be estimated was very limited.

The other approach is to estimate calories from food photos directly without estimating food categories and volumes. Only two works adopted this approach [5,9].

Miyazaki et al. [9] estimated the amount of food calories from food photos directly without estimating food categories and volumes. The biggest difficulty on direct calorie estimation is creating datasets which contains calorie-annotated food images. They hired dietitians to annotate calories on 6512 food photos which up-loaded to the commercial food logging service, Food-Log[1]. In their work, they adopted image-search based calorie estimation, in which they searched the calorie-annotated food photo database for the top k similar images based on conventional hand-crafted features. Since their method ignored information on food categories, their method was applicable for any kinds of foods. However, the number of food images in the database was not enough for the search-based method, and the employed image features was too simple.

On the other hand, we proposed a CNN-based direct food calorie estimation [5]. They employed multi-task CNNs for simultaneous estimation of food categories and calories from food photos. In [5], we collected calorie annotated recipe data from the online cooking recipe sites, and trained multi-task CNN that outputs food calories and food categories from a food photo that contained only one dish. Since there exists strong correlation between food categories and calories, we expected that simultaneous training of both brought performance boosting compared to independent single training. we were inspired by the work of Chen and Ngo [2] in which we proposed a multi-task CNN to estimate food categories and food ingredients at the same time, and proved that simultaneous estimation boosted estimation performance on both tasks. In [5], the recipe sites has various kind of foods, but we used only 15 food categories in the recipe dataset for multi-task learning of food calories and food categories. In addition, there is no fair comparison with previous works.

In this paper, regarding two representative methods on direct food calorie estimation, we compare CNN-based estimation [5] and search-based estimation [9] with the same datasets. To do that, we construct a calorie-annotated 68,774 food image dataset without food category. In addition, for the search-based method, we use CNN features instead of hand-crafted features used in [9].

---

[1] http://www.foodlog.jp/

2   Method

In this work we compare two methods. This section briefly describes the details of the two methods.

2.1   CNN-based food calorie estimation

As a direct calorie regression method, we estimate food calories from a food photos by CNN according to [5]. They collected calorie annotated recipe data from the online cooking recipe sites, and trained multi-task CNN that outputs food calories and food categories directly from a food photo that contained only one dish. According to [5], we train the network shown in Fig. 1 by the recipe dataset for food calorie estimation. This network is a single-task CNN that outputs food calories only. Initially, each layer is pre-trained by the ImageNet 1000-class dataset. The architecture of this network is based on VGG16 [14]. As shown in Fig. 1, only the output layer (fc8) is replaced by a single unit which outputs food calories.

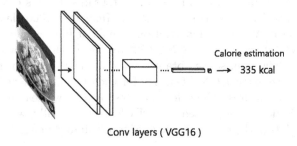

Fig. 1. The architecture for CNN-based direct food calorie estimation ([5]).

According to [5], we use a loss function as shown below for food calorie estimation task.

$$L = \lambda_{re}L_{re} + \lambda_{ab}L_{ab} \tag{1}$$

L_{ab} and L_{re} are absolute error and relative error. The absolute error is the absolute value of the difference between the estimated value and the ground-truth, and the relative error is the ratio of the absolute error to ground-truth. Generally, in the regression problem, a mean square error is used as the loss function, however in [5] we used this loss function. This loss function improves performance. where λ_{re} and λ_{ab} are the weight on the loss function, and it is usually determined so that all loss terms converge to the same value. In this work, λ_{re} and λ_{ab} are determined as follows. Firstly, the weights of the loss terms are set to 1 and train once. In the training, the values of the losses for each iteration are preserved. Finally, the reciprocal of the average value of the loss in all iterations is used as the weight for the loss term of each task. In this experiments, we fixed λ_{re} to 1.

Let y_i as the estimated value of an image x_i and g_i as the ground-truth, L_{ab} and L_{re} are defined as following:

$$L_{ab} = |y_i - g_i| \tag{2}$$

$$L_{re} = \frac{|y_i - g_i|}{g_i} \tag{3}$$

2.2 Search-based food calorie estimation

In [9], Miyazaki et al. adopted image-search based calorie estimation, in which they searched the calorie-annotated food photo database for the top k similar images based on conventional hand-crafted features such as SURF-based BoF and color histograms and estimated food calories by averaging the food calories of the top k food photos.

As an image-search based calorie estimation method, we follow this search-based method in [9]. However we use CNN features instead of conventional features such as SURF-based BoF and color histograms. In this experiments, we use VGG16 [14] which is pre-trained with the ImageNet 1000-class dataset for a feature extractor. We extract activation signals of fully connected layers (fc layers) of the VGG16 network as CNN features. Both fc6 layer and fc7 layer of VGG16 [14] are 4096-dim, so we obtain a 4096-dim feature vector for each food image. Initially, we extract CNN features for each training image and create a database of CNN features. Then, for each test image, we search the database for the top k similar images based on CNN features. Finally, we obtain a food calorie by calculating their average value of top k similar images.

3 Dataset

The datasets used in [5,9] are small. Then, we did not perform fair comparison of CNN-base [5] and search-base [9] with 15 categories dataset used in [5]. Therefore in this work we use following two datasets for comparison between CNN-base [5] and search-base [9].

3.1 15 categories dataset

In this work, we used calorie-annotated recipe data in [5] for food calorie estimation. It costs too much to create calorie-annotated food image dataset by hand. In [5], we focused on using commercial cooking recipe sites on the web and collected recipe data which has food calorie information for one person. Then we manually collected data on 15 categories, and created a total of 4877 images dataset. In this experiment, we used this dataset for food calorie estimation by both CNN-based method and search-based method.

3.2   All recipe dataset

In [5], we used only 15 food categories in the recipe dataset for multi-task learning of food calories and food categories. In this work, in order to correspond to every category, we used all recipe data. Then, we excluded photos of multiple dishes, and photos lower than 256×256. For excluding photos with more than one dishes, we used Faster R-CNN [13] trained by UEC FOOD-100 [8] which is the food image dataset annotated bounding boxes for each image. Faster R-CNN is the basis of the latest research on object detection using CNN, and achieves high-speed and highly accurate detection. In the end, we created 68,774 food images dataset.

4   Experiments

In this experiments we compared CNN-based method and search-based method for 15 categories dataset and all recipe dataset respectively. In CNN-based method, for the test, 10 models obtained at the 100 iteration intervals from the last 1000 iterations in training were used, and the average value of the estimated values obtained from each model was taken as the final estimated value. In search-based method, we searched the database for the top k similar images based on CNN features ($k = 1, 5, 10$). Also, we used fc6 and fc7 features of VGG16 [14] as CNN features in this experiments.

4.1   Calorie estimation with 15 categories dataset

In this experiment, we used 15 categories dataset for food calorie estimation.

In CNN-based method, according to [5], we used 70% of the dataset for training of single-task CNN in Fig. 1 and multi-task CNN, and the rest for testing. For optimization of the CNN, we used Momentum SGD, the momentum value 0.9. Then we used 0.001 of the learning rate for 50,000 iterations, and then 0.0001 for 20,000 iterations with size of mini-batch 8.

In search-based method, initially, we created CNN features database by 70% of the dataset, then the rest of the dataset was used for testing.

In addition, in this experiment, we estimated food calories by CNN-based classification and treated this as a baseline method. Initially, we calculated an average value of food calories for each food category using 70% of the dataset. Then for each test image, we estimated food category by CNN, and regarded the average calorie values over the estimated category as the estimated food calorie. In baseline, we finetuned VGG16 [14] for 15-class food classification. Then we used 0.001 of the learning rate for 20,000 iterations with size of mini-batch 8.

Table 1 shows the result of food calorie estimation with 15 categories dataset. We show the average of the relative error representing the ratio between the estimated values and the ground-truth, and the absolute error representing the differences between both. In addition we show the correlation coefficient between estimated value and ground-truth and the ratio of the estimated value within the relative error of 20% and 40%.

Figure 2(b) shows the relation between the ground truth values and the estimated calorie values by search-based method, while Fig. 2(c) shows the relation between that by the CNN-based method.

Table 1 indicates the performance improve by single-task CNN. Compared with search-base method (fc6, $k = 15$), in single-task CNN, 18.3% and 8.8 kcal were reduced on the relative error and the absolute error, and 0.069 and 8.1% were increased on the correlation coefficient and the ratio of the estimated calories within 40% error. However, single-task CNN is not much different from the baseline.

Table 1. Comparison of CNN-based method and search-based method with 15 categories dataset. In search-based method, we used fc6 and fc7 feature vectors and the top k similar images. The feature vector of fc6+fc7 means that fc6 and fc7 are concatenated. Multi-task CNN [5] is simultaneous learning of food categories and calories.

	rel. err.(%)	abs. err.(kcal)	correlation	20% err.(%) $\vee$|	40% err.(%) $\vee$|
Baseline	32.4	93.6	0.784	50.0	76.8
fc6 (4096-d), k=5	47.9	117.2	0.673	43.1	68.8
fc6 (4096-d), k=10	47.4	111.9	0.699	45.4	70.1
fc6 (4096-d), k=15	47.4	110.4	0.707	45.6	70.5
fc7 (4096-d), k=5	52.5	119.2	0.657	42.8	69.3
fc7 (4096-d), k=10	52.3	116.5	0.675	44.2	69.7
fc7 (4096-d), k=15	54.0	116.3	0.672	44.0	69.2
fc6+fc7 (8192-d), k=5	48.2	117.4	0.673	43.0	69.4
fc6+fc7 (8192-d), k=10	47.4	112.2	0.698	45.3	70.1
fc6+fc7 (8192-d), k=15	47.6	110.7	0.706	45.5	71.1
Single-task CNN [5]	29.1	101.6	0.776	45.5	78.6
Multi-task CNN [5]	27.2	96.2	0.805	48.3	80.2

4.2   Calorie estimation with all recipe dataset

In this experiment, we used all recipe dataset. In CNN-based method, we trained single-task CNN in Fig. 1 by 80% of the dataset. In this case, since we cannot use food category, we use only single-task without multi-task. We used 0.001 of the learning rate for 150,000 iterations, and then used 0.0001 for 50,000 iterations. In search-based method, initially, we created CNN features database by 80% of the dataset, then the rest of the dataset was used for testing.

Table 2 shows the result of food calorie estimation with all recipe dataset. In Table 2, similar to 15 categories dataset, it was confirmed that the CNN-based regression is superior that the search-based methods. However, their difference is not so significant.

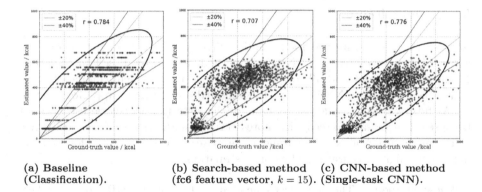

(a) Baseline
(Classification).

(b) Search-based method
(fc6 feature vector, $k = 15$).

(c) CNN-based method
(Single-task CNN).

Fig. 2. The relation between the ground-truth values and the estimated calorie values.

Table 2. Comparison of CNN-based method and search-based method with all recipe dataset. In search-based method, we used fc6 and fc7 feature vectors and the top k similar images. The feature vector of fc6+fc7 means that fc6 and fc7 are concatenated.

	rel. err. (%)	abs. err. (kcal)	correlation	$\leq$ 20% err. (%)	$\leq$ 40% err. (%)
fc6 (4096-d), k=15	122.5	141.6	0.353	25.1	47.8
fc7 (4096-d), k=15	128.4	144.7	0.329	24.2	46.8
fc6+fc7 (8192-d), k=15	122.3	141.6	0.350	25.1	47.6
Single-task CNN [5]	60.0	132.0	0.436	23.5	48.0

5 Discussion

Compared with search-base method, the CNN-based method showed improvement in performance. However, in calorie estimation with 15 categories dataset, single-task CNN is not much different from the baseline. Compared with the performance of single-task CNN with 15 categories dataset, that with all recipe dataset was significantly lower. Because of these facts, it seems that it is effective to consider food category for food calorie estimation, because there are strong correlation between food calories and food categories. In addition, for calorie estimation, we think it is necessary to recognize food ingredients and sizes explicitly as well as food categories. In order to realize highly accurate food calorie estimation, it is considered to be urgent to create high-quality datasets. It is biggest issue how to build a large-scale calorie-annotated food photo dataset.

6 Conclusion

In this paper, we estimated food calories directly from a food photo. In this experiments we compared CNN-based method and search-based method for 15 categories dataset and all recipe dataset respectively. Then, compared with search-base method, CNN-based method showed improvement in performance.

As future work, we plan to combine object detection to calorie estimation, because it is necessary to recognize more detailed information such as food ingredients and multiple objects. In parallel we prepare a calorie-annotated food image dataset for highly accurate food calorie estimation.

Acknowledgments. This work was supported by JSPS KAKENHI Grant Number 15H05915, 17H01745, 17H05972, 17H06026 and 17H06100.

References

1. Bettadapura, V., Thomaz, E., Parnami, A., Abowd, D.G., Essa, A.: Leveraging context to support automated food recognition in restaurant. In: Proceedings of the 2015 IEEE Winter Conference on Applications of Computer Vision (WACV) (2015)
2. Chen, J., Ngo, C.W.: Deep-based ingredient recognition for cooking recipe retrival. In: Proceedings of ACM International Conference Multimedia (2016)
3. Chen, M., Yang, Y., Ho, C., Wang, S., Liu, E., Chang, E., Yeh, C., Ouhyoung, M.: Automatic Chinese food identification and quantity estimation. In: Proceedings of SIGGRAPH Asia Technical Briefs, p. 29 (2012)
4. Dehais, J., Anthimopoulos, M., Mougiakakou, S.: Gocarb: a smartphone application for automatic assessment of carbohydrate intake. In: Proceedings of ACM MM Workshop on Multimedia Assisted Dietary Management (2016)
5. Ege, T., Yanai, K.: Simultaneous estimation of food categories and calories with multi-task CNN. In: Proceedings of IAPR International Conference on Machine Vision Applications(MVA) (2017)
6. Kong, F., Tan, J.: Dietcam: automatic dietary assessment with mobile camera phones. In: Proceedings of Pervasive and Mobile Computing, pp. 147–163 (2012)
7. Martinel, N., Foresti, G.L., Micheloni, C.: Wide-slice residual networks for food recognition (2016). arXiv preprint: arXiv:1612.06543
8. Matsuda, Y., Hajime, H., Yanai, K.: Recognition of multiple-food images by detecting candidate regions. In: Proceedings of IEEE International Conference on Multimedia and Expo. (2012)
9. Miyazaki, T., Chaminda, G., Silva, D., Aizawa, K.: Image - based calorie content estimation for dietary assessment. In: Proceedings of IEEE ISM Workshop on Multimedia for Cooking and Eating Activities (2011)
10. Myers, A., Johnston, N., Rathod, V., Korattikara, A., Gorban, A., Silberman, N., Guadarrama, S., Papandreou, G., Huang, J., Murphy, P.K.: Im2calories: towards an automated mobile vision food diary. In: Proceedings of IEEE International Conference on Computer Vision (2015)
11. Okamoto, K., Yanai, K.: An automatic calorie estimation system of food images on a smartphone. In: Proceedings of ACM MM Workshop on Multimedia Assisted Dietary Management (2016)

12. Pouladzadeh, P., Shirmohammadi, S., Almaghrabi, R.: Measuring calorie and nutrition from food image. IEEE Trans. Instrum. Measur. **63**, 1947–1956 (2014)
13. Ren, S., He, K., Girshick, R., Sun, J.: Faster R-CNN: towards real-time object detection with region proposal networks. IEEE Trans. Pattern Anal. Mach. Intell. **39**, 1137–1149 (2016)
14. Simonyan, K., Zisserman, A.: Very deep convolutional networks for large-scale image recognition (2014). arXiv preprint: arXiv:1409.1556
15. Tanno, R., Okamoto, K., Yanai, K.: Deepfoodcam: A DCNN-based real-time mobile food recognition system. In: Proceedings of ACM MM Workshop on Multimedia Assisted Dietary Management (2016)
16. Yanai, K., Kawano, Y.: Food image recognition using deep convolutional network with pre-training and fine-tuning. In: Proceedings of IEEE International Conference on Multimedia and Expo. (2015)

Distinguishing Nigerian Food Items and Calorie Content with Hyperspectral Imaging

Xinzuo Wang[1], Neda Rohani[1], Adwaiy Manerikar[1], Aggelos Katsagellos[1], Oliver Cossairt[1], and Nabil Alshurafa[1,2(✉)]

[1] Department of EECS, Northwestern University, Evanston, IL, USA
{XinzuoWang2018,nedarohani,AdwaiyManerikar2019}@u.northwestern.edu,
aggk@eecs.northwestern.edu, {oliver.cossairt,nabil}@northwestern.edu
[2] Feinberg School of Medicine, Northwestern University, Chicago, IL, USA

Abstract. Identifying food types consumed and their calorie composition is one of the central tasks of dietary assessment. Traditional automated image processing methods learn to map images to an existing food database with known caloric composition. However, even when the correct food type is identified, caloric makeup can vary depending on its ingredients, and using true-color images proves insufficient to distinguish within food type variability. In this paper, we show that hyperspectral imaging provides useful information and promise in distinguishing caloric composition within the same food type. We collect data using a hyperspectral camera from Nigerian foods cooked with varying degrees of fat content, and capture images under different intensities of light. We apply Principle Component Analysis (PCA) to reduce the dimensionality, and train a Support Vector Machine (SVM) classifier using a Radial Basis Function kernel and show that applying this technique on hyperspectral images can more readily distinguish calorie composition. Furthermore, compared with methods that only use true-color based features, our method shows that a classifier trained using features from hyperspectral images is significantly more predictive of within-food caloric content, and by fusing results from two classifiers trained separately using hyperspectral and RGB imagery we obtain the greatest predictive power.

Keywords: Hyperspectral imaging · Food identification Calorie detection

1 Introduction

Food crisis and undernutrition have been critical issues in many low and middle income countries. One promising way to address this problem is to provide targeted delivery of health and supplementary nutrition (like the Plumpy'Nut project in East Africa), food fortification, and empowering local villages to grow nutritious foods.

However, aside from daily food diaries and reports from local health workers, there is no reliable automated method to identify foods consumed and their

© Springer International Publishing AG 2017
S. Battiato et al. (Eds.): ICIAP 2017 International Workshops, LNCS 10590, pp. 462–470, 2017.
https://doi.org/10.1007/978-3-319-70742-6_45

caloric content. A method is needed to detect - for every food consumed - a unique food signature that is invariant to light, heat, and slight variations in visual appearance.

Despite several efforts in the field of image recognition, conventional imaging technologies that only acquire morphology are not adequate for the accurate detection and assessment of intrinsic properties of a food. Spectroscopic imaging covering the visible and near-IR spectrum (from 400 nm to 1100 nm) can help identify unique spectral features that readily discriminate between foods. In this paper, through feature extraction and classification on hyperspectral images of real food, we show that hyperspectral imaging provides useful information and promise in distinguishing caloric composition within the same food type.

2   Related Works

Throughout the past decade, food images have been widely studied. For food image segmentation, Zhu et al. [13] employs connected component analysis and normalized cuts. Anthimopoulos et al. [1] uses mean-shift algorithm. Kong et al. [6] extracts Scale Invariant Feature Transform (SIFT) points. Matsuda et al. [8] provides a method to segment food images containing multiple food items by using Felzenszwalb's deformable part model (DPM) and JSEG region segmentation. For food feature extraction, Gabor features [13], simple color and text features [12] have been explored on food images. In Dehais et al. [3], SIFT and Speeded Up Robust Features (SURF) detectors are used.

Meanwhile, hyperspectral imaging has developed wide uses for identifying the chemical and physical properties of food. Some of these uses include predicting color [9], detecting damage [4], and analyzing quality attributes [5]. Also many works have been focused on bruises detection [2,7], and food quality classification [10] by using PCA.

However, for food image recognition, while these methods have been successful in various data sets, they are all based on true color images which only focus on RGB channels. In this paper, we argue that RGB channels can be insufficient in many natural settings where foods and dishes are more complex (i.e. food in restaurants). To solve this problem, we take advantage of hyperspectral images which contain information from multiple spectra. In hyperspectral image analysis, only a few methods have been proposed to detect calorie contents of real-world foods. This work provides a method to distinguish calorie content of food types using hyperspectral imaging.

3   Methods

In this section we introduce our hyperspectral image processing technique. To begin, we first introduce our data (foods cooked), then our image acquisition system, followed by our food type identification and within-food calorie discriminant techniques.

3.1   Food Samples and the Hyperspectral Imaging System

To simulate real-world foods in low income countries, we prepared food samples using traditional Nigerian recipes. Three separate dishes were made with three different levels of fat content, for a total of nine samples. The three dishes were white rice, chicken stew, and spiced yams. The fat content was adjusted by using various quantities of oil during cooking. The low-fat rice was prepared without butter while the medium- and high-fat rice dishes were prepared using one and four tablespoons of butter, respectively. Similarly, for the low-fat yam and stew no oil was used. One tablespoon of oil was used for the medium fat dishes, and four tablespoons of oil were used for the high fat dishes. The nutritional information for each dish was calculated based on the nutritional value of the ingredients. The nutritional information can be viewed in Table 1. During the measurement process, the system was shielded from outside light in order to decrease the interference of ambient light. The size of the recorded images is 240 wavebands with a resolution of 640×244 pixels. Image sizes varied slightly depending on the location of the camera at the beginning of each image acquisition. Data was collected for each pixel in the wavelength range of 393 nm to 892 nm.

Table 1. Nutritional information for food samples.

Dish	Rice			Yams			Stew		
	Low fat	Med fat	High fat	Low fat	Med fat	High fat	Low fat	Med fat	High fat
Total fat (kcal)	204	306	612	249	351	657	577	697	1057

3.2   Hyperspectral Image Acquisition

A total number of 30 images were taken. For each dish, three images were taken: one in each light setting. This led to a total of 27 images (9×3), followed by three extra reference images taken in between light adjustments to calibrate the system to the newer lighting settings. The images were acquired using a laboratory hyperspectral system. Only halogen lights were used, and all other light sources in the room were turned off. During image acquisition, 100 g of each sample were placed in straw fiber bowls.

Due to the variant intensity of the light source, calibration with light and dark references was necessary in order to obtain accurate hyperspectral images. The dark reference was used in order to remove dark current effects. This image was collected by placing a black cap over the camera lens and turning off all lights in the room. The light reference was obtained by taking an image of a reflective white sheet of paper. The corrected image can be calculated by $R = R_o - R_d / R_r - R_d$ where R_o is the acquired original hyperspectral image, R_r is the white reference image, R_d is the dark image.

This procedure was repeated twice more, and each time the two light sources were moved to a greater distance from the sample. Each time, the light source was adjusted, the images used for references had to be retaken in order to maintain an accurate reference measurement. The exposure time and camera speed remained the same for all images.

3.3   Feature Extraction for Food Item Detection

To identify between food types, we perform preprocessing, feature extraction, and classification, each section is described below:

Preprocessing. The whole preprocessing procedure includes three steps: data cleaning, dimension reduction, and patch selection. During data cleaning we remove noisy bands between 360 nm to 480 nm (first 30 channels), so the wavelength range used for feature extraction is between 480 nm and 892 nm. The resulting data set includes 30 images (644 × 244 pixel resolution each) with 210 wavebands.

To further reduce the dimension of the data, we merge 210 wavebands into seven larger wavebands. That is, for each pixel, we calculate the mean for every 30 wavebands. Therefore, each pixel is represented by a seven-dimensional vector. Finally, we select 40 30 × 30 pixels patches from each image at each waveband to expand our data set and also enrich the training of our model.

Feature Extraction. The left side of Fig. 1 shows different food items we used for feature extraction. From the image, we can easily see that the visual appearance of different food items is largely different, while the same food items almost look alike and are homogeneous. This reminds us that simple statistical features such as mean and standard deviation from the visible light spectrum are enough for food type detection, particularly with a low selection of food types.

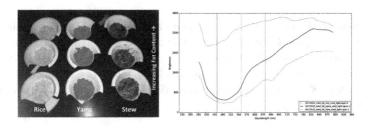

Fig. 1. Left side: Picture of our food samples. Right side: Average spectrum for three kinds of food items under the same light condition and fat content.

Classification. For food item detection, we extract the mean, standard deviation, max and min from the first three wavebands for a total of 12 features. We then build a random forest classifier using these features to classify three kinds of food items.

3.4   Feature Extraction for Calorie Content Detection

After classifying the food type, we need to classify the food calorie content. The variation in calorie content is represented in three labels of low, medium, and high fat. As mentioned before, the images have been captured under different light conditions: high, medium, and low light. Images captured with different fat content and different light conditions of stew and yams have very similar spectra which makes distinguishing between them very challenging. In Fig. 2, the spectra of stew with medium and high fat in three different light conditions are provided and as can be observed they have very similar shapes and intensities. For fat content classification, for each food, we use nine images: three images under different light conditions for each fat condition. Before classifying the calorie content we apply different preprocessing and feature extraction described below.

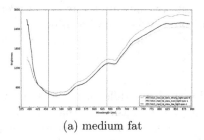 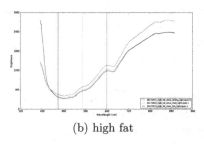

(a) medium fat   (b) high fat

Fig. 2. Images of stews with medium and high fat content captured under different light conditions. Even though the system was calibrated between each light condition, there are still differences in the spectra based on the intensity of light.

Preprocessing. First, we crop each image and select a rectangle of the image that contains the food. Then, we remove the first 30 noisy bands. To have a more meaningful data representation in a lower dimensional space, we apply PCA and select the first k-components which accounts for much of the variance in the data (accounting for 98% variance of the information). We selected 16, 51 and 43 PCs for rice, yams and stew, respectively.

Feature Extraction. After preprocessing the images, we divide the data into train and test sets. The images in two different light conditions (e.g. low and high) are considered as training images and the images in another light condition (e.g. medium) are used as test images. Now that we have training and test images, we extract patches of size $30 \times 30 \times k$ from each image and use the "mean" spectrum over the patch pixels as the new feature vector (size k).

4   Experiments and Results

In this section we apply classification methods to the food data sets to evaluate selected features.

4.1   Food Item Classification

The random forest yielded best performance with 10 trees and a maximum depth of 10. The confusion matrix for three labels is shown in Table 2. Results show that the classifier achieves more than 98% accuracy.

Table 2. Confusion matrix and F-measure for food item classification.

Classified as	Yams	Rice	Stew
	(F-measure: 0.976)	(F-measure: 0.997)	(F-measure: 0.977)
Yams	346	0	14
Rice	0	359	1
Stew	3	1	356

4.2   Food Calorie Content Classification

For the fat content classification, we use Radial Basis Function (RBF) kernel SVM which has been used widely for classification problems. In RBF, the kernel function is: $K(x_i, x_j) = \exp(-\gamma \| x_i - x_j \|_2^2)$. The optimal values of hyper parameters of RBF classifier are obtained by using n-fold cross validation. The optimal γ values have been found as $1.1e-2$, $1.9e-2$ and $2.3e-2$, for rice, yams and stew respectively. Then, the classifiers are trained with the optimal hyper parameters and tested on the test dataset.

We also apply the same procedure with true-color RGB images to compare against the hyperspectral images. We extracted $30 \times 30 \times 3$ patches from the images and calculated the "mean" vector over pixel patches and trained RBF kernel SVMs. Table 3 shows confusion matrices for each food type using RGB images and hyperspectral images. As can be observed from these tables, using hyperspectral images provides us with more discriminant information to classify foods compared to RGB images. However, if we look at the Yams' confusion matrices, it seems that RGB-based features yield higher recall (but lower precision) when testing on the low fat class while hyperspectral features work better for the other two classes. To use the outputs obtained by both set of the features, we used the simple Arithmetic Mean Rule (AMR) [11] to combine the probability outputs of two classifiers. It was found that using AMR, increases the accuracy from 81.66% to 85.0%. The confusion matrix from this approach is given in Table 4. As can be observed from Table 4, in the new approach more samples of low fat and medium fat are classified correctly (yielding higher recall and precision).

Table 3. Results for food calorie content identification using RGB and hyper-spectral images.

RGB images	Rice			Yams			Stew		
	(Accuracy: 91.66%)			(Accuracy: 65.83%)			(Accuracy: 54.44%)		
Classified as	Low fat	Med fat	High fat	Low fat	Med fat	High fat	Low fat	Med fat	High fat
Low fat	60	0	0	33	7	0	43	2	15
Med fat	14	45	1	17	19	4	31	20	9
High fat	0	0	60	6	7	27	25	13	22
Precision	0.81	1	0.98	0.59	0.58	0.87	0.43	0.57	0.47
Recall	1	0.75	1	0.82	0.47	0.67	0.71	0.33	0.36
Hyper-spectral images	Rice			Yams			Stew		
	(Accuracy: 99.44%)			(Accuracy: 81.66%)			(Accuracy: 82.77%)		
Classified as	Low fat	Med fat	High fat	Low fat	Med fat	High fat	Low fat	Med fat	High fat
Low fat	60	0	0	27	11	2	45	0	15
Med fat	0	59	1	6	31	3	3	50	7
High fat	0	0	60	0	0	40	13	3	44
Precision	1	1	1	0.81	0.73	0.88	0.73	0.94	0.66
Recall	1	0.93	1	0.67	0.77	1	0.75	0.83	0.73

Table 4. Results for food calorie content identification in yams using RGB and hyper-spectral images.

Classified as	Low fat	Med fat	High fat
Low fat	29	11	0
Med fat	6	33	1
High fat	0	0	40
Precision	0.87	0.75	0.97
Recall	0.72	0.82	1

5   Conclusion and Discussion

In this paper we demonstrated that hyperspectral imaging is able to aid in distinguishing between food calorie content with varying percentage of fat. For food type detection, we generated features from the visible spectrum only and achieved a 97% F-measure. When distinguishing calorie content, our method using PCA and SVM with an RBF kernel on hyperspectral images was able to improve our ability to distinguish calorie content, compared to using only true-color RGB images. We further show potential for improving classification by augmenting data from both hyperspectral and RGB images. Such findings show that further expanding existing databases of food images with hyperspectral images may further advance automated image-based calorie detection. However, there remain some limitations in this work, which we are inspired to address in the future. First of all we use a limited number of food types, and only vary fat content. We also only analyze hyperspectral data with wavelengths ranging from 393 to 892 nm. Moreover, while our food is cooked in a home environment, our images are extracted in a laboratory environment. Our results inspire further research in the use of hyperspectral imaging to advance automated estimation of calorie content.

Acknowledgements. We would like to thank Shirlene Wang and Susan Hood for preparing the food imaged by the hyperspectral camera. Their work enabled the success of the project and facilitated the experiment greatly. Furthermore, we would like to thank Marc Sebastian Walton, Emeline Pouyet, and Amy Marquardt for providing us access and assistance with their hyperspectral imaging system.

References

1. Anthimopoulos, M., Dehais, J., Diem, P., Mougiakakou, S.: Segmentation and recognition of multi-food meal images for carbohydrate counting. In: 2013 IEEE 13th International Conference on Bioinformatics and Bioengineering (BIBE), pp. 1–4. IEEE (2013)
2. Ariana, D.P., Lu, R.: Evaluation of internal defect and surface color of whole pickles using hyperspectral imaging. J. Food Eng. **96**(4), 583–590 (2010)
3. Dehais, J., Shevchik, S., Diem, P., Mougiakakou, S.G.: Food volume computation for self dietary assessment applications. In: 2013 IEEE 13th International Conference on Bioinformatics and Bioengineering (BIBE), pp. 1–4. IEEE (2013)
4. ElMasry, G., Wang, N., Vigneault, C.: Detecting chilling injury in red delicious apple using hyperspectral imaging and neural networks. Postharvest Biol. Technol. **52**(1), 1–8 (2009)
5. Kamruzzaman, M., ElMasry, G., Sun, D.-W., Allen, P.: Prediction of some quality attributes of lamb meat using near-infrared hyperspectral imaging and multivariate analysis. Analytica Chimica Acta **714**, 57–67 (2012)
6. Kong, F., Tan, J.: Dietcam: automatic dietary assessment with mobile camera phones. Pervasive Mob. Comput. **8**(1), 147–163 (2012)
7. Li, J., Rao, X., Ying, Y.: Detection of common defects on oranges using hyperspectral reflectance imaging. Comput. Electron. Agric. **78**(1), 38–48 (2011)
8. Matsuda, Y., Hoashi, H., Yanai, K.: Recognition of multiple-food images by detecting candidate regions. In: 2012 IEEE International Conference on Multimedia and Expo (ICME), pp. 25–30. IEEE (2012)
9. Qiao, J., Wang, N., Ngadi, M.O., Gunenc, A., Monroy, M., Gariepy, C., Prasher, S.O.: Prediction of drip-loss, ph, and color for pork using a hyperspectral imaging technique. Meat Sci. **76**(1), 1–8 (2007)
10. Qiao, J., Ngadi, M.O., Wang, N., Gariépy, C., Prasher, S.O.: Pork quality and marbling level assessment using a hyperspectral imaging system. J. Food Eng. **83**(1), 10–16 (2007)
11. Ross, A., Jain, A.: Information fusion in biometrics. Pattern Recogn. Lett. **24**(13), 2115–2125 (2003)

12. Shroff, G., Smailagic, A., Siewiorek, D.P.: Wearable context-aware food recognition for calorie monitoring. In: 12th IEEE International Symposium on Wearable Computers, ISWC 2008, pp. 119–120. IEEE (2008)
13. Zhu, F., Bosch, M., Woo, I., Kim, S.Y., Boushey, C.J., Ebert, D.S., Delp, E.J.: The use of mobile devices in aiding dietary assessment and evaluation. IEEE J. Sel. Topics Sig. Process. 4(4), 756–766 (2010)

A Multimedia Database for Automatic Meal Assessment Systems

Dario Allegra[1], Marios Anthimopoulos[2,3], Joachim Dehais[2], Ya Lu[2],
Filippo Stanco[1], Giovanni Maria Farinella[1],
and Stavroula Mougiakakou[2,4(✉)]

[1] Department of Mathematics and Computer Science, University of Catania,
Catania, Italy
{allegra,fstanco,gfarinella}@dmi.unict.it
[2] ARTORG Center for Biomedical Engineering Research, University of Bern,
Bern, Switzerland
{marios.anthimopoulos,joachim.dehais,ya.lu,
stavroula.mougiakakou}@artorg.unibe.ch
[3] Department of Emergency Medicine, Bern University Hospital,
Bern, Switzerland
[4] Department of Endocrinology, Diabetes and Clinical Nutrition,
Bern University Hospital, Bern, Switzerland

Abstract. A healthy diet is crucial for maintaining overall health and for controlling food-related chronic diseases, like diabetes and obesity. Proper diet management however, relies on the rather challenging task of food intake assessment and monitoring. To facilitate this procedure, several systems have been recently proposed for automatic meal assessment on mobile devices using computer vision methods. The development and validation of these systems requires large amounts of data and although some public datasets already exist, they don't cover the entire spectrum of inputs and/or uses. In this paper, we introduce a database, which contains RGB images of meals together with the corresponding depth maps, 3D models, segmentation and recognition maps, weights and volumes. We also present a number of experiments on the new database to provide baselines performances in the context of food segmentation, depth and volume estimation.

1 Introduction

Automatic diet assessment refers to the use of information technology for the ad-hoc translation of food intake into nutrient information in an accurate and intuitive way. Over the last years there have been a number of systems that use visual meal information to output nutrient content, mainly calories and carbohydrates [1–5], with only few of them being validated by end-users [6, 7]. Typically, once the visual information is available, a number of computer vision steps is executed: food detection, segmentation, recognition, and volume estimation. By knowing the food type and its volume and by using food composition databases the contained nutrients are estimated. Key element in the development and technical validation of the computer vision steps is the

© Springer International Publishing AG 2017
S. Battiato et al. (Eds.): ICIAP 2017 International Workshops, LNCS 10590, pp. 471–478, 2017.
https://doi.org/10.1007/978-3-319-70742-6_46

data availability. However, the currently available food image datasets addresses needs related to the food recognition step.

Scope of the paper is to introduce a database that contains annotated and labelled RGB and RGB-D images from 80 different central-European meals served on a round dish accompanied by accelerometer data. Each meal consists of two to four different food items (e.g. vegetables, meat) of know weight, volume and nutrient composition. The newly introduced database offers resources to improve the current methods, compare among different approaches and hopefully progress the field of automatic diet assessment.

2 Food Image Datasets

One of the first datasets to address food recognition is the PFID [8]. It includes 4545 still images, 606 stereo image pairs, and 303 videos that cover a 360° angle around the food. It contains meals from 11 fast food restaurants that belong to 101 different food categories. In [9], the UECFOOD-100 was proposed: a dataset, which includes 9060 Japanese food images across 100 classes. This dataset was extended in [10] with 156 new classes (UECFOOD-256). In [11], a dataset of 50 classes with 100 Asian food images per class was introduced. The authors also presented preliminary results on food quantity estimation by using depth maps acquired through a Microsoft Kinect. In [12], the UNICT-FD889 was presented. The dataset intended to be used for near duplicate image retrieval and includes 3583 food images of real-life meals belonging to 889 classes, whereas in [13] the dataset was extended to 1200 classes and 4754 images. In [14], two new datasets to address food vs non-food classification were introduced, while in [15], a large-scale dataset with 101 classes and 1000 images per class was proposed (Food-101). The dataset was created by downloading images from the website foodspotting.com. This dataset was then partially labeled and annotated to perform food segmentation and recognition. The same 101 classes have been considered in the UPCM Food-101 dataset [16], which includes images combined with a textual description. A smaller dataset named FooDD has been proposed in [17] and consists of 3000 images of various meals acquired in restaurants under different illumination conditions. Finally, in [18], a dataset containing food images from, and geolocation of, six restaurants in Asia was presented.

3 Data Collection and Processing

Each of the 80 meals was placed on a table with a fully visible reference card next to it for color and geometric calibration. The acquisition procedure was conducted in the environment of a laboratory following two setups: (i) constrained and (ii) unconstrained. For each setup, the following systems were used: Intel® RealSense™ Camera SR300 and GoCARB App [7] installed on a Samsung Galaxy S4. Finally, the LG Nexus 5X was used to get a 3D multiview reconstruction used as ground truth for computing the food items' volume.

3.1   Constrained Setup

The dish was placed in a small table with a rotating bracket mount with limited degrees of freedom, in order to control distance and angle. The acquisition device was attached at the top of the bracket. Data were acquired at two different distances (40 cm and 60 cm) and four angles (0°, 30°, 60°, 90°). Thus, for each dish a total of eight captures / device was acquired.

- *Intel® RealSense™ Camera SR300:* From the depth sensor, we got four different types of images per capture:

  1. A 24-bit RGB image at 1920 × 1080;
  2. A 16-bit depth 640 × 480 image, where the pixel values is the distance from the sensor in tenth of millimeters;
  3. A depth image aligned with the RGB one;
  4. An RGB image masked with the related aligned depth map.

- *GoCARB App installed in a Samsung Galaxy S4:* From the GoCARB system for each capture we get a 4128 × 3096 RGB image and the information about calibration, as well as the gravity vector.

3.2   Unconstrained Setup

In the unconstrained setup, the device was placed freely in front of the dish and data were acquired at a randomly chosen distance and angle in the range of 40 cm to 60 cm and 45° to 90° respectively.

- *Intel® RealSense™ Camera SR300:* From the depth sensor, 200 consecutive RGBD frames at 10 fps were captured.
- *GoCARB App installed in a Samsung Galaxy S4:* Three image pairs were captured, each of them with the characteristics mentioned in the constrained setup.

Finally, approximately 50 images with resolution 4032 × 3024 were captured from all possible angles above the table (360° view) using the LG Nexus 5X. The images were used to build the ground truth 3D model of each meal. The acquisition information is summarized in Table 1.

3.3   Data Processing

Image labeling and annotation: For a subset of the acquired RGB and RGB-D images, segmentation and recognition maps are provided after manual manipulation. Details are presented in Table 1, while a sample of the proposed database in given in Fig. 1.

Ground truth estimation: The set of photos obtained with the LG Nexus 5X has been used to create a 3D reconstruction of the dish, through the online Autodesk Recap 360 service. The resulting 3D models were manually cleaned, rotated to a horizontal alignment, and rescaled by using the real size as obtained from the calibration card. In this clean model, we manually separated the food items. Hence, we have computed the individual volumes, in order to use it as ground truth for volume estimation algorithms.

Table 1. A summary of the acquired RGB and RGB-D data, along with the provided maps. For each meal served on a round dish the weight and volume of each food items is available, as well as information from smartphone's accelerometer.

Sensors	Setup	Images	Distance (cm)	Angle	Maps	
					Recognition	Segmentation
Intel® RealSense™ Camera SR300	Constrained	8 RGB-D	40	0°	-	
				30°	-	
				60°	X	1
				90°	X	1
			60	0°	-	
				30°	-	
				60°	X	1
				90°	X	1
	Unconstrained	200 RGB-D	[40–60]	[45° –90°]	X	2
Samsung Galaxy S4 (using GoCARB)	Constrained	8 RGB	40	0°	-	
				30°	-	
				60°	X	1
				90°	X	1
			60	0°	-	
				30°	-	
				60°	X	1
				90°	X	1
	Unconstrained	6 RGB	[40–60]	[45° –90°]	X	1
LG Nexus	Unconstrained	~50 RGB	[40–60]	360° view	X	1
Total/ dish		**~272 (208 RGB-D; ~64 RGB)**			X	**12**
Total for the 80 dishes		**21807 (16640 RGB-D; 5167 RGB)**			X	**960**

4   Baseline Methods

The images of the proposed database were used to benchmark some state of the art methods for food segmentation, depth and volume estimation.

4.1   Segmentation

Food segmentation is a challenging task due to the great variability in food types, shapes and colors. Here, we investigate whether the use of depth-map information could improve the segmentation result. To this end, we applied a method similar to [19] and compared the results with and without considering the depth as input. The method consists of two main steps: border maps extraction by a convolutional neural network

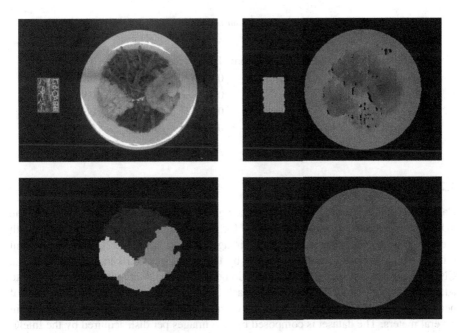

Fig. 1. On the top-left, the RGB acquisition performed with Real Sense at 40cm and 90° (top view). On the top-right, the corresponding depth map. On the bottom-left, the segmentation map for the image in the top-left. On the bottom-right, the plate map for the same images, got under the same constrains. Intensities were rescaled for visualization.

(CNN) and region growing segmentation. In our experiments, we altered the first step by utilizing different CNN architectures (SegNet [20] and U-Net [21]) and using the depth map as additional input. Specifically, the top view (40 cm and 90°) acquisition performed with Intel® RealSense™ Camera SR300 was used, after being inverted to represent the distance from the table. Finally, all the data have been normalized and automatically cropped to 256 × 256 by employing the plate map. We used 60 images for training, 10 for validation and 10 for testing. To increase the image variability, we augmented the dataset by considering two flips and four rotations. The results, confirm that depth-map information can reduce the error for borders extraction step and consequently for segmentation. Online augmentation (column AUG RGB-D in Table 2), has been performed by randomly modifying for each image at each iteration of the training data. Specifically, we add a random number from a normal distribution with mean 0 and standard deviation 0.01, to the color channels, while we multiply the depth map with a random number with mean 1 and standard deviation 0.1. The metrics used to assess the performance are the same used in [19]. We tested different architectures (SegNet, Unet), loss functions (mean square error - MSE and mean absolute error - MAE) and batch normalization strategy (per feature-map, mode 0; per batch, mode 2). Best results have been achieved with Unet, with no batch normalization e by training the CNN with online augmentation. As expected the best result has been obtained with depth information, moreover data augmentation with the smallest standard deviation has increased the training generalization.

Table 2. Segmentation results (MSE: Mean square error; MAE: Mean absolute error).

CNN	Loss	AUG RGB-D	RGB		RGB-D	
			Min Fscore	Total Fscore	Min Fscore	Total Fscore
Segnet	MSE	No	0.7329	0.9326	0.7059	0.9288
Unet	MAE	No	0.6889	0.9268	0.7351	0.9342
Unet	MSE	No	0.6875	0.9247	0.7332	0.9328
Unet	MAE	Yes	0.6893	0.9281	**0.7426**	**0.9369**

4.2 Depth Estimation

Calculating the depth of a food image is a significant component in understanding the 3D geometry of a meal, which is essential for food volume estimation. However, depth prediction is usually performed by stereo images or motion as in [22]. Here, we present a method that performs depth estimation by using just one RGB image, as input to a CNN. The method is inspired by [23], although some modifications have been made to adapt it to our problem. The considered task focuses on the estimation of the depth of near distance objects (within 1 meter), whereas the scenarios in [23] range within several meters. The dataset is composed by two images per dish acquired by the Intel® RealSense™ Camera SR300 in unconstrained setup: 60 dishes used for training, 10 for validation and 10 for testing, resulting in 120, 20 and 20 images, respectively. The training data were augmented by flipping the images left-to-right. The chosen network architecture is similar to Segnet-Basic [20], which consists of four encoding and four decoding convolutional layers. Each convolutional layer has 64 kernels and is followed by batch normalization and a ReLU activation, while the last layer uses the sigmoid activation function as a loss function, we use the mean absolute difference (MAD) between the estimated depth map and the ground truth from the depth sensor. For optimization, we used Adam with learning rate of 0.0005.

Table 3 reports the quantitative comparison of the depth prediction on the proposed dataset, where only the pixels inside the plate are evaluated. Apart from MAD value, the absolute relative difference (ARD) with respect to ground truth is also provided for the sake of clarity. As expected, in food depth prediction scenario, the result obtained using standard algorithm of [23] shows relatively poor performance. However, by using the proposed method, the performance is significantly improved. For further demonstration, the prediction result performed by our method is shown in Fig. 2(b), revealing a good agreement with the ground truth depicted in Fig. 2(a).

Table 3. Comparison on the proposed dataset (MAD: Mean absolute difference; ARD: Absolute relative difference).

Method	MAD (mm)	ARD (%)
NYU [23]	37.09	7.53
Proposed	**8.64**	**1.76**

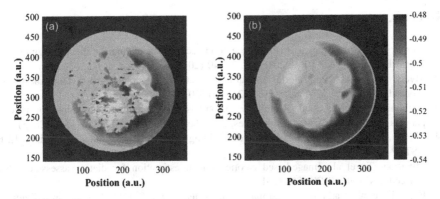

Fig. 2. (a): Depth map captured by the Intel® RealSense™ Camera SR300; (b): Depth map predicted by the proposed network. Color bar is in meter. (Color figure online)

4.3   Volume Estimation

Knowing the food volume is critical to estimate its nutritional value. In this experiment, we compare the performance of the GoCARB system in two different scenarios. As first we estimate the volume of each food item by reconstructing a 3D model as in [22]. The second experiment is aimed to assess the importance of depth map in volume estimation. We replace the depth estimation step as calculated in [22] with the depth obtained from the RGB-D images captured by depth sensor. In this case, we have to estimate the vertical direction and the table plane from the depth map to calculate the volume. To do so, we modify the table plane estimation method of [22]. First, we detect the plate through RGB channels, then sample the depth map at its border, and fit a plane to the selected points to find the ellipse plane. To find the table plane, we select all the points outside of the plate, and shift the ellipse plane to their modal height. To measure the performance the mean absolute percentage error, as defined in [22], was used.

In these conditions, the average error using stereo reconstruction was 13.8%, and 14% using RGB-D images. The two methods provide comparable results, however it has to be noted that the RGB-D sensor baseline (distance between the two elements of the stereo reconstruction module) is quite small, reducing its accuracy, while already developed algorithms were employed without any prior optimization the specific problem. However, these results indicate that a monocular RGB-D image can replace stereo pairs for volume estimation without performance drop.

5   Conclusions

In this paper, we have introduced a new multimedia food database that contains images, depth maps, weight/volume measurements of served meals, nutrient content together with the corresponding annotations, labels and accelerometer data. Furthermore, the results of some baseline methods on food segmentation and depth/volume estimation have been presented.

References

1. Merler, M., et al.: Snap, Eat, RepEat: a food recognition engine for dietary logging. In: Proceedings of the MADiMa 2016, pp. 31–40 (2016)
2. Myers, A., et al.: Im2Calories: towards an automated mobile vision food diary. In: Proceedings of the ICCV 2015, pp. 1233–124 (2015)
3. Anthimopoulos, M., et al.: Computer vision-based carbohydrate estimation for type 1 patients with diabetes using smartphones. J. Diabetes Sci. Technol. **3**, 507–515 (2015)
4. Zhu, F., et al.: The use of mobile devices in aiding dietary assessment and evaluation. IEEE J-STSP **4**(4), 756–766 (2010)
5. Miyazaki, T., et al.: Image-based calorie content estimation for dietary assessment. In: Proceedings of the IEEE ISM (2011)
6. Bally, L., et al.: Carbohydrate estimation supported by the GoCARB system in individuals with type 1 diabetes – a randomized prospective pilot study. Diabetes Care **40**(2), e6–e7 (2016). dc162173
7. Rhyner, D., et al.: Carbohydrate estimation by a mobile phone-based system versus self-estimations of individuals with type 1 diabetes mellitus: a comparative study. J. Med. Internet Res. **18**(5), e101 (2016)
8. Chen, M., et al.: PFID: Pittsburgh fast-food image dataset. In: Proceedings of the ICIP 2009, pp. 289–292 (2009)
9. Matsuda, Y., et al.: Recognition of multiple-food images by detecting candidate regions. In: Proceedings of the ICME 2012, pp. 25–30 (2012)
10. Kawano, Y., et al.: Automatic expansion of a food image dataset leveraging existing categories with domain adaptation. ECCV **2014**(8927), 3–17 (2014)
11. Chen, M.-Y., et al.: Automatic chinese food identification and quantity estimation. In: Proceedings of the SIGGRAPH Asia Technical Briefs, pp. 1–4 (2012)
12. Farinella, G.M., et al.: A benchmark dataset to study the representation of food images. ACVR **2014**(8927), 584–599 (2014)
13. Farinella, G.M., et al.: Retrieval and classification of food images. Comput. Biol. Med. **77**, 23–39 (2016)
14. Farinella, G.M., et al.: On the exploitation of one class classification to distinguish food vs non-food images. MADiMa **2015**(9281), 375–383 (2015)
15. Bossard, L., et al.: Food-101 - mining discriminative components with random forests. ECCV **8694**, 446–461 (2014)
16. Wang, X., et al.: Recipe recognition with large multimodal food dataset. In: Proceedings of the IEEE ICMEW 2015, pp, 1–6 (2015)
17. Pouladzadeh, P., et al.: FooDD: food detection dataset for calorie measurement using food images. MADiMa **2015**(9281), 441–448 (2015)
18. Herranz, L., et al.: A probabilistic model for food image recognition in restaurants. In: Proceedings of the ICME 2015, pp. 1–6 (2015)
19. Dehais, J., et al.: Food image segmentation for dietary assessment. In: Proceedings of the MADiMa 2016, pp. 23–28 (2016)
20. Badrinarayanan, V., et al.: SegNet: a deep convolutional encoder-decoder architecture for scene segmentation. In: Proceedings of the IEEE TPAMI (2017)
21. Ronneberger, O., et al.: U-Net: convolutional networks for biomedical image segmentation. MICCAI **9351**, 234–241 (2015)
22. Dehais, J., et al.: Two-View 3D reconstruction for food volume estimation. IEEE TMM **19** (5), 1090–1099 (2017)
23. Eigen, D., et. al.: Depth map prediction from a single image using a multi-scale deep network. In: Proceedings of the NIPS 2014, pp. 2366–2374 (2014)

Author Index

480   Author Index